Introduction 1

CHAPTER OBJECTIVES

> Describe the relationship between hardware and software.

> Define various types of software and how they are used.

> Identify the core hardware components of a computer and explain their roles.

> Explain how the hardware components interact to execute programs and manage data.

> Describe how computers are connected into networks to share information.

> Introduce the Java programming language.

> Describe the steps involved in program compilation and execution.

> Present an overview of object-oriented principles.

This book is about writing well-designed software. To understand software, we must first have a fundamental understanding of its role in a computer system. Hardware and software cooperate in a computer system to accomplish complex tasks. The purpose of various hardware components, and the way those components are connected into networks, are important prerequisites to the study of software development. This chapter first discusses basic computer processing, and then begins our exploration of software development by introducing the Java programming language and the principles of object-oriented programming.

1.1   COMPUTER PROCESSING

We begin our exploration of computer systems with an overview of computer processing, defining some fundamental terminology and showing how the key pieces of a computer system interact.

A computer system is made up of hardware and software. The *hardware* components of a computer system are the physical, tangible pieces that support the computing effort. They include chips, boxes, wires, keyboards, speakers, disks, cables, plugs, printers, mice, monitors, and so on. If you can physically touch it and it can be considered part of a computer system, then it is computer hardware.

The hardware components of a computer are essentially useless without instructions to tell them what to do. A *program* is a series of instructions that the hardware executes one after another. *Software* consists of programs and the data those programs use. Software is the intangible counterpart to the physical hardware components. Together they form a tool that we can use to solve problems.

The key hardware components in a computer system are:

> central processing unit (CPU)
> input/output (I/O) devices
> main memory
> secondary memory devices

Each of these hardware components is described in detail in the next section. For now, let's simply examine their basic roles. The *central processing unit* (CPU) is the device that executes the individual commands of a program. *Input/output (I/O) devices*, such as the keyboard, mouse, and monitor, allow a human being to interact with the computer.

Programs and data are held in storage devices called memory, which fall into two categories: main memory and secondary memory. *Main memory* is the storage device that holds the software while it is being processed by the CPU. *Secondary memory* devices store software in a relatively permanent manner. The most important secondary memory device of a typical computer system is the hard disk that resides inside the main computer box. A floppy disk is similar to a hard disk, but it cannot store nearly as much information as a hard disk. Floppy disks have the advantage of portability; they can be removed temporarily or moved from computer to computer as needed. Other portable secondary memory devices include zip disks and compact discs (CDs).

Figure 1.1 shows how information moves among the basic hardware components of a computer. Suppose you have an executable program you wish to run. The program is stored on some secondary memory device, such as a hard disk.

When you instruct the computer to execute your program, a copy of the program is brought in from secondary memory and stored in main memory. The CPU reads the individual program instructions from main memory. The CPU then executes the instructions one at a time until the program ends. The data that the instructions use,

Key Concept

The CPU reads the program instructions from main memory, executing them one at a time until the program ends.

such as two numbers that will be added together, are also stored in main memory. They are either brought in from secondary memory or read from an input device such as the keyboard. During execution, the progam may display information to an output device such as a monitor.

The process of executing a program is fundamental to the operation of a computer. All computer systems basically work in the same way.

Software Categories

Software can be classified into many categories using various criteria. At this point we will simply differentiate between system programs and application programs.

The *operating system* is the core software of a computer. It performs two important functions. First, it provides a *user interface* that allows the user to interact with the machine. Second, the operating system manages computer resources such as the CPU and main memory. It determines when programs are allowed to run, where they are loaded into memory, and how hardware devices communicate. It is the operating system's job to make the computer easy to use and to ensure that it runs efficiently.

Several popular operating systems are in use today. Windows 2000 and Windows XP are two versions of the operating system developed by Microsoft for personal computers. Various versions of the Unix operating system are also quite popular, especially in larger

Key Concept

The operating system provides a user interface and manages computer resources.

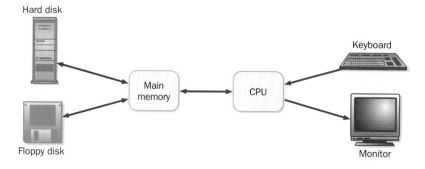

FIGURE 1.1   A simplified view of a computer system

computer systems. A version of Unix called Linux was developed as an open source project, which means that many people contributed to its development and its code is freely available. Because of that, Linux has become a particular favorite among some users. Mac OS is the operating system used for computing systems developed by Apple Computers.

An *application* is a generic term for just about any software other than the operating system. Word processors, missile control systems, database managers, Web browsers, and games can all be considered application programs. Each application program has its own user interface that allows the user to interact with that particular program.

The user interface for most modern operating systems and applications is a *graphical user interface* (GUI), which, as the name implies, make use of graphical screen elements. These elements include:

> *windows,* which are used to separate the screen into distinct work areas
> *icons,* which are small images that represent computer resources, such as a file
> *pull-down menus,* which provide the user with lists of options
> *scroll bars,* which allow the user to move up and down in a particular window
> *buttons,* which can be "pushed" with a mouse click to indicate a user selection

The mouse is the primary input device used with GUIs; thus, GUIs are sometimes called *point-and-click interfaces.* The screen shot in Figure 1.2 shows an example of a GUI.

Key Concept

As far as the user is concerned, the interface *is* the program.

The interface to an application or operating system is an important part of the software because it is the only part of the program with which the user directly interacts. To the user, the interface *is* the program. Throughout this book we discuss the design and implementation of graphical user interfaces.

The focus of this book is the development of high-quality application programs. We explore how to design and write software that will perform calculations, make decisions, and control graphics. We use the Java programming language throughout the text to demonstrate various computing concepts.

Digital Computers

Two fundamental techniques are used to store and manage information: analog and digital. *Analog* information is continuous, in direct proportion to the source of the information. For example, a mercury thermometer is an analog device for

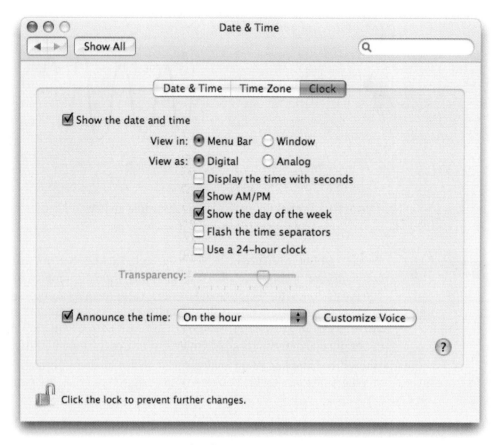

FIGURE 1.2   An example of a graphical user interface (GUI)

measuring temperature. The mercury rises in a tube in direct proportion to the temperature outside the tube. Another example of analog information is an electronic signal used to represent the vibrations of a sound wave. The signal's voltage varies in direct proportion to the original sound wave. A stereo amplifier sends this kind of electronic signal to its speakers, which vibrate to reproduce the sound. We use the term analog because the signal is directly analogous to the information it represents. Figure 1.3 graphically depicts a sound wave captured by a microphone and represented as an electronic signal.

Digital technology breaks information into discrete pieces and represents those pieces as numbers. The music on a compact disc is stored digitally, as a series of numbers. Each number represents the voltage level of one specific instance of the recording. Many of these measurements are taken in a short period of time,

Sound wave   Analog signal of the sound wave

FIGURE 1.3 A sound wave and an electronic analog signal that represents the wave

perhaps 40,000 measurements every second. The number of measurements per second is called the *sampling rate*. If samples are taken often enough, the discrete voltage measurements can be used to generate a continuous analog signal that is "close enough" to the original. In most cases, the goal is to create a reproduction of the original signal that is good enough to satisfy the human senses.

Figure 1.4 shows the sampling of an analog signal. When analog information is converted to a digital format by breaking it into pieces, we say it has been *dig-*

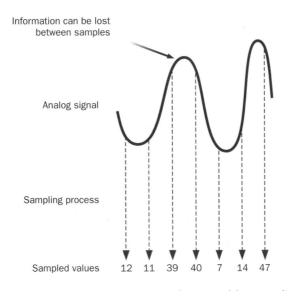

Information can be lost between samples

Analog signal

Sampling process

Sampled values   12   11   39   40   7   14   47

FIGURE 1.4 Digitizing an analog signal by sampling

itized. Because the changes that occur in a signal between samples are lost, the sampling rate must be sufficiently fast.

Sampling is only one way to digitize information. For example, a sentence of text is stored on a computer as a series of numbers, where each number represents a single character in the sentence. Every letter, digit, and punctuation symbol has been assigned a number. Even the space character is assigned a number. Consider the following sentence:

Hi, Heather.

The characters of the sentence are represented as a series of 12 numbers, as shown in Figure 1.5. When a character is repeated, such as the uppercase 'H', the same representation number is used. Note that the uppercase version of a letter is stored as a different number from the lowercase version, such as the 'H' and 'h' in the word Heather. They are considered separate and distinct characters.

Modern electronic computers are digital. Every kind of information, including text, images, numbers, audio, video, and even program instructions, is broken into pieces. Each piece is represented as a number. The information is stored by storing those numbers.

Binary Numbers

A digital computer stores information as numbers, but those numbers are not stored as *decimal* values. All information in a computer is stored and managed as *binary* values. Unlike the decimal system, which has 10 digits (0 through 9), the binary number system has only two digits (0 and 1). A single binary digit is called a *bit*.

All number systems work according to the same rules. The *base value* of a number system dictates how many digits we have to work with and indicates the place value of each digit in a number. The decimal number system is base 10,

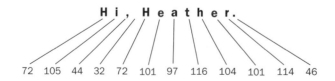

FIGURE 1.5 Text is stored by mapping each character to a number

whereas the binary number system is base 2. Appendix B contains a detailed discussion of number systems.

Modern computers use binary numbers because the devices that store and move information are less expensive and more reliable if they have to represent only one of two possible values. Other than this characteristic, there is nothing special about the binary number system. Computers have been created that use other number systems to store information, but they aren't as convenient.

Some computer memory devices, such as hard drives, are magnetic in nature. Magnetic material can be polarized easily to one extreme or the other, but intermediate levels are difficult to distinguish. Therefore, magnetic devices can be used to represent binary values quite efficiently—a magnetized area represents a binary 1 and a demagnetized area represents a binary 0. Other computer memory devices are made up of tiny electrical circuits. These devices are easier to create and are less likely to fail if they have to switch between only two states. We're better off reproducing millions of these simple devices than creating fewer, more complicated ones.

Binary values and digital electronic signals go hand in hand. They improve our ability to transmit information reliably along a wire. As we've seen, an analog signal has continuously varying voltage, but a digital signal is *discrete*, which means the voltage changes dramatically between one extreme (such as +5 volts) and the other (such as –5 volts). At any point, the voltage of a digital signal is considered to be either "high," which represents a binary 1, or "low," which represents a binary 0. Figure 1.6 compares these two types of signals.

As a signal moves down a wire, it gets weaker and degrades due to environmental conditions. That is, the voltage levels of the original signal change slightly. The trouble with an analog signal is that as it fluctuates, it loses its original information. Since the information is directly analogous to the signal, any change in

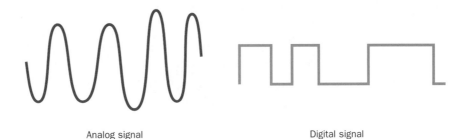

Analog signal   Digital signal

FIGURE 1.6   An analog signal vs. a digital signal

the signal changes the information. The changes in an analog signal cannot be recovered because the degraded signal is just as valid as the original. A digital signal degrades just as an analog signal does, but because the digital signal is originally at one of two extremes, it can be reinforced before any information is lost. The voltage may change slightly from its original value, but it still can be interpreted as either high or low.

The number of bits we use in any given situation determines the number of unique items we can represent. A single bit has two possible values, 0 and 1, and therefore can represent two possible items or situations. If we want to represent the state of a light bulb (off or on), one bit will suffice, because we can interpret 0 as the light bulb being off and 1 as the light bulb being on. If we want to represent more than two things, we need more than one bit.

Two bits, taken together, can represent four possible items because there are exactly four combinations of two bits: 00, 01, 10, and 11. Suppose we want to represent the gear that a car is in (park, drive, reverse, or neutral). We would need only two bits, and could set up a mapping between the bit combinations and the gears. For instance, we could say that 00 represents park, 01 represents drive, 10 represents reverse, and 11 represents neutral. In this case, it wouldn't matter if we switched that mapping around, though in some cases the relationships between the bit combinations and what they represent is important.

Three bits can represent eight unique items, because there are eight combinations of three bits. Similarly, four bits can represent 16 items, five bits can represent 32 items, and so on. Figure 1.7 shows the relationship between the number of bits used and the number of items they can represent. In general, N bits can represent 2^N unique items. For every bit added, the number of items that can be represented doubles.

> **Key Concept**
>
> There are exactly 2^N combinations of N bits. Therefore, N bits can represent up to 2^N unique items.

We've seen how a sentence of text is stored on a computer by mapping characters to numeric values. Those numeric values are stored as binary numbers. Suppose we want to represent character strings in a language that contains 256 characters and symbols. We would need to use eight bits to store each character because there are 256 unique permutations of eight bits (2^8 equals 256). Each bit permutation, or binary value, is mapped to a specific character.

Ultimately, representing information on a computer boils down to the number of items there are to represent and determining the way those items are mapped to binary values.

1 bit 2 items	2 bits 4 items	3 bits 8 items	4 bits 16 items	5 bits 32 items	
0	00	000	0000	00000	10000
1	01	001	0001	00001	10001
	10	010	0010	00010	10010
	11	011	0011	00011	10011
		100	0100	00100	10100
		101	0101	00101	10101
		110	0110	00110	10110
		111	0111	00111	10111
			1000	01000	11000
			1001	01001	11001
			1010	01010	11010
			1011	01011	11011
			1100	01100	11100
			1101	01101	11101
			1110	01110	11110
			1111	01111	11111

FIGURE 1.7   The number of bits used determines the number of items that can be represented

1.2   HARDWARE COMPONENTS

Let's examine the hardware components of a computer system in more detail. Consider the computer described in Figure 1.8. What does it all mean? Is the system capable of running the software you want it to? How does it compare to other systems? These terms are explained throughout this section.

- 2.8 GHz Intel Pentium 4 processor

- 512 MB RAM

- 80 GB Hard Drive

- 48x CD-RW / DVD-ROM Combo Drive

- 17" Flat Screen Video Display with 1280 x 1024 resolution

- 56 Kb/s Modem

FIGURE 1.8   The hardware specification of a particular computer

Computer Architecture

The architecture of a house defines its structure. Similarly, we use the term *computer architecture* to describe how the hardware components of a computer are put together. Figure 1.9 illustrates the basic architecture of a generic computer system. Information travels between components across a group of wires called a *bus*.

The CPU and the main memory make up the core of a computer. As we mentioned earlier, main memory stores programs and data that are in active use, and the CPU methodically executes program instructions one at a time.

Suppose we have a program that computes the average of a list of numbers. The program and the numbers must reside in main memory while the program runs. The CPU reads one program instruction from main memory and executes it. If an instruction needs data, such as a number in the list, to perform its task, the CPU reads that information as well. This process repeats until the program ends. The average, when computed, is stored in main memory to await further processing or long-term storage in secondary memory.

Almost all devices in a computer system other than the CPU and main memory are called *peripherals;* they operate at the periphery, or outer edges, of the system (although they may be in the same box). Users don't interact directly with the

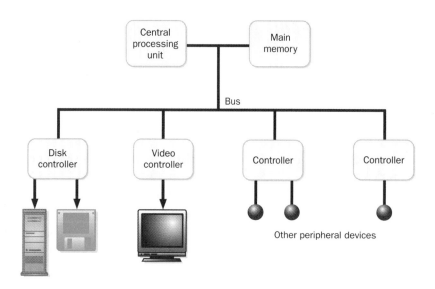

FIGURE 1.9   Basic computer architecture

CPU or main memory. Although they form the essence of the machine, the CPU and main memory would not be useful without peripheral devices.

Controllers are devices that coordinate the activities of specific peripherals. Every device has its own particular way of formatting and communicating data, and part of the controller's role is to handle these idiosyncrasies and isolate them from the rest of the computer hardware. Furthermore, the controller often handles much of the actual transmission of information, allowing the CPU to focus on other activities.

Input/output (I/O) devices and secondary memory devices are considered peripherals. Another category of peripherals includes *data transfer devices*, which allow information to be sent and received between computers. The computer specified in Figure 1.8 includes a data transfer device called a *modem*, which allows information to be sent across a telephone line. The modem in the example can transfer data at a maximum rate of 56 *kilobits* (Kb) per second, or approximately 56,000 *bits per second* (bps).

In some ways, secondary memory devices and data transfer devices can be thought of as I/O devices because they represent a source of information (input) and a place to send information (output). For our discussion, however, we define I/O devices as those devices that allow the user to interact with the computer.

Input/Output Devices

Let's examine some I/O devices in more detail. The most common input devices are the keyboard and the mouse. Others include:

> *bar code readers*, such as the ones used at a grocery store checkout
> *joysticks*, often used for games and advanced graphical applications
> *microphones*, used by voice recognition systems that interpret simple voice commands
> *virtual reality devices*, such as gloves that interpret the movement of the user's hand
> *scanners*, which convert text, photographs, and graphics into machine-readable form

Monitors and printers are the most common output devices. Others include:

> *plotters*, which move pens across large sheets of paper (or vice versa)
> *speakers*, for audio output
> *goggles*, for virtual reality display

Some devices can provide both input and output capabilities. A *touch screen* system can detect the user touching the screen at a particular place. Software can then use the screen to display text and graphics in response to the user's touch. Touch screens are particularly useful in situations where the interface to the machine must be simple, such as at an information booth.

The computer described in Figure 1.8 includes a monitor with a 17-inch diagonal display area. It is a flat screen, which makes use of newer liquid crystal display (LCD) technology rather than the older cathode ray tube (CRT) monitors that take up much more space on a desk. A picture is represented in a computer by breaking it up into separate picture elements, or *pixels*. The monitor can display a grid of 1280 by 1024 pixels. Representing and managing graphical data is discussed in more detail in Chapter 2.

Main Memory and Secondary Memory

Main memory is made up of a series of small, consecutive *memory locations*, as shown in Figure 1.10. Associated with each memory location is a unique number called an *address*.

> **Key Concept**
>
> An address is a unique number associated with each memory location.

When data is stored in a memory location, it overwrites and destroys any information that was previously stored at that location. However, data is read from a memory location without affecting it.

On many computers, each memory location consists of eight bits, or one *byte*, of information. If we need to store a value that cannot be represented in a single

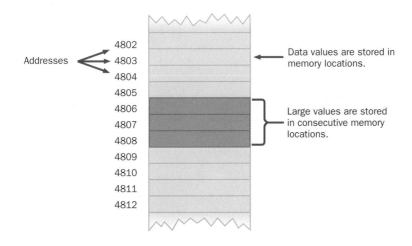

Addresses

4802 — Data values are stored in memory locations.
4803
4804
4805
4806 ⎫
4807 ⎬ Large values are stored in consecutive memory locations.
4808 ⎭
4809
4810
4811
4812

FIGURE 1.10 Memory locations

byte, such as a large number, then multiple, consecutive bytes are used to store the data.

The *storage capacity* of a device such as main memory is the total number of bytes it can hold. Devices can store thousands or millions of bytes, so you should become familiar with larger units of measure. Because computer memory is based on the binary number system, all units of storage are powers of two. A *kilobyte* (KB) is 1024, or 2^{10}, bytes. Some larger units of storage are a *megabyte* (MB), a *gigabyte* (GB), and a *terabyte* (TB), as listed in Figure 1.11. It's usually easier to think about these capacities by rounding them off. For example, most computer users think of a kilobyte as approximately one thousand bytes, a megabyte as approximately one million bytes, and so forth.

Many personal computers have 512 megabytes or 1 gigabyte of main memory, or RAM, such as the system described in Figure 1.8 (we discuss RAM in more detail later in this chapter). A large main memory allows large programs, or multiple programs, to run efficiently because they don't have to retrieve information from secondary memory as often.

> **Key Concept**
>
> Main memory is volatile, meaning the stored information is maintained only as long as electric power is supplied.

Main memory is usually *volatile*, meaning that the information stored in it will be lost if its electric power supply is turned off. When you are working on a computer, you should often save your work onto a secondary memory device such as a disk in case the power goes out. Secondary memory devices are usually *nonvolatile*; the information is retained even if the power supply is turned off.

The most common secondary storage devices are hard disks and floppy disks. A high-density floppy disk can store 1.44 MB of information. The storage capacities of hard drives vary, but on personal computers, capacities typically range between 40 and 160 GB, such as in the system described in Figure 1.8.

A disk is a magnetic medium on which bits are represented as magnetized particles. A read/write head passes over the spinning disk, reading or writing infor-

Unit	Symbol	Number of Bytes
byte		$2^{0} = 1$
kilobyte	KB	$2^{10} = 1024$
megabyte	MB	$2^{20} = 1,048,576$
gigabyte	GB	$2^{30} = 1,073,741,824$
terabyte	TB	$2^{40} = 1,099,511,627,776$

FIGURE 1.11 Units of binary storage

mation as appropriate. A hard disk drive might actually contain several disks in a vertical column with several read/write heads, such as the one shown in Figure 1.12.

To get an intuitive feel for how much information these devices can store, consider that all the information in this book, including pictures and formatting, requires about 7 MB of storage.

Magnetic tapes are also used as secondary storage but are considerably slower than disks because of the way information is accessed. A disk is a *direct access device* since the read/write head can move, in general, directly to the information needed. The terms direct access and *random access* are often used interchangeably. However, information on a tape can be accessed only after first getting past the intervening data. A tape must be rewound or fast-forwarded to get to the appropriate position. A tape is therefore considered a *sequential access device*. Tapes are usually used only to store information when it is no longer used frequently, or to provide a backup copy of the information on a disk.

Two other terms are used to describe memory devices: *random access memory* (RAM) and *read-only memory* (ROM). It's important to understand these terms because they are used often, and their names can be misleading. The terms RAM and main memory are basically interchangeable. When contrasted with ROM, however, the term RAM seems to imply something it shouldn't. Both RAM and ROM are direct (or random) access devices. RAM should probably be called read-write memory, since data can be both written to it and read from it. This feature distinguishes it from ROM. After information is stored on ROM, it cannot be altered (as the term "read-only" implies). ROM chips are often embedded into the main circuit board of a computer and used to provide the preliminary instructions needed when the computer is initially turned on.

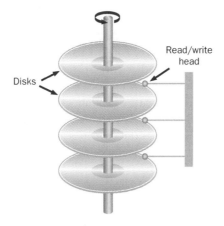

FIGURE 1.12   A hard disk drive with multiple disks and read/write heads

A *CD-ROM* is a portable secondary memory device. CD stands for compact disc. It is accurately called ROM because information is stored permanently when the CD is created and cannot be changed. Like its musical CD counterpart, a CD-ROM stores information in binary format. When the CD is initially created, a microscopic pit is pressed into the disc to represent a binary 1, and the disc is left smooth to represent a binary 0. The bits are read by shining a low-intensity laser beam onto the spinning disc. The laser beam reflects strongly from a smooth area on the disc but weakly from a pitted area. A sensor receiving the reflection determines whether each bit is a 1 or a 0 accordingly. A typical CD-ROM's storage capacity is approximately 650 MB.

Variations on basic CD technology have emerged quickly. It is now common for a home computer to be equipped with a *CD-Recordable* (CD-R) drive. A CD-R can be used to create a CD for music or for general computer storage. Once created, you can use a CD-R disc in a standard CD player, but you can't change the information on a CD-R disc once it has been "burned." Music CDs that you buy in a store are pressed from a mold, whereas CD-Rs are burned with a laser.

A *CD-Rewritable* (CD-RW) disc can be erased and reused. They can be reused because the pits and flat surfaces of a normal CD are simulated on a CD-RW by coating the surface of the disc with a material that, when heated to one temperature becomes amorphous (and therefore nonreflective) and when heated to a different temperature becomes crystalline (and therefore reflective). The CD-RW media doesn't work in all players, but CD-RW drives can create both CD-R and CD-RW discs.

CDs were initially a popular format for music; they later evolved to be used as a general computer storage device. Similarly, the *DVD* format was originally created for video and is now making headway as a general format for computer data. DVD once stood for digital video disc or digital versatile disc, but now the acronym generally stands on its own. A DVD has a tighter format (more bits per square inch) than a CD and can therefore store much more information. It is likely that DVD-ROMs eventually will replace CD-ROMs completely because there is a compatible migration path, meaning that a DVD drive can read a CD-ROM. Similar to CD-R and CD-RW, there are DVD-R and DVD-RW discs. The drive listed in Figure 1.8 allows the user to read and write CD-RW discs and read DVD-ROMs. This, of course, includes the ability to play music CDs and watch DVD videos.

The speed of a CD or DVD drive is expressed in multiples of x, which represents a data transfer speed of 153,600 bytes of data per second. The drive described in Figure 1.8 has a maximum data access speed of 48x, though it probably writes data at much slower speeds.

The capacity of storage devices changes continually as technology improves. A general rule in the computer industry suggests that storage capacity approximately doubles every 18 months. However, this progress eventually will slow down as capacities approach absolute physical limits.

The Central Processing Unit

The central processing unit (CPU) interacts with main memory to perform all fundamental processing in a computer. The CPU interprets and executes instructions, one after another, in a continuous cycle. It is made up of three important components, as shown in Figure 1.13. The *control unit* coordinates the processing steps, the *registers* provide a small amount of storage space in the CPU itself, and the *arithmetic/logic unit* performs calculations and makes decisions.

The control unit coordinates the transfer of data and instructions between main memory and the registers in the CPU. It also coordinates the execution of the circuitry in the arithmetic/logic unit to perform operations on data stored in particular registers.

In most CPUs, some registers are reserved for special purposes. For example, the *instruction register* holds the current instruction being executed. The *program counter* is a register that holds the address of the next instruction to be executed. In addition to these and other special-purpose registers, the CPU also contains a set of general-purpose registers that are used for temporary storage of values as needed.

The concept of storing both program instructions and data together in main memory is the underlying principle of the *von Neumann architecture* of computer design, named after John von Neumann, who first advanced this programming concept in 1945. These computers continually follow the *fetch-decode-execute*

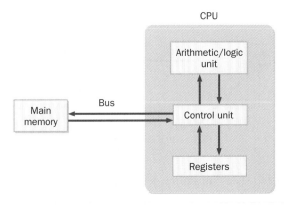

FIGURE 1.13   CPU components and main memory

cycle depicted in Figure 1.14. An instruction is fetched from main memory at the address stored in the program counter and is put into the instruction register. The program counter is incremented at this point to prepare for the next cycle. Then the instruction is decoded electronically to determine which operation to carry out. Finally, the control unit activates the correct circuitry to carry out the instruction, which may load a data value into a register or add two values together, for example.

The CPU is constructed on a chip called a *microprocessor,* a device that is part of the main circuit board of the computer. This board also contains ROM chips and communication sockets to which device controllers, such as the controller that manages the video display, can be connected.

Another crucial component of the main circuit board is the *system clock.* The clock generates an electronic pulse at regular intervals, which synchronizes the events of the CPU. The rate at which the pulses occur is called the *clock speed,* and it varies depending on the processor. The computer described in Figure 1.8 includes a Pentium 4 processor that runs at a clock speed of 2.8 gigahertz (GHz), or approximately 2.8 billion pulses per second. The speed of the system clock provides a rough measure of how fast the CPU executes instructions. Similar to storage capacities, the speed of processors is constantly increasing with advances in technology.

1.3   NETWORKS

A single computer can accomplish a great deal, but connecting several computers together into networks can dramatically increase productivity and facilitate the sharing of information. A *network* is two or more computers connected together so they can exchange

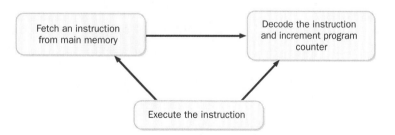

FIGURE 1.14   The continuous fetch-decode-execute cycle

information. Using networks has become the normal mode of commercial computer operation. New technologies are emerging every day to capitalize on the connected environments of modern computer systems.

Figure 1.15 shows a simple computer network. One of the devices on the network is a printer, which allows any computer connected to the network to print a document on that printer. One of the computers on the network is designated as a *file server,* which is dedicated to storing programs and data that are needed by many network users. A file server usually has a large amount of secondary memory. When a network has a file server, each individual computer doesn't need its own copy of a program.

Network Connections

If two computers are directly connected, they can communicate in basically the same way that information moves across wires inside a single machine. When connecting two geographically close computers, this solution works well and is called a *point-to-point connection.* However, consider the task of connecting many computers together across large distances. If point-to-point connections are used, every computer is directly connected by a wire to every other computer in the network. A separate wire for each connection is not a workable solution because every time a new computer is added to the network, a new communication line will have to be installed for each computer already in the network. Furthermore, a single computer can handle only a small number of direct connections.

Figure 1.16 shows multiple point-to-point connections. Consider the number of communication lines that would be needed if two or three additional computers were added to the network.

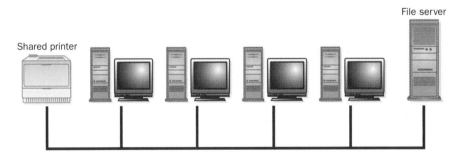

FIGURE 1.15   A simple computer network

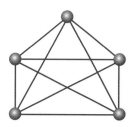

FIGURE 1.16 Point-to-point connections

Compare the diagrams in Figure 1.15 and Figure 1.16. All of the computers shown in Figure 1.15 share a single communication line. Each computer on the network has its own *network address,* which uniquely identifies it. These addresses are similar in concept to the addresses in main memory except that they identify individual computers on a network instead of individual memory locations inside a single computer. A message is sent across the line from one computer to another by specifying the network address of the computer for which it is intended.

Sharing a communication line is cost effective and makes adding new computers to the network relatively easy. However, a shared line introduces delays. The computers on the network cannot use the communication line at the same time. They have to take turns sending information, which means they have to wait when the line is busy.

One technique to improve network delays is to divide large messages into segments, called *packets,* and then send the individual packets across the network intermixed with pieces of other messages sent by other users. The packets are collected at the destination and reassembled into the original message. This situation is similar to a group of people using a conveyor belt to move a set of boxes from one place to another. If only one person were allowed to use the conveyor belt at a time, and that person had a large number of boxes to move, the others would be waiting a long time before they could use it. By taking turns, each person can put one box on at a time, and they all can get their work done. It's not as fast as having a conveyor belt of your own, but it's not as slow as having to wait until everyone else is finished.

Local-Area Networks and Wide-Area Networks

A *local-area network* (LAN) is designed to span short distances and connect a relatively small number of computers. Usually a LAN connects the machines in only

one building or in a single room. LANs are convenient to install and manage and are highly reliable. As computers became increasingly small and versatile, LANs became an inexpensive way to share information throughout an organization. However, having a LAN is like having a telephone system that allows you to call only the people in your own town. We need to be able to share information across longer distances.

> **Key Concept**
>
> A local-area network (LAN) is an effective way to share information and resources throughout an organization.

A *wide-area network* (WAN) connects two or more LANs, often across long distances. Usually one computer on each LAN is dedicated to handling the communication across a WAN. This technique relieves the other computers in a LAN from having to perform the details of long-distance communication. Figure 1.17 shows several LANs connected into a WAN. The LANs connected by a WAN are often owned by different companies or organizations, and might even be located in different countries.

The impact of networks on computer systems has been dramatic. Computing resources can now be shared among many users, and computer-based communication across the entire world is now possible. In fact, the use of networks is now so pervasive that some computers require network resources in order to operate.

The Internet

Throughout the 1970s, a United States government organization called the Advanced Research Projects Agency (ARPA) funded several projects to explore

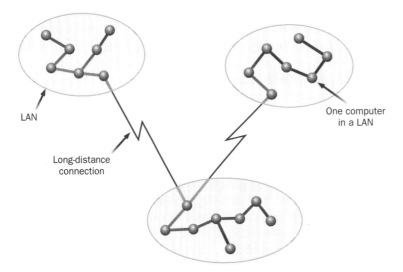

FIGURE 1.17   LANs connected into a WAN

network technology. One result of these efforts was the ARPANET, a WAN that eventually became known as the Internet. The *Internet* is a network of networks. The term Internet comes from the WAN concept of *internetworking*—connecting many smaller networks together.

From the mid 1980s through the present day, the Internet has grown incredibly. In 1983, there were fewer than 600 computers connected to the Internet. By the year 2000, that number had reached over 10 million. As more and more computers connect to the Internet, the task of keeping up with the larger number of users and heavier traffic has been difficult. New technologies have replaced the ARPANET several times since the initial development, each time providing more capacity and faster processing.

A *protocol* is a set of rules that governs how two things communicate. The software that controls the movement of messages across the Internet must conform to a set of protocols called TCP/IP (pronounced by spelling out the letters, T-C-P-I-P). TCP stands for *Transmission Control Protocol*, and IP stands for *Internet Protocol*. The IP software defines how information is formatted and transferred from the source to the destination. The TCP software handles problems such as pieces of information arriving out of their original order or information getting lost, which can happen if too much information converges at one location at the same time.

Every computer connected to the Internet has an *IP address* that uniquely identifies it among all other computers on the Internet. An example of an IP address is 204.192.116.2. Fortunately, the users of the Internet rarely have to deal with IP addresses. The Internet allows each computer to be given a name. Like IP addresses, the names must be unique. The Internet name of a computer is often referred to as its *Internet address*. Two examples of Internet addresses are spencer.villanova.edu and kant.gestalt-llc.com.

The first part of an Internet address is the local name of a specific computer. The rest of the address is the *domain name*, which indicates the organization to which the computer belongs. For example, villanova.edu is the domain name for the network of computers at Villanova University, and spencer is the name of a particular computer on that campus. Because the domain names are unique, many organizations can have a computer named spencer without confusion. Individual departments might be assigned *subdomains* that are added to the basic domain name to uniquely distinguish their set of computers within the larger organization. For example, the csc.villanova.edu subdomain is devoted to the Department of Computing Sciences at Villanova University.

The last part of each domain name, called a *top-level domain* (TLD), usually indicates the type of organization to which the computer belongs. The TLD edu indicates an educational institution. The TLD com refers to a commercial business. For example, gestalt-llc.com refers to Gestalt, LLC, a company specializing in software technologies. Another common TLD is org, used mostly by nonprofit organizations. Many computers, especially those outside of the United States, use a TLD that denotes the country of origin, such as uk for the United Kingdom or au for Australia. Recently, in response to a diminishing supply of domain names, some new top-level domain names have been created, such as biz, info, and name.

When an Internet address is referenced, it gets translated to its corresponding IP address, which is used from that point on. The software that does this translation is called the *Domain Name System* (DNS). Each organization connected to the Internet operates a *domain server* that maintains a list of all computers at that organization and their IP addresses. It works somewhat like telephone directory assistance in that you provide the name, and the domain server gives back a number. If the local domain server does not have the IP address for the name, it contacts another domain server that does.

The Internet has revolutionized computer processing. Initially, the primary use of interconnected computers was to send electronic mail, but Internet capabilities continue to improve. One of the most significant uses of the Internet is the World Wide Web.

The World Wide Web

The Internet gives us the capability to exchange information. The *World Wide Web* (also known as WWW or simply the Web) makes the exchange of information easy. Web software provides a common user interface through which many different types of information can be accessed with the click of a mouse.

> **Key Concept**
>
> The World Wide Web is software that makes sharing information across a network easy.

The Web is based on the concepts of hypertext and hypermedia. The term *hypertext* was first used in 1965 to describe a way to organize information so that the flow of ideas was not constrained to a linear progression. In fact, that concept was entertained as a way to manage large amounts of information as early as the 1940s. Researchers on the Manhattan Project, who were developing the first atomic bomb, envisioned such an approach. The underlying idea is that documents can be linked at various points according to natural relationships so that the reader can jump from one document to another, following the appropriate path for that reader's needs. When other media components are incorporated, such as graphics, sound, animations, and video, the resulting organization is called *hypermedia*.

The terms Internet and World Wide Web are sometimes used interchangeably, but there are important differences between the two. The Internet makes it possible to communicate via computers around the world. The Web makes that communication a straightforward and enjoyable activity. The Web is essentially a distributed information service and is based on a set of software applications. It is not a network. Although it is used effectively with the Internet, it is not inherently bound to it. The Web can be used on a LAN that is not connected to any other network or even on a single machine to display HTML documents.

A *browser* is a software tool that loads and formats Web documents for viewing. *Mosaic,* the first graphical interface browser for the Web, was released in 1993. The designer of a Web document defines *links* to other Web information that might be anywhere on the Internet. Some of the people who developed Mosaic went on to found the Netscape Communications Corporation and create the Netscape Navigator browser. It is currently one of the most popular systems for accessing information on the Web. Microsoft's Internet Explorer is another popular browser.

A computer dedicated to providing access to Web documents is called a *Web server.* Browsers load and interpret documents provided by a Web server. Many such documents are formatted using the *HyperText Markup Language* (HTML). The Java programming language has an intimate relationship with Web processing because links to Java programs can be embedded in HTML documents and executed through Web browsers. We explore this relationship in more detail in Chapter 2.

Uniform Resource Locators

Information on the Web is found by identifying a *Uniform Resource Locator* (URL). A URL uniquely specifies documents and other information for a browser to obtain and display. The following is an example URL:

http://www.google.com

The Web site at this particular URL is a popular *search engine,* which enables you to search the Web for information using particular words or phrases.

> **Key Concept**
>
> A URL uniquely specifies documents and other information found on the Web for a browser to obtain and display.

A URL contains several pieces of information. The first piece is a protocol, which determines the way the browser transmits and processes information. The second piece is the Internet address of the machine on which the document is stored. The third piece of information is the file name of interest. If no file name

is given, as is the case with the Google URL, the Web server usually provides a default page (such as index.html).

Let's look at another example URL:

http://www.gestalt-llc.com/vision.html

In this URL, the protocol is http, which stands for *HyperText Transfer Protocol.* The machine referenced is www (a typical reference to a Web server), found at domain gestalt-llc.com. Finally, vision.html is a file to be transferred to the browser for viewing. Many other forms for URLs exist, but this form is the most common.

1.4 THE JAVA PROGRAMMING LANGUAGE

Let's now turn our attention to the software that makes a computer system useful. A program is written in a particular *programming language* that uses specific words and symbols to express the problem solution. A programming language defines a set of rules that determines exactly how a programmer can combine the words and symbols of the language into *programming statements,* which are the instructions that are carried out when the program is executed.

Since the inception of computers, many programming languages have been created. We use the Java language in this book to demonstrate various programming concepts and techniques. Although our main goal is to learn these underlying software development concepts, an important side effect will be to become proficient in the development of Java programs.

Java is a relatively new programming language compared to many others. It was developed in the early 1990s by James Gosling at Sun Microsystems. Java was introduced to the public in 1995 and has gained tremendous popularity since.

Java has undergone various changes since its creation. The most recent Java technology is generally referred to as the *Java 2 Platform,* which is organized into three major groups:

> Java 2 Platform, Standard Edition (J2SE)
> Java 2 Platform, Enterprise Edition (J2EE)
> Java 2 Platform, Micro Edition (J2ME)

This book focuses on the Standard Edition, which, as the name implies, is the mainstream version of the language and associated tools. Furthermore, this book is based on the most recent version of the Standard Edition, which is J2SE 5.0.

Some parts of early Java technologies have been *deprecated*, which means they are considered old-fashioned and should not be used. When it is important, we point out deprecated elements and discuss their preferred alternatives.

One reason Java got some initial attention was because it was the first programming language to deliberately embrace the concept of writing programs that can be executed using the Web. The original hype about Java's Web capabilities initially obscured the far more important features that make it a useful general-purpose programming language.

> **Key Concept**
>
> This book focuses on the principles of object-oriented programming.

Java is an *object-oriented programming language.* Objects are the fundamental elements that make up a program. The principles of object-oriented software development are the cornerstone of this book. We explore object-oriented programming concepts later in this chapter and throughout the rest of the book.

The Java language is accompanied by a library of extra software that we can use when developing programs. This software, referred to as the Java *standard class library,* provides the ability to create graphics, communicate over networks, and interact with databases, among many other features. The standard library that supports Java programming is huge and quite versatile. Although we won't be able to cover all aspects of the library, we will explore many of them.

Java is used in commercial environments all over the world. It is one of the fastest growing programming technologies of all time. So not only is it a good language in which to learn programming concepts, it is also a practical language that will serve you well in the future.

A Java Program

Let's look at a simple but complete Java program. The program in Listing 1.1 prints two sentences to the screen. This particular program prints a quote by Abraham Lincoln. The output is shown below the program listing.

All Java applications have a similar basic structure. Despite its small size and simple purpose, this program contains several important features. Let's carefully dissect it and examine its pieces.

> **Key Concept**
>
> Comments do not affect a program's processing; instead, they serve to facilitate human comprehension.

The first few lines of the program are comments, which start with the // symbols and continue to the end of the line. Comments don't affect what the program does but are included to make the program easier to understand by humans. Programmers can and should include comments as needed throughout a program to clearly identify the purpose of the program and describe any special processing. Any written comments or documents, including a user's guide and

Listing 1.1

```
//************************************************************
//  Lincoln.java      Author: Lewis/Loftus
//
//  Demonstrates the basic structure of a Java application.
//************************************************************

public class Lincoln
{
    //----------------------------------------------------------
    //  Prints a presidential quote.
    //----------------------------------------------------------
    public static void main (String[] args)
    {
        System.out.println ("A quote by Abraham Lincoln:");

        System.out.println ("Whatever you are, be a good one.");
    }
}
```

Output

```
A quote by Abraham Lincoln:
Whatever you are, be a good one.
```

technical references, are called *documentation*. Comments included in a program are called *inline documentation*.

The rest of the program is a *class definition*. This class is called `Lincoln`, though we could have named it just about anything we wished. The class definition runs from the first opening brace ({) to the final closing brace (}) on the last line of the program. All Java programs are defined using class definitions.

Inside the class definition are some more comments describing the purpose of the `main` method, which is defined directly below the comments. A *method* is a group of programming statements that is given a name. In this case, the name of the method is `main` and it contains only two programming statements. Like a class definition, a method is also delimited by braces.

All Java applications have a `main` method, which is where processing begins. Each programming statement in the `main` method is executed, one at a time in order, until the end of the method is reached. Then the program ends, or *terminates*. The `main` method definition in a Java program is always preceded by the

words `public`, `static`, and `void`, which we examine later in the text. The use of `String` and `args` does not come into play in this particular program. We describe these later also.

The two lines of code in the `main` method invoke another method called `println` (pronounced print line). We *invoke*, or *call*, a method when we want it to execute. The `println` method prints the specified characters to the screen. The characters to be printed are represented as a *character string*, enclosed in double quote characters (″). When the program is executed, it calls the `println` method to print the first statement, calls it again to print the second statement, and then, because that is the last line in the `main` method, the program terminates.

The code executed when the `println` method is invoked is not defined in this program. The `println` method is part of the `System.out` object, which is part of the Java standard class library. It's not technically part of the Java language, but is always available for use in any Java program. We explore the `println` method in more detail in Chapter 2.

Comments

Let's examine comments in more detail. Comments are the only language feature that allows programmers to compose and communicate their thoughts independent of the code. Comments should provide insight into the programmer's original intent. A program is often used for many years, and often many modifications are made to it over time. The original programmer often will not remember the details of a particular program when, at some point in the future, modifications are required. Furthermore, the original programmer is not always available to make the changes; thus, someone completely unfamiliar with the program will need to understand it. Good documentation is therefore essential.

As far as the Java programming language is concerned, the content of comments can be any text whatsoever. Comments are ignored by the computer; they do not affect how the program executes.

The comments in the `Lincoln` program represent one of two types of comments allowed in Java. The comments in `Lincoln` take the following form:

```
// This is a comment.
```

This type of comment begins with a double slash (//) and continues to the end of the line. You cannot have any characters between the two slashes. The computer ignores any text after the double slash to the end of the line. A comment

can follow code on the same line to document that particular line, as in the following example:

```
System.out.println ("Monthly Report"); // always use this title
```

The second form a Java comment may have is the following:

```
/*  This is another comment.  */
```

This comment type does not use the end of a line to indicate the end of the comment. Anything between the initiating slash-asterisk (/*) and the terminating asterisk-slash (*/) is part of the comment, including the invisible *newline* character that represents the end of a line. Therefore, this type of comment can extend over multiple lines. No space can be between the slash and the asterisk.

If there is a second asterisk following the /* at the beginning of a comment, the content of the comment can be used to automatically generate external documentation about your program by using a tool called *javadoc*. More information about javadoc is given in Appendix I.

The two basic comment types can be used to create various documentation styles, such as:

```
// This is a comment on a single line.

//------------------------------------------------------------
// Some comments such as those above methods or classes
// deserve to be blocked off to focus special attention
// on a particular aspect of your code.  Note that each of
// these lines is technically a separate comment.
//------------------------------------------------------------

/*
   This is one comment
   that spans several lines.
*/
```

Programmers often concentrate so much on writing code that they focus too little on documentation. You should develop good commenting practices and follow them habitually. Comments should be well written, often in complete sentences. They should not belabor the obvious but should provide appropriate insight into the intent of the code. The following examples are *not* good comments:

```
System.out.println ("hello"); // prints hello
System.out.println ("test");  // change this later
```

The first comment paraphrases the obvious purpose of the line and does not add any value to the statement. It is better to have no comment than a useless one. The second comment is ambiguous. What should be changed later? When is later? Why should it be changed?

Identifiers and Reserved Words

The various words used when writing programs are called *identifiers*. The identifiers in the `Lincoln` program are `class`, `Lincoln`, `public`, `static`, `void`, `main`, `String`, `args`, `System`, `out`, and `println`. These fall into three categories:

> words that we make up when writing a program (`Lincoln` and `args`)
> words that another programmer chose (`String`, `System`, `out`, `println`, and `main`)
> words that are reserved for special purposes in the language (`class`, `public`, `static`, and `void`)

While writing the program, we simply chose to name the class `Lincoln`, but we could have used one of many other possibilities. For example, we could have called it `Quote`, or `Abe`, or `GoodOne`. The identifier `args` (which is short for arguments) is often used in the way we use it in `Lincoln`, but we could have used just about any other identifier in its place.

The identifiers `String`, `System`, `out`, and `println` were chosen by other programmers. These words are not part of the Java language. They are part of the Java standard library of predefined code, a set of classes and methods that someone has already written for us. The authors of that code chose the identifiers in that code—we're just making use of them.

Reserved words are identifiers that have a special meaning in a programming language and can only be used in predefined ways. A reserved word cannot be used for any other purpose, such as naming a class or method. In the `Lincoln` program, the reserved words used are `class`, `public`, `static`, and `void`. Throughout the book, we show Java reserved words in blue type. Figure 1.18 lists all of the Java reserved words in alphabetical order. The words marked with an asterisk are reserved for possible future use in later versions of the language but currently have no meaning in Java.

An identifier that we make up for use in a program can be composed of any combination of letters, digits, the underscore character (_), and the dollar sign ($), but it cannot begin with a digit. Identifiers may be of any length. Therefore, `total`, `label7`, `nextStockItem`, `NUM_BOXES`, and `$amount` are all valid identifiers, but `4th_word` and `coin#value` are not valid.

abstract	default	goto*	package	this
assert	do	if	private	throw
boolean	double	implements	protected	throws
break	else	import	public	transient
byte	enum	instanceof	return	true
case	extends	int	short	try
catch	false	interface	static	void
char	final	long	strictfp	volatile
class	finally	native	super	while
const*	float	new	switch	
continue	for	null	synchronized	

FIGURE 1.18   Java reserved words

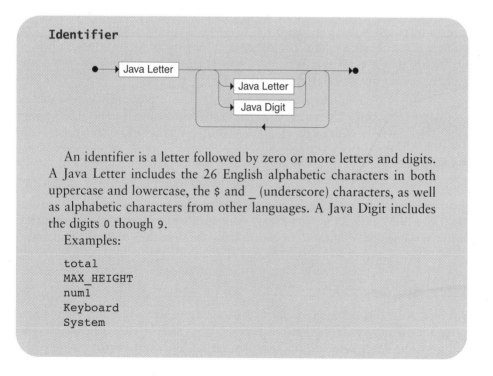

Identifier

An identifier is a letter followed by zero or more letters and digits. A Java Letter includes the 26 English alphabetic characters in both uppercase and lowercase, the $ and _ (underscore) characters, as well as alphabetic characters from other languages. A Java Digit includes the digits 0 though 9.

Examples:

```
total
MAX_HEIGHT
num1
Keyboard
System
```

Both uppercase and lowercase letters can be used in an identifier, and the difference is important. Java is *case sensitive*, which means that two identifier names that differ only in the case of their letters are considered to be different

identifiers. Therefore, `total`, `Total`, `ToTaL`, and `TOTAL` are all different identifiers. As you can imagine, it is not a good idea to use multiple identifiers that differ only in their case, because they can be easily confused.

Although the Java language doesn't require it, using a consistent case format for each kind of identifier makes your identifiers easier to understand. There are various Java conventions regarding identifiers that should be followed, though technically they don't have to be. For example, we use *title case* (uppercase for the first letter of each word) for class names. Throughout the text, we describe the preferred case style for each type of identifier when it is first encountered.

While an identifier can be of any length, you should choose your names carefully. They should be descriptive but not verbose. You should avoid meaningless names such as `a` or `x`. An exception to this rule can be made if the short name is actually descriptive, such as using `x` and `y` to represent (x, y) coordinates on a two-dimensional grid. Likewise, you should not use unnecessarily long names, such as the identifier `theCurrentItemBeingProcessed`. The name `currentItem` would serve just as well. As you might imagine, the use of identifiers that are verbose is a much less prevalent problem than the use of names that are not descriptive.

You should always strive to make your programs as readable as possible. Therefore, you should always be careful when abbreviating words. You might think `curStVal` is a good name to represent the current stock value, but another person trying to understand the code may have trouble figuring out what you meant. It might not even be clear to you two months after writing it.

A *name* in Java is a series of identifiers separated by the dot (period) character. The name `System.out` is the way we designate the object through which we invoked the `println` method. Names appear quite regularly in Java programs.

White Space

All Java programs use *white space* to separate the words and symbols used in a program. White space consists of blanks, tabs, and newline characters. The phrase white space refers to the fact that, on a white sheet of paper with black printing, the space between the words and symbols is white. The way a programmer uses white space is important because it can be used to emphasize parts of the code and can make a program easier to read.

Except when it's used to separate words, the computer ignores white space. It does not affect the execution of a program. This fact gives programmers a great deal of flexibility in how they format a program. The lines of a program should be divided in logical places and certain lines should be indented and aligned so that the program's underlying structure is clear.

> **Key Concept**
>
> Appropriate use of white space makes a program easier to read and understand.

Because white space is ignored, we can write a program in many different ways. For example, taking white space to one extreme, we could put as many words as possible on each line. The code in Listing 1.2, the `Lincoln2` program, is formatted quite differently from `Lincoln` but prints the same message.

Taking white space to the other extreme, we could write almost every word and symbol on a different line with varying amounts of spaces, such as `Lincoln3`, shown in Listing 1.3.

All three versions of `Lincoln` are technically valid and will execute in the same way, but they are radically different from a reader's point of view. Both of the latter examples show poor style and make the program difficult to understand. You may be asked to adhere to particular guidelines when you write your programs. A software development company often has a programming style policy that it requires its programmers to follow. In any case, you should adopt and consistently use a set of style guidelines that increase the readability of your code.

> **Key Concept**
>
> You should adhere to a set of guidelines that establish the way you format and document your programs.

Listing 1.2

```java
//********************************************************************
//  Lincoln2.java       Author: Lewis/Loftus
//
//  Demonstrates a poorly formatted, though valid, program.
//********************************************************************

public class Lincoln2{public static void main(String[]args){
System.out.println("A quote by Abraham Lincoln:");
System.out.println("Whatever you are, be a good one.");}}
```

Output

```
A quote by Abraham Lincoln:
Whatever you are, be a good one.
```

Listing 1.3

```
//*************************************************************************
//   Lincoln3.java         Author: Lewis/Loftus
//
//   Demonstrates another valid program that is poorly formatted.
//*************************************************************************

        public          class
     Lincoln3
  {
                  public
   static
        void
  main
          (
String
          [ ]
    args                            )
  {
  System.out.println          (
"A quote by Abraham Lincoln:"              )
  ;         System.out.println
          (
      "Whatever you are, be a good one."
      )
   ;
}
          }
```

Output

```
A quote by Abraham Lincoln:
Whatever you are, be a good one.
```

1.5 PROGRAM DEVELOPMENT

The process of getting a program running involves various activities. The program has to be written in the appropriate programming language, such as Java. That program has to be translated into a form that the computer can execute. Errors can occur at various stages of this process and must be fixed. Various software tools can be used to help with all parts of the development process as well. Let's explore these issues in more detail.

Programming Language Levels

Suppose a particular person is giving travel directions to a friend. That person might explain those directions in any one of several languages, such as English, Russian, or Italian. The directions are the same no matter which language is used to explain them, but the manner in which the directions are expressed is different. The friend must be able understand the language being used in order to follow the directions.

Similarly, a problem can be solved by writing a program in one of many programming languages, such as Java, Ada, C, C++, C#, Pascal, and Smalltalk. The purpose of the program is essentially the same no matter which language is used, but the particular statements used to express the instructions, and the overall organization of those instructions, vary with each language. A computer must be able to understand the instructions in order to carry them out.

Programming languages can be categorized into the following four groups. These groups basically reflect the historical development of computer languages.

> machine language
> assembly language
> high-level languages
> fourth-generation languages

In order for a program to run on a computer, it must be expressed in that computer's *machine language*. Each type of CPU has its own language. For that reason, we can't run a program specifically written for a Sun Workstation, with its Sparc processor, on a Dell PC, with its Intel processor.

Each machine language instruction can accomplish only a simple task. For example, a single machine language instruction might copy a value into a register or compare a value to zero. It might take four separate machine language instructions to add two numbers together and to store the result. However, a computer can do millions of these instructions in a second, and therefore many simple commands can be executed quickly to accomplish complex tasks.

> **Key Concept**
>
> All programs must be translated to a particular CPU's machine language in order to be executed.

Machine language code is expressed as a series of binary digits and is extremely difficult for humans to read and write. Originally, programs were entered into the computer by using switches or some similarly tedious method. Early programmers found these techniques to be time consuming and error prone.

These problems gave rise to the use of *assembly language*, which replaced binary digits with *mnemonics*, short English-like words that represent commands or data. It is much easier for programmers to deal with words than with binary

digits. However, an assembly language program cannot be executed directly on a computer. It must first be translated into machine language.

Generally, each assembly language instruction corresponds to an equivalent machine language instruction. Therefore, similar to machine language, each assembly language instruction accomplishes only a simple operation. Although assembly language is an improvement over machine code from a programmer's perspective, it is still tedious to use. Both assembly language and machine language are considered *low-level languages*.

> **Key Concept**
>
> High-level languages allow a programmer to ignore the underlying details of machine language.

Today, most programmers use a *high-level language* to write software. A high-level language is expressed in English-like phrases, and thus is easier for programmers to read and write. A single high-level language programming statement can accomplish the equivalent of many—perhaps hundreds—of machine language instructions. The term high-level refers to the fact that the programming statements are expressed in a way that is far removed from the machine language that is ultimately executed. Java is a high-level language, as are Ada, C++, Smalltalk, and many others.

Figure 1.19 shows equivalent expressions in a high-level language, assembly language, and machine language. The expressions add two numbers together. The assembly language and machine language in this example are specific to a Sparc processor.

The high-level language expression in Figure 1.19 is readable and intuitive for programmers. It is similar to an algebraic expression. The equivalent assembly language code is somewhat readable, but it is more verbose and less intuitive. The machine language is basically unreadable and much longer. In fact, only a small portion of the binary machine code to add two numbers together is shown in

High-Level Language	Assembly Language	Machine Language
a + b	ld [%fp–20], %o0	. . .
	ld [%fp–24], %o1	1101 0000 0000 0111
	add %o0, %o1, %o0	1011 1111 1110 1000
		1101 0010 0000 0111
		1011 1111 1110 1000
		1001 0000 0000 0000
		. . .

FIGURE 1.19 A high-level expression and its assembly language and machine language equivalent

Figure 1.19. The complete machine language code for this particular expression is over 400 bits long.

A high-level language insulates programmers from needing to know the underlying machine language for the processor on which they are working. But high-level language code must be translated into machine language in order to be executed.

Some programming languages are considered to operate at an even higher level than high-level languages. They might include special facilities for automatic report generation or interaction with a database. These languages are called *fourth-generation languages*, or simply 4GLs, because they followed the first three generations of computer programming: machine, assembly, and high-level.

Editors, Compilers, and Interpreters

Several special-purpose programs are needed to help with the process of developing new programs. They are sometimes called software tools because they are used to build programs. Examples of basic software tools include an editor, a compiler, and an interpreter.

Initially, you use an *editor* as you type a program into a computer and store it in a file. There are many different editors with many different features. You should become familiar with the editor you will use regularly because it can dramatically affect the speed at which you enter and modify your programs.

Figure 1.20 shows a very basic view of the program development process. After editing and saving your program, you attempt to translate it from high-level code into a form that can be executed. That translation may result in errors, in which case you return to the editor to make changes to the code to fix the problems. Once the translation occurs successfully, you can execute the program and evaluate the results. If the results are not what you want, or if you want to enhance your existing program, you again return to the editor to make changes.

The translation of source code into (ultimately) machine language for a particular type of CPU can occur in a variety of ways. A *compiler* is a program that

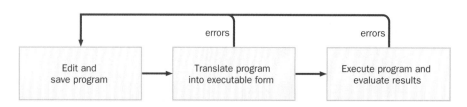

FIGURE 1.20   Editing and running a program

translates code in one language to equivalent code in another language. The original code is called *source code*, and the language into which it is translated is called the *target language*. For many traditional compilers, the source code is translated directly into a particular machine language. In that case, the translation process occurs once (for a given version of the program), and the resulting executable program can be run whenever needed.

An *interpreter* is similar to a compiler but has an important difference. An interpreter interweaves the translation and execution activities. A small part of the source code, such as one statement, is translated and executed. Then another statement is translated and executed, and so on. One advantage of this technique is that it eliminates the need for a separate compilation phase. However, the program generally runs more slowly because the translation process occurs during each execution.

> ### Key Concept
> A Java compiler translates Java source code into Java bytecode, a low-level, architecture-neutral representation of the program.

The process generally used to translate and execute Java programs combines the use of a compiler and an interpreter. This process is pictured in Figure 1.21. The Java compiler translates Java source code into Java *bytecode*, which is a representation of the program in a low-level form similar to machine language code. The Java interpreter reads Java bytecode and executes it on a specific machine. Another compiler could translate the bytecode into a particular machine language for efficient execution on that machine.

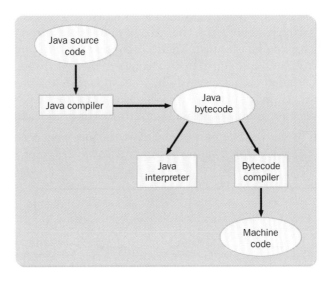

FIGURE 1.21 The Java translation and execution process

The difference between Java bytecode and true machine language code is that Java bytecode is not tied to any particular processor type. This approach has the distinct advantage of making Java *architecture neutral,* and therefore easily portable from one machine type to another. The only restriction is that there must be a Java interpreter or a bytecode compiler for each processor type on which the Java bytecode is to be executed.

Since the compilation process translates the high-level Java source code into a low-level representation, the interpretation process is more efficient than interpreting high-level code directly. Executing a program by interpreting its bytecode is still slower than executing machine code directly, but it is fast enough for most applications. Note that for efficiency, Java bytecode could be compiled into machine code.

Development Environments

A software *development environment* is the set of tools used to create, test, and modify a program. Some development environments are available for free while others, which may have advanced features, must be purchased. Some environments are referred to as *integrated development environments* (IDEs) because they integrate various tools into one software program.

Any development environment will contain certain key tools, such as a Java compiler and interpreter. Some will include a *debugger,* which helps you find errors in a program. Other tools that may be included are documentation generators, archiving tools, and tools that help you visualize your program structure.

Sun Microsystems, the creator of the Java programming language, provides the Java *Software Development Kit* (SDK), which is sometimes referred to simply as the *Java Development Kit* (JDK). The SDK can be downloaded free of charge for various hardware platforms from Sun's Java Web site, java.sun.com, and is also included on the CD that accompanies this book.

The SDK tools are not an integrated environment. The commands for compilation and interpretation are executed on the command line. That is, the SDK does not have a GUI. It also does not include an editor, although any editor that can save a document as simple text can be used.

Sun also has a Java IDE called NetBeans (www.netbeans.org) that incorporates the development tools of the SDK into one convenient GUI-based program. IBM promotes a similar IDE called Eclipse (www.eclipse.org). Both NetBeans and Eclipse are *open source* projects, meaning that they are developed by a wide collection of programmers and are available for free.

> **Key Concept**
>
> Many different development environments exist to help you create and modify Java programs.

A research group at Auburn University has developed jGRASP, a free Java IDE that is included on the CD that accompanies this book. It can also be downloaded from www.jgrasp.com. In addition to fundamental development tools, jGRASP contains tools that graphically display program elements.

Various other Java development environments are available. A Web search will unveil dozens of them. The choice of which development environment to use is important. The more you know about the capabilities of your environment, the more productive you can be during program development.

Syntax and Semantics

Each programming language has its own unique *syntax*. The syntax rules of a language dictate exactly how the vocabulary elements of the language can be combined to form statements. These rules must be followed in order to create a program. We've already discussed several Java syntax rules. For instance, the fact that an identifier cannot begin with a digit is a syntax rule. The fact that braces are used to begin and end classes and methods is also a syntax rule. Appendix L formally defines the basic syntax rules for the Java programming language, and specific rules are highlighted throughout the text.

During compilation, all syntax rules are checked. If a program is not syntactically correct, the compiler will issue error messages and will not produce byte-code. Java has a similar syntax to the programming languages C and C++, and therefore the look and feel of the code is familiar to people with a background in those languages.

The *semantics* of a statement in a programming language define what will happen when that statement is executed. Programming languages are generally unambiguous, which means the semantics of a program are well defined. That is, there is one and only one interpretation for each statement. On the other hand, the *natural languages* that humans use to communicate, such as English and Italian, are full of ambiguities. A sentence can often have two or more different meanings. For example, consider the following sentence:

Time flies like an arrow.

The average human is likely to interpret this sentence as a general observation: that time moves quickly in the same way that an arrow moves quickly. However, if we interpret the word *time* as a verb (as in "run the 50-yard dash and I'll time you") and the word *flies* as a noun (the plural of fly), the interpretation changes completely. We know that arrows don't time things, so we wouldn't normally interpret the sentence that way, but it is a valid interpretation of the words in the

sentence. A computer would have a difficult time trying to determine which meaning is intended. Moreover, this sentence could describe the preferences of an unusual insect known as a "time fly," which might be found near an archery range. After all, fruit flies like a banana.

> **Key Concept**
>
> Syntax rules dictate the form of a program. Semantics dictate the meaning of the program statements.

The point is that one specific English sentence can have multiple valid meanings. A computer language cannot allow such ambiguities to exist. If a programming language instruction could have two different meanings, a computer would not be able to determine which one should be carried out.

Errors

Several different kinds of problems can occur in software, particularly during program development. The term computer error is often misused and varies in meaning depending on the situation. From a user's point of view, anything that goes awry when interacting with a machine can be called a computer error. For example, suppose you charged a $23 item to your credit card, but when you received the bill, the item was listed at $230. After you have the problem fixed, the credit card company apologizes for the "computer error." Did the computer arbitrarily add a zero to the end of the number, or did it perhaps multiply the value by 10? Of course not. A computer follows the commands we give it and operates on the data we provide. If our programs are wrong or our data inaccurate, then we cannot expect the results to be correct. A common phrase used to describe this situation is "garbage in, garbage out."

> **Key Concept**
>
> The programmer is responsible for the accuracy and reliability of a program.

You will encounter three kinds of errors as you develop programs:

> compile-time error
> run-time error
> logical error

The compiler checks to make sure you are using the correct syntax. If you have any statements that do not conform to the syntactic rules of the language, the compiler will produce a *syntax error*. The compiler also tries to find other problems, such as the use of incompatible types of data. The syntax might be technically correct, but you may be attempting to do something that the language doesn't semantically allow. Any error identified by the compiler is called a *compile-time error*. If a compile-time error occurs, an executable version of the program is not created.

> **Key Concept**
>
> A Java program must be syntactically correct or the compiler will not produce bytecode.

The second kind of problem occurs during program execution. It is called a *run-time error* and causes the program to terminate abnormally. For example, if we attempt to divide by zero, the program will "crash" and halt execution at that point. Because the requested operation is undefined, the system simply abandons its attempt to continue processing your program. The best programs are *robust*; that is, they avoid as many run-time errors as possible. For example, the program code could guard against the possibility of dividing by zero and handle the situation appropriately if it arises. In Java, many run-time problems are called *exceptions* that can be caught and dealt with accordingly.

The third kind of software problem is a *logical error.* In this case, the software compiles and executes without complaint, but it produces incorrect results. For example, a logical error occurs when a value is calculated incorrectly or when a graphical button does not appear in the correct place. A programmer must test the program thoroughly, comparing the expected results to those that actually occur. When defects are found, they must be traced back to the source of the problem in the code and corrected. The process of finding and correcting defects in a program is called *debugging.* Logical errors can manifest themselves in many ways, and the actual root cause might be difficult to discover.

1.6   OBJECT-ORIENTED PROGRAMMING

As we stated earlier in this chapter, Java is an object-oriented (OO) language. As the name implies, an *object* is a fundamental entity in a Java program. This book is focused on the idea of developing software by defining objects that interact with each other.

The principles of object-oriented software development have been around for many years, essentially as long as high-level programming languages have been used. The programming language Simula, developed in the 1960s, had many characteristics that define the modern OO approach to software development. In the 1980s and 1990s, object-oriented programming became wildly popular, due in large part to the development of programming languages like C++ and Java. It is now the dominant approach used in commercial software development.

One of the most attractive characteristics of the object-oriented approach is the fact that objects can be used quite effectively to represent real-world entities. We can use a software object to represent an employee in a company, for instance. We'd create one object per employee, each with behaviors and characteristics that we need to represent. In this way, object-oriented programming allows us to map our programs to the real situations that the programs represent. That is, the object-oriented approach makes it easier to solve problems, which is the point of writing a program in the first place.

Let's discuss the general issues related to problem solving, then explore the specific characteristics of the object-oriented approach that helps us solve those problems.

Problem Solving

In general, problem solving consists of multiple steps:

1. Understanding the problem.
2. Designing a solution.
3. Considering alternatives to the solution and refining the solution.
4. Implementing the solution.
5. Testing the solution and fixing any problems that exist.

Although this approach applies to any kind of problem solving, it works particularly well when developing software. These steps aren't purely linear. That is, some of the activities will overlap others. But at some point, all of these steps should be carefully addressed.

The first step, understanding the problem, may sound obvious, but a lack of attention to this step has been the cause of many misguided software development efforts. If we attempt to solve a problem we don't completely understand, we often end up solving the wrong problem or at least going off on improper tangents. Each problem has a *problem domain,* the real-world issues that are key to our solution. For example, if we are going to write a program to score a bowling match, then the problem domain includes the rules of bowling. To develop a good solution, we must thoroughly understand the problem domain.

The key to designing a problem solution is breaking it down into manageable pieces. A solution to any problem can rarely be expressed as one big task. Instead, it is a series of small cooperating tasks that interact to perform a larger task. When developing software, we don't write one big program. We design separate pieces that are responsible for certain parts of the solution, then integrate them with the other parts.

Our first inclination toward a solution may not be the best one. We must always consider alternatives and refine the solution as necessary. The earlier we consider alternatives, the easier it is to modify our approach.

Implementing the solution is the act of taking the design and putting it in a usable form. When developing a software solution to a problem, the implementation stage is the process of actually writing the program. Too often programming is thought of as writing code. But in most cases, the act of designing the program should be far more interesting and creative than the process of implementing the design in a particular programming language.

At many points in the development process, we should test our solution to find any errors that exist so that we can fix them. Testing cannot guarantee that there aren't still problems yet to be discovered, but it can raise our confidence that we have a viable solution.

Throughout this text we explore techniques that allow us to design and implement elegant programs. Although we will often get immersed in these details, we should never forget that our primary goal is to solve problems.

Object-Oriented Software Principles

Object-oriented programming ultimately requires a solid understanding of the following terms:

> object
> attribute
> method
> class
> encapsulation
> inheritance
> polymorphism

In addition to these terms, there are many associated concepts that allow us to tailor our solutions in innumerable ways. This book is designed to help you evolve your understanding of these concepts gradually and naturally. This section provides an overview of these ideas at a high level to establish some terminology and provide the big picture.

We mentioned earlier that an *object* is a fundamental element in a program. A software object often represents a real object in our problem domain, such as a bank account. Every object has a *state* and a set of *behaviors*. By "state" we mean state of being—fundamental characteristics that currently define the object. For example, part of a bank account's state is its current balance. The behaviors of an object are the activities associated with the object. Behaviors associated with a bank account probably include the ability to make deposits and withdrawals.

In addition to objects, a Java program also manages primitive data. *Primitive data* includes fundamental values such as numbers and characters. Objects usually represent more interesting or complex entities.

An object's *attributes* are the values it stores internally, which may be represented as primitive data or as other objects. For example, a bank account object may store a floating point number (a primitive value) that represents the balance of the account. It may contain other attributes, such as the name of the account owner. Collectively, the values of an object's attributes define its current state.

As mentioned earlier in this chapter, a *method* is a group of programming statements that is given a name. When a method is invoked, its statements are executed. A set of methods is associated with an object. The methods of an object define its potential behaviors. To define the ability to make a deposit into a bank account, we define a method containing programming statements that will update the account balance accordingly.

An object is defined by a *class*. A class is the model or blueprint from which an object is created. Consider the blueprint created by an architect when designing a house. The blueprint defines the important characteristics of the house—its walls, windows, doors, electrical outlets, and so on. Once the blueprint is created, several houses can be built using it, as depicted in Figure 1.22.

In one sense, the houses built from the blueprint are different. They are in different locations, have different addresses, contain different furniture, and are inhabited by different people. Yet in many ways they are the "same" house. The layout of the rooms and other crucial characteristics are the same in each. To create a different house, we would need a different blueprint.

A class is a blueprint of an object. It establishes the kind of data an object of that type will hold and defines the methods that represent the behavior of such objects. However, a class is not an object any more than a blueprint is a house.

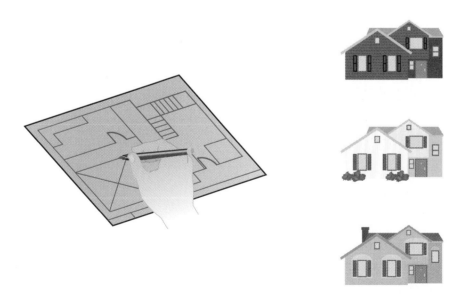

FIGURE 1.22   A house blueprint and three houses created from it

In general, a class contains no space to store data. Each object has space for its own data, which is why each object can have its own state.

Once a class has been defined, multiple objects can be created from that class. For example, once we define a class to represent the concept of a bank account, we can create multiple objects that represent specific, individual bank accounts. Each bank account object would keep track of its own balance.

An object should be *encapsulated,* which means it protects and manages its own information. That is, an object should be self-governing. The only changes made to the state of the object should be accomplished by that object's methods. We should design objects so that other objects cannot "reach in" and change its state.

Classes can be created from other classes by using *inheritance.* That is, the definition of one class can be based on another class that already exists. Inheritance is a form of *software reuse,* capitalizing on the similarities between various kinds of classes that we may want to create. One class can be used to derive several new classes. Derived classes can then be used to derive even more classes. This creates a hierarchy of classes, where the attributes and methods defined in one class are inherited by its children, which in turn pass them on to their children, and so on. For example, we might create a hierarchy of classes that represent various types of accounts. Common characteristics are defined in high-level classes, and specific differences are defined in derived classes.

Polymorphism is the idea that we can refer to multiple types of related objects over time in consistent ways. It gives us the ability to design powerful and elegant solutions to problems that deal with multiple objects.

Some of the core object-oriented concepts are depicted in Figure 1.23. We don't expect you to understand these ideas fully at this point. Most of this book is designed to flesh out these ideas. This overview is intended only to set the stage.

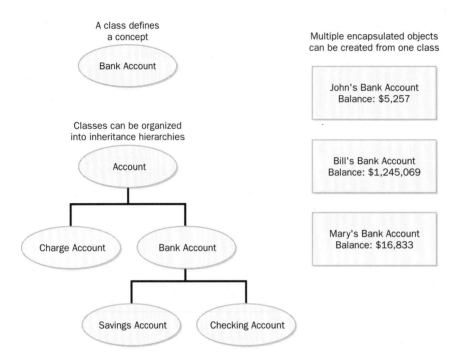

FIGURE 1.23   Various aspects of object-oriented software

Summary of Key Concepts

> A computer system consists of hardware and software that work in concert to help us solve problems.

> The CPU reads the program instructions from main memory, executing them one at a time until the program ends.

> The operating system provides a user interface and manages computer resources.

> As far as the user is concerned, the interface *is* the program.

> Digital computers store information by breaking it into pieces and representing each piece as a number.

> Binary is used to store information in a computer because the devices that store and manipulate binary data are inexpensive and reliable.

> There are exactly 2^N combinations of N bits. Therefore, N bits can represent up to 2^N unique items.

> The core of a computer is made up of main memory, which stores programs and data, and the CPU, which executes program instructions one at a time.

> An address is a unique number associated with each memory location.

> Main memory is volatile, meaning the stored information is maintained only as long as electric power is supplied.

> The surface of a CD has both smooth areas and small pits. A pit represents a binary 1 and a smooth area represents a binary 0.

> A rewritable CD simulates the pits and smooth areas of a regular CD by using a coating that can be made amorphous or crystalline as needed.

> The fetch-decode-execute cycle forms the foundation of computer processing.

> A network consists of two or more computers connected together so that they can exchange information.

> Sharing a communication line creates delays, but it is cost effective and simplifies adding new computers to the network.

> A local-area network (LAN) is an effective way to share information and resources throughout an organization.

> The Internet is a wide-area network (WAN) that spans the globe.

> Every computer connected to the Internet has an IP address that uniquely identifies it.

> The World Wide Web is software that makes sharing information across a network easy.

> A URL uniquely specifies documents and other information found on the Web for a browser to obtain and display.

> This book focuses on the principles of object-oriented programming.

> Comments do not affect a program's processing; instead, they serve to facilitate human comprehension.

> Inline documentation should provide insight into your code. It should not be ambiguous or belabor the obvious.

> Java is case sensitive. The uppercase and lowercase versions of a letter are distinct.

> Identifier names should be descriptive and readable.

> Appropriate use of white space makes a program easier to read and understand.

> You should adhere to a set of guidelines that establish the way you format and document your programs.

> All programs must be translated to a particular CPU's machine language in order to be executed.

> High-level languages allow a programmer to ignore the underlying details of machine language.

> A Java compiler translates Java source code into Java bytecode, a low-level, architecture-neutral representation of the program.

> Many different development environments exist to help you create and modify Java programs.

> Syntax rules dictate the form of a program. Semantics dictate the meaning of the program statements.

> The programmer is responsible for the accuracy and reliability of a program.

> A Java program must be syntactically correct or the compiler will not produce bytecode.

> Object-oriented programming helps us solve problems, which is the purpose of writing a program.

> Program design involves breaking a solution down into manageable pieces.

> Each object has a state, defined by its attributes, and a set of behaviors, defined by its methods.

> A class is a blueprint of an object. Multiple objects can be created from one class definition.

Self-Review Questions

SR 1.1   What is hardware? What is software?

SR 1.2   What are the two primary functions of an operating system?

SR 1.3   What happens to information when it is stored digitally?

SR 1.4   How many unique items can be represented with the following?

    a. 2 bits

    b. 4 bits

    c. 5 bits

    d. 7 bits

SR 1.5   How many bits are there in each of the following?

    a. 8 bytes

    b. 2 KB

    c. 4 MB

SR 1.6   What are the two primary hardware components in a computer? How do they interact?

SR 1.7   What is a memory address?

SR 1.8   What does volatile mean? Which memory devices are volatile and which are nonvolatile?

SR 1.9   What is a file server?

SR 1.10   What is the total number of communication lines needed for a fully connected point-to-point network of five computers? Six computers?

SR 1.11   What is the origin of the word Internet?

SR 1.12   Explain the parts of the following URLs:

    a. duke.csc.villanova.edu/jss/examples.html

    b. java.sun.com/products/index.html

SR 1.13   What is the relationship between a high-level language and machine language?

SR 1.14   What is Java bytecode?

SR 1.15   What is white space? How does it affect program execution? How does it affect program readability?

SR 1.16   Which of the following are not valid Java identifiers? Why?

a. `RESULT`

b. `result`

c. `12345`

d. `x12345y`

e. `black&white`

f. `answer_7`

SR 1.17   What do we mean by the syntax and semantics of a programming language?

SR 1.18   What are the primary concepts that support object-oriented programming?

Exercises

EX 1.1   Describe the hardware components of your personal computer or of a computer in a lab to which you have access. Include the processor type and speed, storage capacities of main and secondary memory, and types of I/O devices. Explain how you determined your answers.

EX 1.2   Why do we use the binary number system to store information on a computer?

EX 1.3   How many unique items can be represented with each of the following?

a. 1 bit

b. 3 bits

c. 6 bits

d. 8 bits

e. 10 bits

f. 16 bits

EX 1.4   If a picture is made up of 128 possible colors, how many bits would be needed to store each pixel of the picture? Why?

EX 1.5   If a language uses 240 unique letters and symbols, how many bits would be needed to store each character of a document? Why?

EX 1.6   How many bits are there in each of the following? How many bytes are there in each?

a. 12 KB

b. 5 MB

c. 3 GB

d. 2 TB

EX 1.7   Explain the difference between random access memory (RAM) and read-only memory (ROM).

EX 1.8   A disk is a random-access device but it is not RAM (random access memory). Explain.

EX 1.9   Determine how your computer, or a computer in a lab to which you have access, is connected to others across a network. Is it linked to the Internet? Draw a diagram to show the basic connections in your environment.

EX 1.10   Explain the differences between a local-area network (LAN) and a wide-area network (WAN). What is the relationship between them?

EX 1.11   What is the total number of communication lines needed for a fully connected point-to-point network of eight computers? Nine computers? Ten computers? What is a general formula for determining this result?

EX 1.12   Explain the difference between the Internet and the World Wide Web.

EX 1.13   List and explain the parts of the URLs for:

a. your school

b. the Computer Science department of your school

c. your instructor's Web page

EX 1.14 Use a Web browser to access information through the Web about the following topics. For each one, explain the process you used to find the information and record the specific URLs you found.

    a. the Philadelphia Phillies baseball team

    b. wine production in California

    c. the subway systems in two major cities

    d. vacation opportunities in the Caribbean

EX 1.15 Give examples of the two types of Java comments and explain the differences between them.

EX 1.16 Which of the following are not valid Java identifiers? Why?

    a. `Factorial`

    b. `anExtremelyLongIdentifierIfYouAskMe`

    c. `2ndLevel`

    d. `level2`

    e. `MAX_SIZE`

    f. `highest$`

    g. `hook&ladder`

EX 1.17 Why are the following valid Java identifiers not considered good identifiers?

    a. `q`

    b. `totVal`

    c. `theNextValueInTheList`

EX 1.18 Java is case sensitive. What does that mean?

EX 1.19 What do we mean when we say that the English language is ambiguous? Give two examples of English ambiguity (other than the example used in this chapter) and explain the ambiguity. Why is ambiguity a problem for programming languages?

EX 1.20   Categorize each of the following situations as a compile-time error, run-time error, or logical error.

a. multiplying two numbers when you meant to add them

b. dividing by zero

c. forgetting a semicolon at the end of a programming statement

d. spelling a word wrong in the output

e. producing inaccurate results

f. typing a { when you should have typed (

Programming Projects

PP 1.1   Enter, compile, and run the following application:

```
public class Test
{
    public static void main (String[] args)
    {
        System.out.println ("An Emergency Broadcast");
    }
}
```

PP 1.2   Introduce the following errors, one at a time, to the program from the programming project 1.1. Record any error messages that the compiler produces. Fix the previous error each time before you introduce a new one. If no error messages are produced, explain why. Try to predict what will happen before you make each change.

a. change Test to test

b. change Emergency to emergency

c. remove the first quotation mark in the string

d. remove the last quotation mark in the string

e. change main to man

f. change println to bogus

g. remove the semicolon at the end of the println statement

h. remove the last brace in the program

PP 1.3   Write an application that prints, on separate lines, your name, your birthday, your hobbies, your favorite book, and your favorite movie. Label each piece of information in the output.

PP 1.4   Write an application that prints the phrase `Knowledge is Power`:

a. on one line

b. on three lines, one word per line, with the words centered relative to each other

c. inside a box made up of the characters = and |

PP 1.5   Write an application that prints a list of four or five web sites that you enjoy. Print both the site name and the URL.

PP 1.6   Write an application that prints the first few verses of a song (your choice). Label the chorus.

PP 1.7   Write an application that prints the following diamond shape. Don't print any unneeded characters. (That is, don't make any character string longer than it has to be.)

```
        *
       ***
      *****
     *******
    *********
     *******
      *****
       ***
        *
```

PP 1.8   Write an application that displays your initials in large block letters. Make each large letter out of the corresponding regular character. For example:

```
JJJJJJJJJJJJJJJ    AAAAAAAAA    LLLL
JJJJJJJJJJJJJJJ   AAAAAAAAAAA   LLLL
         JJJJ     AAA     AAA   LLLL
         JJJJ     AAA     AAA   LLLL
         JJJJ     AAAAAAAAAAA   LLLL
J        JJJJ     AAAAAAAAAAA   LLLL
JJ       JJJJ     AAA     AAA   LLLL
 JJJJJJJJJJJ      AAA     AAA   LLLLLLLLLLLLLL
  JJJJJJJJJ       AAA     AAA   LLLLLLLLLLLLLL
```

Answers to Self-Review Questions

SR 1.1   The hardware of a computer system consists of its physical components such as a circuit board, monitor, or keyboard. Computer software are the programs that are executed by the hardware and the data that those programs use. Hardware is tangible, whereas software is intangible. In order to be useful, hardware requires software and software requires hardware.

SR 1.2   The operating system provides a user interface and efficiently coordinates the use of resources such as main memory and the CPU.

SR 1.3   The information is broken into pieces, and those pieces are represented as numbers.

SR 1.4   In general, N bits can represent 2^N unique items. Therefore:

a. 2 bits can represent 4 items because $2^2 = 4$.

b. 4 bits can represent 16 items because $2^4 = 16$.

c. 5 bits can represent 32 items because $2^5 = 32$.

d. 7 bits can represent 128 items because $2^7 = 128$.

SR 1.5   There are eight bits in a byte. Therefore:

a. 8 bytes = 8 * 8 bits = 64 bits

b. 2 KB = 2 * 1,024 bytes = 2,048 bytes = 2,048 * 8 bits = 16,384 bits

c. 4 MB = 4 * 1,048,576 bytes = 4,194,304 bytes = 4,194,304 * 8 bits = 33,554,432 bits

SR 1.6   The two primary hardware components are main memory and the CPU. Main memory holds the currently active programs and data. The CPU retrieves individual program instructions from main memory, one at a time, and executes them.

SR 1.7   A memory address is a number that uniquely identifies a particular memory location in which a value is stored.

SR 1.8   Main memory is volatile, which means the information that is stored in it will be lost if the power supply to the computer is turned off. Secondary memory devices are nonvolatile; therefore the information that is stored on them is retained even if the power goes off.

SR 1.9   A file server is a network computer that is dedicated to storing and providing programs and data that are needed by many network users.

SR 1.10   Counting the number of unique connections in Figure 1.16, there are 10 communication lines needed to fully connect a point-to-point network of five computers. Adding a sixth computer to the network will require that it be connected to the original five, bringing the total to 15 communication lines.

SR 1.11   The word Internet comes from the word internetworking, a concept related to wide-area networks (WANs). An internetwork connects one network to another. The Internet is a WAN.

SR 1.12   Breaking down the parts of each URL:

a. duke is the name of a computer within the csc subdomain (the Department of Computing Sciences) of the villanova.edu domain, which represents Villanova University. The edu top-level domain indicates that it is an educational organization. This URL is requesting a file called examples.html from within a subdirectory called jss.

b. java is the name of a computer (Web server) at the sun.com domain, which represents Sun Microsystems, Inc. The com top-level domain indicates that it is a commercial business. This URL is requesting a file called index.html from within a subdirectory called products.

SR 1.13   High-level languages allow a programmer to express a series of program instructions in English-like terms that are relatively easy to read and use. However, in order to execute, a program must be expressed in a particular computer's machine language, which consists of a series of bits that are basically unreadable by humans. A high-level language program must be translated into machine language before it can be run.

SR 1.14   Java bytecode is a low-level representation of a Java source code program. The Java compiler translates the source code into bytecode, which can then be executed using the Java interpreter. The bytecode might be transported across the Web before being executed by a Java interpreter that is part of a Web browser.

SR 1.15 White space is a term that refers to the spaces, tabs, and newline characters that separate words and symbols in a program. The compiler ignores extra white space; therefore, it doesn't affect execution. However, it is crucial to use white space appropriately to make a program readable to humans.

SR 1.16 All of the identifiers shown are valid except `12345` (since an identifier cannot begin with a digit) and `black&white` (since an identifier cannot contain the character &). The identifiers `RESULT` and `result` are both valid, but should not be used together in a program because they differ only by case. The underscore character (as in `answer_7`) is a valid part of an identifier.

SR 1.17 Syntax rules define how the symbols and words of a programming language can be put together. The semantics of a programming language instruction determine what will happen when that instruction is executed.

SR 1.18 The primary elements that support object-oriented programming are objects, classes, encapsulation, and inheritance. An object is defined by a class, which contains methods that define the operations on those objects (the services that they perform). Objects are encapsulated such that they store and manage their own data. Inheritance is a reuse technique in which one class can be derived from another.

Data and Expressions

2

CHAPTER OBJECTIVES

> Discuss the use of character strings, concatenation, and escape sequences.

> Explore the declaration and use of variables.

> Describe the Java primitive data types.

> Discuss the syntax and processing of expressions.

> Define the types of data conversions and the mechanisms for accomplishing them.

> Introduce the Scanner class to create interactive programs.

> Explore basic graphics concepts and the techniques for drawing shapes.

> Introduce the concept of a Java applet.

This chapter explores some of the basic types of data used in a Java program and the use of expressions to perform calculations. It discusses the conversion of data from one type to another, and how to read input interactively from the user running a program. This chapter also begins the Graphics Track for the book, in which we introduce the concepts of graphical programming, explore the relationship between Java and the Web, and delve into Java's abilities to manipulate color and draw shapes.

2.1 CHARACTER STRINGS

In Chapter 1 we discussed the basic structure of a Java program, including the use of comments, identifiers, and white space, using the Lincoln program as an example. Chapter 1 also included an overview of the various concepts involved in object-oriented programming, such as objects, classes, and methods. Take a moment to review these ideas if necessary.

A character string is an object in Java, defined by the class String. Because strings are so fundamental to computer programming, Java provides the ability to use a *string literal*, delimited by double quotation characters, as we've seen in previous examples. We explore the String class and its methods in more detail in Chapter 3. For now, let's explore the use of string literals in more detail.

The following are all examples of valid string literals:

```
"The quick brown fox jumped over the lazy dog."
"602 Greenbriar Court, Chalfont PA 18914"
"x"
""
```

A string literal can contain any valid characters, including numeric digits, punctuation, and other special characters. The last example in the list above contains no characters at all.

The print and println Methods

In the Lincoln program in Chapter 1, we invoked the println method as follows:

```
System.out.println ("Whatever you are, be a good one.");
```

This statement demonstrates the use of objects. The System.out object represents an output device or file, which by default is the monitor screen. To be more precise, the object's name is out and it is stored in the System class. We explore that relationship in more detail at the appropriate point in the text.

The println method is a service that the System.out object performs for us. Whenever we request it, the object will print a character string to the screen. We can say that we send the println message to the System.out object to request that some text be printed.

Each piece of data that we send to a method is called a *parameter*. In this case, the println method takes only one parameter: the string of characters to be printed.

The `System.out` object also provides another service we can use: the `print` method. The difference between `print` and `println` is small but important. The `println` method prints the information sent to it, then moves to the beginning of the next line. The `print` method is similar to `println`, but does not advance to the next line when completed.

> **Key Concept**
>
> The `print` and `println` methods represent two services provided by the `System.out` object.

The program shown in Listing 2.1 is called `Countdown`, and it invokes both the `print` and `println` methods.

Carefully compare the output of the `Countdown` program, shown at the bottom of the program listing, to the program code. Note that the word `Liftoff` is printed on the same line as the first few words, even though it is printed using the `println` method. Remember that the `println` method moves to the beginning of the next line *after* the information passed to it is printed.

Listing 2.1

```java
//********************************************************************
//  Countdown.java        Author: Lewis/Loftus
//
//  Demonstrates the difference between print and println.
//********************************************************************

public class Countdown
{
   //-----------------------------------------------------------------
   //  Prints two lines of output representing a rocket countdown.
   //-----------------------------------------------------------------
   public static void main (String[] args)
   {
      System.out.print ("Three... ");
      System.out.print ("Two... ");
      System.out.print ("One... ");
      System.out.print ("Zero... ");

      System.out.println ("Liftoff!"); // appears on first output line

      System.out.println ("Houston, we have a problem.");
   }
}
```

Output

```
Three... Two... One... Zero... Liftoff!
Houston, we have a problem.
```

String Concatenation

A string literal cannot span multiple lines in a program. The following program statement is improper syntax and would produce an error when attempting to compile:

```
// The following statement will not compile
System.out.println ("The only stupid question is
the one that's not asked.");
```

When we want to print a string that is too long to fit on one line in a program, we can rely on *string concatenation* to append one string to the end of another. The string concatenation operator is the plus sign (+). The following expression concatenates one character string to another, producing one long string:

```
"The only stupid question is " + "the one that's not asked."
```

The program called `Facts` shown in Listing 2.2 contains several `println` statements. The first one prints a sentence that is somewhat long and will not fit on one line of the program. Since a character literal cannot span two lines in a program, we split the string into two and use string concatenation to append them. Therefore, the string concatenation operation in the first `println` statement results in one large string that is passed to the method to be printed.

Note that we don't have to pass any information to the `println` method, as shown in the second line of the `Facts` program. This call does not print any visible characters, but it does move to the next line of output. So in this case calling `println` with no parameters has the effect of printing a blank line.

The last three calls to `println` in the `Facts` program demonstrate another interesting thing about string concatenation: Strings can be concatenated with numbers. Note that the numbers in those lines are not enclosed in double quotes and are therefore not character strings. In these cases, the number is automatically converted to a string, and then the two strings are concatenated.

Because we are printing particular values, we simply could have included the numeric value as part of the string literal, such as:

```
"Speed of ketchup: 40 km per year"
```

Digits are characters and can be included in strings as needed. We separate them in the `Facts` program to demonstrate the ability to concatenate a string and a number. This technique will be useful in upcoming examples.

As you can imagine, the + operator is also used for arithmetic addition. Therefore, what the + operator does depends on the types of data on which it

This book is dedicated to our families.
Sharon, Justin, and Kayla Lewis
and
Veena, Isaac, and Dévi Loftus

Publisher	Greg Tobin
Senior Acquisitions Editor	Michael Hirsch
Editorial Assistant	Lindsey Triebel
Production Supervisor	Marilyn Lloyd
Digital Assets Manager	Marianne Groth
Marketing Manager	Michelle Brown
Marketing Assistant	Dana Lopreato
Senior Prepress Supervisor	Caroline Fell
Senior Media Buyer	Ginny Michaud
Cover Design	Suzanne Heiser/Night & Day Design
Project Management, Composition, and Illustrations	Argosy Publishing
Cover Design Supervisor	Joyce Cosentino Wells
Cover Image	© 2005 Brand X Pictures

Access the latest information about Addison-Wesley titles from our World Wide Web site: http://www.aw-bc.com/computing.

Many of the designations used by manufacturers and sellers to distinguish their products are claimed as trademarks. Where those designations appear in this book, and Addison-Wesley was aware of a trademark claim, the designations have been printed in initial caps or all caps.

The programs and applications presented in this book have been included for their instructional value. They have been tested with care, but are not guaranteed for any particular purpose. The publisher does not offer any warranties or representations, nor does it accept any liabilities with respect to the programs or applications.

Library of Congress Cataloging-in-Publication Data

Lewis, John, 1963-
  Java software solutions : foundations of program design / John Lewis, William Loftus.-- 5th ed.
      p. cm.
  1. Java (Computer program language) 2. Object-oriented programming (Computer science) I. Loftus, William. II. Title.
  QA76.73.J38L49 2006
  005.13'3--dc22

                              2005034748

For information on obtaining permission for use of material in this work, please submit a written request to Pearson Education, Inc., Rights and Contracts Department, 75 Arlington Street, Suite 300, Boston, MA 02116, fax your request to 617-848-7047, or e-mail at http://www.pearsoned.com/legal/permissions.htm.

ISBN 0-321-40949-3

1 2 3 4 5 6 7 8 9 10—QWT—09 08 07 06

SOFTWARE SOLUTIONS
foundations of program design
fifth edition

JOHN LEWIS
Villanova University

WILLIAM LOFTUS
Gestalt, LLC

PEARSON

Addison
Wesley

Boston San Francisco New York
London Toronto Sydney Tokyo Singapore Madrid
Mexico City Munich Paris Cape Town Hong Kong Montreal

java™
SOFTWARE SOLUTIONS
foundations of program design
fifth edition

Contents

Exercises. These intermediate problems require computations, the analysis or writing of code fragments, and probing questions about the chapter content. While the exercises may deal with code, they generally do not require any online activity.

Programming Projects. These problems require the design and implementation of Java programs. They vary widely in level of difficulty.

Addison-Wesley's MyCodeMate. Working online, students can view, compile, run, and edit select programming problems and all code listings from the textbook. Look for this MyCodeMate icon to see which Programming Projects are available with your included online subscription to MyCodeMate.

Summary of Key Concepts

> An object, with its well-defined interface, is a perfect mechanism for implementing a collection.

> The size of a dynamic data structure grows and shrinks as needed.

> A dynamically linked list is managed by storing and updating references to objects.

> Insert and delete operations can be implemented by carefully manipulating object references.

> Many variations on the implementation of dynamically linked lists can be defined.

> A queue is a linear data structure that manages data in a first-in, first-out manner.

> A stack is a linear data structure that manages data in a last-in, first-out manner.

> A tree is a non-linear data structure that organizes data into a hierarchy.

> A graph is a non-linear data structure that connects nodes using generic edges.

> The Java Collections API defines several collection classes implemented in various ways.

> The classes of the Java Collections API are implemented as generic types.

Summary of Key Concepts. The Key Concepts presented throughout a chapter are summarized at the end of the chapter.

Self-Review Questions and Answers. These short-answer questions review the fundamental ideas and terms established in the chapter. They are designed to allow students to assess their own basic grasp of the material. The answers to these questions can be found at the end of the problem sets.

Self-Review Questions

SR 12.1   What is a collection?

SR 12.2   Why are objects particularly well suited for implementing abstract data types?

SR 12.3   What is a dynamic data structure?

SR 12.4   Describe the steps, depicted in Figure 12.2, to insert a node into a list. What special cases exist?

Answers to Self-Review Questions

SR 12.1   A collection is an object whose purpose is to store and organize primitive data or other objects. Some collections represent classic data structures that are helpful in particular problem solving situations.

SR 12.2   An abstract data type (ADT) is a collection of data and the operations that can be performed on that data. An object is essentially the same thing in that we encapsulate related vari-

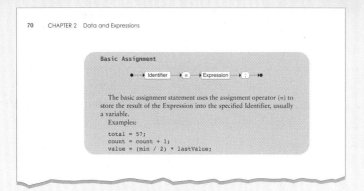

Basic Assignment

The basic assignment statement uses the assignment operator (=) to store the result of the Expression into the specified Identifier, usually a variable.
Examples:

```
total = 57;
count = count + 1;
value = (min / 2) * lastValue;
```

Syntax Diagrams. At appropriate points in the text, syntactic elements of the Java language are discussed in special highlighted sections with diagrams that clearly identify the valid forms for a statement or construct. Syntax diagrams for the entire Java language are presented in Appendix L.

Graphics Track. All processing that involves graphics and graphical user interfaces is discussed in one or two sections at the end of each chapter that we collectively refer to as the Graphics Track. This material can be skipped without loss of continuity, or focused on specifically as desired. The material in any Graphics Track section relates to the main topics of the chapter in which it is found. Graphics Track sections are indicated by a patterned border on the edge of the page.

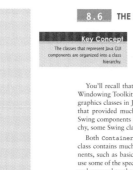

8.6   THE COMPONENT CLASS HIERARCHY

Key Concept

The classes that represent Java GUI components are organized into a class hierarchy.

All of the Java classes that define GUI components are part of a class hierarchy, shown in part in Figure 8.7. Almost all Swing GUI components are derived from the JComponent class, which defines how all components work in general. JComponent is derived from the Container class, which in turn is derived from the Component class.

You'll recall that there are two primary GUI APIs used in Java: the Abstract Windowing Toolkit (AWT) and the Swing classes. The AWT is the original set of graphics classes in Java. Swing classes were introduced later, adding components that provided much more functionality than their AWT counterparts. We use Swing components in our examples in this book. In the component class hierarchy, some Swing classes are ultimately derived from AWT classes.

Both Container and Component are original AWT classes. The Component class contains much of the general functionality that applies to all GUI components, such as basic painting and event handling. So although we may prefer to use some of the specific Swing components, they are based on core AWT concepts and respond to the same events as AWT components. Because they are derived from Container, many Swing components can serve as containers, though in most circumstances those abilities are curtailed. For example, we've seen that a JLabel object can contain an image, but it cannot be used as a generic container to which any component can be added.

Many features that apply to all Swing components are defined in the JComponent class and are inherited into its descendants. For example, we have the ability to put a border on any Swing component (as we saw in Chapter 6). This ability is defined once in the JComponent class and is inherited by any class that is derived, directly or indirectly, from it.

Feature Walkthrough

Key Concepts. Throughout the text, the Key Concept boxes highlight fundamental ideas and important guidelines. These concepts are summarized at the end of each chapter.

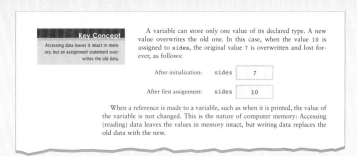

Key Concept

Accessing data leaves it intact in memory, but an assignment statement overwrites the old data.

A variable can store only one value of its declared type. A new value overwrites the old one. In this case, when the value 10 is assigned to sides, the original value 7 is overwritten and lost forever, as follows:

After initialization:	sides	7
After first assignment:	sides	10

When a reference is made to a variable, such as when it is printed, the value of the variable is not changed. This is the nature of computer memory: Accessing (reading) data leaves the values in memory intact, but writing data replaces the old data with the new.

Listing 10.3

```
//********************************************************************
//  Propagation.java       Author: Lewis/Loftus
//
//  Demonstrates exception propagation.
//********************************************************************

public class Propagation
{
    //-----------------------------------------------------------------
    //  Invokes the level1 method to begin the exception demonstration.
    //-----------------------------------------------------------------
    static public void main (String[] args)
    {
        ExceptionScope demo = new ExceptionScope();

        System.out.println("Program beginning.");
        demo.level1();
        System.out.println("Program ending.");
    }
}
```

Output

```
Program beginning.
Level 1 beginning.
Level 2 beginning.
Level 3 beginning.

The exception message is: / by zero

The call stack trace:
java.lang.ArithmeticException: / by zero
        at ExceptionScope.level3(ExceptionScope.java:54)
        at ExceptionScope.level2(ExceptionScope.java:41)
        at ExceptionScope.level1(ExceptionScope.java:18)
        at Propagation.main(Propagation.java:17)

Level 1 ending.
Program ending.
```

Listings. All programming examples are presented in clearly labeled listings, followed by the program output, a sample run, or screen shot display as appropriate. The code is colored to visually distinguish comments and reserved words.

Many other people have helped in various ways. They include Ken Arnold, Mike Czepiel, John Loftus, Sebastian Niezgoda, and Sammy Perugini. Our apologies to anyone we may have forgotten.

The ACM Special Interest Group on Computer Science Education (SIGCSE) is a tremendous resource. Their conferences provide an opportunity for educators from all levels and all types of schools to share ideas and materials. If you are an educator in any area of computing and are not involved with SIGCSE, you're missing out.

Hans-Peter Bischof	Rochester Institute of Technology
Robert Burton	Brigham Young University
James Cross	Auburn University
Robert Cohen	University of Massachusetts, Boston
Eman El-Sheikh	University of West Florida
Christopher Eliot	University of Massachusetts, Amherst
Matt Evett	Eastern Michigan University
John Gauch	University of Kansas
Chris Haynes	Indiana University
Laurie Hendren	McGill University
James Heliotis	Rochester Institute of Technology
Mike Higgs	Austin College
Karen Kluge	Dartmouth College
Jason Levy	University of Hawaii
Peter MacKenzie	McGill University
Blayne Mayfield	Oklahoma State University
Faye Navabi-Tadayon	Arizona State University
Lawrence Osborne	Lamar University
Barry Pollack	City College of San Francisco
B. Ravikumar	University of Rhode Island
David Riley	University of Wisconsin (La Crosse)
Jerry Ross	Lane Community College
Carolyn Schauble	Colorado State University
Arjit Sengupta	Georgia State University
Vijay Srinivasan	JavaSoft, Sun Microsystems, Inc.
Katherine St. John	Lehman College, CUNY
Ed Timmerman	University of Maryland, University College
Shengru Tu	University of New Orleans
Paul Tymann	Rochester Institute of Technology
John J. Wegis	JavaSoft, Sun Microsystems, Inc.
Linda Wilson	Dartmouth College
David Wittenberg	Brandeis University
Wang-Chan Wong	California State University (Dominguez Hills)

Thanks also go to my colleagues at Villanova University who have provided so much wonderful feedback. They include Bob Beck, Cathy Helwig, Dan Joyce, Anany Levitin, Najib Nadi, Beth Taddei, and Barbara Zimmerman.

Special thanks go to Pete DePasquale of The College of New Jersey for the design and evolution of the PaintBox project, as well as the original Java Class Library appendix.

Instructor Resources

The following supplements are available to qualified instructors only. Visit the Addison-Wesley Instructor Resource Center (www.aw.com/irc) or send an e-mail to computing@aw.com for information on how to access them:

> Presentation Slides—in PowerPoint.
> Solutions—includes solutions to exercises and programming projects.
> Test Bank with powerful test generator software—includes a wealth of free response, multiple-choice, and true/false type questions.
> Lab Manual—lab exercises are designed to accompany the topic progression in the text. A printed version of this manual is also available.

Acknowledgments

We are most grateful to the faculty and students from around the world who have provided their feedback on previous editions of this book. We are pleased to see the depth of the faculty's concern for their students and the students' thirst for knowledge. Your comments and questions are always welcome.

We continue to be amazed at the talent and effort demonstrated by the team at Addison-Wesley. Michael Hirsch, our editor, has amazing insight and commitment. His assistant, Lindsey Triebel, is a source of consistent and helpful support. Marketing Manager Michelle Brown makes sure that instructors understand the pedagogical advantages of the text. The cover and interior design were designed by the skilled talents of Joyce Wells. Marilyn Lloyd led the production effort. The Addison-Wesley folks are supported by a phenomenal team at Argosy Publishing, including Megan Schwenke and Edalin Michael. We thank all of these people for ensuring that this book meets the highest quality standards.

Special thanks go to the following people who provided valuable advice to us about this book via their participation in focus groups, interviews, and reviews: Robert Burton—Brigham Young University; John Chandler—Oklahoma State University; Dave Musicant—Carleton College; Patricia Roth—Southern Polytechnic State University; Saroja Kanchi—Kettering University; Elizabeth Adams—James Madison University; Stuart Steiner—Eastern Washington University; Laurie Murphy—Pacific Lutheran University; Dodi Coreson—Linn Benton Community College.

The reviewers of previous editions of this text, as well as many other instructors and friends, have provided valuable feedback. They include:

Lewis Barnett   University of Richmond
Tom Bennet   Mississippi College
Gian Mario Besana   DePaul University

Chapter 11 (Recursion) covers the concept, implementation, and proper use of recursion. Several examples from various domains are used to demonstrate how recursive techniques make certain types of processing elegant.

Chapter 12 (Data Structures) introduces the idea of a collection and its underlying data structure. Abstraction is revisited in this context and the classic data structures are explored. Generic types are introduced as well. This chapter serves as an introduction to a CS2 course.

Supplements

Student CD

This CD includes:

> Source code for all the programs in the text.
> Various Java development environments.

If a CD did not come with your book or you can't locate your CD, you can access most of these items at www.aw.com/cssupport

Other CDs Upon Request

Professors using this book in a course may want to order it with one of many other available Java development environments. Contact your campus Addison-Wesley representative for a list of current IDEs and their specific ISBNs to order.

MyCodeMate—Your Own T.A. Just a Click Away

Addison-Wesley's *MyCodeMate* is a book-specific Web resource that provides tutorial help and evaluation of student programs. Example programs throughout the book and selected Programming Projects from every chapter have been integrated into *MyCodeMate*. Using this tool, a student is able to write and compile programs from any computer with Internet access, and receive guidance and feedback on how to proceed and on how to address compiler error messages. Instructors can track each student's progress on Programming Projects from the text or can develop projects of their own. **A complementary subscription of *MyCodeMate* is offered when the access code is ordered in a package with a new copy of this text.** Subscriptions can also be purchased online. For more information visit www.mycodemate.com, or contact your campus Addison-Wesley representative.

Chapter 2 (Data and Expressions) explores some of the basic types of data used in a Java program and the use of expressions to perform calculations. It discusses the conversion of data from one type to another, and how to read input interactively from the user with the help of the standard `Scanner` class.

Chapter 3 (Using Classes and Objects) explores the use of predefined classes and the objects that can be created from them. Classes and objects are used to manipulate character strings, produce random numbers, perform complex calculations, and format output. Enumerated types are also discussed.

Chapter 4 (Writing Classes) explores the basic issues related to writing classes and methods. Topics include instance data, visibility, scope, method parameters, and return types. Encapsulation and constructors are covered as well. Some of the more involved topics are deferred to or revisited in Chapter 6.

Chapter 5 (Conditionals and Loops) covers the use of boolean expressions to make decisions. All related statements for conditionals and loops are discussed, including the enhanced version of the `for` loop. The `Scanner` class is revisited for iterative input parsing and reading text files.

Chapter 6 (Object-Oriented Design) reinforces and extends the coverage of issues related to the design of classes. Techniques for identifying the classes and objects needed for a problem and the relationships among them are discussed. This chapter also covers static class members, interfaces, and the design of enumerated type classes. Method design issues and method overloading are also discussed.

Chapter 7 (Arrays) contains extensive coverage of arrays and array processing. Topics include command-line arguments, variable length parameter lists, and multidimensional arrays. The `ArrayList` class and its use as a generic type is explored as well.

Chapter 8 (Inheritance) covers class derivations and associated concepts such as class hierarchies, overriding, and visibility. Strong emphasis is put on the proper use of inheritance and its role in software design.

Chapter 9 (Polymorphism) explores the concept of binding and how it relates to polymorphism. Then we examine how polymorphic references can be accomplished using either inheritance or interfaces. Sorting is used as an example of polymorphism. Design issues related to polymorphism are examined as well.

Chapter 10 (Exceptions) explores the class hierarchy from the Java standard library used to define exceptions, as well as the ability to define our own exception objects. We also discuss the use of exceptions when dealing with input and output, and examine an example that writes a text file.

Cornerstones of the Text

This text is based on the following basic ideas that we believe make for a sound introductory text:

> *True object-orientation.* A text that really teaches a solid object-oriented approach must use what we call object-speak. That is, all processing should be discussed in object-oriented terms. That does not mean, however, that the first program a student sees must discuss the writing of multiple classes and methods. A student should learn to use objects before learning to write them. This text uses a natural progression that culminates in the ability to design real object-oriented solutions.

> *Sound programming practices.* Students should not be taught how to program; they should be taught how to write good software. There's a difference. Writing software is not a set of cookbook actions, and a good program is more than a collection of statements. This text integrates practices that serve as the foundation of good programming skills. These practices are used in all examples and are reinforced in the discussions. Students learn how to solve problems as well as how to implement solutions. We introduce and integrate basic software engineering techniques throughout the text.

> *Examples.* Students learn by example. This text is filled with fully implemented examples that demonstrate specific concepts. We have intertwined small, readily understandable examples with larger, more realistic ones. There is a balance between graphics and nongraphics programs.

> *Graphics and GUIs.* Graphics can be a great motivator for students, and their use can serve as excellent examples of object-orientation. As such, we use them throughout the text in a well-defined set of sections that we call the Graphics Track. This coverage includes the use of event processing and GUIs. Students learn to build GUIs in the appropriate way by using a natural progression of topics. The Graphics Track can be avoided entirely for those who do not choose to use graphics.

Chapter Breakdown

Chapter 1 (Introduction) introduces computer systems in general, including basic architecture and hardware, networking, programming, and language translation. Java is introduced in this chapter, and the basics of general program development, as well as object-oriented programming, are discussed. This chapter contains broad introductory material that can be covered while students become familiar with their development environment.

Preface

Welcome to the Fifth Edition of *Java Software Solutions, Foundations of Program Design*. We are pleased that this book has served the needs of so many students and faculty over the years. This edition is designed to further enhance the pedagogy of introductory computing, particularly with enhanced support for the instructor.

The overall vision of the book has not changed significantly from that of previous editions. Feedback from both instructors and students has made it clear that we are hitting the mark in that regard. The emphasis remains on presenting underlying core concepts. The Graphics Track sections in each chapter still segregate the coverage of graphics and graphical user interfaces, giving extreme flexibility in how that material gets covered. The casual writing style and entertaining examples still rule the day.

One of the significant enhancements in this edition is an improved set of end-of-chapter materials. Additional problem sets have been added to the Self-Review Questions, Exercises, and Programming Projects in each chapter. Furthermore, they have been carefully organized to present a nice flow given the topics they address and their level of challenge.

Some key additions and improvements to the text itself have also been made, including a new introductory section in Chapter 4. These additions were designed to strengthen the existing flow of discussion, rather than modifying it. In addition, we've made a complete pass through the text, making numerous minor adjustments to eliminate ambiguities and bolster understanding.

One other key change was made for this edition: we chose to remove the API reference material in Appendix M from the printed text. It is still available online as a supplement for those who'd like to use it. However, the main reason for removing it was to guide students instead to the official API documentation available from the java.sun.com Web site. That resource is much more complete than the abbreviated version we were able to include in the text. Furthermore, it represents the proper, state-of-the-practice technique for looking up API details that professional programmers use every day. We should encourage our students to become familiar with and actively use that official resource.

Listing 2.2

```java
//********************************************************************
//  Facts.java       Author: Lewis/Loftus
//
//  Demonstrates the use of the string concatenation operator and the
//  automatic conversion of an integer to a string.
//********************************************************************

public class Facts
{
   //-----------------------------------------------------------------
   //  Prints various facts.
   //-----------------------------------------------------------------
   public static void main (String[] args)
   {
      // Strings can be concatenated into one long string
      System.out.println ("We present the following facts for your "
                          + "extracurricular edification:");

      System.out.println ();

      // A string can contain numeric digits
      System.out.println ("Letters in the Hawaiian alphabet: 12");

      // A numeric value can be concatenated to a string
      System.out.println ("Dialing code for Antarctica: " + 672);

      System.out.println ("Year in which Leonardo da Vinci invented "
                          + "the parachute: " + 1515);

      System.out.println ("Speed of ketchup: " + 40 + " km per year");
   }
}
```

Output

```
We present the following facts for your extracurricular edification:

Letters in the Hawaiian alphabet: 12
Dialing code for Antarctica: 672
Year in which Leonardo da Vinci invented the parachute: 1515
Speed of ketchup: 40 km per year
```

operates. If either or both of the operands of the + operator are strings, then string concatenation is performed.

The `Addition` program shown in Listing 2.3 demonstrates the distinction between string concatenation and arithmetic addition. The `Addition` program uses the + operator four times. In the first call to `println`, both + operations perform string concatenation, because the operators are executed left to right. The first operator concatenates the string with the first number (24), creating a larger string. Then that string is concatenated with the second number (45), creating an even larger string, which gets printed.

In the second call to `println`, we use parentheses to group the + operation with the two numeric operands. This forces that operation to happen first. Because both operands are numbers, the numbers are added in the arithmetic sense, producing the result 69. That number is then concatenated with the string, producing a larger string that gets printed.

Listing 2.3

```
//********************************************************************
//  Addition.java       Author: Lewis/Loftus
//
//  Demonstrates the difference between the addition and string
//  concatenation operators.
//********************************************************************

public class Addition
{
   //-----------------------------------------------------------------
   //  Concatenates and adds two numbers and prints the results.
   //-----------------------------------------------------------------
   public static void main (String[] args)
   {
      System.out.println ("24 and 45 concatenated: " + 24 + 45);

      System.out.println ("24 and 45 added: " + (24 + 45));
   }
}
```

Output

```
24 and 45 concatenated: 2445
24 and 45 added: 69
```

We revisit this type of situation later in this chapter when we formalize the precedence rules that define the order in which operators get evaluated.

Escape Sequences

Because the double quotation character (") is used in the Java language to indicate the beginning and end of a string, we must use a special technique to print the quotation character. If we simply put it in a string ("""), the compiler gets confused because it thinks the second quotation character is the end of the string and doesn't know what to do with the third one. This results in a compile-time error.

To overcome this problem, Java defines several *escape sequences* to represent special characters. An escape sequence begins with the backslash character (\), which indicates that the character or characters that follow should be interpreted in a special way. Figure 2.1 lists the Java escape sequences.

> **Key Concept**
>
> An escape sequence can be used to represent a character that would otherwise cause compilation problems.

The program in Listing 2.4, called `Roses`, prints some text resembling a poem. It uses only one `println` statement to do so, despite the fact that the poem is several lines long. Note the escape sequences used throughout the string. The \n escape sequence forces the output to a new line, and the \t escape sequence represents a tab character. The \" escape sequence ensures that the quote character is treated as part of the string, not the termination of it, which enables it to be printed as part of the output.

Escape Sequence	Meaning
\b	backspace
\t	tab
\n	newline
\r	carriage return
\"	double quote
\'	single quote
\\	backslash

FIGURE 2.1 Java escape sequences

Listing 2.4

```java
//********************************************************************
//  Roses.java         Author: Lewis/Loftus
//
//  Demonstrates the use of escape sequences.
//********************************************************************

public class Roses
{
   //-----------------------------------------------------------------
   //  Prints a poem (of sorts) on multiple lines.
   //-----------------------------------------------------------------
   public static void main (String[] args)
   {
      System.out.println ("Roses are red,\n\tViolets are blue,\n" +
         "Sugar is sweet,\n\tBut I have \"commitment issues\",\n\t" +
         "So I'd rather just be friends\n\tAt this point in our " +
         "relationship.");
   }
}
```

Output

```
Roses are red,
        Violets are blue,
Sugar is sweet,
        But I have "commitment issues",
        So I'd rather just be friends
        At this point in our relationship.
```

2.2   VARIABLES AND ASSIGNMENT

Most of the information we manage in a program is represented by variables. Let's examine how we declare and use them in a program.

> **Key Concept**
>
> A variable is a name for a memory location used to hold a value of a particular data type.

Variables

A *variable* is a name for a location in memory used to hold a data value. A variable declaration instructs the compiler to reserve a portion of main memory space large enough to hold a particular type of value and indicates the name by which we refer to that location.

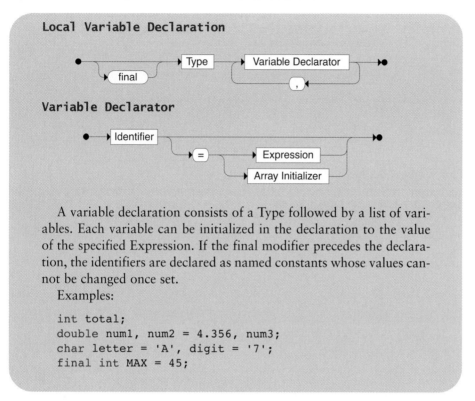

Local Variable Declaration

Variable Declarator

A variable declaration consists of a Type followed by a list of variables. Each variable can be initialized in the declaration to the value of the specified Expression. If the final modifier precedes the declaration, the identifiers are declared as named constants whose values cannot be changed once set.

Examples:

```
int total;
double num1, num2 = 4.356, num3;
char letter = 'A', digit = '7';
final int MAX = 45;
```

Consider the program `PianoKeys`, shown in Listing 2.5. The first line of the main method is the declaration of a variable named `keys` that holds an integer (`int`) value. The declaration also gives `keys` an initial value of 88. If an initial value is not specified for a variable, the value is undefined. Most Java compilers give errors or warnings if you attempt to use a variable before you've explicitly given it a value.

The `keys` variable, with its value, could be pictured as follows:

keys   88

In the `PianoKeys` program, two pieces of information are used in the call to the `println` method. The first is a string, and the second is the variable `keys`. When a variable is referenced, the value currently stored in it is used. Therefore, when the call to `println` is executed, the value of `keys`, which is 88, is obtained.

Listing 2.5

```
//********************************************************************
//  PianoKeys.java        Author: Lewis/Loftus
//
//  Demonstrates the declaration, initialization, and use of an
//  integer variable.
//********************************************************************

public class PianoKeys
{
   //-----------------------------------------------------------------
   //  Prints the number of keys on a piano.
   //-----------------------------------------------------------------
   public static void main (String[] args)
   {
      int keys = 88;

      System.out.println ("A piano has " + keys + " keys.");
   }
}
```

Output

```
A piano has 88 keys.
```

Because that value is an integer, it is automatically converted to a string and concatenated with the initial string. The concatenated string is passed to `println` and printed.

A variable declaration can have multiple variables of the same type declared on one line. Each variable on the line can be declared with or without an initializing value. For example:

```
int count, minimum = 0, result;
```

The Assignment Statement

Let's examine a program that changes the value of a variable. Listing 2.6 shows a program called `Geometry`. This program first declares an integer variable called `sides` and initializes it to 7. It then prints out the current value of `sides`.

Listing 2.6

```java
//********************************************************************
//  Geometry.java       Author: Lewis/Loftus
//
//  Demonstrates the use of an assignment statement to change the
//  value stored in a variable.
//********************************************************************

public class Geometry
{
    //-----------------------------------------------------------------
    //  Prints the number of sides of several geometric shapes.
    //-----------------------------------------------------------------
    public static void main (String[] args)
    {
        int sides = 7;  // declaration with initialization
        System.out.println ("A heptagon has " + sides + " sides.");

        sides = 10;  // assignment statement
        System.out.println ("A decagon has " + sides + " sides.");

        sides = 12;
        System.out.println ("A dodecagon has " + sides + " sides.");
    }
}
```

Output

```
A heptagon has 7 sides.
A decagon has 10 sides.
A dodecagon has 12 sides.
```

The next line in main changes the value stored in the variable sides:

```
sides = 10;
```

This is called an *assignment statement* because it assigns a value to a variable. When executed, the expression on the right-hand side of the assignment operator (=) is evaluated, and the result is stored in the memory location indicated by the variable on the left-hand side. In this example, the expression is simply a number, 10. We discuss expressions that are more involved than this in the next section.

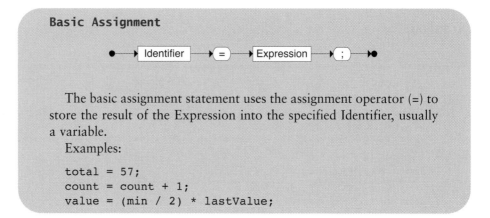

Basic Assignment

Identifier → = → Expression → ;

The basic assignment statement uses the assignment operator (=) to store the result of the Expression into the specified Identifier, usually a variable.
Examples:

```
total = 57;
count = count + 1;
value = (min / 2) * lastValue;
```

A variable can store only one value of its declared type. A new value overwrites the old one. In this case, when the value 10 is assigned to sides, the original value 7 is overwritten and lost forever, as follows:

After initialization: sides | 7 |

After first assignment: sides | 10 |

When a reference is made to a variable, such as when it is printed, the value of the variable is not changed. This is the nature of computer memory: Accessing (reading) data leaves the values in memory intact, but writing data replaces the old data with the new.

The Java language is *strongly typed,* meaning that we are not allowed to assign a value to a variable that is inconsistent with its declared type. Trying to combine incompatible types will generate an error when you attempt to compile the program. Therefore, the expression on the right-hand side of an assignment statement must evaluate to a value compatible with the type of the variable on the left-hand side.

Constants

Sometimes we use data that is constant throughout a program. For instance, we might write a program that deals with a theater that can hold no more than 427 people. It is often helpful to give a constant value a name, such as

MAX_OCCUPANCY, instead of using a literal value, such as 427, throughout the code. The purpose and meaning of literal values such as 427 is often confusing to someone reading the code. By giving the value a name, you help explain its role in the program.

Constants are identifiers and are similar to variables except that they hold a particular value for the duration of their existence. Constants are, to use the English meaning of the words, not variable. Their value doesn't change.

> **Key Concept**
>
> Constants hold a particular value for the duration of their existence.

In Java, if you precede a declaration with the reserved word `final`, the identifier is made a constant. By convention, uppercase letters are used when naming constants to distinguish them from regular variables, and individual words are separated using the underscore character. For example, the constant describing the maximum occupancy of a theater could be declared as follows:

```java
final int MAX_OCCUPANCY = 427;
```

The compiler will produce an error message if you attempt to change the value of a constant once it has been given its initial value. This is another good reason to use constants. Constants prevent inadvertent coding errors because the only valid place to change their value is in the initial assignment.

There is a third good reason to use constants. If a constant is used throughout a program and its value needs to be modified, then you have to change it in only one place. For example, if the capacity of the theater changes (because of a renovation) from 427 to 535, then you have to change only one declaration, and all uses of MAX_OCCUPANCY automatically reflect the change. If the literal 427 had been used throughout the code, each use would have to be found and changed. If you were to miss any uses of the literal value, problems would surely arise.

2.3   PRIMITIVE DATA TYPES

There are eight *primitive data types* in Java: four subsets of integers, two subsets of floating point numbers, a character data type, and a boolean data type. Everything else is represented using objects. Let's examine these eight primitive data types in some detail.

Integers and Floating Points

Java has two basic kinds of numeric values: integers, which have no fractional part, and floating points, which do. There are four integer data types (`byte`, `short`, `int`, and `long`) and two floating point data types (`float` and `double`).

All of the numeric types differ by the amount of memory space used to store a value of that type, which determines the range of values that can be represented. The size of each data type is the same for all hardware platforms. All numeric types are *signed,* meaning that both positive and negative values can be stored in them. Figure 2.2 summarizes the numeric primitive types.

Recall from our discussion in Chapter 1 that a bit can be either a 1 or a 0. Because each bit can represent two different states, a string of N bits can be used to represent 2^N different values. Appendix B describes number systems and these kinds of relationships in more detail.

When designing programs, we sometimes need to be careful about picking variables of appropriate size so that memory space is not wasted. This occurs in situations where memory space is particularly restricted, such as a program that runs on a personal data assistant (PDA). In such cases, we can choose a variable's data type accordingly. For example, if the value of a particular variable will not vary outside of a range of 1 to 1000, then a two-byte integer (short) is large enough to accommodate it. On the other hand, when it's not clear what the range of a particular variable will be, we should provide a reasonable, even generous, amount of space. In most situations memory space is not a serious restriction, and we can usually afford generous assumptions.

Note that even though a float value supports very large (and very small) numbers, it only has seven significant digits. Therefore, if it is important to accurately maintain a value such as 50341.2077, we need to use a double.

As we've already discussed, a *literal* is an explicit data value used in a program. The various numbers used in programs such as Facts and Addition and PianoKeys are all *integer literals*. Java assumes all integer literals are of type int, unless an L or l is appended to the end of the value to indicate that it should be considered a literal of type long, such as 45L.

Type	Storage	Min Value	Max Value
byte	8 bits	–128	127
short	16 bits	–32,768	32,767
int	32 bits	–2,147,483,648	2,147,483,647
long	64 bits	–9,223,372,036,854,775,808	9,223,372,036,854,775,807
float	32 bits	Approximately –3.4E+38 with 7 significant digits	Approximately 3.4E+38 with 7 significant digits
double	64 bits	Approximately –1.7E+308 with 15 significant digits	Approximately 1.7E+308 with 15 significant digits

FIGURE 2.2   The Java numeric primitive types

Likewise, Java assumes that all *floating point literals* are of type `double`. If we need to treat a floating point literal as a `float`, we append an `F` or `f` to the end

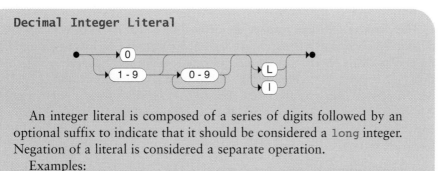

Decimal Integer Literal

An integer literal is composed of a series of digits followed by an optional suffix to indicate that it should be considered a `long` integer. Negation of a literal is considered a separate operation.
Examples:

```
5
2594
4920328L
```

of the value, as in `2.718F` or `123.45f`. Numeric literals of type `double` can be followed by a `D` or `d` if desired.

The following are examples of numeric variable declarations in Java:

```
int answer = 42;
byte smallNumber1, smallNumber2;
long countedStars = 86827263927L;
float ratio = 0.2363F;
double delta = 453.523311903;
```

Characters

Characters are another fundamental type of data used and managed on a computer. Individual characters can be treated as separate data items, and, as we've seen in several examples, they can be combined to form character strings.

A *character literal* is expressed in a Java program with single quotes, such as `'b'` or `'J'` or `';'`. You will recall that *string literals* are delineated using double quotation marks, and that the `String` type is not a primitive data type in Java, it is a class name. We discuss the `String` class in detail in the next chapter.

Note the difference between a digit as a character (or part of a string) and a digit as a number (or part of a larger number). The number `602` is a numeric value that can be used in an arithmetic calculation. But in the string "602 Greenbriar Court" the 6, 0, and 2 are characters, just like the rest of the characters that make up the string.

The characters we can manage are defined by a *character set,* which is simply a list of characters in a particular order. Each programming language supports a particular character set that defines the valid values for a character variable in that language. Several character sets have been proposed, but only a few have been used regularly over the years. The *ASCII character set* is a popular choice. ASCII stands for the American Standard Code for Information Interchange. The basic ASCII set uses seven bits per character, providing room to support 128 different characters, including:

> uppercase letters, such as 'A', 'B', and 'C'
> lowercase letters, such as 'a', 'b', and 'c'
> punctuation, such as the period ('.'), semicolon (';'), and comma (',')
> the digits '0' through '9'
> the space character, ' '
> special symbols, such as the ampersand ('&'), vertical bar ('|'), and backslash ('\')
> control characters, such as the carriage return, null, and end-of-text marks

The *control characters* are sometimes called nonprinting or invisible characters because they do not have a specific symbol that represents them. Yet they are as valid as any other character and can be stored and used in the same ways. Many control characters have special meaning to certain software applications.

As computing became a worldwide endeavor, users demanded a more flexible character set containing other language alphabets. ASCII was extended to use eight bits per character, and the number of characters in the set doubled to 256. The extended ASCII contains many accented and diacritical characters used in languages other than English.

However, even with 256 characters, the ASCII character set cannot represent the world's alphabets, especially given the various Asian alphabets and their many thousands of ideograms. Therefore, the developers of the Java programming language chose the *Unicode character set,* which uses 16 bits per character, supporting 65,536 unique characters. The characters and symbols from many languages are included in the Unicode definition. ASCII is a subset of the Unicode character set. Appendix C discusses the Unicode character set in more detail.

Key Concept

Java uses the 16-bit Unicode character set to represent character data.

A character set assigns a particular number to each character, so by definition the characters are in a particular order. This is referred to as lexicographic order. In the ASCII and Unicode ordering, the digit characters '0' through '9' are continuous (no other characters intervene) and in order. Similarly, the lowercase alphabetic characters `'a'` through `'z'` are continuous and in order, as are the uppercase alphabetic characters `'A'` through `'Z'`. These characteristics make it relatively easy to keep things in alphabetical order.

In Java, the data type `char` represents a single character. The following are some examples of character variable declarations in Java:

```java
char topGrade = 'A';
char symbol1, symbol2, symbol3;
char terminator = ';', separator = ' ';
```

Booleans

A boolean value, defined in Java using the reserved word `boolean`, has only two valid values: `true` and `false`. A boolean variable is usually used to indicate whether a particular condition is true, but it can also be used to represent any situation that has two states, such as a light bulb being on or off.

A boolean value cannot be converted to any other data type, nor can any other data type be converted to a boolean value. The words `true` and `false` are reserved in Java as *boolean literals* and cannot be used outside of this context.

The following are some examples of boolean variable declarations in Java:

```java
boolean flag = true;
boolean tooHigh, tooSmall, tooRough;
boolean done = false;
```

2.4   EXPRESSIONS

An *expression* is a combination of one or more operators and operands that usually perform a calculation. The value calculated does not have to be a number, but often is. The operands used in the operations might be literals, constants, variables, or other sources of data. The manner in which expressions are evaluated and used is fundamental to programming. For now we will focus on arithmetic expressions that use numeric operands and produce numeric results.

> **Key Concept**
>
> Expressions are combinations of operators and operands used to perform a calculation.

Arithmetic Operators

The usual arithmetic operations are defined for both integer and floating point numeric types, including addition (+), subtraction (–), multiplication (*), and division (/). Java also has another arithmetic operation: The *remainder operator* (%) returns the remainder after dividing the second operand into the first. The remainder operator is sometimes called the modulus operator. The sign of the result of a remainder operation is the sign of the numerator. Therefore:

Operation	Result
17 % 4	1
–20 % 3	–2
10 % –5	0
3 % 8	3

As you might expect, if either or both operands to any numeric operator are floating point values, the result is a floating point value. However, the division operator produces results that are less intuitive, depending on the types of the operands. If both operands are integers, the / operator performs *integer division*, meaning that any fractional part of the result is discarded. If one or the other or both operands are floating point values, the / operator performs *floating point division*, and the fractional part of the result is kept. For example, the result of 10/4 is 2, but the results of 10.0/4 and 10/4.0 and 10.0/4.0 are all 2.5.

A *unary operator* has only one operand, while a *binary operator* has two. The + and – arithmetic operators can be either unary or binary. The binary versions accomplish addition and subtraction, and the unary versions represent positive and negative numbers. For example, –1 is an example of using the unary negation operator to make the value negative. The unary + operator is rarely used.

Java does not have a built-in operator for raising a value to an exponent. However, the Math class provides methods that perform exponentiation and many other mathematical functions. The Math class is discussed in Chapter 3.

Operator Precedence

Operators can be combined to create more complex expressions. For example, consider the following assignment statement:

```
result = 14 + 8 / 2;
```

The entire right-hand side of the assignment is evaluated, and then the result is stored in the variable. But what is the result? If the addition is performed first, the result is 11; if the division operation is performed first, the result is 18. The order of operator evaluation makes a big difference. In this case, the division is performed before the addition, yielding a result of 18.

Note that in this and subsequent examples, we use literal values rather than variables to simplify the expression. The order of operator evaluation is the same if the operands are variables or any other source of data.

All expressions are evaluated according to an *operator precedence hierarchy* that establishes the rules that govern the order in which operations are evaluated. The arithmetic operators generally follow the same rules you learned in algebra. Multiplication, division, and the remainder operator all have equal precedence and are performed before (have higher precedence than) addition and subtraction. Addition and subtraction have equal precedence.

> **Key Concept**
>
> Java follows a well-defined set of precedence rules that governs the order in which operators will be evaluated in an expression.

Any arithmetic operators at the same level of precedence are performed left to right. Therefore we say the arithmetic operators have a *left-to-right association*.

Precedence, however, can be forced in an expression by using parentheses. For instance, if we really wanted the addition to be performed first in the previous example, we could write the expression as follows:

```
result = (14 + 8) / 2;
```

Any expression in parentheses is evaluated first. In complicated expressions, it is good practice to use parentheses even when it is not strictly necessary, to make it clear how the expression is evaluated.

Parentheses can be nested, and the innermost nested expressions are evaluated first. Consider the following expression:

```
result = 3 * ((18 - 4) / 2);
```

In this example, the result is 21. First, the subtraction is performed, forced by the inner parentheses. Then, even though multiplication and division are at the same level of precedence and usually would be evaluated left to right, the division is performed first because of the outer parentheses. Finally, the multiplication is performed.

After the arithmetic operations are complete, the computed result is stored in the variable on the left-hand side of the assignment operator (=). In other words, the assignment operator has a lower precedence than any of the arithmetic operators.

The evaluation of a particular expression can be shown using an *expression tree,* such as the one in Figure 2.3. The operators are executed from the bottom up, creating values that are used in the rest of the expression. Therefore, the operations lower in the tree have a higher precedence than those above, or they are forced to be executed earlier using parentheses.

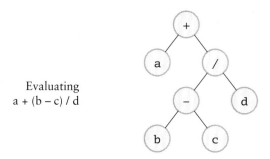

Evaluating
a + (b − c) / d

FIGURE 2.3   An expression tree

The parentheses used in expressions are actually operators themselves. Parentheses have a higher precedence than almost any other operator. Figure 2.4 shows a precedence table with the relationships between the arithmetic operators, parentheses, and the assignment operator. Appendix D includes a full precedence table showing all Java operators.

For an expression to be syntactically correct, the number of left parentheses must match the number of right parentheses and they must be properly nested. The following examples are *not* valid expressions:

```
result = ((19 + 8) % 3) − 4);    // not valid
result = (19 (+ 8 %) 3 − 4);     // not valid
```

Precedence Level	Operator	Operation	Associates
1	+	unary plus	R to L
	−	unary minus	
2	*	multiplication	L to R
	/	division	
	%	remainder	
3	+	addition	L to R
	−	subtraction	
	+	string concatenation	
4	=	assignment	R to L

FIGURE 2.4   Precedence among some of the Java operators

Keep in mind that when a variable is referenced in an expression, its current value is used to perform the calculation. In the following assignment statement, the current value of the variable count is added to the current value of the variable total, and the result is stored in the variable sum:

```
sum = count + total;
```

The original value contained in sum before this assignment is overwritten by the calculated value. The values stored in count and total are not changed.

The same variable can appear on both the left-hand side and the right-hand side of an assignment statement. Suppose the current value of a variable called count is 15 when the following assignment statement is executed:

```
count = count + 1;
```

Because the right-hand expression is evaluated first, the original value of count is obtained and the value 1 is added to it, producing the result 16. That result is then stored in the variable count, overwriting the original value of 15 with the new value of 16. Therefore, this assignment statement *increments*, or adds 1 to, the variable count.

Let's look at another example of expression processing. The program in Listing 2.7, called TempConverter, converts a particular Celsius temperature value to its equivalent Fahrenheit value using an expression that computes the following formula:

$$\text{Fahrenheit} = \frac{9}{5} \text{ Celsius} + 32$$

Note that in the temperature conversion program, the operands to the division operation are floating point literals to ensure that the fractional part of the number is kept. The precedence rules dictate that the multiplication happens before the addition in the final conversion computation.

The TempConverter program is not very useful because it converts only one data value that we included in the program as a constant (24 degrees Celsius). Every time the program is run it produces the same result. A far more useful version of the program would obtain the value to be converted from the user each time the program is executed. Interactive programs that read user input are discussed later in this chapter.

Listing 2.7

```java
//********************************************************************
//  TempConverter.java        Author: Lewis/Loftus
//
//  Demonstrates the use of primitive data types and arithmetic
//  expressions.
//********************************************************************

public class TempConverter
{
   //-----------------------------------------------------------------
   //  Computes the Fahrenheit equivalent of a specific Celsius
   //  value using the formula F = (9/5)C + 32.
   //-----------------------------------------------------------------
   public static void main (String[] args)
   {
      final int BASE = 32;
      final double CONVERSION_FACTOR = 9.0 / 5.0;

      double fahrenheitTemp;
      int celsiusTemp = 24;   // value to convert

      fahrenheitTemp = celsiusTemp * CONVERSION_FACTOR + BASE;

      System.out.println ("Celsius Temperature: " + celsiusTemp);
      System.out.println ("Fahrenheit Equivalent: " + fahrenheitTemp);
   }
}
```

Output

```
Celsius Temperature: 24
Fahrenheit Equivalent: 75.2
```

Increment and Decrement Operators

There are two other useful arithmetic operators. The *increment operator* (++) adds 1 to any integer or floating point value. The two plus signs that make up the operator cannot be separated by white space. The *decrement operator* (--) is similar except that it subtracts 1 from the value. They are both unary operators because they operate on only one operand. The following statement causes the value of count to be incremented:

```
count++;
```

The result is stored back into the variable count. Therefore it is functionally equivalent to the following statement, which we discussed in the previous section:

```
count = count + 1;
```

The increment and decrement operators can be applied after the variable (such as count++ or count--), creating what is called the *postfix form* of the operator. They can also be applied before the variable (such as ++count or --count), in what is called the *prefix form*. When used alone in a statement, the prefix and postfix forms are functionally equivalent. That is, it doesn't matter if you write

```
count++;
```

or

```
++count;
```

However, when such a form is written as a statement by itself, it is usually written in its postfix form.

When the increment or decrement operator is used in a larger expression, it can yield different results depending on the form used. For example, if the variable count currently contains the value 15, the following statement assigns the value 15 to total and the value 16 to count:

```
total = count++;
```

However, the following statement assigns the value 16 to both total and count:

```
total = ++count;
```

The value of count is incremented in both situations, but the value used in the larger expression depends on whether a prefix or postfix form of the increment operator is used.

Because of the subtle differences between the prefix and postfix forms of the increment and decrement operators, they should be used with care. As always, favor the side of readability.

Assignment Operators

As a convenience, several *assignment operators* have been defined in Java that combine a basic operation with assignment. For example, the += operator can be used as follows:

```
total += 5;
```

This performs the same operation as the following statement:

```
total = total + 5;
```

The right-hand side of the assignment operator can be a full expression. The expression on the right-hand side of the operator is evaluated, then that result is added to the current value of the variable on the left-hand side, and that value is stored in the variable. Therefore, the following statement:

```
total += (sum - 12) / count;
```

is equivalent to:

```
total = total + ((sum - 12) / count);
```

Many similar assignment operators are defined in Java, including those that perform subtraction (-=), multiplication (*=), division (/=), and remainder (%=). The entire set of Java operators is discussed in Appendix D.

All of the assignment operators evaluate the entire expression on the right-hand side first, then use the result as the right operand of the other operation. Therefore, the following statement:

```
result *= count1 + count2;
```

is equivalent to:

```
result = result * (count1 + count2);
```

Likewise, the following statement:

```
result %= (highest - 40) / 2;
```

is equivalent to:

```
result = result % ((highest - 40) / 2);
```

Some assignment operators perform particular functions depending on the types of the operands, just as their corresponding regular operators do. For example, if the operands to the += operator are strings, then the assignment operator performs string concatenation.

2.5   DATA CONVERSION

Because Java is a strongly typed language, each data value is associated with a particular type. It is sometimes helpful or necessary to convert a data value of one type to another type, but we must be careful that we don't lose important information in the process. For example, suppose a short variable that holds the number 1000 is converted to a byte value. Because a byte does not have enough bits to represent the value 1000, some bits would be lost in the conversion, and the number represented in the byte would not keep its original value.

A conversion between one primitive type and another falls into one of two categories: widening conversions and narrowing conversions. *Widening conversions* are the safest because they usually do not lose information. They are called widening conversions because they go from one data type to another type that uses an equal or greater amount of space to store the value. Figure 2.5 lists the Java widening conversions.

For example, it is safe to convert from a byte to a short because a byte is stored in 8 bits and a short is stored in 16 bits. There is no loss of information. All widening conversions that go from an integer type to another integer type, or from a floating point type to another floating point type, preserve the numeric value exactly.

Although widening conversions do not lose any information about the magnitude of a value, the widening conversions that result in a floating point value can lose precision. When converting from an int or a long to a float, or from a

From	To
byte	short, int, long, float, or double
short	int, long, float, or double
char	int, long, float, or double
int	long, float, or double
long	float or double
float	double

FIGURE 2.5   Java widening conversions

long to a double, some of the least significant digits may be lost. In this case, the resulting floating point value will be a rounded version of the integer value, following the rounding techniques defined in the IEEE 754 floating point standard.

Narrowing conversions are more likely to lose information than widening conversions are. They often go from one type to a type that uses less space to store a value, and therefore some of the information may be compromised. Narrowing conversions can lose both numeric magnitude and precision. Therefore, in general, they should be avoided. Figure 2.6 lists the Java narrowing conversions.

An exception to the space-shrinking situation in narrowing conversions is when we convert a byte (8 bits) or short (16 bits) to a char (16 bits). These are still considered narrowing conversions because the sign bit is incorporated into the new character value. Since a character value is unsigned, a negative integer will be converted into a character that has no particular relationship to the numeric value of the original integer.

Note that boolean values are not mentioned in either widening or narrowing conversions. A boolean value cannot be converted to any other primitive type and vice versa.

Conversion Techniques

In Java, conversions can occur in three ways:

> assignment conversion
> promotion
> casting

From	To
byte	char
short	byte or char
char	byte or short
int	byte, short, or char
long	byte, short, char, or int
float	byte, short, char, int, or long
double	byte, short, char, int, long, or float

FIGURE 2.6 Java narrowing conversions

Assignment conversion occurs when a value of one type is assigned to a variable of another type during which the value is converted to the new type. Only widening conversions can be accomplished through assignment. For example, if money is a float variable and dollars is an int variable, then the following assignment statement automatically converts the value in dollars to a float:

```
money = dollars;
```

Therefore, if dollars contains the value 25, after the assignment, money contains the value 25.0. However, if we attempt to assign money to dollars, the compiler will issue an error message alerting us to the fact that we are attempting a narrowing conversion that could lose information. If we really want to do this assignment, we have to make the conversion explicit by using a cast.

Conversion via *promotion* occurs automatically when certain operators need to modify their operands in order to perform the operation. For example, when a floating point value called sum is divided by an integer value called count, the value of count is promoted to a floating point value automatically, before the division takes place, producing a floating point result:

```
result = sum / count;
```

A similar conversion is taking place when a number is concatenated with a string. The number is first converted (promoted) to a string, then the two strings are concatenated.

Casting is the most general form of conversion in Java. If a conversion can be accomplished at all in a Java program, it can be accomplished using a cast. A cast is a Java operator that is specified by a type name in parentheses. It is placed in front of the value to be converted. For example, to convert money to an integer value, we could put a cast in front of it:

```
dollars = (int) money;
```

The cast returns the value in money, truncating any fractional part. If money contained the value 84.69, then after the assignment, dollars would contain the value 84. Note, however, that the cast does not change the value in money. After the assignment operation is complete, money still contains the value 84.69.

Casts are helpful in many situations where we need to treat a value temporarily as another type. For example, if we want to divide the integer value total by the integer value count and get a floating point result, we could do it as follows:

```
result = (float) total / count;
```

First, the cast operator returns a floating point version of the value in `total`. This operation does not change the value in `total`. Then, `count` is treated as a floating point value via arithmetic promotion. Now the division operator will perform floating point division and produce the intended result. If the cast had not been included, the operation would have performed integer division and truncated the answer before assigning it to `result`. Also note that because the cast operator has a higher precedence than the division operator, the cast operates on the value of `total`, not on the result of the division.

2.6   INTERACTIVE PROGRAMS

It is often useful to design a program to read data from the user interactively during execution. That way, new results can be computed each time the program is run, depending on the data that is entered.

The `Scanner` Class

The `Scanner` class, which is part of the standard Java class library, provides convenient methods for reading input values of various types. The input could come from various sources, including data typed interactively by the user or data stored in a file. The `Scanner` class can also be used to parse a character string into separate pieces. Figure 2.7 lists some of the methods provided by the `Scanner` class.

We must first create a `Scanner` object in order to invoke its methods. Objects in Java are created using the `new` operator. The following declaration creates a `Scanner` object that reads input from the keyboard:

```
Scanner scan = new Scanner (System.in);
```

This declaration creates a variable called scan that represents a `Scanner` object. The object itself is created by the `new` operator and a call to a special method called a *constructor* to set up the object. The `Scanner` constructor accepts a parameter that indicates the source of the input. The `System.in` object represents the *standard input stream*, which by default is the keyboard. Creating objects using the new operator is discussed further in the next chapter.

Unless specified otherwise, a `Scanner` object assumes that white space characters (space characters, tabs, and new lines) are used to separate the elements of the input, called *tokens*, from each other. These characters are called the input *delimiters*. The set of delimiters can be changed if the input tokens are separated by characters other than white space.

```
Scanner (InputStream source)
Scanner (File source)
Scanner (String source)
        Constructors: sets up the new scanner to scan values from the specified source.

String next()
        Returns the next input token as a character string.

String nextLine()
        Returns all input remaining on the current line as a character string.

boolean nextBoolean()
byte nextByte()
double nextDouble()
float nextFloat()
int nextInt()
long nextLong()
short nextShort()
        Returns the next input token as the indicated type. Throws
        InputMismatchException if the next token is inconsistent with the type.

boolean hasNext()
        Returns true if the scanner has another token in its input.

Scanner useDelimiter (String pattern)
Scanner useDelimiter (Pattern pattern)
        Sets the scanner's delimiting pattern.

Pattern delimiter()
        Returns the pattern the scanner is currently using to match delimiters.

String findInLine (String pattern)
String findInLine (Pattern pattern)
        Attempts to find the next occurrence of the specified pattern, ignoring delimiters.
```

FIGURE 2.7   Some methods of the Scanner class

The next method of the Scanner class reads the next input token as a string and returns it. Therefore, if the input consisted of a series of words separated by spaces, each call to next would return the next word. The nextLine method reads all of the input until the end of the line is found, and returns it as one string.

The program Echo, shown in Listing 2.8, simply reads a line of text typed by the user, stores it in a variable that holds a character string, then echoes it back to the screen.

The import statement above the definition of the Echo class tells the program that we will be using the Scanner class in this program. The Scanner class is part

Listing 2.8

```
//********************************************************************
//   Echo.java         Author: Lewis/Loftus
//
//   Demonstrates the use of the nextLine method of the Scanner class
//   to read a string from the user.
//********************************************************************

import java.util.Scanner;

public class Echo
{
    //-----------------------------------------------------------------
    //   Reads a character string from the user and prints it.
    //-----------------------------------------------------------------
    public static void main (String[] args)
    {
        String message;
        Scanner scan = new Scanner (System.in);

        System.out.println ("Enter a line of text:");

        message = scan.nextLine();

        System.out.println ("You entered: \"" + message + "\"");
    }
}
```

Output

```
Enter a line of text:
Set your laser printer on stun!
You entered: "Set your laser printer on stun!"
```

of the `java.util` class library. The use of the `import` statement is discussed further in Chapter 3.

Various `Scanner` methods such as `nextInt` and `nextDouble` are provided to read data of particular types. The `GasMileage` program, shown in Listing 2.9,

---

Listing 2.9

```java
//********************************************************************
//  GasMileage.java        Author: Lewis/Loftus
//
//  Demonstrates the use of the Scanner class to read numeric data.
//********************************************************************

import java.util.Scanner;

public class GasMileage
{
    //-----------------------------------------------------------------
    //  Calculates fuel efficiency based on values entered by the
    //  user.
    //-----------------------------------------------------------------
    public static void main (String[] args)
    {
        int miles;
        double gallons, mpg;

        Scanner scan = new Scanner (System.in);

        System.out.print ("Enter the number of miles: ");
        miles = scan.nextInt();

        System.out.print ("Enter the gallons of fuel used: ");
        gallons = scan.nextDouble();

        mpg = miles / gallons;

        System.out.println ("Miles Per Gallon: " + mpg);
    }
}
```

Output

```
Enter the number of miles: 328
Enter the gallons of fuel used: 11.2
Miles Per Gallon: 29.28571428571429
```

reads the number of miles traveled as an integer, and the number of gallons of fuel consumed as a double, then computes the gas mileage.

As you can see by the output of the `GasMileage` program, the calculation produces a floating point result that is accurate to several decimal places. In the next chapter we discuss classes that help us format our output in various ways, including rounding a floating point value to a particular number of decimal places.

A `Scanner` object processes the input one token at a time, based on the methods used to read the data and the delimiters used to separate the input values. Therefore, multiple values can be put on the same line of input or can be separated over multiple lines, as appropriate for the situation.

In Chapter 5 we use the `Scanner` class to read input from a data file and modify the delimiters it uses to parse the data. Appendix H explores how to use the `Scanner` class to analyze its input using patterns called *regular expressions*.

2.7 GRAPHICS

Graphics play a crucial role in computer systems. Throughout this book we explore various aspects of graphics and discuss how they are accomplished. In fact, the last one or two sections of each chapter are devoted to graphics topics. We refer to this as the *Graphics Track* through the book. These sections can be skipped without losing continuity through the rest of the text, incorporated into the regular flow of the chapters, or explored as a group.

> **Key Concept**
>
> Graphical data is represented by dividing it into many small pieces called pixels.

A picture, like all other information stored on a computer, must be digitized by breaking the information into pieces and representing those pieces as numbers. In the case of pictures, we break the picture into *pixels* (picture elements). A pixel is a tiny region that represents a very small piece of the picture. The complete picture is stored by storing the color of each individual pixel.

A digitized picture can be reproduced when needed by reassembling its pixels. The more pixels used to represent a picture, the more realistic it looks when it is reproduced. The number of pixels used to represent a picture is called the *picture resolution*. The number of pixels that can be displayed by a monitor is called the *monitor resolution*.

A black and white picture can be stored by representing each pixel using a single bit. If the bit is 0, that pixel is white; if the bit is 1, it is black. Figure 2.8 shows a black and white picture that has been stored digitally and an enlargement of a portion of that picture, which shows the individual pixels.

 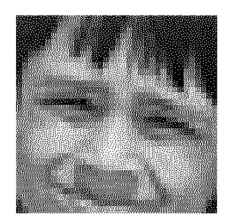

FIGURE 2.8   A digitized picture with a small portion magnified

Coordinate Systems

When drawn, each pixel of a picture is mapped to a pixel on the monitor screen. Each computer system and programming language defines a coordinate system so that we can refer to particular pixels.

A traditional two-dimensional Cartesian coordinate system has two axes that meet at the origin. Values on either axis can be negative or positive. The Java programming language has a relatively simple coordinate system in which all of the visible coordinates are positive. Figure 2.9 compares a traditional coordinate system to the Java coordinate system.

Each point in the Java coordinate system is represented using an (x, y) pair of values. The top-left corner of any Java drawing area has coordinates (0, 0). The x-axis coordinates get larger as you move to the right, and the y-axis coordinates get larger as you move down.

> **Key Concept**
>
> Java's coordinate system has the origin in the upper-left corner and all visible coordinates are positive.

As we've seen in previous examples, a Java program does not have to be graphical in nature. However, if it is, each graphical component in the program has its own coordinate system, with the origin (0, 0) in the top-left corner. This consistent approach makes it relatively easy to manage various graphical elements.

Representing Color

Color pictures are divided into pixels, just as black and white pictures are. However, because each pixel can be one of many possible colors, it is not sufficient

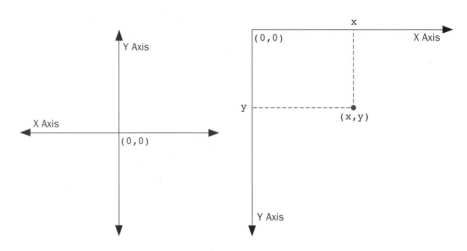

FIGURE 2.9   A traditional coordinate system and the Java coordinate system

to represent each pixel using only one bit. There are various ways to represent the color of a pixel. Let's briefly discuss one popular technique.

Every color can be represented as a mix of three *primary colors*: red, green, and blue. In Java, as in many other computer languages, colors are specified by three numbers that are collectively referred to as an *RGB value*. RGB stands for Red-Green-Blue. Each number represents the contribution of a primary color. Using one byte (eight bits) to store each of the three numbers, the numbers can range from 0 to 255. The level of each primary color determines the overall color. For example, high values of red and green combined with a low level of blue results in a shade of yellow.

In Java, a programmer uses the Color class, which is part of the java.awt package, to define and manage colors. Each object of the Color class represents a single color. The class contains several instances of itself to provide a basic set of predefined colors. Figure 2.10 lists the predefined colors of the Color class. It also contains methods to define and manage many other colors.

Color	Object	RGB Value
black	`Color.black`	0, 0, 0
blue	`Color.blue`	0, 0, 255
cyan	`Color.cyan`	0, 255, 255
gray	`Color.gray`	128, 128, 128
dark gray	`Color.darkGray`	64, 64, 64
light gray	`Color.lightGray`	192, 192, 192
green	`Color.green`	0, 255, 0
magenta	`Color.magenta`	255, 0, 255
orange	`Color.orange`	255, 200, 0
pink	`Color.pink`	255, 175, 175
red	`Color.red`	255, 0, 0
white	`Color.white`	255, 255, 255
yellow	`Color.yellow`	255, 255, 0

FIGURE 2.10   Predefined colors in the `Color` class

2.8   APPLETS

There are two kinds of Java programs: Java applets and Java applications. A Java *applet* is a Java program that is intended to be embedded into an HTML document, transported across a network, and executed using a Web browser. A Java *application* is a stand-alone program that can be executed using a Java interpreter. All programs presented thus far in this book have been Java applications.

> **Key Concept**
>
> Applets are Java programs that are usually transported across a network and executed using a Web browser.

The Web enables users to send and receive various types of media, such as text, graphics, and sound, using a point-and-click interface that is extremely convenient and easy to use. A Java applet was the first kind of executable program that could be retrieved using Web software. Java applets are considered just another type of media that can be exchanged across the Web.

Though Java applets are generally intended to be transported across a network, they don't have to be. They can be viewed locally using a Web browser. For that matter, they don't even have to be executed through a Web browser at all. A tool in Sun's Java Software Development Kit called *appletviewer* can be used to interpret and execute an applet. We use appletviewer to display applets in this book. However, usually the point of making a Java applet is to provide a link to it on a Web page and allow it to be retrieved and executed by Web users anywhere in the world.

Java bytecode (not Java source code) is linked to an HTML document and sent across the Web. A version of the Java interpreter embedded in a Web browser is used to execute the applet once it reaches its destination. A Java applet must be compiled into bytecode format before it can be used with the Web.

There are some important differences between the structure of a Java applet and the structure of a Java application. Because the Web browser that executes an applet is already running, applets can be thought of as a part of a larger program. As such they do not have a `main` method where execution starts. The `paint` method in an applet is automatically invoked by the applet. Consider the program in Listing 2.10, in which the `paint` method is used to draw a few shapes and write a quotation by Albert Einstein to the screen.

The two `import` statements at the beginning of the program explicitly indicate the packages that are used in the program. In this example, we need the `JApplet` class, which is part of the `javax.swing` package, and various graphics capabilities defined in the `java.awt` package. Chapter 3 explores `import` statements further.

A class that defines an applet extends the `JApplet` class, as indicated in the header line of the class declaration. This process is making use of the object-oriented concept of inheritance, which we discussed in Chapter 1 and explore in more detail later in the book. Applet classes must also be declared as `public`.

The `paint` method is one of several applet methods that have particular significance. It is invoked automatically whenever the graphic elements of the applet need to be painted to the screen, such as when the applet is first run or when another window that was covering it is moved.

Note that the `paint` method accepts a `Graphics` object as a parameter. A `Graphics` object defines a particular *graphics context* with which we can interact. The graphics context passed into an applet's `paint` method represents the entire applet window. Each graphics context has its own coordinate system. In later examples, we will have multiple components, each with its own graphics context.

A `Graphics` object allows us to draw various shapes using methods such as `drawRect`, `drawOval`, `drawLine`, and `drawString`. The parameters passed to the drawing methods specify the coordinates and sizes of the shapes to be drawn. We explore these and other methods that draw shapes in the next section.

Listing 2.10

```java
//********************************************************************
//  Einstein.java        Author: Lewis/Loftus
//
//  Demonstrates a basic applet.
//********************************************************************

import javax.swing.JApplet;
import java.awt.*;

public class Einstein extends JApplet
{
   //-----------------------------------------------------------------
   //  Draws a quotation by Albert Einstein among some shapes.
   //-----------------------------------------------------------------
   public void paint (Graphics page)
   {
      page.drawRect (50, 50, 40, 40);       // square
      page.drawRect (60, 80, 225, 30);      // rectangle
      page.drawOval (75, 65, 20, 20);       // circle
      page.drawLine (35, 60, 100, 120);     // line

      page.drawString ("Out of clutter, find simplicity.", 110, 70);
      page.drawString ("-- Albert Einstein", 130, 100);
   }
}
```

Display

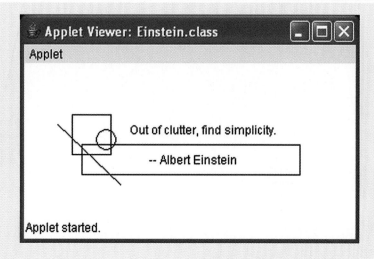

Executing Applets Using the Web

In order for the applet to be transmitted over the Web and executed by a browser, it must be referenced in a HyperText Markup Language (HTML) document. An HTML document contains *tags* that specify formatting instructions and identify the special types of media that are to be included in a document. A Java program is considered a specific media type, just as text, graphics, and sound are.

An HTML tag is enclosed in angle brackets. The following is an example of an applet tag:

```
<applet code="Einstein.class" width="350" height="175">
</applet>
```

This tag dictates that the bytecode stored in the file `Einstein.class` should be transported over the network and executed on the machine that wants to view this particular HTML document. The applet tag also indicates the width and height of the applet.

There are other tags that can be used to reference an applet in an HTML file, including the `<object>` tag and the `<embed>` tag. The `<object>` tag is actually the tag that should be used, according to the World Wide Web Consortium (W3C). However, browser support for the `<object>` tag is not consistent. For now, the most reliable solution is to use the `<applet>` tag.

Note that the applet tag refers to the bytecode file of the `Einstein` applet, not to the source code file. Before an applet can be transported using the Web, it must be compiled into its bytecode format. Then, as shown in Figure 2.11, the docu-

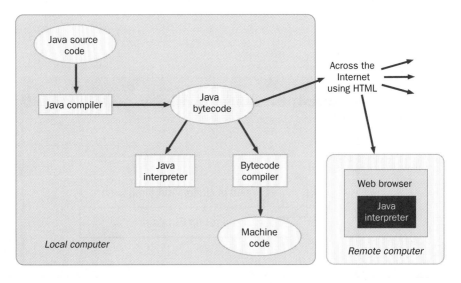

FIGURE 2.11   The Java translation and execution process, including applets

ment can be loaded using a Web browser, which will automatically interpret and execute the applet.

2.9   DRAWING SHAPES

The Java standard class library provides many classes that let us present and manipulate graphical information. The `Graphics` class is fundamental to all such processing.

The `Graphics` Class

The `Graphics` class is defined in the `java.awt` package. It contains various methods that allow us to draw shapes, including lines, rectangles, and ovals. Figure 2.12 lists some of the fundamental drawing methods of the `Graphics` class. Note that these methods also let us draw circles and squares, which are just specific types of ovals and rectangles, respectively. We discuss additional drawing methods of the `Graphics` class later in the book at appropriate points.

The methods of the `Graphics` class allow us to specify whether we want a shape filled or unfilled. An unfilled shape shows only the outline of the shape and is otherwise transparent (you can see any underlying graphics). A filled shape is solid between its boundaries and covers any underlying graphics.

> **Key Concept**
>
> Most shapes can be drawn filled (opaque) or unfilled (as an outline).

All of these methods rely on the Java coordinate system, which we discussed earlier in this chapter. Recall that point (0,0) is in the upper-left corner, such that *x* values get larger as we move to the right, and *y* values get larger as we move down. Any shapes drawn at coordinates that are outside the visible area will not be seen.

Many of the `Graphics` drawing methods are self-explanatory, but some require a little more discussion. Note, for instance, that an oval drawn by the `drawOval` method is defined by the coordinate of the upper-left corner and dimensions that specify the width and height of a *bounding rectangle*. Shapes with curves, such as ovals, are often defined by a rectangle that encompasses their perimeters. Figure 2.13 depicts a bounding rectangle for an oval.

> **Key Concept**
>
> A bounding rectangle is used to define the position and size of curved shapes such as ovals.

An arc can be thought of as a segment of an oval. To draw an arc, we specify the oval of which the arc is a part and the portion of the oval in which we're interested. The starting point of the arc is defined by the *start angle* and the ending

```
void drawLine (int x1, int y1, int x2, int y2)
    Paints a line from point (x1, y1) to point (x2, y2).

void drawRect (int x, int y, int width, int height)
    Paints a rectangle with upper left corner (x, y) and dimensions width and
    height.

void drawOval (int x, int y, int width, int height)
    Paints an oval bounded by the rectangle with an upper left corner of (x, y) and
    dimensions width and height.

void drawString (String str, int x, int y)
    Paints the character string str at point (x, y), extending to the right.

void drawArc (int x, int y, int width, int height, int
startAngle, int arcAngle)
    Paints an arc along the oval bounded by the rectangle defined by x, y, width,
    and height. The arc starts at startAngle and extends for a distance defined by
    arcAngle.

void fillRect (int x, int  y, int width, int height)
    Same as their draw counterparts, but filled with the current foreground color.

void fillOval (int x, int y, int width, int height)

void fillArc (int x, int y, int width, int height,
int startAngle, int arcAngle)

Color getColor ()
    Returns this graphics context's foreground color.

void setColor (Color color)
    Sets this graphics context's foreground color to the specified color.
```

FIGURE 2.12 Some methods of the `Graphics` class

Key Concept

An arc is a segment of an oval beginning at a specific start angle and extending for a distance specified by the arc angle.

point of the arc is defined by the *arc angle*. The arc angle does not indicate where the arc ends, but rather its range. The start angle and the arc angle are measured in degrees. The origin for the start angle is an imaginary horizontal line passing through the center of the oval and can be referred to as 0°, as shown in Figure 2.14.

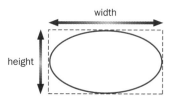

FIGURE 2.13   An oval and its bounding rectangle

Every graphics context has a current *foreground color* that is used whenever shapes or strings are drawn. Every surface that can be drawn on has a *background color*. The foreground color is set using the setColor method of the Graphics class, and the background color is set using the setBackground method of the component on which we are drawing, such as the applet.

Listing 2.11 shows an applet called Snowman. It uses various drawing and color methods to draw a winter scene featuring a snowman. Review the code carefully to note how each shape is drawn to create the overall picture.

Note that the snowman figure is based on two constant values called MID and TOP, which define the midpoint of the snowman (left to right) and the top of the snowman's head. The entire snowman figure is drawn relative to these values. Using constants like these makes it easier to create the snowman and to make modifications later. For example, to shift the snowman to the right or left in our picture, only one constant declaration would have to change.

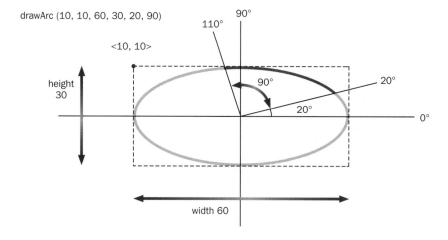

FIGURE 2.14   An arc defined by an oval, a start angle, and an arc angle

Listing 2.11

```
//********************************************************************
//   Snowman.java       Author: Lewis/Loftus
//
//   Demonstrates basic drawing methods and the use of color.
//********************************************************************

import javax.swing.JApplet;
import java.awt.*;

public class Snowman extends JApplet
{
   //-----------------------------------------------------------------
   //  Draws a snowman.
   //-----------------------------------------------------------------
   public void paint (Graphics page)
   {
      final int MID = 150;
      final int TOP = 50;

      setBackground (Color.cyan);

      page.setColor (Color.blue);
      page.fillRect (0, 175, 300, 50);   // ground

      page.setColor (Color.yellow);
      page.fillOval (-40, -40, 80, 80);   // sun

      page.setColor (Color.white);
      page.fillOval (MID-20, TOP, 40, 40);        // head
      page.fillOval (MID-35, TOP+35, 70, 50);   // upper torso
      page.fillOval (MID-50, TOP+80, 100, 60);   // lower torso

      page.setColor (Color.black);
      page.fillOval (MID-10, TOP+10, 5, 5);   // left eye
      page.fillOval (MID+5, TOP+10, 5, 5);    // right eye

      page.drawArc (MID-10, TOP+20, 20, 10, 190, 160);   // smile
```

Listing 2.11   continued

```
    page.drawLine (MID-25, TOP+60, MID-50, TOP+40);   // left arm
    page.drawLine (MID+25, TOP+60, MID+55, TOP+60);   // right arm

    page.drawLine (MID-20, TOP+5, MID+20, TOP+5);    // brim of hat
    page.fillRect (MID-15, TOP-20, 30, 25);          // top of hat
  }
}
```

Display

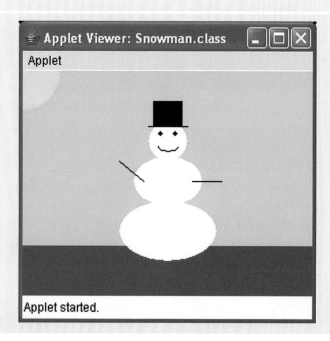

Summary of Key Concepts

> The `print` and `println` methods represent two services provided by the `System.out` object.

> An escape sequence can be used to represent a character that would otherwise cause compilation problems.

> A variable is a name for a memory location used to hold a value of a particular data type.

> Accessing data leaves it intact in memory, but an assignment statement overwrites the old data.

> We cannot assign a value of one type to a variable of an incompatible type.

> Constants hold a particular value for the duration of their existence.

> Java has two kinds of numeric values: integer and floating point. There are four integer data types and two floating point data types.

> Java uses the 16-bit Unicode character set to represent character data.

> Expressions are combinations of operators and operands used to perform a calculation.

> Java follows a well-defined set of precedence rules that governs the order in which operators will be evaluated in an expression.

> Narrowing conversions should be avoided because they can lose information.

> The `Scanner` class provides methods for reading input of various types from various sources.

> Graphical data is represented by dividing it into many small pieces called pixels.

> Java's coordinate system has the origin in the upper-left corner and all visible coordinates are positive.

> Colors are represented in Java using an RGB value—three values that represent the contributions of the primary colors red, green, and blue.

> The `Color` class contains several predefined colors that are commonly used, and can be used to define many others.

> Applets are Java programs that are usually transported across a network and executed using a Web browser.

> Most shapes can be drawn filled (opaque) or unfilled (as an outline).

> A bounding rectangle is used to define the position and size of curved shapes such as ovals.

> An arc is a segment of an oval beginning at a specific start angle and extending for a distance specified by the arc angle.

Self-Review Questions

SR 2.1   What is primitive data? How are primitive data types different from objects?

SR 2.2   What is a string literal?

SR 2.3   What is the difference between the print and println methods?

SR 2.4   What is a parameter?

SR 2.5   What is an escape sequence? Give some examples.

SR 2.6   What is a variable declaration?

SR 2.7   How many values can be stored in an integer variable?

SR 2.8   What are the four integer data types in Java? How are they different?

SR 2.9   What is a character set?

SR 2.10   What is operator precedence?

SR 2.11   What is the result of 19%5 when evaluated in a Java expression? Explain.

SR 2.12   What is the result of 13/4 when evaluated in a Java expression? Explain.

SR 2.13   If an integer variable diameter currently holds the value 5, what is its value after the following statement is executed? Explain.

```
diameter = diameter * 4;
```

SR 2.14   If an integer variable weight currently holds the value 100, what is its value after the following statement is executed? Explain.

```
weight -= 17;
```

SR 2.15   Why are widening conversions safer than narrowing conversions?

SR 2.16 How can a black and white picture be represented using 1s and 0s?

SR 2.17 What is the difference between a Java application and a Java applet?

SR 2.18 What is a bounding rectangle?

Exercises

EX 2.1 Explain the following programming statement in terms of objects and the services they provide:

```
System.out.println ("I gotta be me!");
```

EX 2.2 What output is produced by the following code fragment? Explain.

```
System.out.print ("Here we go!");
System.out.println ("12345");
System.out.print ("Test this if you are not sure.");
System.out.print ("Another.");
System.out.println ();
System.out.println ("All done.");
```

EX 2.3 What is wrong with the following program statement? How can it be fixed?

```
System.out.println ("To be or not to be, that
is the question.");
```

EX 2.4 What output is produced by the following statement? Explain.

```
System.out.println ("50 plus 25 is " + 50 + 25);
```

EX 2.5 What is the output produced by the following statement? Explain.

```
System.out.println ("He thrusts his fists\n\tagainst" +
" the post\nand still insists\n\the sees the \"ghost\"");
```

EX 2.6 What value is contained in the integer variable size after the following statements are executed?

```
size = 18;
size = size + 12;
size = size * 2;
size = size / 4;
```

EX 2.7   What value is contained in the floating point variable depth after the following statements are executed?

```
depth = 2.4;
depth = 20 - depth * 4;
depth = depth / 5;
```

EX 2.8   What value is contained in the integer variable length after the following statements are executed?

```
length = 5;
length *= 2;
length *= length;
length /= 100;
```

EX 2.9   Write four different program statements that increment the value of an integer variable total.

EX 2.10 Given the following declarations, what result is stored in each of the listed assignment statements?

```
int iResult, num1 = 25, num2 = 40, num3 = 17, num4 = 5;
double fResult, val1 = 17.0, val2 = 12.78;
```

a. iResult = num1 / num4;
b. fResult = num1 / num4;
c. iResult = num3 / num4;
d. fResult = num3 / num4;
e. fResult = val1 / num4;
f. fResult = val1 / val2;
g. iResult = num1 / num2;
h. fResult = (double) num1 / num2;
i. fResult = num1 / (double) num2;
j. fResult = (double) (num1 / num2);
k. iResult = (int) (val1 / num4);
l. fResult = (int) (val1 / num4);
m. fResult = (int) ((double) num1 / num2);
n. iResult = num3 % num4;
o. iResult = num2 % num3;
p. iResult = num3 % num2;
q. iResult = num2 % num4;

EX 2.11 For each of the following expressions, indicate the order in which the operators will be evaluated by writing a number beneath each operator.

a. a − b − c − d
b. a − b + c − d
c. a + b / c / d
d. a + b / c * d
e. a / b * c * d
f. a % b / c * d
g. a % b % c % d
h. a − (b − c) − d
i. (a − (b − c)) − d
j. a − ((b − c) − d)
k. a % (b % c) * d * e
l. a + (b − c) * d − e
m. (a + b) * c + d * e
n. (a + b) * (c / d) % e

EX 2.12 Explain the role played by the Web in the translation and execution of some Java programs.

EX 2.13 Compare and contrast a traditional coordinate system and the coordinate system used by Java graphical components.

EX 2.14 How many bits are needed to store a color picture that is 400 pixels wide and 250 pixels high? Assume color is represented using the RGB technique described in this chapter and that no special compression is done.

EX 2.15 Assuming you have a `Graphics` object called `page`, write a statement that will draw a line from point (20, 30) to point (50, 60).

EX 2.16 Assuming you have a `Graphics` object called `page`, write a statement that will draw a rectangle with height 70 and width 35, such that its upper-left corner is at point (10, 15).

EX 2.17 Assuming you have a `Graphics` object called `page`, write a statement that will draw a circle *centered* on point (50, 50) with a radius of 20 pixels.

EX 2.18 The following lines of code draw the eyes of the snowman in the `Snowman` applet. The eyes seem centered on the face when drawn, but the first parameters of each call are not equally offset from the midpoint. Explain.

```
page.fillOval (MID-10, TOP+10, 5, 5);
page.fillOval (MID+5, TOP+10, 5, 5);
```

Programming Projects

PP 2.1 Create a revised version of the `Lincoln` application from Chapter 1 such that quotes appear around the quotation.

PP 2.2 Write an application that reads three integers and prints their average.

PP 2.3 Write an application that reads two floating point numbers and prints their sum, difference, and product.

PP 2.4 Create a version of the `TempConverter` application to convert from Fahrenheit to Celsius. Read the Fahrenheit temperature from the user.

PP 2.5 Write an application that converts miles to kilometers. (One mile equals 1.60935 kilometers.) Read the miles value from the user as a floating point value.

PP 2.6 Write an application that reads values representing a time duration in hours, minutes, and seconds, and then prints the equivalent total number of seconds. (For example, 1 hour, 28 minutes, and 42 seconds is equivalent to 5322 seconds.)

PP 2.7 Create a version of the previous project that reverses the computation. That is, read a value representing a number of seconds, then print the equivalent amount of time as a combination of hours, minutes, and seconds. (For example, 9999 seconds is equivalent to 2 hours, 46 minutes, and 39 seconds.)

PP 2.8 Write an application that determines the value of the coins in a jar and prints the total in dollars and cents. Read integer values that represent the number of quarters, dimes, nickels, and pennies.

PP 2.9 Write an application that prompts for and reads a `double` value representing a monetary amount. Then determine the fewest number of each bill and coin needed to represent that amount, starting with the highest (assume that a ten dollar bill is the maximum size needed). For example, if the value entered is

47.63 (forty-seven dollars and sixty-three cents), then the program should print the equivalent amount as:

```
4 ten dollar bills
1 five dollar bills
2 one dollar bills
2 quarters
1 dimes
0 nickles
3 pennies
```

PP 2.10   Write an application that prompts for and reads an integer representing the length of a square's side, then prints the square's perimeter and area.

PP 2.11   Write an application that prompts for and reads the numerator and denominator of a fraction as integers, then prints the decimal equivalent of the fraction.

PP 2.12   Create a revised version of the Snowman applet with the following modifications:

> Add two red buttons to the upper torso.
> Make the snowman frown instead of smile.
> Move the sun to the upper-right corner of the picture.
> Display your name in the upper-left corner of the picture.
> Shift the entire snowman 20 pixels to the right.

PP 2.13   Write an applet that writes your name using the drawString method. Embed a link to your applet in an HTML document and view it using a Web browser.

PP 2.14   Write an applet that draws the Big Dipper. Add some extra stars in the night sky.

PP 2.15   Write an applet that draws some balloons tied to strings. Make the balloons various colors.

PP 2.16   Write an applet that draws the Olympic logo. The circles in the logo should be colored, from left to right, blue, yellow, black, green, and red.

PP 2.17   Write an applet that draws a house with a door (and doorknob), windows, and a chimney. Add some smoke coming out of the chimney and some clouds in the sky.

PP 2.18   Write an applet that displays a business card of your own design. Include both graphics and text.

PP 2.19   Write an applet that displays your name in shadow text by drawing your name in black, then drawing it again slightly offset in a lighter color.

PP 2.20   Write an applet that shows a pie chart with eight equal slices, all colored differently.

Answers to Self-Review Questions

SR 2.1   Primitive data are basic values such as numbers or characters. Objects are more complex entities that usually contain primitive data that help define them.

SR 2.2   A string literal is a sequence of characters delimited by double quotes.

SR 2.3   Both the `print` and `println` methods of the `System.out` object write a string of characters to the monitor screen. The difference is that, after printing the characters, the `println` performs a carriage return so that whatever's printed next appears on the next line. The `print` method allows subsequent output to appear on the same line.

SR 2.4   A parameter is data that is passed into a method when it is invoked. The method usually uses that data to accomplish the ser-vice that it provides. For example, the parameter to the `println` method indicate what characters should be printed. The two numeric operands to the `Math.pow` method are the operands to the power function that is computed and returned.

SR 2.5   An escape sequence is a series of characters that begins with the backslash (\) and that implies that the following characters should be treated in some special way. Examples: \n represents the newline character, \t represents the tab character, and \" represents the quotation character (as opposed to using it to terminate a string).

SR 2.6   A variable declaration establishes the name of a variable and the type of data that it can contain. A declaration may also have an optional initialization, which gives the variable an initial value.

SR 2.7   An integer variable can store only one value at a time. When a new value is assigned to it, the old one is overwritten and lost.

SR 2.8   The four integer data types in Java are `byte`, `short`, `int`, and `long`. They differ in how much memory space is allocated for each and therefore how large a number they can hold.

SR 2.9   A character set is a list of characters in a particular order. A character set defines the valid characters that a particular type of computer or programming language will support. Java uses the Unicode character set.

SR 2.10 Operator precedence is the set of rules that dictates the order in which operators are evaluated in an expression.

SR 2.11 The result of `19%5` in a Java expression is 4. The remainder operator `%` returns the remainder after dividing the second operand into the first. Five goes into 19 three times, with 4 left over.

SR 2.12 The result of `13/4` in a Java expression is 3 (not 3.25). The result is an integer because both operands are integers. Therefore the `/` operator performs integer division, and the fractional part of the result is truncated.

SR 2.13 After executing the statement, `diameter` holds the value 20. First the current value of `diameter` (5) is multiplied by 4, and then the result is stored back in `diameter`.

SR 2.14 After executing the statement, `weight` holds the value 83. The assignment operator `-=` modifies `weight` by first subtracting 17 from the current value (100), then storing the result back into `weight`.

SR 2.15 A widening conversion tends to go from a small data value, in terms of the amount of space used to store it, to a larger one. A narrowing conversion does the opposite. Information is more likely to be lost in a narrowing conversion, which is why narrowing conversions are considered to be less safe than widening ones.

SR 2.16 A black and white picture can be drawn using a series of dots, called pixels. Pixels that correspond to a value of 0 are displayed in white and pixels that correspond to a value of 1 are displayed in black. By using thousands of pixels, a realistic black and white photo can be produced on a computer screen.

SR 2.17   A Java applet is a Java program that can be executed using a Web browser. Usually, the bytecode form of the Java applet is pulled across the Internet from another computer and executed locally. A Java application is a Java program that can stand on its own. It does not require a Web browser in order to execute.

SR 2.18   A bounding rectangle is an imaginary rectangle that surrounds a curved shape, such as an oval, in order to define the shape's width, height, and upper left corner.

Using Classes and Objects

3

CHAPTER OBJECTIVES

> Discuss the creation of objects and the use of object reference variables.

> Explore the services provided by the `String` class.

> Describe how the Java standard class library is organized into packages.

> Explore the services provided by the `Random` and `Math` classes.

> Discuss ways to format output using the `NumberFormat` and `DecimalFormat` classes.

> Introduce enumerated types.

> Discuss wrapper classes and the concept of autoboxing.

> Introduce components and containers used in graphical user interfaces.

> Describe a label component and the use of images.

This chapter further explores the use of predefined classes and the objects we can create from them. Using classes and objects for the services they provide is a fundamental part of object-oriented software, and sets the stage for writing classes of our own. In this chapter, we use classes and objects to manipulate character strings, produce random numbers, perform complex calculations, and format output. This chapter also introduces the concept of an enumerated type, which is a special kind of class in Java, and discusses the concept of a wrapper class. In the Graphics Track of this chapter, we lay the foundation for developing graphical user interfaces for our programs, and discuss how to display images.

3.1   CREATING OBJECTS

At the end of Chapter 1 we presented an overview of object-oriented concepts, including the basic relationship between classes and objects. Then in Chapter 2, in addition to discussing primitive data, we provided some examples of using objects for the services they provide. This chapter explores these ideas further.

In previous examples, we've used the `println` method many times. As we mentioned in Chapter 2, the `println` method is a service provided by the `System.out` object, which represents the standard output stream. To be more precise, the identifier `out` is an object variable that is stored in the `System` class. It has been predefined and set up for us as part of the Java standard class library. We can simply use it.

In Chapter 2 we also used the `Scanner` class, which represents an object that allows us to read input from the keyboard or a file. We created a `Scanner` object using the `new` operator. Once the object was created, we were able to use it for the various services it provides. That is, we were able to invoke its methods.

Let's carefully examine the idea of creating an object. In Java, a variable name represents either a primitive value or an object. Like variables that hold primitive types, a variable that refers to an object must be declared. The class used to define an object can be thought of as the type of an object. The declarations of object variables have a similar structure to the declarations of primitive variables.

Consider the following two declarations:

```
int num;
String name;
```

The first declaration creates a variable that holds an integer value, as we've seen many times before. The second declaration creates a `String` variable that holds a *reference* to a `String` object. An object variable doesn't hold an object itself, it holds the address of an object.

Initially, the two variables declared above don't contain any data. We say they are *uninitialized,* which can be depicted as follows:

num | – |

name | – |

As we pointed out in Chapter 2, it is always important to make sure a variable is initialized before using it. For an object variable, that means we must make sure it refers to a valid object prior to using it. In most situations the compiler will issue an error if you attempt to use a variable before initializing it.

An object variable can also be set to `null`, which is a reserved word in Java. A null reference specifically indicates that a variable does not refer to an object.

Note that, although we've declared a `String` reference variable, no `String` object actually exists yet. The act of creating an object using the `new` operator is called *instantiation*. An object is said to be an *instance* of a particular class. To instantiate an object, we can use the `new` operator, which returns the address of the new object. The following two assignment statements give values to the two variables declared above:

```
num = 42;
name = new String("James Gosling");
```

After the `new` operator creates the object, a *constructor* is invoked to help set it up initially. A constructor is a special method that has the same name as the class. In this example, the parameter to the constructor is a string literal that specifies the characters that the string object will hold. After these assignments are executed, the variables can be depicted as:

> **Key Concept**
>
> The `new` operator returns a reference to a newly created object.

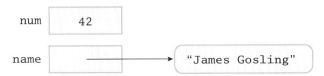

Since an object reference variable holds the address of the object, it can be thought of as a *pointer* to the location in memory where the object is held. We could show the numeric address, but the actual address value is irrelevant—what's important is that the variable refers to a particular object.

After an object has been instantiated, we use the *dot operator* to access its methods. We've used the dot operator many times already, such as in calls to `System.out.println`. The dot operator is appended directly after the object reference, followed by the method being invoked. For example, to invoke the `length` method defined in the `String` class, we can use the dot operator on the `name` reference variable:

```
count = name.length()
```

The `length` method does not take any parameters, but the parentheses are still necessary to indicate that a method is being invoked. Some methods produce a value that is *returned* when the method completes. The purpose of the `length` method of the `String` class is to determine and return the length of the string (the number of characters it contains). In this example, the returned value is assigned to the variable `count`. For the string `"James Gosling"`, the `length` method returns `13`, which includes the space between the first and last names. Some methods do not return a value. Other `String` methods are discussed in the next section.

The act of declaring the object reference variable and creating the object itself can be combined into one step by initializing the variable in the declaration, just as we do with primitive types:

```
String title = new String("Java Software Solutions");
```

Even though they are not primitive types, character strings are so fundamental and so often used that Java defines string literals delimited by double quotation marks, as we've seen in various examples. This is a shortcut notation. Whenever a string literal appears, a `String` object is created automatically. Therefore the following declaration is valid:

```
String city = "London";
```

That is, for `String` objects, the explicit use of the `new` operator and the call to the constructor can be eliminated. In most cases, we will use this simplified syntax.

Aliases

Because an object reference variable stores an address, a programmer must be careful when managing objects. First, let's review the effect of assignment on primitive values. Suppose we have two integer variables, `num1`, initialized to 5, and `num2`, initialized to 12:

num1 | 5
num2 | 12

In the following assignment statement, a copy of the value that is stored in `num1` is stored in `num2`:

```
num2 = num1;
```

```
String (String str)
   Constructor: creates a new string object with the same characters as str.

char charAt (int index)
   Returns the character at the specified index.

int compareTo (String str)
   Returns an integer indicating if this string is lexically before (a negative return
   value), equal to (a zero return value), or lexically after (a positive return value),
   the string str.

String concat (String str)
   Returns a new string consisting of this string concatenated with str.

boolean equals (String str)
   Returns true if this string contains the same characters as str (including
   case) and false otherwise.

boolean equalsIgnoreCase (String str)
   Returns true if this string contains the same characters as str (without
   regard to case) and false otherwise.

int length ()
   Returns the number of characters in this string.

String replace (char oldChar, char newChar)
   Returns a new string that is identical with this string except that every
   occurrence of oldChar is replaced by newChar.

String substring (int offset, int endIndex)
   Returns a new string that is a subset of this string starting at index offset
   and extending through endIndex-1.

String toLowerCase ()
   Returns a new string identical to this string except all uppercase letters are
   converted to their lowercase equivalent.

String toUpperCase ()
   Returns a new string identical to this string except all lowercase letters are
   converted to their uppercase equivalent.
```

FIGURE 3.1   Some methods of the String class

After printing the original phrase and its length, the concat method is executed to create a new string object referenced by the variable mutation1:

mutation1 ───────────▶ "Change is inevitable, except from vending machines."

Listing 3.1

```java
//********************************************************************
//   StringMutation.java       Author: Lewis/Loftus
//
//   Demonstrates the use of the String class and its methods.
//********************************************************************

public class StringMutation
{
   //-----------------------------------------------------------------
   //  Prints a string and various mutations of it.
   //-----------------------------------------------------------------
   public static void main (String[] args)
   {
      String phrase = "Change is inevitable";
      String mutation1, mutation2, mutation3, mutation4;

      System.out.println ("Original string: \"" + phrase + "\"");
      System.out.println ("Length of string: " + phrase.length());

      mutation1 = phrase.concat (", except from vending machines.");
      mutation2 = mutation1.toUpperCase();
      mutation3 = mutation2.replace ('E', 'X');
      mutation4 = mutation3.substring (3, 30);

      // Print each mutated string
      System.out.println ("Mutation #1: " + mutation1);
      System.out.println ("Mutation #2: " + mutation2);
      System.out.println ("Mutation #3: " + mutation3);
      System.out.println ("Mutation #4: " + mutation4);

      System.out.println ("Mutated length: " + mutation4.length());
   }
}
```

Output

```
Original string: "Change is inevitable"
Length of string: 20
Mutation #1: Change is inevitable, except from vending machines.
Mutation #2: CHANGE IS INEVITABLE, EXCEPT FROM VENDING MACHINES.
Mutation #3: CHANGX IS INXVITABLX, XXCXPT FROM VXNDING MACHINXS.
Mutation #4: NGX IS INXVITABLX, XXCXPT F
Mutated length: 27
```

Then the `toUpperCase` method is executed on the `mutation1` object, and the resulting string is stored in `mutation2`:

mutation2 → "CHANGE IS INEVITABLE, EXCEPT FROM VENDING MACHINES"

Notice that the `length` and `concat` methods are executed on the `phrase` object, but the `toUpperCase` method is executed on the `mutation1` object. Any method of the `String` class can be executed on any `String` object, but for any given invocation, a method is executed on a particular object. The results of executing `toUpperCase` on `mutation1` would be very different than the results of executing `toUpperCase` on `phrase`. Remember, each object has its own state, which often affects the results of method calls.

Finally, the `String` object variables `mutation3` and `mutation4` are initialized by the calls to `mutation2.replace` and `mutation3.substring`, respectively:

mutation3 → "CHANGX IS INXVITABLX, XXCXPT FROM VXNDING MACHINXS"

mutation4 → "NGX IS INXVITABLX, XXCXPT F"

3.3 PACKAGES

We mentioned earlier that the Java language is supported by a standard class library that we can make use of as needed. Let's examine that idea further.

A *class library* is a set of classes that supports the development of programs. A compiler or development environment often comes with a class library. Class libraries can also be obtained separately through third-party vendors. The classes in a class library contain methods that are often valuable to a programmer because of the special functionality they offer. In fact, programmers often become dependent on the methods in a class library and begin to think of them as part of the language. However, technically, they are not in the language itself.

The `String` class, for instance, is not an inherent part of the Java language. It is part of the Java standard class library that can be found in any Java development environment. The classes that make up the library were created by employees at Sun Microsystems, the people who created the Java language.

The class library is made up of several clusters of related classes, which are sometimes called Java APIs, or *application programming interfaces*. For example, we may refer to the Java Database API when we're talking about the set of classes that helps us write programs that interact with a database. Another example of an API is the Java Swing API, which refers to a set of classes that defines special graphical components used in a graphical user interface. Sometimes the entire standard library is referred to generically as the Java API.

> ### Key Concept
> The Java standard class library is organized into packages.

The classes of the Java standard class library are also grouped into *packages*. Each class is part of a particular package. The `String` class, for example, is part of the `java.lang` package. The `System` class is part of the `java.lang` package as well. We mentioned in Chapter 2 that the `Scanner` class is part of the `java.util` package.

The package organization is more fundamental and language-based than the API names. Though there is a general correspondence between package and API names, the groups of classes that make up a given API might cross packages. In this book, we primarily refer to classes in terms of their package organization.

Figure 3.2 describes some of the packages that are part of the Java standard class library. These packages are available on any platform that supports Java software development. Some of these packages support highly specific programming techniques and will not come into play in the development of basic programs.

Various classes of the Java standard class library are discussed throughout this book.

The `import` Declaration

The classes of the `java.lang` package are automatically available for use when writing a Java program. To use classes from any other package, however, we must either *fully qualify* the reference or use an *import declaration*. Recall that the example programs that use the `Scanner` class include an `import` declaration.

When you want to use a class from a class library in a program, you could use its fully qualified name, including the package name, every time it is referenced. For example, every time you want to refer to the `Scanner` class that is defined in the `java.util` package, you could write `java.util.Scanner`. However, completely specifying the package and class name every time it is needed quickly becomes tiring. Java provides the `import` declaration to simplify these references.

The `import` declaration specifies the packages and classes that will be used in a program so that the fully qualified name is not necessary with each reference. As we've seen, the following is an example of an `import` declaration:

```
import java.util.Scanner;
```

Package	Provides support to
`java.applet`	Create programs (applets) that are easily transported across the Web.
`java.awt`	Draw graphics and create graphical user interfaces; AWT stands for Abstract Windowing Toolkit.
`java.beans`	Define software components that can be easily combined into applications.
`java.io`	Perform a wide variety of input and output functions.
`java.lang`	General support; it is automatically imported into all Java programs.
`java.math`	Perform calculations with arbitrarily high precision.
`java.net`	Communicate across a network.
`java.rmi`	Create programs that can be distributed across multiple computers; RMI stands for Remote Method Invocation.
`java.security`	Enforce security restrictions.
`java.sql`	Interact with databases; SQL stands for Structured Query Language.
`java.text`	Format text for output.
`java.util`	General utilities.
`javax.swing`	Create graphical user interfaces with components that extend the AWT capabilities.
`javax.xml.parsers`	Process XML documents; XML stands for eXtensible Markup Language.

FIGURE 3.2   Some packages in the Java standard class library

This declaration asserts that the `Scanner` class of the `java.util` package may be used in the program. Once this `import` declaration is made, it is sufficient to use the simple name `Scanner` when referring to that class in the program.

If two classes from two different packages have the same name, `import` declarations will not suffice because the compiler won't be able to figure out which class is being referenced in the flow of the code. When such situations arise, which is rare, the fully qualified names should be used in the code.

Another form of the `import` declaration uses an asterisk (`*`) to indicate that any class inside the package might be used in the program. Therefore, the following declaration allows all classes in the `java.util` package to be referenced in the program without qualifying each reference:

```
import java.util.*;
```

If only one class of a particular package will be used in a program, it is usually better to name the class specifically in the `import` declaration. However, if two or more will be used, the * notation is usually fine.

The classes of the `java.lang` package are automatically imported because they are fundamental and can be thought of as basic extensions to the language. Therefore, any class in the `java.lang` package, such as `System` and `String`, can be used without an explicit `import` declaration. It's as if all program files automatically contain the following declaration:

```
import java.lang.*;
```

3.4   THE Random CLASS

The need for random numbers occurs frequently when writing software. Games often use a random number to represent the roll of a die or the shuffle of a deck of cards. A flight simulator may use random numbers to determine how often a simulated flight has engine trouble. A program designed to help high school students prepare for the SATs may use random numbers to choose the next question to ask.

The `Random` class, which is part of the `java.util` class, represents a *pseudorandom number generator*. A random number generator picks a number at random out of a range of values. A program that serves this role is technically pseudorandom, because a program has no means to actually pick a number randomly. A pseudorandom number generator performs a series of complicated calculations, based on an initial *seed value*, and produces a number. Though they are technically not random (because they are calculated), the values produced by a pseudorandom number generator usually appear random, at least random enough for most situations.

Figure 3.3 lists some of the methods of the `Random` class. The `nextInt` method can be called with no parameters, or we can pass it a single integer value. The version that takes no parameters generates a random number across the entire range of `int` values, including negative numbers. Usually, though, we need a random number within a more specific range. For instance, to simulate the roll of a die, we might want a random number in the range of 1 to 6. The `nextInt` method returns a value that's in the range from 0 to one less than its parameter. For example, if we pass in 100, we'll get a return value that is greater than or equal to 0 and less than or equal to 99.

```
Random ()
   Constructor: creates a new pseudorandom number generator.

float nextFloat ()
   Returns a random number between 0.0 (inclusive) and 1.0 (exclusive).

int nextInt ()
   Returns a random number that ranges over all possible int values (positive
   and negative).

int nextInt (int num)
   Returns a random number in the range 0 to num-1.
```

FIGURE 3.3   Some methods of the Random class

Note that the value that we pass to the nextInt method is also the number of possible values we can get in return. We can shift the range as needed by adding or subtracting the proper amount. To get a random number in the range 1 to 6, we can call nextInt(6) to get a value from 0 to 5, and then add 1.

The nextFloat method of the Random class returns a float value that is greater than or equal to 0.0 and less than 1.0. If desired, we can use multiplication to scale the result, cast it into an int value to truncate the fractional part, and then shift the range as we do with integers.

The program shown in Listing 3.2 produces several random numbers in various ranges.

Listing 3.2

```java
//********************************************************************
//   RandomNumbers.java          Author: Lewis/Loftus
//
//   Demonstrates the creation of pseudo-random numbers using the
//   Random class.
//********************************************************************

import java.util.Random;

public class RandomNumbers
{
    //-----------------------------------------------------------------
    //   Generates random numbers in various ranges.
    //-----------------------------------------------------------------
```

Listing 3.2 continued

```java
public static void main (String[] args)
{
    Random generator = new Random();
    int num1;
    float num2;

    num1 = generator.nextInt();
    System.out.println ("A random integer: " + num1);

    num1 = generator.nextInt(10);
    System.out.println ("From 0 to 9: " + num1);

    num1 = generator.nextInt(10) + 1;
    System.out.println ("From 1 to 10: " + num1);

    num1 = generator.nextInt(15) + 20;
    System.out.println ("From 20 to 34: " + num1);

    num1 = generator.nextInt(20) - 10;
    System.out.println ("From -10 to 9: " + num1);

    num2 = generator.nextFloat();
    System.out.println ("A random float (between 0-1): " + num2);

    num2 = generator.nextFloat() * 6;   // 0.0 to 5.999999
    num1 = (int)num2 + 1;
    System.out.println ("From 1 to 6: " + num1);
}
}
```

Output

```
A random integer: 1773351873
From 0 to 9: 8
From 1 to 10: 6
From 20 to 34: 20
From -10 to 9: -6
A random float (between 0-1): 0.71058085
From 1 to 6: 3
```

3.5   THE Math CLASS

The Math class provides a large number of basic mathematical functions that are often helpful in making calculations. The Math class is defined in the java.lang package of the Java standard class library. Figure 3.4 lists several of its methods.

All the methods in the Math class are *static methods* (also called *class methods*), which means they can be invoked through the name of the class in which they are defined, without having to instantiate an object of the class first. We've seen a static method used in previous examples when invoking the create method of the Scanner class. Static methods are discussed further in Chapter 6.

> ### Key Concept
> All methods of the Math class are static, meaning they are invoked through the class name.

The methods of the Math class return values, which can be used in expressions as needed. For example, the following statement computes the absolute value of the number stored in total, adds it to the value of count raised to the fourth power, and stores the result in the variable value:

```
value = Math.abs(total) + Math.pow(count, 4);
```

Note that you can pass an integer value to a method that accepts a double parameter. This is a form of assignment conversion, which was discussed in Chapter 2.

The Quadratic program, shown in Listing 3.3, uses the Math class to compute the roots of a quadratic equation. Recall that a quadratic equation has the following general form:

```
ax² + bx + c
```

The Quadratic program reads values that represent the coefficients in a quadratic equation (a, b, and c), and then evaluates the quadratic formula to determine the roots of the equation. The quadratic formula is:

$$\text{roots} = \frac{-b \pm \sqrt{b^2 - 4ac}}{2a}$$

Note that this program assumes that the discriminant (the value under the square root) is positive. If it's not, the results will not be a valid number, which Java represents as NAN, which stands for Not A Number. In Chapter 5 we will see how we can handle this type of situation gracefully.

```
static int abs (int num)
   Returns the absolute value of num.

static double acos (double num)

static double asin (double num)

static double atan (double num)
   Returns the arc cosine, arc sine, or arc tangent of num.

static double cos (double angle)

static double sin (double angle)

static double tan (double angle)
   Returns the angle cosine, sine, or tangent of angle, which is measured
   in radians.

static double ceil (double num)
   Returns the ceiling of num, which is the smallest whole number greater
   than or equal to num.

static double exp (double power)
   Returns the value e raised to the specified power.

static double floor (double num)
   Returns the floor of num, which is the largest whole number less than
   or equal to num.

static double pow (double num, double power)
   Returns the value num raised to the specified power.

static double random ()
   Returns a random number between 0.0 (inclusive) and 1.0 (exclusive).

static double sqrt (double num)
   Returns the square root of num, which must be positive.
```

FIGURE 3.4   Some methods of the Math class

Listing 3.3

```java
//********************************************************************
//  Quadratic.java        Author: Lewis/Loftus
//
//  Demonstrates the use of the Math class to perform a calculation
//  based on user input.
//********************************************************************

import java.util.Scanner;

public class Quadratic
{
    //-----------------------------------------------------------------
    //  Determines the roots of a quadratic equation.
    //-----------------------------------------------------------------
    public static void main (String[] args)
    {
        int a, b, c;   // ax^2 + bx + c
        double discriminant, root1, root2;

        Scanner scan = new Scanner (System.in);

        System.out.print ("Enter the coefficient of x squared: ");
        a = scan.nextInt();

        System.out.print ("Enter the coefficient of x: ");
        b = scan.nextInt();

        System.out.print ("Enter the constant: ");
        c = scan.nextInt();

        // Use the quadratic formula to compute the roots.
        // Assumes a positive discriminant.

        discriminant = Math.pow(b, 2) - (4 * a * c);
        root1 = ((-1 * b) + Math.sqrt(discriminant)) / (2 * a);
        root2 = ((-1 * b) - Math.sqrt(discriminant)) / (2 * a);
```

Listing 3.3 **continued**

```
        System.out.println ("Root #1: " + root1);
        System.out.println ("Root #2: " + root2);
    }
}
```

Output

```
Enter the coefficient of x squared: 3
Enter the coefficient of x: 8
Enter the constant: 4
Root #1: -0.6666666666666666
Root #2: -2.0
```

3.6   FORMATTING OUTPUT

The NumberFormat class and the DecimalFormat class are used to format information so that it looks appropriate when printed or displayed. They are both part of the Java standard class library and are defined in the java.text package.

The NumberFormat Class

The NumberFormat class provides generic formatting capabilities for numbers. You don't instantiate a NumberFormat object by using the new operator. Instead, you request an object from one of the static methods that you invoke through the class name itself. Figure 3.5 lists some of the methods of the NumberFormat class.

```
String format (double number)
    Returns a string containing the specified number formatted according to
    this object's pattern.

static NumberFormat getCurrencyInstance()
    Returns a NumberFormat object that represents a currency format for the
    current locale.

static NumberFormat getPercentInstance()
    Returns a NumberFormat object that represents a percentage format for
    the current locale.
```

FIGURE 3.5   Some methods of the NumberFormat class

Two of the methods in the NumberFormat class, getCurrencyInstance and getPercentInstance, return an object that is used to format numbers. The getCurrencyInstance method returns a formatter for monetary values, and the getPercentInstance method returns an object that formats a percentage. The format method is invoked through a formatter object and returns a String that contains the number formatted in the appropriate manner.

The Purchase program shown in Listing 3.4 uses both types of formatters. It reads in a sales transaction and computes the final price, including tax.

Listing 3.4

```java
//********************************************************************
//   Purchase.java        Author: Lewis/Loftus
//
//   Demonstrates the use of the NumberFormat class to format output.
//********************************************************************

import java.util.Scanner;
import java.text.NumberFormat;

public class Purchase
{
   //-----------------------------------------------------------------
   //   Calculates the final price of a purchased item using values
   //   entered by the user.
   //-----------------------------------------------------------------
   public static void main (String[] args)
   {
      final double TAX_RATE = 0.06;  // 6% sales tax

      int quantity;
      double subtotal, tax, totalCost, unitPrice;

      Scanner scan = new Scanner (System.in);

      NumberFormat fmt1 = NumberFormat.getCurrencyInstance();
      NumberFormat fmt2 = NumberFormat.getPercentInstance();

      System.out.print ("Enter the quantity: ");
      quantity = scan.nextInt();

      System.out.print ("Enter the unit price: ");
      unitPrice = scan.nextDouble();
```

Listing 3.4   **continued**

```
        subtotal = quantity * unitPrice;
        tax = subtotal * TAX_RATE;
        totalCost = subtotal + tax;

        // Print output with appropriate formatting
        System.out.println ("Subtotal: " + fmt1.format(subtotal));
        System.out.println ("Tax: " + fmt1.format(tax) + " at "
                            + fmt2.format(TAX_RATE));
        System.out.println ("Total: " + fmt1.format(totalCost));
    }
}
```

Output

```
Enter the quantity: 5
Enter the unit price: 3.87
Subtotal: $19.35
Tax: $1.16 at 6%
Total: $20.51
```

The DecimalFormat Class

Unlike the NumberFormat class, the DecimalFormat class is instantiated in the traditional way using the new operator. Its constructor takes a string that represents the pattern that will guide the formatting process. We can then use the format method to format a particular value. At a later point, if we want to change the pattern that the formatter object uses, we can invoke the applyPattern method. Figure 3.6 describes these methods.

```
DecimalFormat (String pattern)
   Constructor: creates a new DecimalFormat object with the specified pattern.

void applyPattern (String pattern)
   Applies the specified pattern to this DecimalFormat object.

String format (double number)
   Returns a string containing the specified number formatted according to the
   current pattern.
```

FIGURE 3.6   Some methods of the DecimalFormat class

The pattern defined by the string that is passed to the `DecimalFormat` constructor can get fairly elaborate. Various symbols are used to represent particular formatting guidelines. The pattern defined by the string `"0.###"`, for example, indicates that at least one digit should be printed to the left of the decimal point and should be a zero if the integer portion of the value is zero. It also indicates that the fractional portion of the value should be rounded to three digits.

This pattern is used in the `CircleStats` program, shown in Listing 3.5, which reads the radius of a circle from the user and computes its area and circumference. Trailing zeros, such as in the circle's area of 78.540, are not printed.

The `printf` Method

In addition to `print` and `println`, the `System` class has another output method called `printf`, which allows the user to print a formatted string containing data values. The first parameter to the method represents the format string, and the remaining parameters specify the values that are inserted into the format string.

For example, the following line of code prints an ID number and a name:

```
System.out.printf ("ID: %5d\tName: %s", id, name);
```

The first parameter specifies the format of the output and includes literal characters that label the output values as well as escape characters such as `\t`. The pattern `%5d` indicates that the corresponding numeric value (`id`) should be printed in a field of five characters. The pattern `%s` matches the string parameter `name`. The values of `id` and `name` are inserted into the string, producing a result such as:

```
ID: 24036     Name: Larry Flagelhopper
```

The `printf` method was added to Java to mirror a similar function used in programs written in the C programming language. It makes it easier for a programmer to translate (or *migrate*) an existing C program into Java.

Older software that still has value is called a *legacy system*. Maintaining a legacy system is often a costly effort because, among other things, it is based on older technologies. But in many cases, maintaining a legacy system is still more cost-effective than migrating it to new technology, such as writing it in a newer language. Adding the `printf` method is an attempt to make such migrations easier, and therefore less costly, by providing the same kind of output statement that C programmers have come to rely on.

> **Key Concept**
>
> The `printf` method was added to Java to support the migration of legacy systems.

However, using the `printf` method is not a particularly clean object-oriented solution to the problem of formatting output, so we avoid its use in this book.

Listing 3.5

```java
//********************************************************************
//  CircleStats.java       Author: Lewis/Loftus
//
//  Demonstrates the formatting of decimal values using the
//  DecimalFormat class.
//********************************************************************

import java.util.Scanner;
import java.text.DecimalFormat;

public class CircleStats
{
   //-----------------------------------------------------------------
   //  Calculates the area and circumference of a circle given its
   //  radius.
   //-----------------------------------------------------------------
   public static void main (String[] args)
   {
      int radius;
      double area, circumference;

      Scanner scan = new Scanner (System.in);

      System.out.print ("Enter the circle's radius: ");
      radius = scan.nextInt();

      area = Math.PI * Math.pow(radius, 2);
      circumference = 2 * Math.PI * radius;

      // Round the output to three decimal places
      DecimalFormat fmt = new DecimalFormat ("0.###");

      System.out.println ("The circle's area: " + fmt.format(area));
      System.out.println ("The circle's circumference: "
                          + fmt.format(circumference));
   }
}
```

Output

```
Enter the circle's radius: 5
The circle's area: 78.54
The circle's circumference: 31.416
```

3.7 ENUMERATED TYPES

Java provides the ability to define an enumerated type, which can then be used as the type of a variable when it is declared. An enumerated type establishes all possible values of a variable of that type by listing, or enumerating, them. The values are identifiers, and can be anything desired.

For example, the following declaration defines an enumerated type called `Season` whose possible values are `winter`, `spring`, `summer`, and `fall`:

```
enum Season {winter, spring, summer, fall}
```

There is no limit to the number of values that you can list for an enumerated type. Once the type is defined, a variable can be declared of that type:

```
Season time;
```

The variable `time` is now restricted in the values it can take on. It can hold one of the four `Season` values, but nothing else. Java enumerated types are considered to be *type-safe*, meaning that any attempt to use a value other than one of the enumerated values will result in a compile-time error.

> **Key Concept**
>
> Enumerated types are type-safe, ensuring that invalid values will not be used.

The values are accessed through the name of the type. For example:

```
time = Season.spring;
```

Enumerated types can be quite helpful in situations in which you have a relatively small number of distinct values that a variable can assume. For example, suppose we wanted to represent the various letter grades a student could earn. We might declare the following enumerated type:

```
enum Grade {A, B, C, D, F}
```

Any initialized variable that holds a `Grade` is guaranteed to have one of those valid grades. That's better than using a simple character or string variable to represent the grade, which could take on any value.

Suppose we also wanted to represent plus and minus grades, such as A– and B+. We couldn't use A– or B+ as values, because they are not valid identifiers (the characters '–' and '+' cannot be part of an identifier in Java). However, the same values could be represented using the identifiers `Aminus`, `Bplus`, etc.

Internally, each value in an enumerated type is stored as an integer, which is referred to as its *ordinal value*. The first value in an enumerated type has an ordinal value of 0, the second one has an ordinal value of 1, the third one 2, and so on. The ordinal values are used internally only. You cannot assign a numeric value to an enumerated type, even if it corresponds to a valid ordinal value.

An enumerated type is a special kind of class, and the variables of an enumerated type are object variables. As such, there are a few methods associated with all enumerated types. The `ordinal` method returns the numeric value associated with a particular enumerated type value. The `name` method returns the name of the value, which is the same as the identifier that defines the value.

Listing 3.6 shows a program called `IceCream` that declares an enumerated type and exercises some of its methods. Because enumerated types are special types of classes, they are not defined within a method. They can be defined either at the class level (within the class but outside a method), as in this example, or at the outermost level.

We explore enumerated types further in Chapter 6.

Listing 3.6

```
//********************************************************************
//   IceCream.java        Author: Lewis/Loftus
//
//   Demonstrates the use of enumerated types.
//********************************************************************

public class IceCream
{
    enum Flavor {vanilla, chocolate, strawberry, fudgeRipple, coffee,
                 rockyRoad, mintChocolateChip, cookieDough}

    //-----------------------------------------------------------------
    //   Creates and uses variables of the Flavor type.
    //-----------------------------------------------------------------
    public static void main (String[] args)
    {
        Flavor cone1, cone2, cone3;

        cone1 = Flavor.rockyRoad;
        cone2 = Flavor.chocolate;
```

Listing 3.6   **continued**

```
        System.out.println ("cone1 value: " + cone1);
        System.out.println ("cone1 ordinal: " + cone1.ordinal());
        System.out.println ("cone1 name: " + cone1.name());

        System.out.println ();
        System.out.println ("cone2 value: " + cone2);
        System.out.println ("cone2 ordinal: " + cone2.ordinal());
        System.out.println ("cone2 name: " + cone2.name());

        cone3 = cone1;

        System.out.println ();
        System.out.println ("cone3 value: " + cone3);
        System.out.println ("cone3 ordinal: " + cone3.ordinal());
        System.out.println ("cone3 name: " + cone3.name());
    }
}
```

Output

```
cone1 value: rockyRoad
cone1 ordinal: 5
cone1 name: rockyRoad

cone2 value: chocolate
cone2 ordinal: 1
cone2 name: chocolate

cone3 value: rockyRoad
cone3 ordinal: 5
cone3 name: rockyRoad
```

3.8   WRAPPER CLASSES

As we've discussed previously, Java represents data by using primitive types (such as int, double, char, and boolean) in addition to classes and objects. Having two categories of data to manage (primitive values and object references) can present a challenge in some circumstances. For example, we might create an object that serves as a container to hold various types of other objects. However, in a specific situation, we may want it to hold a simple integer value. In these cases we need to "wrap" a primitive value into an object.

A *wrapper class* represents a particular primitive type. For instance, the `Integer` class represents a simple integer value. An object created from the `Integer` class stores a single `int` value. The constructors of the wrapper classes accept the primitive value to store. For example:

```
Integer ageObj = new Integer(40);
```

Once this declaration and instantiation are performed, the `ageObj` object effectively represents the integer 40 as an object. It can be used wherever an object is needed in a program rather than a primitive type.

For each primitive type in Java there exists a corresponding wrapper class in the Java class library. All wrapper classes are defined in the `java.lang` package. Figure 3.7 shows the wrapper class that corresponds to each primitive type.

Note that there is even a wrapper class that represents the type `void`. However, unlike the other wrapper classes, the `Void` class cannot be instantiated. It simply represents the concept of a void reference.

Wrapper classes also provide various methods related to the management of the associated primitive type. For example, the `Integer` class contains methods that return the `int` value stored in the object and that convert the stored value to other primitive types. Figure 3.8 lists some of the methods found in the `Integer` class. The other wrapper classes have similar methods.

Note that the wrapper classes also contain static methods that can be invoked independent of any instantiated object. For example, the `Integer` class contains a static method called `parseInt` to convert an integer that is stored in a `String` to its corresponding `int` value. If the `String` object `str` holds the string "987",

Primitive Type	Wrapper Class
byte	Byte
short	Short
int	Integer
long	Long
float	Float
double	Double
char	Character
boolean	Boolean
void	Void

FIGURE 3.7   Wrapper classes in the Java class library

```
Integer (int value)
   Constructor: creates a new Integer object storing the specified value.

byte byteValue ()
double doubleValue ()
float floatValue ()
int intValue ()
long longValue ()
   Return the value of this Integer as the corresponding primitive type.

static int parseInt (String str)
   Returns the int corresponding to the value stored in the
   specified string.

static String toBinaryString (int num)
static String tohexString (int num)
static String toOctalString (int num)
   Returns a string representation of the specified integer value in the
   corresponding base.
```

FIGURE 3.8   Some methods of the `Integer` class

the following line of code converts the string into the integer value 987 and stores that value the `int` variable num:

```
num = Integer.parseInt(str);
```

The Java wrapper classes often contain static constants that are helpful as well. For example, the `Integer` class contains two constants, `MIN_VALUE` and `MAX_VALUE`, that hold the smallest and largest `int` values, respectively. The other wrapper classes contain similar constants for their types.

Autoboxing

Autoboxing is the automatic conversion between a primitive value and a corresponding wrapper object. For example, in the following code, an `int` value is assigned to an `Integer` object reference variable:

```
Integer obj1;
int num1 = 69;
obj1 = num1;  // automatically creates an Integer object
```

The reverse conversion, called unboxing, also occurs automatically when needed. For example:

```
Integer obj2 = new Integer(69);
int num2;
num2 = obj2;   // automatically extracts the int value
```

Assignments between primitive types and object types are generally incompatible. The ability to autobox occurs only between primitive types and corresponding wrapper classes. In any other case, attempting to assign a primitive value to an object reference variable, or vice versa, will cause a compile-time error.

3.9 COMPONENTS AND CONTAINERS

In the Graphics Track sections of Chapter 2 we introduced the Java capabilities to draw shapes using the `Graphics` and `Color` classes from the Java standard class library. We also defined the concept of an applet, a Java program that is intended to be embedded in a Web page and executed through a browser. Recall that, in contrast to applets, Java applications are stand-alone programs that are not executed through the Web.

Most of the example programs we've looked at so far have been Java applications. More specifically, they have been *command-line applications,* which interact with the user only through simple text prompts. A Java application can have graphical components as well. Throughout the rest of the book, in the Graphics Track sections at the end of each chapter, we will explore the capabilities of Java to create programs with graphical user interfaces (GUIs). In this chapter we establish the basic issues regarding graphics-based applications.

A GUI *component* is an object that represents a screen element that is used to display information or to allow the user to interact with the program in a certain way. GUI components include labels, buttons, text fields, scroll bars, and menus.

Java components and other GUI-related classes are defined primarily in two packages: `java.awt` and `javax.swing`. (Note the x in `javax.swing`.) The *Abstract Windowing Toolkit* (AWT) was the original Java GUI package. It still contains many important classes, such as the `Color` class that we used in Chapter 2. The *Swing* package was added later and provides components that are more versatile than those of the AWT package. Both packages are needed for GUI development, but we will use Swing components whenever there is an option.

A *container* is a special type of component that is used to hold and organize other components. Frames and panels are two examples of Java containers. Let's explore them in more detail.

> **Key Concept**
>
> Containers are special GUI components that hold and organize other components.

Frames and Panels

A *frame* is a container that is used to display GUI-based Java applications. A frame is displayed as a separate window with its own title bar. It can be repositioned on the screen and resized as needed by dragging it with the mouse. It contains small buttons in the corner of the frame that allow the frame to be minimized, maximized, and closed. A frame is defined by the `JFrame` class.

A *panel* is also a container. However, unlike a frame, it cannot be displayed on its own. A panel must be added to another container for it to be displayed. Generally a panel doesn't move unless you move the container that it's in. Its primary role is to help organize the other components in a GUI. A panel is defined by the `JPanel` class.

> **Key Concept**
>
> A frame is displayed as a separate window, but a panel can only be displayed as part of another container.

We can classify containers as either heavyweight or lightweight. A *heavyweight container* is one that is managed by the underlying operating system on which the program is run, whereas a *lightweight container* is managed by the Java program itself. Occasionally this distinction will be important as we explore GUI development. A frame is a heavyweight component, and a panel is a lightweight component.

Heavyweight components are more complex than lightweight components in general. A frame, for example, has multiple *panes,* which are responsible for various characteristics of the frame window. All visible elements of a Java interface are displayed in a frame's *content pane.*

Generally, we can create a Java GUI-based application by creating a frame in which the program interface is displayed. The interface is often organized onto a primary panel, which is added to the frame's content pane. The components in the primary panel are often organized using other panels as needed.

Containers are generally not useful unless they help us organize and display other components. Let's examine another fundamental GUI component. A *label* is a component that displays a line of text in a GUI. A label can also display an image, a topic discussed later in this chapter. Usually, labels are used to display information or identify other components in the GUI. Labels can be found in almost every GUI-based program.

Let's look at an example that uses frames, panels, and labels. When the program in Listing 3.7 is executed, a new window appears on the screen displaying a phrase. The text of the phrase is displayed using two label components. The labels are organized in a panel, and the panel is displayed in the content pane of the frame.

The `JFrame` constructor takes a string as a parameter, which it displays in the title bar of the frame. The call to the `setDefaultCloseOperation` method determines what will happen when the close button (the `X`) in the corner of the frame is clicked. In most cases we'll simply let that button terminate the program, as indicated by the `EXIT_ON_CLOSE` constant.

A panel is created by instantiating the `JPanel` class. The background color of the panel is set using the `setBackground` method. The `setPreferredSize` method accepts a `Dimension` object as a parameter, which is used to indicate the width and height of the component in pixels. The size of many components can be set this way, and most also have `setMinimumSize` and `setMaximumSize` methods to help control the look of the interface.

The labels are created by instantiating the `JLabel` class, passing to its constructor the text of the label. In this program two separate label components are created.

Containers have an `add` method that allows other components to be added to them. Both labels are added to the primary panel, and are from that point on considered to be part of that panel. The order in which components are added to a container often matters. In this case, it determines which label appears above the other.

Finally, the content pane of the frame is obtained using the `getContentPane` method, immediately after which the `add` method of the content pane is called to add the panel. The `pack` method of the frame sets its size appropriately based on its contents—in this case the frame is sized to accommodate the size of the panel it contains. This is a better approach than trying to set the size of the frame explicitly, which should change as the components within the frame change. The call to the `setVisible` method causes the frame to be displayed on the monitor screen.

The `Authority` program is not interactive. In general, labels do not allow the user to interact with a program. We will examine interactive GUI components in the next chapter.

However, you can interact with the frame itself in various ways. You can move the entire frame to another point on the desktop by grabbing the title bar of the frame and dragging it with the mouse. You can also resize the frame by dragging the bottom-right corner of the frame. Note what happens when the frame is made wider: the second label pops up next to the first label.

Listing 3.7

```java
//********************************************************************
//  Authority.java        Author: Lewis/Loftus
//
//  Demonstrates the use of frames, panels, and labels.
//********************************************************************

import java.awt.*;
import javax.swing.*;

public class Authority
{
    //-----------------------------------------------------------------
    //  Displays some words of wisdom.
    //-----------------------------------------------------------------
    public static void main (String[] args)
    {
        JFrame frame = new JFrame ("Authority");

        frame.setDefaultCloseOperation (JFrame.EXIT_ON_CLOSE);

        JPanel primary = new JPanel();
        primary.setBackground (Color.yellow);
        primary.setPreferredSize (new Dimension(250, 75));

        JLabel label1 = new JLabel ("Question authority,");
        JLabel label2 = new JLabel ("but raise your hand first.");

        primary.add (label1);
        primary.add (label2);

        frame.getContentPane().add(primary);
        frame.pack();
        frame.setVisible(true);
    }
}
```

Display

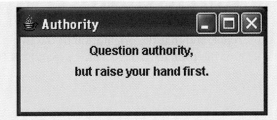

Every container is managed by an object called a *layout manager* that determines how the components in the container are laid out. The layout manager is consulted when important things happen to the interface, such as when the frame is resized.

Unless you specify otherwise, the components in a panel will try to arrange themselves next to one another in a row, and a component will move down to the next row only when the width of the panel won't accommodate it. Experiment with this program to see how the layout manager changes the organization of the labels as the window size is changed. Layout managers are discussed in more detail in the Graphics Track sections of Chapter 6.

3.10   NESTED PANELS

In the previous section, we saw an example in which two labels were contained in a panel that was contained in a frame. Such relationships make up the *containment hierarchy* of an interface, which can be as intricate as needed to create the visual effect desired.

In particular, it is common to have multiple layers of nested panels to organize and group components in various ways. While you shouldn't include unnecessary components in the containment hierarchy, don't hesitate to include extra scaffolding in the creation of an interface to help achieve the effect you want.

The program in Listing 3.8, `NestedPanels`, creates two subpanels, each containing a label. Both subpanels are put onto another panel, which is then added to the content pane of the frame.

Note that the primary panel in the program was not explicitly sized. It sized itself as needed to accommodate the two panels contained in it. Also note that the subpanels have a buffer around them through which the blue of the primary panel can be seen. Such spacing is a function of the layout manager that is used to govern the container, and the characteristics set for the components themselves. These issues are explored further in later Graphics Track sections.

As you did with the previous example, execute and experiment with this one. Resize the frame to see the effect on the components. Note that the size of the subpanels stays fixed, and that the orientation of the two panels changes depending on the width of the primary panel (which expands as the frame expands).

After you are comfortable with the way the components are laid out relative to each other, change the background color of all panels to the same color (say, green) to see how the distinction between panels can be invisible if the interface is designed accordingly.

Listing 3.8

```java
//********************************************************************
//   NestedPanels.java        Author: Lewis/Loftus
//
//   Demonstrates a basic component hierarchy.
//********************************************************************

import java.awt.*;
import javax.swing.*;

public class NestedPanels
{
   //-----------------------------------------------------------------
   //  Presents two colored panels nested within a third.
   //-----------------------------------------------------------------
   public static void main (String[] args)
   {
      JFrame frame = new JFrame ("Nested Panels");
      frame.setDefaultCloseOperation (JFrame.EXIT_ON_CLOSE);

      // Set up first subpanel
      JPanel subPanel1 = new JPanel();
      subPanel1.setPreferredSize (new Dimension(150, 100));
      subPanel1.setBackground (Color.green);
      JLabel label1 = new JLabel ("One");
      subPanel1.add (label1);

      // Set up second subpanel
      JPanel subPanel2 = new JPanel();
      subPanel2.setPreferredSize (new Dimension(150, 100));
      subPanel2.setBackground (Color.red);
      JLabel label2 = new JLabel ("Two");
      subPanel2.add (label2);

      // Set up primary panel
      JPanel primary = new JPanel();
      primary.setBackground (Color.blue);
      primary.add (subPanel1);
      primary.add (subPanel2);
```

Listing 3.8   **continued**

```
        frame.getContentPane().add(primary);
        frame.pack();
        frame.setVisible(true);
    }
}
```

Display

3.11   IMAGES

Images often play an important role in graphics-based software. Java has the ability to use JPEG and GIF images in various ways. The Graphics class contains a drawImage method that allows you to draw the image just as you would draw a shape or character string. An image can also be incorporated into a label component. Let's explore the relationship between images and labels in more detail.

Key Concept

A label can contain text, an image, or both.

As we've seen in previous sections, a label defined by the JLabel class can be used to provide information to the user or to describe other components in an interface. A JLabel can also contain an image. That is, a label can be composed of text, an image, or both.

The ImageIcon class is used to represent an image that is included in a label. The ImageIcon constructor takes the name of the image file and loads it into the object. ImageIcon objects can be made using either JPEG or GIF images.

The alignment of the text and image within the label can be set explicitly, using either the JLabel constructor or specific methods. Similarly, we can set the position of the text relative to the image.

The `LabelDemo` program shown in Listing 3.9 displays several labels. Each
label shows its text and image in different orientations.

Listing 3.9

```
//********************************************************************
//  LabelDemo.java        Author: Lewis/Loftus
//
//  Demonstrates the use of image icons in labels.
//********************************************************************

import java.awt.*;
import javax.swing.*;

public class LabelDemo
{
    //----------------------------------------------------------------
    //  Creates and displays the primary application frame.
    //----------------------------------------------------------------
    public static void main (String[] args)
    {
        JFrame frame = new JFrame ("Label Demo");
        frame.setDefaultCloseOperation (JFrame.EXIT_ON_CLOSE);

        ImageIcon icon = new ImageIcon ("devil.gif");

        JLabel label1, label2, label3;

        label1 = new JLabel ("Devil Left", icon, SwingConstants.CENTER);

        label2 = new JLabel ("Devil Right", icon, SwingConstants.CENTER);
        label2.setHorizontalTextPosition (SwingConstants.LEFT);
        label2.setVerticalTextPosition (SwingConstants.BOTTOM);

        label3 = new JLabel ("Devil Above", icon, SwingConstants.CENTER);
        label3.setHorizontalTextPosition (SwingConstants.CENTER);
        label3.setVerticalTextPosition (SwingConstants.BOTTOM);

        JPanel panel = new JPanel();
        panel.setBackground (Color.cyan);
        panel.setPreferredSize (new Dimension (200, 250));
        panel.add (label1);
        panel.add (label2);
        panel.add (label3);
```

Listing 3.9   **continued**

```
        frame.getContentPane().add(panel);
        frame.pack();
        frame.setVisible(true);
    }
}
```

Display

The third parameter passed to the JLabel constructor defines the horizontal positioning of the label within the space allowed for the label in the panel. The SwingConstants interface contains several constants used by various Swing components, making it easier to refer to them.

The orientation of the label's text and image is explicitly set using the setHorizontalTextPosition and setVerticalTextPosition methods. As shown in the case of the first label, the default horizontal position for text is on the right (image on the left), and the default vertical position for text is centered relative to the image.

Don't confuse the horizontal positioning of the label in the container with the setting of the orientation between the text and the image. The third parameter of the constructor determines the first, and the explicit method calls determine the second.

By putting an image in a label, it becomes part of a component that gets laid out with all other components in a container, instead of being drawn in a particular place. This is an appropriate design decision: whether to draw an image using the `drawImage` method of the `Graphics` class or to use a label to display an image. Your choice should be based on the particular needs of the program.

Summary of Key Concepts

> The `new` operator returns a reference to a newly created object.

> Multiple reference variables can refer to the same object.

> Usually a method is executed on a particular object, which affects the results.

> A class library provides useful support when developing programs.

> The Java standard class library is organized into packages.

> All classes of the `java.lang` package are automatically imported for every program.

> A pseudorandom number generator performs a complex calculation to create the illusion of randomness.

> All methods of the `Math` class are static, meaning they are invoked through the class name.

> The `printf` method was added to Java to support the migration of legacy systems.

> Enumerated types are type-safe, ensuring that invalid values will not be used.

> A wrapper class allows a primitive value to be managed as an object.

> Autoboxing provides automatic conversions between primitive values and corresponding wrapper objects.

> Containers are special GUI components that hold and organize other components.

> A frame is displayed as a separate window, but a panel can only be displayed as part of another container.

> Every container is managed by a layout manager.

> Panels can be nested to create an intricate containment hierarchy of components.

> A label can contain text, an image, or both.

Self-Review Questions

SR 3.1   What does the `new` operator accomplish?

SR 3.2   What is a null reference?

SR 3.3   What is an alias? How does it relate to garbage collection?

SR 3.4   Write a declaration for a `String` variable called `author` and initialize it to the string `"Fred Brooks"`. Draw a graphic representation of the variable and its value.

SR 3.5   Write a statement that prints the value of a `String` object called `title` in all uppercase letters.

SR 3.6   Write a declaration for a `String` variable called `front` and initialize it to the first 10 characters of another `String` object called `description`.

SR 3.7   What is a Java package?

SR 3.8   What does the `java.net` package contain? The `javax.swing` package?

SR 3.9   What package contains the `Scanner` class? The `String` class? The `Random` class? The `Math` class?

SR 3.10   What does an import statement accomplish?

SR 3.11   Why doesn't the `String` class have to be specifically imported into our programs?

SR 3.12   Given a `Random` object called `rand`, what does the call `rand.nextInt()` return?

SR 3.13   Given a `Random` object called `rand`, what does the call `rand.nextInt(20)` return?

SR 3.14   What is a class method (also called a static method)?

SR 3.15   Write a statement that prints the sine of an angle measuring 1.23 radians.

SR 3.16   Write a declaration for a `double` variable called `result` and initialize it to 5 raised to the power 2.5.

SR 3.17   What are the steps to output a floating-point value as a percentage using Java's formatting classes?

SR 3.18   Write the declaration of an enumerated type that represents movie ratings.

SR 3.19   How can we represent a primitive value as an object?

SR 3.20   What is the difference between a frame and a panel?

SR 3.21   What is the containment hierarchy of a Java graphical user interface?

Exercises

EX 3.1   Write a statement that prints the number of characters in a `String` object called `overview`.

EX 3.2   Write a statement that prints the 8th character of a `String` object called `introduction`.

EX 3.3   Write a declaration for a `String` variable called `change` and initialize it to the same characters stored in another `String` object called `original` with all `'e'` characters changed to `'j'`.

EX 3.4   What output is produced by the following code fragment?

```
String m1, m2, m3;
m1 = "Quest for the Holy Grail";
m2 = m1.toLowerCase();
m3 = m1 + " " + m2;
System.out.println (m3.replace('h', 'z'));
```

EX 3.5   What is the effect of the following import statement?

```
import java.awt.*;
```

EX 3.6   Assuming that a `Random` object has been created called `generator`, what is the range of the result of each of the following expressions?

a. `generator.nextInt(20)`

b. `generator.nextInt(8) + 1`

c. `generator.nextInt(45) + 10`

d. `generator.nextInt(100) - 50`

EX 3.7   Write code to declare and instantiate an object of the `Random` class (call the object reference variable `rand`). Then write a list of expressions using the `nextInt` method that generates random numbers in the following specified ranges, including the endpoints. Use the version of the `nextInt` method that accepts a single integer parameter.

a. 0 to 10

b. 0 to 500

c. 1 to 10

d. 1 to 500

e. 25 to 50

f. −10 to 15

EX 3.8   Write an assignment statement that computes the square root of the sum of num1 and num2 and assigns the result to num3.

EX 3.9   Write a single statement that computes and prints the absolute value of total.

EX 3.10 Write code statements to create a DecimalFormat object that will round a formatted value to 4 decimal places. Then write a statement that uses that object to print the value of result, properly formatted.

EX 3.11 Write code statements that prompt for and read a double value from the user, and then print the result of raising that value to the fourth power. Output the results to 3 decimal places.

EX 3.12 Write a declaration for an enumerated type that represents the days of the week.

Programming Projects

PP 3.1   Write an application that prompts for and reads the user's first and last name (separately). Then print a string composed of the first letter of the user's first name, followed by (no more than) the first five characters of the user's last name, followed by a random number in the range 10 to 99. Similar algorithms are sometimes used to generate usernames for new computer accounts.

PP 3.2   Write an application that prints the sum of cubes. Prompt for and read two integer values and print the sum of each value raised to the third power.

PP 3.3   Write an application that creates and prints a random phone number of the form xxx-xxx-xxxx. Include the dashes in the output. Do not let the first three digits contain an 8 or 9 (but don't be more restrictive than that), and make sure that the second set of three digits is not greater than 742. *Hint:* Think through the easiest way to construct the phone number. Each digit does not have to be determined separately.

PP 3.4   Write an application that reads the (x,y) coordinates for two points. Compute the distance between the two points using the following formula:

Distance = $\sqrt{(x_2 - x_1)^2 + (y_2 - y_1)^2}$

PP 3.5   Write an application that reads the radius of a sphere and prints its volume and surface area. Use the following formulas. Print the output to four decimal places. r represents the radius.

$$\text{Volume} = \tfrac{4}{3}\pi r^3$$

Surface area $= 4\pi r^2$

PP 3.6   Write an application that reads the lengths of the sides of a triangle from the user. Compute the area of the triangle using Heron's formula (below), in which s represents half of the perimeter of the triangle, and a, b, and c represent the lengths of the three sides. Print the area to three decimal places.

$$\text{Area} = \sqrt{s(s-a)(s-b)(s-c)}$$

PP 3.7   Write an application that displays a frame containing two labels that display your name, one for your first name and one for your last. Experiment with the size of the window to see the labels change their orientation to each other.

PP 3.8   Write an application that displays a frame containing two panels. Each panel should contain two images (use four unique images—your choice). Fix the size of the first panel so that both of its images remain side by side. Allow the other panel to change size as needed. Experiment with the size of the window to see the images change orientation. Make sure you understand why the application behaves as it does.

PP 3.9   Modify the `LabelDemo` program so that it displays a fourth label, with the text of the label centered above the image.

Answers to Self-Review Questions

SR 3.1   The `new` operator creates a new instance (an object) of the specified class. The constructor of the class is then invoked to help set up the newly created object.

SR 3.2   A null reference is a reference that does not refer to any object. The reserved word `null` can be used to check for null references before following them.

SR 3.3   Two references are aliases of each other if they refer to the same object. Changing the state of the object through one reference changes it for the other because there is actually only one object. An object is marked for garbage collection only when there are no valid references to it.

SR 3.4   The following declaration creates a `String` variable called `author` and initializes it:

```
String author = new String ("Fred Brooks");
```

For strings, this declaration could have been abbreviated as follows:

```
String author = "Fred Brooks";
```

This object reference variable and its value can be depicted as follows:

```
author                    "Fred Brooks"
```

SR 3.5   The following statement prints the value of a `String` object in all uppercase letters:

```
System.out.println (title.toUpperCase());
```

SR 3.6   The following declaration creates a `String` object and sets it equal to the first 10 characters of the `String` description:

```
String front = description.substring(0, 10);
```

SR 3.7   A Java package is a collection of related classes. The Java standard class library is a group of packages that support common programming tasks.

SR 3.8   Each package contains a set of classes that support particular programming activities. The classes in the `java.net` package support network communication, and the classes in the `javax.swing` class support the development of graphical user interfaces.

SR 3.9   The `Scanner` class and the `Random` class are part of the `java.util` package. The `String` and `Math` classes are part of the `java.lang` package.

SR 3.10 An import statement establishes the fact that a program uses a particular class, specifying what package that class is a part of. This allows the programmer to use the class name (such as `Random`) without having to fully qualify the reference (such as `java.util.Random`) every time.

SR 3.11   The String class is part of the java.lang package, which is automatically imported into any Java program. Therefore, no separate import declaration is needed.

SR 3.12   A call to the nextInt method of a Random object returns a random integer in the range of all possible int values, both positive and negative.

SR 3.13   Passing a positive integer parameter x to the nextInt method of a Random object returns a random number in the range of 0 to $x-1$. So a call to nextInt(20) will return a random number in the range 0 to 19, inclusive.

SR 3.14   A class or static method can be invoked through the name of the class that contains it, such as Math.abs. If a method is not static, it can be executed only through an instance (an object) of the class.

SR 3.15   The following statement prints the sine of 1.23 radians:

```
System.out.println (Math.sin(1.23));
```

SR 3.16   The following declaration creates a double variable and initializes it to 5 raised to the power 2.5:

```
double result = Math.pow(5, 2.5);
```

SR 3.17   To output a floating-point value as a percentage, you first obtain a NumberFormat object using a call to the static method getPercentageInstance of the NumberFormat class. Then you pass the value to be formatted to the format method of the formatter object, which returns a properly formatted string. For example:

```
NumberFormat fmt = NumberFormat.getPercentageInstance();
System.out.println (fmt.format(value));
```

SR 3.18   The following is a declaration of an enumerated type for movie ratings:

```
enum Ratings {G, PG, PG13, R, NC17}
```

SR 3.19   A wrapper class is defined in the Java standard class library for each primitive type. In situations where objects are called for, an object created from a wrapper class may suffice.

SR 3.20   Both a frame and a panel are containers that can hold GUI elements. However, a frame is displayed as a separate window with a title bar, whereas a panel cannot be displayed on its own. A panel is often displayed inside a frame.

SR 3.21   The containment hierarchy of a graphical user interface identifies the nesting of elements within the GUI. For example, in a particular GUI suppose some labels and buttons are contained within a panel that is contained within another panel that is contained within a frame. The containment hierarchy can be represented as a tree that indicates how all the elements of a GUI are nested within each other.

Writing Classes 4

> Discuss the structure and content of a class definition.

> Establish the concept of object state using instance data.

> Describe the effect of visibility modifiers on methods and data.

> Explore the structure of a method definition, including parameters and return values.

> Discuss the structure and purpose of a constructor.

> Explore the creation of graphical objects.

> Introduce the concepts needed to create an interactive graphical user interface.

> Explore some basic GUI components and events.

In Chapter 3 we used classes and objects for the various services they provide. That is, we used the predefined classes in the Java class library that are provided to us to make the process of writing programs easier. In this chapter we address the heart of object-oriented programming: writing our own classes to define our own objects. This chapter explores the basics of class definitions, including the structure of methods and the scope and encapsulation of data. The Graphics Track sections of this chapter discuss how to write classes that have graphical representations and introduce the issues necessary to create a truly interactive graphical user interface.

4.1   CLASSES AND OBJECTS REVISITED

In Chapter 1 we introduced basic object-oriented concepts, including a brief overview of objects and classes. In Chapter 3 we used several predefined classes from the Java standard class library to create objects and use them for the particular functionality they provided.

In this chapter we turn our attention to writing our own classes. Although existing class libraries provide many useful classes, the essence of object-oriented program development is the process of designing and implementing our own classes to suit our specific needs.

Recall the basic relationship between an object and a class: a class is a blueprint of an object. The class represents the concept of an object, and any object created from that class is a realization of that concept.

For example, from Chapter 3 we know that the `String` class represents a concept of a character string, and that each `String` object represents a particular string that contains specific characters.

Let's consider another example. Suppose a class called `Student` represents a student at a university. An object created from the `Student` class would represent a particular student. The `Student` class represents the general concept of a student, and every object created from that class represents an actual student attending the school. In a system that helps manage the business of a university, we would have one `Student` class and thousands of `Student` objects.

Recall that an object has a *state*, which is defined by the values of the *attributes* associated with that object. The attributes of a student may include the student's name, address, major, and grade point average. The `Student` class establishes that each student has these attributes. Each `Student` object stores the values of these attributes for a particular student. In Java, an object's attributes are defined by variables declared within a class.

An object also has *behaviors*, which are defined by the *operations* associated with that object. The operations of a student would include the ability to update that student's address and compute that student's current grade point average. The `Student` class defines the operations, such as the details of how a grade point average is computed. These operations can then be executed on (or by) a particular `Student` object. Note that the behaviors of an object may modify the state of that object. In Java, an object's operations are defined by methods declared within a class.

Figure 4.1 lists some examples of classes, with some attributes and operations that might be defined for objects of those classes. It's up to the program designer

Class	Attributes	Operations
Student	Name Address Major Grade point average	Set address Set major Compute grade point average
Rectangle	Length Width Color	Set length Set width Set color
Aquarium	Material Length Width Height	Set material Set length Set width Set height Compute volume Compute filled weight
Flight	Airline Flight number Origin city Destination city Current status	Set airline Set flight number Determine status
Employee	Name Department Title Salary	Set department Set title Set salary Compute wages Compute bonus Compute taxes

FIGURE 4.1   Examples of classes and some possible attributes and operations

to determine what attributes and operations are needed, which depends on the purpose of the program and the role a particular object plays in that purpose. Consider other attributes and operations you might include for these examples.

4.2   ANATOMY OF A CLASS

In all of our previous examples, we've written a single class containing a single main method. These classes represent small but complete programs. These programs often instantiated objects using predefined classes from the Java class library and used those objects for the services they provide. Those predefined classes are part of the program too, but we never really concern ourselves with them other than to know how to interact with them. We simply trust them to provide the services they promise.

Let's look at another, similar example. The RollingDice class shown in Listing 4.1 contains a main method that instantiates two Die objects (as in the singular of dice). It then rolls the dice and prints the results. It also calls several other methods provided by the `Die` class, such as the ability to explicitly set and get the current face value of a die.

The primary difference between this example and previous examples is that the `Die` class is not a predefined part of the Java class library. We have to write the `Die` class ourselves, defining the services we want `Die` objects to perform, if this program is to compile and run.

Every class can contain data declarations and method declarations, as depicted in Figure 4.2. The data declarations represent the data that will be stored in each object of the class. The method declarations define the services that those objects will provide. Collectively, the data and methods of a class are called the *members* of a class.

The classes we've written in previous examples follow this model as well, but contain no data at the class level and contain only one method (the `main` method). We'll continue to define classes like this, such as the `RollingDice` class, to define the starting point of a program.

True object-oriented programming, however, comes from defining classes that represent objects with well-defined state and behavior. For example, at any given moment a `Die` object is showing a particular face value, which we could refer to as the state of the die. A `Die` object also has various methods we can invoke on it, such as the ability to roll the die or get its face value. These methods represent the behavior of a die.

> **Key Concept**
>
> The heart of object-oriented programming is defining classes that represent objects with well-defined state and behavior.

The `Die` class is shown in Listing 4.2. It contains two data values: an integer constant (`MAX`) that represents the maximum face value of the die, and an integer variable (`faceValue`) that represents the current face value of the die. It also contains a constructor called `Die` and four regular methods: `roll`, `setFaceValue`, `getFaceValue`, and `toString`.

You will recall from Chapters 2 and 3 that constructors are special methods that have the same name as the class. The `Die` constructor gets called when the `new` operator is used to create a new instance of the `Die` class. The rest of the methods in the `Die` class define the various services provided by `Die` objects.

We use a header block of documentation to explain the purpose of each method in the class. This practice is not only crucial for anyone trying to understand the software, it also separates the code visually so that it's easy for the eye to jump from one method to the next while reading the code.

Figure 4.3 lists the methods of the `Die` class. From this point of view, it looks no different from any other class that we've used in previous examples. The only important difference is that the `Die` class was not provided for us by the Java standard class library. We wrote it ourselves.

Listing 4.1

```java
//********************************************************************
//  RollingDice.java       Author: Lewis/Loftus
//
//  Demonstrates the creation and use of a user-defined class.
//********************************************************************

public class RollingDice
{
   //-----------------------------------------------------------------
   //  Creates two Die objects and rolls them several times.
   //-----------------------------------------------------------------
   public static void main (String[] args)
   {
      Die die1, die2;
      int sum;

      die1 = new Die();
      die2 = new Die();

      die1.roll();
      die2.roll();
      System.out.println ("Die One: " + die1 + ", Die Two: " + die2);

      die1.roll();
      die2.setFaceValue(4);
      System.out.println ("Die One: " + die1 + ", Die Two: " + die2);

      sum = die1.getFaceValue() + die2.getFaceValue();
      System.out.println ("Sum: " + sum);

      sum = die1.roll() + die2.roll();
      System.out.println ("Die One: " + die1 + ", Die Two: " + die2);
      System.out.println ("New sum: " + sum);
   }
}
```

Output

```
Die One: 5, Die Two: 2
Die One: 1, Die Two: 4
Sum: 5
Die One: 4, Die Two: 2
New sum: 6
```

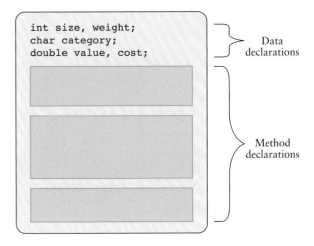

FIGURE 4.2   The members of a class: data and method declarations

Listing 4.2

```
//************************************************************************
//   Die.java          Author: Lewis/Loftus
//
//   Represents one die (singular of dice) with faces showing values
//   between 1 and 6.
//************************************************************************

public class Die
{
    private final int MAX = 6;   // maximum face value

    private int faceValue;   // current value showing on the die

    //-----------------------------------------------------------------
    //   Constructor: Sets the initial face value.
    //-----------------------------------------------------------------
    public Die()
    {
        faceValue = 1;
    }
```

Listing 4.2   continued

```java
//-----------------------------------------------------------------
//  Rolls the die and returns the result.
//-----------------------------------------------------------------
public int roll()
{
   faceValue = (int)(Math.random() * MAX) + 1;

   return faceValue;
}

//-----------------------------------------------------------------
//  Face value mutator.
//-----------------------------------------------------------------
public void setFaceValue (int value)
{
   faceValue = value;
}

//-----------------------------------------------------------------
//  Face value accessor.
//-----------------------------------------------------------------
public int getFaceValue()
{
   return faceValue;
}

//-----------------------------------------------------------------
//  Returns a string representation of this die.
//-----------------------------------------------------------------
public String toString()
{
   String result = Integer.toString(faceValue);

   return result;
}
}
```

The methods of the `Die` class include the ability to roll the die, producing a new random face value. The `roll` method returns the new face value to the calling method, but you can also get the current face value at any time using the `getFaceValue` method. The `setFaceValue` method sets the face value explicitly, as if you had reached over and turned the die to whatever face you wanted. The `toString` method of any object gets called automatically whenever you pass the object to a `print` or `println` method, to obtain a string description of the object to print. Therefore it's usually a good idea to define a `toString` method for most classes. The definitions of these methods have various parts, and we'll dissect them as we proceed through this chapter.

For the examples in this book, we usually store each class in its own file. Java allows multiple classes to be stored in one file. If a file contains multiple classes, only one of those classes can be declared using the reserved word `public`. Furthermore, the name of the public class must correspond to the name of the file. For instance, class `Die` is stored in a file called `Die.java`.

Instance Data

Note that in the `Die` class, the constant `MAX` and the variable `faceValue` are declared inside the class, but not inside any method. The location at which a variable is declared defines its *scope,* which is the area within a program in which that variable can be referenced. By being declared at the class level (not within a method), these variables and constants can be referenced in any method of the class.

`Die()`
  Constructor: Sets the initial face value of the die to 1.

`int roll()`
  Rolls the die by setting the face value to a random number in the appropriate range.

`void setFaceValue (int value)`
  Sets the face value of the die to the specified value.

`int getFaceValue()`
  Returns the current face value of the die.

`String toString()`
  Returns a string representation of the die indicating its current face value.

FIGURE 4.3 Some methods of the `Die` class

Attributes such as the variable `faceValue` are called *instance data* because memory space is created for each instance of the class that is created. Each `Die` object has its own `faceValue` variable with its own data space. That's how each `Die` object can have its own state. We see that in the output of the `RollingDice` program: one die has a face value of 5 and the other has a face value of 2. That's possible only because the memory space for the `faceValue` variable is created for each `Die` object.

We can depict this situation as follows:

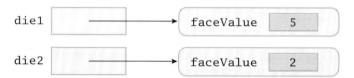

The `die1` and `die2` reference variables point to (that is, contain the address of) their respective `Die` objects. Each object contains a `faceValue` variable with its own memory space. Thus each object can store different values for its instance data.

Java automatically initializes any variables declared at the class level. For example, all variables of numeric types such as `int` and `double` are initialized to zero. However, despite the fact that the language performs this automatic initialization, it is good practice to initialize variables explicitly (usually in a constructor) so that anyone reading the code will clearly understand the intent.

UML Class Diagrams

Throughout this book we use *UML diagrams* to visualize relationships among classes and objects. UML stands for the *Unified Modeling Language,* which has become the most popular notation for representing the design of an object-oriented program.

Several types of UML diagrams exist, each designed to show specific aspects of object-oriented programs. We focus primarily on UML *class diagrams* in this book to show the contents of classes and the relationships among them.

In a UML diagram, each class is represented as a rectangle, possibly containing three sections to show the class name, its attributes (data), and its operations (methods). Figure 4.4 shows a class diagram containing the classes of the `RollingDice` program.

The arrow connecting the `RollingDice` and `Die` classes in Figure 4.4 indicates that a relationship exists between the classes. A dotted arrow indicates that one class *uses* the methods of the other class. Other types of object-oriented relationships between classes are shown with different types of connecting lines and arrows. We'll discuss these other relationships as we explore the appropriate topics in the book.

Keep in mind that UML is not designed specifically for Java programmers. It is intended to be language independent. Therefore the syntax used in a UML diagram is not necessarily the same as Java. For example, the type of a variable is shown after the variable name, separated by a colon. Return types of methods are shown the same way.

UML diagrams are versatile. We can include whatever appropriate information is desired, depending on the goal of a particular diagram. We might leave out the data and method sections of a class, for instance, if those details aren't relevant for a particular diagram.

UML diagrams allow you to visualize a program's design. As our programs get larger, made up of more and more classes, these visualizations become increasingly helpful. We will explore new aspects of UML diagrams as the situation dictates.

4.3 ENCAPSULATION

We mentioned in our overview of object-oriented concepts in Chapter 1 that an object should be *self-governing*. That is, the instance data of an object should be modified only by that object. For example, the methods of the `Die` class should be solely responsible for changing the value of the `faceValue` variable. We

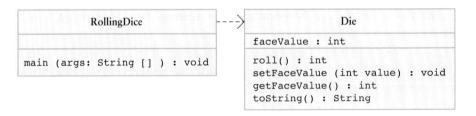

FIGURE 4.4   A UML class diagram showing the classes involved in the `RollingDice` program

should make it difficult, if not impossible, for code outside of a class to "reach in" and change the value of a variable that is declared inside that class. This characteristic is called *encapsulation.*

An object should be encapsulated from the rest of the system. It should interact with other parts of a program only through the specific set of methods that define the services that that object provides. These methods define the *interface* between that object and the program that uses it.

Encapsulation is depicted graphically in Figure 4.5. The code that uses an object, sometimes called the *client* of an object, should not be allowed to access variables directly. The client should call an object's methods, and those methods then interact with the data encapsulated within the object. For example, the `main` method in the `RollingDice` program calls the `roll` method of the die objects. The `main` method should not (and in fact cannot) access the `faceValue` variable directly.

In Java, we accomplish object encapsulation using *modifiers.* A modifier is a Java reserved word that is used to specify particular characteristics of a programming language construct. In Chapter 2 we discussed the `final` modifier, which is used to declare a constant. Java has several modifiers that can be used in various ways. Some modifiers can be used together, but some combinations are invalid. We discuss various Java modifiers at appropriate points throughout this book, and all of them are summarized in Appendix E.

Visibility Modifiers

Some of the Java modifiers are called *visibility modifiers* because they control access to the members of a class. The reserved words `public` and `private` are visibility modifiers that can be applied to the variables and methods of a class. If

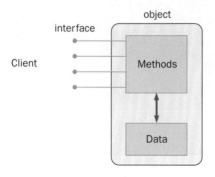

FIGURE 4.5   A client interacting with the methods of an object

a member of a class has *public visibility*, it can be directly referenced from outside of the object. If a member of a class has *private visibility*, it can be used anywhere inside the class definition but cannot be referenced externally. A third visibility modifier, `protected`, is relevant only in the context of inheritance. We discuss it in Chapter 8.

Public variables violate encapsulation. They allow code external to the class in which the data is defined to reach in and access or modify the value of the data. Therefore instance data should be defined with private visibility. Data that is declared as `private` can be accessed only by the methods of the class.

The visibility we apply to a method depends on the purpose of that method. Methods that provide services to the client must be declared with public visibility so that they can be invoked by the client. These methods are sometimes referred to as *service methods*. A `private` method cannot be invoked from outside the class. The only purpose of a `private` method is to help the other methods of the class do their job. Therefore they are sometimes referred to as *support methods*.

The table in Figure 4.6 summarizes the effects of public and private visibility on both variables and methods.

Giving constants public visibility is generally considered acceptable because, although their values can be accessed directly, they cannot be changed because they were declared using the `final` modifier. Keep in mind that encapsulation means that data values should not be able to be *changed* directly by another part of the code. Because constants, by definition, cannot be changed, the encapsulation issue is largely moot.

	public	**private**
Variables	Violate encapsulation	Enforce encapsulation
Methods	Provide services to clients	Support other methods in the class

FIGURE 4.6   The effects of public and private visibility

UML class diagrams can show the visibility of a class member by preceding it with a particular character. A member with public visibility is preceded by a plus sign (+), and a member with private visibility is preceded by a minus sign (-).

Accessors and Mutators

Because instance data is generally declared with private visibility, a class usually provides services to access and modify data values. A method such as getFaceValue is called an *accessor method* because it provides read-only access to a particular value. Likewise, a method such as setFaceValue is called a *mutator method* because it changes a particular value.

> **Key Concept**
>
> Most objects contain accessor and mutator methods to allow the client to manage data in a controlled manner.

Generally, accessor method names have the form getX, where X is the value to which it provides access. Likewise, mutator method names have the form setX, where X is the value they are setting. Therefore these types of methods are sometimes referred to as "getters" and "setters."

For example, if a class contains the instance variable height, it should also probably contain the methods getHeight and setHeight. Note that this naming convention capitalizes the first letter of the variable when used in the method names, which is consistent with how method names are written in general.

Some methods may provide accessor and/or mutator capabilities as a side effect of their primary purpose. For example, the roll method of the Die class changes the faceValue of the die, and returns that new value as well. Note that the code of the roll method is careful to keep the face value of the die in the valid range (1 to MAX). Service methods must be carefully designed to permit only appropriate access and valid changes.

This points out a flaw in the design of the Die class. Note that there is no restriction on the setFaceValue method—a client could use it to set the die value to a number such as 20, which is outside the valid range. The code of the setFaceValue method should allow only valid modifications to the face value of a die. We explore how that kind of control can be accomplished in the next chapter.

4.4   ANATOMY OF A METHOD

We've seen that a class is composed of data declarations and method declarations. Let's examine method declarations in more detail.

As we stated in Chapter 1, a method is a group of programming language statements that is given a name. A *method declaration* specifies the code that is executed when the method is invoked. Every method in a Java program is part of a particular class.

When a method is called, the flow of control transfers to that method. One by one, the statements of that method are executed. When that method is done, control returns to the location where the call was made and execution continues.

The *called method* (the one that is invoked) might be part of the same class as the *calling method* that invoked it. If the called method is part of the same class, only the method name is needed to invoke it. If it is part of a different class, it is invoked through the name of an object of that other class, as we've seen many times. Figure 4.7 shows the flow of execution as methods are called.

We've defined the `main` method of a program many times in previous examples. Its definition follows the same syntax as all methods. The header of a method includes the type of the return value, the method name, and a list of parameters that the method accepts. The statements that make up the body of the method are defined in a block delimited by braces. The rest of this section discusses issues related to method declarations in more detail.

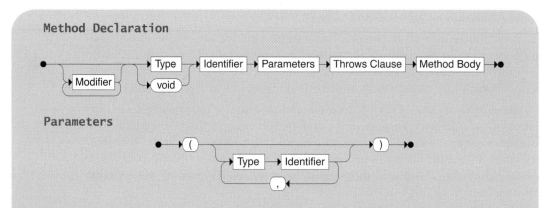

A method is defined by optional modifiers, followed by a return Type, followed by an Identifier that determines the method name, followed by a list of Parameters, followed by the Method Body. The return Type indicates the type of value that will be returned by the method, which may be void. The Method Body is a block of statements that executes when the method is invoked. The Throws Clause is optional and indicates the exceptions that may be thrown by this method.

Example:

```
public void instructions (int count)
{
    System.out.println ("Follow all instructions.");
    System.out.println ("Use no more than " + count +
                    " turns.");
}
```

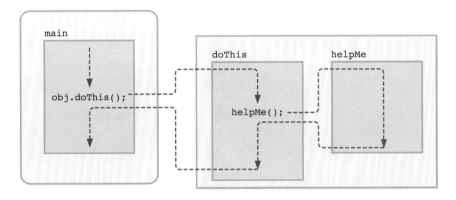

FIGURE 4.7 The flow of control following method invocations

The `return` Statement

The return type specified in the method header can be a primitive type, class name, or the reserved word `void`. When a method does not return any value, `void` is used as the return type, as is always done with the `main` method. The `setFaceValue` method of the `Die` class also has a return type of void.

A method that returns a value must have a *return statement.* When a `return` statement is executed, control is immediately returned to the statement in the calling method, and processing continues there. A `return` statement consists of the reserved word `return` followed by an expression that dictates the value to be returned. The expression must be consistent with the return type in the method header.

The `getFaceValue` method of the `Die` class returns an `int` value that represents the current value of the die. The `roll` method does the same, returning the new value to which `faceValue` was just randomly set. The `toString` method returns a `String` object.

A method that does not return a value does not usually contain a `return` statement. The method automatically returns to the calling method when the end of the method is reached. Such methods may contain a `return` statement without an expression.

It is usually not good practice to use more than one `return` statement in a method, even though it is possible to do so. In general, a method should have one `return` statement as the last line of the method body, unless that makes the method overly complex.

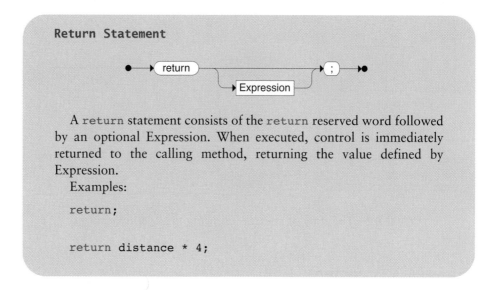

Return Statement

A `return` statement consists of the `return` reserved word followed by an optional Expression. When executed, control is immediately returned to the calling method, returning the value defined by Expression.

Examples:

```
return;
```

```
return distance * 4;
```

The value that is returned from a method can be ignored in the calling method. For example, in the `main` method of the `RollingDice` class, the value that is returned from the `roll` method is ignored in several calls, while in others the return value is used in a calculation.

Constructors do not have a return type (not even `void`) and therefore cannot return a value. We discuss constructors in more detail later in this chapter.

Parameters

As we defined in Chapter 2, a parameter is a value that is passed into a method when it is invoked. The *parameter list* in the header of a method specifies the types of the values that are passed and the names by which the called method will refer to those values.

The names of the parameters in the header of the method declaration are called *formal parameters*. In an invocation, the values passed into a method are called *actual parameters*. The actual parameters are also called the *arguments* to the method.

A method invocation and definition always give the parameter list in parentheses after the method name. If there are no parameters, an empty set of parentheses is used, as is the case in the `roll` and `getFaceValue` methods. The `Die` constructor also takes no parameters, although constructors often do.

The formal parameters are identifiers that serve as variables inside the method and whose initial values come from the actual parameters in the invocation. When a method is called, the value in each actual parameter is copied and stored in the corresponding formal parameter. Actual parameters can be literals, variables, or full expressions. If an expression is used as an actual parameter, it is fully evaluated before the method call and the result is passed as the parameter.

The only method in the `Die` class that accepts any parameters is the `setFaceValue` method, which accepts a single `int` parameter. The formal parameter name is `value`. In the `main` method, the value of 4 is passed into it as the actual parameter.

The parameter lists in the invocation and the method declaration must match up. That is, the value of the first actual parameter is copied into the first formal parameter, the second actual parameter into the second formal parameter, and so on, as shown in Figure 4.8. The types of the actual parameters must be consistent with the specified types of the formal parameters.

Other details regarding parameter passing are discussed in Chapter 6.

Local Data

As we described earlier in this chapter, the scope of a variable or constant is the part of a program in which a valid reference to that variable can be made. A variable can be declared inside a method, making it *local data* as opposed to instance data. Recall that instance data is declared in a class but not inside any particular method.

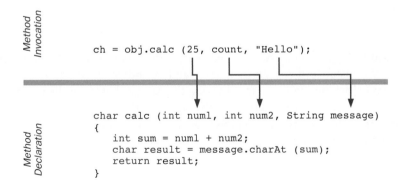

FIGURE 4.8 Passing parameters from the method invocation to the declaration

Key Concept

A variable declared in a method is local to that method and cannot be used outside of it.

Local data has scope limited to only the method in which it is declared. The variable `result` declared in the `toString` method of the `Die` class is local data. Any reference to `result` in any other method of the `Die` class would have caused the compiler to issue an error message. A local variable simply does not exist outside of the method in which it is declared. On the other hand, instance data, declared at the class level, has a scope of the entire class; any method of the class can refer to it.

Because local data and instance data operate at different levels of scope, it's possible to declare a local variable inside a method with the same name as an instance variable declared at the class level. Referring to that name in the method will reference the local version of the variable. This naming practice obviously has the potential to confuse anyone reading the code, so it should be avoided.

The formal parameter names in a method header serve as local data for that method. They don't exist until the method is called, and they cease to exist when the method is exited. For example, the formal parameter `value` in the `setFaceValue` method comes into existence when the method is called and goes out of existence when the method finishes executing.

Bank Account Example

Let's look at another example of a class and its use. The `Transactions` class shown in Listing 4.3 contains a `main` method that creates a few `Account` objects and invokes their services.

The `Account` class, shown in Listing 4.4, represents a basic bank account. It contains instance data representing the account number, the account's current balance, and the name of the account's owner. Note that instance data can be an object reference variable (not just a primitive type), such as the account owner's name, which is a reference to a `String` object. The interest rate for the account is stored as a constant.

The constructor of the `Account` class accepts three parameters that are used to initialize the instance data. The `deposit` and `withdraw` methods perform the basic transactions on the account, adjusting the balance based on the parameters. There is also an `addInterest` method that updates the balance by adding in the interest earned. These methods represent valid ways to change the balance, so a classic mutator such as `setBalance` is not provided.

Listing 4.3

```java
//********************************************************************
//   Transactions.java        Author: Lewis/Loftus
//
//   Demonstrates the creation and use of multiple Account objects.
//********************************************************************

public class Transactions
{
   //-----------------------------------------------------------------
   //  Creates some bank accounts and requests various services.
   //-----------------------------------------------------------------
   public static void main (String[] args)
   {
      Account acct1 = new Account ("Ted Murphy", 72354, 102.56);
      Account acct2 = new Account ("Jane Smith", 69713, 40.00);
      Account acct3 = new Account ("Edward Demsey", 93757, 759.32);

      acct1.deposit (25.85);

      double smithBalance = acct2.deposit (500.00);
      System.out.println ("Smith balance after deposit: " +
                          smithBalance);

      System.out.println ("Smith balance after withdrawal: " +
                          acct2.withdraw (430.75, 1.50));

      acct1.addInterest();
      acct2.addInterest();
      acct3.addInterest();

      System.out.println ();
      System.out.println (acct1);
      System.out.println (acct2);
      System.out.println (acct3);
   }
}
```

Output

```
Smith balance after deposit: 540.0
Smith balance after withdrawal: 107.75

72354    Ted Murphy       $132.90
69713    Jane Smith       $111.52
93757    Edward Demsey    $785.90
```

Listing 4.4

```java
//********************************************************************
//  Account.java        Author: Lewis/Loftus
//
//  Represents a bank account with basic services such as deposit
//  and withdraw.
//********************************************************************

import java.text.NumberFormat;

public class Account
{
   private final double RATE = 0.035;  // interest rate of 3.5%

   private long acctNumber;
   private double balance;
   private String name;

   //-----------------------------------------------------------------
   //  Sets up the account by defining its owner, account number,
   //  and initial balance.
   //-----------------------------------------------------------------
   public Account (String owner, long account, double initial)
   {
      name = owner;
      acctNumber = account;
      balance = initial;
   }

   //-----------------------------------------------------------------
   //  Deposits the specified amount into the account. Returns the
   //  new balance.
   //-----------------------------------------------------------------
   public double deposit (double amount)
   {
      balance = balance + amount;

      return balance;
   }
```

Listing 4.4   **continued**

```java
//----------------------------------------------------------------
//  Withdraws the specified amount from the account and applies
//  the fee. Returns the new balance.
//----------------------------------------------------------------
public double withdraw (double amount, double fee)
{
   balance = balance - amount - fee;

   return balance;
}

//----------------------------------------------------------------
//  Adds interest to the account and returns the new balance.
//----------------------------------------------------------------
public double addInterest ()
{
   balance += (balance * RATE);
   return balance;
}

//----------------------------------------------------------------
//  Returns the current balance of the account.
//----------------------------------------------------------------
public double getBalance ()
{
   return balance;
}

//----------------------------------------------------------------
//  Returns a one-line description of the account as a string.
//----------------------------------------------------------------
public String toString ()
{
   NumberFormat fmt = NumberFormat.getCurrencyInstance();

   return acctNumber + "\t" + name + "\t" + fmt.format(balance);
}
}
```

The status of the three `Account` objects just after they were created in the `Transactions` program could be depicted as follows:

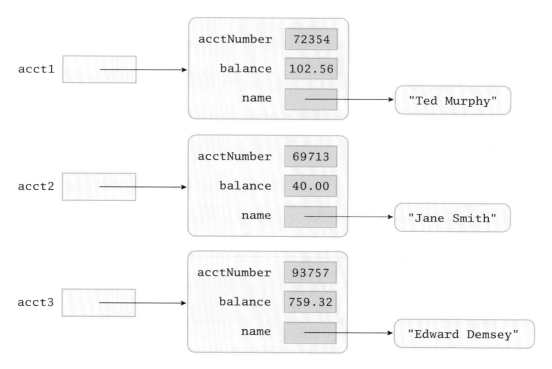

The various methods that update the balance of the account could be more rigorously designed. Checks should be made to ensure that the parameter values are valid, such as preventing the withdrawal of a negative amount (which would essentially be a deposit). This processing is discussed in the next chapter.

4.5   CONSTRUCTORS REVISITED

As we stated in Chapter 2, a constructor is similar to a method that is invoked when an object is instantiated. When we define a class, we usually define a constructor to help us set up the class. In particular, we often use a constructor to initialize the variables associated with each object.

A constructor differs from a regular method in two ways. First, the name of a constructor is the same name as the class. Therefore the name of the constructor in the `Die` class is `Die`, and the name of the constructor in the `Account` class is

Account. Second, a constructor cannot return a value and does not have a return type specified in the method header.

A common mistake made by programmers is to put a void return type on a constructor. As far as the compiler is concerned, putting any return type on a constructor, even void, turns it into a regular method that happens to have the same name as the class. As such, it cannot be invoked as a constructor. This leads to error messages that are sometimes difficult to decipher.

Generally, a constructor is used to initialize the newly instantiated object. For instance, the constructor of the Die class sets the face value of the die to 1 initially. The constructor of the Account class sets the values of the instance variables to the values passed in as parameters to the constructor.

We don't have to define a constructor for every class. Each class has a *default constructor* that takes no parameters. The default constructor is used if we don't provide our own. This default constructor generally has no effect on the newly created object.

4.6   GRAPHICAL OBJECTS

Some objects have a graphical representation, meaning that their state and behaviors include information about what the object looks like visually. A graphical object might contain data about its size and color, for instance, and it may contain methods to draw it.

In Chapter 3 we instantiated and used graphical components such as frames, panels, labels, and images. Certainly these components can be considered graphical objects. This section examines some of them in more detail and explores how to define our own objects that have graphical characteristics.

The program in Listing 4.5 displays a smiling face and a text caption. The main method in the SmilingFace class does not deal with all of those details, however. Instead, the main method sets up the frame for the program and uses it to display an instantiation of the SmilingFacePanel class.

The SmilingFacePanel class is shown in Listing 4.6. It defines two constants on which the drawing is based (BASEX and BASEY), a constructor that sets up the key aspects of the panel, and a method called paintComponent that draws the face that we see when the program is executed. In this case, instead of adding GUI components to this panel, we are simply drawing on it.

Listing 4.5

```java
//********************************************************************
//  SmilingFace.java        Author: Lewis/Loftus
//
//  Demonstrates the use of a separate panel class.
//********************************************************************

import javax.swing.JFrame;

public class SmilingFace
{
   //-----------------------------------------------------------------
   //  Creates the main frame of the program.
   //-----------------------------------------------------------------
   public static void main (String[] args)
   {
      JFrame frame = new JFrame ("Smiling Face");
      frame.setDefaultCloseOperation (JFrame.EXIT_ON_CLOSE);

      SmilingFacePanel panel = new SmilingFacePanel();

      frame.getContentPane().add(panel);

      frame.pack();
      frame.setVisible(true);
   }
}
```

Display

Listing 4.6

```java
//************************************************************************
//  SmilingFacePanel.java          Author: Lewis/Loftus
//
//  Demonstrates the use of a separate panel class.
//************************************************************************

import javax.swing.JPanel;
import java.awt.*;

public class SmilingFacePanel extends JPanel
{
   private final int BASEX = 120, BASEY = 60; // base point for head

   //-------------------------------------------------------------------
   //  Constructor: Sets up the main characteristics of this panel.
   //-------------------------------------------------------------------
   public SmilingFacePanel ()
   {
      setBackground (Color.blue);
      setPreferredSize (new Dimension(320, 200));
      setFont (new Font("Arial", Font.BOLD, 16));
   }

   //-------------------------------------------------------------------
   //  Draws a face.
   //-------------------------------------------------------------------
   public void paintComponent (Graphics page)
   {
      super.paintComponent (page);

      page.setColor (Color.yellow);
      page.fillOval (BASEX, BASEY, 80, 80);     // head
      page.fillOval (BASEX-5, BASEY+20, 90, 40);   // ears

      page.setColor (Color.black);
      page.drawOval (BASEX+20, BASEY+30, 15, 7);   // eyes
      page.drawOval (BASEX+45, BASEY+30, 15, 7);

      page.fillOval (BASEX+25, BASEY+31, 5, 5);    // pupils
      page.fillOval (BASEX+50, BASEY+31, 5, 5);
```

Listing 4.6   **continued**

```
        page.drawArc (BASEX+20, BASEY+25, 15, 7, 0, 180);   // eyebrows
        page.drawArc (BASEX+45, BASEY+25, 15, 7, 0, 180);

        page.drawArc (BASEX+35, BASEY+40, 15, 10, 180, 180);   // nose
        page.drawArc (BASEX+20, BASEY+50, 40, 15, 180, 180);   // mouth

        page.setColor (Color.white);
        page.drawString ("Always remember that you are unique!",
                     BASEX-105, BASEY-15);
        page.drawString ("Just like everyone else.", BASEX-45, BASEY+105);
    }
}
```

Note that the SmilingFacePanel class extends the JPanel class. As we mentioned in Chapter 2 in our discussion of applets, the extends clause establishes an inheritance relationship. The SmilingFacePanel class inherits the characteristics of the JPanel class. That is, a SmilingFacePanel *is* a JPanel. At this point that's all you really need to know about inheritance, which is discussed in detail in Chapter 8.

The constructor of the SmilingFacePanel class sets the background color and preferred size of the panel, as well as setting the panel's default font. Note that these calls are not made to some other object, as we did in Chapter 3 when we created a separate JPanel object. When a method is called without being invoked through a particular object, you can think of it as the object "talking to itself." The calls in the constructor are made to the object represented by the SmilingFacePanel class.

The paintComponent method accepts a Graphics object as a parameter, which, as we discussed in Chapter 2, represents the graphics context for a component. Graphics are drawn on the panel by making method calls to the panel's graphics context (the page parameter).

Every JPanel object has a paintComponent method that automatically gets called to draw the panel. In this case we are adding to the definition of paintComponent—telling it that in addition to drawing the background of the panel, it should also draw the face and words as defined by the various calls made in the paintComponent method. The first line of the paintComponent method is a call to super.paintComponent, which represents the regular JPanel version of the paintComponent method, which handles the painting of the background. We will almost always use this as the first line of code in a paintComponent method.

Let's look at another example. The Splat class shown in Listing 4.7 contains a main method that creates and displays the frame for the program. Visually, this program simply draws a few filled circles. The interesting thing about this program is not what it does, but how it does it—each circle drawn in this program is represented by its own object.

The main method instantiates a SplatPanel object and adds it to the frame. The SplatPanel class is shown in Listing 4.8. Like the SmilingFacePanel class in the previous example, the SplatPanel class is derived from JPanel. It holds as instance data five Circle objects, which are instantiated in the constructor.

The paintComponent method in the SplatPanel class draws the panel by calling the draw method of each circle. Essentially, the SplatPanel class asks each circle to draw itself.

The Circle class is shown in Listing 4.9. It defines instance data to store the size of the circle, its (*x*, *y*) location, and its color. These values are set using the constructor, and the class contains all the appropriate accessor and mutator methods. The draw method of the Circle class simply draws the circle based on the values of its instance data (its current state).

The Splat program embodies fundamental object-oriented thinking. Each circle manages itself and will draw itself in whatever graphics context you pass it. Each Circle object maintains its own state. The Circle class is defined in a way that can be used in other situations and programs.

Listing 4.7

```
//********************************************************************
//  Splat.java         Author: Lewis/Loftus
//
//  Demonstrates the use of graphical objects.
//********************************************************************

import javax.swing.*;
import java.awt.*;

public class Splat
{
```

Listing 4.7   continued

```
//---------------------------------------------------------------
//   Presents a collection of circles.
//---------------------------------------------------------------
public static void main (String[] args)
{
    JFrame frame = new JFrame ("Splat");
    frame.setDefaultCloseOperation (JFrame.EXIT_ON_CLOSE);

    frame.getContentPane().add(new SplatPanel());

    frame.pack();
    frame.setVisible(true);
}
}
```

Display

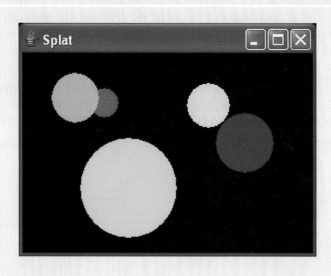

Listing 4.8

```java
//********************************************************************
//  SplatPanel.java         Author: Lewis/Loftus
//
//  Demonstrates the use of graphical objects.
//********************************************************************

import javax.swing.*;
import java.awt.*;

public class SplatPanel extends JPanel
{
   private Circle circle1, circle2, circle3, circle4, circle5;

   //-----------------------------------------------------------------
   //  Constructor: Creates five Circle objects.
   //-----------------------------------------------------------------
   public SplatPanel()
   {
      circle1 = new Circle (30, Color.red, 70, 35);
      circle2 = new Circle (50, Color.green, 30, 20);
      circle3 = new Circle (100, Color.cyan, 60, 85);
      circle4 = new Circle (45, Color.yellow, 170, 30);
      circle5 = new Circle (60, Color.blue, 200, 60);

      setPreferredSize (new Dimension(300, 200));
      setBackground (Color.black);
   }

   //-----------------------------------------------------------------
   //  Draws this panel by requesting that each circle draw itself.
   //-----------------------------------------------------------------
   public void paintComponent (Graphics page)
   {
      super.paintComponent(page);

      circle1.draw(page);
      circle2.draw(page);
      circle3.draw(page);
      circle4.draw(page);
      circle5.draw(page);
   }
}
```

Listing 4.9

```java
//********************************************************************
//  Circle.java        Author: Lewis/Loftus
//
//  Represents a circle with a particular position, size, and color.
//********************************************************************

import java.awt.*;

public class Circle
{
   private int diameter, x, y;
   private Color color;

   //-----------------------------------------------------------------
   //  Constructor: Sets up this circle with the specified values.
   //-----------------------------------------------------------------
   public Circle (int size, Color shade, int upperX, int upperY)
   {
      diameter = size;
      color = shade;
      x = upperX;
      y = upperY;
   }

   //-----------------------------------------------------------------
   //  Draws this circle in the specified graphics context.
   //-----------------------------------------------------------------
   public void draw (Graphics page)
   {
      page.setColor (color);
      page.fillOval (x, y, diameter, diameter);
   }

   //-----------------------------------------------------------------
   //  Diameter mutator.
   //-----------------------------------------------------------------
   public void setDiameter (int size)
   {
      diameter = size;
   }
```

Listing 4.9   **continued**

```java
//-----------------------------------------------------------------
//   Color mutator.
//-----------------------------------------------------------------
public void setColor (Color shade)
{
   color = shade;
}

//-----------------------------------------------------------------
//   X mutator.
//-----------------------------------------------------------------
public void setX (int upperX)
{
   x = upperX;
}


//-----------------------------------------------------------------
//   Y mutator.
//-----------------------------------------------------------------
public void setY (int upperY)
{
   y = upperY;
}

//-----------------------------------------------------------------
//   Diameter accessor.
//-----------------------------------------------------------------
public int getDiameter ()
{
   return diameter;
}

//-----------------------------------------------------------------
//   Color accessor.
//-----------------------------------------------------------------
public Color getColor ()
{
   return color;
}
```

Listing 4.9   **continued**

```
//-----------------------------------------------------------
//   X accessor.
//-----------------------------------------------------------
public int getX ()
{
   return x;
}

//-----------------------------------------------------------
//   Y accessor.
//-----------------------------------------------------------
public int getY ()
{
   return y;
}
}
```

4.7   GRAPHICAL USER INTERFACES

In Chapters 2 and 3 we introduced a few key components that are helpful in the design of graphics-based programs. What we need now is true user interaction, which is the heart of a graphical user interface (GUI). This section introduces the concepts needed to create interactive GUI-based programs. It lays the groundwork for all GUI discussions throughout the book.

At least three kinds of objects are needed to create a graphical user interface in Java:

> components
> events
> listeners

As we mentioned in Chapter 3, a GUI *component* is an object that defines a screen element to display information or allow the user to interact with a program in a certain way. Examples of GUI components include push buttons, text fields, labels, scroll bars, and menus. A *container* is a special type of component that is used to hold and organize other components. We've already used containers such as frames and panels, and have explored the use of labels as well.

An *event* is an object that represents some occurrence in which we may be interested. Often, events correspond to user actions, such as pressing a mouse button or typing a key on the keyboard. Most GUI components generate events to indicate a user action related to that component. For example, a button component will generate an event to indicate that the button has been pushed. A program that is oriented around a GUI, responding to events from the user, is called *event-driven*.

A *listener* is an object that "waits" for an event to occur and responds in some way when it does. We must carefully establish the relationships among the listener, the event it listens for, and the component that will generate the event.

> **Key Concept**
>
> A GUI is made up of components, events that represent user actions, and listeners that respond to those events.

For the most part, we will use components and events that are predefined by classes in the Java class library. We will tailor the behavior of the components, but their basic roles have been established. We will, however, write listener classes to perform whatever actions we desire when events occur.

Specifically, to create a Java program that uses a GUI, we must:

> instantiate and set up the necessary components,
> implement listener classes that define what happens when particular events occur, and
> establish the relationship between the listeners and the components that generate the events of interest.

In some respects, once you have a basic understanding of event-driven programming, the rest is just detail. There are many types of components you can use that produce many types of events that you may want to acknowledge. But they all work in the same basic way. They all have the same core relationships to one another.

The following sections introduce some more components and present examples of GUI-based programs that allow true user interaction.

4.8   BUTTONS

The `PushCounter` program shown in Listing 4.10 presents the user with a single push button (labeled "`Push Me!`"). Each time the button is pushed, a counter is updated and displayed.

The components used in this program include a button, a label to display the count, a panel to organize the GUI, and a frame to display the panel. The panel is defined by the `PushCounterPanel` class, shown in Listing 4.11.

Listing 4.10

```java
//********************************************************************
//  PushCounter.java        Author: Lewis/Loftus
//
//  Demonstrates a graphical user interface and an event listener.
//********************************************************************

import javax.swing.JFrame;

public class PushCounter
{
   //-----------------------------------------------------------------
   //  Creates the main program frame.
   //-----------------------------------------------------------------
   public static void main (String[] args)
   {
      JFrame frame = new JFrame ("Push Counter");
      frame.setDefaultCloseOperation (JFrame.EXIT_ON_CLOSE);

      frame.getContentPane().add(new PushCounterPanel());

      frame.pack();
      frame.setVisible(true);
   }
}
```

Display

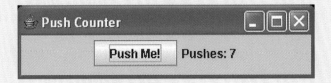

Listing 4.11

```java
//********************************************************************
//   PushCounterPanel.java        Author: Lewis/Loftus
//
//   Demonstrates a graphical user interface and an event listener.
//********************************************************************

import java.awt.*;
import java.awt.event.*;
import javax.swing.*;

public class PushCounterPanel extends JPanel
{
   private int count;
   private JButton push;
   private JLabel label;

   //-----------------------------------------------------------------
   //   Constructor: Sets up the GUI.
   //-----------------------------------------------------------------
   public PushCounterPanel ()
   {
      count = 0;

      push = new JButton ("Push Me!");
      push.addActionListener (new ButtonListener());

      label = new JLabel ("Pushes: " + count);

      add (push);
      add (label);

      setPreferredSize (new Dimension(300, 40));
      setBackground (Color.cyan);
   }

   //********************************************************************
   //   Represents a listener for button push (action) events.
   //********************************************************************
   private class ButtonListener implements ActionListener
   {
```

Listing 4.11   continued

```
//-----------------------------------------------------------------
//  Updates the counter and label when the button is pushed.
//-----------------------------------------------------------------
public void actionPerformed (ActionEvent event)
{
    count++;
    label.setText("Pushes: " + count);
}
    }
}
```

A push button is a component that allows the user to initiate an action with a press of the mouse. There are other types of button components that we explore in later chapters. A push button is defined by the JButton class.

The PushCounterPanel constructor sets up the GUI. The call to the JButton constructor takes a String parameter that specifies the text shown on the button. The button and the label are added to the panel.

The only event of interest in this program occurs when the button is pushed. To respond to the event, we must create a listener object for that event, so we must write a class that represents the listener.

A JButton generates an *action event* when it is pushed. Therefore the listener class we write will be an action event listener. In this program, we define a class called ButtonListener to represent the listener for this event.

> **Key Concept**
>
> Listeners are often defined as inner classes because of the intimate relationship between the listener and the GUI components.

We could write the ButtonListener class in its own file, or even in the same file but outside of the PushCounterPanel class. However, then we would have to set up a way to communicate between the listener and the components of the GUI that the listener updates. Instead, we define the ButtonListener class as an *inner class,* which is a class defined within another class. As such, it automatically has access to the members of the class that contains it. You should only create inner classes in situations in which there is an intimate relationship between the two classes and in which the inner class is not accessed by any other class. The relationship between a listener and its GUI is one of the few situations in which an inner class is appropriate.

Listener classes are written by implementing an *interface,* which is a list of methods that the implementing class must define. The Java standard class library contains interfaces for many types of events. An action listener is created by implementing the `ActionListener` interface, therefore we include the `implements` clause in the `ButtonListener` class. Interfaces are discussed in more detail in Chapter 6.

The only method listed in the `ActionListener` interface is the `actionPerformed` method, so that's the only method that the `ButtonListener` class must implement. The component that generates the action event (in this case the button) will call the `actionPerformed` method when the event occurs, passing in an `ActionEvent` object that represents the event. Sometimes we will use the event object, and other times it is simply sufficient to know that the event occurred. In this case, we have no need to interact with the event object. When the event occurs, the listener increments the `count` and resets the text of the label by using the `setText` method.

Remember, we not only have to create a listener for an event, we must also set up the relationship between the listener and the component that will generate the event. To do so, we add the listener to the component by calling the appropriate method. In the `PushCounterPanel` constructor, we call the `addActionListener` method, passing in a newly instantiated `ButtonListener` object.

Review this example carefully, noting how it accomplishes the three key steps to creating an interactive GUI-based program. It creates and sets up the GUI components, creates the appropriate listener for the event of interest, and sets up the relationship between the listener and the component that will generate the event.

4.9   TEXT FIELDS

Let's look at another example that uses another component: a text field. The `Fahrenheit` program shown in Listing 4.12 presents a GUI that includes a text field into which the user can type a Fahrenheit temperature. When the user presses the Enter (or Return) key, the equivalent Celsius temperature is displayed.

The interface for the `Fahrenheit` program is set up in the `FahrenheitPanel` class. The text field is an object of the `JTextField` class. The `JTextField` constructor takes an integer parameter that specifies the size of the field in number of characters based on the current default font.

The text field and various labels are added to the panel to be displayed. Remember that a panel is governed by a layout manager called flow layout, which puts as many components on a line as it can fit. So if you resize the frame,

Listing 4.12

```
//********************************************************************
//   Fahrenheit.java         Author: Lewis/Loftus
//
//   Demonstrates the use of text fields.
//********************************************************************

import javax.swing.JFrame;

public class Fahrenheit
{
   //-----------------------------------------------------------------
   //   Creates and displays the temperature converter GUI.
   //-----------------------------------------------------------------
   public static void main (String[] args)
   {
      JFrame frame = new JFrame ("Fahrenheit");
      frame.setDefaultCloseOperation (JFrame.EXIT_ON_CLOSE);

      FahrenheitPanel panel = new FahrenheitPanel();

      frame.getContentPane().add(panel);
      frame.pack();
      frame.setVisible(true);
   }
}
```

Display

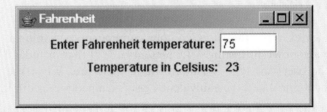

Listing 4.13

```java
//********************************************************************
//   FahrenheitPanel.java        Author: Lewis/Loftus
//
//   Demonstrates the use of text fields.
//********************************************************************

import java.awt.*;
import java.awt.event.*;
import javax.swing.*;

public class FahrenheitPanel extends JPanel
{
    private JLabel inputLabel, outputLabel, resultLabel;
    private JTextField fahrenheit;

    //-----------------------------------------------------------------
    //  Constructor: Sets up the main GUI components.
    //-----------------------------------------------------------------
    public FahrenheitPanel()
    {
        inputLabel = new JLabel ("Enter Fahrenheit temperature:");
        outputLabel = new JLabel ("Temperature in Celsius: ");
        resultLabel = new JLabel ("---");

        fahrenheit = new JTextField (5);
        fahrenheit.addActionListener (new TempListener());

        add (inputLabel);
        add (fahrenheit);
        add (outputLabel);
        add (resultLabel);

        setPreferredSize (new Dimension(300, 75));
        setBackground (Color.yellow);
    }
```

Listing 4.13   continued

```java
//************************************************************
//  Represents an action listener for the temperature input field.
//************************************************************
private class TempListener implements ActionListener
{
    //----------------------------------------------------------
    //  Performs the conversion when the enter key is pressed in
    //  the text field.
    //----------------------------------------------------------
    public void actionPerformed (ActionEvent event)
    {
        int fahrenheitTemp, celsiusTemp;

        String text = fahrenheit.getText();

        fahrenheitTemp = Integer.parseInt (text);
        celsiusTemp = (fahrenheitTemp-32) * 5/9;

        resultLabel.setText (Integer.toString (celsiusTemp));
    }
}
}
```

the orientation of the labels and text field may change. We examine layout managers in detail in Chapter 6, providing more options for controlling the layout of the components.

If the cursor is currently in the text field, the text field component generates an action event when the Enter or Return key is pressed. Therefore we need to set up a listener object to respond to action events. As we did in the PushCounter program in the previous section, we define the listener as an inner class that implements the ActionListener interface.

The text field component calls the actionPerformed method when the user presses the Enter key. The method first retrieves the text from the text field by calling its getText method, which returns a character string. The text is converted to an integer using the parseInt method of the Integer wrapper class. Then the method performs the calculation to determine the equivalent Celsius temperature and sets the text of the appropriate label with the result.

Note that a push button and a text field generate the same kind of event: an action event. So an alternative to the `Fahrenheit` program design is to add a `JButton` object to the GUI that causes the conversion to occur when the user uses the mouse to press the button. For that matter, the same listener object can be used to listen to multiple components at the same time. So the listener could be added to both the text field and the button, giving the user the option. Pressing either the button or the Enter key will cause the conversion to be performed. These variations are left as programming projects.

Summary of Key Concepts

> The heart of object-oriented programming is defining classes that represent objects with well-defined state and behavior.

> The scope of a variable, which determines where it can be referenced, depends on where it is declared.

> A UML class diagram helps us visualize the contents of and relationships among the classes of a program.

> An object should be encapsulated, guarding its data from inappropriate access.

> Instance variables should be declared with private visibility to promote encapsulation.

> Most objects contain accessor and mutator methods to allow the client to manage data in a controlled manner.

> The value returned from a method must be consistent with the return type specified in the method header.

> When a method is called, the actual parameters are copied into the formal parameters.

> A variable declared in a method is local to that method and cannot be used outside of it.

> A constructor cannot have any return type, even `void`.

> A GUI is made up of components, events that represent user actions, and listeners that respond to those events.

> Listeners are often defined as inner classes because of the intimate relationship between the listener and the GUI components.

Self-Review Questions

SR 4.1   What is an attribute?

SR 4.2   What is an operation?

SR 4.3   What is the difference between an object and a class?

SR 4.4   What is the scope of a variable?

SR 4.5   What are UML diagrams designed to do?

SR 4.6   Objects should be self-governing. Explain.

SR 4.7   What is a modifier?

SR 4.8   Why might a constant be given public visibility?

SR 4.9   Describe each of the following:

    a. public method

    b. private method

    c. public variable

    d. private variable

SR 4.10   What is the interface to an object?

SR 4.11   Why is a method invoked through (or on) a particular object? What is the exception to that rule?

SR 4.12   What does it mean for a method to return a value?

SR 4.13   What does the `return` statement do?

SR 4.14   Is a return statement required?

SR 4.15   Explain the difference between an actual parameter and a formal parameter.

SR 4.16   What are constructors used for? How are they defined?

SR 4.17   What is the relationship between an event and a listener?

SR 4.18   Can we add any kind of listener to any component? Explain.

SR 4.19   What type of event does a push button (a `JButton` object) generate?

Exercises

EX 4.1   For each of the following pairs, which represents a class and which represents an object of that class?

    a. Superhero, Superman

    b. Justin, Person

    c. Rover, Pet

    d. Magazine, Time

    e. Christmas, Holiday

EX 4.2   List some attributes and operations that might be defined for a class called `PictureFrame` that represents a picture frame.

EX 4.3   List some attributes and operations that might be defined for a class called `Meeting` that represents a business meeting.

EX 4.4 List some attributes and operations that might be defined for a class called `Course` that represents a college course (not a particular offering of a course, just the course in general).

EX 4.5 Write a method called `lyrics` that prints the lyrics of a song when invoked. The method should accept no parameters and return no value.

EX 4.6 Write a method called `cube` that accepts one integer parameter and returns that value raised to the third power.

EX 4.7 Write a method called `random100` that returns a random integer in the range of 1 to 100 (inclusive).

EX 4.8 Write a method called `randomInRange` that accepts two integer parameters representing a range. The method should return a random integer in the specified range (inclusive). Assume that the first parameter is greater than the second.

EX 4.9 Write a method called `randomColor` that creates and returns a `Color` object that represents a random color. Recall that a `Color` object can be defined by three integer values between 0 and 255, representing the contributions of red, green, and blue (its RGB value).

EX 4.10 Draw a UML class diagram that shows the relationships among the classes used in the `Transactions` program.

EX 4.11 Draw a UML class diagram that shows the relationships among the classes used in the `PushCounter` program.

EX 4.12 Draw a UML class diagram that shows the relationships among the classes used in the `Fahrenheit` program.

Programming Projects

PP 4.1 Design and implement a class called `Sphere` that contains instance data that represents the sphere's diameter. Define the `Sphere` constructor to accept and initialize the diameter, and include getter and setter methods for the diameter. Include methods that calculate and return the volume and surface area of the sphere (see Programming Project 3.5 for the formulas). Include a `toString` method that returns a one-line description of the sphere. Create a driver class called `MultiSphere`, whose `main` method instantiates and updates several `Sphere` objects.

PP 4.2 Design and implement a class called Dog that contains instance data that represents the dog's name and age. Define the Dog constructor to accept and initialize instance data. Include getter and setter methods for the name and age. Include a method to compute and return the age of the dog in "person years" (seven times the dogs age). Include a toString method that returns a one-line description of the dog. Create a driver class called Kennel, whose main method instantiates and updates several Dog objects.

PP 4.3 Design and implement a class called Box that contains instance data that represents the height, width, and depth of the box. Also include a boolean variable called full as instance data that represents if the box is full or not. Define the Box constructor to accept and initialize the height, width, and depth of the box. Each newly created Box is empty (the constructor should initialize full to false). Include getter and setter methods for all instance data. Include a toString method that returns a one-line description of the box. Create a driver class called BoxTest, whose main method instantiates and updates several Box objects.

PP 4.4 Design and implement a class called Book that contains instance data for the title, author, publisher, and copyright date. Define the Book constructor to accept and initialize this data. Include setter and getter methods for all instance data. Include a toString method that returns a nicely formatted, multi-line description of the book. Create a driver class called Bookshelf, whose main method instantiates and updates several Book objects.

PP 4.5 Design and implement a class called Flight that represents an airline flight. It should contain instance data that represents the airline name, flight number, and the flight's origin and destination cities. Define the Flight constructor to accept and initialize all instance data. Include getter and setter methods for all instance data. Include a toString method that returns a one-line description of the flight. Create a driver class called FlightTest, whose main method instantiates and updates several Flight objects.

PP 4.6 Design and implement a class called Bulb that represents a light bulb that can be turned on and off. Create a driver class called Lights whose main method instantiates and turns on some Bulb objects.

PP 4.7   Using the Die class defined in this chapter, design and implement a class called PairOfDice, composed of two Die objects. Include methods to set and get the individual die values, a method to roll the dice, and a method that returns the current sum of the two die values. Create a driver class called RollingDice2 to instantiate and use a PairOfDice object.

PP 4.8   Design and implement a class called Building that represents a graphical depiction of a building. Allow the parameters to the constructor to specify the building's width and height. Each building should be colored black, and contain a few random windows of yellow. Create a program that draws a random skyline of buildings.

PP 4.9   Write a program that displays a graphical seating chart for a dinner party. Create a class called Diner (as in one who dines) that stores the person's name, gender, and location at the dinner table. A diner is graphically represented as a circle, color-coded by gender, with the person's name printed in the circle.

PP 4.10   Create a class called Crayon that represents one crayon of a particular color and length (height). Design and implement a program that draws a box of crayons.

PP 4.11   Create a class called Star that represents a graphical depiction of a star. Let the constructor of the star accept the number of points in the star (4, 5, or 6), the radius of the star, and the center point location. Write a program that draws a sky containing various types of stars.

PP 4.12   Modify the Fahrenheit program from this chapter so that it displays a button that, when pressed, also causes the conversion calculation to take place. That is, the user will now have the option of pressing enter in the text field or pressing the button. Have the listener that is already defined for the text field also listen for the button push.

PP 4.13   Design and implement an application that displays a button and a label. Every time the button is pushed, the label should display a random number between 1 and 100, inclusive.

PP 4.14   Design and implement an application that presents two buttons and a label to the user. Label the buttons Increment and Decrement, respectively. Display a numeric value (initially 50) using the label. Each time the increment button is pushed, increment the value displayed. Likewise, each time the decrement button is pressed, decrement the value displayed.

PP 4.15   Design and implement an application that draws a traffic light and uses a push button to change the state of the light. Derive the drawing surface from the JPanel class and use another panel to organize the drawing surface and the button.

PP 4.16   Develop an application that implements a prototype user interface for composing an email message. The application should have text fields for the To, CC, and Bcc address lists and subject line, and one for the message body. Include a button labeled Send. When the Send button is pushed, the program should print the contents of all fields to standard output using println statements.

Answers to Self-Review Questions

SR 4.1   An attribute is a data value stored in an object and defines a particular characteristic of that object. For example, one attribute of a Student object might be that student's current grade point average. Collectively, the values of an object's attributes determine that object's current state.

SR 4.2   An operation is a function that can be done to or done by an object. For example, one operation of a Student object might be to compute that student's current grade point average. Collectively, an object's operations are referred to as the object's behaviors.

SR 4.3   A class is the blueprint of an object. It defines the variables and methods that will be a part of every object that is instantiated from it. But a class reserves no memory space for variables. Each object has its own data space and therefore its own state.

SR 4.4   The scope of a variable is the area within a program in which the variable can be referenced. An instance variable, declared at the class level, can be referenced in any method of the class. Local variables, including the formal parameters, declared within a particular method, can be referenced only in that method.

SR 4.5   A UML diagram helps us visualize the entities (classes and objects) in a program as well as the relationships among them. UML diagrams are tools that help us capture the design of a program prior to writing it.

SR 4.6   A self-governing object is one that controls the values of its own data. Encapsulated objects, which don't allow an external client to reach in and change its data, are self-governing.

SR 4.7   A modifier is a Java reserved word that can be used in the definition of a variable or method and that specifically defines certain characteristics of its use. For example, by declaring a variable with private visibility, the variable cannot be directly accessed outside of the object in which it is defined.

SR 4.8   A constant might be declared with public visibility because that would not violate encapsulation. Because the value of a constant cannot be changed, it is not generally a problem for another object to access it directly.

SR 4.9   The modifiers affect the methods and variables in the following ways:

a. A public method is called a service method for an object because it defines a service that the object provides.
b. A private method is called a support method because it cannot be invoked from outside the object and is used to support the activities of other methods in the class.
c. A public variable is a variable that can be directly accessed and modified by a client. This explicitly violates the principle of encapsulation and therefore should be avoided.
d. A private variable is a variable that can be accessed and modified only from within the class. Variables almost always are declared with private visibility.

SR 4.10   An object's interface is the set of public operations (methods) defined on it. That is, the interface establishes the set of services the object will perform for the rest of the system.

SR 4.11   Although a method is defined in a class, it is invoked through a particular object to indicate which object of that class is being affected. For example, the Student class may define the operation that computes the grade point average of a student, but the operation is invoked through a particular Student object to compute the GPA for that student. The exception to this rule is the invocation of a static method (see Chapter 3), which is executed through the class name and does not affect any particular object.

SR 4.12 An invoked method may return a value, which means it computes a value and provides that value to the calling method. The calling method usually uses the invocation, and thus its return value, as part of a larger expression.

SR 4.13 An explicit `return` statement is used to specify the value that is returned from a method. The type of the return value must match the return type specified in the method definition.

SR 4.14 A return statement is required in methods that have a return type other than void. A method that does not return a value could use a return statement without an expression, but it is not necessary. Only one return statement should be used in a method.

SR 4.15 An actual parameter is a value sent to a method when it is invoked. A formal parameter is the corresponding variable in the header of the method declaration; it takes on the value of the actual parameter so that it can be used inside the method.

SR 4.16 Constructors are special methods in an object that are used to initialize the object when it is instantiated. A constructor has the same name as its class, and it does not return a value.

SR 4.17 Events usually represent user actions. A listener object is set up to listen for a certain event to be generated from a particular component.

SR 4.18 No, we cannot add any listener to any component. Each component generates a certain set of events, and only listeners of those types can be added to the component.

SR 4.19 A `JButton` object generates an action event when the button is pushed. When that occurs, the `actionPerformed` method of the action listener associated with that button is invoked.

Conditionals and Loops 5

CHAPTER OBJECTIVES

> Define the flow of control through a method.

> Explore boolean expressions that can be used to make decisions.

> Perform basic decision making using if and switch statements.

> Discuss issues pertaining to the comparison of certain types of data.

> Execute statements repetitively using while, do, and for loops.

> Discuss the concept of an iterator object and use one to read a text file.

> Draw with the aid of conditionals and loops.

> Explore more GUI components and events.

All programming languages have statements that allow you to make decisions to determine what to do next. Some of those statements allow you to repeat a certain activity multiple times. This chapter discusses several such statements, as well as exploring some issues related to comparing data and objects. It includes a discussion of boolean expressions, which form the basis of any decision. The Graphics Track sections of this chapter explore new drawing options and several new components and events.

5.1   BOOLEAN EXPRESSIONS

The order in which statements are executed in a running program is called the *flow of control*. Unless otherwise specified, the execution of a program proceeds in a linear fashion. That is, a running program starts at the first programming statement and moves down one statement at a time until the program is complete. A Java application begins executing with the first line of the main method and proceeds step by step until it gets to the end of the main method.

Invoking a method alters the flow of control. When a method is called, control jumps to the code defined for that method. When the method completes, control returns to the place in the calling method where the invocation was made and processing continues from there.

> **Key Concept**
>
> Conditionals and loops allow us to control the flow of execution through a method.

Within a given method, we can alter the flow of control through the code by using certain types of programming statements. Statements that control the flow of execution through a method fall into two categories: conditionals and loops.

A *conditional statement* is sometimes called a *selection statement* because it allows us to choose which statement will be executed next. The conditional statements in Java are the if statement, the if-else statement, and the switch statement. These statements allow us to decide which statement to execute next. Each decision is based on a *boolean expression* (also called a *condition*), which is an expression that evaluates to either true or false. The result of the expression determines which statement is executed next.

The following is an example of an if statement:

```
if (count > 20)
    System.out.println ("Count exceeded");
```

> **Key Concept**
>
> An if statement allows a program to choose whether to execute a particular statement.

The condition in this statement is count > 20. That expression evaluates to a boolean (true or false) result. Either the value stored in count is greater than 20 or it's not. If it is, the println statement is executed. If it's not, the println statement is skipped and processing continues with whatever code follows it. The if statement and other conditionals are explored in detail in this chapter.

The ability to make decisions like this come up all the time in programming situations. For example, the cost of life insurance might be dependent on whether the insured person is a smoker. If the person smokes, we calculate the cost using a particular formula; if not, we calculate it using another. The role of a conditional statement is to evaluate a boolean condition (whether the person smokes) and then to execute the proper calculation accordingly.

A *loop*, or *repetition statement*, allows us to execute a programming statement over and over again. Like a conditional, a loop is based on a boolean expression that determines how many times the statement is executed.

> **Key Concept**
>
> A loop allows a program to execute a statement multiple times.

For example, suppose we wanted to calculate the grade point average of every student in a class. The calculation is the same for each student; it is just performed on different data. We would set up a loop that repeats the calculation for each student until there are no more students to process.

Java has three types of loop statements: the `while` statement, the `do` statement, and the `for` statement. Each type of loop statement has unique characteristics that distinguish it from the others.

All conditionals and loops are based on boolean expressions, which use equality operators, relational operators, and logical operators to make decisions. Before we discuss the conditional and loop statements, let's explore these operators.

Equality and Relational Operators

The `==` and `!=` operators are called *equality operators*. They test whether two values are equal or not equal, respectively. Note that the equality operator consists of two equal signs side by side and should not be mistaken for the assignment operator that uses only one equal sign.

The following `if` statement prints a sentence only if the variables `total` and `sum` contain the same value:

```
if (total == sum)
    System.out.println ("total equals sum");
```

Likewise, the following `if` statement prints a sentence only if the variables `total` and `sum` do *not* contain the same value:

```
if (total != sum)
    System.out.println ("total does NOT equal sum");
```

Java also has several *relational operators* that let us decide relative ordering between values. Earlier in this section we used the greater than operator (>) to decide if one value was greater than another. We can ask such questions using various operators, depending on the relationship. These include less than (<), greater than or equal to (>=), and less than or equal to (<=). Figure 5.1 lists the Java equality and relational operators.

Operator	Meaning
==	equal to
!=	not equal to
<	less than
<=	less than or equal to
>	greater than
>=	greater than or equal to

FIGURE 5.1   Java equality and relational operators

The equality and relational operators have precedence lower than the arithmetic operators. Therefore, arithmetic operations are evaluated first, followed by equality and relational operations. As always, parentheses can be used to explicitly specify the order of evaluation.

We'll see more examples of relational operators as we examine conditional and loop statements throughout this chapter.

Logical Operators

In addition to the equality and relational operators, Java has three *logical operators* that produce boolean results. They also take boolean operands. Figure 5.2 lists and describes the logical operators.

The ! operator is used to perform the *logical NOT* operation, which is also called the *logical complement*. The logical complement of a boolean value yields its opposite value. That is, if a boolean variable called found has the value false, then !found is true. Likewise, if found is true, then !found is false. The logical NOT operation does not change the value stored in found.

Operator	Description	Example	Result
!	logical NOT	! a	true if a is false and false if a is true
&&	logical AND	a && b	true if a and b are both true and false otherwise
||	logical OR	a || b	true if a or b or both are true and false otherwise

FIGURE 5.2   Java logical operators

A logical operation can be described by a *truth table* that lists all possible combinations of values for the variables involved in an expression. Because the logical NOT operator is unary, there are only two possible values for its one operand, true or false. Figure 5.3 shows a truth table that describes the ! operator.

The && operator performs a *logical AND* operation. The result is true if both operands are true, but false otherwise. Compare that to the result of the *logical OR* operator (||), which is true if one or the other or both operands are true, but false otherwise.

The AND and OR operators are both binary operators since each uses two operands. Therefore there are four possible combinations to consider: both operands are true, both are false, one is true and the other false, and vice versa. Figure 5.4 depicts a truth table that shows both the && and || operators.

The logical NOT has the highest precedence of the three logical operators, followed by logical AND, then logical OR.

Consider the following if statement:

```
if (!done && (count > MAX))
    System.out.println ("Completed.");
```

Under what conditions would the println statement be executed? The value of the boolean variable done is either true or false, and the NOT operator reverses that value. The value of count is either greater than MAX or it isn't. The truth table in Figure 5.5 breaks down all of the possibilities.

An important characteristic of the && and || operators is that they are "short-circuited." That is, if their left operand is sufficient to decide the boolean result of the operation, the right operand is not evaluated. This situation can occur with both operators, but for different reasons. If the left operand of the && operator is false, then the result of the operation will be false no matter what the value of the right operand is. Likewise, if the left operand of the || is true, then the result of the operation is true no matter what the value of the right operand is.

> **Key Concept**
>
> Logical operators are often used to construct sophisticated conditions.

a	!a
false	true
true	false

FIGURE 5.3   Truth table describing the logical NOT operator

a	b	a && b	a || b
false	false	false	false
false	true	false	true
true	false	false	true
true	true	true	true

FIGURE 5.4 Truth table describing the logical AND and OR operators

done	count > MAX	!done	!done && (count > MAX)
false	false	true	false
false	true	true	true
true	false	false	false
true	true	false	false

FIGURE 5.5 A truth table for a specific condition

Sometimes you can capitalize on the fact that the operation is short-circuited. For example, the condition in the following `if` statement will not attempt to divide by zero if the left operand is false. If count has the value zero, the left side of the `&&` operation is false; therefore the whole expression is false and the right side is not evaluated.

```
if (count != 0 && total/count > MAX)
    System.out.println ("Testing.");
```

You should consider carefully whether or not to rely on these kinds of subtle programming language characteristics. Not all programming languages work the same way. As we have stressed before, you should always strive to make extremely clear to the reader exactly how the logic of your program works.

5.2 THE `if` STATEMENT

We've used a basic `if` statement in earlier examples in this chapter. Let's now explore it in detail.

An *if statement* consists of the reserved word `if` followed by a boolean expression, followed by a statement. The condition is enclosed in parentheses and must evaluate to true or false. If the condition is true, the statement is executed and processing continues with the next statement. If the condition is false, the statement is skipped and processing continues immediately with the next statement. Figure 5.6 shows this processing.

Key Concept

Proper indentation is important for human readability; it shows the relationship between one statement and another.

Consider the following example of an `if` statement:

```
if (total > amount)
    total = total + (amount + 1);
```

In this example, if the value in `total` is greater than the value in `amount`, the assignment statement is executed; otherwise the assignment statement is skipped.

Note that the assignment statement in this example is indented under the header line of the `if` statement. This communicates that the assignment statement is part of the `if` statement; it implies that the `if` statement governs whether the assignment statement will be executed. This indentation is extremely important for the human reader, although it is ignored by the compiler.

The example in Listing 5.1 reads the age of the user and then makes a decision as to whether to print a particular sentence based on the age that is entered.

The `Age` program echoes the age value that is entered in all cases. If the age is less than the value of the constant `MINOR`, the statement about youth is printed. If the age is equal to or greater than the value of `MINOR`, the `println` statement is skipped. In either case, the final sentence about age being a state of mind is printed.

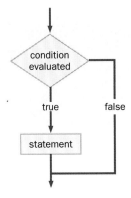

FIGURE 5.6   The logic of an `if` statement

Listing 5.1

```java
//********************************************************************
//  Age.java         Author: Lewis/Loftus
//
//  Demonstrates the use of an if statement.
//********************************************************************

import java.util.Scanner;

public class Age
{
    //-----------------------------------------------------------------
    //  Reads the user's age and prints comments accordingly.
    //-----------------------------------------------------------------
    public static void main (String[] args)
    {
        final int MINOR = 21;

        Scanner scan = new Scanner (System.in);

        System.out.print ("Enter your age: ");
        int age = scan.nextInt();

        System.out.println ("You entered: " + age);

        if (age < MINOR)
            System.out.println ("Youth is a wonderful thing. Enjoy.");

        System.out.println ("Age is a state of mind.");
    }
}
```

Output

```
Enter your age: 40
You entered: 40
Age is a state of mind.
```

Let's look at a few more examples of basic `if` statements. The following `if` statement causes the variable `size` to be set to zero if its current value is greater than or equal to the value in the constant `MAX`:

```
if (size >= MAX)
    size = 0;
```

The condition of the following `if` statement first adds three values together, then compares the result to the value stored in `numBooks`:

```
if (numBooks < stackCount + inventoryCount + duplicateCount)
    reorder = true;
```

If `numBooks` is less than the other three values combined, the boolean variable `reorder` is set to `true`. The addition operations are performed before the less than operator because the arithmetic operators have a higher precedence than the relational operators.

Assuming `generator` refers to an object of the `Random` class, the following `if` statement examines the value returned from a call to `nextInt` to determine a random winner:

```
if (generator.nextInt(CHANCE) == 0)
    System.out.println ("You are a randomly selected winner!");
```

The odds of this code picking a winner are based on the value of the `CHANCE` constant. That is, if `CHANCE` contains 20, the odds of winning are 1 in 20. The fact that the condition is looking for a return value of 0 is arbitrary; any value between 0 and `CHANCE-1` would have worked.

The `if-else` Statement

Sometimes we want to do one thing if a condition is true and another thing if that condition is false. We can add an *else clause* to an `if` statement, making it an *if-else statement,* to handle this kind of situation. The following is an example of an `if-else` statement:

```
if (height <= MAX)
    adjustment = 0;
else
    adjustment = MAX - height;
```

If the condition is true, the first assignment statement is executed; if the condition is false, the second assignment statement is executed. Only one or the other will be executed, because a boolean condition

> **Key Concept**
>
> An `if-else` statement allows a program to do one thing if a condition is true and another thing if the condition is false.

evaluates to either true or false. Note that proper indentation is used again to communicate that the statements are part of the governing `if` statement.

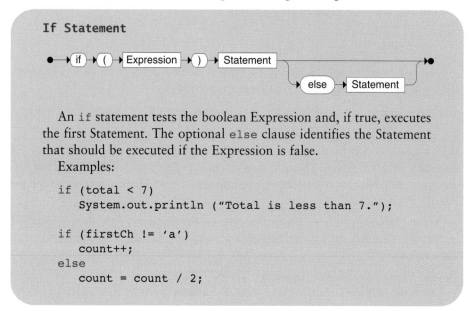

If Statement

An `if` statement tests the boolean Expression and, if true, executes the first Statement. The optional `else` clause identifies the Statement that should be executed if the Expression is false.

Examples:

```
if (total < 7)
    System.out.println ("Total is less than 7.");

if (firstCh != 'a')
    count++;
else
    count = count / 2;
```

The `Wages` program shown in Listing 5.2 uses an `if-else` statement to compute the proper payment amount for an employee.

In the `Wages` program, if an employee works over 40 hours in a week, the payment amount takes into account the overtime hours. An `if-else` statement is used to determine whether the number of hours entered by the user is greater than 40. If it is, the extra hours are paid at a rate one and a half times the normal rate. If there are no overtime hours, the total payment is based simply on the number of hours worked and the standard rate.

Let's look at another example of an `if-else` statement:

```
if (roster.getSize() == FULL)
    roster.expand();
else
    roster.addName (name);
```

This example makes use of an object called `roster`. Even without knowing what `roster` represents, or from what class it was created, we can see that it has at least three methods: `getSize`, `expand`, and `addName`. The condition of the `if` statement calls `getSize` and compares the result to the constant `FULL`. If the condition is true, the `expand` method is invoked (apparently to expand the size of the

Listing 5.2

```java
//********************************************************************
//  Wages.java       Author: Lewis/Loftus
//
//  Demonstrates the use of an if-else statement.
//********************************************************************

import java.text.NumberFormat;
import java.util.Scanner;

public class Wages
{
   //-----------------------------------------------------------------
   //  Reads the number of hours worked and calculates wages.
   //-----------------------------------------------------------------
   public static void main (String[] args)
   {
      final double RATE = 8.25;  // regular pay rate
      final int STANDARD = 40;   // standard hours in a work week

      Scanner scan = new Scanner (System.in);

      double pay = 0.0;

      System.out.print ("Enter the number of hours worked: ");
      int hours = scan.nextInt();

      System.out.println ();

      // Pay overtime at "time and a half"
      if (hours > STANDARD)
         pay = STANDARD * RATE + (hours-STANDARD) * (RATE * 1.5);
      else
         pay = hours * RATE;

      NumberFormat fmt = NumberFormat.getCurrencyInstance();
      System.out.println ("Gross earnings: " + fmt.format(pay));
   }
}
```

Output

```
Enter the number of hours worked: 46

Gross earnings: $404.25
```

roster). If the roster is not yet full, the variable name is passed as a parameter to the addName method.

The program in Listing 5.3 instantiates a Coin object, flips the coin by calling the flip method, then uses an if-else statement to determine which of two sentences gets printed based on the result.

The Coin class is shown in Listing 5.4. It stores two integer constants (HEADS and TAILS) that represent the two possible states of the coin, and an instance variable called face that represents the current state of the coin. The Coin constructor initially flips the coin by calling the flip method, which determines the new state of the coin by randomly choosing a number (either 0 or 1). The

Listing 5.3

```
//********************************************************************
//  CoinFlip.java          Author: Lewis/Loftus
//
//  Demonstrates the use of an if-else statement.
//********************************************************************

public class CoinFlip
{
    //----------------------------------------------------------------
    //  Creates a Coin object, flips it, and prints the results.
    //----------------------------------------------------------------
    public static void main (String[] args)
    {
        Coin myCoin = new Coin();

        myCoin.flip();

        System.out.println (myCoin);

        if (myCoin.isHeads())
            System.out.println ("You win.");
        else
            System.out.println ("Better luck next time.");
    }
}
```

Output

```
Tails
Better luck next time.
```

Listing 5.4

```java
//********************************************************************
//  Coin.java          Author: Lewis/Loftus
//
//  Represents a coin with two sides that can be flipped.
//********************************************************************

public class Coin
{
   private final int HEADS = 0;
   private final int TAILS = 1;

   private int face;

   //-----------------------------------------------------------------
   //  Sets up the coin by flipping it initially.
   //-----------------------------------------------------------------
   public Coin ()
   {
      flip();
   }

   //-----------------------------------------------------------------
   //  Flips the coin by randomly choosing a face value.
   //-----------------------------------------------------------------
   public void flip ()
   {
      face = (int) (Math.random() * 2);
   }

   //-----------------------------------------------------------------
   //  Returns true if the current face of the coin is heads.
   //-----------------------------------------------------------------
   public boolean isHeads ()
   {
      return (face == HEADS);
   }
```

Listing 5.4   **continued**

```
//-------------------------------------------------------------
//  Returns the current face of the coin as a string.
//-------------------------------------------------------------
public String toString()
{
    String faceName;

    if (face == HEADS)
        faceName = "Heads";
    else
        faceName = "Tails";

    return faceName;
}
}
```

isHeads method returns a boolean value based on the current face value of the coin. The toString method uses an if-else statement to determine which character string to return to describe the coin. The toString method is automatically called when the myCoin object is passed to println in the main method.

Using Block Statements

We may want to do more than one thing as the result of evaluating a boolean condition. In Java, we can replace any single statement with a *block statement*. A block statement is a collection of statements enclosed in braces. We've used these braces many times in previous examples to delimit method and class definitions.

The program called Guessing, shown in Listing 5.5, uses an if-else statement in which the statement of the else clause is a block statement.

If the guess entered by the user equals the randomly chosen answer, an appropriate acknowledgement is printed. However, if the answer is incorrect, two statements are printed, one that states that the guess is wrong and one that prints the actual answer. A programming project at the end of this chapter expands the concept of this example into the Hi-Lo game.

Note that if the block braces were not used, the sentence stating that the answer is incorrect would be printed if the answer was wrong, but the sentence

Listing 5.5

```java
//********************************************************************
//   Guessing.java          Author: Lewis/Loftus
//
//   Demonstrates the use of a block statement in an if-else.
//********************************************************************

import java.util.*;

public class Guessing
{
   //-----------------------------------------------------------------
   //   Plays a simple guessing game with the user.
   //-----------------------------------------------------------------
   public static void main (String[] args)
   {
      final int MAX = 10;
      int answer, guess;

      Scanner scan = new Scanner (System.in);
      Random generator = new Random();

      answer = generator.nextInt(MAX) + 1;

      System.out.print ("I'm thinking of a number between 1 and "
                        + MAX + ". Guess what it is: ");

      guess = scan.nextInt();

      if (guess == answer)
         System.out.println ("You got it! Good guessing!");
      else
      {
         System.out.println ("That is not correct, sorry.");
         System.out.println ("The number was " + answer);
      }
   }
}
```

Output

```
I'm thinking of a number between 1 and 10. Guess what it is: 7
That is not correct, sorry.
The number was 5
```

revealing the correct answer would be printed in all cases. That is, only the first statement would be considered part of the else clause.

Remember that indentation means nothing except to the human reader. Statements that are not blocked properly can lead to the programmer making improper assumptions about how the code will execute. For example, the following code is misleading:

```
if (depth > 36.238)
    delta = 100;
else
    System.out.println ("WARNING: Delta is being reset to ZERO");
    delta = 0;   // not part of the else clause!
```

The indentation (not to mention the logic of the code) implies that the variable delta is reset only when depth is less than 36.238. However, without using a block, the assignment statement that resets delta to zero is not governed by the if-else statement at all. It is executed in either case, which is clearly not what is intended.

A block statement can be used anywhere a single statement is called for in Java syntax. For example, the if portion of an if-else statement could be a block, or the else portion could be a block (as we saw in the Guessing program), or both parts could be block statements. For example:

```
if (boxes != warehouse.getCount())
{
    System.out.println ("Inventory and warehouse do NOT match.");
    System.out.println ("Beginning inventory process again!");
    boxes = 0;
}
else
{
    System.out.println ("Inventory and warehouse MATCH.");
    warehouse.ship();
}
```

In this if-else statement, the value of boxes is compared to a value obtained by calling the getCount method of the warehouse object (whatever that is). If they do not match exactly, two println statements and an assignment statement are executed. If they do match, a different message is printed and the ship method of warehouse is invoked.

The Conditional Operator

The Java *conditional operator* is similar to an if-else statement in some ways. It is a *ternary operator* because it requires three operands. The symbol for the conditional operator is usually written ?:, but it is not like other operators in that the two symbols that make it up are always separated. The following is an example of an expression that contains the conditional operator:

```
(total > MAX) ? total + 1 : total * 2;
```

Preceding the ? is a boolean condition. Following the ? are two expressions separated by the : symbol. The entire conditional expression returns the value of the first expression if the condition is true, and returns the value of the second expression if the condition is false.

Keep in mind that this is an expression that returns a value, and usually we want to do something with that value, such as assign it to a variable:

```
total = (total > MAX) ? total + 1 : total * 2;
```

In many ways, the ?: operator serves like an abbreviated if-else statement. The previous statement is functionally equivalent to, but sometimes more convenient than, the following:

```
if (total > MAX)
    total = total + 1;
else
    total = total * 2;
```

Now consider the following declaration:

```
int larger = (num1 > num2) ? num1 : num2;
```

If num1 is greater than num2, the value of num1 is returned and used to initialize the variable larger. If not, the value of num2 is returned and used to initialize larger. Similarly, the following statement prints the smaller of the two values:

```
System.out.println ("Smaller: " + ((num1 < num2) ? num1 : num2));
```

The conditional operator is occasionally helpful to evaluate a short condition and return a result. It is not a replacement for an if-else statement, however, because the operands to the ?: operator are expressions, not necessarily full statements. Even when the conditional operator is a viable alternative, you should use it sparingly because it is often less readable than an if-else statement.

Nested `if` Statements

The statement executed as the result of an `if` statement could be another `if` statement. This situation is called a *nested if*. It allows us to make another decision after determining the results of a previous decision. The program in Listing 5.6, called `MinOfThree`, uses nested `if` statements to determine the smallest of three integer values entered by the user.

Carefully trace the logic of the `MinOfThree` program, using various input sets with the minimum value in all three positions, to see how it determines the lowest value.

An important situation arises with nested `if` statements. It may seem that an `else` clause after a nested `if` could apply to either `if` statement. For example:

```
if (code == 'R')
    if (height <= 20)
        System.out.println ("Situation Normal");
    else
        System.out.println ("Bravo!");
```

> **Key Concept**
>
> In a nested `if` statement, an `else` clause is matched to the closest unmatched `if`.

Is the `else` clause matched to the inner `if` statement or the outer `if` statement? The indentation in this example implies that it is part of the inner `if` statement, and that is correct. An `else` clause is always matched to the closest unmatched `if` that preceded it. However, if we're not careful, we can easily mismatch it in our mind and misalign the indentation. This is another reason why accurate, consistent indentation is crucial.

Braces can be used to specify the `if` statement to which an `else` clause belongs. For example, if the previous example should have been structured so that the string `"Bravo!"` is printed if `code` is not equal to `'R'`, we could force that relationship (and properly indent) as follows:

```
if (code == 'R')
{
    if (height <= 20)
        System.out.println ("Situation Normal");
}
else
    System.out.println ("Bravo!");
```

By using the block statement in the first `if` statement, we establish that the `else` clause belongs to it.

Listing 5.6

```java
//********************************************************************
//   MinOfThree.java          Author: Lewis/Loftus
//
//   Demonstrates the use of nested if statements.
//********************************************************************

import java.util.Scanner;

public class MinOfThree
{
    //-----------------------------------------------------------------
    //   Reads three integers from the user and determines the smallest
    //   value.
    //-----------------------------------------------------------------
    public static void main (String[] args)
    {
        int num1, num2, num3, min = 0;

        Scanner scan = new Scanner (System.in);

        System.out.println ("Enter three integers: ");
        num1 = scan.nextInt();
        num2 = scan.nextInt();
        num3 = scan.nextInt();

        if (num1 < num2)
            if (num1 < num3)
                min = num1;
            else
                min = num3;
        else
            if (num2 < num3)
                min = num2;
            else
                min = num3;

        System.out.println ("Minimum value: " + min);
    }
}
```

Output

```
Enter three integers:
45   22   69
Minimum value: 22
```

5.3   COMPARING DATA

When comparing data using boolean expressions, it's important to understand some nuances that arise depending on the type of data being examined. Let's look at a few key situations.

Comparing Floats

An interesting situation occurs when comparing floating point data. Two floating point values are equal, according to the == operator, only if all the binary digits of their underlying representations match. If the compared values are the results of computation, it may be unlikely that they are exactly equal even if they are close enough for the specific situation. Therefore, you should rarely use the equality operator (==) when comparing floating point values.

A better way to check for floating point equality is to compute the absolute value of the difference between the two values and compare the result to some tolerance level. For example, we may choose a tolerance level of 0.00001. If the two floating point values are so close that their difference is less than the tolerance, then we are willing to consider them equal. Comparing two floating point values, f1 and f2, could be accomplished as follows:

```
if (Math.abs(f1 - f2) < TOLERANCE)
    System.out.println ("Essentially equal.");
```

The value of the constant TOLERANCE should be appropriate for the situation.

Comparing Characters

We know what it means when we say that one number is less than another, but what does it mean to say one character is less than another? As we discussed in Chapter 2, characters in Java are based on the Unicode character set, which defines an ordering of all possible characters that can be used. Because the character 'a' comes before the character 'b' in the character set, we can say that 'a' is less than 'b'.

We can use the equality and relational operators on character data. For example, if two character variables ch1 and ch2 hold two characters, we might determine their relative ordering in the Unicode character set with an if statement as follows:

```
if (ch1 > ch2)
    System.out.println (ch1 + " is greater than " + ch2);
else
    System.out.println (ch1 + " is NOT greater than " + ch2);
```

The Unicode character set is structured so that all lowercase alphabetic characters ('a' through 'z') are contiguous and in alphabetical order. The same is true of uppercase alphabetic characters ('A' through 'Z') and characters that represent digits ('0' through '9'). The digits precede the uppercase alphabetic characters, which precede the lowercase alphabetic characters. Before, after, and in between these groups are other characters. See the chart in Appendix C for details.

Comparing Objects

The Unicode relationships among characters make it easy to sort characters and strings of characters. If you have a list of names, for instance, you can put them in alphabetical order based on the inherent relationships among characters in the character set.

However, you should not use the equality or relational operators to compare String objects. The String class contains a method called equals that returns a boolean value that is true if the two strings being compared contain exactly the same characters, and is false otherwise. For example:

```
if (name1.equals(name2))
    System.out.println ("The names are the same.");
else
    System.out.println ("The names are not the same.");
```

Assuming that name1 and name2 are String objects, this condition determines whether the characters they contain are an exact match. Because both objects were created from the String class, they both respond to the equals message. Therefore the condition could have been written as name2.equals(name1) and the same result would occur.

> **Key Concept**
>
> The compareTo method can be used to determine the relative order of strings.

It is valid to test the condition (name1 == name2), but that actually tests to see whether both reference variables refer to the same String object. For any object, the == operator tests whether both reference variables are aliases of each other (whether they contain the same address). That's different than testing to see whether two different String objects contain the same characters.

Keep in mind that a string literal (such as "Howdy") is a convenience, and is actually a shorthand technique for creating a String object. An interesting issue related to string comparisons is the fact that Java only creates a unique object for string literals when needed. That is, if the string literal `"Hi"` is used multiple times in a method, only one `String` object is created to represent it. Therefore, the conditions of both `if` statements in the following code are true:

```
String str = "software";
if (str == "software")
    System.out.println ("References are the same");
if (str.equals("software"))
    System.out.println ("Characters are the same");
```

The first time the string literal `"software"` is used, a `String` object is created to represent it, and the reference variable `str` is set to its address. Each subsequent time the literal is used, the original object is referenced.

To determine the relative ordering of two strings, use the `compareTo` method of the `String` class. The `compareTo` method is more versatile than the `equals` method. Instead of returning a `boolean` value, the `compareTo` method returns an integer. The return value is negative if the `String` object through which the method is invoked precedes (is less than) the string that is passed in as a parameter. The return value is zero if the two strings contain the same characters. The return value is positive if the `String` object through which the method is invoked follows (is greater than) the string that is passed in as a parameter. For example:

```
int result = name1.compareTo(name2);
if (result < 0)
    System.out.println (name1 + " comes before " + name2);
else
    if (result == 0)
        System.out.println ("The names are equal.");
    else
        System.out.println (name1 + " follows " + name2);
```

Keep in mind that comparing characters and strings is based on the Unicode character set (see Appendix C). This is called a *lexicographic ordering*. If all alphabetic characters are in the same case (upper or lower), the lexicographic ordering will be alphabetic ordering as well. However, when comparing two strings, such as "able" and "Baker", the `compareTo` method will conclude that "Baker" comes first because all of the uppercase letters come before all of the lowercase letters in the Unicode character set. A string that is the prefix of another, longer string is considered to precede the longer string. For example, when comparing two strings such as "horse" and "horsefly", the `compareTo` method will conclude that "horse" comes first.

5.4   THE switch STATEMENT

Another conditional statement in Java is called the *switch statement*, which causes the executing program to follow one of several paths based on a single value. We also discuss the *break statement* in this section because it is usually used with a switch statement.

The switch statement evaluates an expression to determine a value and then matches that value with one of several possible *cases*. Each case has statements associated with it. After evaluating the expression, control jumps to the statement associated with the first case that matches the value. Consider the following example:

```
switch (idChar)
{
    case 'A':
        aCount = aCount + 1;
        break;
    case 'B':
        bCount = bCount + 1;
        break;
    case 'C':
        cCount = cCount + 1;
        break;
    default:
        System.out.println ("Error in Identification Character.");
}
```

First, the expression is evaluated. In this example, the expression is a simple char variable. Execution then transfers to the first statement identified by the case value that matches the result of the expression. Therefore, if idChar contains an 'A', the variable aCount is incremented. If it contains a 'B', the case for 'A' is skipped and processing continues where bCount is incremented.

If no case value matches that of the expression, execution continues with the optional *default case*, indicated by the reserved word default. If no default case exists, no statements in the switch statement are executed and processing continues with the statement after the switch statement. It is often a good idea to include a default case, even if you don't expect it to be executed.

When a break statement is encountered, processing jumps to the statement following the switch statement. A break statement is usually used to break out of each case of a switch statement. Without a break statement, processing continues into the next case of the switch. Therefore if the break statement at the end of the

> **Key Concept**
>
> A break statement is usually used at the end of each case alternative of a switch statement.

'A' case in the previous example was not there, both the aCount and bCount variables would be incremented when the idChar contains an 'A'. Usually we want to perform only one case, so a break statement is almost always used. Occasionally, though, the "pass through" feature comes in handy.

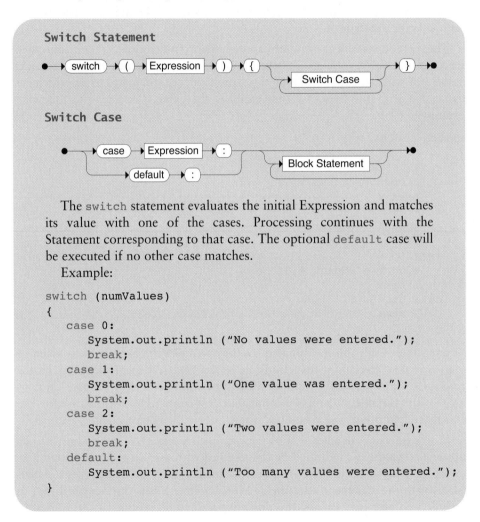

Switch Statement

Switch Case

The switch statement evaluates the initial Expression and matches its value with one of the cases. Processing continues with the Statement corresponding to that case. The optional default case will be executed if no other case matches.

Example:

```
switch (numValues)
{
    case 0:
        System.out.println ("No values were entered.");
        break;
    case 1:
        System.out.println ("One value was entered.");
        break;
    case 2:
        System.out.println ("Two values were entered.");
        break;
    default:
        System.out.println ("Too many values were entered.");
}
```

The expression evaluated at the beginning of a switch statement must be of type char, byte, short, or int. In particular, it cannot be a boolean, or a floating point value, or a String. Furthermore, the value of each case must be a constant; it cannot be a variable or other expression.

Note that the implicit boolean condition of a switch statement is based on equality. The expression at the beginning of the statement is compared to each case value to determine which one it equals. A switch statement cannot be used to determine other relational operations (such as less than), unless some preliminary processing is done. For example, the GradeReport program in Listing 5.7 prints a comment based on a numeric grade that is entered by the user.

Listing 5.7

```java
//********************************************************************
//   GradeReport.java         Author: Lewis/Loftus
//
//   Demonstrates the use of a switch statement.
//********************************************************************

import java.util.Scanner;

public class GradeReport
{
    //-----------------------------------------------------------------
    //  Reads a grade from the user and prints comments accordingly.
    //-----------------------------------------------------------------
    public static void main (String[] args)
    {
        int grade, category;

        Scanner scan = new Scanner (System.in);

        System.out.print ("Enter a numeric grade (0 to 100): ");
        grade = scan.nextInt();

        category = grade / 10;

        System.out.print ("That grade is ");

        switch (category)
        {
            case 10:
                System.out.println ("a perfect score. Well done.");
                break;
            case 9:
                System.out.println ("well above average. Excellent.");
                break;
```

Listing 5.7   **continued**

```
            case 8:
                System.out.println ("above average. Nice job.");
                break;
            case 7:
                System.out.println ("average.");
                break;
            case 6:
                System.out.println ("below average. You should see the");
                System.out.println ("instructor to clarify the material "
                                            + "presented in class.");
                break;
            default:
                System.out.println ("not passing.");
        }
    }
}
```

Output

```
Enter a numeric grade (0 to 100): 86
That grade is above average. Nice job.
```

In `GradeReport`, the category of the grade is determined by dividing the grade by 10 using integer division, resulting in an integer value between 0 and 10 (assuming a valid grade is entered). This result is used as the expression of the `switch`, which prints various messages for grades 60 or higher and a default sentence for all other values.

Note that any `switch` statement could be implemented as a set of nested `if` statements. However, nested `if` statements quickly become difficult for a human reader to understand and are error prone to implement and debug. But because a `switch` can evaluate only equality, sometimes nested `if` statements are necessary. It depends on the situation.

5.5   THE while STATEMENT

As we discussed in the introduction of this chapter, a repetition statement (or loop) allows us to execute another statement multiple times. A *while statement* is a loop that evaluates a boolean condition just like an `if` statement does and executes a statement (called the *body* of the loop) if the condition is true. However, unlike the if statement, after the body is executed, the condition is evaluated again. If it is still true, the body is executed again. This repetition continues until the condition becomes false; then processing continues with the statement after the body of the while loop. Figure 5.7 shows this processing.

> **Key Concept**
>
> A while statement executes the same statement until its condition becomes false.

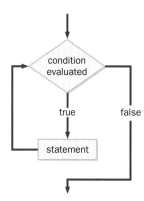

FIGURE 5.7   The logic of a while loop

While Statement

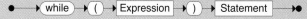

The while loop repeatedly executes the specified Statement as long as the boolean Expression is true. The Expression is evaluated first; therefore the Statement might not be executed at all. The Expression is evaluated again after each execution of Statement until the Expression becomes false.
Example:

```
while (total > max)
{
    total = total / 2;
    System.out.println ("Current total: " + total);
}
```

The following loop prints the values from 1 to 5. Each iteration through the loop prints one value, then increments the counter.

```
int count = 1;
while (count <= 5)
{
    System.out.println (count);
    count++;
}
```

Note that the body of the `while` loop is a block containing two statements. The entire block is repeated on each iteration of the loop.

Let's look at another program that uses a `while` loop. The `Average` program shown in Listing 5.8 reads a series of integer values from the user, sums them up, and computes their average.

We don't know how many values the user may enter, so we need to have a way to indicate that the user is done entering numbers. In this program, we designate zero to be a *sentinel value* that indicates the end of the input. The `while` loop continues to process input values until the user enters zero. This assumes that zero is not one of the valid numbers that should contribute to the average. A sentinel value must always be outside the normal range of values entered.

Note that in the `Average` program, a variable called `sum` is used to maintain a *running sum,* which means it is the sum of the values entered thus far. The variable `sum` is initialized to zero, and each value read is added to and stored back into `sum`.

We also have to count the number of values that are entered so that after the loop concludes we can divide by the appropriate value to compute the average. Note that the sentinel value is not counted. Consider the unusual situation in which the user immediately enters the sentinel value before entering any valid values. The `if` statement at the end of the program avoids a divide-by-zero error.

Let's examine yet another program that uses a `while` loop. The `WinPercentage` program shown in Listing 5.9 computes the winning percentage of a sports team based on the number of games won.

We use a `while` loop in the `WinPercentage` program to *validate the input,* meaning we guarantee that the user enters a value that we consider to be valid. In this example, that means that the number of games won must be greater than or equal to zero and less than or equal to the total number of games played. The `while` loop continues to execute, repeatedly prompting the user for valid input, until the entered number is indeed valid.

We generally want our programs to be *robust,* which means that they handle potential problems as elegantly as possible. Validating input data and avoiding

Listing 5.8

```java
//********************************************************************
//   Average.java         Author: Lewis/Loftus
//
//   Demonstrates the use of a while loop, a sentinel value, and a
//   running sum.
//********************************************************************

import java.text.DecimalFormat;
import java.util.Scanner;

public class Average
{
   //-----------------------------------------------------------------
   //   Computes the average of a set of values entered by the user.
   //   The running sum is printed as the numbers are entered.
   //-----------------------------------------------------------------
   public static void main (String[] args)
   {
      int sum = 0, value, count = 0;
      double average;

      Scanner scan = new Scanner (System.in);

      System.out.print ("Enter an integer (0 to quit): ");
      value = scan.nextInt();

      while (value != 0)  // sentinel value of 0 to terminate loop
      {
         count++;

         sum += value;
         System.out.println ("The sum so far is " + sum);

         System.out.print ("Enter an integer (0 to quit): ");
         value = scan.nextInt();
      }

      System.out.println ();
```

Listing 5.8   **continued**

```
        if (count == 0)
            System.out.println ("No values were entered.");
        else
        {
            average = (double)sum / count;

            DecimalFormat fmt = new DecimalFormat ("0.###");
            System.out.println ("The average is " + fmt.format(average));
        }
    }
}
```

Output

```
Enter an integer (0 to quit): 25
The sum so far is 25
Enter an integer (0 to quit): 164
The sum so far is 189
Enter an integer (0 to quit): -14
The sum so far is 175
Enter an integer (0 to quit): 84
The sum so far is 259
Enter an integer (0 to quit): 12
The sum so far is 271
Enter an integer (0 to quit): -35
The sum so far is 236
Enter an integer (0 to quit): 0

The average is 39.333
```

errors such as dividing by zero are situations that we should consciously address when designing a program. Loops and conditionals help us recognize and deal with such situations.

Infinite Loops

It is the programmer's responsibility to ensure that the condition of a loop will eventually become false. If it doesn't, the loop body will execute forever, or at least until the program is interrupted. This situation, referred to as an *infinite loop*, is a common mistake.

Listing 5.9

```java
//********************************************************************
//  WinPercentage.java        Author: Lewis/Loftus
//
//  Demonstrates the use of a while loop for input validation.
//********************************************************************

import java.text.NumberFormat;
import java.util.Scanner;

public class WinPercentage
{
    //-----------------------------------------------------------------
    //  Computes the percentage of games won by a team.
    //-----------------------------------------------------------------
    public static void main (String[] args)
    {
        final int NUM_GAMES = 12;
        int won;
        double ratio;

        Scanner scan = new Scanner (System.in);

        System.out.print ("Enter the number of games won (0 to "
                            + NUM_GAMES + "): ");
        won = scan.nextInt();

        while (won < 0 || won > NUM_GAMES)
        {
            System.out.print ("Invalid input. Please reenter: ");
            won = scan.nextInt();
        }

        ratio = (double)won / NUM_GAMES;

        NumberFormat fmt = NumberFormat.getPercentInstance();

        System.out.println ();
        System.out.println ("Winning percentage: " + fmt.format(ratio));
    }
}
```

Listing 5.9 **continued**

Output

```
Enter the number of games won (0 to 12): -5
Invalid input. Please reenter: 13
Invalid input. Please reenter: 7

Winning percentage: 58%
```

The following is an example of an infinite loop:

```
int count = 1;
while (count <= 25)   // Warning: this is an infinite loop!
{
    System.out.println (count);
    count = count - 1;
}
```

If you execute this loop, you should be prepared to interrupt it. On most systems, pressing the Control-C keyboard combination (hold down the Control key and press C) terminates a running program.

> **Key Concept**
>
> We must design our programs carefully to avoid infinite loops.

In this example, the initial value of count is 1 and it is decremented in the loop body. The while loop will continue as long as count is less than or equal to 25. Because count gets smaller with each iteration, the condition will always be true, or at least until the value of count gets so small that an underflow error occurs. The point is that the logic of the code is clearly wrong.

Let's look at some other examples of infinite loops:

```
int count = 1;
while (count != 50)   // infinite loop
    count += 2;
```

In this code fragment, the variable count is initialized to 1 and is moving in a positive direction. However, note that it is being incremented by 2 each time. This loop will never terminate because count will never equal 50. It begins at 1 and then changes to 3, then 5, and so on. Eventually it reaches 49, then changes to 51, then 53, and continues forever.

Now consider the following situation:

```
double num = 1.0;
while (num != 0.0)    // infinite loop
    num = num - 0.1;
```

Once again, the value of the loop control variable seems to be moving in the correct direction. And, in fact, it seems like num will eventually take on the value 0.0. However, this loop is infinite (at least on most systems) because num will never have a value *exactly* equal to 0.0. This situation is similar to one we discussed earlier in this chapter when we explored the idea of comparing floating point values in the condition of an if statement. Because of the way the values are represented in binary, minute computational errors occur internally, making it problematic to compare two floating point values for equality.

Nested Loops

The body of a loop can contain another loop. This situation is called a *nested loop*. Keep in mind that for each iteration of the outer loop, the inner loop executes completely. Consider the following code fragment. How many times does the string "Here again" get printed?

```
int count1, count2;
count1 = 1;
while (count1 <= 10)
{
    count2 = 1;
    while (count2 <= 50)
    {
        System.out.println ("Here again");
        count2++;
    }
    count1++;
}
```

The println statement is inside the inner loop. The outer loop executes 10 times, as count1 iterates between 1 and 10. The inner loop executes 50 times, as count2 iterates between 1 and 50. For each iteration of the outer loop, the inner loop executes completely. Therefore the println statement is executed 500 times.

As with any loop situation, we must be careful to scrutinize the conditions of the loops and the initializations of variables. Let's consider some small changes to this code. What if the condition of the outer loop were (count1 < 10) instead of (count1 <= 10)? How would that change the total number of lines printed?

Well, the outer loop would execute 9 times instead of 10, so the `println` statement would be executed 450 times. What if the outer loop were left as it was originally defined, but `count2` were initialized to 10 instead of 1 before the inner loop? The inner loop would then execute 40 times instead of 50, so the total number of lines printed would be 400.

Let's look at another example that uses a nested loop. A *palindrome* is a string of characters that reads the same forward or backward. For example, the following strings are palindromes:

> radar
> drab bard
> ab cde xxxx edc ba
> kayak
> deified
> able was I ere I saw elba

Note that some palindromes have an even number of characters, whereas others have an odd number of characters. The `PalindromeTester` program shown in Listing 5.10 tests to see whether a string is a palindrome. The user may test as many strings as desired.

The code for `PalindromeTester` contains two loops, one inside the other. The outer loop controls how many strings are tested, and the inner loop scans through each string, character by character, until it determines whether the string is a palindrome.

The variables `left` and `right` store the indexes of two characters. They initially indicate the characters on either end of the string. Each iteration of the inner loop compares the two characters indicated by `left` and `right`. We fall out of the inner loop when either the characters don't match, meaning the string is not a palindrome, or when the value of `left` becomes equal to or greater than the value of `right`, which means the entire string has been tested and it is a palindrome.

Note that the following phrases would not be considered palindromes by the current version of the program:

> A man, a plan, a canal, Panama.
> Dennis and Edna sinned.
> Rise to vote, sir.
> Doom an evil deed, liven a mood.
> Go hang a salami; I'm a lasagna hog.

Listing 5.10

```java
//********************************************************************
//  PalindromeTester.java        Author: Lewis/Loftus
//
//  Demonstrates the use of nested while loops.
//********************************************************************

import java.util.Scanner;

public class PalindromeTester
{
    //-----------------------------------------------------------------
    //  Tests strings to see if they are palindromes.
    //-----------------------------------------------------------------
    public static void main (String[] args)
    {
        String str, another = "y";
        int left, right;

        Scanner scan = Scanner.create (System.in);

        while (another.equalsIgnoreCase("y")) // allows y or Y
        {
            System.out.println ("Enter a potential palindrome:");
            str = scan.nextLine();

            left = 0;
            right = str.length() - 1;

            while (str.charAt(left) == str.charAt(right) && left < right)
            {
                left++;
                right--;
            }

            System.out.println();

            if (left < right)
                System.out.println ("That string is NOT a palindrome.");
            else
                System.out.println ("That string IS a palindrome.");
```

Listing 5.10   **continued**

```
        System.out.println();
        System.out.print ("Test another palindrome (y/n)? ");
        another = scan.nextLine();
      }
    }
  }
```

Output

```
Enter a potential palindrome:
radar

That string IS a palindrome.

Test another palindrome (y/n)? y
Enter a potential palindrome:
able was I ere I saw elba

That string IS a palindrome.

Test another palindrome (y/n)? y
Enter a potential palindrome:
abcddcba

That string IS a palindrome.

Test another palindrome (y/n)? y
Enter a potential palindrome:
abracadabra

That string is NOT a palindrome.

Test another palindrome (y/n)? n
```

These strings fail our current criteria for a palindrome because of the spaces, punctuation marks, and changes in uppercase and lowercase. However, if these characteristics were removed or ignored, these strings read the same forward and backward. Consider how the program could be changed to handle these situations. These modifications are included as a programming project at the end of the chapter.

Other Loop Controls

We've seen how the break statement can be used to break out of the cases of a switch statement. The break statement can also be placed in the body of any loop, even though this is usually inappropriate. Its effect on a loop is similar to its effect on a switch statement. The execution of the loop is stopped, and the statement following the loop is executed.

It is never necessary to use a break statement in a loop. An equivalent loop can always be written without it. Because the break statement causes program flow to jump from one place to another, using a break in a loop is not good practice. Its use is tolerated in a switch statement because an equivalent switch statement cannot be written without it. However, you can and should avoid it in a loop.

A *continue statement* has a similar effect on loop processing. The continue statement is similar to a break, but the loop condition is evaluated again, and the loop body is executed again if it is still true. Like the break statement, the continue statement can always be avoided in a loop, and for the same reasons, it should be.

5.6   ITERATORS

An *iterator* is an object that has methods that allow you to process a collection of items one at a time. That is, an iterator lets you step through each item and interact with it as needed. For example, your goal may be to compute the dues for each member of a club, or print the distinct parts of a URL. The key is that an iterator provides a consistent and simple mechanism for systematically processing a group of items. Since it is inherently a repetitive process, it is closely related to the idea of loops.

> **Key Concept**
>
> An iterator is an object that helps you process a group of related items.

Technically an iterator object in Java is defined using the Iterator interface, which is discussed in the next chapter. For now it is simply helpful to know that such objects exist and that they can make the processing of a collection of items easier.

Every iterator object has a method called hasNext that returns a boolean value indicating if there is at least one more item to process. Therefore the hasNext method can be used as a condition of a loop to control the processing of each item. An iterator also has a method called next to retrieve the next item in the collection to process.

There are several classes in the Java standard class library that define iterator objects. One of these is Scanner, a class we've used several times in previous examples to help us read data from the user. The `hasNext` method of the `Scanner` class returns true if there is another input token to process. And, as we've seen previously, it has a `next` method that returns the next input token as a string.

The `Scanner` class also has specific variations of the `hasNext` method, such as the `hasNextInt` and `hasNextDouble` methods, which allow you to determine if the next input token is a particular type. Likewise, as we've seen, there are variations of the `next` method, such as `nextInt` and `nextDouble`, that retrieve values of specific types.

When reading input interactively from the standard input stream, the `hasNext` method of the `Scanner` class will wait until there is input available, then return true. That is, interactive input read from the keyboard is always thought to have more data to process—it just hasn't arrived yet until the user types it in. That's why in previous examples we've used special sentinel values to determine the end of interactive input.

However, the fact that a `Scanner` object is an iterator is particularly helpful when the scanner is being used to process input from a source that has a specific end point, such as processing the lines of a data file or processing the parts of a character string. Let's examine an example of this type of processing.

Reading Text Files

Suppose we have an input file called `urls.inp` that contains a list of URLs that we want to process in some way. The following are the first few lines of `urls.inp`:

```
www.google.com
java.sun.com/j2se/5.0
www.linux.org/info/gnu.html
duke.csc.villanova.edu/lewis/
www.csc.villanova.edu/academics/index.jsp
```

The program shown in Listing 5.11 reads the URLs from this file and dissects them to show the various parts of the path. It uses a `Scanner` object to process the input. In fact, it uses multiple `Scanner` objects—one to read the lines of the data file, and another to process each URL string.

There are two `while` loops in this program, one nested within the other. The outer loop processes each line in the file, and the inner loop processes each token in the current line.

Listing 5.11

```java
//********************************************************************
//   URLDissector.java        Author: Lewis/Loftus
//
//   Demonstrates the use of Scanner to read file input and parse it
//   using alternative delimiters.
//********************************************************************

import java.util.Scanner;
import java.io.*;

public class URLDissector
{
   //-----------------------------------------------------------------
   //   Reads urls from a file and prints their path components.
   //-----------------------------------------------------------------
   public static void main (String[] args) throws IOException
   {
      String url;
      Scanner fileScan, urlScan;

      fileScan = new Scanner (new File("urls.inp"));

      // Read and process each line of the file
      while (fileScan.hasNext())
      {
         url = fileScan.nextLine();
         System.out.println ("URL: " + url);

         urlScan = new Scanner (url);
         urlScan.useDelimiter("/");

         //  Print each part of the url
         while (urlScan.hasNext())
            System.out.println ("    " + urlScan.next());

         System.out.println();
      }
   }
}
```

Listing 5.11 **continued**

Output

```
URL: www.google.com
   www.google.com

URL: java.sun.com/j2se/5.0
   java.sun.com
   j2se
   5.0

URL: www.linux.org/info/gnu.html
   www.linux.org
   info
   gnu.html

URL: duke.csc.villanova.edu/lewis/
   duke.csc.villanova.edu
   lewis

URL: www.csc.villanova.edu/academics/index.jsp
   www.csc.villanova.edu
   academics
   index.jsp
```

The variable `fileScan` is created as a scanner that operates on the input file names `urls.inp`. Instead of passing `System.in` into the `Scanner` constructor, we instantiate a `File` object that represents the input file and pass it into the `Scanner` constructor. At that point, the `fileScan` object is ready to read and process input from the input file.

If for some reason there is a problem finding or opening the input file, the attempt to create a `File` object will throw an `IOException`, which is why we've added the `throws IOException` clause to the `main` method header. (Processing I/O exceptions is discussed further in Chapter 10.)

The body of the outer `while` loop will be executed as long as the `hasNext` method of the input file scanner returns true—that is, as long as there is more input in the data file to process. Each iteration through the loop reads one line (one URL) from the input file and prints it out.

For each URL, a new `Scanner` object is set up to parse the pieces of the URL string, which is passed into the `create` method of `Scanner` when instantiating the `urlScan` object. The inner `while` loop prints each token of the URL on a separate line.

Recall that, by default, a `Scanner` object assumes that white space (spaces, tabs, and new lines) is used as the delimiters separating the input tokens. That works in this example for the scanner that is reading each line of the input file. However, if the default delimiters do not suffice, as in the processing of a URL in this example, they can be changed.

> **Key Concept**
> The delimiters used to separate tokens in a `Scanner` object can be explicitly set as needed.

In this case, we are interested in each part of the path separated by the slash (/) character. A call to the `useDelimiter` method of the scanner sets the delimiter to a slash prior to processing the URL string.

If you want to use more than one alternate delimiter character, or if you want to parse the input in more complex ways, the `Scanner` class can process patterns called *regular expressions,* which are discussed in Appendix H.

5.7   THE do STATEMENT

The *do statement* is similar to the `while` statement except that its termination condition is at the end of the loop body. Like the `while` loop, the do loop executes the statement in the loop body until the condition becomes false. The condition is written at the end of the loop to indicate that it is not evaluated until the loop body is executed. Note that the body of a do loop is always executed at least once. Figure 5.8 shows this processing.

The following code prints the numbers from 1 to 5 using a do loop. Compare this code with the similar example earlier in this chapter that uses a `while` loop to accomplish the same task.

```
int count = 0;
do
{
   count++;
   System.out.println (count);
} while (count < 5);
```

Note that the do loop begins simply with the reserved word do. The body of the do loop continues until the *while clause* that contains the boolean condition that determines whether the loop body will be executed again. Sometimes it is difficult to determine whether a line of code that begins with the reserved word `while` is the beginning of a `while` loop or the end of a do loop.

> **Key Concept**
> A do statement executes its loop body at least once.

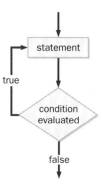

FIGURE 5.8   The logic of a do loop

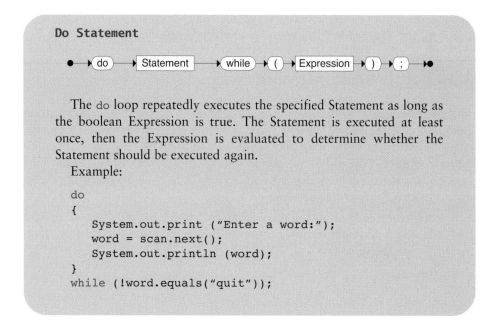

Do Statement

The do loop repeatedly executes the specified Statement as long as the boolean Expression is true. The Statement is executed at least once, then the Expression is evaluated to determine whether the Statement should be executed again.

Example:

```
do
{
    System.out.print ("Enter a word:");
    word = scan.next();
    System.out.println (word);
}
while (!word.equals("quit"));
```

Let's look at another example of the do loop. The program called ReverseNumber, shown in Listing 5.12, reads an integer from the user and reverses its digits mathematically.

Listing 5.12

```java
//********************************************************************
//   ReverseNumber.java          Author: Lewis/Loftus
//
//   Demonstrates the use of a do loop.
//********************************************************************

import java.util.Scanner;

public class ReverseNumber
{
   //-----------------------------------------------------------------
   //   Reverses the digits of an integer mathematically.
   //-----------------------------------------------------------------
   public static void main (String[] args)
   {
      int number, lastDigit, reverse = 0;

      Scanner scan = new Scanner (System.in);

      System.out.print ("Enter a positive integer: ");
      number = scan.nextInt();

      do
      {
         lastDigit = number % 10;
         reverse = (reverse * 10) + lastDigit;
         number = number / 10;
      }
      while (number > 0);

      System.out.println ("That number reversed is " + reverse);
   }
}
```

Output

```
Enter a positive integer: 2896
That number reversed is 6982
```

The do loop in the ReverseNumber program uses the remainder operation to determine the digit in the 1's position, then adds it into the reversed number, then truncates that digit from the original number using integer division. The do loop terminates when we run out of digits to process, which corresponds to the point when the variable number reaches the value zero. Carefully trace the logic of this program with a few examples to see how it works.

If you know you want to perform the body of a loop at least once, then you probably want to use a do statement. A do loop has many of the same properties as a while statement, so it must also be checked for termination conditions to avoid infinite loops.

5.8   THE for STATEMENT

The while and the do statements are good to use when you don't initially know how many times you want to execute the loop body. The *for statement* is another repetition statement that is particularly well suited for executing the body of a loop a specific number of times that can be determined before the loop is executed.

The following code prints the numbers 1 through 5 using a for loop, just as we did using a while loop and a do loop in previous examples:

```
for (int count=1; count <= 5; count++)
    System.out.println (count);
```

The header of a for loop contains three parts separated by semicolons. Before the loop begins, the first part of the header, called the *initialization*, is executed. The second part of the header is the boolean condition, which is evaluated before the loop body (like the while loop). If true, the body of the loop is executed, followed by the execution of the third part of the header, which is called the *increment*. Note that the initialization part is executed only once, but the increment part is executed after each iteration of the loop. Figure 5.9 shows this processing.

A for loop can be a bit tricky to read until you get used to it. The execution of the code doesn't follow a "top to bottom, left to right" reading. The increment code executes after the body of the loop even though it is in the header.

In this example, the initialization portion of the for loop header is used to declare the variable count as well as to give it an initial value. We are not required to declare a variable there, but it is common practice in situations where the variable is not needed outside of the loop. Because count is declared in the for loop header, it exists only inside the loop body and cannot be referenced elsewhere. The loop control variable is set up, checked, and modified by the actions in the loop header. It can be referenced inside the loop body, but it should not be modified except by the actions defined in the loop header.

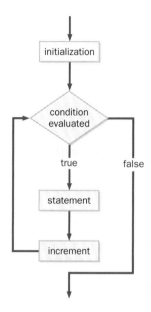

FIGURE 5.9   The logic of a `for` loop

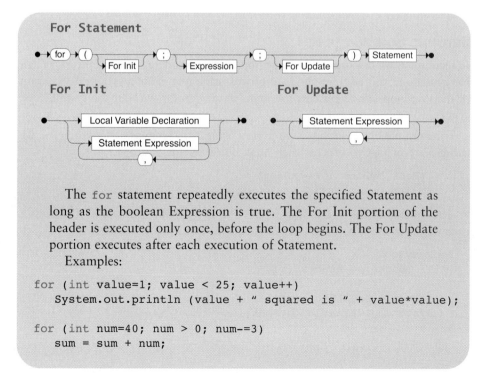

For Statement

The `for` statement repeatedly executes the specified Statement as long as the boolean Expression is true. The For Init portion of the header is executed only once, before the loop begins. The For Update portion executes after each execution of Statement.

Examples:

```
for (int value=1; value < 25; value++)
    System.out.println (value + " squared is " + value*value);

for (int num=40; num > 0; num-=3)
    sum = sum + num;
```

The increment portion of the `for` loop header, despite its name, could decrement a value rather than increment it. For example, the following loop prints the integer values from 100 down to 1:

```
for (int num = 100; num > 0; num--)
    System.out.println (num);
```

In fact, the increment portion of the `for` loop can perform any calculation, not just a simple increment or decrement. Consider the program shown in Listing 5.13, which prints multiples of a particular value up to a particular limit.

The increment portion of the `for` loop in the `Multiples` program adds the value entered by the user after each iteration. The number of values printed per line is controlled by counting the values printed and then moving to the next line whenever `count` is evenly divisible by the `PER_LINE` constant.

The `Stars` program in Listing 5.14 shows the use of nested `for` loops. The output is a triangle shape made of asterisk characters. The outer loop executes exactly 10 times. Each iteration of the outer loop prints one line of the output. The inner loop performs a different number of iterations depending on the line value controlled by the outer loop. Each iteration of the inner loop prints one star on the current line. Writing programs that print variations on this triangle configuration are included in the programming projects at the end of the chapter.

Iterators and `for` Loops

In section 5.6 we discussed that some objects are considered to be iterators, which have `hasNext` and `next` methods to process each item from a group. A variation of the `for` loop lets us process the items in an iterator without the complicated syntax.

For example, if `bookList` is an iterator object that manages `Book` objects, we can use a `for` loop to process each `Book` object in the iterator as follows:

```
for (Book myBook : bookList)
    System.out.println (myBook);
```

This version of the `for` loop is referred to as a *foreach statement*. It processes each object in the iterator in turn. It is equivalent to the following:

```
Book myBook;
while (bookList.hasNext())
{
    myBook = bookList.next();
    System.out.println (myBook);
}
```

Listing 5.13

```java
//********************************************************************
//  Multiples.java         Author: Lewis/Loftus
//
//  Demonstrates the use of a for loop.
//********************************************************************

import java.util.Scanner;

public class Multiples
{
   //-----------------------------------------------------------------
   //  Prints multiples of a user-specified number up to a user-
   //  specified limit.
   //-----------------------------------------------------------------
   public static void main (String[] args)
   {
      final int PER_LINE = 5;
      int value, limit, mult, count = 0;

      Scanner scan = new Scanner (System.in);

      System.out.print ("Enter a positive value: ");
      value = scan.nextInt();

      System.out.print ("Enter an upper limit: ");
      limit = scan.nextInt();

      System.out.println ();
      System.out.println ("The multiples of " + value + " between " +
                          value + " and " + limit + " (inclusive) are:");

      for (mult = value; mult <= limit; mult += value)
      {
         System.out.print (mult + "\t");

         // Print a specific number of values per line of output
         count++;
         if (count % PER_LINE == 0)
            System.out.println();
      }
   }
}
```

Listing 5.13   continued

Output

```
Enter a positive value: 7
Enter an upper limit: 400

The multiples of 7 between 7 and 400 (inclusive) are:
7          14          21          28          35
42         49          56          63          70
77         84          91          98          105
112        119         126         133         140
147        154         161         168         175
182        189         196         203         210
217        224         231         238         245
252        259         266         273         280
287        294         301         308         315
322        329         336         343         350
357        364         371         378         385
392        399
```

This version of the `for` loop can also be used on arrays, which are discussed in Chapter 7. We use the `foreach` loop as appropriate in various situations throughout the rest of the book.

Comparing Loops

The three loop statements (`while`, `do`, and `for`) are functionally equivalent. Any particular loop written using one type of loop can be written using either of the other two loop types. Which type of loop we use depends on the situation.

Listing 5.14

```java
//********************************************************************
//   Stars.java          Author: Lewis/Loftus
//
//   Demonstrates the use of nested for loops.
//********************************************************************

public class Stars
{
    //-----------------------------------------------------------------
    //   Prints a triangle shape using asterisk (star) characters.
    //-----------------------------------------------------------------
    public static void main (String[] args)
    {
        final int MAX_ROWS = 10;

        for (int row = 1; row <= MAX_ROWS; row++)
        {
            for (int star = 1; star <= row; star++)
                System.out.print ("*");

            System.out.println();
        }
    }
}
```

Output

```
*
**
***
****
*****
******
*******
********
*********
**********
```

As we mentioned earlier, the primary difference between a `while` loop and a `do` loop is when the condition is evaluated. If we know we want to execute the loop body at least once, a `do` loop is usually the better choice. The body of a `while` loop, on the other hand, might not be executed at all if the condition is initially false. Therefore we say that the body of a `while` loop is executed zero or more times, but the body of a `do` loop is executed one or more times.

A `for` loop is like a `while` loop in that the condition is evaluated before the loop body is executed. We generally use a `for` loop when the number of times we want to iterate through a loop is fixed or can be easily calculated. In many situations, it is simply more convenient to separate the code that sets up and controls the loop iterations inside the `for` loop header from the body of the loop.

5.9 DRAWING WITH LOOPS AND CONDITIONALS

Conditionals and loops greatly enhance our ability to generate interesting graphics.

The `Bullseye` program shown in Listing 5.15 draws a target. The drawing actually occurs in the `BullseyePanel` class, shown in Listing 5.16. The `paintComponent` of the `BullseyePanel` class uses an `if` statement to alternate the colors between black and white.

Note that each ring is actually drawn as a filled circle (an oval of equal width and length). Because we draw the circles on top of each other, the inner circles cover the inner part of the larger circles, creating the ring effect. At the end, a final red circle is drawn for the bull's-eye.

Let's look at another example. Listing 5.17 shows the `Boxes` class, which instantiates and displays `BoxesPanel`, shown in Listing 5.18. The purpose of this program is to draw several randomly sized rectangles in random locations. If the width of a rectangle is below a certain thickness (5 pixels), the box is filled with the color yellow. If the height is less than the same minimal thickness, the box is filled with the color green. Otherwise, the box is drawn, unfilled, in white.

Listing 5.15

```
//********************************************************************
//   Bullseye.java         Author: Lewis/Loftus
//
//   Demonstrates the use of loops to draw.
//********************************************************************

import javax.swing.JFrame;

public class Bullseye
{
   //-----------------------------------------------------------------
   //   Creates the main frame of the program.
   //-----------------------------------------------------------------
   public static void main (String[] args)
   {
      JFrame frame = new JFrame ("Bullseye");
      frame.setDefaultCloseOperation (JFrame.EXIT_ON_CLOSE);

      BullseyePanel panel = new BullseyePanel();

      frame.getContentPane().add(panel);
      frame.pack();
      frame.setVisible(true);
   }
}
```

Display

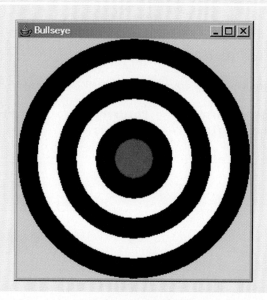

Listing 5.16

```java
//********************************************************************
//  BullseyePanel.java         Author: Lewis/Loftus
//
//  Demonstrates the use of conditionals and loops to guide drawing.
//********************************************************************

import javax.swing.JPanel;
import java.awt.*;

public class BullseyePanel extends JPanel
{
    private final int MAX_WIDTH = 300, NUM_RINGS = 5, RING_WIDTH = 25;

    //-----------------------------------------------------------------
    //  Sets up the bullseye panel.
    //-----------------------------------------------------------------
    public BullseyePanel ()
    {
        setBackground (Color.cyan);
        setPreferredSize (new Dimension(300,300));
    }

    //-----------------------------------------------------------------
    //  Paints a bullseye target.
    //-----------------------------------------------------------------
    public void paintComponent (Graphics page)
    {
        super.paintComponent (page);

        int x = 0, y = 0, diameter = MAX_WIDTH;

        page.setColor (Color.white);

        for (int count = 0; count < NUM_RINGS; count++)
        {
            if (page.getColor() == Color.black)  // alternate colors
                page.setColor (Color.white);
            else
                page.setColor (Color.black);
```

Listing 5.16   **continued**

```
            page.fillOval (x, y, diameter, diameter);

            diameter -= (2 * RING_WIDTH);
            x += RING_WIDTH;
            y += RING_WIDTH;
        }

        // Draw the red bullseye in the center
        page.setColor (Color.red);
        page.fillOval (x, y, diameter, diameter);
    }
}
```

5.10   DETERMINING EVENT SOURCES

In Chapter 4 we began our exploration of creating programs with a truly interactive graphical user interface (GUI). You'll recall that interactive GUIs require that we create listener objects and set up the relationship between listeners and the components that generate the events of interest.

Let's look at an example in which one listener object is used to listen to two different components. The program represented by the LeftRight class, shown in Listing 5.19, displays a label and two buttons. When the left button is pressed, the label displays the word Left and when the right button is pressed the label displays the word Right.

The LeftRightPanel class, shown in Listing 5.20, creates one instance of the ButtonListener object, then adds that listener to both buttons. Therefore, when either button is pressed, the actionPerformed method of the ButtonListener class is invoked.

On each invocation, the actionPerformed method uses an if-else statement to determine which button generated the event. The getSource method is called on the ActionEvent object that the button passes into the actionPerformed method. The getSource method returns a reference to the component that generated the event. The condition of the if statement compares the event source to the reference to the left button. If they don't match, then the event must have been generated by the right button.

Listing 5.17

```
//********************************************************************
//   Boxes.java          Author: Lewis/Loftus
//
//   Demonstrates the use of loops to draw.
//********************************************************************

import javax.swing.JFrame;

public class Boxes
{
    //----------------------------------------------------------------
    //   Creates the main frame of the program.
    //----------------------------------------------------------------
    public static void main (String[] args)
    {
        JFrame frame = new JFrame ("Boxes");
        frame.setDefaultCloseOperation (JFrame.EXIT_ON_CLOSE);

        BoxesPanel panel = new BoxesPanel();

        frame.getContentPane().add(panel);
        frame.pack();
        frame.setVisible(true);
    }
}
```

Display

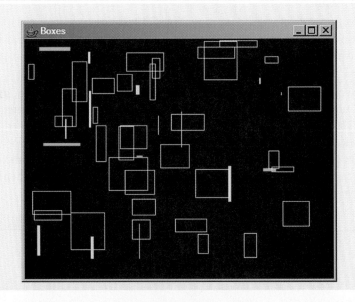

Listing 5.18

```java
//********************************************************************
//  BoxesPanel.java        Author: Lewis/Loftus
//
//  Demonstrates the use of conditionals and loops to guide drawing.
//********************************************************************

import javax.swing.JPanel;
import java.awt.*;
import java.util.Random;

public class BoxesPanel extends JPanel
{
   private final int NUM_BOXES = 50, THICKNESS = 5, MAX_SIDE = 50;
   private final int MAX_X = 350, MAX_Y = 250;
   private Random generator;

   //-----------------------------------------------------------------
   //  Sets up the drawing panel.
   //-----------------------------------------------------------------
   public BoxesPanel ()
   {
      generator = new Random();

      setBackground (Color.black);
      setPreferredSize (new Dimension(400, 300));
   }

   //-----------------------------------------------------------------
   //  Paints boxes of random width and height in a random location.
   //  Narrow or short boxes are highlighted with a fill color.
   //-----------------------------------------------------------------
   public void paintComponent(Graphics page)
   {
      super.paintComponent (page);

      int x, y, width, height;

      for (int count = 0; count < NUM_BOXES; count++)
      {
         x = generator.nextInt(MAX_X) + 1;
         y = generator.nextInt(MAX_Y) + 1;
```

Listing 5.18   **continued**

```
            width = generator.nextInt(MAX_SIDE) + 1;
            height = generator.nextInt(MAX_SIDE) + 1;

            if (width <= THICKNESS)   // check for narrow box
            {
               page.setColor (Color.yellow);
               page.fillRect (x, y, width, height);
            }
            else
               if (height <= THICKNESS)   // check for short box
               {
                  page.setColor (Color.green);
                  page.fillRect (x, y, width, height);
               }
               else
               {
                  page.setColor (Color.white);
                  page.drawRect (x, y, width, height);
               }
         }
      }
}
```

We could have created two separate listener classes, one to listen to the left button and another to listen to the right. In that case the `actionPerformed` method would not have to determine the source of the event. Whether to have multiple listeners or determine the event source when it occurs is a design decision that should be made depending on the situation.

Note that the two buttons are put on the same panel called `buttonPanel`, which is separate from the panel represented by the `LeftRightPanel` class. By putting both buttons on one panel, we can guarantee their visual relationship to each other even when the frame is resized in various ways. For buttons labeled Left and Right, that may be important.

Listing 5.19

```
//********************************************************************
//   LeftRight.java          Author: Lewis/Loftus
//
//   Demonstrates the use of one listener for multiple buttons.
//********************************************************************

import javax.swing.JFrame;

public class LeftRight
{
   //-----------------------------------------------------------------
   //   Creates the main program frame.
   //-----------------------------------------------------------------
   public static void main (String[] args)
   {
      JFrame frame = new JFrame ("Left Right");
      frame.setDefaultCloseOperation (JFrame.EXIT_ON_CLOSE);

      frame.getContentPane().add(new LeftRightPanel());

      frame.pack();
      frame.setVisible(true);
   }
}
```

Display

Listing 5.20

```java
//********************************************************************
//  LeftRightPanel.java          Author: Lewis/Loftus
//
//  Demonstrates the use of one listener for multiple buttons.
//********************************************************************

import java.awt.*;
import java.awt.event.*;
import javax.swing.*;

public class LeftRightPanel extends JPanel
{
    private JButton left, right;
    private JLabel label;
    private JPanel buttonPanel;

    //-----------------------------------------------------------------
    //  Constructor: Sets up the GUI.
    //-----------------------------------------------------------------
    public LeftRightPanel ()
    {
        left = new JButton ("Left");
        right = new JButton ("Right");

        ButtonListener listener = new ButtonListener();
        left.addActionListener (listener);
        right.addActionListener (listener);

        label = new JLabel ("Push a button");

        buttonPanel = new JPanel();
        buttonPanel.setPreferredSize (new Dimension(200, 40));
        buttonPanel.setBackground (Color.blue);
        buttonPanel.add (left);
        buttonPanel.add (right);

        setPreferredSize (new Dimension(200, 80));
        setBackground (Color.cyan);
        add (label);
        add (buttonPanel);
    }
```

Listing 5.20   **continued**

```
//************************************************************
//   Represents a listener for both buttons.
//************************************************************
private class ButtonListener implements ActionListener
{
    //----------------------------------------------------------
    //   Determines which button was pressed and sets the label
    //   text accordingly.
    //----------------------------------------------------------
    public void actionPerformed (ActionEvent event)
    {
        if (event.getSource() == left)
            label.setText("Left");
        else
            label.setText("Right");
    }
}
}
```

5.11   DIALOG BOXES

A component called a dialog box can be helpful to assist in GUI processing. A *dialog box* is a graphical window that pops up on top of any currently active window so that the user can interact with it. A dialog box can serve a variety of purposes, such as conveying some information, confirming an action, or allowing the user to enter some information. Usually a dialog box has a solitary purpose, and the user's interaction with it is brief.

The Swing package of the Java class library contains a class called JOptionPane that simplifies the creation and use of basic dialog boxes. Figure 5.10 lists some of the methods of JOptionPane.

The basic formats for a JOptionPane dialog box fall into three categories. A *message dialog box* simply displays an output string. An *input dialog box* presents a prompt and a single input text field into which the user can enter one string of data. A *confirm dialog box* presents the user with a simple yes-or-no question.

Let's look at a program that uses each of these types of dialog boxes. Listing 5.21 shows a program that first presents the user with an input dialog box that

```
static String showInputDialog (Object msg)
   Displays a dialog box containg the specified message and an input text
field. The contents of the text field are returned.

static int showConfirmDialog (Component parent, Object msg)
   Displays a dialog box containing the specified message and Yes/No
button options. If the parent component is null, the box is centered on the screen.

static void showMessageDialog (Component parent, Object msg)
   Displays a dialog box containing the specified message. If the parent
component is null, the box is centered on the screen.
```

FIGURE 5.10   Some methods of the `JOptionPane` class

Listing 5.21

```java
//********************************************************************
//   EvenOdd.java          Author: Lewis/Loftus
//
//   Demonstrates the use of the JOptionPane class.
//********************************************************************

import javax.swing.JOptionPane;

public class EvenOdd
{
   //-----------------------------------------------------------------
   //   Determines if the value input by the user is even or odd.
   //   Uses multiple dialog boxes for user interaction.
   //-----------------------------------------------------------------
   public static void main (String[] args)
   {
      String numStr, result;
      int num, again;

      do
      {
         numStr = JOptionPane.showInputDialog ("Enter an integer: ");

         num = Integer.parseInt(numStr);
```

Listing 5.21   **continued**

```
        result = "That number is " + ((num%2 == 0) ? "even" : "odd");

        JOptionPane.showMessageDialog (null, result);

        again = JOptionPane.showConfirmDialog (null, "Do Another?");
    }
    while (again == JOptionPane.YES_OPTION);
  }
}
```

Display

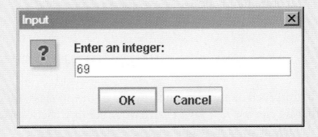

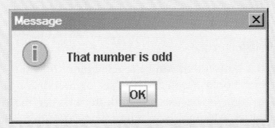

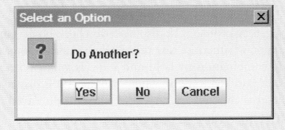

requests the user to enter an integer. After the user presses the OK button on the input dialog box, a second dialog box (this time a message dialog box) appears, informing the user whether the number entered was even or odd. After the user dismisses that box, a third dialog box appears, to determine whether the user would like to test another number. If the user presses the button labeled Yes, the series of dialog boxes repeats. Otherwise the program terminates.

The first parameter to the showMessageDialog and the showConfirmDialog methods specifies the governing parent component for the dialog box. Using a null reference as this parameter causes the dialog box to appear centered on the screen.

Many of the JOptionPane methods allow the programmer to tailor the contents of the dialog box. Furthermore, the showOptionDialog method can be used to create dialog boxes that combine characteristics of the three basic formats for more elaborate interactions.

5.12   MORE BUTTON COMPONENTS

A push button such as those defined by the JButton class are only one kind of button that we can use in a Java GUI. Two others are check boxes and radio buttons. Let's look at these in detail.

Check Boxes

A *check box* is a button that can be toggled on or off using the mouse, indicating that a particular boolean condition is set or unset. For example, a check box labeled Collate might be used to indicate whether the output of a print job should be collated. Although you might have a group of check boxes indicating a set of options, each check box operates independently. That is, each can be set to on or off and the status of one does not influence the others.

The program in Listing 5.22 displays two check boxes and a label. The check boxes determine whether the text of the label is displayed in bold, italic, both, or neither. Any combination of bold and italic is valid. For example, both check boxes could be checked (on), in which case the text is displayed in both bold and italic. If neither is checked, the text of the label is displayed in a plain style.

The GUI for the StyleOptions program is embodied in the StyleOptionsPanel class shown in Listing 5.23. A check box is represented by the JCheckBox class. When a check box changes state from selected (checked) to

Listing 5.22

```java
//********************************************************************
//   StyleOptions.java        Author: Lewis/Loftus
//
//   Demonstrates the use of check boxes.
//********************************************************************

import javax.swing.JFrame;

public class StyleOptions
{
   //-----------------------------------------------------------------
   //   Creates and presents the program frame.
   //-----------------------------------------------------------------
   public static void main (String[] args)
   {
      JFrame frame = new JFrame ("Style Options");
      frame.setDefaultCloseOperation (JFrame.EXIT_ON_CLOSE);

      StyleOptionsPanel panel = new StyleOptionsPanel();
      frame.getContentPane().add (panel);

      frame.pack();
      frame.setVisible(true);
   }
}
```

Display

Listing 5.23

```java
//********************************************************************
//   StyleOptionsPanel.java          Author: Lewis/Loftus
//
//   Demonstrates the use of check boxes.
//********************************************************************

import javax.swing.*;
import java.awt.*;
import java.awt.event.*;

public class StyleOptionsPanel extends JPanel
{
    private JLabel saying;
    private JCheckBox bold, italic;

    //-----------------------------------------------------------------
    //   Sets up a panel with a label and some check boxes that
    //   control the style of the label's font.
    //-----------------------------------------------------------------
    public StyleOptionsPanel()
    {
        saying = new JLabel ("Say it with style!");
        saying.setFont (new Font ("Helvetica", Font.PLAIN, 36));

        bold = new JCheckBox ("Bold");
        bold.setBackground (Color.cyan);
        italic = new JCheckBox ("Italic");
        italic.setBackground (Color.cyan);

        StyleListener listener = new StyleListener();
        bold.addItemListener (listener);
        italic.addItemListener (listener);

        add (saying);
        add (bold);
        add (italic);

        setBackground (Color.cyan);
        setPreferredSize (new Dimension(300, 100));
    }
```

Listing 5.23   **continued**

```
//**************************************************************
//   Represents the listener for both check boxes.
//**************************************************************
private class StyleListener implements ItemListener
{
    //---------------------------------------------------------
    //   Updates the style of the label font style.
    //---------------------------------------------------------
    public void itemStateChanged (ItemEvent event)
    {
        int style = Font.PLAIN;

        if (bold.isSelected())
            style = Font.BOLD;

        if (italic.isSelected())
            style += Font.ITALIC;

        saying.setFont (new Font ("Helvetica", style, 36));
    }
}
}
```

deselected (unchecked), or vice versa, it generates an *item event*. The ItemListener interface contains a single method called itemStateChanged. In this example, we use the same listener object to handle both check boxes.

This program also uses the Font class, which represents a particular *character font*. A Font object is defined by the font name, the font style, and the font size. The font name establishes the general visual characteristics of the characters. We are using the Helvetica font in this program. The style of a Java font can be plain, bold, italic, or bold and italic combined. The check boxes in our GUI are set up to change the characteristics of our font style.

The style of a font is represented as an integer, and integer constants defined in the Font class are used to represent the various aspects of the style. The constant PLAIN is used to represent a plain style. The constants BOLD and ITALIC are used to represent bold and italic, respectively. The sum of the BOLD and ITALIC constants indicates a style that is both bold and italic.

The `itemStateChanged` method of the listener determines what the revised style should be now that one of the check boxes has changed state. It initially sets the style to be plain. Then each check box is consulted in turn using the `isSelected` method, which returns a boolean value. First, if the bold check box is selected (checked), then the style is set to bold. Then, if the italic check box is selected, the `ITALIC` constant is added to the `style` variable. Finally, the font of the label is set to a new font with its revised style.

Note that, given the way the listener is written in this program, it doesn't matter which check box was clicked to generate the event. Both check boxes are processed by the same listener. It also doesn't matter whether the changed check box was toggled from selected to unselected or vice versa. The state of both check boxes is examined if either is changed.

Radio Buttons

A *radio button* is used with other radio buttons to provide a set of mutually exclusive options. Unlike a check box, a radio button is not particularly useful by itself. It has meaning only when it is used with one or more other radio buttons. Only one option out of the group is valid. At any point in time, one and only one button of the group of radio buttons is selected (on). When a radio button from the group is pushed, the other button in the group that is currently on is automatically toggled off.

The term "radio buttons" comes from the way the buttons worked on an old-fashioned car radio. At any point, one button was pushed to specify the current choice of station; when another was pushed, the current one automatically popped out.

The `QuoteOptions` program, shown in Listing 5.24, displays a label and a group of radio buttons. The radio buttons determine which quote is displayed in the label. Because only one of the quotes can be displayed at a time, the use of radio buttons is appropriate. For example, if the `Comedy` radio button is selected, the comedy quote is displayed in the label. If the `Philosophy` button is then pressed, the `Comedy` radio button is automatically toggled off and the comedy quote is replaced by a philosophical one.

The `QuoteOptionsPanel` class, shown in Listing 5.25, sets up and displays the GUI components. A radio button is represented by the `JRadioButton` class. Because the radio buttons in a set work together, the `ButtonGroup` class is used to define a set of related radio buttons.

Listing 5.24

```
//********************************************************************
//   QuoteOptions.java        Author: Lewis/Loftus
//
//   Demonstrates the use of radio buttons.
//********************************************************************

import javax.swing.JFrame;

public class QuoteOptions
{
   //-----------------------------------------------------------------
   //   Creates and presents the program frame.
   //-----------------------------------------------------------------
   public static void main (String[] args)
   {
      JFrame frame = new JFrame ("Quote Options");
      frame.setDefaultCloseOperation (JFrame.EXIT_ON_CLOSE);

      QuoteOptionsPanel panel = new QuoteOptionsPanel();
      frame.getContentPane().add (panel);

      frame.pack();
      frame.setVisible(true);
   }
}
```

Display

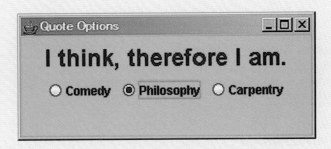

Listing 5.25

```java
//********************************************************************
//   QuoteOptionsPanel.java          Author: Lewis/Loftus
//
//   Demonstrates the use of radio buttons.
//********************************************************************

import javax.swing.*;
import java.awt.*;
import java.awt.event.*;

public class QuoteOptionsPanel extends JPanel
{
    private JLabel quote;
    private JRadioButton comedy, philosophy, carpentry;
    private String comedyQuote, philosophyQuote, carpentryQuote;

    //-----------------------------------------------------------------
    //   Sets up a panel with a label and a set of radio buttons
    //   that control its text.
    //-----------------------------------------------------------------
    public QuoteOptionsPanel()
    {
        comedyQuote = "Take my wife, please.";
        philosophyQuote = "I think, therefore I am.";
        carpentryQuote = "Measure twice. Cut once.";

        quote = new JLabel (comedyQuote);
        quote.setFont (new Font ("Helvetica", Font.BOLD, 24));

        comedy = new JRadioButton ("Comedy", true);
        comedy.setBackground (Color.green);
        philosophy = new JRadioButton ("Philosophy");
        philosophy.setBackground (Color.green);
        carpentry = new JRadioButton ("Carpentry");
        carpentry.setBackground (Color.green);

        ButtonGroup group = new ButtonGroup();
        group.add (comedy);
        group.add (philosophy);
        group.add (carpentry);
```

Listing 5.25   continued

```java
        QuoteListener listener = new QuoteListener();
        comedy.addActionListener (listener);
        philosophy.addActionListener (listener);
        carpentry.addActionListener (listener);

        add (quote);
        add (comedy);
        add (philosophy);
        add (carpentry);

        setBackground (Color.green);
        setPreferredSize (new Dimension(300, 100));
    }

    //*****************************************************************
    //   Represents the listener for all radio buttons.
    //*****************************************************************
    private class QuoteListener implements ActionListener
    {
        //--------------------------------------------------------------
        //   Sets the text of the label depending on which radio
        //   button was pressed.
        //--------------------------------------------------------------
        public void actionPerformed (ActionEvent event)
        {
            Object source = event.getSource();

            if (source == comedy)
                quote.setText (comedyQuote);
            else
                if (source == philosophy)
                    quote.setText (philosophyQuote);
                else
                    quote.setText (carpentryQuote);
        }
    }
}
```

Note that each button is added to the button group, and also that each button is added individually to the panel. A `ButtonGroup` object is not a container to organize and display components; it is simply a way to define the group of radio buttons that work together to form a set of dependent options. The `ButtonGroup` object ensures that the currently selected radio button is turned off when another in the group is selected.

A radio button produces an action event when it is selected. The `actionPerformed` method of the listener first retrieves the source of the event using the `getSource` method, and then compares it to each of the three radio buttons in turn. Depending on which button was selected, the text of the label is set to the appropriate quote.

Note that unlike push buttons, both check boxes and radio buttons are *toggle buttons,* meaning that at any time they are either on or off. The difference is in how they are used. Independent options (choose any combination) are controlled with check boxes. Dependent options (choose one of a set) are controlled with radio buttons. If there is only one option to be managed, a check box can be used by itself. As we mentioned earlier, a radio button, on the other hand, makes sense only in conjunction with one or more other radio buttons.

Also note that check boxes and radio buttons produce different types of events. A check box produces an item event and a radio button produces an action event. The use of different event types is related to the differences in button functionality. A check box produces an event when it is selected or deselected, and the listener could make the distinction if desired. A radio button, on the other hand, produces an event only when it is selected (the currently selected button from the group is deselected automatically).

Summary of Key Concepts

> Conditionals and loops allow us to control the flow of execution through a method.

> An `if` statement allows a program to choose whether to execute a particular statement.

> A loop allows a program to execute a statement multiple times.

> Logical operators are often used to construct sophisticated conditions.

> Proper indentation is important for human readability; it shows the relationship between one statement and another.

> An `if-else` statement allows a program to do one thing if a condition is true and another thing if the condition is false.

> In a nested `if` statement, an `else` clause is matched to the closest unmatched `if`.

> The relative order of characters in Java is defined by the Unicode character set.

> The `compareTo` method can be used to determine the relative order of strings.

> A `break` statement is usually used at the end of each case alternative of a `switch` statement.

> A `while` statement executes the same statement until its condition becomes false.

> We must design our programs carefully to avoid infinite loops.

> An iterator is an object that helps you process a group of related items.

> The delimiters used to separate tokens in a `Scanner` object can be explicitly set as needed.

> A `do` statement executes its loop body at least once.

> A `for` statement is usually used when a loop will be executed a set number of times.

> Radio buttons operate as a group, providing a set of mutually exclusive options.

Self-Review Questions

SR 5.1   What is meant by the flow of control through a program?

SR 5.2   What type of conditions are conditionals and loops based on?

SR 5.3   What are the equality operators? The relational operators?

SR 5.4   What is a nested `if` statement? A nested loop?

SR 5.5   How do block statements help us in the construction of conditionals and loops?

SR 5.6   What happens if a case in a `switch` does not end with a `break` statement?

SR 5.7   What is a truth table?

SR 5.8   How do we compare strings for equality?

SR 5.9   Why must we be careful when comparing floating point values for equality?

SR 5.10   What is an assignment operator?

SR 5.11   What is an infinite loop? Specifically, what causes it?

SR 5.12   Compare and contrast a `while` loop and a `do` loop.

SR 5.13   When would we use a `for` loop instead of a `while` loop?

SR 5.14   What is a dialog box?

SR 5.15   Compare and contrast check boxes and radio buttons.

Exercises

EX 5.1   What happens in the `MinOfThree` program if two or more of the values are equal? If exactly two of the values are equal, does it matter whether the equal values are lower or higher than the third?

EX 5.2   What is wrong with the following code fragment? Rewrite it so that it produces correct output.

```
if (total == MAX)
   if (total < sum)
      System.out.println ("total == MAX and < sum.");
else
   System.out.println ("total is not equal to MAX");
```

EX 5.3   What is wrong with the following code fragment? Will this code compile if it is part of an otherwise valid program? Explain.

```
if (length = MIN_LENGTH)
   System.out.println ("The length is minimal.");
```

EX 5.4   What output is produced by the following code fragment?

```
int num = 87, max = 25;
if (num >= max*2)
    System.out.println ("apple");
    System.out.println ("orange");
System.out.println ("pear");
```

EX 5.5   What output is produced by the following code fragment?

```
int limit = 100, num1 = 15, num2 = 40;
if (limit <= limit)
{
    if (num1 == num2)
        System.out.println ("lemon");
    System.out.println ("lime");
}
System.out.println ("grape");
```

EX 5.6   Put the following list of strings in lexicographic order as if determined by the compareTo method of the String class. Consult
the Unicode chart in Appendix C.

```
"fred"
"Ethel"
"?-?-?-?"
"{([])}"
"Lucy"
"ricky"
"book"
"******"
"12345"
"          "
"HEPHALUMP"
"bookkeeper"
"6789"
";+<?"
"^^^^^^^^^^^"
"hephalump"
```

EX 5.7   What output is produced by the following code fragment?

```
int num = 0, max = 20;
while (num < max)
{
    System.out.println (num);
    num += 4;
}
```

EX 5.8   What output is produced by the following code fragment?

```
int num = 1, max = 20;
while (num < max)
{
   if (num%2 == 0)
      System.out.println (num);
   num++;
}
```

EX 5.9   What output is produced by the following code fragment?

```
for (int num = 0; num <= 200; num += 2)
   System.out.println (num);
```

EX 5.10 What output is produced by the following code fragment?

```
for(int val = 200; val >= 0; val -= 1)
   if (val % 4 != 0)
      System.out.println (val);
```

EX 5.11 Transform the following while loop into an equivalent do loop
(make sure it produces the same output).

```
int num = 1;
while (num < 20)
{
   num++;
   System.out.println (num);
}
```

EX 5.12 Transform the while loop from the previous exercise into an
equivalent for loop (make sure it produces the same output).

EX 5.13 What is wrong with the following code fragment? What are
three distinct ways it could be changed to remove the flaw?

```
count = 50;
while (count >= 0)
{
   System.out.println (count);
   count = count + 1;
}
```

EX 5.14 Write a while loop that verifies that the user enters a positive
integer value.

EX 5.15   Write a `do` loop that verifies that the user enters an even integer value.

EX 5.16   Write a code fragment that reads and prints integer values entered by a user until a particular sentinel value (stored in `SENTINEL`) is entered. Do not print the sentinel value.

EX 5.17   Write a `for` loop to print the odd numbers from 1 to 99 (inclusive).

EX 5.18   Write a `for` loop to print the multiples of 3 from 300 down to 3.

EX 5.19   Write a code fragment that reads 10 integer values from the user and prints the highest value entered.

EX 5.20   Write a code fragment that determines and prints the number of times the character 'a' appears in a `String` object called `name`.

EX 5.21   Write a code fragment that prints the characters stored in a `String` object called `str` backward.

EX 5.22   Write a code fragment that prints every other character in a `String` object called `word` starting with the first character.

EX 5.23   Write a method called `powersOfTwo` that prints the first 10 powers of 2 (starting with 2). The method takes no parameters and doesn't return anything.

EX 5.24   Write a method called `alarm` that prints the string "`Alarm!`" multiple times on separate lines. The method should accept an integer parameter that specifies how many times the string is printed. Print an error message if the parameter is less than 1.

EX 5.25   Write a method called `sum100` that returns the sum of the integers from 1 to 100, inclusive.

EX 5.26   Write a method called `maxOfTwo` that accepts two integer parameters and returns the larger of the two.

EX 5.27   Write a method called `sumRange` that accepts two integer parameters that represent a range. Issue an error message and return zero if the second parameter is less than the first. Otherwise, the method should return the sum of the integers in that range (inclusive).

EX 5.28   Write a method called `larger` that accepts two floating point parameters (of type `double`) and returns true if the first parameter is greater than the second, and false otherwise.

EX 5.29 Write a method called countA that accepts a String parameter and returns the number of times the character 'A' is found in the string.

EX 5.30 Write a method called evenlyDivisible that accepts two integer parameters and returns true if the first parameter is evenly divisible by the second, or vice versa, and false otherwise. Return false if either parameter is zero.

EX 5.31 Write a method called isAlpha that accepts a character parameter and returns true if that character is either an uppercase or lowercase alphabetic letter.

EX 5.32 Write a method called floatEquals that accepts three floating point values as parameters. The method should return true if the first two parameters are equal within the tolerance of the third parameter.

EX 5.33 Write a method called reverse that accepts a String parameter and returns a string that contains the characters of the parameter in reverse order. Note that there is a method in the String class that performs this operation, but for the sake of this exercise, you are expected to write your own.

EX 5.34 Write a method called isIsosceles that accepts three integer parameters that represent the lengths of the sides of a triangle. The method returns true if the triangle is iosceles but not equilateral (meaning that exactly two of the sides have an equal length), and false otherwise.

EX 5.35 Explain what would happen if the radio buttons used in the QuoteOptions program were not organized into a ButtonGroup object. Modify the program to test your answer.

Programming Projects

PP 5.1 Design and implement an application that reads an integer value representing a year from the user. The purpose of the program is to determine if the year is a leap year (and therefore has 29 days in February) in the Gregorian calendar. A year is a leap year if it is divisible by 4, unless it is also divisible by 100 but not 400. For example, the year 2003 is not a leap year, but 2004 is. The year 1900 is not a leap year because it is divisible by 100, but the year 2000 is a leap year because even though it is divisible by 100, it is also divisible by 400. Produce an error message for

any input value less than 1582 (the year the Gregorian calendar was adopted).

PP 5.2   Modify the solution to the previous project so that the user can evaluate multiple years. Allow the user to terminate the program using an appropriate sentinel value. Validate each input value to ensure it is greater than or equal to 1582.

PP 5.3   Design and implement an application that reads an integer value and prints the sum of all even integers between 2 and the input value, inclusive. Print an error message if the input value is less than 2. Prompt accordingly.

PP 5.4   Design and implement an application that reads a string from the user and prints it one character per line.

PP 5.5   Design and implement an application that determines and prints the number of odd, even, and zero digits in an integer value read from the keyboard.

PP 5.6   Design and implement an application that produces a multiplication table, showing the results of multiplying the integers 1 through 12 by themselves.

PP 5.7   Design and implement an application that prints the first few verses of the traveling song "One Hundred Bottles of Beer." Use a loop such that each iteration prints one verse. Read the number of verses to print from the user. Validate the input. The following are the first two verses of the song:

> 100 bottles of beer on the wall
> 100 bottles of beer
> If one of those bottles should happen to fall
> 99 bottles of beer on the wall
>
> 99 bottles of beer on the wall
> 99 bottles of beer
> If one of those bottles should happen to fall
> 98 bottles of beer on the wall

PP 5.8   Design and implement an application that plays the Hi-Lo guessing game with numbers. The program should pick a random number between 1 and 100 (inclusive), then repeatedly prompt the user to guess the number. On each guess, report to the user that he or she is correct or that the guess is high or low. Continue accepting guesses until the user guesses correctly or

chooses to quit. Use a sentinel value to determine whether the user wants to quit. Count the number of guesses and report that value when the user guesses correctly. At the end of each game (by quitting or a correct guess), prompt to determine whether the user wants to play again. Continue playing games until the user chooses to stop.

PP 5.9   Create a modified version of the `PalindromeTester` program so that the spaces, punctuation, and changes in uppercase and lowercase are not considered when determining whether a string is a palindrome. *Hint*: These issues can be handled in several ways. Think carefully about your design.

PP 5.10   Using the `PairOfDice` class from Programming Project 4.7, design and implement an application that rolls a pair of dice 1000 times, counting the number of box cars (two sixes) that occur.

PP 5.11   Using the `Coin` class defined in this chapter, design and implement a driver class called `CountFlips` whose `main` method flips a coin 100 times and counts how many times each side comes up. Print the results.

PP 5.12   Using the `Coin` class defined in this chapter, design and implement a driver class called `FlipRace` whose `main` method creates two `Coin` objects, then continually flips them both to see which coin first comes up heads three flips in a row. Continue flipping the coins until one of the coins wins the race, and consider the possibility that they might tie. Print the results of each turn, and at the end print the winner and total number of flips that were required.

PP 5.13   Create modified versions of the `Stars` program to print the following patterns. Create a separate program to produce each pattern. *Hint*: Parts b, c, and d require several loops, some of which print a specific number of spaces.

```
a. **********  b.              *  c.**********  d.           *
   ********                 **     ********              ***
   *******                 ***     *******             *****
   *******                ****     *******            *******
   ******                *****     ******            ********
   *****                ******     *****            *********
   ****                *******     ****              *******
   ***                ********     ***                *****
   **                *********     **                  ***
   *                **********     *                    *
```

PP 5.14 Design and implement an application that prints a table showing a subset of the Unicode characters and their numeric values. Print five number/character pairs per line, separated by tab characters. Print the table for numeric values from 32 (the space character) to 126 (the ~ character), which corresponds to the printable ASCII subset of the Unicode character set. Compare your output to the table in Appendix C. Unlike the table in Appendix C, the values in your table can increase as they go across a row.

PP 5.15 Design and implement an application that reads a string from the user, then determines and prints how many of each lower-case vowel (a, e, i, o, and u) appear in the entire string. Have a separate counter for each vowel. Also count and print the number of nonvowel characters.

PP 5.16 Design and implement an application that plays the Rock-Paper-Scissors game against the computer. When played between two people, each person picks one of three options (usually shown by a hand gesture) at the same time, and a winner is determined. In the game, Rock beats Scissors, Scissors beats Paper, and Paper beats Rock. The program should randomly choose one of the three options (without revealing it), then prompt for the user's selection. At that point, the program reveals both choices and prints a statement indicating if the user won, the computer won, or if it was a tie. Continue playing until the user chooses to stop, then print the number of user wins, losses, and ties.

PP 5.17 Design and implement an application that prints the verses of the song "The Twelve Days of Christmas," in which each verse adds one line. The first two verses of the song are:

> On the 1st day of Christmas my true love gave to me
> A partridge in a pear tree.
> On the 2nd day of Christmas my true love gave to me
> Two turtle doves, and
> A partridge in a pear tree.

Use a switch statement in a loop to control which lines get printed. *Hint:* Order the cases carefully and avoid the break statement. Use a separate switch statement to put the appropriate suffix on the day number (1st, 2nd, 3rd, etc.). The final verse of the song involves all 12 days, as follows:

On the 12th day of Christmas, my true love gave to me
Twelve drummers drumming,
Eleven pipers piping,
Ten lords a leaping,
Nine ladies dancing,
Eight maids a milking,
Seven swans a swimming,
Six geese a laying,
Five golden rings,
Four calling birds,
Three French hens,
Two turtle doves, and
A partridge in a pear tree.

PP 5.18   Design and implement an application that simulates a simple slot machine in which three numbers between 0 and 9 are randomly selected and printed side by side. Print an appropriate statement if all three of the numbers are the same, or if any two of the numbers are the same. Continue playing until the user chooses to stop.

PP 5.19   Design and implement a program that counts the number of integer values in a text input file. Produce a table listing the values you identify as integers from the input file.

PP 5.20   Design and implement a program that draws 20 horizontal, evenly spaced parallel lines of random length.

PP 5.21   Design and implement a program that draws the side view of stair steps from the lower left to the upper right.

PP 5.22   Design and implement a program that draws 100 circles of random color and random diameter in random locations. Ensure that in each case the entire circle appears in the visible area of the applet.

PP 5.23   Design and implement a program that draws 10 concentric circles of random radius.

PP 5.24   Design and implement a program that draws a brick wall pattern in which each row of bricks is offset from the row above and below it.

PP 5.25   Design and implement a program that draws a quilt in which a simple pattern is repeated in a grid of squares.

PP 5.26   Modify the previous problem such that it draws a quilt using a separate class called `Pattern` that represents a particular pattern. Allow the constructor of the `Pattern` class to vary some characteristics of the pattern, such as its color scheme. Instantiate two separate `Pattern` objects and incorporate them in a checkerboard layout in the quilt.

PP 5.27   Design and implement a program that draws a simple fence with vertical, equally spaced slats backed by two horizontal support boards. Behind the fence show a simple house in the background. Make sure the house is visible between the slats in the fence.

PP 5.28   Design and implement a program that draws a rainbow. Use tightly spaced concentric arcs to draw each part of the rainbow in a particular color.

PP 5.29   Design and implement a program that draws 20,000 points in random locations within the visible area. Make the points on the left half of the panel appear in red and the points on the right half of the panel appear in green. Draw each point by drawing a line with a length of only one pixel.

PP 5.30   Design and implement a program that draws 10 circles of random radius in random locations. Fill in the largest circle in red.

PP 5.31   Design and implement an application that uses dialog boxes to obtain two integer values (one dialog box for each value) and display the sum and product of the values. Use another dialog box to see whether the user wants to process another pair of values.

PP 5.32   Modify the `Die` class from Chapter 4 so that the `setFaceValue` method does nothing if the parameter is outside of the valid range of values.

PP 5.33   Modify the `Account` class from Chapter 4 so that it performs validity checks on the deposit and withdraw operations. Specifically, don't allow the deposit of a negative number or a withdrawal that exceeds the current balance. Print appropriate error messages if these problems occur.

PP 5.34   Redesign and implement a version of the `PalindromeTester` program so that it uses dialog boxes to obtain the input string, display the results, and prompt to continue.

PP 5.35   Modify the `StyleOptions` program in this chapter to allow the user to specify the size of the font. Use a text field to obtain the size.

PP 5.36 Design and implement a program to process golf scores. The scores of four golfers are stored in a text file. Each line represents one hole, and the file contains 18 lines. Each line contains five values: par for the hole followed by the number of strokes each golfer used on that hole. Determine the winner and produce a table showing how well each golfer did (compared to par).

PP 5.37 Design and implement a program that compares two text input files, line by line, for equality. Print any lines that are not equivalent.

PP 5.38 Design and implement a program that counts the number of punctuation marks in a text input file. Produce a table that shows how many times each symbol occurred.

PP 5.39 Develop a simple tool for calculating basic statistics for a segment of text. The application should have a single window with a scrolling text box (a JTextArea) and a stats box. The stats box should be a panel with a titled border, containing labeled fields that display the number of words in the text box and the average word length, as well as any other statistics that you would like to add. The stats box should also contain a button that, when pressed, re-computes the statistics for the current contents of the text field.

PP 5.40 Using the PairOfDice class from Programming Project 4.7, design and implement a class to play a game called Pig. In this game, the user competes against the computer. On each turn, the current player rolls a pair of dice and accumulates points. The goal is to reach 100 points before your opponent does. If, on any turn, the player rolls a 1, all points accumulated for that round are forfeited and control of the dice moves to the other player. If the player rolls two 1s in one turn, the player loses all points accumulated thus far in the game and loses control of the dice. The player may voluntarily turn over the dice after each roll. Therefore the player must decide to either roll again (be a pig) and risk losing points, or relinquish control of the dice, possibly allowing the other player to win. Implement the computer player such that it always relinquishes the dice after accumulating 20 or more points in any given round.

PP 5.41   Design and implement a class called `Card` that represents a standard playing card. Each card has a suit and a face value. Create a program that deals 5 random cards.

Answers to Self-Review Questions

SR 5.1   The flow of control through a program determines the program statements that will be executed on a given run of the program.

SR 5.2   Each conditional and loop is based on a boolean condition that evaluates to either true or false.

SR 5.3   The equality operators are equal (`==`) and not equal (`!=`). The relational operators are less than (`<`), less than or equal to (`<=`), greater than (`>`), and greater than or equal to (`>=`).

SR 5.4   A nested `if` occurs when the statement inside an `if` or `else` clause is an `if` statement. A nested `if` lets the programmer make a series of decisions. Similarly, a nested loop is a loop within a loop.

SR 5.5   A block statement groups several statements together. We use them to define the body of an `if` statement or loop when we want to do multiple things based on the boolean condition.

SR 5.6   If a case does not end with a `break` statement, processing continues into the statements of the next case. We usually want to use `break` statements in order to jump to the end of the `switch`.

SR 5.7   A truth table is a table that shows all possible results of a boolean expression, given all possible combinations of variables and conditions.

SR 5.8   We compare strings for equality using the `equals` method of the `String` class, which returns a boolean result. The `compareTo` method of the `String` class can also be used to compare strings. It returns a positive, 0, or negative integer result depending on the relationship between the two strings.

SR 5.9   Because they are stored internally as binary numbers, comparing floating point values for exact equality will be true only if they are the same bit-by-bit. It's better to use a reasonable tolerance value and consider the difference between the two values.

SR 5.10   An assignment operator combines an operation with assignment. For example, the `+=` operator performs an addition, then stores the value back into the variable on the right-hand side.

SR 5.11   An infinite loop is a repetition statement that never terminates. Specifically, the body of the loop never causes the condition to become false.

SR 5.12   A `while` loop evaluates the condition first. If it is true, it executes the loop body. The `do` loop executes the body first and then evaluates the condition. Therefore the body of a `while` loop is executed zero or more times, and the body of a `do` loop is executed one or more times.

SR 5.13   A `for` loop is usually used when we know, or can calculate, how many times we want to iterate through the loop body. A `while` loop handles a more generic situation.

SR 5.14   A dialog box is a small window that appears for the purpose of conveying information, confirming an action, or accepting input. Generally, dialog boxes are used in specific situations for brief user interactions.

SR 5.15   Both check boxes and radio buttons show a toggled state: either on or off. However, radio buttons work as a group in which only one can be toggled on at any point in time. Check boxes, on the other hand, represent independent options. They can be used alone or in a set in which any combination of toggled states is valid.

Object-Oriented Design 6

CHAPTER OBJECTIVES

> Establish key issues related to the design of object-oriented software.

> Explore techniques for identifying the classes and objects needed in a program.

> Discuss the relationships among classes.

> Describe the effect of the `static` modifier on methods and data.

> Discuss the creation of a formal object interface.

> Further explore the definition of enumerated type classes.

> Discuss issues related to the design of methods, including method overloading.

> Explore issues related to the design of graphical user interfaces, including layout managers.

This chapter extends our discussion of the design of object-oriented software. We first focus on the stages of software development and the process of identifying classes and objects in the problem domain. We then discuss various issues that affect the design of a class, including static members, class relationships, interfaces, and enumerated types. We also explore design issues at the method level and introduce the concept of method overloading. A discussion of testing strategies rounds out these issues. In the Graphics Track sections of this chapter we focus on GUI design concepts, including layout managers and containment hierarchies.

6.1   SOFTWARE DEVELOPMENT ACTIVITIES

Creating software involves much more than just writing code. As the problems you tackle get bigger, and the solutions include more classes, it becomes crucial to carefully think through the design of the software. Any proper software development effort consists of four basic *development activities*:

> establishing the requirements
> creating a design
> implementing the design
> testing

It would be nice if these activities, in this order, defined a step-by-step approach for developing software. However, although they may seem to be sequential, they are almost never completely linear in reality. They overlap and interact. Let's discuss each development activity briefly.

Software requirements specify *what* a program must accomplish. They indicate the tasks that a program should perform, not how it performs them. Often requirements are expressed in a document called a *functional specification*.

We discussed in Chapter 1 the basic premise that programming is really about problem solving; we create a program to solve a particular problem. Requirements are the clear expression of that problem. Until we truly know what problem we are trying to solve, we can't actually solve it.

The person or group who wants a software product developed (the *client*) will often provide an initial set of requirements. However, these initial requirements are often incomplete, ambiguous, and perhaps even contradictory. The software developer must work with the client to refine the requirements until all key decisions about what the system will do have been addressed.

Requirements often address user interface issues such as output format, screen layouts, and graphical interface components. Essentially, the requirements establish the characteristics that make the program useful for the end user. They may also apply constraints to your program, such as how fast a task must be performed.

A *software design* indicates *how* a program will accomplish its requirements. The design specifies the classes and objects needed in a program and defines how they interact. It also specifies the relationships among the classes. Low-level design issues deal with how individual methods accomplish their tasks.

A civil engineer would never consider building a bridge without designing it first. The design of software is no less essential. Many problems that occur in software are directly attributable to a lack of good design effort. It has been shown time and again that the effort spent on the design of a program is well worth it, saving both time and money in the long run.

During software design, alternatives need to be considered and explored. Often, the first attempt at a design is not the best solution. Fortunately, changes are relatively easy to make during the design stage.

Implementation is the process of writing the source code that will solve the problem. More precisely, implementation is the act of translating the design into a particular programming language. Too many programmers focus on implementation exclusively when actually it should be the least creative of all development activities. The important decisions should be made when establishing the requirements and creating the design.

Testing is the act of ensuring that a program will solve the intended problem given all of the constraints under which it must perform. Testing includes running a program multiple times with various inputs and carefully scrutinizing the results. But it means far more than that. We revisit the issues related to testing in section 6.9.

6.2   IDENTIFYING CLASSES AND OBJECTS

A fundamental part of object-oriented software design is determining the classes that will contribute to the program. We have to carefully consider how we want to represent the various elements that make up the overall solution. These classes determine the objects that we will manage in the system.

One way to identify potential classes is to identify the objects discussed in the program requirements. Objects are generally nouns. You literally may want to scrutinize a problem description, or a functional specification if available, to identify the nouns found in it. For example, Figure 6.1 shows part of a problem description with the nouns circled.

Of course, not every noun in the problem specification will correspond to a class in your program. This activity is just a starting point that allows you to think about the types of objects a program will manage.

```
The user must be allowed to specify each
product by its primary characteristics,
including its name and product number. If the
bar code does not match the product, then an
error should be generated to the message window
and entered into the error log. The summary
report of all transactions must be structured
as specified in section 7.A.
```

FIGURE 6.1   A partial problem description with the nouns circled

Remember that a class represents a group of objects with similar behavior. A plural noun in the specification, such as products, may indicate the need for a class that represents one of those items, such as `Product`. Even if there is only one of a particular kind of object needed in your system, it may best be represented as a class.

Classes that represent objects should generally be given names that are singular nouns, such as `Coin`, `Student`, and `Message`. A class represents a single item from which we are free to create as many instances as we choose.

Another key decision is whether to represent something as an object or as a primitive attribute of another object. For example, we may initially think that an employee's salary should be represented as an integer, and that may work for much of the system's processing. But upon further reflection we might realize that the salary is based on the person's rank, which has upper and lower salary bounds that must be managed with care. Therefore the final conclusion may be that we'd be better off representing all of that data and the associated behavior as a separate class.

Given the needs of a particular program, we want to strike a good balance between classes that are too general and those that are too specific. For example, it may complicate our design unnecessarily to create a separate class for each type of appliance that exists in a house. It may be sufficient to have a single `Appliance` class, with perhaps a piece of instance data that indicates what type of appliance it is. Then again, it may not. It all depends on what the software is going to accomplish.

In addition to classes that represent objects from the problem domain, we likely will need classes that support the work necessary to get the job done. For example, in addition to `Member` objects, we may want a separate class to help us manage all of the members of a club.

Keep in mind that when producing a real system, some of the classes we identify during design may already exist. Even if nothing matches exactly, there may be an old class that's similar enough to serve as the basis for our new class. The existing class my be part of the Java standard class library, part of a solution to a problem we've solved previously, or part of a library that can be bought from a third party. These are all examples of software reuse.

Assigning Responsibilities

Part of the process of identifying the classes needed in a program is the process of assigning responsibilities to each class. Each class represents an object with certain behaviors that are defined by the methods of the class. Any activity that the program must accomplish must be represented somewhere in the behaviors of the classes. That is, each class is responsible for carrying out certain activities, and those responsibilities must be assigned as part of designing a program.

The behaviors of a class perform actions that make up the functionality of a program. Thus we generally use verbs for the names of behaviors and the methods that accomplish them.

Sometimes it is challenging to determine which is the best class to carry out a particular responsibility. Consider multiple possibilities. Sometimes such analysis makes you realize that you could benefit from defining another class to shoulder the responsibility.

It's not necessary in the early stages of a design to identify all the methods that a class will contain. It is often sufficient to assign primary responsibilities, and consider how those responsibilities translate to particular methods.

6.3   STATIC CLASS MEMBERS

We've used static methods in various situations in previous examples in the book. For example, all the methods of the `Math` class are static. Recall that a static method is one that is invoked through its class name, instead of through an object of that class.

Not only can methods be static, but variables can be static as well. We declare static class members using the `static` modifier.

Deciding whether to declare a method or variable as static is a key step in class design. Let's examine the implications of static variables and methods more closely.

Static Variables

So far, we've seen two categories of variables: local variables that are declared inside a method, and instance variables that are declared in a class but not inside a method. The term *instance variable* is used because each instance of the class has its own version of the variable. That is, each object has distinct memory space for each variable so that each object can have a distinct value for that variable.

A *static variable*, which is sometimes called a *class variable*, is shared among all instances of a class. There is only one copy of a static variable for all objects of the class. Therefore, changing the value of a static variable in one object changes it for all of the others. The reserved word `static` is used as a modifier to declare a static variable as follows:

> **Key Concept**
>
> A static variable is shared among all instances of a class.

```
private static int count = 0;
```

Memory space for a static variable is established when the class that contains it is referenced for the first time in a program. A local variable declared within a method cannot be static.

Constants, which are declared using the `final` modifier, are often declared using the `static` modifier. Because the value of constants cannot be changed, there might as well be only one copy of the value across all objects of the class.

Static Methods

In Chapter 3 we briefly introduced the concept of a *static method* (also called a *class method*). Static methods can be invoked through the class name. We don't have to instantiate an object of the class in order to invoke the method. In Chapter 3 we noted that all the methods of the `Math` class are static methods. For example, in the following line of code the `sqrt` method is invoked through the `Math` class name:

```
System.out.println ("Square root of 27: " + Math.sqrt(27));
```

The methods in the `Math` class perform basic computations based on values passed as parameters. There is no object state to maintain in these situations; therefore there is no good reason to force us to create an object in order to request these services.

A method is made static by using the `static` modifier in the method declaration. As we've seen many times, the `main` method of a Java program must be declared with the `static` modifier; this is done so that `main` can be executed by the interpreter without instantiating an object from the class that contains `main`.

Because static methods do not operate in the context of a particular object, they cannot reference instance variables, which exist only in an instance of a class. The compiler will issue an error if a static method attempts to use a nonstatic variable. A static method can, however, reference static variables because static variables exist independent of specific objects. Therefore, the `main` method can access only static or local variables.

The program in Listing 6.1 instantiates several objects of the `Slogan` class, printing each one out in turn. At the end of the program it invokes a method called `getCount` through the class name, which returns the number of `Slogan` objects that were instantiated in the program.

Listing 6.2 shows the `Slogan` class. The constructor of `Slogan` increments a static variable called `count`, which is initialized to zero when it is declared. Therefore, `count` serves to keep track of the number of instances of `Slogan` that are created.

Listing 6.1

```java
//********************************************************************
//  SloganCounter.java       Author: Lewis/Loftus
//
//  Demonstrates the use of the static modifier.
//********************************************************************

public class SloganCounter
{
   //-----------------------------------------------------------------
   //  Creates several Slogan objects and prints the number of
   //  objects that were created.
   //-----------------------------------------------------------------
   public static void main (String[] args)
   {
      Slogan obj;

      obj = new Slogan ("Remember the Alamo.");
      System.out.println (obj);

      obj = new Slogan ("Don't Worry. Be Happy.");
      System.out.println (obj);

      obj = new Slogan ("Live Free or Die.");
      System.out.println (obj);

      obj = new Slogan ("Talk is Cheap.");
      System.out.println (obj);

      obj = new Slogan ("Write Once, Run Anywhere.");
      System.out.println (obj);

      System.out.println();
      System.out.println ("Slogans created: " + Slogan.getCount());
   }
}
```

Output

```
Remember the Alamo.
Don't Worry. Be Happy.
Live Free or Die.
Talk is Cheap.
Write Once, Run Anywhere.

Slogans created: 5
```

Listing 6.2

```java
//********************************************************************
//  Slogan.java        Author: Lewis/Loftus
//
//  Represents a single slogan string.
//********************************************************************

public class Slogan
{
   private String phrase;
   private static int count = 0;

   //-----------------------------------------------------------------
   //  Constructor: Sets up the slogan and counts the number of
   //  instances created.
   //-----------------------------------------------------------------
   public Slogan (String str)
   {
      phrase = str;
      count++;
   }

   //-----------------------------------------------------------------
   //  Returns this slogan as a string.
   //-----------------------------------------------------------------
   public String toString()
   {
      return phrase;
   }

   //-----------------------------------------------------------------
   //  Returns the number of instances of this class that have been
   //  created.
   //-----------------------------------------------------------------
   public static int getCount ()
   {
      return count;
   }
}
```

The getCount method of Slogan is also declared as static, which allows it to be invoked through the class name in the main method. Note that the only data referenced in the getCount method is the integer variable count, which is static. As a static method, getCount cannot reference any nonstatic data.

The getCount method could have been declared without the static modifier, but then its invocation in the main method would have to have been done through an instance of the Slogan class instead of the class itself.

6.4 CLASS RELATIONSHIPS

The classes in a software system have various types of relationships to each other. Three of the more common relationships are dependency, aggregation, and inheritance.

We've seen dependency relationships in many examples in which one class "uses" another. This section revisits the dependency relationship and explores the situation where a class depends on itself. We then explore aggregation, in which the objects of one class contain objects of another, creating a "has-a" relationship. Inheritance, which we introduced in Chapter 1, creates an "is-a" relationship between classes. We defer our detailed examination of inheritance until Chapter 8.

Dependency

In many previous examples, we've seen the idea of one class being dependent on another. This means that one class relies on another in some sense. Often the methods of one class will invoke the methods of the other class. This establishes a "uses" relationship.

Generally, if class A uses class B, then one or more methods of class A invoke one or more methods of class B. If an invoked method is static, then A merely references B by name. If the invoked method is not static, then A must have access to a specific instance of class B in order to invoke the method. That is, A must have a reference to an object of class B.

The way in which one object gains access to an object of another class is an important design decision. It occurs when one class instantiates the objects of another, but that's often the basis of an aggregation relationship. The access can also be accomplished by passing one object to another as a method parameter.

In general, we want to minimize the number of dependencies among classes. The less dependent our classes are on each other, the less impact changes and errors will have on the system.

Dependencies Among Objects of the Same Class

In some cases, a class depends on itself. That is, an object of one class interacts with another object of the same class. To accomplish this, a method of the class may accept as a parameter an object of the same class. Designing such a class drives home the idea that a class represents a particular object.

The concat method of the String class is an example of this situation. The method is executed through one String object and is passed another String object as a parameter. For example:

```
str3 = str1.concat(str2);
```

The String object executing the method (str1) appends its characters to those of the String passed as a parameter (str2). A new String object is returned as a result and stored as str3.

The RationalTester program shown in Listing 6.3 demonstrates a similar situation. A rational number is a value that can be represented as a ratio of two

Listing 6.3

```java
//********************************************************************
//  RationalTester.java         Author: Lewis/Loftus
//
//  Driver to exercise the use of multiple Rational objects.
//********************************************************************

public class RationalTester
{
   //-----------------------------------------------------------------
   //  Creates some rational number objects and performs various
   //  operations on them.
   //-----------------------------------------------------------------
   public static void main (String[] args)
   {
      RationalNumber r1 = new RationalNumber (6, 8);
      RationalNumber r2 = new RationalNumber (1, 3);
      RationalNumber r3, r4, r5, r6, r7;

      System.out.println ("First rational number: " + r1);
      System.out.println ("Second rational number: " + r2);

      if (r1.equals(r2))
         System.out.println ("r1 and r2 are equal.");
```

Listing 6.3   **continued**

```
            else
                System.out.println ("r1 and r2 are NOT equal.");

            r3 = r1.reciprocal();
            System.out.println ("The reciprocal of r1 is: " + r3);

            r4 = r1.add(r2);
            r5 = r1.subtract(r2);
            r6 = r1.multiply(r2);
            r7 = r1.divide(r2);

            System.out.println ("r1 + r2: " + r4);
            System.out.println ("r1 - r2: " + r5);
            System.out.println ("r1 * r2: " + r6);
            System.out.println ("r1 / r2: " + r7);
        }
    }
```

Output

```
First rational number: 3/4
Second rational number: 1/3
r1 and r2 are NOT equal.
The reciprocal of r1 is: 4/3
r1 + r2: 13/12
r1 - r2: 5/12
r1 * r2: 1/4
r1 / r2: 9/4
```

integers (a fraction). The RationalTester program creates two objects representing rational numbers and then performs various operations on them to produce new rational numbers.

The RationalNumber class is shown in Listing 6.4. Keep in mind as you examine this class that each object created from the RationalNumber class represents a single rational number. The RationalNumber class contains various operations on rational numbers, such as addition and subtraction.

The methods of the RationalNumber class, such as add, subtract, multiply, and divide, use the RationalNumber object that is executing the method as the first (left) operand and the RationalNumber object passed as a parameter as the second (right) operand.

Listing 6.4

```java
//********************************************************************
//  RationalNumber.java        Author: Lewis/Loftus
//
//  Represents one rational number with a numerator and denominator.
//********************************************************************

public class RationalNumber
{
   private int numerator, denominator;

   //-----------------------------------------------------------------
   //  Constructor: Sets up the rational number by ensuring a nonzero
   //  denominator and making only the numerator signed.
   //-----------------------------------------------------------------
   public RationalNumber (int numer, int denom)
   {
      if (denom == 0)
         denom = 1;

      // Make the numerator "store" the sign
      if (denom < 0)
      {
         numer = numer * -1;
         denom = denom * -1;
      }

      numerator = numer;
      denominator = denom;

      reduce();
   }

   //-----------------------------------------------------------------
   //  Returns the numerator of this rational number.
   //-----------------------------------------------------------------
   public int getNumerator ()
   {
      return numerator;
   }
```

Listing 6.4   continued

```java
//----------------------------------------------------------
//  Returns the denominator of this rational number.
//----------------------------------------------------------
public int getDenominator ()
{
   return denominator;
}

//----------------------------------------------------------
//  Returns the reciprocal of this rational number.
//----------------------------------------------------------
public RationalNumber reciprocal ()
{
   return new RationalNumber (denominator, numerator);
}

//----------------------------------------------------------
//  Adds this rational number to the one passed as a parameter.
//  A common denominator is found by multiplying the individual
//  denominators.
//----------------------------------------------------------
public RationalNumber add (RationalNumber op2)
{
   int commonDenominator = denominator * op2.getDenominator();
   int numerator1 = numerator * op2.getDenominator();
   int numerator2 = op2.getNumerator() * denominator;
   int sum = numerator1 + numerator2;

   return new RationalNumber (sum, commonDenominator);
}

//----------------------------------------------------------
//  Subtracts the rational number passed as a parameter from this
//  rational number.
//----------------------------------------------------------
public RationalNumber subtract (RationalNumber op2)
{
   int commonDenominator = denominator * op2.getDenominator();
   int numerator1 = numerator * op2.getDenominator();
   int numerator2 = op2.getNumerator() * denominator;
   int difference = numerator1 - numerator2;

   return new RationalNumber (difference, commonDenominator);
}
```

Listing 6.4 **continued**

```java
//----------------------------------------------------------------
//  Multiplies this rational number by the one passed as a
//  parameter.
//----------------------------------------------------------------
public RationalNumber multiply (RationalNumber op2)
{
    int numer = numerator * op2.getNumerator();
    int denom = denominator * op2.getDenominator();

    return new RationalNumber (numer, denom);
}

//----------------------------------------------------------------
//  Divides this rational number by the one passed as a parameter
//  by multiplying by the reciprocal of the second rational.
//----------------------------------------------------------------
public RationalNumber divide (RationalNumber op2)
{
    return multiply (op2.reciprocal());
}

//----------------------------------------------------------------
//  Determines if this rational number is equal to the one passed
//  as a parameter.  Assumes they are both reduced.
//----------------------------------------------------------------
public boolean isLike (RationalNumber op2)
{
    return ( numerator == op2.getNumerator() &&
             denominator == op2.getDenominator() );
}

//----------------------------------------------------------------
//  Returns this rational number as a string.
//----------------------------------------------------------------
public String toString ()
{
    String result;

    if (numerator == 0)
        result = "0";
    else
        if (denominator == 1)
            result = numerator + "";
```

Listing 6.4   **continued**

```java
        else
            result = numerator + "/" + denominator;

    return result;
    }

    //-----------------------------------------------------------------
    //  Reduces this rational number by dividing both the numerator
    //  and the denominator by their greatest common divisor.
    //-----------------------------------------------------------------
    private void reduce ()
    {
        if (numerator != 0)
        {
            int common = gcd (Math.abs(numerator), denominator);

            numerator = numerator / common;
            denominator = denominator / common;
        }
    }

    //-----------------------------------------------------------------
    //  Computes and returns the greatest common divisor of the two
    //  positive parameters. Uses Euclid's algorithm.
    //-----------------------------------------------------------------
    private int gcd (int num1, int num2)
    {
        while (num1 != num2)
            if (num1 > num2)
                num1 = num1 - num2;
            else
                num2 = num2 - num1;

        return num1;
    }
}
```

The `isLike` method of the `RationalNumber` class is used to determine if two rational numbers are essentially equal. It's tempting, therefore, to call that method `equals`, similar to the method used to compare `String` objects (discussed in Chapter 5). However, in Chapter 8 we will discuss how the `equals` method is somewhat special due to inheritance, and that it should be implemented in a particular way. So to avoid confusion we call this method `isLike` for now.

Note that some of the methods in the `RationalNumber` class, including `reduce` and `gcd`, are declared with private visibility. These methods are `private` because we don't want them executed directly from outside a `RationalNumber` object. They exist only to support the other services of the object.

Aggregation

Some objects are made up of other objects. A car, for instance, is made up of its engine, its chassis, its wheels, and several other parts. Each of these other parts could be considered a separate object. Therefore we can say that a car is an *aggregation*—it is composed, at least in part, of other objects. Aggregation is sometimes described as a *"has-a" relationship*. For instance, a car has a chassis.

In the software world, we define an *aggregate object* as any object that contains references to other objects as instance data. For example, an `Account` object contains, among other things, a `String` object that represents the name of the account owner. We sometimes forget that strings are objects, but technically that makes each `Account` object an aggregate object.

Aggregation is a special type of dependency. That is, a class that is defined in part by another class is dependent on that class. The methods of the aggregate object generally invoke the methods of the objects from which it is composed.

Let's consider another example. The program `StudentBody` shown in Listing 6.5 creates two `Student` objects. Each `Student` object is composed, in part, of two `Address` objects, one for the student's address at school and another for the student's home address. The `main` method does nothing more than create the `Student` objects and print them out. Once again we are passing objects to the `println` method, relying on the automatic call to the `toString` method to create a valid representation of the object that is suitable for printing.

The `Student` class shown in Listing 6.6 represents a single student. This class would have to be greatly expanded if it were to represent all aspects of a student. We deliberately keep it simple for now so that the object aggregation is clearly shown. The instance data of the `Student` class includes two references to `Address` objects. We refer to those objects in the `toString` method as we create

Listing 6.5

```java
//********************************************************************
//  StudentBody.java        Author: Lewis/Loftus
//
//  Demonstrates the use of an aggregate class.
//********************************************************************

public class StudentBody
{
   //-----------------------------------------------------------------
   //  Creates some Address and Student objects and prints them.
   //-----------------------------------------------------------------
   public static void main (String[] args)
   {
      Address school = new Address ("800 Lancaster Ave.", "Villanova",
                                    "PA", 19085);

      Address jHome = new Address ("21 Jump Street", "Lynchburg",
                                   "VA", 24551);
      Student john = new Student ("John", "Smith", jHome, school);


      Address mHome = new Address ("123 Main Street", "Euclid", "OH",
                                   44132);
      Student marsha = new Student ("Marsha", "Jones", mHome, school);

      System.out.println (john);
      System.out.println ();
      System.out.println (marsha);
   }
}
```

Output

```
John Smith
Home Address:
21 Jump Street
Lynchburg, VA  24551
School Address:
800 Lancaster Ave.
Villanova, PA  19085
```

Listing 6.5   **continued**

```
Marsha Jones
Home Address:
123 Main Street
Euclid, OH  44132
School Address:
800 Lancaster Ave.
Villanova, PA  19085
```

a string representation of the student. By concatenating an `Address` object to another string, the `toString` method in `Address` is automatically invoked.

The `Address` class is shown in Listing 6.7. It represents a street address. Note that nothing about the `Address` class indicates that it is part of a `Student` object. The `Address` class is kept generic by design and therefore could be used in any situation in which a street address is needed.

The more complex an object, the more likely it will need to be represented as an aggregate object. In UML, aggregation is represented by a connection between two classes, with an open diamond at the end near the class that is the aggregate. Figure 6.2 shows a UML class diagram for the `StudentBody` program.

Note that in previous UML diagram examples and in Figure 6.2, strings are not represented as separate classes with aggregation relationships, though technically they could be. Strings are so fundamental to programming that often they are represented as if they are a primitive type in a UML diagram.

The `this` Reference

Before we leave the topic of relationships among classes, we should examine another special reference used in Java programs called the `this` reference. The word `this` is a reserved word in Java. It allows an object to refer to itself. As we have discussed, a nonstatic method is invoked through (or by) a particular object or class. Inside that method, the `this` reference can be used to refer to the currently executing object.

Listing 6.6

```java
//********************************************************************
//   Student.java        Author: Lewis/Loftus
//
//   Represents a college student.
//********************************************************************

public class Student
{
   private String firstName, lastName;
   private Address homeAddress, schoolAddress;

   //-----------------------------------------------------------------
   //   Constructor: Sets up this student with the specified values.
   //-----------------------------------------------------------------
   public Student (String first, String last, Address home,
                   Address school)
   {
      firstName = first;
      lastName = last;
      homeAddress = home;
      schoolAddress = school;
   }

   //-----------------------------------------------------------------
   //   Returns a string description of this Student object.
   //-----------------------------------------------------------------
   public String toString()
   {
      String result;

      result = firstName + " " + lastName + "\n";
      result += "Home Address:\n" + homeAddress + "\n";
      result += "School Address:\n" + schoolAddress;

      return result;
   }
}
```

Listing 6.7

```java
//********************************************************************
//  Address.java        Author: Lewis/Loftus
//
//  Represents a street address.
//********************************************************************

public class Address
{
   private String streetAddress, city, state;
   private long zipCode;

   //----------------------------------------------------------------
   //  Constructor: Sets up this address with the specified data.
   //----------------------------------------------------------------
   public Address (String street, String town, String st, long zip)
   {
      streetAddress = street;
      city = town;
      state = st;
      zipCode = zip;
   }

   //----------------------------------------------------------------
   //  Returns a description of this Address object.
   //----------------------------------------------------------------
   public String toString()
   {
      String result;

      result = streetAddress + "\n";
      result += city + ", " + state + "   " + zipCode;

      return result;
   }
}
```

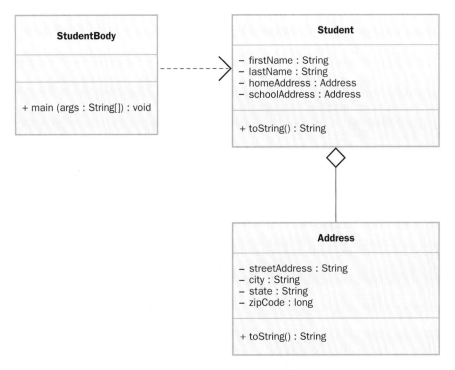

FIGURE 6.2   A UML class diagram showing aggregation

For example, in a class called `ChessPiece` there could be a method called move, which could contain the following line:

```
if (this.position == piece2.position)
   result = false;
```

In this situation, the `this` reference is being used to clarify which position is being referenced. The `this` reference refers to the object through which the method was invoked. So when the following line is used to invoke the method, the `this` reference refers to bishop1:

```
bishop1.move();
```

However, when another object is used to invoke the method, the `this` reference refers to it. Therefore, when the following invocation is used, the `this` reference in the move method refers to bishop2:

```
bishop2.move();
```

Often, the `this` reference is used to distinguish the parameters of a constructor from their corresponding instance variables with the same names. For example, the constructor of the `Account` class was presented in Chapter 4 as follows:

```
public Account (String owner, long account, double initial)
{
    name = owner;
    acctNumber = account;
    balance = initial;
}
```

When writing this constructor, we deliberately came up with different names for the parameters to distinguish them from the instance variables `name`, `acctNumber`, and `balance`. This distinction is arbitrary. The constructor could have been written as follows using the `this` reference:

```
public Account (String name, long acctNumber, double balance)
{
    this.name = name;
    this.acctNumber = acctNumber;
    this.balance = balance;
}
```

In this version of the constructor, the `this` reference specifically refers to the instance variables of the object. The variables on the right-hand side of the assignment statements refer to the formal parameters. This approach eliminates the need to come up with different yet equivalent names. This situation sometimes occurs in other methods but comes up often in constructors.

6.5   INTERFACES

We've used the term interface to refer to the set of public methods through which we can interact with an object. That definition is consistent with our use of it in this section, but now we are going to formalize this concept using a particular language construct in Java.

> **Key Concept**
>
> An interface is a collection of abstract methods and therefore cannot be instantiated.

A Java *interface* is a collection of constants and abstract methods. An *abstract method* is a method that does not have an implementation. That is, there is no body of code defined for an abstract method. The header of the method, including its parameter list, is simply followed by a semicolon. An interface cannot be instantiated.

Listing 6.8 shows an interface called `Complexity`. It contains two abstract methods: `setComplexity` and `getComplexity`.

Listing 6.8

```java
//********************************************************************
//  Complexity.java        Author: Lewis/Loftus
//
//  Represents the interface for an object that can be assigned an
//  explicit complexity.
//********************************************************************

public interface Complexity
{
    public void setComplexity (int complexity);
    public int getComplexity();
}
```

An abstract method can be preceded by the reserved word abstract, though in interfaces it usually is not. Methods in interfaces have public visibility by default.

A class *implements* an interface by providing method implementations for each of the abstract methods defined in the interface. A class that implements an interface uses the reserved word implements followed by the interface name in the class header. If a class asserts that it implements a particular interface, it must provide a definition for all methods in the interface. The compiler will produce errors if any of the methods in the interface are not given a definition in the class.

The Question class, shown in Listing 6.9, implements the Complexity interface. Both the setComplexity and getComplexity methods are implemented. They must be declared with the same signatures as their abstract counterparts in the interface. In the Question class, the methods are defined simply to set or return a numeric value representing the complexity level of the question that the object represents.

Note that the Question class also implements additional methods that are not part of the Complexity interface. Specifically, it defines methods called getQuestion, getAnswer, answerCorrect, and toString, which have nothing to do with the interface. The interface guarantees that the class implements certain methods, but it does not restrict it from having others. It is common for a class that implements an interface to have other methods.

Listing 6.9

```java
//********************************************************************
//  Question.java        Author: Lewis/Loftus
//
//  Represents a question (and its answer).
//********************************************************************

public class Question implements Complexity
{
   private String question, answer;
   private int complexityLevel;

   //-----------------------------------------------------------------
   //  Constructor: Sets up the question with a default complexity.
   //-----------------------------------------------------------------
   public Question (String query, String result)
   {
      question = query;
      answer = result;
      complexityLevel = 1;
   }

   //-----------------------------------------------------------------
   //  Sets the complexity level for this question.
   //-----------------------------------------------------------------
   public void setComplexity (int level)
   {
      complexityLevel = level;
   }

   //-----------------------------------------------------------------
   //  Returns the complexity level for this question.
   //-----------------------------------------------------------------
   public int getComplexity()
   {
      return complexityLevel;
   }

   //-----------------------------------------------------------------
   //  Returns the question.
   //-----------------------------------------------------------------
   public String getQuestion()
   {
      return question;
   }
```

Listing 6.9   continued

```java
//------------------------------------------------------------
//  Returns the answer to this question.
//------------------------------------------------------------
public String getAnswer()
{
    return answer;
}


//------------------------------------------------------------
//  Returns true if the candidate answer matches the answer.
//------------------------------------------------------------
public boolean answerCorrect (String candidateAnswer)
{
    return answer.equals(candidateAnswer);
}


//------------------------------------------------------------
//  Returns this question (and its answer) as a string.
//------------------------------------------------------------
public String toString()
{
    return question + "\n" + answer;
}
}
```

Listing 6.10 shows a program called MiniQuiz, which uses some Question objects.

An interface and its relationship to a class that implements it can be shown in a UML class diagram. An interface is represented similarly to a class node except that the designation <<interface>> is inserted above the class name. A dotted arrow with a closed arrowhead is drawn from the class to the interface that it implements. Figure 6.3 shows a UML class diagram for the MiniQuiz program.

Multiple classes can implement the same interface, providing alternative definitions for the methods. For example, we could implement a class called Task that also implements the Complexity interface. In it we could choose to manage the complexity of a task in a different way (though it would still have to implement all the methods of the interface).

Listing 6.10

```java
//********************************************************************
//  MiniQuiz.java       Author: Lewis/Loftus
//
//  Demonstrates the use of a class that implements an interface.
//********************************************************************

import java.util.Scanner;

public class MiniQuiz
{
    //-----------------------------------------------------------------
    //  Presents a short quiz.
    //-----------------------------------------------------------------
    public static void main (String[] args)
    {
        Question q1, q2;
        String possible;

        Scanner scan = new Scanner (System.in);

        q1 = new Question ("What is the capital of Jamaica?",
                           "Kingston");
        q1.setComplexity (4);

        q2 = new Question ("Which is worse, ignorance or apathy?",
                           "I don't know and I don't care");
        q2.setComplexity (10);

        System.out.print (q1.getQuestion());
        System.out.println (" (Level: " + q1.getComplexity() + ")");
        possible = scan.nextLine();
        if (q1.answerCorrect(possible))
            System.out.println ("Correct");
        else
            System.out.println ("No, the answer is " + q1.getAnswer());

        System.out.println();
        System.out.print (q2.getQuestion());
        System.out.println (" (Level: " + q2.getComplexity() + ")");
        possible = scan.nextLine();
        if (q2.answerCorrect(possible))
```

Listing 6.10   **continued**

```
        System.out.println ("Correct");
    else
        System.out.println ("No, the answer is " + q2.getAnswer());
    }
}
```

Output

```
What is the capital of Jamaica? (Level: 4)
Kingston
Correct

Which is worse, ignorance or apathy? (Level: 10)
apathy
No, the answer is I don't know and I don't care
```

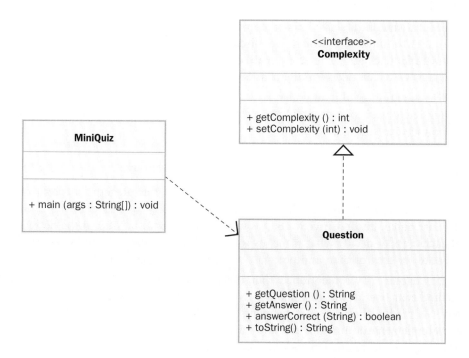

FIGURE 6.3 A UML class diagram for the MiniQuiz program

A class can implement more than one interface. In these cases, the class must provide an implementation for all methods in all interfaces listed. To show that a class implements multiple interfaces, they are listed in the `implements` clause, separated by commas. For example:

```
class ManyThings implements interface1, interface2, interface3
{
    // contains all methods of all interfaces
}
```

In addition to, or instead of, abstract methods, an interface can also contain constants, defined using the `final` modifier. When a class implements an interface, it gains access to all the constants defined in it.

The interface construct formally defines the ways in which we can interact with a class. It also serves as a basis for a powerful programming technique called polymorphism, which we discuss in Chapter 9.

The `Comparable` Interface

The Java standard class library contains interfaces as well as classes. The `Comparable` interface, which we discussed in Chapter 5, is defined in the `java.lang` package. The `Comparable` interface contains only one method, `compareTo`, which takes an object as a parameter and returns an integer.

The intention of this interface is to provide a common mechanism for comparing one object to another. One object calls the method and passes another as a parameter as follows:

```
if (obj1.compareTo(obj2) < 0)
    System.out.println ("obj1 is less than obj2");
```

As specified by the documentation for the interface, the integer that is returned from the `compareTo` method should be negative if `obj1` is less than `obj2`, 0 if they are equal, and positive if `obj1` is greater than `obj2`. It is up to the designer of each class to decide what it means for one object of that class to be less than, equal to, or greater than another.

In Chapter 5, we mentioned that the `String` class contains a `compareTo` method that operates in this manner. Now we can clarify that the `String` class has this method because it implements the `Comparable` interface. The `String` class implementation of this method bases the comparison on the lexicographic ordering defined by the Unicode character set.

The `Iterator` Interface

The `Iterator` interface is another interface defined as part of the Java standard class library. It is used by a class that represents a collection of objects, providing a means to move through the collection one object at a time.

In Chapter 5 we defined the concept of an iterator, using a loop to process all elements in the collection. Most iterators, including objects of the `Scanner` class, are defined using the `Iterator` interface.

The two primary methods in the `Iterator` interface are `hasNext`, which returns a boolean result, and `next`, which returns an object. Neither of these methods takes any parameters. The `hasNext` method returns true if there are items left to process, and `next` returns the next object. It is up to the designer of the class that implements the `Iterator` interface to decide the order in which objects will be delivered by the `next` method.

We should note that, according to the spirit of the interface, the `next` method does not remove the object from the underlying collection; it simply returns a reference to it. The `Iterator` interface also has a method called `remove`, which takes no parameters and has a `void` return type. A call to the `remove` method removes the object that was most recently returned by the `next` method from the underlying collection.

6.6　ENUMERATED TYPES REVISITED

In Chapter 3 we introduced the concept of an enumerated type, which defines a new data type and lists all possible values of that type. We gave an example that defined an enumerated type called `Season`, which was declared as follows:

```
enum Season {winter, spring, summer, fall}
```

We mentioned that an enumerated type is a special kind of class, and that the values of the enumerated type are objects. The values are, in fact, instances of its own enumerated type. For example, `winter` is an object of the `Season` class. Let's explore this concept a bit further.

Suppose we declare a variable of the `Season` type as follows:

```
Season time;
```

Because an enumerated type is a special kind of class, the variable `time` is an object reference variable. Furthermore, as an enumerated type, it can be assigned only the values listed in the `Season` defini-

> **Key Concept**
>
> The values of an enumerated type are static variables of that type.

tion. These values (`winter`, `spring`, `summer`, and `fall`) are actually references to `Season` objects that are stored as `public static` variables within the `Season` class. Thus we can make an assignment such as the following:

```
time = Season.spring;
```

Now let's take this idea a step further. In Listing 6.11 we redefine the `Season` type, giving it a more substantial definition. Note that we still use the `enum`

Listing 6.11

```
//***********************************************************************
//   Season.java        Author: Lewis/Loftus
//
//   Enumerates the values for Season.
//***********************************************************************

public enum Season
{
    winter ("December through February"),
    spring ("March through May"),
    summer ("June through August"),
    fall ("September through November");

    private String span;

    //--------------------------------------------------------------------
    //   Constructor: Sets up each value with an associated string.
    //--------------------------------------------------------------------
    Season (String months)
    {
        span = months;
    }

    //--------------------------------------------------------------------
    //   Returns the span message for this value.
    //--------------------------------------------------------------------
    public String getSpan()
    {
        return span;
    }
}
```

reserved word to declare the enumerated type, and we still list all possible values of the type. In addition, in this definition we add a private `String` called `span`, a constructor for the `Season` class, and a method named `getSpan`. Each value in the list of values for the enumerated type invokes the constructor, passing it a character string that is then stored in the `span` variable of each value.

The `main` method of the `SeasonTester` class, shown in Listing 6.12, prints each value of the `Season` enumerated type, as well as the span statement for each. Every enumerated type contains a static method called `values` that returns a list of all possible values for that type. This list is an iterator, so we can use the enhanced version of a `for` loop to process each value.

In addition to the list of possible values defined in every enumerated type, we can include any number of attributes or methods of our own choosing. This provides various opportunities for creative class design.

> **Key Concept**
>
> We can add attributes and methods to the definition of an enumerated type.

Listing 6.12

```
//********************************************************************
//   SeasonTester.java        Author: Lewis/Loftus
//
//   Demonstrates the use of a full enumerated type.
//********************************************************************

public class SeasonTester
{
   //-----------------------------------------------------------------
   //   Iterates through the values of the Season enumerated type.
   //-----------------------------------------------------------------
   public static void main (String[] args)
   {
      for (Season time : Season.values())
         System.out.println (time + "\t" + time.getSpan());
   }
}
```

Output

```
winter   December through February
spring   March through May
summer   June through August
fall     September through November
```

6.7   **METHOD DESIGN**

Once you have identified classes and assigned basic responsibilities, the design of each method will determine how exactly the class will define its behaviors. Some methods are straightforward and require little thought. Others are more interesting and require careful planning.

An *algorithm* is a step-by-step process for solving a problem. A recipe is an example of an algorithm. Travel directions are another example of an algorithm. Every method implements an algorithm that determines how that method accomplishes its goals.

An algorithm is often described using *pseudocode,* which is a mixture of code statements and English phrases. Pseudocode provides enough structure to show how the code will operate, without getting bogged down in the syntactic details of a particular programming language or becoming prematurely constrained by the characteristics of particular programming constructs.

This section discusses two important aspects of program design at the method level: method decomposition and the implications of passing objects as parameters.

Method Decomposition

Key Concept

A complex service provided by an object can be decomposed to make use of private support methods.

Occasionally, a service that an object provides is so complicated that it cannot reasonably be implemented using one method. Therefore we sometimes need to decompose a method into multiple methods to create a more understandable design. As an example, let's examine a program that translates English sentences into Pig Latin.

Pig Latin is a made-up language in which each word of a sentence is modified, in general, by moving the initial sound of the word to the end and adding an "ay" sound. For example, the word *happy* would be written and pronounced *appyhay* and the word *birthday* would become *irthdaybay*. Words that begin with vowels simply have a "yay" sound added on the end, turning the word *enough* into *enoughyay*. Consonant blends such as "ch" and "st" at the beginning of a word are moved to the end together before adding the "ay" sound. Therefore the word *grapefruit* becomes *apefruitgray*.

The `PigLatin` program shown in Listing 6.13 reads one or more sentences, translating each into Pig Latin.

Listing 6.13

```java
//********************************************************************
//  PigLatin.java        Author: Lewis/Loftus
//
//  Demonstrates the concept of method decomposition.
//********************************************************************

import java.util.Scanner;

public class PigLatin
{
   //-----------------------------------------------------------------
   //  Reads sentences and translates them into Pig Latin.
   //-----------------------------------------------------------------
   public static void main (String[] args)
   {
      String sentence, result, another;

      Scanner scan = new Scanner (System.in);

      do
      {
         System.out.println ();
         System.out.println ("Enter a sentence (no punctuation):");
         sentence = scan.nextLine();

         System.out.println ();
         result = PigLatinTranslator.translate (sentence);
         System.out.println ("That sentence in Pig Latin is:");
         System.out.println (result);

         System.out.println ();
         System.out.print ("Translate another sentence (y/n)? ");
         another = scan.nextLine();
      }
      while (another.equalsIgnoreCase("y"));
   }
}
```

The workhorse behind the PigLatin program is the PigLatinTranslator class, shown in Listing 6.14. The PigLatinTranslator class provides one fundamental service, a static method called translate, which accepts a string and

Listing 6.13   **continued**

Output

```
Enter a sentence (no punctuation):
Do you speak Pig Latin

That sentence in Pig Latin is:
oday ouyay eakspay igpay atinlay

Translate another sentence (y/n)? y

Enter a sentence (no punctuation):
Play it again Sam

That sentence in Pig Latin is:
ayplay ityay againyay amsay

Translate another sentence (y/n)? n
```

translates it into Pig Latin. Note that the `PigLatinTranslator` class does not contain a constructor because none is needed.

The act of translating an entire sentence into Pig Latin is not trivial. If written in one big method, it would be very long and difficult to follow. A better solution, as implemented in the `PigLatinTranslator` class, is to decompose the `translate` method and use several other support methods to help with the task.

The `translate` method uses a `Scanner` object to separate the string into words. Recall that one role of the `Scanner` class (discussed in Chapter 3) is to separate a string into smaller elements called tokens. In this case, the tokens are separated by space characters so we can use the default white space delimiters. The `PigLatin` program assumes that no punctuation is included in the input.

The `translate` method passes each word to the private support method `translateWord`. Even the job of translating one word is somewhat involved, so the `translateWord` method makes use of two other private methods, `beginsWithVowel` and `beginsWithBlend`.

The `beginsWithVowel` method returns a `boolean` value that indicates whether the word passed as a parameter begins with a vowel. Note that instead of checking each vowel separately, the code for this method declares a string that contains all the vowels, and then invokes the `String` method `indexOf` to determine

Listing 6.14

```java
//********************************************************************
//  PigLatinTranslator.java        Author: Lewis/Loftus
//
//  Represents a translator from English to Pig Latin. Demonstrates
//  method decomposition.
//********************************************************************

import java.util.Scanner;

public class PigLatinTranslator
{
   //-----------------------------------------------------------------
   //  Translates a sentence of words into Pig Latin.
   //-----------------------------------------------------------------
   public static String translate (String sentence)
   {
      String result = "";

      sentence = sentence.toLowerCase();

      Scanner scan = new Scanner (sentence);

      while (scan.hasNext())
      {
         result += translateWord (scan.next());
         result += " ";
      }

      return result;
   }

   //-----------------------------------------------------------------
   //  Translates one word into Pig Latin. If the word begins with a
   //  vowel, the suffix "yay" is appended to the word.  Otherwise,
   //  the first letter or two are moved to the end of the word,
   //  and "ay" is appended.
   //-----------------------------------------------------------------
   private static String translateWord (String word)
   {
      String result = "";

      if (beginsWithVowel(word))
         result = word + "yay";
```

Listing 6.14   **continued**

```java
      else
         if (beginsWithBlend(word))
            result = word.substring(2) + word.substring(0,2) + "ay";
         else
            result = word.substring(1) + word.charAt(0) + "ay";

      return result;
   }

   //-----------------------------------------------------------------
   //  Determines if the specified word begins with a vowel.
   //-----------------------------------------------------------------
   private static boolean beginsWithVowel (String word)
   {
      String vowels = "aeiou";

      char letter = word.charAt(0);

      return (vowels.indexOf(letter) != -1);
   }

   //-----------------------------------------------------------------
   //  Determines if the specified word begins with a particular
   //  two-character consonant blend.
   //-----------------------------------------------------------------
   private static boolean beginsWithBlend (String word)
   {
      return ( word.startsWith ("bl") || word.startsWith ("sc") ||
               word.startsWith ("br") || word.startsWith ("sh") ||
               word.startsWith ("ch") || word.startsWith ("sk") ||
               word.startsWith ("cl") || word.startsWith ("sl") ||
               word.startsWith ("cr") || word.startsWith ("sn") ||
               word.startsWith ("dr") || word.startsWith ("sm") ||
               word.startsWith ("dw") || word.startsWith ("sp") ||
               word.startsWith ("fl") || word.startsWith ("sq") ||
               word.startsWith ("fr") || word.startsWith ("st") ||
               word.startsWith ("gl") || word.startsWith ("sw") ||
               word.startsWith ("gr") || word.startsWith ("th") ||
               word.startsWith ("kl") || word.startsWith ("tr") ||
               word.startsWith ("ph") || word.startsWith ("tw") ||
               word.startsWith ("pl") || word.startsWith ("wh") ||
               word.startsWith ("pr") || word.startsWith ("wr") );
   }
}
```

whether the first character of the word is in the vowel string. If the specified character cannot be found, the `indexOf` method returns a value of −1.

The `beginsWithBlend` method also returns a `boolean` value. The body of the method contains only a `return` statement with one large expression that makes several calls to the `startsWith` method of the `String` class. If any of these calls returns true, then the `beginsWithBlend` method returns true as well.

Note that the `translateWord`, `beginsWithVowel`, and `beginsWithBlend` methods are all declared with private visibility. They are not intended to provide services directly to clients outside the class. Instead, they exist to help the `translate` method, which is the only true service method in this class, to do its job. By declaring them with private visibility, they cannot be invoked from outside this class. If the `main` method of the `PigLatin` class attempted to invoke the `translateWord` method, for instance, the compiler would issue an error message.

Figure 6.4 shows a UML class diagram for the `PigLatin` program. Note the notation showing the visibility of various methods.

Whenever a method becomes large or complex, we should consider decomposing it into multiple methods to create a more understandable class design. First, however, we must consider how other classes and objects can be defined to create better overall system design. In an object-oriented design, method decomposition must be subordinate to object decomposition.

Method Parameters Revisited

Another important issue related to method design involves the way parameters are passed into a method. In Java, all parameters are passed *by value*. That is, the current value of the actual parameter (in the invocation) is copied into the formal parameter in the method header. We mentioned this issue in Chapter 4; let's examine it now in more detail.

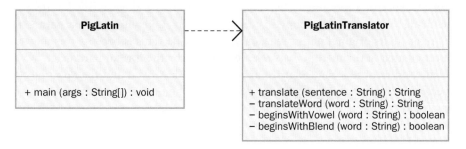

FIGURE 6.4 A UML class diagram for the `PigLatin` program

Essentially, parameter passing is like an assignment statement, assigning to the formal parameter a copy of the value stored in the actual parameter. This issue must be considered when making changes to a formal parameter inside a method. The formal parameter is a separate copy of the value that is passed in, so any changes made to it have no effect on the actual parameter. After control returns to the calling method, the actual parameter will have the same value as it did before the method was called.

However, when we pass an object to a method, we are actually passing a reference to that object. The value that gets copied is the address of the object. Therefore the formal parameter and the actual parameter become aliases of each other. If we change the state of the object through the formal parameter reference inside the method, we are changing the object referenced by the actual parameter, because they refer to the same object. On the other hand, if we change the formal parameter reference itself (to make it point to a new object, for instance), we have not changed the fact that the actual parameter still refers to the original object.

The program in Listing 6.15 illustrates the nuances of parameter passing. Carefully trace the processing of this program and note the values that are output. The `ParameterTester` class contains a `main` method that calls the `changeValues` method in a `ParameterModifier` object. Two of the parameters to `changeValues` are `Num` objects, each of which simply stores an integer value. The other parameter is a primitive integer value.

Listing 6.16 shows the `ParameterModifier` class, and Listing 6.17 shows the `Num` class. Inside the `changeValues` method, a modification is made to each of the three formal parameters: the integer parameter is set to a different value, the value stored in the first `Num` parameter is changed using its `setValue` method, and a new `Num` object is created and assigned to the second `Num` parameter. These changes are reflected in the output printed at the end of the `changeValues` method.

However, note the final values that are printed after returning from the method. The primitive integer was not changed from its original value because the change was made to a copy inside the method. Likewise, the last parameter still refers to its original object with its original value. This is because the new `Num` object created in the method was referred to only by the formal parameter. When the method returned, that formal parameter was destroyed and the `Num` object it referred to was marked for garbage collection. The only change that is "permanent" is the change made to the state of the second parameter. Figure 6.5 shows the step-by-step processing of this program.

Listing 6.15

```java
//********************************************************************
//  ParameterTester.java        Author: Lewis/Loftus
//
//  Demonstrates the effects of passing various types of parameters.
//********************************************************************

public class ParameterTester
{
    //-----------------------------------------------------------------
    //  Sets up three variables (one primitive and two objects) to
    //  serve as actual parameters to the changeValues method. Prints
    //  their values before and after calling the method.
    //-----------------------------------------------------------------
    public static void main (String[] args)
    {
        ParameterModifier modifier = new ParameterModifier();

        int a1 = 111;
        Num a2 = new Num (222);
        Num a3 = new Num (333);

        System.out.println ("Before calling changeValues:");
        System.out.println ("a1\ta2\ta3");
        System.out.println (a1 + "\t" + a2 + "\t" + a3 + "\n");

        modifier.changeValues (a1, a2, a3);

        System.out.println ("After calling changeValues:");
        System.out.println ("a1\ta2\ta3");
        System.out.println (a1 + "\t" + a2 + "\t" + a3 + "\n");
    }
}
```

Listing 6.15 **continued**

Output

```
Before calling changeValues
a1       a2       a3
111      222      333

Before changing the values:
f1       f2       f3
111      222      333

After changing the values:
f1       f2       f3
999      888      777

After calling changeValues:
a1       a2       a3
111      888      333
```

6.8 METHOD OVERLOADING

As we've discussed, when a method is invoked, the flow of control transfers to the code that defines the method. After the method has been executed, control returns to the location of the call, and processing continues.

Often the method name is sufficient to indicate which method is being called by a specific invocation. But in Java, as in other object-oriented languages, you can use the same method name with different parameter lists for multiple methods. This technique is called *method overloading*. It is useful when you need to perform similar methods on different types of data.

> **Key Concept**
>
> The versions of an overloaded method are distinguished by the number, type, and order of their parameters.

The compiler must still be able to associate each invocation to a specific method declaration. If the method name for two or more methods is the same, additional information is used to uniquely identify the version that is being invoked. In Java, a method name can be used for multiple methods as long as the number of parameters, the types of those parameters, and/or the order of the types of parameters is distinct.

Listing 6.16

```java
//********************************************************************
//  ParameterModifier.java      Author: Lewis/Loftus
//
//  Demonstrates the effects of changing parameter values.
//********************************************************************

public class ParameterModifier
{
   //-----------------------------------------------------------------
   //  Modifies the parameters, printing their values before and
   //  after making the changes.
   //-----------------------------------------------------------------
   public void changeValues (int f1, Num f2, Num f3)
   {
      System.out.println ("Before changing the values:");
      System.out.println ("f1\tf2\tf3");
      System.out.println (f1 + "\t" + f2 + "\t" + f3 + "\n");

      f1 = 999;
      f2.setValue(888);
      f3 = new Num (777);

      System.out.println ("After changing the values:");
      System.out.println ("f1\tf2\tf3");
      System.out.println (f1 + "\t" + f2 + "\t" + f3 + "\n");
   }
}
```

For example, we could declare a method called sum as follows:

```java
public int sum (int num1, int num2)
{
   return num1 + num2;
}
```

Listing 6.17

```java
//********************************************************************
//  Num.java         Author: Lewis/Loftus
//
//  Represents a single integer as an object.
//********************************************************************

public class Num
{
   private int value;

   //-------------------------------------------------------------------
   //  Sets up the new Num object, storing an initial value.
   //-------------------------------------------------------------------
   public Num (int update)
   {
      value = update;
   }

   //-------------------------------------------------------------------
   //  Sets the stored value to the newly specified value.
   //-------------------------------------------------------------------
   public void setValue (int update)
   {
      value = update;
   }

   //-------------------------------------------------------------------
   //  Returns the stored integer value as a string.
   //-------------------------------------------------------------------
   public String toString ()
   {
      return value + "";
   }
}
```

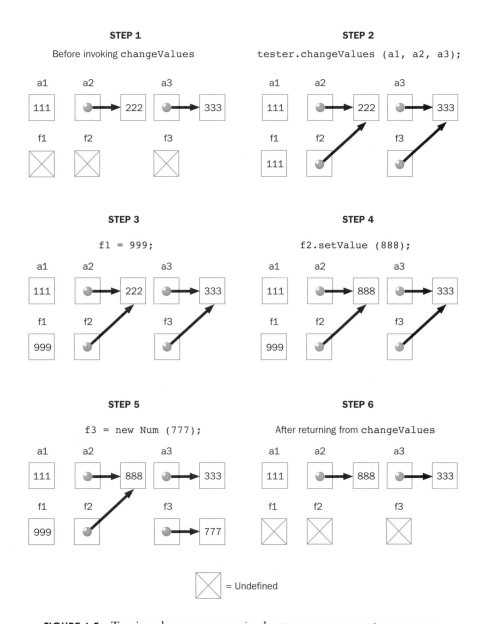

FIGURE 6.5   Tracing the parameters in the ParameterTesting program

Then we could declare another method called sum, within the same class, as follows:

```
public int sum (int num1, int num2, int num3)
{
    return num1 + num2 + num3;
}
```

Now, when an invocation is made, the compiler looks at the number of parameters to determine which version of the sum method to call. For instance, the following invocation will call the second version of the sum method:

```
sum (25, 69, 13);
```

A method's name, along with the number, type, and order of its parameters, is called the method's *signature*. The compiler uses the complete method signature to *bind* a method invocation to the appropriate definition.

The compiler must be able to examine a method invocation to determine which specific method is being invoked. If you attempt to specify two method names with the same signature, the compiler will issue an appropriate error message and will not create an executable program. There can be no ambiguity.

Note that the return type of a method is not part of the method signature. That is, two overloaded methods cannot differ only by their return type. This is because the value returned by a method can be ignored by the invocation. The compiler would not be able to distinguish which version of an overloaded method is being referenced in such situations.

The println method is an example of a method that is overloaded several times, each accepting a single type. The following is a partial list of its various signatures:

> println (String s)

> println (int i)

> println (double d)

> println (char c)

> println (boolean b)

The following two lines of code actually invoke different methods that have the same name:

```
System.out.println ("Number of students: ");
System.out.println (count);
```

The first line invokes the version of `println` that accepts a string. The second line, assuming `count` is an integer variable, invokes the version of `println` that accepts an integer.

We often use a `println` statement that prints several distinct types, such as:

```
System.out.println ("Number of students: " + count);
```

Remember, in this case the plus sign is the string concatenation operator. First, the value in the variable `count` is converted to a string representation, then the two strings are concatenated into one longer string, and finally the definition of `println` that accepts a single string is invoked.

Constructors can be overloaded, and often are. By providing multiple versions of a constructor, we provide multiple ways to set up an object.

6.9   TESTING

The term *testing* can be applied in many ways to software development. Testing certainly includes its traditional definition: the act of running a completed program with various inputs to discover problems. But it also includes any evaluation that is performed by human or machine to assess the quality of the evolving system. These evaluations should occur long before a single line of code is written.

The goal of testing is to find errors. By finding errors and fixing them, we improve the quality of our program. It's likely that later on someone else will find any errors that remain hidden during development. The earlier the errors are found, the easier and cheaper they are to fix. Taking the time to uncover problems as early as possible is almost always worth the effort.

Running a program with specific input and producing the correct results establishes only that the program works for that particular input. As more and more test cases execute without revealing errors, our confidence in the program rises, but we can never really be sure that all errors have been eliminated. There could always be another error still undiscovered. Because of that, it is important to thoroughly test a program in as many ways as possible and with well-designed test cases.

> **Key Concept**
>
> Testing a program can never guarantee the absence of errors.

It is possible to prove that a program is correct, but that technique is enormously complex for large systems, and errors can be made in the proof itself. Therefore we generally rely on testing to determine the quality of a program.

After determining that an error exists, we determine the cause of the error and fix it. After a problem is fixed, we should run previous tests again to make sure that while fixing the problem we didn't create another. This technique is called *regression testing*.

Reviews

One technique used to evaluate design or code is called a *review*, which is a meeting in which several people carefully examine a design document or section of code. Presenting our design or code to others causes us to think more carefully about it and permits others to share their suggestions with us. The participants discuss its merits and problems, and create a list of issues that must be addressed. The goal of a review is to identify problems, not to solve them, which usually takes much more time.

A design review should determine whether the requirements are addressed. It should also assess the way the system is decomposed into classes and objects. A code review should determine how faithfully the design satisfies the requirements and how faithfully the implementation represents the design. It should identify any specific problems that would cause the design or the implementation to fail in its responsibilities.

Sometimes a review is called a *walkthrough* because its goal is to step carefully through a document and evaluate each section.

Defect Testing

Since the goal of testing is to find errors, it is often referred to as *defect testing*. With that goal in mind, a good test is one that uncovers any deficiencies in a pro-

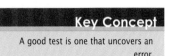

gram. This might seem strange, because we ultimately don't want to have problems in our system. But keep in mind that errors almost certainly exist. Our testing efforts should make every attempt to find them. We want to increase the reliability of our program by finding and fixing the errors that exist, rather than letting users discover them.

A *test case* is a set of inputs, user actions, or other initial conditions, and the expected output. A test case should be appropriately documented so that it can be repeated later as needed. Developers often create a complete *test suite*, which is a set of test cases that covers various aspects of the system.

Because programs operate on a large number of possible inputs, it is not feasible to create test cases for all possible input or user actions. Nor is it usually necessary to test every single situation. Two specific test cases may be so similar that they actually do not test unique aspects of the program. To do both would be a wasted effort. We'd rather execute a test case that stresses the program in some new way. Therefore we want to choose our test cases carefully. To that end, let's examine two approaches to defect testing: black-box testing and white-box testing.

As the name implies, *black-box testing* treats the thing being tested as a black box. In black-box testing, test cases are developed without regard to the internal workings. Black-box tests are based on inputs and outputs. An entire program can be tested using a black-box technique, in which case the inputs are the user-provided information and user actions such as button pushes. A test case is successful only if the input produces the expected output. A single class can also be tested using a black-box technique, which focuses on the system interface (its public methods) of the class. Certain parameters are passed in, producing certain results. Black-box test cases are often derived directly from the requirements of the system or from the stated purpose of a method.

The input data for a black-box test case are often selected by defining equivalence categories. An *equivalence category* is a collection of inputs that are expected to produce similar outputs. Generally, if a method will work for one value in the equivalence category, we have every reason to believe it will work for the others. For example, the input to a method that computes the square root of an integer can be divided into two equivalence categories: nonnegative integers and negative integers. If it works appropriately for one nonnegative value, it will likely work for all nonnegative values. Likewise, if it works appropriately for one negative value, it will likely work for all negative values.

Equivalence categories have defined boundaries. Because all values of an equivalence category essentially test the same features of a program, only one test case inside the equivalence boundary is needed. However, because programming often produces "off by one" errors, the values on and around the boundary should be tested exhaustively. For an integer boundary, a good test suite would include at least the exact value of the boundary, the boundary minus 1, and the boundary plus 1. Test cases that use these cases, plus at least one from within the general field of the category, should be defined.

Let's look at an example. Consider a method whose purpose is to validate that a particular integer value is in the range 0 to 99, inclusive. There are three equivalence categories in this case: values below 0, values in the range of 0 to 99, and values above 99. Black-box testing dictates that we use test values that surround and fall on the boundaries, as well as some general values from the equivalence categories. Therefore, a set of black-box test cases for this situation might be: −500, −1, 0, 1, 50, 98, 99, 100, and 500.

White-box testing, also known as *glass-box testing*, exercises the internal structure and implementation of a method. A white-box test case is based on the logic of the code. The goal is to ensure that every path through a program is executed at least once. A white-box test maps the possible paths through the code and ensures that the test cases cause every path to be executed. This type of testing is often called *statement coverage*.

Paths through code are controlled by various control flow statements that use conditional expressions, such as `if` statements. In order to have every path through the program executed at least once, the input data values for the test cases need to control the values for the conditional expressions. The input data of one or more test cases should cause the condition of an `if` statement to evaluate to `true` in at least one case and to `false` in at least one case. Covering both true and false values in an `if` statement guarantees that both the paths through the `if` statement will be executed. Similar situations can be created for loops and other constructs.

In both black-box and white-box testing, the expected output for each test should be established prior to running the test. It's too easy to be persuaded that the results of a test are appropriate if you haven't first carefully determined what the results should be.

6.10   GUI DESIGN

As we focus on the details that allow us to create GUIs, we may sometimes lose sight of the big picture. As we continue to explore GUI construction, we should keep in mind that our goal is to solve a problem. Specifically, we want to create software that is useful. Knowing the details of components, events, and other language elements gives us the tools to put GUIs together, but we must guide that knowledge with the following fundamental ideas of good GUI design:

> Know the user.
> Prevent user errors.
> Optimize user abilities.
> Be consistent.

> **Key Concept**
>
> The design of any GUI should adhere to basic guidelines regarding consistency and usability.

The software designer must understand the user's needs and potential activities in order to develop an interface that will serve that user well. Keep in mind that, to the user, the interface *is* the software. It is the only way the user interacts with the system. As such, the interface must satisfy the user's needs.

Whenever possible, we should design interfaces so that the user can make as few mistakes as possible. In many situations, we have the flexibility to choose one of several components to accomplish a specific task. We should always try to choose components that will prevent inappropriate actions and avoid invalid input. For example, if an input value must be one of a set of particular values, we should use components that allow the user to make only a valid choice. That is, constraining the user to a few valid choices with, for instance, a set of radio buttons is better than allowing the user to type arbitrary and possibly invalid data into a text field. We cover additional components appropriate for specific situations in this chapter.

Not all users are alike. Some are more adept than others at using a particular GUI or GUI components in general. We shouldn't design with only the lowest common denominator in mind. For example, we should provide shortcuts whenever reasonable. That is, in addition to a normal series of actions that will allow a user to accomplish a task, we should also provide redundant ways to accomplish the same task. Using keyboard shortcuts (mnemonics) is a good example. Sometimes these additional mechanisms are less intuitive, but they may be faster for the experienced user.

Finally, consistency is important when dealing with large systems or multiple systems in a common environment. Users become familiar with a particular organization or color scheme; these should not be changed arbitrarily.

6.11   LAYOUT MANAGERS

In addition to the components, events, and listeners that comprise the backbone of a GUI, the most important activity in GUI design is the use of layout managers. A *layout manager* is an object that governs how components are arranged in a container. It determines the size and position of each component and may take many factors into account to do so. Every container has a default layout manager, although we can replace it if we prefer another one.

> **Key Concept**
>
> The layout manager of a container determines how components are visually presented.

A container's layout manager is consulted whenever a change to the visual appearance of its contents might be needed. When the size of a container is adjusted, for example, the layout manager is consulted to determine how all of the components in the container should appear in the resized container. Every time a component is added to a container, the layout manager determines how the addition affects all of the existing components.

> **Key Concept**
>
> When changes occur, the components in a container reorganize themselves according to the layout manager's policy.

The table in Figure 6.6 describes several of the predefined layout managers provided by the Java standard class library.

Every layout manager has its own particular properties and rules governing the layout of components. For some layout managers, the order in which you add the components affects their positioning, whereas others provide more specific control. Some layout managers take a component's preferred size or alignment into account, whereas others don't. To develop good GUIs in Java, it is important to become familiar with features and characteristics of various layout managers.

We can use the `setLayout` method of a container to change its layout manager. We've done this a few times in previous examples. For example, the following code sets the layout manager of a `JPanel`, which has a flow layout by default, so that it uses a border layout instead:

```
JPanel panel = new JPanel();
panel.setLayout (new BorderLayout());
```

> **Key Concept**
>
> The layout manager for each container can be explicitly set.

Let's explore some of these layout managers in more detail. We'll focus on the most popular layout managers at this point: flow, border, box, and grid. The class presented in Listing 6.18 contains the `main` method of an application that demonstrates the use and effects of these layout managers.

The `LayoutDemo` program introduces the use of a *tabbed pane*, a container that allows the user to select (by clicking on a tab) which of several panes is currently visible. A tabbed pane is defined by the `JTabbedPane` class. The `addTab` method creates a tab, specifying the name that appears on the tab and the component to be displayed on that pane when it achieves focus by being "brought to the front" and made visible to the user.

Layout Manager	Description
Border Layout	Organizes components into five areas (North, South, East, West and Center).
Box Layout	Organizes components into a single row or column.
Card Layout	Organizes components into one area such that only one is visible at any time.
Flow Layout	Organizes components from left to right, starting new rows as necessary.
Grid Layout	Organizes components into a grid of rows and columns.
GridBag Layout	Organizes components into a grid of cells, allowing components to span more than one cell.

FIGURE 6.6 Some predefined Java layout managers

Listing 6.18

```java
//********************************************************************
//  LayoutDemo.java        Author: Lewis/Loftus
//
//  Demonstrates the use of flow, border, grid, and box layouts.
//********************************************************************

import javax.swing.*;

public class LayoutDemo
{
   //-----------------------------------------------------------------
   //  Sets up a frame containing a tabbed pane. The panel on each
   //  tab demonstrates a different layout manager.
   //-----------------------------------------------------------------
   public static void main (String[] args)
   {
      JFrame frame = new JFrame ("Layout Manager Demo");
      frame.setDefaultCloseOperation (JFrame.EXIT_ON_CLOSE);

      JTabbedPane tp = new JTabbedPane();
      tp.addTab ("Intro", new IntroPanel());
      tp.addTab ("Flow", new FlowPanel());
      tp.addTab ("Border", new BorderPanel());
      tp.addTab ("Grid", new GridPanel());
      tp.addTab ("Box", new BoxPanel());

      frame.getContentPane().add(tp);
      frame.pack();
      frame.setVisible(true);
   }
}
```

Interestingly, there is an overlap in the functionality provided by tabbed panes and the card layout manager. Similar to the tabbed pane, a card layout allows several layers to be defined, and only one of those layers is displayed at any given point. However, a container managed by a card layout can be adjusted only under program control, whereas tabbed panes allow the user to indicate directly which tab should be displayed.

In this example, each tab of the tabbed pane contains a panel that is controlled by a different layout manager. The first tab simply contains a panel with an introductory message, as shown in Listing 6.19. As we explore each layout manager in more detail, we examine the class that defines the corresponding panel of this program and discuss its visual effect.

Listing 6.19

```
//********************************************************************
//  IntroPanel.java          Author: Lewis/Loftus
//
//  Represents the introduction panel for the LayoutDemo program.
//********************************************************************

import java.awt.*;
import javax.swing.*;

public class IntroPanel extends JPanel
{
    //-----------------------------------------------------------------
    //  Sets up this panel with two labels.
    //-----------------------------------------------------------------
    public IntroPanel()
    {
        setBackground (Color.green);

        JLabel l1 = new JLabel ("Layout Manager Demonstration");
        JLabel l2 = new JLabel ("Choose a tab to see an example of " +
                                "a layout manager.");

        add (l1);
        add (l2);
    }
}
```

Display

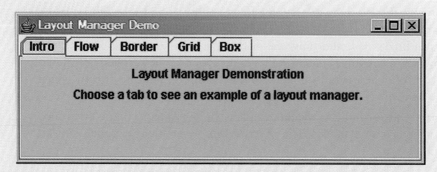

Flow Layout

Flow layout is one of the easiest layout managers to use. The `JPanel` class uses flow layout by default. Flow layout puts as many components as possible on a row, at their preferred size. When a component cannot fit on a row, it is put on the next row. As many rows as needed are added to fit all components that have been added to the container. Figure 6.7 depicts a container governed by a flow layout manager.

The class in Listing 6.20 represents the panel that demonstrates the flow layout in the `LayoutDemo` program. It explicitly sets the layout to be a flow layout (though in this case that is unnecessary because `JPanel` defaults to flow layout). The buttons are then created and added to the panel.

The size of each button is made large enough to accommodate the size of the label that is put on it. As we mentioned earlier, flow layout puts as many of these buttons as possible on one row within the panel, and then starts putting components on another row. When the size of the frame is widened (by dragging the lower-right corner with the mouse, for example), the panel grows as well, and more buttons can fit on a row. When the frame is resized, the layout manager is consulted and the components are reorganized automatically. Note that on each row the components are centered within the window by default.

The constructor of the `FlowLayout` class is overloaded to allow the programmer to tailor the characteristics of the layout manager. Within each row, components are either centered, left aligned, or right aligned. The alignment defaults to centered. The horizontal and vertical gap size between components also can be specified when the layout manager is created. The `FlowLayout` class also has methods to set the alignment and gap sizes after the layout manager is created.

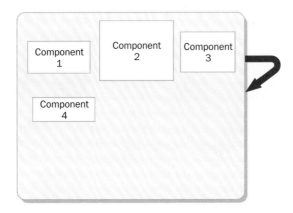

FIGURE 6.7   Flow layout puts as many components as possible on a row

Listing 6.20

```java
//********************************************************************
//  FlowPanel.java        Author: Lewis/Loftus
//
//  Represents the panel in the LayoutDemo program that demonstrates
//  the flow layout manager.
//********************************************************************

import java.awt.*;
import javax.swing.*;

public class FlowPanel extends JPanel
{
   //-----------------------------------------------------------------
   //  Sets up this panel with some buttons to show how flow layout
   //  affects their position.
   //-----------------------------------------------------------------
   public FlowPanel ()
   {
      setLayout (new FlowLayout());

      setBackground (Color.green);

      JButton b1 = new JButton ("BUTTON 1");
      JButton b2 = new JButton ("BUTTON 2");
      JButton b3 = new JButton ("BUTTON 3");
      JButton b4 = new JButton ("BUTTON 4");
      JButton b5 = new JButton ("BUTTON 5");

      add (b1);
      add (b2);
      add (b3);
      add (b4);
      add (b5);
   }
}
```

Listing 6.20   continued

Display

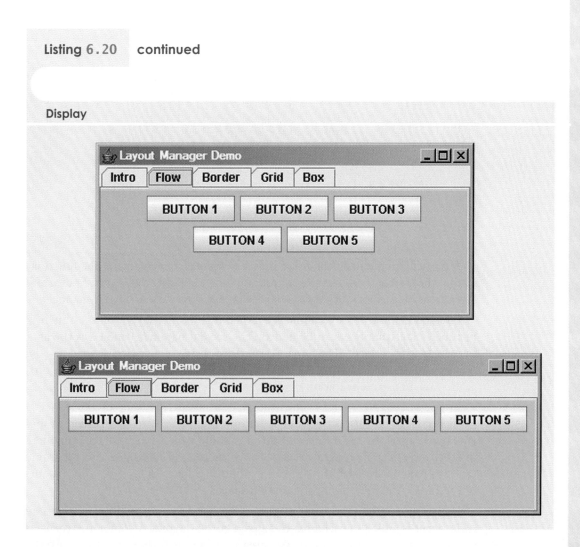

Border Layout

A *border layout* has five areas to which components can be added: North, South, East, West, and Center. The areas have a particular positional relationship to each other, as shown in Figure 6.8.

The four outer areas become as big as needed in order to accommodate the component they contain. If no components are added to the North, South, East, or West areas, these areas do not take up any room in the overall layout. The Center area expands to fill any available space.

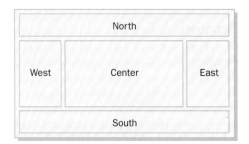

FIGURE 6.8 Border layout organizes components in five areas

A particular container might use only a few areas, depending on the functionality of the system. For example, a program might use only the Center, South, and West areas. This versatility makes border layout a very useful layout manager.

The add method for a container governed by a border layout takes as its first parameter the component to be added. The second parameter indicates the area to which it is added. The area is specified using constants defined in the BorderLayout class. Listing 6.21 shows the panel used by the LayoutDemo program to demonstrate the border layout.

In the BorderPanel class constructor, the layout manager of the panel is explicitly set to be border layout. The buttons are then created and added to specific panel areas. By default, each button is made wide enough to accommodate its label and tall enough to fill the area to which it has been assigned. As the frame (and the panel) is resized, the size of each button adjusts as needed, with the button in the Center area filling any unused space.

Each area in a border layout displays only one component. That is, only one component is added to each area of a given border layout. A common error is to add two components to a particular area of a border layout, in which case the first component added is replaced by the second, and only the second is seen when the container is displayed. To add multiple components to an area within a border layout, we first add the components to another container, such as a JPanel, then add the panel to the area.

Note that although the panel used to display the buttons has a green background, no green is visible in the display for Listing 6.21. By default there are no horizontal or vertical gaps between the areas of a border layout. These gaps can be set with an overloaded constructor or with explicit methods of the BorderLayout class. If the gaps are increased, the underlying panel will show through.

Listing 6.21

```
//********************************************************************
//   BorderPanel.java        Author: Lewis/Loftus
//
//   Represents the panel in the LayoutDemo program that demonstrates
//   the border layout manager.
//********************************************************************

import java.awt.*;
import javax.swing.*;

public class BorderPanel extends JPanel
{
    //-----------------------------------------------------------------
    //  Sets up this panel with a button in each area of a border
    //  layout to show how it affects their position, shape, and size.
    //-----------------------------------------------------------------
    public BorderPanel()
    {
        setLayout (new BorderLayout());

        setBackground (Color.green);

        JButton b1 = new JButton ("BUTTON 1");
        JButton b2 = new JButton ("BUTTON 2");
        JButton b3 = new JButton ("BUTTON 3");
        JButton b4 = new JButton ("BUTTON 4");
        JButton b5 = new JButton ("BUTTON 5");

        add (b1, BorderLayout.CENTER);
        add (b2, BorderLayout.NORTH);
        add (b3, BorderLayout.SOUTH);
        add (b4, BorderLayout.EAST);
        add (b5, BorderLayout.WEST);
    }
}
```

Listing 6.21   continued

Display

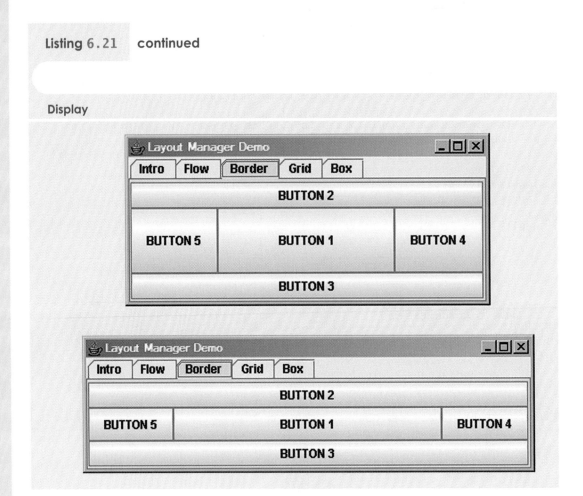

Grid Layout

A *grid layout* presents a container's components in a rectangular grid of rows and columns. One component is placed in each grid cell, and all cells are the same size. Figure 6.9 shows the general organization of a grid layout.

The number of rows and columns in a grid layout is established using parameters to the constructor when the layout manager is created. The class in Listing 6.22 shows the panel used by the LayoutDemo program to demonstrate a grid layout. It specifies that the panel should be managed using a grid of two rows and three columns.

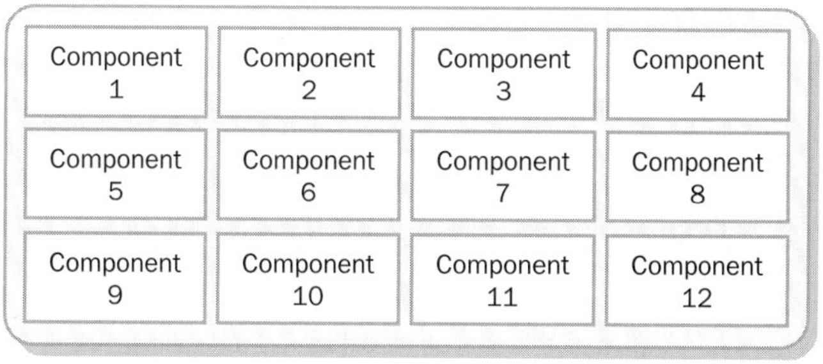

FIGURE 6.9   Grid layout creates a rectangular grid of equal-sized cells

As buttons are added to the container, they fill the grid (by default) from left to right and top to bottom. There is no way to explicitly assign a component to a particular location in the grid other than the order in which they are added to the container.

The size of each cell is determined by the container's overall size. When the container is resized, all of the cells change size proportionally to fill the container.

If the value used to specify either the number of rows or the number of columns is zero, the grid expands as needed in that dimension to accommodate the number of components added to the container. The values for the number of rows and columns cannot both be zero.

By default, there are no horizontal and vertical gaps between the grid cells. The gap sizes can be specified using an overloaded constructor or with the appropriate `GridLayout` methods.

Box Layout

A *box layout* organizes components either vertically or horizontally, in one row or one column, as shown in Figure 6.10. It is easy to use, yet when combined with other box layouts, it can produce complex GUI designs similar to those that can be accomplished with a `GridBagLayout`, which in general is far more difficult to master.

Listing 6.22

```java
//************************************************************************
//  GridPanel.java        Author: Lewis/Loftus
//
//  Represents the panel in the LayoutDemo program that demonstrates
//  the grid layout manager.
//************************************************************************

import java.awt.*;
import javax.swing.*;

public class GridPanel extends JPanel
{
    //---------------------------------------------------------------
    //  Sets up this panel with some buttons to show how grid
    //  layout affects their position, shape, and size.
    //---------------------------------------------------------------
    public GridPanel()
    {
        setLayout (new GridLayout (2, 3));

        setBackground (Color.green);

        JButton b1 = new JButton ("BUTTON 1");
        JButton b2 = new JButton ("BUTTON 2");
        JButton b3 = new JButton ("BUTTON 3");
        JButton b4 = new JButton ("BUTTON 4");
        JButton b5 = new JButton ("BUTTON 5");

        add (b1);
        add (b2);
        add (b3);
        add (b4);
        add (b5);
    }
}
```

Listing 6.22   continued

Display

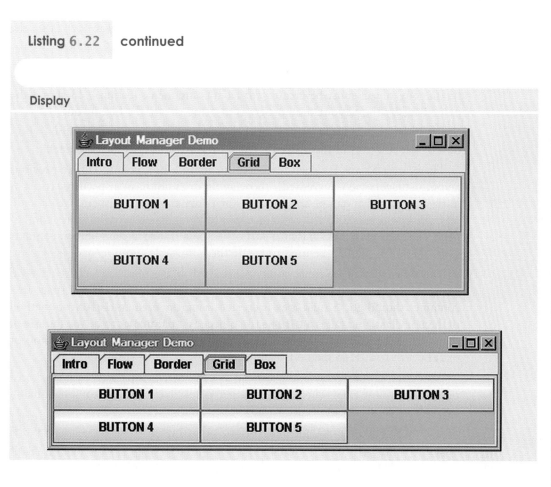

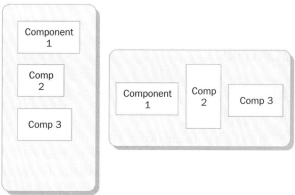

FIGURE 6.10   Box layout organizes components either vertically or horizontally

When a `BoxLayout` object is created, we specify that it will follow either the X axis (horizontal) or the Y axis (vertical), using constants defined in the `BoxLayout` class. Unlike other layout managers, the constructor of a `BoxLayout` takes as its first parameter the component that it will govern. Therefore a new `BoxLayout` object must be created for each component. Listing 6.23 shows the panel used by the `LayoutDemo` program to demonstrate the box layout.

Components in containers governed by a box layout are organized (top to bottom or left to right) in the order in which they are added to the container.

There are no gaps between the components in a box layout. Unlike previous layout managers we've explored, a box layout does not have a specific vertical or horizontal gap that can be specified for the entire container. Instead, we can add *invisible components* to the container that take up space between other components. The `Box` class, which is also part of the Java standard class library, contains static methods that can be used to create these invisible components.

The two types of invisible components used in the `BoxPanel` class are *rigid areas,* which have a fixed size, and *glue,* which specifies where excess space in a container should go. A rigid area is created using the `createRigidArea` method of the `Box` class, and takes a `Dimension` object as a parameter to define the size of the invisible area. Glue is created using the `createHorizontalGlue` method or `createVerticalGlue` method, as appropriate.

Note that in our example, the space between buttons separated by a rigid area remains constant even when the container is resized. Glue, on the other hand, expands or contracts as needed to fill the space.

A box layout—more than most of the other layout managers—respects the alignments and the minimum, maximum, and preferred sizes of the components it governs. Therefore, setting the characteristics of the components that go into the container is another way to tailor the visual effect.

6.12 BORDERS

Java provides the ability to put a *border* around any Swing component. A border is not a component itself but rather defines how the edge of any component should be drawn and has an important effect on the design of a GUI. A border provides visual cues as to how GUI components are organized, and can be used to give titles to components. Figure 6.11 lists the predefined borders in the Java standard class library.

Listing 6.23

```
//********************************************************************
//  BoxPanel.java        Author: Lewis/Loftus
//
//  Represents the panel in the LayoutDemo program that demonstrates
//  the box layout manager.
//********************************************************************

import java.awt.*;
import javax.swing.*;

public class BoxPanel extends JPanel
{
    //-----------------------------------------------------------------
    //  Sets up this panel with some buttons to show how a vertical
    //  box layout (and invisible components) affects their position.
    //-----------------------------------------------------------------
    public BoxPanel()
    {
        setLayout (new BoxLayout (this, BoxLayout.Y_AXIS));

        setBackground (Color.green);

        JButton b1 = new JButton ("BUTTON 1");
        JButton b2 = new JButton ("BUTTON 2");
        JButton b3 = new JButton ("BUTTON 3");
        JButton b4 = new JButton ("BUTTON 4");
        JButton b5 = new JButton ("BUTTON 5");

        add (b1);
        add (Box.createRigidArea (new Dimension (0, 10)));
        add (b2);
        add (Box.createVerticalGlue());
        add (b3);
        add (b4);
        add (Box.createRigidArea (new Dimension (0, 20)));
        add (b5);
    }
}
```

Listing 6.23   **continued**

Display

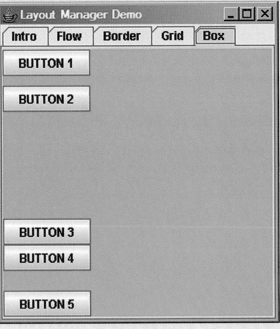

Border	Description
Empty Border	Puts buffering space around the edge of a component, but otherwise has no visual effect.
Line Border	A simple line surrounding the component.
Etched Border	Creates the effect of an etched groove around a component.
Bevel Border	Creates the effect of a component raised above the surface or sunken below it.
Titled Border	Includes a text title on or around the border.
Matte Border	Allows the size of each edge to be specified. Uses either a soild color or an image.
Compound Border	A combination of two borders.

FIGURE 6.11 Component borders

The `BorderFactory` class is useful for creating borders for components. It has many methods for creating specific types of borders. A border is applied to a component by using the component's `setBorder` method.

The program in Listing 6.24 demonstrates several types of borders. It simply creates several panels, sets a different border for each, and then displays them in a larger panel by using a grid layout.

Let's look at each type of border created in this program. An *empty border* is applied to the larger panel that holds all the others, to create a buffer of space around the outer edge of the frame. The sizes of the top, left, bottom, and right edges of the empty border are specified in pixels. The *line border* is created using a particular color and specifies the line thickness in pixels (3 in this case). The line thickness defaults to 1 pixel if left unspecified. The *etched border* created in this program uses default colors for the highlight and shadow of the etching, but both could be explicitly set if desired.

A *bevel border* can be either raised or lowered. The default coloring is used in this program, although the coloring of each aspect of the bevel can be tailored as desired, including the outer highlight, inner highlight, outer shadow, and inner shadow. Each of these aspects could be a different color if desired.

A *titled border* places a title on or around the border. The default position for the title is on the border at the top-left edge. Using the `setTitleJustification` method of the `TitledBorder` class, this position can be set to many other places above, below, on, or to the left, right, or center of the border.

Listing 6.24

```java
//********************************************************************
//  BorderDemo.java       Author: Lewis/Loftus
//
//  Demonstrates the use of various types of borders.
//********************************************************************

import java.awt.*;
import javax.swing.*;
import javax.swing.border.*;

public class BorderDemo
{
   //-----------------------------------------------------------------
   //  Creates several bordered panels and displays them.
   //-----------------------------------------------------------------
   public static void main (String[] args)
   {
      JFrame frame = new JFrame ("Border Demo");
      frame.setDefaultCloseOperation (JFrame.EXIT_ON_CLOSE);

      JPanel panel = new JPanel();
      panel.setLayout (new GridLayout (0, 2, 5, 10));
      panel.setBorder (BorderFactory.createEmptyBorder (8, 8, 8, 8));

      JPanel p1 = new JPanel();
      p1.setBorder (BorderFactory.createLineBorder (Color.red, 3));
      p1.add (new JLabel ("Line Border"));
      panel.add (p1);

      JPanel p2 = new JPanel();
      p2.setBorder (BorderFactory.createEtchedBorder ());
      p2.add (new JLabel ("Etched Border"));
      panel.add (p2);

      JPanel p3 = new JPanel();
      p3.setBorder (BorderFactory.createRaisedBevelBorder ());
      p3.add (new JLabel ("Raised Bevel Border"));
      panel.add (p3);

      JPanel p4 = new JPanel();
      p4.setBorder (BorderFactory.createLoweredBevelBorder ());
      p4.add (new JLabel ("Lowered Bevel Border"));
      panel.add (p4);
```

Listing 6.24   **continued**

```java
      JPanel p5 = new JPanel();
      p5.setBorder (BorderFactory.createTitledBorder ("Title"));
      p5.add (new JLabel ("Titled Border"));
      panel.add (p5);

      JPanel p6 = new JPanel();
      TitledBorder tb = BorderFactory.createTitledBorder ("Title");
      tb.setTitleJustification (TitledBorder.RIGHT);
      p6.setBorder (tb);
      p6.add (new JLabel ("Titled Border (right)"));
      panel.add (p6);

      JPanel p7 = new JPanel();
      Border b1 = BorderFactory.createLineBorder (Color.blue, 2);
      Border b2 = BorderFactory.createEtchedBorder ();
      p7.setBorder (BorderFactory.createCompoundBorder (b1, b2));
      p7.add (new JLabel ("Compound Border"));
      panel.add (p7);

      JPanel p8 = new JPanel();
      Border mb = BorderFactory.createMatteBorder (1, 5, 1, 1,
                                            Color.red);
      p8.setBorder (mb);
      p8.add (new JLabel ("Matte Border"));
      panel.add (p8);

      frame.getContentPane().add (panel);
      frame.pack();
      frame.setVisible(true);
   }
}
```

Listing 6.24 continued

Display

A *compound border* is a combination of two or more borders. The example in this program creates a compound border using a line border and an etched border. The `createCompoundBorder` method accepts two borders as parameters and makes the first parameter the outer border and the second parameter the inner border. Combinations of three or more borders are created by first creating a compound border using two borders, then making another compound border using it and yet another one.

A *matte border* specifies the sizes, in pixels, of the top, left, bottom, and right edges of the border. Those edges can be composed of a single color, as they are in this example, or an image icon can be used.

Borders should be used carefully. They can be helpful in drawing attention to appropriate parts of your GUI and can conceptually group related items together. However, if used inappropriately, they can also detract from the elegance of the presentation. Borders should enhance the interface, not complicate or compete with it.

6.13 CONTAINMENT HIERARCHIES

The way components are grouped into containers, and the way those containers are nested within each other, establishes the *containment hierarchy* for a GUI. We introduced this concept in Chapter 3. By carefully designing the containment hierarchy, a GUI can be tailored to have a precise visual effect.

For any Java program, there is generally one primary container, called a *top-level container,* such as a frame or applet. The top-level container of a program often contains one or more other containers, such as panels. These panels may contain other panels to organize the other components as desired.

Each container can have its own layout manager. The final appearance of a GUI is a function of the layout managers chosen for each of the containers and the design of the containment hierarchy. Many combinations are possible, and there is rarely a single best option. As always, we should be guided by the desired system goals and general GUI design guidelines.

> **Key Concept**
>
> A GUI's appearance is a function of the containment hierarchy and the layout managers of each container.

Figure 6.12 shows a GUI application that has been annotated to describe its containment hierarchy. Several components used in this program have been discussed previously in this text; others are discussed in later chapters.

Note that in many cases, the use of some containers is not obvious just by looking at the GUI. A panel, in particular, is invisible unless we draw attention to it in some way, such as by giving it a border. We can also use invisible components to provide specific spacing between components. These elements are all part of the containment hierarchy, even though they are not visible to the user.

A particular program's containment hierarchy can be represented as a tree structure, such as the one shown in Figure 6.13. The root of the tree is the top-level container. Each level of the tree shows the containers and components held in the containers of the level above.

When changes are made that might affect the visual layout of the components in a program, the layout managers of each container are consulted in turn. The changes in one may affect another. These changes ripple through the containment hierarchy as needed.

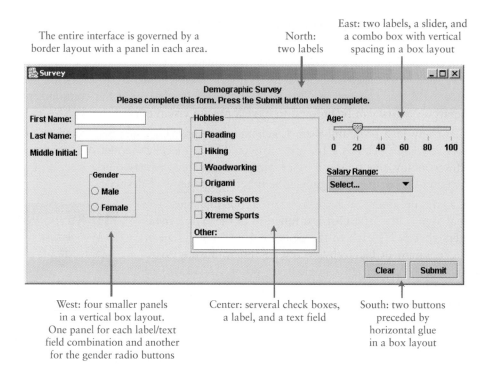

The entire interface is governed by a border layout with a panel in each area.

North: two labels

East: two labels, a slider, and a combo box with vertical spacing in a box layout

West: four smaller panels in a vertical box layout. One panel for each label/text field combination and another for the gender radio buttons

Center: serveral check boxes, a label, and a text field

South: two buttons preceded by horizontal glue in a box layout

FIGURE 6.12 The containment hierarchy of a GUI

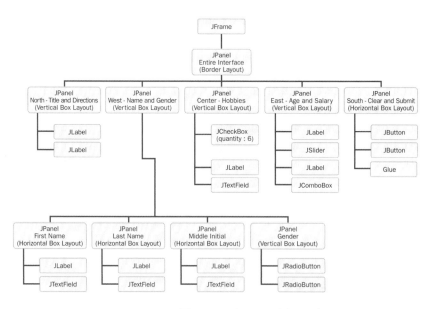

FIGURE 6.13 The containment hierarchy tree

Summary of Key Concepts

> The effort put into design is both crucial and cost-effective.

> The nouns in a problem description may indicate some of the classes and objects needed in a program.

> A static variable is shared among all instances of a class.

> An aggregate object is composed of other objects, forming a has-a relationship.

> An interface is a collection of abstract methods and therefore cannot be instantiated.

> The values of an enumerated type are static variables of that type.

> We can add attributes and methods to the definition of an enumerated type.

> A complex service provided by an object can be decomposed to make use of private support methods.

> When an object is passed to a method, the actual and formal parameters become aliases.

> The versions of an overloaded method are distinguished by the number, type, and order of their parameters.

> Testing a program can never guarantee the absence of errors.

> A good test is one that uncovers an error.

> It is not feasible to exhaustively test a program for all possible input and user actions.

> The design of any GUI should adhere to basic guidelines regarding consistency and usability.

> The layout manager of a container determines how components are visually presented.

> When changes occur, the components in a container reorganize themselves according to the layout manager's policy.

> The layout manager for each container can be explicitly set.

> Borders can be applied to Swing components to group objects and focus attention.

> A GUI's appearance is a function of the containment hierarchy and the layout managers of each container.

Self-Review Questions

SR 6.1   Name the four basic activities that are involved in a software development process.

SR 6.2   What is the difference between a static variable and an instance variable?

SR 6.3   What kinds of variables can the `main` method of any program reference? Why?

SR 6.4   Describe a dependency relationship between two classes.

SR 6.5   How are overloaded methods distinguished from each other?

SR 6.6   What is method decomposition?

SR 6.7   Explain how a class can have an association with itself.

SR 6.8   What is an aggregate object?

SR 6.9   What does the `this` reference refer to?

SR 6.10   How are objects passed as parameters?

SR 6.11   What is the difference between a class and an interface?

SR 6.12   What general guidelines for GUI design are presented in this chapter?

SR 6.13   When is a layout manager consulted?

SR 6.14   How does the flow layout manager behave?

SR 6.15   Describe the areas of a border layout.

SR 6.16   What effect does a glue component in a box layout have?

SR 6.17   What is the role of the `BorderFactory` class?

SR 6.18   What is the containment hierarchy for a GUI?

Exercises

EX 6.1   Write a method called `average` that accepts two integer parameters and returns their average as a floating point value.

EX 6.2   Overload the `average` method of Exercise 6.1 such that if three integers are provided as parameters, the method returns the average of all three.

EX 6.3   Overload the `average` method of Exercise 6.1 to accept four integer parameters and return their average.

EX 6.4   Write a method called `multiConcat` that takes a `String` and an integer as parameters. Return a `String` that consists of the string parameter concatenated with itself `count` times, where `count` is the integer parameter. For example, if the parameter values are `"hi"` and 4, the return value is `"hihihihi"`. Return the original string if the integer parameter is less than 2.

EX 6.5   Overload the `multiConcat` method from Exercise 6.4 such that if the integer parameter is not provided, the method returns the string concatenated with itself. For example, if the parameter is `"test"`, the return value is `"testtest"`.

EX 6.6   Write a method called `drawCircle` that draws a circle based on the method's parameters: a `Graphics` object through which to draw the circle, two integer values representing the (x, y) coordinates of the center of the circle, another integer that represents the circle's radius, and a `Color` object that defines the circle's color. The method does not return anything.

EX 6.7   Overload the `drawCircle` method of Exercise 6.6 such that if the `Color` parameter is not provided, the circle's color will default to black.

EX 6.8   Overload the `drawCircle` method of Exercise 6.6 such that if the radius is not provided, a random radius in the range 10 to 100 (inclusive) will be used.

EX 6.9   Overload the `drawCircle` method of Exercise 6.6 such that if both the color and the radius of the circle are not provided, the color will default to red and the radius will default to 40.

EX 6.10   Discuss the manner in which Java passes parameters to a method. Is this technique consistent between primitive types and objects? Explain.

EX 6.11   Explain why a static method cannot refer to an instance variable.

EX 6.12   Can a class implement two interfaces that each contains the same method signature? Explain.

EX 6.13   Create an interface called `Visible` that includes two methods: `makeVisible` and `makeInvisible`. Both methods should take no parameters and should return a `boolean` result. Describe how a class might implement this interface.

EX 6.14   Draw a UML class diagram that shows the relationships among the elements of Exercise 6.13.

EX 6.15 Create an interface called VCR that has methods that represent the standard operations on a video cassette recorder (play, stop, etc.). Define the method signatures any way you desire. Describe how a class might implement this interface.

EX 6.16 Draw a UML class diagram that shows the relationships among the elements of Exercise 6.15.

EX 6.17 Draw the containment hierarchy tree for the LayoutDemo program.

EX 6.18 What visual effect would result by changing the horizontal and vertical gaps on the border layout used in the LayoutDemo program? Make the change to test your answer.

EX 6.19 Write the lines of code that will define a compound border using three borders. Use a line border on the inner edge, an etched border on the outer edge, and a raised bevel border in between.

Programming Projects

PP 6.1 Modify the Account class from Chapter 4 so that it also permits an account to be opened with just a name and an account number, assuming an initial balance of zero. Modify the main method of the Transactions class to demonstrate this new capability.

PP 6.2 Modify the Student class presented in this chapter as follows. Each student object should also contain the scores for three tests. Provide a constructor that sets all instance values based on parameter values. Overload the constructor such that each test score is assumed to be initially zero. Provide a method called setTestScore that accepts two parameters: the test number (1 through 3) and the score. Also provide a method called getTestScore that accepts the test number and returns the appropriate score. Provide a method called average that computes and returns the average test score for this student. Modify the toString method such that the test scores and average are included in the description of the student. Modify the driver class main method to exercise the new Student methods.

PP 6.3 Design and implement a class called Course that represents a course taken at a school. A course object should keep track of up to five students, as represented by the modified Student class from the previous programming project. The constructor of the

Course class should accept only the name of the course. Provide a method called addStudent that accepts one Student parameter (the Course object should keep track of how many valid students have been added to the course). Provide a method called average that computes and returns the average of all students' test score averages. Provide a method called roll that prints all students in the course. Create a driver class with a main method that creates a course, adds several students, prints a roll, and prints the overall course test average.

PP 6.4   Modify the RationalNumber class so that it implements the Comparable interface. To perform the comparison, compute an equivalent floating point value from the numerator and denominator for both Rational objects, then compare them using a tolerance value of 0.0001. Write a main driver to test your modifications.

PP 6.5   Design a Java interface called Priority that includes two methods: setPriority and getPriority. The interface should define a way to establish numeric priority among a set of objects. Design and implement a class called Task that represents a task (such as on a to-do list) that implements the Priority interface. Create a driver class to exercise some Task objects.

PP 6.6   Modify the Task class from Programming Project 6.5 so that it also implements the Complexity interface defined in this chapter. Modify the driver class to show these new features of Task objects.

PP 6.7   Modify the Task class from Programming Projects 6.5 and 6.6 so that it also implements the Comparable interface from the Java standard class library. Implement the interface such that the tasks are ranked by priority. Create a driver class whose main method shows these new features of Task objects.

PP 6.8   Design a Java interface called Lockable that includes the following methods: setKey, lock, unlock, and locked. The setKey, lock, and unlock methods take an integer parameter that represents the key. The setKey method establishes the key. The lock and unlock methods lock and unlock the object, but only if the key passed in is correct. The locked method returns a boolean that indicates whether or not the object is locked. A Lockable object represents an object whose regular methods are protected: if the object is locked, the methods cannot be

invoked; if it is unlocked, they can be invoked. Redesign and implement a version of the `Coin` class from Chapter 5 so that it is `Lockable`.

PP 6.9 Redesign and implement a version of the `Account` class from Chapter 4 so that it is `Lockable` as defined by Programming Project 6.8.

PP 6.10 Redesign and implement a version of the `PigLatin` program so that it uses a GUI. Accept the sentence using a text field and display the results using a label.

PP 6.11 Modify the `IntroPanel` class of the `LayoutDemo` program so that it uses a box layout manager. Use invisible components to put space before and between the two labels on the panel.

PP 6.12 Modify the `QuoteOptions` program from Chapter 5 to change its visual appearance. Present the radio buttons in a vertical column with a surrounding border to the left of the quote label.

PP 6.13 Design and implement a program that displays a numeric keypad that might appear on a phone. Above the keypad buttons, show a label that displays the numbers as they are picked. To the right of the keypad buttons, include another button to clear the display. Use a border layout to manage the overall presentation, and a grid layout to manage the keypad buttons. Put a border around the keypad buttons to group them visually, and a border around the display.

PP 6.14 Design and implement an application that helps a pizza restaurant take orders. Use a tabbed pane for different categories of food (pizza, beverages, special items). Collect information about quantity and size. Display the cost of the order as information is gathered. Use appropriate components for collecting the various kinds of information. Structure the interface carefully using the containment hierarchy and layout managers.

Answers to Self-Review Questions

SR 6.1 The four basic activities in software development are requirements analysis (deciding what the program should do), design (deciding how to do it), implementation (writing the solution in source code), and testing (validating the implementation).

SR 6.2   Memory space for an instance variable is created for each object that is instantiated from a class. A static variable is shared among all objects of a class.

SR 6.3   The main method of any program is static, and can refer only to static or local variables. Therefore, a main method could not refer to instance variables declared at the class level.

SR 6.4   A dependency relationship between two classes occurs when one class relies on the functionality of the other. It is often referred to as a "uses" relationship.

SR 6.5   Overloaded methods are distinguished by having a unique signature, which includes the number, order, and type of the parameters. The return type is not part of the signature.

SR 6.6   Method decomposition is the process of dividing a complex method into several support methods to get the job done. This simplifies and facilitates the design of the program.

SR 6.7   A method executed through an object might take as a parameter another object created from the same class. For example, the concat method of the String class is executed through one String object and takes another String object as a parameter.

SR 6.8   An aggregate object is an object that has other objects as instance data. That is, an aggregate object is one that is made up of other objects.

SR 6.9   The this reference always refers to the currently executing object. A non-static method of a class is written generically for all objects of the class, but it is invoked through a particular object. The this reference, therefore, refers to the object through which that method is currently being executed.

SR 6.10   Objects are passed to methods by copying the reference to the object (its address). Therefore the actual and formal parameters of a method become aliases of each other.

SR 6.11   A class can be instantiated; an interface cannot. An interface contains a set of abstract methods for which a class provides the implementation.

SR 6.12   The general guidelines for GUI design include: know the needs and characteristics of the user, prevent user errors when possible, optimize user abilities by providing shortcuts and other redundant means to accomplish a task, and be consistent in GUI layout and coloring schemes.

SR 6.13   A layout manager is consulted whenever the visual appearance of its components might be affected, such as when the container is resized or when a new component is added to the container.

SR 6.14   Flow layout attempts to put as many components on a row as possible. Multiple rows are created as needed.

SR 6.15   Border layout is divided into five areas: North, South, East, West, and Center. The North and South areas are at the top and bottom of the container, respectively, and span the entire width of the container. Sandwiched between them, from left to right, are the West, Center, and East areas. Any unused area takes up no space, and the others fill in as needed.

SR 6.16   A glue component in a box layout dictates where any extra space in the layout should go. It expands as necessary, but takes up no space if there is no extra space to distribute.

SR 6.17   The `BorderFactory` class contains several methods used to create borders that can be applied to components.

SR 6.18   The containment hierarchy for a GUI is the set of nested containers and the other components they contain. The containment hierarchy can be described as a tree.

Arrays 7

CHAPTER OBJECTIVES

> Define and use arrays for basic data organization.

> Discuss bounds checking and techniques for managing capacity.

> Discuss the issues related to arrays as objects and arrays of objects.

> Explore the use of command-line arguments.

> Describe the syntax and use of variable-length parameter lists.

> Discuss the creation and use of multidimensional arrays.

> Examine the `ArrayList` class and its generic parameter.

> Explore mouse and keyboard events.

In our programming efforts, we often want to organize objects or primitive data in a form that is easy to access and modify. This chapter introduces arrays, which are programming constructs that group data into lists. Arrays are a fundamental component of most high-level languages. We also explore the `ArrayList` class in the Java standard class library, which provides capabilities similar to arrays, with additional features. In the Graphics Track sections of this chapter, we explore methods that let us draw complex multisided figures, and examine the events generated by the mouse and the keyboard.

7.1   ARRAY ELEMENTS

An *array* is a simple but powerful programming language construct used to group and organize data. When writing a program that manages a large amount of information, such as a list of 100 names, it is not practical to declare separate variables for each piece of data. Arrays solve this problem by letting us declare one variable that can hold multiple, individually accessible values.

An array is a list of values. Each value is stored at a specific, numbered position in the array. The number corresponding to each position is called an *index* or a *subscript*. Figure 7.1 shows an array of integers and the indexes that correspond to each position. The array is called `height`; it contains integers that represent several peoples' heights in inches.

In Java, array indexes always begin at zero. Therefore the value stored at index 5 is actually the sixth value in the array. The array shown in Figure 7.1 has 11 values, indexed from 0 to 10.

> **Key Concept**
>
> An array of size *N* is indexed from 0 to *N*–1.

To access a value in an array, we use the name of the array followed by the index in square brackets. For example, the following expression refers to the ninth value in the array `height`:

```
height[8]
```

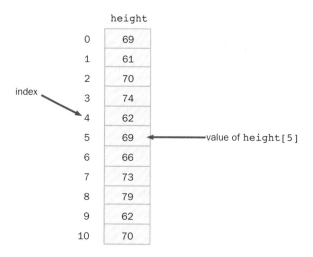

FIGURE 7.1   An array called `height` containing integer values

According to Figure 7.1, `height[8]` (pronounced height-sub-eight) contains the value 79. Don't confuse the value of the index, in this case 8, with the value stored in the array at that index, in this case 79.

The expression `height[8]` refers to a single integer stored at a particular memory location. It can be used wherever an integer variable can be used. Therefore you can assign a value to it, use it in calculations, print its value, and so on. Furthermore, because array indexes are integers, you can use integer expressions to specify the index used to access an array. These concepts are demonstrated in the following lines of code:

```
height[2] = 72;
height[count] = feet * 12;
average = (height[0] + height[1] + height[2]) / 3;
System.out.println ("The middle value is " + height[MAX/2]);
pick = height[rand.nextInt(11)];
```

7.2   DECLARING AND USING ARRAYS

In Java, arrays are objects. To create an array, the reference to the array must be declared. The array can then be instantiated using the `new` operator, which allocates memory space to store values. The following code represents the declaration for the array shown in Figure 7.1:

> **Key Concept**
>
> In Java, an array is an object that must be instantiated.

```
int[] height = new int[11];
```

The variable `height` is declared to be an array of integers whose type is written as `int[]`. All values stored in an array have the same type (or are at least compatible). For example, we can create an array that can hold integers or an array that can hold strings, but not an array that can hold both integers and strings. An array can be set up to hold any primitive type or any object (class) type. A value stored in an array is sometimes called an *array element*, and the type of values that an array holds is called the *element type* of the array.

Note that the type of the array variable (`int[]`) does not include the size of the array. The instantiation of `height`, using the `new` operator, reserves the memory space to store 11 integers indexed from 0 to 10. Once an array is declared to be a certain size, the number of values it can hold cannot be changed.

The example shown in Listing 7.1 creates an array called `list` that can hold 15 integers, which it loads with successive increments of 10. It then changes the value of the sixth element in the array (at index 5). Finally, it prints all values stored in the array.

Listing 7.1

```java
//********************************************************************
//  BasicArray.java        Author: Lewis/Loftus
//
//  Demonstrates basic array declaration and use.
//********************************************************************

public class BasicArray
{
   //-----------------------------------------------------------------
   //  Creates an array, fills it with various integer values,
   //  modifies one value, then prints them out.
   //-----------------------------------------------------------------
   public static void main (String[] args)
   {
      final int LIMIT = 15, MULTIPLE = 10;

      int[] list = new int[LIMIT];

      //  Initialize the array values
      for (int index = 0; index < LIMIT; index++)
         list[index] = index * MULTIPLE;

      list[5] = 999;   // change one array value

      //  Print the array values
      for (int value : list)
         System.out.print (value + "   ");
   }
}
```

Output

```
0   10   20   30   40   999   60   70   80   90   100   110   120   130   140
```

Figure 7.2 shows the array as it changes during the execution of the BasicArray program. It is often convenient to use for loops when handling arrays because the number of positions in the array is constant. Note that a constant called LIMIT is used in several places in the BasicArray program. This constant is used to declare the size of the array and to control the for loop that initializes the array values

The iterator version of the for loop is used to print the values in the array. Recall from Chapter 5 that this version of the for loop extracts each value in the

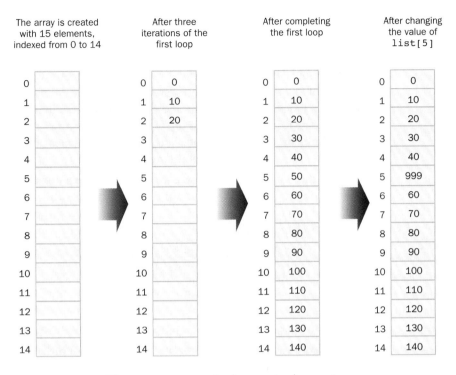

The array is created with 15 elements, indexed from 0 to 14	After three iterations of the first loop	After completing the first loop	After changing the value of `list[5]`

FIGURE 7.2   The array `list` as it changes in the `BasicArray` program

specified iterator. Every Java array is an iterator, so this type of loop can be used whenever we want to process every element stored in an array.

The square brackets used to indicate the index of an array are treated as an operator in Java. Therefore, just like the + operator or the <= operator, the index operator ([ ]) has a precedence relative to the other Java operators that determines when it is executed. It has the highest precedence of all Java operators.

Bounds Checking

The index operator performs automatic *bounds checking*, which ensures that the index is in range for the array being referenced. Whenever a reference to an array element is made, the index must be greater than or equal to zero and less than the size of the array. For example, suppose an array called `prices` is created with 25 elements. The valid indexes for the array are from 0 to 24. Whenever a reference is made to a particular element in the array (such as `prices[count]`), the value of the index is checked. If it is in the valid range of indexes for the array (0 to 24), the reference is carried out. If the index is not valid, an exception called `ArrayIndexOutOfBoundsException` is thrown.

Of course, in our programs we'll want to perform our own bounds checking. That is, we'll want to be careful to remain within the bounds of the array and process every element we intend to. Because array indexes begin at zero and go up to one less than the size of the array, it is easy to create *off-by-one errors* in a program, which are problems created by processing all but one element or by attempting to index one element too many.

One way to check for the bounds of an array is to use the `length` constant, which is held in the array object and stores the size of the array. It is a public constant and therefore can be referenced directly. For example, after the array `prices` is created with 25 elements, the constant `prices.length` contains the value 25. Its value is set once when the array is first created and cannot be changed. The `length` constant, which is an integral part of each array, can be used when the array size is needed without having to create a separate constant. Remember that the length of the array is the number of elements it can hold, thus the maximum index of an array is `length-1`.

Let's look at another example. The program shown in Listing 7.2 reads 10 integers into an array called `numbers`, and then prints them in reverse order.

Note that in the `ReverseOrder` program, the array `numbers` is declared to have 10 elements and therefore is indexed from 0 to 9. The index range is controlled in the `for` loops by using the `length` field of the array object. You should carefully set the initial value of loop control variables and the conditions that terminate loops to guarantee that all intended elements are processed and only valid indexes are used to reference an array element.

The `LetterCount` example, shown in Listing 7.3, uses two arrays and a `String` object. The array called `upper` is used to store the number of times each uppercase alphabetic letter is found in the string. The array called `lower` serves the same purpose for lowercase letters.

Because there are 26 letters in the English alphabet, both the `upper` and `lower` arrays are declared with 26 elements. Each element contains an integer that is initially zero by default. The `for` loop scans through the string one character at a time. The appropriate counter in the appropriate array is incremented for each character found in the string.

Both of the counter arrays are indexed from 0 to 25. We have to map each character to a counter. A logical way to do this is to use `upper[0]` to count the number of `'A'` characters found, `upper[1]` to count the number of `'B'` characters found, and so on. Likewise, `lower[0]` is used to count `'a'` characters,

Listing 7.2

```java
//********************************************************************
//  ReverseOrder.java       Author: Lewis/Loftus
//
//  Demonstrates array index processing.
//********************************************************************

import java.util.Scanner;

public class ReverseOrder
{
   //-----------------------------------------------------------------
   //  Reads a list of numbers from the user, storing them in an
   //  array, then prints them in the opposite order.
   //-----------------------------------------------------------------
   public static void main (String[] args)
   {
      Scanner scan = new Scanner (System.in);

      double[] numbers = new double[10];

      System.out.println ("The size of the array: " + numbers.length);

      for (int index = 0; index < numbers.length; index++)
      {
         System.out.print ("Enter number " + (index+1) + ": ");
         numbers[index] = scan.nextDouble();
      }

      System.out.println ("The numbers in reverse order:");

      for (int index = numbers.length-1; index >= 0; index--)
         System.out.print (numbers[index] + "  ");
   }
}
```

Listing 7.2   continued

Output

```
The size of the array: 10
Enter number 1: 18.36
Enter number 2: 48.9
Enter number 3: 53.5
Enter number 4: 29.06
Enter number 5: 72.404
Enter number 6: 34.8
Enter number 7: 63.41
Enter number 8: 45.55
Enter number 9: 69.0
Enter number 10: 99.18
The numbers in reverse order:
99.18   69.0   45.55   63.41   34.8   72.404   29.06   53.5   48.9   18.36
```

Listing 7.3

```java
//********************************************************************
//  LetterCount.java       Author: Lewis/Loftus
//
//  Demonstrates the relationship between arrays and strings.
//********************************************************************

import java.util.Scanner;

public class LetterCount
{
    //-----------------------------------------------------------------
    //  Reads a sentence from the user and counts the number of
    //  uppercase and lowercase letters contained in it.
    //-----------------------------------------------------------------
    public static void main (String[] args)
    {
        final int NUMCHARS = 26;

        Scanner scan = new Scanner (System.in);
```

Listing 7.3   **continued**

```java
        int[] upper = new int[NUMCHARS];
        int[] lower = new int[NUMCHARS];

        char current;   // the current character being processed
        int other = 0;  // counter for non-alphabetics

        System.out.println ("Enter a sentence:");
        String line = scan.nextLine();

        //  Count the number of each letter occurence
        for (int ch = 0; ch < line.length(); ch++)
        {
           current = line.charAt(ch);
           if (current >= 'A' && current <= 'Z')
              upper[current-'A']++;
           else
              if (current >= 'a' && current <= 'z')
                 lower[current-'a']++;
              else
                 other++;
        }

        //  Print the results
        System.out.println ();
        for (int letter=0; letter < upper.length; letter++)
        {
           System.out.print ( (char) (letter + 'A') );
           System.out.print (": " + upper[letter]);
           System.out.print ("\t\t" + (char) (letter + 'a') );
           System.out.println (": " + lower[letter]);
        }

        System.out.println ();
        System.out.println ("Non-alphabetic characters: " + other);
    }
}
```

Listing 7.3 **continued**

Output

```
Enter a sentence:
In Casablanca, Humphrey Bogart never says "Play it again, Sam."

A: 0          a: 10
B: 1          b: 1
C: 1          c: 1
D: 0          d: 0
E: 0          e: 3
F: 0          f: 0
G: 0          g: 2
H: 1          h: 1
I: 1          i: 2
J: 0          j: 0
K: 0          k: 0
L: 0          l: 2
M: 0          m: 2
N: 0          n: 4
O: 0          o: 1
P: 1          p: 1
Q: 0          q: 0
R: 0          r: 3
S: 1          s: 3
T: 0          t: 2
U: 0          u: 1
V: 0          v: 1
W: 0          w: 0
X: 0          x: 0
Y: 0          y: 3
Z: 0          z: 0

Non-alphabetic characters: 14
```

lower[1] is used to count 'b' characters, and so on. A separate variable called other is used to count any nonalphabetic characters that are encountered.

Note that to determine if a character is an uppercase letter we used the boolean expression (current >= 'A' && current <= 'Z'). A similar expression is used for determining the lowercase letters. We could have used the static methods isUpperCase and isLowerCase in the Character class to make these determinations, but didn't in this example to drive home the point that because characters are based on the Unicode character set, they have a specific numeric value and order that we can use in our programming.

We use the current character to calculate which index in the array to reference. We have to be careful when calculating an index to ensure that it remains within the bounds of the array and matches to the correct element. Remember that in the Unicode character set the uppercase and lowercase alphabetic letters are continuous and in order (see Appendix C). Therefore, taking the numeric value of an uppercase letter such as 'E' (which is 69) and subtracting the numeric value of the character 'A' (which is 65) yields 4, which is the correct index for the counter of the character 'E'. Note that nowhere in the program do we actually need to know the specific numeric values for each letter.

Alternate Array Syntax

Syntactically, there are two ways to declare an array reference in Java. The first technique, which is used in the previous examples and throughout this text, is to associate the brackets with the type of values stored in the array. The second technique is to associate the brackets with the name of the array. Therefore the following two declarations are equivalent:

```
int[] grades;
int grades[];
```

Although there is no difference between these declaration techniques as far as the compiler is concerned, the first is consistent with other types of declarations. The declared type is explicit if the array brackets are associated with the element type, especially if there are multiple variables declared on the same line. Therefore we associate the brackets with the element type throughout this text.

Initializer Lists

You can use an *initializer list* to instantiate an array and provide the initial values for the elements of the array. It is essentially the same idea as initializing a variable of a primitive data type in its declaration except that an array requires several values.

The items in an initializer list are separated by commas and delimited by braces ({}). When an initializer list is used, the new operator is not used. The size of the array is determined by the number of items in the initializer list. For example, the following declaration instantiates the array `scores` as an array of eight integers, indexed from 0 to 7 with the specified initial values:

```
int[] scores = {87, 98, 69, 87, 65, 76, 99, 83};
```

An initializer list can be used only when an array is first declared.

> **Key Concept**
>
> An initializer list can be used to instantiate an array object instead of using the `new` operator.

The type of each value in an initializer list must match the type of the array elements. Let's look at another example:

```
char[] vowels = {'A', 'E', 'I', 'O', 'U'};
```

In this case, the variable `vowels` is declared to be an array of five characters, and the initializer list contains character literals.

The program shown in Listing 7.4 demonstrates the use of an initializer list to instantiate an array.

Arrays as Parameters

> **Key Concept**
>
> An entire array can be passed as a parameter, making the formal parameter an alias of the original.

An entire array can be passed as a parameter to a method. Because an array is an object, when an entire array is passed as a parameter, a copy of the reference to the original array is passed. We discussed this issue as it applies to all objects in Chapter 6.

A method that receives an array as a parameter can permanently change an element of the array because it is referring to the original element value. The method cannot permanently change the reference to the array itself because a copy of the original reference is sent to the method. These rules are consistent with the rules that govern any object type.

An element of an array can be passed to a method as well. If the element type is a primitive type, a copy of the value is passed. If that element is a reference to an object, a copy of the object reference is passed. As always, the impact of changes made to a parameter inside the method depends on the type of the parameter. We discuss arrays of objects further in the next section.

7.3   ARRAYS OF OBJECTS

In the previous examples in this chapter, we used arrays to store primitive types such as integers and characters. Arrays can also store references to objects as ele-

Listing 7.4

```
//********************************************************************
//   Primes.java        Author: Lewis/Loftus
//
//   Demonstrates the use of an initializer list for an array.
//********************************************************************

public class Primes
{
    //-----------------------------------------------------------------
    //  Stores some prime numbers in an array and prints them.
    //-----------------------------------------------------------------
    public static void main (String[] args)
    {
        int[] primeNums = {2, 3, 5, 7, 11, 13, 17, 19};

        System.out.println ("Array length: " + primeNums.length);

        System.out.println ("The first few prime numbers are:");

        for (int prime : primeNums)
            System.out.print (prime + "   ");
    }
}
```

Output

```
Array length: 8
The first few prime numbers are:
2   3   5   7   11   13   17   19
```

ments. Fairly complex information management structures can be created using only arrays and other objects. For example, an array could contain objects, and each of those objects could consist of several variables and the methods that use them. Those variables could themselves be arrays, and so on. The design of a program should capitalize on the ability to combine these constructs to create the most appropriate representation for the information.

Keep in mind that the array itself is an object. So it would be appropriate to picture an array of `int` values called `weight` as follows:

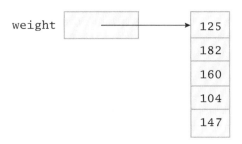

When we store objects in an array, each element is a separate object. That is, an array of objects is really an array of object references. Consider the following declaration:

```
String[] words = new String[5];
```

The variable `words` is an array of references to `String` objects. The `new` operator in the declaration instantiates the array and reserves space for five `String` references. This declaration does not create any `String` objects; it merely creates an array that holds references to `String` objects. Initially, the array looks like this:

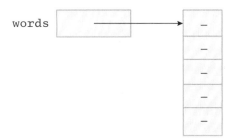

After a few `String` objects are created and put in the array, it might look like this:

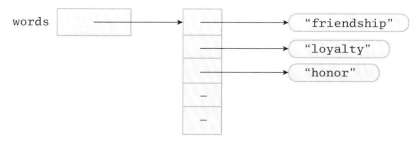

The `words` array is an object, and each character string it holds is its own object. Each object contained in an array has to be instantiated separately.

Keep in mind that `String` objects can be represented as string literals. So the following declaration creates an array called `verbs` and uses an initializer list to populate it with several `String` objects, each instantiated using a string literal:

```
String[] verbs = {"play", "work", "eat", "sleep"};
```

The program called `GradeRange` shown in Listing 7.5 creates an array of `Grade` objects, then prints them. The `Grade` objects are created using several `new` operators in the initialization list of the array.

The `Grade` class is shown in Listing 7.6. Each `Grade` object represents a letter grade for a school course and includes a numerical lower bound. The values for the grade name and lower bound can be set using the `Grade` constructor, or using appropriate mutator methods. Accessor methods are also defined, as is a `toString` method to return a string representation of the grade. The `toString` method is automatically invoked when the grades are printed in the `main` method.

Let's look at another example. Listing 7.7 shows the `Tunes` class, which contains a `main` method that creates, modifies, and examines a compact disc (CD) collection. Each CD added to the collection is specified by its title, artist, purchase price, and number of tracks.

Listing 7.8 shows the `CDCollection` class. It contains an array of `CD` objects representing the collection. It maintains a count of the CDs in the collection and their combined value. It also keeps track of the current size of the collection array so that a larger array can be created if too many CDs are added to the collection.

Listing 7.5

```java
//********************************************************************
//  GradeRange.java       Author: Lewis/Loftus
//
//  Demonstrates the use of an array of objects.
//********************************************************************

public class GradeRange
{
   //-----------------------------------------------------------------
   //  Creates an array of Grade objects and prints them.
   //-----------------------------------------------------------------
   public static void main (String[] args)
   {
      Grade[] grades =
      {
         new Grade("A", 95), new Grade("A-", 90),
         new Grade("B+", 87), new Grade("B", 85), new Grade("B-", 80),
         new Grade("C+", 77), new Grade("C", 75), new Grade("C-", 70),
         new Grade("D+", 67), new Grade("D", 65), new Grade("D-", 60),
         new Grade("F", 0)
      };

      for (Grade letterGrade : grades)
         System.out.println (letterGrade);
   }
}
```

Output

```
A       95
A-      90
B+      87
B       85
B-      80
C+      77
C       75
C-      70
D+      67
D       65
D-      60
F       0
```

Listing 7.6

```java
//********************************************************************
//  Grade.java        Author: Lewis/Loftus
//
//  Represents a school grade.
//********************************************************************

public class Grade
{
   private String name;
   private int lowerBound;

   //-----------------------------------------------------------------
   //  Constructor: Sets up this Grade object with the specified
   //  grade name and numeric lower bound.
   //-----------------------------------------------------------------
   public Grade (String grade, int cutoff)
   {
      name = grade;
      lowerBound = cutoff;
   }

   //-----------------------------------------------------------------
   //  Returns a string representation of this grade.
   //-----------------------------------------------------------------
   public String toString()
   {
      return name + "\t" + lowerBound;
   }

   //-----------------------------------------------------------------
   //  Name mutator.
   //-----------------------------------------------------------------
   public void setName (String grade)
   {
      name = grade;
   }
```

Listing 7.6 **continued**

```java
//-------------------------------------------------------------
//  Lower bound mutator.
//-------------------------------------------------------------
public void setLowerBound (int cutoff)
{
    lowerBound = cutoff;
}

//-------------------------------------------------------------
//  Name accessor.
//-------------------------------------------------------------
public String getName()
{
    return name;
}

//-------------------------------------------------------------
//  Lower bound accessor.
//-------------------------------------------------------------
public int getLowerBound()
{
    return lowerBound;
}
}
```

The `collection` array is instantiated in the `CDCollection` constructor. Every time a CD is added to the collection (using the `addCD` method), a new `CD` object is created and a reference to it is stored in the `collection` array.

Each time a CD is added to the collection, we check to see whether we have reached the current capacity of the `collection` array. If we didn't perform this check, an exception would eventually be thrown when we try to store a new `CD` object at an invalid index. If the current capacity has been reached, the private `increaseSize` method is invoked, which first creates an array that is twice as big as the current `collection` array. Each CD in the existing collection is then

Listing 7.7

```java
//********************************************************************
//  Tunes.java        Author: Lewis/Loftus
//
//  Demonstrates the use of an array of objects.
//********************************************************************

public class Tunes
{
    //-----------------------------------------------------------------
    //  Creates a CDCollection object and adds some CDs to it. Prints
    //  reports on the status of the collection.
    //-----------------------------------------------------------------
    public static void main (String[] args)
    {
        CDCollection music = new CDCollection ();

        music.addCD ("Storm Front", "Billy Joel", 14.95, 10);
        music.addCD ("Come On Over", "Shania Twain", 14.95, 16);
        music.addCD ("Soundtrack", "Les Miserables", 17.95, 33);
        music.addCD ("Graceland", "Paul Simon", 13.90, 11);

        System.out.println (music);

        music.addCD ("Double Live", "Garth Brooks", 19.99, 26);
        music.addCD ("Greatest Hits", "Jimmy Buffet", 15.95, 13);

        System.out.println (music);
    }
}
```

Output

```
~~~~~~~~~~~~~~~~~~~~~~~~~~~~~~~~~~~~~~~~~~~~~~~~~~
My CD Collection

Number of CDs: 4
Total cost: $61.75
Average cost: $15.44
```

Listing 7.7   **continued**

```
CD List:

$14.95  10       Storm Front     Billy Joel
$14.95  16       Come On Over    Shania Twain
$17.95  33       Soundtrack      Les Miserables
$13.90  11       Graceland       Paul Simon


~~~~~~~~~~~~~~~~~~~~~~~~~~~~~~~~~~~~~~~~~~~~~~~
My CD Collection

Number of CDs: 6
Total cost: $97.69
Average cost: $16.28

CD List:

$14.95  10       Storm Front     Billy Joel
$14.95  16       Come On Over    Shania Twain
$17.95  33       Soundtrack      Les Miserables
$13.90  11       Graceland       Paul Simon
$19.99  26       Double Live     Garth Brooks
$15.95  13       Greatest Hits   Jimmy Buffet
```

Listing 7.8

```java
//********************************************************************
//   CDCollection.java        Author: Lewis/Loftus
//
//   Represents a collection of compact discs.
//********************************************************************

import java.text.NumberFormat;

public class CDCollection
{
   private CD[] collection;
   private int count;
   private double totalCost;
```

Listing 7.8   **continued**

```java
//----------------------------------------------------------------
//  Constructor: Creates an initially empty collection.
//----------------------------------------------------------------
public CDCollection ()
{
   collection = new CD[100];
   count = 0;
   totalCost = 0.0;
}

//----------------------------------------------------------------
//  Adds a CD to the collection, increasing the size of the
//  collection if necessary.
//----------------------------------------------------------------
public void addCD (String title, String artist, double cost,
                   int tracks)
{
   if (count == collection.length)
      increaseSize();

   collection[count] = new CD (title, artist, cost, tracks);
   totalCost += cost;
   count++;
}

//----------------------------------------------------------------
//  Returns a report describing the CD collection.
//----------------------------------------------------------------
public String toString()
{
   NumberFormat fmt = NumberFormat.getCurrencyInstance();

   String report = "~~~~~~~~~~~~~~~~~~~~~~~~~~~~~~~~~~~~~~~~~~~~\n";
   report += "My CD Collection\n\n";

   report += "Number of CDs: " + count + "\n";
   report += "Total cost: " + fmt.format(totalCost) + "\n";
   report += "Average cost: " + fmt.format(totalCost/count);

   report += "\n\nCD List:\n\n";
```

Listing 7.8   continued

```
      for (int cd = 0; cd < count; cd++)
         report += collection[cd] + "\n";

      return report;
   }

   //-------------------------------------------------------------------
   //  Increases the capacity of the collection by creating a
   //  larger array and copying the existing collection into it.
   //-------------------------------------------------------------------
   private void increaseSize ()
   {
      CD[] temp = new CD[collection.length * 2];

      for (int cd = 0; cd < collection.length; cd++)
         temp[cd] = collection[cd];

      collection = temp;
   }
}
```

copied into the new array. Finally, the collection reference is set to the larger array. Using this technique, we theoretically never run out of room in our CD collection. The user of the CDCollection object (the main method) never has to worry about running out of space because it's all handled internally.

Figure 7.3 shows a UML class diagram of the Tunes program. Recall that the open diamond indicates aggregation. The cardinality of the relationship is also noted: a CDCollection object contains zero or more CD objects.

The toString method of the CDCollection class returns an entire report summarizing the collection. The report is created, in part, using calls to the toString method of each CD object stored in the collection. Listing 7.9 shows the CD class.

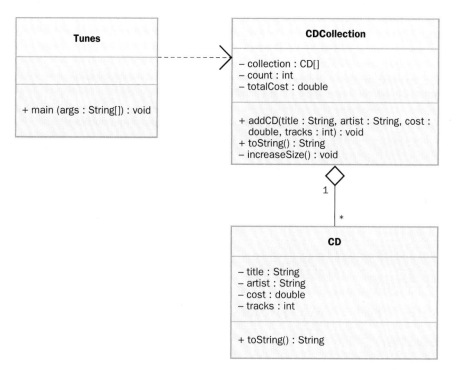

FIGURE 7.3 A UML class diagram of the Tunes program

Listing 7.9

```
//********************************************************************
//  CD.java          Author: Lewis/Loftus
//
//  Represents a compact disc.
//********************************************************************

import java.text.NumberFormat;

public class CD
{
    private String title, artist;
    private double cost;
    private int tracks;
```

Listing 7.9 **continued**

```java
//------------------------------------------------------------
//  Creates a new CD with the specified information.
//------------------------------------------------------------
public CD (String name, String singer, double price, int numTracks)
{
   title = name;
   artist = singer;
   cost = price;
   tracks = numTracks;
}

//------------------------------------------------------------
//  Returns a string description of this CD.
//------------------------------------------------------------
public String toString()
{
   NumberFormat fmt = NumberFormat.getCurrencyInstance();

   String description;

   description = fmt.format(cost) + "\t" + tracks + "\t";
   description += title + "\t" + artist;

   return description;
}
}
```

7.4 COMMAND-LINE ARGUMENTS

The formal parameter to the main method of a Java application is always an array of String objects. We've ignored that parameter in previous examples, but now we can discuss how it might occasionally be useful.

> **Key Concept**
>
> Command-line arguments are stored in an array of String objects and are passed to the main method.

The Java run-time environment invokes the main method when an application is submitted to the interpreter. The String[] parameter, which we typically call args, represents *command-line arguments* that are provided when the interpreter is invoked. Any extra information on the command line when the interpreter is invoked is stored in the `args` array for use by the program. This technique is another way to provide input to a program.

The program shown in Listing 7.10 uses command-line arguments to print a nametag. It assumes the first argument represents some type of greeting and the second argument represents a person's name.

If two strings are not provided on the command line for the `NameTag` program, the `args` array will not contain enough (if any) elements, and the references in the program will cause an `ArrayIndexOutOfBoundsException` to be thrown. If extra information is included on the command line, it will be stored in the `args` array but ignored by the program.

Listing 7.10

```
//********************************************************************
//  NameTag.java         Author: Lewis/Loftus
//
//  Demonstrates the use of command line arguments.
//********************************************************************

public class NameTag
{
   //-----------------------------------------------------------------
   //  Prints a simple name tag using a greeting and a name that is
   //  specified by the user.
   //-----------------------------------------------------------------
   public static void main (String[] args)
   {
      System.out.println ();
      System.out.println ("     " + args[0]);
      System.out.println ("My name is " + args[1]);
   }
}
```

Output

```
> java NameTag Howdy John

     Howdy
My name is John

> java NameTag Hello Bill

     Hello
My name is Bill
```

Remember that the parameter to the `main` method is always an array of `String` objects. If you want numeric information to be input as a command-line argument, the program has to convert it from its string representation.

You also should be aware that in some program development environments a command line is not used to submit a program to the interpreter. In such situations, the command-line information can be specified in some other way. Consult the documentation for these specifics if necessary.

7.5 VARIABLE LENGTH PARAMETER LISTS

Suppose we wanted to design a method that processed a different amount of data from one invocation to the next. For example, let's design a method called `average` that accepts a few integer values and returns their average. In one invocation of the method we might pass in three integers to average:

```
mean1 = average(42, 69, 37);
```

In another invocation of the same method we might pass in seven integers to average:

```
mean2 = average(35, 43, 93, 23, 40, 21, 75);
```

> **Key Concept**
>
> A Java method can be defined to accept a varying number of parameters.

To accomplish this we could define overloaded versions of the `average` method, but that would require that we know the maximum number of parameters there might be and create a separate version of the method for each possibility. Alternatively, we could define the method to accept an array of integers, which could be of different sizes for each call. But that would require packaging the integers into an array in the calling method and passing in one parameter.

Java provides a way to define methods that accept variable length parameter lists. By using some special syntax in the formal parameter list of the method, we can define the method to accept any number of parameters. The parameters are automatically put into an array for easy processing in the method. For example, the `average` method could be written as follows:

```
public double average (int ... list)
{
   double result = 0.0;

   if (list.length != 0)
   {
      int sum = 0;
      for (int num : list)
        sum += num;
      result = (double)sum / list.length;
   }

   return result;
}
```

Note the way the formal parameters are defined. The ellipsis (three periods in a row) indicates that the method accepts a variable number of parameters. In this case, the method accepts any number of int parameters, which it automatically puts into an array called list. In the method, we process the array normally.

We can now pass any number of int parameters to the average method, including none at all. That's why we check to see if the length of the array is zero before we compute the average.

The type of the multiple parameters can be any primitive or object type. For example, the following method accepts and prints multiple Grade objects (we defined the Grade class earlier in this chapter):

```
public void printGrades (Grade ... grades)
{
   for (Grade letterGrade : grades)
      System.out.println (letterGrade);
}
```

A method that accepts a variable number of parameters can also accept other parameters. For example, the following method accepts an int, a String object, and then a variable number of double values that will be stored in an array called nums:

```
public void test (int count, String name, double ... nums)
{
   // whatever
}
```

The varying parameters must come last in the formal arguments. A single method cannot accept two sets of varying parameters.

Constructors can also be set up to accept a varying number of parameters. The program shown in Listing 7.11 creates two Family objects, passing a varying

Listing 7.11

```java
//********************************************************************
//  VariableParameters.java       Author: Lewis/Loftus
//
//  Demonstrates the use of a variable length parameter list.
//********************************************************************

public class VariableParameters
{
   //-----------------------------------------------------------------
   //  Creates two Family objects using a constructor that accepts
   //  a variable number of String objects as parameters.
   //-----------------------------------------------------------------
   public static void main (String[] args)
   {
      Family lewis = new Family ("John", "Sharon", "Justin", "Kayla");

      Family camden = new Family ("Stephen", "Annie", "Matt", "Mary",
         "Simon", "Lucy", "Ruthie", "Sam", "David");

      System.out.println(lewis);
      System.out.println();
      System.out.println(camden);
   }
}
```

Output

```
John
Sharon
Justin
Kayla

Stephen
Annie
Matt
Mary
Simon
Lucy
Ruthie
Sam
David
```

number of strings (representing the family member names) into the `Family` constructor.

The `Family` class is shown in Listing 7.12. The constructor simply stores a reference to the array parameter until it is needed. By using a variable length parameter list for the constructor, we make it easy to create a family of any size.

Listing 7.12

```java
//********************************************************************
//  Family.java       Author: Lewis/Loftus
//
//  Demonstrates the use of variable length parameter lists.
//********************************************************************

public class Family
{
   private String[] members;

   //-----------------------------------------------------------------
   //  Constructor: Sets up this family by storing the (possibly
   //  multiple) names that are passed in as parameters.
   //-----------------------------------------------------------------
   public Family (String ... names)
   {
      members = names;
   }

   //-----------------------------------------------------------------
   //  Returns a string representation of this family.
   //-----------------------------------------------------------------
   public String toString()
   {
      String result = "";

      for (String name : members)
         result += name + "\n";

      return result;
   }
}
```

7.6 TWO-DIMENSIONAL ARRAYS

The arrays we've examined so far have all been *one-dimensional arrays* in the sense that they represent a simple list of values. As the name implies, a *two-dimensional array* has values in two dimensions, which are often thought of as the rows and columns of a table. Figure 7.4 graphically compares a one-dimensional array with a two-dimensional array. We must use two indexes to refer to a value in a two-dimensional array, one specifying the row and another the column.

Brackets are used to represent each dimension in the array. Therefore the type of a two-dimensional array that stores integers is int[][]. Technically, Java represents two-dimensional arrays as an array of arrays. A two-dimensional integer array is really a one-dimensional array of references to one-dimensional integer arrays.

The TwoDArray program shown in Listing 7.13 instantiates a two-dimensional array of integers. As with one-dimensional arrays, the size of the dimensions is specified when the array is created. The size of the dimensions can be different.

Nested for loops are used in the TwoDArray program to load the array with values and also to print those values in a table format. Carefully trace the processing to see how the nested loops eventually visit each element in the two-dimensional array. Note that the outer loops are governed by table.length, which represents the number of rows, and the inner loops are governed by table[row].length, which represents the number of columns in that row.

As with one-dimensional arrays, an initializer list can be used to instantiate a two-dimensional array, where each element is itself an array initializer list. This technique is used in the SodaSurvey program, which is shown in Listing 7.14.

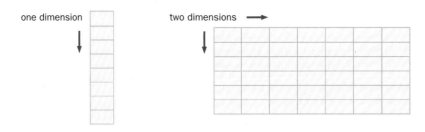

FIGURE 7.4   A one-dimensional array and a two-dimensional array

Listing 7.13

```java
//********************************************************************
//  TwoDArray.java        Author: Lewis/Loftus
//
//  Demonstrates the use of a two-dimensional array.
//********************************************************************

public class TwoDArray
{
   //-----------------------------------------------------------------
   //  Creates a 2D array of integers, fills it with increasing
   //  integer values, then prints them out.
   //-----------------------------------------------------------------
   public static void main (String[] args)
   {
      int[][] table = new int[5][10];

      // Load the table with values
      for (int row=0; row < table.length; row++)
         for (int col=0; col < table[row].length; col++)
            table[row][col] = row * 10 + col;

      // Print the table
      for (int row=0; row < table.length; row++)
      {
         for (int col=0; col < table[row].length; col++)
            System.out.print (table[row][col] + "\t");
         System.out.println();
      }
   }
}
```

Output

0	1	2	3	4	5	6	7	8	9
10	11	12	13	14	15	16	17	18	19
20	21	22	23	24	25	26	27	28	29
30	31	32	33	34	35	36	37	38	39
40	41	42	43	44	45	46	47	48	49

Listing 7.14

```java
//********************************************************************
//  SodaSurvey.java        Author: Lewis/Loftus
//
//  Demonstrates the use of a two-dimensional array.
//********************************************************************

import java.text.DecimalFormat;

public class SodaSurvey
{
    //-----------------------------------------------------------------
    //  Determines and prints the average of each row (soda) and each
    //  column (respondent) of the survey scores.
    //-----------------------------------------------------------------
    public static void main (String[] args)
    {
        int[][] scores = { {3, 4, 5, 2, 1, 4, 3, 2, 4, 4},
                           {2, 4, 3, 4, 3, 3, 2, 1, 2, 2},
                           {3, 5, 4, 5, 5, 3, 2, 5, 5, 5},
                           {1, 1, 1, 3, 1, 2, 1, 3, 2, 4} };

        final int SODAS = scores.length;
        final int PEOPLE = scores[0].length;

        int[] sodaSum = new int[SODAS];
        int[] personSum = new int[PEOPLE];

        for (int soda=0; soda < SODAS; soda++)
            for (int person=0; person < PEOPLE; person++)
            {
                sodaSum[soda] += scores[soda][person];
                personSum[person] += scores[soda][person];
            }

        DecimalFormat fmt = new DecimalFormat ("0.#");
        System.out.println ("Averages:\n");

        for (int soda=0; soda < SODAS; soda++)
            System.out.println ("Soda #" + (soda+1) + ": " +
                        fmt.format ((float)sodaSum[soda]/PEOPLE));
```

Listing 7.14   **continued**

```
        System.out.println ();
        for (int person =0; person < PEOPLE; person++)
            System.out.println ("Person #" + (person+1) + ": " +
                    fmt.format ((float)personSum[person]/SODAS));
    }
}
```

Output

```
Averages:

Soda #1: 3.2
Soda #2: 2.6
Soda #3: 4.2
Soda #4: 1.9

Person #1: 2.2
Person #2: 3.5
Person #3: 3.2
Person #4: 3.5
Person #5: 2.5
Person #6: 3
Person #7: 2
Person #8: 2.8
Person #9: 3.2
Person #10: 3.8
```

Suppose a soda manufacturer held a taste test for four new flavors to see how people liked them. The manufacturer got 10 people to try each new flavor and give it a score from 1 to 5, where 1 equals poor and 5 equals excellent. The two-dimensional array called scores in the SodaSurvey program stores the results of that survey. Each row corresponds to a soda and each column in that row corresponds to the person who tasted it. More generally, each row holds the responses that all testers gave for one particular soda flavor, and each column holds the responses of one person for all sodas.

The SodaSurvey program computes and prints the average responses for each soda and for each respondent. The sums of each soda and person are first stored in one-dimensional arrays of integers. Then the averages are computed and printed.

Multidimensional Arrays

An array can have one, two, three, or even more dimensions. Any array with more than one dimension is called a *multidimensional array*.

It's fairly easy to picture a two-dimensional array as a table. A three-dimensional array could be drawn as a cube. However, once you are past three dimensions, multidimensional arrays might seem hard to visualize. Yet, consider that each subsequent dimension is simply a subdivision of the previous one. It is often best to think of larger multidimensional arrays in this way.

For example, suppose we wanted to store the number of students attending universities across the United States, broken down in a meaningful way. We might represent it as a four-dimensional array of integers. The first dimension represents the state. The second dimension represents the universities in each state. The third dimension represents the colleges in each university. Finally, the fourth dimension represents departments in each college. The value stored at each location is the number of students in one particular department. Figure 7.5 shows these subdivisions.

Two-dimensional arrays are fairly common. However, care should be taken when deciding to create multidimensional arrays in a program. When dealing with large amounts of data that are managed at multiple levels, additional information and the methods needed to manage that information will probably be required. It is far more likely, for instance, that in the previous example, each state would be represented by an object, which may contain, among other things, an array to store information about each university, and so on.

There is one other important characteristic of Java arrays to consider. As we established previously, Java does not directly support multidimensional arrays. Instead, they are represented as arrays of references to array objects. Those arrays could themselves contain references to other arrays. This layering continues for

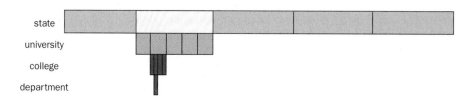

FIGURE 7.5 Visualization of a four-dimensional array

as many dimensions as required. Because of this technique for representing each dimension, the arrays in any one dimension could be of different lengths. These are sometimes called *ragged arrays*. For example, the number of elements in each row of a two-dimensional array may not be the same. In such situations, care must be taken to make sure the arrays are managed appropriately.

7.7   THE `ArrayList` CLASS

The `ArrayList` class is part of the `java.util` package of the Java standard class library. It provides a service similar to an array in that it can store a list of values and reference them by an index. However, whereas an array remains a fixed size throughout its existence, an `ArrayList` object dynamically grows and shrinks as needed. A data element can be inserted into or removed from any location (index) of an `ArrayList` object with a single method invocation.

> **Key Concept**
>
> An `ArrayList` object is similar to an array, but it dynamically changes size as needed, and elements can be inserted and removed.

The `ArrayList` class is part of the Collections API, a group of classes that serve to organize and manage other objects. We discuss collection classes further in Chapter 12.

Unless we specify otherwise, an `ArrayList` is not declared to store a particular type. That is, an `ArrayList` object stores a list of references to the `Object` class, which means that any type of object can be added to an `ArrayList`. Because an `ArrayList` stores references, a primitive value must be stored in an appropriate wrapper class in order to be stored in an `ArrayList`. Figure 7.6 lists several methods of the `ArrayList` class.

The program shown in Listing 7.15 instantiates an `ArrayList` called `band`. The method `add` is used to add several `String` objects to the `ArrayList` in a specific order. Then one particular string is deleted and another is inserted at a particular index. As with any other object, the `toString` method of the `ArrayList` class is automatically called whenever it is sent to the `println` method.

Note that when an element from an `ArrayList` is deleted, the list of elements "collapses" so that the indexes are kept continuous for the remaining elements. Likewise, when an element is inserted at a particular point, the indexes of the other elements are adjusted accordingly.

Specifying an `ArrayList` Element Type

The methods of the `ArrayList` class are designed to accept references to the `Object` class as parameters, thus allowing a reference to any kind of object to be passed to it. Thus, by default, an array can store any type of object. Note that an

```
ArrayList()
    Constructor: creates an initially empty list.

boolean add (Object obj)
    Inserts the specified object to the end of this list.

void add (int index, Object obj)
    Inserts the specified object into this list at the specified index.

void clear()
    Removes all elements from this list.

Object remove (int index)
    Removes the element at the specified index in this list and returns it.

Object get (int index)
    Returns the object at the specified index in this list without removing it.

int indexOf (Object obj)
    Returns the index of the first occurrence of the specified object.

boolean contains (Object obj)
    Returns true if this list contains the specified object.

boolean isEmpty()
    Returns true if this list contains no elements.

int size()
    Returns the number of elements in this list.
```

FIGURE 7.6 Some methods of the `ArrayList` class

implication of this implementation is that the `remove` method's return type is an `Object` reference. In order to retrieve a specific object from the `ArrayList`, the returned object must be cast to its original class. We discuss the `Object` class and its relationship to other classes in Chapter 8.

We can also define an `ArrayList` object to accept particular types of objects. That is, when we instantiate the `ArrayList` object, we can specify that it will be used to hold a certain class of objects. The following line of code creates an `ArrayList` object called `reunion` that stores `Family` objects:

```
ArrayList<Family> reunion = new ArrayList<Family>();
```

Listing 7.15

```java
//********************************************************************
//  Beatles.java        Author: Lewis/Loftus
//
//  Demonstrates the use of a ArrayList object.
//********************************************************************

import java.util.ArrayList;

public class Beatles
{
   //-----------------------------------------------------------------
   //  Stores and modifies a list of band members.
   //-----------------------------------------------------------------
   public static void main (String[] args)
   {
      ArrayList band = new ArrayList();

      band.add ("Paul");
      band.add ("Pete");
      band.add ("John");
      band.add ("George");

      System.out.println (band);

      int location = band.indexOf ("Pete");
      band.remove (location);

      System.out.println (band);
      System.out.println ("At index 1: " + band.get(1));

      band.add (2, "Ringo");

      System.out.println (band);
      System.out.println ("Size of the band: " + band.size());
   }
}
```

Output

```
[Paul, Pete, John, George]
[Paul, John, George]
At index 1: John
[Paul, John, Ringo, George]
Size of the band: 4
```

An `ArrayList` a *generic type*, which formally allows us to specify the type of data on which it operates for each `ArrayList` object we create. We can specify the element type for any class in the Java Collections API in this way. Generics are discussed further in Chapter 12.

The type of the `reunion` object is `ArrayList<Family>`. Given this declaration, the compiler will not allow an object to be added to `reunion` unless it is a `Family` object (or one of its descendents through inheritance). In the `Beatles` program we could have specified that `band` was of type `ArrayList<String>`.

Declaring the element type of an `ArrayList` is usually a good idea because it adds a level of type-checking that we otherwise wouldn't have. It also eliminates the need to cast an object into its true type when it is extracted from the `ArrayList`.

`ArrayList` Efficiency

The `ArrayList` class is implemented, as you might imagine, using an array. That is, the `ArrayList` object stores an array of `Object` references. The methods provided by the class manipulate that array so that the indexes remain continuous as elements are added and removed.

When an `ArrayList` object is instantiated, the internal array is created with an initial capacity that defines the number of references it can currently handle. Elements can be added to the list without needing to allocate more memory until it reaches this capacity. When required, the capacity is expanded to accommodate the new need. We performed a similar operation in the `Tunes` program earlier in this chapter.

When an element is inserted into an `ArrayList`, all of the elements at higher indexes are copied into their new locations to make room for the new element. Figure 7.7 illustrates this process. Similar processing occurs when an element is removed from an `ArrayList`, except that the items are shifted in the other direction, closing the gap created by the deleted element to keep the indexes

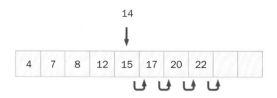

FIGURE 7.7   Inserting an element into an `ArrayList` object

continuous. If several elements are inserted or deleted, this copying is repeated many times over.

If, in general, elements are added to or removed from the end of an `ArrayList`, it's efficiency is not affected. But if elements are added to and/or removed from the front part of a long `ArrayList`, a huge amount of element copying will occur. An `ArrayList`, with its dynamic characteristics, is a useful abstraction of an array, but the abstraction masks some underlying activity that can be fairly inefficient depending on how it is used.

> **Key Concept**
>
> `ArrayList` processing can be inefficient depending on how it is used.

7.8 POLYGONS AND POLYLINES

Arrays are helpful when drawing complex shapes. A polygon, for example, is a multisided shape that is defined in Java using a series of (x, y) points that indicate the vertices of the polygon. Arrays are often used to store the list of coordinates.

Polygons are drawn using methods of the `Graphics` class, similar to how we draw rectangles and ovals. Like these other shapes, a polygon can be drawn filled or unfilled. The methods used to draw a polygon are called `drawPolygon` and `fillPolygon`. Both of these methods are overloaded. One version uses arrays of integers to define the polygon, and the other uses an object of the `Polygon` class to define the polygon. We discuss the `Polygon` class later in this section.

In the version that uses arrays, the `drawPolygon` and `fillPolygon` methods take three parameters. The first is an array of integers representing the x coordinates of the points in the polygon, the second is an array of integers representing the corresponding y coordinates of those points, and the third is an integer that indicates how many points are used from each of the two arrays. Taken together, the first two parameters represent the (x, y) coordinates of the vertices of the polygons.

A polygon is always closed. A line segment is always drawn from the last point in the list to the first point in the list.

Similar to a polygon, a *polyline* contains a series of points connected by line segments. Polylines differ from polygons in that the first and last coordinates are not automatically connected when it is drawn. Since a polyline is not closed, it cannot be filled. Therefore there is only one method, called `drawPolyline`, used to draw a polyline.

> **Key Concept**
>
> A polyline is similar to a polygon except that a polyline is not a closed shape.

As with the `drawPolygon` method, the first two parameters of the `drawPolyline` method are both arrays of integers. Taken together, the first two parameters represent the (x, y) coordinates of the end points of the line segments of the polyline. The third parameter is the number of points in the coordinate list.

The program shown in Listing 7.16 uses polygons to draw a rocket. In the `RocketPanel` class, shown in Listing 7.17, the arrays called `xRocket` and `yRocket` define the points of the polygon that make up the main body of the rocket. The first point in the arrays is the upper tip of the rocket, and they progress clockwise from there. The `xWindow` and `yWindow` arrays specify the points for the polygon that form the window in the rocket. Both the rocket and the window are drawn as filled polygons.

The `xFlame` and `yFlame` arrays define the points of a polyline that are used to create the image of flame shooting out of the tail of the rocket. Because it is drawn as a polyline, and not a polygon, the flame is not closed or filled.

The `Polygon` Class

A polygon can also be defined explicitly using an object of the `Polygon` class, which is defined in the `java.awt` package of the Java standard class library. Two versions of the overloaded `drawPolygon` and `fillPolygon` methods take a single `Polygon` object as a parameter.

A `Polygon` object encapsulates the coordinates of the polygon sides. The constructors of the `Polygon` class allow the creation of an initially empty polygon, or one defined by arrays of integers representing the point coordinates. The `Polygon` class contains methods to add points to the polygon and to determine whether a given point is contained within the polygon shape. It also contains methods to get a representation of a bounding rectangle for the polygon, as well as a method to translate all of the points in the polygon to another position. Figure 7.8 lists these methods.

Listing 7.16

```java
//********************************************************************
//   Rocket.java          Author: Lewis/Loftus
//
//   Demonstrates the use of polygons and polylines.
//********************************************************************

import javax.swing.JFrame;

public class Rocket
{
   //-----------------------------------------------------------------
   //   Creates the main frame of the program.
   //-----------------------------------------------------------------
   public static void main (String[] args)
   {
      JFrame frame = new JFrame ("Rocket");
      frame.setDefaultCloseOperation (JFrame.EXIT_ON_CLOSE);

      RocketPanel panel = new RocketPanel();

      frame.getContentPane().add(panel);
      frame.pack();
      frame.setVisible(true);
   }
}
```

Display

Listing 7.17

```java
//********************************************************************
//  RocketPanel.java          Author: Lewis/Loftus
//
//  Demonstrates the use of polygons and polylines.
//********************************************************************

import javax.swing.JPanel;
import java.awt.*;

public class RocketPanel extends JPanel
{
   private int[] xRocket = {100, 120, 120, 130, 130, 70, 70, 80, 80};
   private int[] yRocket = {15, 40, 115, 125, 150, 150, 125, 115, 40};

   private int[] xWindow = {95, 105, 110, 90};
   private int[] yWindow = {45, 45, 70, 70};

   private int[] xFlame = {70, 70, 75, 80, 90, 100, 110, 115, 120,
                           130, 130};
   private int[] yFlame = {155, 170, 165, 190, 170, 175, 160, 185,
                           160, 175, 155};

   //-----------------------------------------------------------------
   //  Constructor: Sets up the basic characteristics of this panel.
   //-----------------------------------------------------------------
   public RocketPanel()
   {
      setBackground (Color.black);
      setPreferredSize (new Dimension(200, 200));
   }

   //-----------------------------------------------------------------
   //  Draws a rocket using polygons and polylines.
   //-----------------------------------------------------------------
   public void paintComponent (Graphics page)
   {
      super.paintComponent (page);
```

Listing 7.17   continued

```
        page.setColor (Color.cyan);
        page.fillPolygon (xRocket, yRocket, xRocket.length);

        page.setColor (Color.gray);
        page.fillPolygon (xWindow, yWindow, xWindow.length);

        page.setColor (Color.red);
        page.drawPolyline (xFlame, yFlame, xFlame.length);
    }
}
```

Polygon ()
   Constructor: Creates an empty polygon.

Polygon (int[] xpoints, int[] ypoints, int npoints)
   Constructor: Creates a polygon using the (x, y) coordinate pairs
   in corresponding entries of xpoints and ypoints.

void **addPoint** (int x, int y)
   Appends the specified point to this polygon.

boolean **contains** (int x, int y)
   Returns true if the specified point is contained in this polygon.

boolean **contains** (Point p)
   Returns true if the specified point is contained in this polygon.

Rectangle getBounds ()
   Gets the bounding rectangle for this polygon.

void **translate** (int deltaX, int deltaY)
   Translates the vertices of this polygon by deltaX along the x axis
   and deltaY along the y axis.

FIGURE 7.8   Some methods of the Polygon class

7.9 MOUSE EVENTS

Let's examine the events that are generated when using a mouse. Java divides these events into two categories: *mouse events* and *mouse motion events*. The table in Figure 7.9 defines these events.

When you click the mouse button over a Java GUI component, three events are generated: one when the mouse button is pushed down (*mouse pressed*) and two when it is let up (*mouse released* and *mouse clicked*). A mouse click is defined as pressing and releasing the mouse button in the same location. If you press the mouse button down, move the mouse, and then release the mouse button, a mouse clicked event is not generated.

A component will generate a *mouse entered* event when the mouse pointer passes into its graphical space. Likewise, it generates a *mouse exited* event when the mouse pointer leaves.

> **Key Concept**
>
> Moving the mouse and clicking the mouse button generate events to which a program can respond.

Mouse motion events, as the name implies, occur while the mouse is in motion. The *mouse moved* event indicates simply that the mouse is in motion. The *mouse dragged* event is generated when the user has pressed the mouse button down and moved the mouse without releasing the button. Mouse motion events are generated many times, very quickly, while the mouse is in motion.

In a specific situation, we may care about only one or two mouse events. What we listen for depends on what we are trying to accomplish.

Mouse Event	Description
mouse pressed	The mouse button is pressed down.
mouse released	The mouse button is released.
mouse clicked	The mouse button is pressed down and released without moving the mouse in between.
mouse entered	The mouse pointer is moved onto (over) a component.
mouse exited	The mouse pointer is moved off of a component.

Mouse Motion Event	Description
mouse moved	The mouse is moved.
mouse dragged	The mouse is moved while the mouse button is pressed down.

FIGURE 7.9 Mouse events and mouse motion events

The Dots program shown in Listing 7.18 responds to one mouse event. Specifically, it draws a green dot at the location of the mouse pointer whenever the mouse button is pressed.

Listing 7.18

```java
//********************************************************************
//  Dots.java          Author: Lewis/Loftus
//
//  Demonstrates mouse events.
//********************************************************************

import javax.swing.JFrame;

public class Dots
{
   //-----------------------------------------------------------------
   //  Creates and displays the application frame.
   //-----------------------------------------------------------------
   public static void main (String[] args)
   {
      JFrame frame = new JFrame ("Dots");
      frame.setDefaultCloseOperation (JFrame.EXIT_ON_CLOSE);

      frame.getContentPane().add (new DotsPanel());

      frame.pack();
      frame.setVisible(true);
   }
}
```

Display

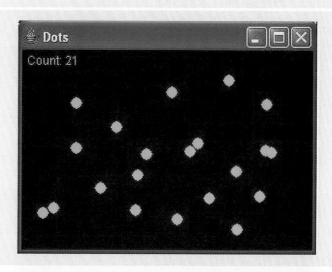

The `main` method of the `Dots` class creates a frame and adds one panel to it. That panel is defined by the `DotsPanel` class shown in Listing 7.19.

Listing 7.19

```java
//********************************************************************
//  DotsPanel.java         Author: Lewis/Loftus
//
//  Represents the primary panel for the Dots program.
//********************************************************************

import java.util.ArrayList;
import javax.swing.JPanel;
import java.awt.*;
import java.awt.event.*;

public class DotsPanel extends JPanel
{
   private final int SIZE = 6;   // radius of each dot

   private ArrayList<Point> pointList;

   //-----------------------------------------------------------------
   //  Constructor: Sets up this panel to listen for mouse events.
   //-----------------------------------------------------------------
   public DotsPanel()
   {
      pointList = new ArrayList<Point>();

      addMouseListener (new DotsListener());

      setBackground (Color.black);
      setPreferredSize (new Dimension(300, 200));
   }

   //-----------------------------------------------------------------
   //  Draws all of the dots stored in the list.
   //-----------------------------------------------------------------
   public void paintComponent (Graphics page)
   {
      super.paintComponent(page);
```

Listing 7.19   **continued**

```java
        page.setColor (Color.green);

        for (Point spot : pointList)
            page.fillOval (spot.x-SIZE, spot.y-SIZE, SIZE*2, SIZE*2);

        page.drawString ("Count: " + pointList.size(), 5, 15);
    }

    //******************************************************************
    //   Represents the listener for mouse events.
    //******************************************************************
    private class DotsListener implements MouseListener
    {
        //--------------------------------------------------------------
        //   Adds the current point to the list of points and redraws
        //   the panel whenever the mouse button is pressed.
        //--------------------------------------------------------------
        public void mousePressed (MouseEvent event)
        {
            pointList.add(event.getPoint());
            repaint();
        }


        //--------------------------------------------------------------
        //   Provide empty definitions for unused event methods.
        //--------------------------------------------------------------
        public void mouseClicked (MouseEvent event) {}
        public void mouseReleased (MouseEvent event) {}
        public void mouseEntered (MouseEvent event) {}
        public void mouseExited (MouseEvent event) {}
    }
}
```

The `DotsPanel` class keeps track of a list of `Point` objects that represent all of the locations at which the user has clicked the mouse. A `Point` class represents the (x, y) coordinates of a given point in two-dimensional space. It provides public access to the instance variables x and y for the point. Each time the panel is painted, all of the points stored in the list are drawn.

The list of `Point` objects is maintained as an `ArrayList` object. More precisely, the type of the `pointList` object is `ArrayList<Point>`, specifying that only `Point` objects can be stored in that `ArrayList`. To draw the points, we use a `for` loop to iterate over all the points stored in the list.

The listener for the mouse pressed event is defined as a private inner class that implements the `MouseListener` interface. The `mousePressed` method is invoked by the panel each time the user presses down on the mouse button while it is over the panel.

A mouse event always occurs at some point in two-dimensional space, and the object that represents that event keeps track of that location. In a mouse listener, we can get and use that point whenever we need it. In the `Dots` program, each time the `mousePressed` method is called, the location of the event is obtained using the `getPoint` method of the `MouseEvent` object. That point is stored in the `ArrayList`, and the panel is then repainted.

> **Key Concept**
>
> A listener may have to provide empty method definitions for unheeded events to satisfy the interface.

Note that, unlike the listener interfaces that we've used in previous examples that contain one method each, the `MouseListener` interface contains five methods. For this program, the only event in which we are interested is the mouse pressed event. Therefore, the only method in which we have any interest is the `mousePressed` method. However, implementing an interface means we must provide definitions for all methods in the interface. Therefore we provide empty methods corresponding to the other events. When those events are generated, the empty methods are called, but no code is executed. In Chapter 8 we discuss a technique for creating listeners that lets us avoid creating such empty methods.

Let's look at an example that responds to two mouse-oriented events. The `RubberLines` program shown in Listing 7.20 draws a line between two points. The first point is determined by the location at which the mouse is first pressed down. The second point changes as the mouse is dragged while the mouse button is held down. When the button is released, the line remains fixed between the first and second points. When the mouse button is pressed again, a new line is started.

The panel on which the lines are drawn is represented by the `RubberLinesPanel` class shown in Listing 7.21. Because we need to listen for both a mouse pressed event and a mouse dragged event, we need a listener that responds to both mouse events and mouse motion events. Note that the listener class in this example implements both the `MouseListener` and `MouseMotionListener` interfaces. It must therefore implement all methods of both interfaces. The two methods of interest, `mousePressed` and `mouseDragged`, are implemented to accomplish our goals, and the other methods are given empty definitions to satisfy the interface contract.

Listing 7.20

```
//********************************************************************
//   RubberLines.java        Author: Lewis/Loftus
//
//   Demonstrates mouse events and rubberbanding.
//********************************************************************

import javax.swing.JFrame;

public class RubberLines
{
   //-----------------------------------------------------------------
   //  Creates and displays the application frame.
   //-----------------------------------------------------------------
   public static void main (String[] args)
   {
      JFrame frame = new JFrame ("Rubber Lines");
      frame.setDefaultCloseOperation (JFrame.EXIT_ON_CLOSE);

      frame.getContentPane().add (new RubberLinesPanel());

      frame.pack();
      frame.setVisible(true);
   }
}
```

Display

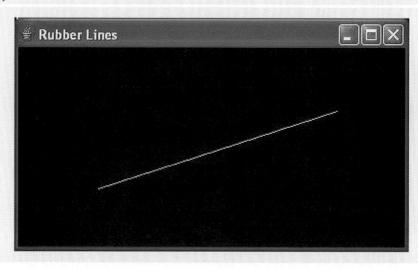

Listing 7.21

```java
//********************************************************************
//  RubberLinesPanel.java          Author: Lewis/Loftus
//
//  Represents the primary drawing panel for the RubberLines program.
//********************************************************************

import javax.swing.JPanel;
import java.awt.*;
import java.awt.event.*;

public class RubberLinesPanel extends JPanel
{
    private Point point1 = null, point2 = null;

    //-----------------------------------------------------------------
    //  Constructor: Sets up this panel to listen for mouse events.
    //-----------------------------------------------------------------
    public RubberLinesPanel()
    {
        LineListener listener = new LineListener();
        addMouseListener (listener);
        addMouseMotionListener (listener);

        setBackground (Color.black);
        setPreferredSize (new Dimension(400, 200));
    }

    //-----------------------------------------------------------------
    //  Draws the current line from the intial mouse-pressed point to
    //  the current position of the mouse.
    //-----------------------------------------------------------------
    public void paintComponent (Graphics page)
    {
        super.paintComponent (page);

        page.setColor (Color.yellow);
        if (point1 != null && point2 != null)
            page.drawLine (point1.x, point1.y, point2.x, point2.y);
    }
```

Listing 7.21   continued

```java
//*****************************************************************
//   Represents the listener for all mouse events.
//*****************************************************************
private class LineListener implements MouseListener,
                                      MouseMotionListener
{
   //-------------------------------------------------------------
   //   Captures the initial position at which the mouse button is
   //   pressed.
   //-------------------------------------------------------------
   public void mousePressed (MouseEvent event)
   {
      point1 = event.getPoint();
   }

   //-------------------------------------------------------------
   //   Gets the current position of the mouse as it is dragged and
   //   redraws the line to create the rubberband effect.
   //-------------------------------------------------------------
   public void mouseDragged (MouseEvent event)
   {
      point2 = event.getPoint();
      repaint();
   }

   //-------------------------------------------------------------
   //   Provide empty definitions for unused event methods.
   //-------------------------------------------------------------
   public void mouseClicked (MouseEvent event) {}
   public void mouseReleased (MouseEvent event) {}
   public void mouseEntered (MouseEvent event) {}
   public void mouseExited (MouseEvent event) {}
   public void mouseMoved (MouseEvent event) {}
}
}
```

When the `mousePressed` method is called, the variable `point1` is set. Then, as the mouse is dragged, the variable `point2` is continually reset and the panel repainted. Therefore the line is constantly being redrawn as the mouse is dragged, giving the appearance that one line is being stretched between a fixed point and a moving point. This effect is called *rubberbanding* and is common in graphical programs.

Note that, in the `RubberLinesPanel` constructor, the listener object is added to the panel twice: once as a mouse listener and once as a mouse motion listener. The method called to add the listener must correspond to the object passed as the parameter. In this case, we had one object that served as a listener for both categories of events. We could have had two listener classes if desired: one listening for mouse events and one listening for mouse motion events. A component can have multiple listeners for various event categories.

Also note that this program draws one line at a time. That is, when the user begins to draw another line with a new mouse click, the previous one disappears. This is because the `paintComponent` method redraws its background, eliminating the line every time. To see the previous lines, we'd have to keep track of them, perhaps using an `ArrayList` as was done in the `Dots` program. This modification to the `RubberLines` program is left as a programming project.

7.10   KEY EVENTS

A *key event* is generated when a keyboard key is pressed. Key events allow a program to respond immediately to the user while he or she is typing or pressing other keyboard keys such as the arrow keys. If key events are being processed the program can respond as soon as the key is pressed; there is no need to wait for the Enter key to be pressed or for some other component (like a button) to be activated.

The `Direction` program shown in Listing 7.22 responds to key events. An image of an arrow is displayed and the image moves across the screen as the arrow keys are pressed. Actually, four different images are used, one for the arrow pointing in each of the primary directions (up, down, right, and left).

The `DirectionPanel` class, shown in Listing 7.23, represents the panel on which the arrow image is displayed. The constructor loads the four arrow images, one of which is always considered to be the current image (the one displayed). The current image is set based on the arrow key that was most recently pressed. For example, if the up arrow is pressed, the image with the arrow pointing up is

Listing 7.22

```java
//********************************************************************
//   Direction.java          Author: Lewis/Loftus
//
//   Demonstrates key events.
//********************************************************************

import javax.swing.JFrame;

public class Direction
{
   //-----------------------------------------------------------------
   //  Creates and displays the application frame.
   //-----------------------------------------------------------------
   public static void main (String[] args)
   {
      JFrame frame = new JFrame ("Direction");
      frame.setDefaultCloseOperation (JFrame.EXIT_ON_CLOSE);

      frame.getContentPane().add (new DirectionPanel());

      frame.pack();
      frame.setVisible(true);
   }
}
```

Display

Listing 7.23

```java
//********************************************************************
//  DirectionPanel.java        Author: Lewis/Loftus
//
//  Represents the primary display panel for the Direction program.
//********************************************************************

import javax.swing.*;
import java.awt.*;
import java.awt.event.*;

public class DirectionPanel extends JPanel
{
   private final int WIDTH = 300, HEIGHT = 200;
   private final int JUMP = 10;  // increment for image movement

   private final int IMAGE_SIZE = 31;

   private ImageIcon up, down, right, left, currentImage;
   private int x, y;

   //-----------------------------------------------------------------
   //  Constructor: Sets up this panel and loads the images.
   //-----------------------------------------------------------------
   public DirectionPanel()
   {
      addKeyListener (new DirectionListener());

      x = WIDTH / 2;
      y = HEIGHT / 2;

      up = new ImageIcon ("arrowUp.gif");
      down = new ImageIcon ("arrowDown.gif");
      left = new ImageIcon ("arrowLeft.gif");
      right = new ImageIcon ("arrowRight.gif");

      currentImage = right;

      setBackground (Color.black);
      setPreferredSize (new Dimension(WIDTH, HEIGHT));
      setFocusable(true);
   }
```

Listing 7.23   **continued**

```java
//-----------------------------------------------------------------
//  Draws the image in the current location.
//-----------------------------------------------------------------
public void paintComponent (Graphics page)
{
    super.paintComponent (page);
    currentImage.paintIcon (this, page, x, y);
}

//*****************************************************************
//  Represents the listener for keyboard activity.
//*****************************************************************
private class DirectionListener implements KeyListener
{
    //-----------------------------------------------------------
    //  Responds to the user pressing arrow keys by adjusting the
    //  image and image location accordingly.
    //-----------------------------------------------------------
    public void keyPressed (KeyEvent event)
    {
        switch (event.getKeyCode())
        {
            case KeyEvent.VK_UP:
                currentImage = up;
                y -= JUMP;
                break;
            case KeyEvent.VK_DOWN:
                currentImage = down;
                y += JUMP;
                break;
            case KeyEvent.VK_LEFT:
                currentImage = left;
                x -= JUMP;
                break;
            case KeyEvent.VK_RIGHT:
                currentImage = right;
                x += JUMP;
                break;
        }

        repaint();
    }
```

Listing 7.23 **continued**

```
    //----------------------------------------------------------------
    // Provide empty definitions for unused event methods.
    //----------------------------------------------------------------
    public void keyTyped (KeyEvent event) {}
    public void keyReleased (KeyEvent event) {}
  }
}
```

displayed. If an arrow key is continually pressed, the appropriate image "moves" in the appropriate direction.

The arrow images are managed as `ImageIcon` objects. In this example, the image is drawn using the `paintIcon` method each time the panel is repainted. The `paintIcon` method takes four parameters: a component to serve as an *image observer*, the graphics context on which the image will be drawn, and the (*x*, *y*) coordinates where the image is drawn. An image observer is a component that serves to manage image loading; in this case we use the panel as the image observer.

The private inner class called `DirectionListener` is set up to respond to key events. It implements the `KeyListener` interface, which defines three methods that we can use to respond to keyboard activity. Figure 7.10 lists these methods.

```
void keyPressed (KeyEvent event)
    Called when a key is pressed.

void keyReleased (KeyEvent event)
    Called when a key is released.

void keyTyped (KeyEvent event)
    Called when a pressed key or key combination produces
    a key character.
```

FIGURE 7.10 The methods of the `KeyListener` interface

Specifically, the `Direction` program responds to key pressed events. Because the listener class must implement all methods defined in the interface, we provide empty methods for the other events.

The `KeyEvent` object passed to the `keyPressed` method of the listener can be used to determine which key was pressed. In the example, we call the `getKeyCode` method of the event object to get a numeric code that represents the key that was pressed. We use a `switch` statement to determine which key was pressed and to respond accordingly. The `KeyEvent` class contains constants that correspond to the numeric code that is returned from the `getKeyCode` method. If any key other than an arrow key is pressed it is ignored.

Key events fire whenever a key is pressed, but most systems enable the concept of *key repetition*. That is, when a key is pressed and held down, it's as if that key is being pressed repeatedly and quickly. Key events are generated in the same way. In the `Direction` program, the user can hold down an arrow key and watch the image move across the screen quickly.

The component that generates key events is the one that currently has the *keyboard focus*. Usually the keyboard focus is held by the primary "active" component. A component usually gets the keyboard focus when the user clicks on it with the mouse. The call to the `setFocusable` method in the panel constructor sets the keyboard focus to the panel.

The `Direction` program sets no boundaries for the arrow image, so it can be moved out of the visible window, then moved back in if desired. You could add code to the listener to stop the image when it reaches one of the window boundaries. This modification is left as a programming project.

Summary of Key Concepts

> An array of size N is indexed from 0 to $N-1$.

> In Java, an array is an object that must be instantiated.

> Bounds checking ensures that an index used to refer to an array element is in range.

> An initializer list can be used to instantiate an array object instead of using the `new` operator.

> An entire array can be passed as a parameter, making the formal parameter an alias of the original.

> Instantiating an array of objects reserves room to store references only. The objects that are stored in each element must be instantiated separately.

> Command-line arguments are stored in an array of `String` objects and are passed to the `main` method.

> A Java method can be defined to accept a varying number of parameters.

> Using an array with more than two dimensions is rare in an object-oriented system.

> An `ArrayList` object is similar to an array, but it dynamically changes size as needed, and elements can be inserted and removed.

> An `ArrayList` is a generic type; therefore, we can specify a specific element type for each `ArrayList` object we create.

> `ArrayList` processing can be inefficient depending on how it is used.

> A polyline is similar to a polygon except that a polyline is not a closed shape.

> Moving the mouse and clicking the mouse button generate events to which a program can respond.

> A listener may have to provide empty method definitions for unheeded events to satisfy the interface.

> Rubberbanding is the graphical effect caused when a shape seems to expand as the mouse is dragged.

> Key events allow a program to respond immediately to the user pressing keyboard keys.

Self-Review Questions

SR 7.1   What is an array?

SR 7.2   How is each element of an array referenced?

SR 7.3   What is an array's element type?

SR 7.4   Explain the concept of array bounds checking. What happens when a Java array is indexed with an invalid value?

SR 7.5   Describe the process of creating an array. When is memory allocated for the array?

SR 7.6   What is an off-by-one error? How does it relate to arrays?

SR 7.7   What does an array initializer list accomplish?

SR 7.8   Can an entire array be passed as a parameter? How is this accomplished?

SR 7.9   How is an array of objects created?

SR 7.10   What is a command-line argument?

SR 7.11   How can Java methods have variable length parameter lists?

SR 7.12   How are multidimensional arrays implemented in Java?

SR 7.13   What are the advantages of using an `ArrayList` object as opposed to an array? What are the disadvantages?

SR 7.14   What type of elements does an `ArrayList` hold?

SR 7.15   What is a polyline? How do we specify its shape?

SR 7.16   What is a mouse event?

SR 7.17   What is a key event?

Exercises

EX 7.1   Which of the following are valid declarations? Which instantiate an array object? Explain your answers.

```
int primes = {2, 3, 4, 5, 7, 11};
float elapsedTimes[] = {11.47, 12.04, 11.72, 13.88};
int[] scores = int[30];
int[] primes = new {2,3,5,7,11};
int[] scores = new int[30];
char grades[] = {'a', 'b', 'c', 'd', 'f'};
char[] grades = new char[];
```

EX 7.2   Describe five programs that would be difficult to implement without using arrays.

EX 7.3   Describe what problem occurs in the following code. What modifications should be made to it to eliminate the problem?

```
int[] numbers = {3, 2, 3, 6, 9, 10, 12, 32, 3, 12, 6};
for (int count = 1; count <= numbers.length; count++)
    System.out.println (numbers[count]);
```

EX 7.4   Write an array declaration and any necessary supporting classes to represent the following statements:

a. students' names for a class of 25 students
b. students' test grades for a class of 40 students
c. credit-card transactions that contain a transaction number, a merchant name, and a charge
d. students' names for a class and homework grades for each student
e. for each employee of the L&L International Corporation: the employee number, hire date, and the amount of the last five raises

EX 7.5   Write code that sets each element of an array called nums to the value of the constant INITIAL.

EX 7.6   Write code that prints the values stored in an array called names backwards.

EX 7.7   Write code that sets each element of a boolean array called flags to alternating values (true at index 0, false at index 1, etc.).

EX 7.8   Write a method called sumArray that accepts an array of floating point values and returns the sum of the values stored in the array.

EX 7.9   Write a method called switchThem that accepts two integer arrays as parameters and switches the contents of the arrays. Take into account that the arrays may be of different sizes.

EX 7.10 Describe a program for which you would use the `ArrayList` class instead of arrays to implement choices. Describe a program for which you would use arrays instead of the `ArrayList` class. Explain your choices.

EX 7.11 What would happen if, in the `Dots` program, we did not provide empty definitions for one or more of the unused mouse events?

EX 7.12 The `Dots` program listens for a mouse pressed event to draw a dot. How would the program behave differently if it listened for a mouse released event instead? A mouse clicked event?

EX 7.13 What would happen if the call to `super.paintComponent` were removed from the `paintComponent` method of the `DotsPanel` class? Remove it and run the program to test your answer.

EX 7.14 What would happen if the call to `super.paintComponent` were removed from the `paintComponent` method of the `RubberLinesPanel` class? Remove it and run the program to test your answer. In what ways is the answer different from the answer to Exercise 7.13?

EX 7.15 Create a UML class diagram for the `Direction` program.

Programming Projects

PP 7.1 Design and implement an application that reads an arbitrary number of integers that are in the range 0 to 50 inclusive and counts how many occurrences of each are entered. After all input has been processed, print all of the values (with the number of occurrences) that were entered one or more times.

PP 7.2 Modify the program from Programming Project 7.1 so that it works for numbers in the range between –25 and 25.

PP 7.3   Design and implement an application that creates a histogram
that allows you to visually inspect the frequency distribution of
a set of values. The program should read in an arbitrary number
of integers that are in the range 1 to 100 inclusive; then produce
a chart similar to the one below that indicates how many input
values fell in the range 1 to 10, 11 to 20, and so on. Print one
asterisk for each value entered.

```
1   - 10   | *****
11  - 20   | **
21  - 30   | *******************
31  - 40   |
41  - 50   | ***
51  - 60   | ********
61  - 70   | **
71  - 80   | *****
81  - 90   | *******
91  - 100  | *********
```

PP 7.4   The lines in the histogram in Programming Project 7.3 will be
too long if a large number of values is entered. Modify the program so that it prints an asterisk for every five values in each
category. Ignore leftovers. For example, if a category had 17 values, print three asterisks in that row. If a category had 4 values,
do not print any asterisks in that row.

PP 7.5   Design and implement an application that computes and prints
the mean and standard deviation of a list of integers x_1 through
x_n. Assume that there will be no more than 50 input values.
Compute both the mean and standard deviation as floating
point values, using the following formulas.

$$\text{mean} = \frac{\sum\limits_{i=1}^{n} x_i}{n}$$

$$\text{sd} = \sqrt{\frac{\sum\limits_{i=1}^{n} (x_i - \text{mean})^2}{n-1}}$$

PP 7.6   The L&L Bank can handle up to 30 customers who have savings accounts. Design and implement a program that manages the accounts. Keep track of key information and allow each customer to make deposits and withdrawals. Produce appropriate error messages for invalid transactions. *Hint*: you may want to base your accounts on the Account class from Chapter 4. Also provide a method to add 3 percent interest to all accounts whenever the method is invoked.

PP 7.7   The programming projects of Chapter 4 discussed a Card class that represents a standard playing card. Create a class called DeckOfCards that stores 52 objects of the Card class. Include methods to shuffle the deck, deal a card, and report the number of cards left in the deck. The shuffle method should assume a full deck. Create a driver class with a main method that deals each card from a shuffled deck, printing each card as it is dealt.

PP 7.8   Design and implement an application that reads a sequence of up to 25 pairs of names and postal (ZIP) codes for individuals. Store the data in an object designed to store a first name (string), last name (string), and postal code (integer). Assume each line of input will contain two strings followed by an integer value, each separated by a tab character. Then, after the input has been read in, sort the list of objects by increasing postal code and print the sorted list in a appropriate format to the screen.

PP 7.9   Modify the program you created in programming problem 7.8 to accomplish the following:

> Support the storing of additional user information: street address (string), city (string), state (string), and 10 digit phone number (long integer, contains area code and does not include special characters such as (,), or -)
> Store the data in an ArrayList object.

PP 7.10   Use the Question class from Chapter 6 to define a Quiz class. A quiz can be composed of up to 25 questions. Define the add method of the Quiz class to add a question to a quiz. Define the giveQuiz method of the Quiz class to present each question in turn to the user, accept an answer for each one, and keep track of the results. Define a class called QuizTime with a main method that populates a quiz, presents it, and prints the final results.

PP 7.11   Modify your answer to Programming Project 7.10 so that the complexity level of the questions given in the quiz is taken into account. Overload the giveQuiz method so that it accepts two integer parameters that specify the minimum and maximum complexity levels for the quiz questions and only presents questions in that complexity range. Modify the main method to demonstrate this feature.

PP 7.12   Design a class that represents a star with a specified radius and color. Use a filled polygon to draw the star. Design and implement a program that draws 10 stars of random radius in random locations.

PP 7.13   Design a class that represents the visual representation of a car. Use polylines and polygons to draw the car in any graphics context and at any location. Create a main driver to display the car.

PP 7.14   Modify the solution to Programming Project 7.13 so that it uses the Polygon class to represent all polygons used in the drawing.

PP 7.15   Modify the QuoteOptions program from Chapter 5 so that it provides three additional quote options. Use an array to store all of the quote strings.

PP 7.16   Design and implement a program that draws 20 circles, with the radius and location of each circle determined at random. If a circle does not overlap any other circle, draw that circle in black. If a circle overlaps one or more other circles, draw it in cyan. Use an array to store a representation of each circle, then determine the color of each circle. Two circles overlap if the distance between their center points is less than the sum of their radii.

PP 7.17   Design and implement a program that draws a checkerboard with five red and eight black checkers on it in various locations. Store the checkerboard as a two-dimensional array.

PP 7.18   Modify the program from Programming Project 7.17 so that the program determines whether any black checkers can jump any red checkers. Under the checkerboard, print (using drawString) the row and column position of all black checkers that have possible jumps.

PP 7.19   Modify the RubberLines program from this chapter so that it shows all of the lines drawn. Show only the final lines (from initial mouse press to mouse release), not the intermediate lines drawn to show the rubberbanding effect. *Hint*: Keep track of a list of objects that represent the lines similar to how the Dots program kept track of multiple dots.

PP 7.20   Design and implement a program that counts the number of times the mouse has been clicked. Display that number in the center of the applet window.

PP 7.21   Design and implement an application that creates a polyline shape dynamically using mouse clicks. Each mouse click adds a new line segment from the previous point. Include a button below the drawing area to clear the current polyline and begin another.

PP 7.22   Design and implement an application that draws a circle using a rubberbanding technique. The circle size is determined by a mouse drag. Use the original mouse click location as a fixed center point. Compute the distance between the current location of the mouse pointer and the center point to determine the current radius of the circle.

PP 7.23   Design and implement an application that serves as a mouse odometer, continually displaying how far, in pixels, the mouse has moved (while it is over the program window). Display the current odometer value using a label. *Hint*: Use the mouse movement event to determine the current position, and compare it to the last position of the mouse. Use the distance formula to see how far the mouse has traveled, and add that to a running total distance.

PP 7.24   Design and implement a program whose background changes color depending on where the mouse pointer is located. If the mouse pointer is on the left half of the applet window, display red; if it is on the right half, display green.

PP 7.25   Design and implement a class that represents a spaceship, which can be drawn (side view) in any particular location. Create a program that displays the spaceship so that it follows the movement of the mouse. When the mouse button is pressed down, have a laser beam shoot out of the front of the spaceship (one continuous beam, not a moving projectile) until the mouse button is released.

PP 7.26 Design and implement a program that helps a hospital analyze the flow of patients through the emergency room. A text input file contains integers that represent the number of patients that entered the emergency room during each hour of each day for four weeks. Read the information and store it in a three dimensional array. Then analyze it to compare the total number of patients per week, per day, and per hour. Display the results of the analysis.

PP 7.27 Modify the `Direction` program from this chapter so that the image is not allowed to move out of the visible area of the panel. Ignore any key event that would cause that to happen.

PP 7.28 Modify the `Direction` program from this chapter so that, in addition to responding to the arrow keys, it also responds to four other keys that move the image in diagonal directions. When the `'t'` key is pressed, move the image up and to the left. Likewise, use `'u'` to move up and right, `'g'` to move down and left, and `'j'` to move down and right. Do not move the image if it has reached a window boundary.

Answers to Self-Review Questions

SR 7.1 An array is an object that stores a list of values. The entire list can be referenced by its name, and each element in the list can be referenced individually based on its position in the array.

SR 7.2 Each element in an array can be referenced by its numeric position, called an index, in the array. In Java, all array indexes begin at zero. Square brackets are used to specify the index. For example, `nums[5]` refers to the sixth element in the array called `nums`.

SR 7.3 An array's element type is the type of values that the array can hold. All values in a particular array have the same type, or are at least of compatible types. So we might have an array of integers, or an array of `boolean` values, or an array of `Dog` objects, etc.

SR 7.4 Whenever a reference is made to a particular array element, the index operator (the brackets that enclose the subscript) ensures that the value of the index is greater than or equal to zero and less than the size of the array. If it is not within the valid range, an `ArrayIndexOutOfBoundsException` is thrown.

SR 7.5   Arrays are objects. Therefore, as with all objects, to create an array we first create a reference to the array (its name). We then instantiate the array itself, which reserves memory space to store the array elements. The only difference between a regular object instantiation and an array instantiation is the bracket syntax.

SR 7.6   An off-by-one error occurs when a program's logic exceeds the boundary of an array (or similar structure) by one. These errors include forgetting to process a boundary element as well as attempting to process a nonexistent element. Array processing is susceptible to off-by-one errors because their indexes begin at zero and run to one less than the size of the array.

SR 7.7   An array initializer list is used in the declaration of an array to set up the initial values of its elements. An initializer list instantiates the array object, so the new operator is not needed.

SR 7.8   An entire array can be passed as a parameter. Specifically, because an array is an object, a reference to the array is passed to the method. Any changes made to the array elements will be reflected outside of the method.

SR 7.9   An array of objects is really an array of object references. The array itself must be instantiated, and the objects that are stored in the array must be created separately.

SR 7.10   A command-line argument is data that is included on the command line when the interpreter is invoked to execute the program. Command-line arguments are another way to provide input to a program. They are accessed using the array of strings that is passed into the main method as a parameter.

SR 7.11   A Java method can be defined to accept a variable number of parameters by using elipses (. . .) in the formal parameter list. When a set of values is passed to the method, they are automatically converted to an array. This allows the method to be written in terms of array processing without forcing the calling method to create the array.

SR 7.12   A multidimensional array is implemented in Java as an array of array objects. The arrays that are elements of the outer array could also contain arrays as elements. This nesting process could continue for as many levels as needed.

SR 7.13   An `ArrayList` keeps the indexes of its objects continuous as they are added and removed, and an `ArrayList` dynamically increases its capacity as needed. In addition, an `ArrayList` is implemented so that it stores references to the `Object` class, which allows any object to be stored in it. A disadvantage of the `ArrayList` class is that it copies a significant amount of data in order to insert and delete elements, and this process is inefficient.

SR 7.14   An `ArrayList` generally holds references to the `Object` class, which means that it can hold any type of object at all (this is discussed further in Chapter 8). A specific type of element can be specified in the `ArrayList` declaration to restrict the type of objects that can be added and eliminate the need to cast the type when extracted.

SR 7.15   A polyline is defined by a series of points that represent its vertices. The `drawPolyline` method takes three parameters to specify its shape. The first is an array of integers that represent the x coordinates of the points. The second is an array of integers that represent the y coordinates of the points. The third parameter is a single integer that indicates the number of points to be used from the arrays.

SR 7.16   A mouse event is an event generated when the user manipulates the mouse in various ways. There are several types of mouse events that may be of interest in a particular situation, including the mouse being moved, a mouse button being pressed, the mouse entering a particular component, and the mouse being dragged.

SR 7.17   A key event is generated when a keyboard key is pressed, which allows a listening program to respond immediately to the user input. The object representing the event holds a code that specifies which key was pressed.

Inheritance 8

CHAPTER OBJECTIVES

- > Explore the derivation of new classes from existing ones.

- > Define the concept and purpose of method overriding.

- > Discuss the design of class hierarchies.

- > Discuss the issue of visibility as it relates to inheritance.

- > Explore the ability to derive one interface from another.

- > Discuss object-oriented design in the context of inheritance.

- > Describe the inheritance structure for GUI components.

- > Explore the creation of listeners by extending adaptor classes.

This chapter explains inheritance, a fundamental technique for organizing and creating classes. It is a simple but powerful idea that influences the way we design object-oriented software and enhances our ability to reuse classes in other situations and programs. In this chapter we explore the technique for creating subclasses and class hierarchies, and we discuss a technique for overriding the definition of an inherited method. We examine the `protected` modifier and discuss the effect all visibility modifiers have on inherited attributes and methods. Finally, we discuss how inheritance affects various issues related to graphical user interfaces (GUIs) in Java, such as the ability to extend an adaptor class to create a listener.

8.1   CREATING SUBCLASSES

In our introduction to object-oriented concepts in Chapter 1 we presented the analogy that a class is to an object what a blueprint is to a house. In subsequent chapters we've reinforced that idea, writing classes that define a set of similar objects. A class establishes the characteristics and behaviors of an object but reserves no memory space for variables (unless those variables are declared as `static`). Classes are the plan, and objects are the embodiment of that plan.

Many houses can be created from the same blueprint. They are essentially the same house in different locations with different people living in them. Now suppose you want a house that is similar to another but with some different or additional features. You want to start with the same basic blueprint but modify it to suit new, slightly different, needs. Many housing developments are created this way. The houses in the development have the same core layout, but they have unique features. For instance, they might all be split-level homes with the same basic room configuration, but some have a fireplace or full basement while others do not, or an upgraded gourmet kitchen instead of the standard version.

It's likely that the housing developer commissioned a master architect to create a single blueprint to establish the basic design of all houses in the development, then a series of new blueprints that include variations designed to appeal to different buyers. The act of creating the series of blueprints was simplified since they all begin with the same underlying structure, while the variations give them unique characteristics that may be important to the prospective owners.

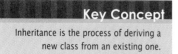

Key Concept

Inheritance is the process of deriving a new class from an existing one.

Creating a new blueprint that is based on an existing blueprint is analogous to the object-oriented concept of *inheritance*, which is the process in which a new class is derived from an existing one. Inheritance is a powerful software development technique and a defining characteristic of object-oriented programming.

Via inheritance, the new class automatically contains the variables and methods in the original class. Then, to tailor the class as needed, the programmer can add new variables and methods to the derived class or modify the inherited ones.

Key Concept

One purpose of inheritance is to reuse existing software.

In general, new classes can be created via inheritance faster, easier, and cheaper than by writing them from scratch. Inheritance is one way to support the idea of *software reuse*. By using existing software components to create new ones, we capitalize on the effort that went into the design, implementation, and testing of the existing software.

Keep in mind that the word *class* comes from the idea of classifying groups of objects with similar characteristics. Classification schemes often use levels of classes that relate to each other. For example, all mammals share certain characteristics:

They are warmblooded, have hair, and bear live offspring. Now consider a subset of mammals, such as horses. All horses are mammals and have all of the characteristics of mammals, but they also have unique features that make them different from other mammals such as dogs.

If we translate this idea into software terms, an existing class called `Mammal` would have certain variables and methods that describe the state and behavior of mammals. A `Horse` class could be derived from the existing `Mammal` class, automatically inheriting the variables and methods contained in `Mammal`. The `Horse` class can refer to the inherited variables and methods as if they had been declared locally in that class. New variables and methods can then be added to the derived class to distinguish a horse from other mammals.

The original class that is used to derive a new one is called the *parent class, superclass,* or *base class.* The derived class is called a *child class,* or *subclass.* Java uses the reserved word `extends` to indicate that a new class is being derived from an existing class.

The process of inheritance should establish an *is-a relationship* between two classes. That is, the child class should be a more specific version of the parent. For example, a horse is a mammal. Not all mammals are horses, but all horses are mammals. For any class X that is derived from class Y, you should be able to say that "X is a Y." If such a statement doesn't make sense, then that relationship is probably not an appropriate use of inheritance.

> **Key Concept**
>
> Inheritance creates an is-a relationship between the parent and child classes.

Let's look at an example. The program shown in Listing 8.1 instantiates an object of class `Dictionary`, which is derived from a class called `Book`. In the `main` method, three methods are invoked through the `Dictionary` object: two that were declared locally in the `Dictionary` class and one that was inherited from the `Book` class.

The `Book` class (see Listing 8.2) is used to derive the `Dictionary` class (see Listing 8.3) using the reserved word `extends` in the header of `Dictionary`. The `Dictionary` class automatically inherits the definition of the `setPages` and `getPages` methods, as well as the `pages` variable. It is as if the those methods and the `pages` variable were declared inside the `Dictionary` class. Note that, in the `Dictionary` class, the `computeRatio` method explicitly references the `pages` variable, even though the variable is declared in the `Book` class.

Also note that although the `Book` class is needed to create the definition of `Dictionary`, no `Book` object is ever instantiated in the program. An instance of a child class does not rely on an instance of the parent class.

Inheritance is a one-way street. The `Book` class cannot use variables or methods that are declared explicitly in the `Dictionary` class. For instance, if we created an object from the `Book` class, it could not be used to invoke the

Listing 8.1

```
//********************************************************************
//   Words.java         Author: Lewis/Loftus
//
//   Demonstrates the use of an inherited method.
//********************************************************************

public class Words
{
    //-----------------------------------------------------------------
    //   Instantiates a derived class and invokes its inherited and
    //   local methods.
    //-----------------------------------------------------------------
    public static void main (String[] args)
    {
        Dictionary webster = new Dictionary();

        System.out.println ("Number of pages: " + webster.getPages());

        System.out.println ("Number of definitions: " +
                            webster.getDefinitions());

        System.out.println ("Definitions per page: " +
                            webster.computeRatio());
    }
}
```

Output

```
Number of pages: 1500
Number of definitions: 52500
Definitions per page: 35.0
```

setDefinitions method. This restriction makes sense because a child class is a more specific version of the parent class. A dictionary has pages because all books have pages; but although a dictionary has definitions, not all books do.

Listing 8.2

```java
//************************************************************
//  Book.java         Author: Lewis/Loftus
//
//  Represents a book. Used as the parent of a derived class to
//  demonstrate inheritance.
//************************************************************

public class Book
{
   protected int pages = 1500;

   //----------------------------------------------------------
   //  Pages mutator.
   //----------------------------------------------------------
   public void setPages (int numPages)
   {
      pages = numPages;
   }

   //----------------------------------------------------------
   //  Pages accessor.
   //----------------------------------------------------------
   public int getPages ()
   {
      return pages;
   }
}
```

Inheritance relationships are often represented in UML class diagrams. Figure 8.1 shows the inheritance relationship between the Book and Dictionary classes. An arrow with an open arrowhead is used to show inheritance in a UML diagram, with the arrow pointing from the child class to the parent class.

Listing 8.3

```java
//********************************************************************
//  Dictionary.java        Author: Lewis/Loftus
//
//  Represents a dictionary, which is a book. Used to demonstrate
//  inheritance.
//********************************************************************

public class Dictionary extends Book
{
   private int definitions = 52500;

   //-----------------------------------------------------------------
   //  Prints a message using both local and inherited values.
   //-----------------------------------------------------------------
   public double computeRatio ()
   {
      return definitions/pages;
   }

   //-----------------------------------------------------------------
   //  Definitions mutator.
   //-----------------------------------------------------------------
   public void setDefinitions (int numDefinitions)
   {
      definitions = numDefinitions;
   }

   //-----------------------------------------------------------------
   //  Definitions accessor.
   //-----------------------------------------------------------------
   public int getDefinitions ()
   {
      return definitions;
   }
}
```

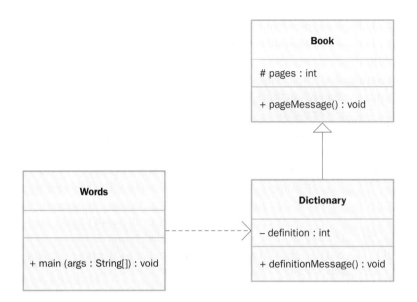

FIGURE 8.1   A UML class diagram showing an inheritance relationship

The protected Modifier

As we've seen, visibility modifiers are used to control access to the members of a class. This effect extends into the process of inheritance as well. Any public method or variable in a parent class can be explicitly referenced by name in the child class, and through objects of that child class. On the other hand, private methods and variables of the parent class cannot be referenced in the child class or through an object of the child class.

However, if we declare a variable with public visibility so that a derived class can reference it, we violate the principle of encapsulation. Therefore, Java provides a third visibility modifier: protected. Note that the variable pages is declared with protected visibility in the Book class. When a variable or method is declared with protected visibility, a derived class can reference it. And protected visibility allows the class to retain some encapsulation properties. The encapsulation with protected visibility is not as tight as it would be if the variable or method were declared private, but it is better than if it were declared public. Specifically, a variable or method declared with protected visibility may be accessed by any class in the same package. The relationships among all Java modifiers are explained completely in Appendix E.

> **Key Concept**
>
> Protected visibility provides the best possible encapsulation that permits inheritance.

In a UML diagram, protected visibility can be indicated by preceding the protected member with a hash mark (#). The pages variable of the Book class has this annotation in Figure 8.1.

Each variable or method retains the effect of its original visibility modifier. For example, the setPages method is still considered to be public in its inherited form in the Dictionary class.

Let's be clear about our terms. All methods and variables, even those declared with private visibility, are inherited by the child class. That is, their definitions exist and memory space is reserved for the variables. It's just that they can't be referenced by name. This issue is explored in more detail in section 8.4.

Constructors, however, are not inherited. Constructors are special methods that are used to set up a particular type of object, so it doesn't make sense for a class called Dictionary to have a constructor called Book. But you can imagine that a child class may want to refer to the constructor of the parent class, which is one of the reasons for the super reference, described next.

The super Reference

The reserved word super can be used in a class to refer to its parent class. Using the super reference, we can access a parent's members. Like the this reference, what the word super refers to depends on the class in which it is used.

One use of the super reference is to invoke a parent's constructor. Let's look at an example. Listing 8.4 shows a modification of the original Words program from Listing 8.1. Similar to the original version, we use a class called Book2 (see Listing 8.5) as the parent of the derived class Dictionary2 (see Listing 8.6). However, unlike earlier versions of these classes, Book2 and Dictionary2 have explicit constructors used to initialize their instance variables. The output of the Words2 program is the same as it is for the original Words program.

The Dictionary2 constructor takes two integer values as parameters, representing the number of pages and definitions in the book. Because the Book2 class already has a constructor that performs the work to set up the parts of the dictionary that were inherited, we rely on that constructor to do that work. However, since the constructor is not inherited, we cannot invoke it directly, and so we use the super reference to get to it in the parent class. The Dictionary2 constructor then proceeds to initialize its definitions variable.

Listing 8.4

```java
//********************************************************************
//  Words2.java        Author: Lewis/Loftus
//
//  Demonstrates the use of the super reference.
//********************************************************************

public class Words2
{
    //-----------------------------------------------------------------
    //  Instantiates a derived class and invokes its inherited and
    //  local methods.
    //-----------------------------------------------------------------
    public static void main (String[] args)
    {
        Dictionary2 webster = new Dictionary2 (1500, 52500);

        System.out.println ("Number of pages: " + webster.getPages());

        System.out.println ("Number of definitions: " +
                            webster.getDefinitions());

        System.out.println ("Definitions per page: " +
                            webster.computeRatio());
    }
}
```

Output

```
Number of pages: 1500
Number of definitions: 52500
Definitions per page: 35.0
```

In this case, it would have been just as easy to set the pages variable explicitly in the Dictionary2 constructor instead of using super to call the Book2 constructor. However, it is good practice to let each class "take care of itself." If we choose to change the way that the Book2 constructor sets up its pages variable, we would also have to remember to make that change in Dictionary2. By using the super reference, a change made in Book2 is automatically reflected in Dictionary2.

Listing 8.5

```java
//********************************************************************
//  Book2.java        Author: Lewis/Loftus
//
//  Represents a book. Used as the parent of a derived class to
//  demonstrate inheritance and the use of the super reference.
//********************************************************************

public class Book2
{
   protected int pages;

   //-----------------------------------------------------------------
   //  Constructor: Sets up the book with the specified number of
   //  pages.
   //-----------------------------------------------------------------
   public Book2 (int numPages)
   {
      pages = numPages;
   }

   //-----------------------------------------------------------------
   //  Pages mutator.
   //-----------------------------------------------------------------
   public void setPages (int numPages)
   {
      pages = numPages;
   }

   //-----------------------------------------------------------------
   //  Pages accessor.
   //-----------------------------------------------------------------
   public int getPages ()
   {
      return pages;
   }
}
```

Listing 8.6

```java
//********************************************************************
//  Dictionary2.java         Author: Lewis/Loftus
//
//  Represents a dictionary, which is a book. Used to demonstrate
//  the use of the super reference.
//********************************************************************

public class Dictionary2 extends Book2
{
   private int definitions;

   //-----------------------------------------------------------------
   //  Constructor: Sets up the dictionary with the specified number
   //  of pages and definitions.
   //-----------------------------------------------------------------
   public Dictionary2 (int numPages, int numDefinitions)
   {
      super(numPages);

      definitions = numDefinitions;
   }

   //-----------------------------------------------------------------
   //  Prints a message using both local and inherited values.
   //-----------------------------------------------------------------
   public double computeRatio ()
   {
      return definitions/pages;
   }

   //-----------------------------------------------------------------
   //  Definitions mutator.
   //-----------------------------------------------------------------
   public void setDefinitions (int numDefinitions)
   {
      definitions = numDefinitions;
   }
```

Listing 8.6   **continued**

```
//-----------------------------------------------------------------
//  Definitions accessor.
//-----------------------------------------------------------------
public int getDefinitions ()
{
   return definitions;
}
}
```

A child's constructor is responsible for calling its parent's constructor. Generally, the first line of a constructor should use the `super` reference call to a constructor of the parent class. If no such call exists, Java will automatically make a call to `super()` at the beginning of the constructor. This rule ensures that a parent class initializes its variables before the child class constructor begins to execute. Using the `super` reference to invoke a parent's constructor can be done only in the child's constructor, and if included it must be the first line of the constructor.

The `super` reference can also be used to reference other variables and methods defined in the parent's class. We use this technique in later sections of this chapter.

Multiple Inheritance

Java's approach to inheritance is called *single inheritance*. This term means that a derived class can have only one parent. Some object-oriented languages allow a child class to have multiple parents. This approach is called *multiple inheritance* and is occasionally useful for describing objects that are in between two categories or classes. For example, suppose we had a class `Car` and a class `Truck` and we wanted to create a new class called `PickupTruck`. A pickup truck is somewhat like a car and somewhat like a truck. With single inheritance, we must decide whether it is better to derive the new class from `Car` or `Truck`. With multiple inheritance, it can be derived from both, as shown in Figure 8.2.

Multiple inheritance works well in some situations, but it comes with a price. What if both `Truck` and `Car` have methods with the same name? Which method

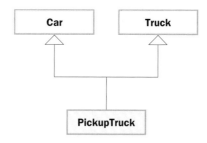

FIGURE 8.2   A UML class diagram showing multiple inheritance

would `PickupTruck` inherit? The answer to this question is complex, and it depends on the rules of the language that supports multiple inheritance.

The designers of the Java language explicitly decided not to support multiple inheritance. Instead, we can rely on interfaces to provide the best features of multiple inheritance, without the added complexity. Although a Java class can be derived from only one parent class, it can implement multiple interfaces. Therefore, we can interact with a particular class in specific ways while inheriting the core information from one parent class.

8.2   OVERRIDING METHODS

When a child class defines a method with the same name and signature as a method in the parent class, we say that the child's version *overrides* the parent's version in favor of its own. The need for overriding occurs often in inheritance situations.

> **Key Concept**
>
> A child class can override (redefine) the parent's definition of an inherited method.

The program in Listing 8.7 provides a simple demonstration of method overriding in Java. The `Messages` class contains a `main` method that instantiates two objects: one from class `Thought` and one from class `Advice`. The `Thought` class is the parent of the `Advice` class.

Both the `Thought` class (see Listing 8.8) and the `Advice` class (see Listing 8.9) contain a definition for a method called `message`. The version of `message` defined in the `Thought` class is inherited by `Advice`, but `Advice` overrides it with an alternative version. The new version of the method prints out an entirely different message and then invokes the parent's version of the `message` method using the `super` reference.

The object that is used to invoke a method determines which version of the method is actually executed. When `message` is invoked using the `parked` object

Listing 8.7

```java
//********************************************************************
//  Messages.java         Author: Lewis/Loftus
//
//  Demonstrates the use of an overridden method.
//********************************************************************

public class Messages
{
    //-----------------------------------------------------------------
    //  Creates two objects and invokes the message method in each.
    //-----------------------------------------------------------------
    public static void main (String[] args)
    {
        Thought parked = new Thought();
        Advice dates = new Advice();

        parked.message();

        dates.message();    // overridden
    }
}
```

Output

```
I feel like I'm diagonally parked in a parallel universe.

Warning: Dates in calendar are closer than they appear.

I feel like I'm diagonally parked in a parallel universe.
```

in the main method, the Thought version of message is executed. When message is invoked using the dates object, the Advice version of message is executed.

A method can be defined with the final modifier. A child class cannot override a final method. This technique is used to ensure that a derived class uses a particular definition of a method.

Method overriding is a key element in object-oriented design. It allows two objects that are related by inheritance to use the same naming conventions for methods that accomplish the same general task in different ways. Overriding becomes even more important when it comes to polymorphism, which is dicussed in Chapter 9.

Listing 8.8

```
//********************************************************************
//   Thought.java        Author: Lewis/Loftus
//
//   Represents a stray thought. Used as the parent of a derived
//   class to demonstrate the use of an overridden method.
//********************************************************************

public class Thought
{
    //-----------------------------------------------------------------
    //   Prints a message.
    //-----------------------------------------------------------------
    public void message()
    {
        System.out.println ("I feel like I'm diagonally parked in a " +
                            "parallel universe.");

        System.out.println();
    }
}
```

Shadowing Variables

It is possible, although not recommended, for a child class to declare a variable with the same name as one that is inherited from the parent. Note the distinction between redeclaring a variable and simply giving an inherited variable a particular value. If a variable of the same name is declared in a child class, it is called a *shadow variable.* It is similar in concept to the process of overriding methods but creates confusing subtleties.

Because an inherited variable is already available to the child class, there is usually no good reason to redeclare it. Someone reading code with a shadowed variable will find two different declarations that seem to apply to a variable used in the child class. This confusion causes problems and serves no useful purpose. A redeclaration of a particular variable name could change its type, but that is usually unnecessary. In general, shadowing variables should be avoided.

Listing 8.9

```java
//********************************************************************
//  Advice.java         Author: Lewis/Loftus
//
//  Represents some thoughtful advice. Used to demonstrate the use
//  of an overridden method.
//********************************************************************

public class Advice extends Thought
{
    //-----------------------------------------------------------------
    //  Prints a message. This method overrides the parent's version.
    //-----------------------------------------------------------------
    public void message()
    {
        System.out.println ("Warning: Dates in calendar are closer " +
                            "than they appear.");

        System.out.println();

        super.message();  // explicitly invokes the parent's version
    }
}
```

8.3   CLASS HIERARCHIES

A child class derived from one parent can be the parent of its own child class. Furthermore, multiple classes can be derived from a single parent. Therefore, inheritance relationships often develop into *class hierarchies*. The diagram in Figure 8.3 shows a class hierarchy that includes the inheritance relationship between the Mammal and Horse classes.

There is no limit to the number of children a class can have or to the number of levels to which a class hierarchy can extend. Two children of the same parent are called *siblings*. Although siblings share the characteristics passed on by their common parent, they are not related by inheritance because one is not used to derive the other.

In class hierarchies, common features should be kept as high in the hierarchy as reasonably possible. That way, the only characteristics explicitly established in

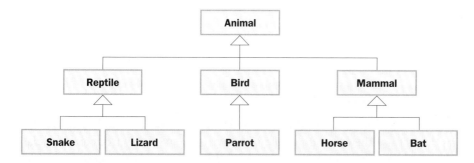

FIGURE 8.3   A UML class diagram showing a class hierarchy

a child class are those that make the class distinct from its parent and from its siblings. This approach maximizes the potential to reuse classes. It also facilitates maintenance activities because when changes are made to the parent, they are automatically reflected in the descendents. Always remember to maintain the is-a relationship when building class hierarchies.

The inheritance mechanism is transitive. That is, a parent passes along a trait to a child class, and that child class passes it along to its children, and so on. An inherited feature might have originated in the immediate parent or possibly several levels higher in a more distant ancestor class.

There is no single best hierarchy organization for all situations. The decisions you make when you are designing a class hierarchy restrict and guide more detailed design decisions and implementation options, so you must make them carefully.

Earlier in this chapter we discussed a class hierarchy that organized animals by their major biological classifications, such as Mammal, Bird, and Reptile. However, in a different situation, the same animals might logically be organized in a different way. For example, as shown in Figure 8.4, the class hierarchy might be organized around a function of the animals, such as their ability to fly. In this case, a Parrot class and a Bat class would be siblings derived from a general

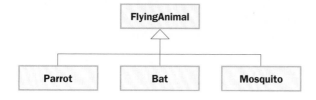

FIGURE 8.4   An alternative hierarchy for organizing animals

FlyingAnimal class. This class hierarchy is as valid and reasonable as the original one. The needs of the programs that use the classes will determine which is best for the particular situation.

The `object` Class

In Java, all classes are derived ultimately from the `Object` class. If a class definition doesn't use the `extends` clause to derive itself explicitly from another class, then that class is automatically derived from the `Object` class by default. Therefore, the following two class definitions are equivalent:

```
class Thing
{
    // whatever
}
```

and

```
class Thing extends Object
{
    // whatever
}
```

> **Key Concept**
>
> All Java classes are derived, directly or indirectly, from the `Object` class.

Because all classes are derived from `Object`, all public methods of `Object` are inherited by every Java class. They can be invoked through any object created in any Java program. The `Object` class is defined in the `java.lang` package of the Java standard class library. Figure 8.5 lists some of the methods of the `Object` class.

As it turns out, we've been using `Object` methods quite often in our examples. The `toString` method, for instance, is defined in the `Object` class, so the `toString` method can be called on any object. As we've seen several times, when a `println` method is called with an object parameter, `toString` is called to determine what to print.

```
boolean equals (Object obj)
    Returns true if this object is an alias of the specified object.

String toString ()
    Returns a string representation of this object.

Object clone ()
    Creates and returns a copy of this object.
```

FIGURE 8.5   Some methods of the `Object` class

Therefore, when we define a toString method in a class, we are actually overriding an inherited definition. The definition for toString that is provided by the Object class returns a string containing the object's class name followed by a numeric value that is unique for that object. Usually, we override the Object version of toString to fit our own needs. The String class has overridden the toString method so that it returns its stored string value.

We are also overriding an inherited method when we define an equals method for a class. As we've discussed previously, the purpose of the equals method is to determine whether two objects are equal. The definition of the equals method provided by the Object class returns true if the two object references actually refer to the same object (that is, if they are aliases). Classes often override the inherited definition of the equals method in favor of a more appropriate definition. For instance, the String class overrides equals so that it returns true only if both strings contain the same characters in the same order.

Abstract Classes

An *abstract class* represents a generic concept in a class hierarchy. An abstract class cannot be instantiated and usually contains one or more *abstract methods*, which have no definition. We've discussed abstract methods in Chapter 6 when they are used to define a Java interface. An abstract class is similar to an interface in some ways. However, unlike interfaces, an abstract class can contain methods that are not abstract. It can also contain data declarations other than constants.

A class is declared as abstract by including the abstract modifier in the class header. Any class that contains one or more abstract methods must be declared as abstract. In abstract classes (unlike interfaces) the abstract modifier must be applied to each abstract method. A class declared as abstract does not have to contain abstract methods.

Abstract classes serve as placeholders in a class hierarchy. As the name implies, an abstract class represents an abstract entity that is usually insufficiently defined to be useful by itself. Instead, an abstract class may contain a partial description that is inherited by all of its descendants in the class hierarchy. Its children, which are more specific, fill in the gaps.

Consider the class hierarchy shown in Figure 8.6. The Vehicle class at the top of the hierarchy may be too generic for a particular application. Therefore we may choose to implement it as an abstract class. In UML diagram, abstract class names are shown in italic.

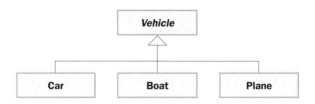

FIGURE 8.6   A vehicle class hierarchy

Concepts that apply to all vehicles can be represented in the `Vehicle` class and are inherited by its descendants. That way, each of its descendants doesn't have to define the same concept redundantly (and perhaps inconsistently). For example, we may say that all vehicles have a particular speed. Therefore we declare a `speed` variable in the `Vehicle` class, and all specific vehicles below it in the hierarchy automatically have that variable because of inheritance. Any change we make to the representation of the speed of a vehicle is automatically reflected in all descendant classes. Similarly, we may declare an abstract method called `fuelConsumption`, whose purpose is to calculate how quickly fuel is being consumed by a particular vehicle. The details of the `fuelConsumption` method must be defined by each type of vehicle, but the `Vehicle` class establishes that all vehicles consume fuel and provides a consistent way to compute that value.

Some concepts don't apply to all vehicles, so we wouldn't represent those concepts at the `Vehicle` level. For instance, we wouldn't include a variable called `numberOfWheels` in the `Vehicle` class, because not all vehicles have wheels. The child classes for which wheels are appropriate can add that concept at the appropriate level in the hierarchy.

There are no restrictions as to where in a class hierarchy an abstract class can be defined. Usually they are located at the upper levels of a class hierarchy. However, it is possible to derive an abstract class from a nonabstract parent.

Usually, a child of an abstract class will provide a specific definition for an abstract method inherited from its parent. Note that this is just a specific case of overriding a method, giving a different definition than the one the parent provides. If a child of an abstract class does not give a definition for every abstract method that it inherits from its parent, then the child class is also considered abstract.

Note that it would be a contradiction for an abstract method to be modified as `final` or `static`. Because a final method cannot be overridden in subclasses, an abstract final method would have no way of being given a definition in subclasses. A static method can be invoked using the class name without declaring an object of the class. Because abstract methods have no implementation, an abstract static method would make no sense.

Choosing which classes and methods to make abstract is an important part of the design process. You should make such choices only after careful consideration. By using abstract classes wisely, you can create flexible, extensible software designs.

Interface Hierarchies

The concept of inheritance can be applied to interfaces as well as classes. That is, one interface can be derived from another interface. These relationships can form an *interface hierarchy,* which is similar to a class hierarchy. Inheritance relationships between interfaces are shown in UML diagrams using the same connection (an arrow with an open arrowhead) as they are with classes.

When a parent interface is used to derive a child interface, the child inherits all abstract methods and constants of the parent. Any class that implements the child interface must implement all of the methods. There are no visibility issues when dealing with inheritance between interfaces (as there are with protected and private members of a class) because all members of an interface are public.

Class hierarchies and interface hierarchies do not overlap. That is, an interface cannot be used to derive a class, and a class cannot be used to derive an interface. A class and an interface interact only when a class is designed to implement a particular interface.

8.4   VISIBILITY

As we discussed earlier in this chapter, all variables and methods, even private members, that are defined in a parent class are inherited by a child class. They exist for an object of a derived class, even though they can't be referenced directly. They can, however, be referenced indirectly.

Let's look at an example that demonstrates this situation. The program shown in Listing 8.10 contains a main method that instantiates a `Pizza` object and invokes a method to determine how many calories the pizza has per serving due to its fat content.

The `FoodItem` class shown in Listing 8.11 represents a generic type of food. The constructor of `FoodItem` accepts the number of grams of fat and the number of servings of that food. The `calories` method returns the number of calories

Listing 8.10

```
//********************************************************************
//   FoodAnalyzer.java         Author: Lewis/Loftus
//
//   Demonstrates indirect access to inherited private members.
//********************************************************************

public class FoodAnalyzer
{
   //-----------------------------------------------------------------
   //   Instantiates a Pizza object and prints its calories per
   //   serving.
   //-----------------------------------------------------------------
   public static void main (String[] args)
   {
      Pizza special = new Pizza (275);

      System.out.println ("Calories per serving: " +
                          special.caloriesPerServing());
   }
}
```

Output

```
Calories per serving: 309
```

due to fat, which the caloriesPerServing method invokes to help compute the number of fat calories per serving.

The Pizza class, shown in Listing 8.12, is derived from the FoodItem class, but it adds no special functionality or data. Its constructor calls the constructor of FoodItem using the super reference, asserting that there are eight servings per pizza.

The Pizza object called special in the main method is used to invoke the method caloriesPerServing, which is defined as a public method of FoodItem. Note that caloriesPerServing calls calories, which is declared with private visibility. Furthermore, calories references the variable fatGrams and the constant CALORIES_PER_GRAM, which are also declared with private visibility.

Listing 8.11

```java
//********************************************************************
//  FoodItem.java         Author: Lewis/Loftus
//
//  Represents an item of food. Used as the parent of a derived class
//  to demonstrate indirect referencing.
//********************************************************************

public class FoodItem
{
   final private int CALORIES_PER_GRAM = 9;
   private int fatGrams;
   protected int servings;

   //-----------------------------------------------------------------
   //  Sets up this food item with the specified number of fat grams
   //  and number of servings.
   //-----------------------------------------------------------------
   public FoodItem (int numFatGrams, int numServings)
   {
      fatGrams = numFatGrams;
      servings = numServings;
   }

   //-----------------------------------------------------------------
   //  Computes and returns the number of calories in this food item
   //  due to fat.
   //-----------------------------------------------------------------
   private int calories()
   {
      return fatGrams * CALORIES_PER_GRAM;
   }

   //-----------------------------------------------------------------
   //  Computes and returns the number of fat calories per serving.
   //-----------------------------------------------------------------
   public int caloriesPerServing()
   {
      return (calories() / servings);
   }
}
```

Listing 8.12

```
//********************************************************************
//  Pizza.java        Author: Lewis/Loftus
//
//  Represents a pizza, which is a food item. Used to demonstrate
//  indirect referencing through inheritance.
//********************************************************************

public class Pizza extends FoodItem
{
   //----------------------------------------------------------------
   //  Sets up a pizza with the specified amount of fat (assumes
   //  eight servings).
   //----------------------------------------------------------------
   public Pizza (int fatGrams)
   {
      super (fatGrams, 8);
   }
}
```

Even though the `Pizza` class cannot explicitly reference `calories`, `fatGrams`, or `CALORIES_PER_GRAM`, they are available for use indirectly when the `Pizza` object needs them. A pizza object cannot be used to invoke the `calories` method, but it can call a method that can. Note that a `FoodItem` object was never created or needed.

8.5   DESIGNING FOR INHERITANCE

Key Concept

Software design must carefully and specifically address inheritance.

As a major characteristic of object-oriented software, inheritance must be carefully and specifically addressed during software design. A little thought about inheritance relationships can lead to a far more elegant design, which pays huge dividends in the long term.

Throughout this chapter, several design issues have been addressed in the discussion of the nuts and bolts of inheritance in Java. The following list summarizes some of the inheritance issues that you should keep in mind during the program design stage:

> Every derivation should be an is-a relationship. The child should be a more specific version of the parent.

> Design a class hierarchy to capitalize on reuse, and potential reuse in the future.
> As classes and objects are identified in the problem domain, find their commonality. Push common features as high in the class hierarchy as appropriate for consistency and ease of maintenance.
> Override methods as appropriate to tailor or change the functionality of a child.
> Add new variables to the child class as needed, but don't shadow (redefine) any inherited variables.
> Allow each class to manage its own data. Therefore use the super reference to invoke a parent's constructor and to call overridden versions of methods if appropriate.
> Use interfaces to create a class that serves multiple roles (simulating multiple inheritance).
> Design a class hierarchy to fit the needs of the application, with attention to how it may be useful in the future.
> Even if there are no current uses for them, override general methods such as toString and equals appropriately in child classes so that the inherited versions don't cause unintentional problems later.
> Use abstract classes to specify a common class interface for the concrete classes lower in the hierarchy.
> Use visibility modifiers carefully to provide the needed access in derived classes without violating encapsulation.

Restricting Inheritance

We've seen the final modifier used in declarations to create constants many times. The other uses of the final modifier involve inheritance and can have a significant influence on software design. Specifically, the final modifier can be used to curtail the abilities related to inheritance.

Earlier in this chapter we mentioned that a method can be declared as final, which means it cannot be overridden in any classes that extend the one it is in. A final method is often used to insist that particular functionality be used in all child classes.

> **Key Concept**
>
> The final modifier can be used to restrict inheritance.

The final modifier can also be applied to an entire class. A final class cannot be extended at all. Consider the following declaration:

```
public final class Standards
{
    // whatever
}
```

Given this declaration, the `Standards` class cannot be used in the `extends` clause of another class. The compiler will generate an error message in such a case. The `Standards` class can be used normally, but it cannot be the parent of another class.

Using the final modifier to restrict inheritance abilities is a key design decision. It should be done in situations in which a child class could possibly be used to change functionality that you, as the designer, specifically want to be handled a certain way. This issue comes up again in the discussion of polymorphism in Chapter 9.

8.6   THE COMPONENT CLASS HIERARCHY

> **Key Concept**
>
> The classes that represent Java GUI components are organized into a class hierarchy.

All of the Java classes that define GUI components are part of a class hierarchy, shown in part in Figure 8.7. Almost all Swing GUI components are derived from the `JComponent` class, which defines how all components work in general. `JComponent` is derived from the `Container` class, which in turn is derived from the `Component` class.

You'll recall that there are two primary GUI APIs used in Java: the Abstract Windowing Toolkit (AWT) and the Swing classes. The AWT is the original set of graphics classes in Java. Swing classes were introduced later, adding components that provided much more functionality than their AWT counterparts. We use Swing components in our examples in this book. In the component class hierarchy, some Swing classes are ultimately derived from AWT classes.

Both `Container` and `Component` are original AWT classes. The `Component` class contains much of the general functionality that applies to all GUI components, such as basic painting and event handling. So although we may prefer to use some of the specific Swing components, they are based on core AWT concepts and respond to the same events as AWT components. Because they are derived from `Container`, many Swing components can serve as containers, though in most circumstances those abilities are curtailed. For example, we've seen that a `JLabel` object can contain an image, but it cannot be used as a generic container to which any component can be added.

Many features that apply to all Swing components are defined in the `JComponent` class and are inherited into its descendants. For example, we have the ability to put a border on any Swing component (as we saw in Chapter 6). This ability is defined once in the `JComponent` class and is inherited by any class that is derived, directly or indirectly, from it.

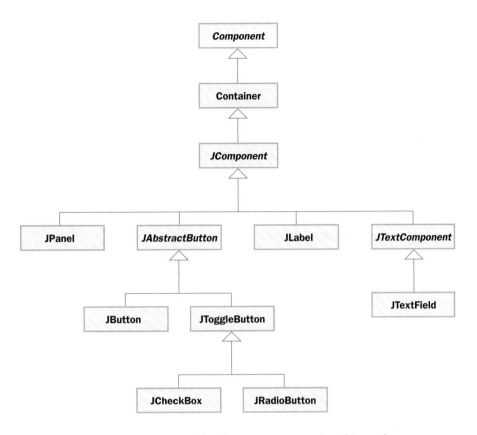

FIGURE 8.7   Part of the GUI component class hierarchy

Some component classes, such as JPanel and JLabel, are derived directly from JComponent. Other component classes are nested further down in the inheritance hierarchy structure. For example, the JAbstractButton class is an abstract class that defines the functionality that applies to all types of GUI buttons. JButton is derived directly from it. However, note that JCheckBox and JRadioButton are both derived from a class called JToggleButton, which embodies the common characteristics for buttons that can be in one of two states. The set of classes that define GUI buttons shows once again how common characteristics are put at appropriately high levels of the class hierarchy rather than duplicated in multiple classes.

The world of text components demonstrates this as well. The JTextField class that we've used in previous examples is one of many Java GUI components that support the management of text data. They are organized under a class called

JTextComponent. Keep in mind that there are many GUI component classes that are not shown in the diagram in Figure 8.7.

In previous chapters we've extended the component class hierarchy further by defining panel and applet classes of our own using inheritance. By extending the JPanel or JApplet class, we create our own classes that automatically have all the characteristics of those components. Sometimes we then overrode the definition of a method, such as the paintComponent method, to behave in a particular way.

Creating our own panel and applet classes is a classic use of inheritance, allowing the parent class to shoulder the responsibilities that apply to all of its descendants. For example, the JApplet class is already designed to handle all of the details concerning applet creation and execution. An applet interacts with a browser, can accept parameters through HTML code, and is constrained by certain security limitations. The JApplet class already takes care of these details in a generic way that applies to all applets. The applet class that we write (the one derived from JApplet) is ready to focus on the purpose of that particular program. In other words, the only issues that we address in our applet code are those that make it different from other applets.

8.7   EXTENDING ADAPTER CLASSES

In previous event-based examples, we've created the listener classes by implementing a particular listener interface. For instance, to create a class that listens for mouse events, we created a listener class that implements the MouseListener interface. As we saw in the Dots and RubberLines programs in Chapter 7, a listener interface often contains event methods that are not important to a particular program, in which case we provided empty definitions to satisfy the interface requirement.

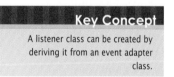

Key Concept

A listener class can be created by deriving it from an event adapter class.

An alternative technique for creating a listener class is to extend an *event adapter class*. Each listener interface that contains more than one method has a corresponding adapter class that already contains empty definitions for all of the methods in the interface. To create a listener, we can derive a new listener class from the appropriate adapter class and override any event methods in which we are interested. Using this technique, we no longer need to provide empty definitions for unused methods.

The program shown in Listing 8.13 displays a panel that responds to mouse click events. Whenever the mouse button is clicked over the panel, a line is drawn

Listing 8.13

```java
//********************************************************************
//  OffCenter.java        Author: Lewis/Loftus
//
//  Demonstrates the use of an event adapter class.
//********************************************************************

import javax.swing.*;

public class OffCenter
{
   //-----------------------------------------------------------------
   //  Creates the main frame of the program.
   //-----------------------------------------------------------------
   public static void main (String[] args)
   {
      JFrame frame = new JFrame ("Off Center");
      frame.setDefaultCloseOperation (JFrame.EXIT_ON_CLOSE);

      frame.getContentPane().add(new OffCenterPanel());
      frame.pack();
      frame.setVisible(true);
   }
}
```

Display

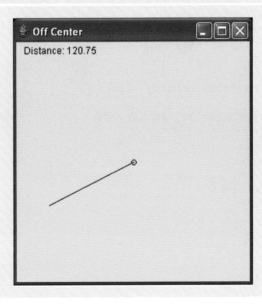

from the location of the mouse pointer to the center of the panel. The distance that line represents in pixels is displayed.

The listener class is implemented as an inner class of the OffCenterPanel class, shown in Listing 8.14. Instead of implementing the MouseListener inter-face directly as we have done in previous examples, this listener extends the MouseAdapter class, which is defined in the java.awt.event package of the Java standard class library. The MouseAdapter class implements the MouseListener interface and contains empty definitions for all of the mouse event methods. In our listener class, we override the definition of the mouseClicked method to suit our needs. Because we inherit the other empty methods corresponding to the rest of the mouse events, we don't have to provide our own empty definitions.

Because of inheritance, we now have a choice when it comes to creating event listeners. We can implement an event listener interface, or we can extend an event adapter class. This is a design decision that should be considered carefully. The best technique depends on the situation.

Listing 8.14

```
//********************************************************************
//  OffCenterPanel.java         Author: Lewis/Loftus
//
//  Represents the primary drawing panel for the OffCenter program.
//********************************************************************

import java.awt.*;
import java.awt.event.*;
import java.text.DecimalFormat;
import javax.swing.*;

public class OffCenterPanel extends JPanel
{
    private final int WIDTH=300, HEIGHT=300;

    private DecimalFormat fmt;
    private Point current;
    private int centerX, centerY;
    private double length;
```

Listing 8.14   **continued**

```java
//---------------------------------------------------------------
//  Constructor: Sets up the panel and necessary data.
//---------------------------------------------------------------
public OffCenterPanel()
{
   addMouseListener (new OffCenterListener());

   centerX = WIDTH / 2;
   centerY = HEIGHT / 2;

   fmt = new DecimalFormat ("0.##");

   setPreferredSize (new Dimension(WIDTH, HEIGHT));
   setBackground (Color.yellow);
}

//---------------------------------------------------------------
//  Draws a line from the mouse pointer to the center point of
//  the panel and displays the distance.
//---------------------------------------------------------------
public void paintComponent (Graphics page)
{
   super.paintComponent (page);

   page.setColor (Color.black);
   page.drawOval (centerX-3, centerY-3, 6, 6);

   if (current != null)
   {
      page.drawLine (current.x, current.y, centerX, centerY);
      page.drawString ("Distance: " + fmt.format(length), 10, 15);
   }
}
```

Listing 8.14   continued

```java
//***********************************************************
//  Represents the listener for mouse events. Demonstrates the
//  ability to extend an adapter class.
//***********************************************************
private class OffCenterListener extends MouseAdapter
{
   //-----------------------------------------------------------
   //  Computes the distance from the mouse pointer to the center
   //  point of the applet.
   //-----------------------------------------------------------
   public void mouseClicked (MouseEvent event)
   {
      current = event.getPoint();
      length = Math.sqrt(Math.pow((current.x-centerX), 2) +
                         Math.pow((current.y-centerY), 2));
      repaint();
   }
}
}
```

8.8   THE Timer CLASS

A *timer* object, created from the Timer class of the javax.swing package, can be thought of as a GUI component. However, unlike other components, it does not have a visual representation that appears on the screen. Instead, as the name implies, it helps us manage an activity over time.

A timer object generates an action event at regular intervals. To perform an animation, we set up a timer to generate an action event periodically, then update the animation graphics in the action listener. The methods of the Timer class are shown in Figure 8.8.

> **Key Concept**
>
> A Timer object generates action events at regular intervals and can be used to control an animation.

The program shown in Listing 8.15 displays the image of a smiling face that seems to glide across the program window at an angle, bouncing off of the window edges.

The constructor of the ReboundPanel class, shown in Listing 8.16, creates a Timer object. The first parameter to the Timer constructor is the delay in milliseconds. The

```
Timer (int delay, ActionListener listener)
     Constructor: Creates a timer that generates an action event at
     regular intervals, specified by the delay. The event will be handled
     by the specified listener.

void addActionListener (ActionListener listener)
     Adds an action listener to the timer.

boolean isRunning ()
     Returns true if the timer is running.

void setDelay (int delay)
     Sets the delay of the timer.

void start ()
     Starts the timer, causing it to generate action events.

void stop ()
     Stops the timer, causing it to stop generating action events.
```

FIGURE 8.8   Some methods of the Timer class

second parameter to the constructor is the listener that handles the action events of the timer. The constructor also sets up the initial position for the image and the number of pixels it will move, in both the vertical and horizontal directions, each time the image is redrawn.

The actionPerformed method of the listener updates the current *x* and *y* coordinate values, then checks to see if those values cause the image to "run into" the edge of the panel. If so, the movement is adjusted so that the image will make future moves in the opposite direction horizontally, vertically, or both. Note that this calculation takes the image size into account.

The speed of the animation in this program is a function of two factors: the pause between the action events and the distance the image is shifted each time. In this example, the timer is set to generate an action event every 20 milliseconds, and the image is shifted 3 pixels each time it is updated. You can experiment with these values to change the speed of the animation. The goal should be to create the illusion of movement that is pleasing to the eye.

Listing 8.15

```
//********************************************************************
//   Rebound.java        Author: Lewis/Loftus
//
//   Demonstrates an animation and the use of the Timer class.
//********************************************************************

import java.awt.*;
import java.awt.event.*;
import javax.swing.*;

public class Rebound
{
   //-----------------------------------------------------------------
   //   Displays the main frame of the program.
   //-----------------------------------------------------------------
   public static void main (String[] args)
   {
      JFrame frame = new JFrame ("Rebound");
      frame.setDefaultCloseOperation (JFrame.EXIT_ON_CLOSE);

      frame.getContentPane().add(new ReboundPanel());
      frame.pack();
      frame.setVisible(true);
   }
}
```

Display

Listing 8.16

```java
//********************************************************************
//   ReboundPanel.java        Author: Lewis/Loftus
//
//   Represents the primary panel for the Rebound program.
//********************************************************************

import java.awt.*;
import java.awt.event.*;
import javax.swing.*;

public class ReboundPanel extends JPanel
{
   private final int WIDTH = 300, HEIGHT = 100;
   private final int DELAY = 20, IMAGE_SIZE = 35;

   private ImageIcon image;
   private Timer timer;
   private int x, y, moveX, moveY;

   //-----------------------------------------------------------------
   //  Sets up the panel, including the timer for the animation.
   //-----------------------------------------------------------------
   public ReboundPanel()
   {
      timer = new Timer(DELAY, new ReboundListener());

      image = new ImageIcon ("happyFace.gif");

      x = 0;
      y = 40;
      moveX = moveY = 3;

      setPreferredSize (new Dimension(WIDTH, HEIGHT));
      setBackground (Color.black);
      timer.start();
   }

   //-----------------------------------------------------------------
   //  Draws the image in the current location.
   //-----------------------------------------------------------------
```

Listing 8.16   continued

```java
    public void paintComponent (Graphics page)
    {
        super.paintComponent (page);
        image.paintIcon (this, page, x, y);
    }

    //*****************************************************************
    //  Represents the action listener for the timer.
    //*****************************************************************
    private class ReboundListener implements ActionListener
    {
        //-------------------------------------------------------------
        //  Updates the position of the image and possibly the direction
        //  of movement whenever the timer fires an action event.
        //-------------------------------------------------------------
        public void actionPerformed (ActionEvent event)
        {
            x += moveX;
            y += moveY;

            if (x <= 0 || x >= WIDTH-IMAGE_SIZE)
                moveX = moveX * -1;

            if (y <= 0 || y >= HEIGHT-IMAGE_SIZE)
                moveY = moveY * -1;

            repaint();
        }
    }
}
```

Summary of Key Concepts

> Inheritance is the process of deriving a new class from an existing one.

> One purpose of inheritance is to reuse existing software.

> Inheritance creates an is-a relationship between the parent and child classes.

> Protected visibility provides the best possible encapsulation that permits inheritance.

> A parent's constructor can be invoked using the `super` reference.

> A child class can override (redefine) the parent's definition of an inherited method.

> The child of one class can be the parent of one or more other classes, creating a class hierarchy.

> Common features should be located as high in a class hierarchy as is reasonably possible.

> All Java classes are derived, directly or indirectly, from the `Object` class.

> The `toString` and `equals` methods are inherited by every class in every Java program.

> An abstract class cannot be instantiated. It represents a concept on which other classes can build their definitions.

> A class derived from an abstract parent must override all of its parent's abstract methods, or the derived class will also be considered abstract.

> Inheritance can be applied to interfaces so that one interface can be derived from another.

> Private members are inherited by the child class, but cannot be referenced directly by name. They may be used indirectly, however.

> Software design must carefully and specifically address inheritance.

> The `final` modifier can be used to restrict inheritance.

> The classes that represent Java GUI components are organized into a class hierarchy.

> A listener class can be created by deriving it from an event adapter class.

> A `Timer` object generates action events at regular intervals and can be used to control an animation.

Self-Review Questions

SR 8.1   Describe the relationship between a parent class and a child class.

SR 8.2   How does inheritance support software reuse?

SR 8.3   What relationship should every class derivation represent?

SR 8.4   What does the `protected` modifier accomplish?

SR 8.5   Why is the `super` reference important to a child class?

SR 8.6   What is the difference between single inheritance and multiple inheritance?

SR 8.7   Why would a child class override one or more of the methods of its parent class?

SR 8.8   What is the significance of the `Object` class?

SR 8.9   What is the role of an abstract class?

SR 8.10   Are all members of a parent class inherited by the child? Explain.

SR 8.11   What is an interface hierarchy?

SR 8.12   How can the `final` modifier be used to restrict inheritance?

SR 8.13   What is an adapter class?

SR 8.14   What does a `Timer` object do?

Exercises

EX 8.1   Draw a UML class diagram showing an inheritance hierarchy containing classes that represent different types of clocks. Show the variables and method names for two of these classes.

EX 8.2   Show an alternative diagram for the hierarchy in Exercise 8.1. Explain why it may be a better or worse approach than the original.

EX 8.3   Draw a UML class diagram showing an inheritance hierarchy containing classes that represent different types of cars, organized first by manufacturer. Show some appropriate variables and method names for at least two of these classes.

EX 8.4   Show an alternative diagram for the hierarchy in Exercise 8.3 in which the cars are organized first by type (sports car, sedan, SUV, etc.). Show some appropriate variables and method names for at least two of these classes. Compare and contrast the two approaches.

EX 8.5   Draw a UML class diagram showing an inheritance hierarchy containing classes that represent different types of airplanes. Show some appropriate variables and method names for at least two of these classes.

EX 8.6   Draw a UML class diagram showing an inheritance hierarchy containing classes that represent different types of trees (oak, elm, etc.). Show some appropriate variables and method names for at least two of these classes.

EX 8.7   Draw a UML class diagram showing an inheritance hierarchy containing classes that represent different types of payment transactions at a store (cash, credit card, etc). Show some appropriate variables and method names for at least two of these classes.

EX 8.8   Experiment with a simple derivation relationship between two classes. Put `println` statements in constructors of both the parent and child classes. Do not explicitly call the constructor of the parent in the child. What happens? Why? Change the child's constructor to explicitly call the constructor of the parent. Now what happens?

Programming Projects

PP 8.1   Design and implement a class called `MonetaryCoin` that is derived from the `Coin` class presented in Chapter 5. Store a value in the monetary coin that represents its value and add a method that returns its value. Create a `main` driver class to instantiate and compute the sum of several `MonetaryCoin` objects. Demonstrate that a monetary coin inherits its parent's ability to be flipped.

PP 8.2   Design and implement a set of classes that define the employees of a hospital: doctor, nurse, administrator, surgeon, receptionist, janitor, and so on. Include methods in each class that are named according to the services provided by that person and that print an appropriate message. Create a main driver class to instantiate and exercise several of the classes.

PP 8.3   Design and implement a set of classes that define various types of reading material: books, novels, magazines, technical journals, textbooks, and so on. Include data values that describe various attributes of the material, such as the number of pages and the names of the primary characters. Include methods that are named appropriately for each class and that print an appropriate message. Create a main driver class to instantiate and exercise several of the classes.

PP 8.4   Design and implement a set of classes that keeps track of various sports statistics. Have each low-level class represent a specific sport. Tailor the services of the classes to the sport in question, and move common attributes to the higher-level classes as appropriate. Create a main driver class to instantiate and exercise several of the classes.

PP 8.5   Design and implement a set of classes that keeps track of demographic information about a set of people, such as age, nationality, occupation, income, and so on. Design each class to focus on a particular aspect of data collection. Create a main driver class to instantiate and exercise several of the classes.

PP 8.6   Modify the Rebound program from this chapter such that when the mouse button is clicked the animation stops, and when it is clicked again the animation resumes.

PP 8.7   Design and implement an application that displays an animation of a car (side view) moving across the screen from left to right. Create a Car class that represents the car (or use one that was created for a programming project in Chapter 7).

PP 8.8   Design and implement an application that displays an animation of a horizontal line segment moving across the screen, eventually passing across a vertical line. As the vertical line is passed, the horizontal line should change color. The change of color should occur while the horizontal line crosses the vertical one; therefore, while crossing, the horizontal line will be two different colors.

PP 8.9   Design and implement an application that plays a game called
Catch-the-Creature. Use an image to represent the creature.
Have the creature appear at a random location for a random
duration, then disappear and reappear somewhere else. The
goal is to "catch" the creature by pressing the mouse button
while the mouse pointer is on the creature image. Create a separate class to represent the creature, and include in it a method
that determines if the location of the mouse click corresponds
to the current location of the creature. Display a count of the
number of times the creature is caught.

PP 8.10   Design and implement an application that works as a stopwatch. Include a display that shows the time (in seconds) as it
increments. Include buttons that allow the user to start and stop
the time, and reset the display to zero. Arrange the components
to present a nice interface. *Hint*: use the `Timer` class (described
in Chapter 8) to control the timing of the stopwatch.

PP 8.11   Design and implement a set of classes that define a series of
three-dimensional geometric shapes. For each store fundamental data about their size and provide methods to access and
modify this data. In addition, provide appropriate methods to
compute each shape's circumference, area, and volume. In your
design, consider how shapes are related and thus where inheritance can be implemented. Create a main `driver` class to
instantiate several shapes of differing types and exercise the
behavior you provided.

PP 8.12   Design and implement a set of classes that define various types
of electronics equipment (computers, cell phones, pagers, digital cameras, etc.). Include data values that describe various
attributes of the electronics, such as the weight, cost, power
usage, and the names of the manufacturers. Include methods
that are named appropriately for each class and that print an
appropriate message. Create a main `driver` class to instantiate
and exercise several of the classes.

PP 8.13   Design and implement a set of classes that define various
courses in your curriculum. Include information about each
course such as the title, number, description, and department
which teaches the course. Consider the categories of classes
that comprise your curriculum when designing your inheritance
structure. Create a main `driver` class to instantiate and exercise several of the classes.

Answers to Self-Review Questions

SR 8.1   A child class is derived from a parent class using inheritance. The methods and variables of the parent class automatically become a part of the child class, subject to the rules of the visibility modifiers used to declare them.

SR 8.2   Because a new class can be derived from an existing class, the characteristics of the parent class can be reused without the error-prone process of copying and modifying code.

SR 8.3   Each inheritance derivation should represent an is-a relationship: the child *is-a* more specific version of the parent. If this relationship does not hold, then inheritance is being used improperly.

SR 8.4   The `protected` modifier establishes a visibility level (like public and private) that takes inheritance into account. A variable or method declared with protected visibility can be referenced by name in the derived class, while retaining some level of encapsulation. Protected visibility allows access from any class in the same package.

SR 8.5   The `super` reference can be used to call the parent's constructor, which cannot be invoked directly by name. It can also be used to invoke the parent's version of an overridden method.

SR 8.6   With single inheritance, a class is derived from only one parent, whereas with multiple inheritance, a class can be derived from multiple parents, inheriting the properties of each. The problem with multiple inheritance is that collisions must be resolved in the cases when two or more parents contribute an attribute or method with the same name. Java only supports single inheritance.

SR 8.7   A child class may prefer its own definition of a method in favor of the definition provided for it by its parent. In this case, the child overrides (redefines) the parent's definition with its own.

SR 8.8   All classes in Java are derived, directly or indirectly, from the `Object` class. Therefore all public methods of the `Object` class, such as `equals` and `toString`, are available to every object.

SR 8.9   An abstract class is a representation of a general concept. Common characteristics and method signatures can be defined in an abstract class so that they are inherited by child classes derived from it.

SR 8.10   A class member is not inherited if it has private visibility, meaning that it cannot be referenced by name in the child class. However, such members do exist for the child and can be referenced indirectly.

SR 8.11   A new interface can be derived from an existing interface using inheritance, just as a new class can be derived from an existing class.

SR 8.12   The `final` modifier can be applied to a particular method, which keeps that method from being overridden in a child class. It can also be applied to an entire class, which keeps that class from being extended at all.

SR 8.13   An adapter class is a class that implements a listener interface, providing empty definitions for all of its methods. A listener class can be created by extending the appropriate adapter class and overriding the methods of interest.

SR 8.14   An object created from the `Timer` class produces an action event at regular intervals. It can be used to control the speed of an animation.

Polymorphism 9

CHAPTER OBJECTIVES

> Define polymorphism and explore its benefits.

> Discuss the concept of dynamic binding.

> Use inheritance relationships to create polymorphic references.

> Use interfaces to create polymorphic references.

> Explore sorting and searching using polymorphic implementations.

> Discuss object-oriented design in the context of polymorphism.

> Discuss the processing of events as an example of polymorphism.

> Examine more GUI components.

This chapter discusses polymorphism, another fundamental principle of object-oriented software. We first explore the concept of binding and discuss how it relates to polymorphism. Then we examine how polymorphic references can be accomplished using either inheritance or interfaces. Design issues related to polymorphism are examined. The Graphics Track of this chapter discusses how event processing in a graphical user interface is an example of polymorphism. We also examine several new GUI components.

9.1   LATE BINDING

Often, the type of a reference variable matches the class of the object to which it refers exactly. For example, consider the following reference:

```
ChessPiece bishop;
```

The `bishop` variable may be used to point to an object that is created by instantiating the `ChessPiece` class. However, it doesn't have to. The variable type and the object it refers to must be compatible, but their types need not be exactly the same. The relationship between a reference variable and the object it refers to is more flexible than that.

> **Key Concept**
>
> A polymorphic reference can refer to different types of objects over time.

The term *polymorphism* can be defined as "having many forms." A *polymorphic reference* is a reference variable that can refer to different types of objects at different points in time. The specific method invoked through a polymorphic reference can change from one invocation to the next.

Consider the following line of code:

```
obj.doIt();
```

If the reference `obj` is polymorphic, it can refer to different types of objects at different times. So if that line of code is in a loop, or if it's in a method that is called more than once, that line of code could call a different version of the `doIt` method each time it is invoked.

At some point, the commitment is made to execute certain code to carry out a method invocation. This commitment is referred to as *binding* a method invocation to a method definition. In many situations, the binding of a method invocation to a method definition can occur at compile time. For polymorphic references, however, the decision cannot be made until run time. The method definition that is used is based on the object that is being referred to by the reference variable at that moment. This deferred commitment is called *late binding* or *dynamic binding*. It is less efficient than binding at compile time because the decision must be made during the execution of the program. This overhead is generally acceptable in light of the flexibility that a polymorphic reference provides.

> **Key Concept**
>
> The binding of a method invocation to its definition is performed at run time for a polymorphic reference.

We can create a polymorphic reference in Java in two ways: using inheritance and using interfaces. Let's look at each in turn.

9.2   POLYMORPHISM VIA INHERITANCE

When we declare a reference variable using a particular class name, it can be used to refer to any object of that class. In addition, it can also refer to any object of any class that is related to its declared type by inheritance. For example, if the class Mammal is the parent of the class Horse, then a Mammal reference can be used to refer to any object of class Horse. This ability is shown in the following code segment:

```
Mammal pet;
Horse secretariat = new Horse();
pet = secretariat;  // a valid assignment
```

> **Key Concept**
>
> A reference variable can refer to any object created from any class related to it by inheritance.

The reverse operation, assigning the Mammal object to a Horse reference, can also be done but it requires an explicit cast. Assigning a reference in this direction is generally less useful and more likely to cause problems because although a horse has all the functionality of a mammal (because a horse *is-a* mammal), the reverse is not necessarily true.

This relationship works throughout a class hierarchy. If the Mammal class were derived from a class called Animal, the following assignment would also be valid:

```
Animal creature = new Horse();
```

Carrying this to the limit, an Object reference can be used to refer to any object because ultimately all classes are descendants of the Object class. An ArrayList, for example, uses polymorphism in that it is designed to hold Object references. That's why an ArrayList can be used to store any kind of object. In fact, a particular ArrayList can be used to hold several different types of objects at one time because, by inheritance, they are all Object objects.

The reference variable creature can be polymorphic because at any point in time it can refer to an Animal object, a Mammal object, or a Horse object. Suppose that all three of these classes have a method called move that is implemented in different ways (because the child class overrode the definition it inherited). The following invocation calls the move method, but the particular version of the method it calls is determined at run time:

```
creature.move();
```

> **Key Concept**
>
> The type of the object, not the type of the reference, is used to determine which version of a method to invoke.

When this line is executed, if creature currently refers to an Animal object, the move method of the Animal class is invoked. Likewise, if creature currently refers to a Mammal object, the

Mammal version of move is invoked. Likewise if it currently refers to a Horse object.

Of course, since Animal and Mammal represent general concepts, they may be defined as abstract classes. This situation does not eliminate the ability to have polymorphic references. Suppose the move method in the Mammal class is abstract, and is given unique definitions in the Horse, Dog, and Whale classes (all derived from Mammal). A Mammal reference variable can be used to refer to any objects created from any of the Horse, Dog, and Whale classes, and can be used to execute the move method on any of them.

Let's look at another situation. Consider the class hierarchy shown in Figure 9.1. The classes in it represent various types of employees that might be employed at a particular company. Let's explore an example that uses this hierarchy to pay a set of employees of various types.

The Firm class shown in Listing 9.1 contains a main driver that creates a Staff of employees and invokes the payday method to pay them all. The program output includes information about each employee and how much each is paid (if anything).

The Staff class shown in Listing 9.2 maintains an array of objects that represent individual employees of various kinds. Note that the array is declared to hold StaffMember references, but it is actually filled with objects created from several other classes, such as Executive and Employee. These classes are all descendants of the StaffMember class, so the assignments are valid. The staffList array is filled with polymorphic references.

The payday method of the Staff class scans through the list of employees, printing their information and invoking their pay methods to determine how much each employee should be paid. The invocation of the pay method is polymorphic because each class has its own version of the pay method.

The StaffMember class shown in Listing 9.3 is abstract. It does not represent a particular type of employee and is not intended to be instantiated. Rather, it serves as the ancestor of all employee classes and contains information that applies to all employees. Each employee has a name, address, and phone number, so variables to store these values are declared in the StaffMember class and are inherited by all descendants.

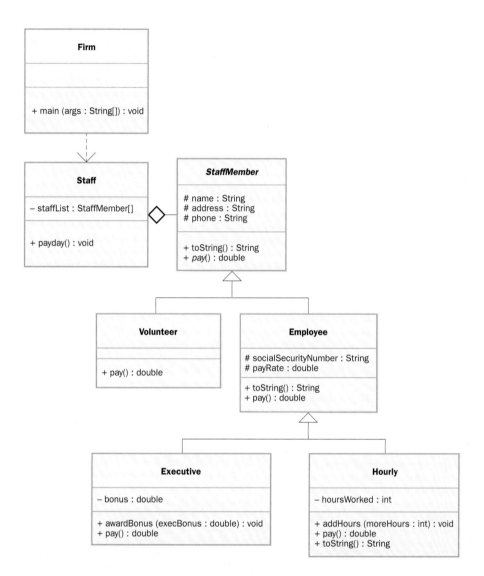

FIGURE 9.1   A class hierarchy of employees

Listing 9.1

```java
//********************************************************************
//  Firm.java        Author: Lewis/Loftus
//
//  Demonstrates polymorphism via inheritance.
//********************************************************************

public class Firm
{
   //-----------------------------------------------------------------
   //  Creates a staff of employees for a firm and pays them.
   //-----------------------------------------------------------------
   public static void main (String[] args)
   {
      Staff personnel = new Staff();

      personnel.payday();
   }
}
```

Output

```
Name: Sam
Address: 123 Main Line
Phone: 555-0469
Social Security Number: 123-45-6789
Paid: 2923.07
------------------------------------
Name: Carla
Address: 456 Off Line
Phone: 555-0101
Social Security Number: 987-65-4321
Paid: 1246.15
------------------------------------
Name: Woody
Address: 789 Off Rocker
Phone: 555-0000
Social Security Number: 010-20-3040
Paid: 1169.23
------------------------------------
```

Listing 9.1   continued

```
Name: Diane
Address: 678 Fifth Ave.
Phone: 555-0690
Social Security Number: 958-47-3625
Current hours: 40
Paid: 422.0
------------------------------------
Name: Norm
Address: 987 Suds Blvd.
Phone: 555-8374
Thanks!
------------------------------------
Name: Cliff
Address: 321 Duds Lane
Phone: 555-7282
Thanks!
------------------------------------
```

Listing 9.2

```java
//********************************************************************
//  Staff.java        Author: Lewis/Loftus
//
//  Represents the personnel staff of a particular business.
//********************************************************************

public class Staff
{
   private StaffMember[] staffList;

   //-----------------------------------------------------------------
   //  Constructor: Sets up the list of staff members.
   //-----------------------------------------------------------------
   public Staff ()
   {
      staffList = new StaffMember[6];

      staffList[0] = new Executive ("Sam", "123 Main Line",
         "555-0469", "123-45-6789", 2423.07);
```

Listing 9.2 **continued**

```java
      staffList[1] = new Employee ("Carla", "456 Off Line",
         "555-0101", "987-65-4321", 1246.15);
      staffList[2] = new Employee ("Woody", "789 Off Rocker",
         "555-0000", "010-20-3040", 1169.23);

      staffList[3] = new Hourly ("Diane", "678 Fifth Ave.",
         "555-0690", "958-47-3625", 10.55);

      staffList[4] = new Volunteer ("Norm", "987 Suds Blvd.",
         "555-8374");
      staffList[5] = new Volunteer ("Cliff", "321 Duds Lane",
         "555-7282");

      ((Executive)staffList[0]).awardBonus (500.00);

      ((Hourly)staffList[3]).addHours (40);
   }

   //-----------------------------------------------------------------
   //  Pays all staff members.
   //-----------------------------------------------------------------
   public void payday ()
   {
      double amount;

      for (int count=0; count < staffList.length; count++)
      {
         System.out.println (staffList[count]);

         amount = staffList[count].pay();   // polymorphic

         if (amount == 0.0)
            System.out.println ("Thanks!");
         else
            System.out.println ("Paid: " + amount);

         System.out.println ("------------------------------------");
      }
   }
}
```

Listing 9.3

```java
//********************************************************************
//  StaffMember.java        Author: Lewis/Loftus
//
//  Represents a generic staff member.
//********************************************************************

abstract public class StaffMember
{
   protected String name;
   protected String address;
   protected String phone;

   //-----------------------------------------------------------------
   //  Constructor: Sets up this staff member using the specified
   //  information.
   //-----------------------------------------------------------------
   public StaffMember (String eName, String eAddress, String ePhone)
   {
      name = eName;
      address = eAddress;
      phone = ePhone;
   }

   //-----------------------------------------------------------------
   //  Returns a string including the basic employee information.
   //-----------------------------------------------------------------
   public String toString()
   {
      String result = "Name: " + name + "\n";

      result += "Address: " + address + "\n";
      result += "Phone: " + phone;

      return result;
   }

   //-----------------------------------------------------------------
   //  Derived classes must define the pay method for each type of
   //  employee.
   //-----------------------------------------------------------------
   public abstract double pay();
}
```

The `StaffMember` class contains a `toString` method to return the information managed by the `StaffMember` class. It also contains an abstract method called `pay`, which takes no parameters and returns a value of type `double`. At the generic `StaffMember` level, it would be inappropriate to give a definition for this method. However, the descendants of `StaffMember` each provide their own specific definition for `pay`. By defining `pay` abstractly in `StaffMember`, the `payday` method of `Staff` can polymorphically pay each employee.

This is the essence of polymorphism. Each class knows best how it should handle a specific behavior, in this case paying an employee. Yet in one sense it's all the same behavior—the employee is getting paid. Polymorphism lets us treat similar objects in consistent but unique ways.

The `Volunteer` class shown in Listing 9.4 represents a person that is not compensated monetarily for his or her work. We keep track only of a volunteer's basic information, which is passed into the constructor of `Volunteer`, which in turn passes it to the `StaffMember` constructor using the `super` reference. The `pay` method of `Volunteer` simply returns a zero pay value. If `pay` had not been overridden, the `Volunteer` class would have been considered abstract and could not have been instantiated.

Note that when a volunteer gets "paid" in the `payday` method of `Staff`, a simple expression of thanks is printed. In all other situations, where the pay value is greater than zero, the payment itself is printed.

The `Employee` class shown in Listing 9.5 represents an employee that gets paid at a particular rate each pay period. The pay rate, as well as the employee's social security number, is passed along with the other basic information to the `Employee` constructor. The basic information is passed to the constructor of `StaffMember` using the `super` reference.

The `toString` method of `Employee` is overridden to concatenate the additional information that `Employee` manages to the information returned by the parent's version of `toString`, which is called using the `super` reference. The `pay` method of an `Employee` simply returns the pay rate for that employee.

The `Executive` class shown in Listing 9.6 represents an employee that may earn a bonus in addition to his or her normal pay rate. The `Executive` class is derived from `Employee` and therefore inherits from both `StaffMember` and `Employee`. The constructor of `Executive` passes along its information to the `Employee` constructor and sets the executive bonus to zero.

A bonus is awarded to an executive using the `awardBonus` method. This method is called in the `payday` method in `Staff` for the only executive that is part of the `staffList` array. Note that the generic `StaffMember` reference must be cast into an `Executive` reference to invoke the `awardBonus` method (which doesn't exist for a `StaffMember`).

Listing 9.4

```
//********************************************************************
//  Volunteer.java        Author: Lewis/Loftus
//
//  Represents a staff member that works as a volunteer.
//********************************************************************

public class Volunteer extends StaffMember
{
   //-----------------------------------------------------------------
   //  Constructor: Sets up this volunteer using the specified
   //  information.
   //-----------------------------------------------------------------
   public Volunteer (String eName, String eAddress, String ePhone)
   {
      super (eName, eAddress, ePhone);
   }

   //-----------------------------------------------------------------
   //  Returns a zero pay value for this volunteer.
   //-----------------------------------------------------------------
   public double pay()
   {
      return 0.0;
   }
}
```

The `Executive` class overrides the `pay` method so that it first determines the payment as it would for any employee, then adds the bonus. The `pay` method of the `Employee` class is invoked using `super` to obtain the normal payment amount. This technique is better than using just the `payRate` variable because if we choose to change how `Employee` objects get paid, the change will automatically be reflected in `Executive`. After the bonus is awarded, it is reset to zero.

The `Hourly` class shown in Listing 9.7 represents an employee whose pay rate is applied on an hourly basis. It keeps track of the number of hours worked in the current pay period, which can be modified by calls to the `addHours` method. This method is called from the `payday` method of `Staff`. The `pay` method of `Hourly` determines the payment based on the number of hours worked, and then resets the hours to zero.

Listing 9.5

```java
//********************************************************************
//  Employee.java       Author: Lewis/Loftus
//
//  Represents a general paid employee.
//********************************************************************

public class Employee extends StaffMember
{
   protected String socialSecurityNumber;
   protected double payRate;

   //-----------------------------------------------------------------
   //  Constructor: Sets up this employee with the specified
   //  information.
   //-----------------------------------------------------------------
   public Employee (String eName, String eAddress, String ePhone,
                    String socSecNumber, double rate)
   {
      super (eName, eAddress, ePhone);

      socialSecurityNumber = socSecNumber;
      payRate = rate;
   }

   //-----------------------------------------------------------------
   //  Returns information about an employee as a string.
   //-----------------------------------------------------------------
   public String toString()
   {
      String result = super.toString();

      result += "\nSocial Security Number: " + socialSecurityNumber;

      return result;
   }
```

Listing 9.5   **continued**

```
   //-----------------------------------------------------------------
   //  Returns the pay rate for this employee.
   //-----------------------------------------------------------------
   public double pay()
   {
      return payRate;
   }
}
```

Listing 9.6

```
//********************************************************************
//  Executive.java        Author: Lewis/Loftus
//
//  Represents an executive staff member, who can earn a bonus.
//********************************************************************

public class Executive extends Employee
{
   private double bonus;

   //-----------------------------------------------------------------
   //  Constructor: Sets up this executive with the specified
   //  information.
   //-----------------------------------------------------------------
   public Executive (String eName, String eAddress, String ePhone,
                     String socSecNumber, double rate)
   {
      super (eName, eAddress, ePhone, socSecNumber, rate);

      bonus = 0;  // bonus has yet to be awarded
   }
```

Listing 9.6   continued

```java
//-----------------------------------------------------------------
//  Awards the specified bonus to this executive.
//-----------------------------------------------------------------
public void awardBonus (double execBonus)
{
   bonus = execBonus;
}

//-----------------------------------------------------------------
//  Computes and returns the pay for an executive, which is the
//  regular employee payment plus a one-time bonus.
//-----------------------------------------------------------------
public double pay()
{
   double payment = super.pay() + bonus;

   bonus = 0;

   return payment;
}
}
```

Listing 9.7

```java
//********************************************************************
//  Hourly.java       Author: Lewis/Loftus
//
//  Represents an employee that gets paid by the hour.
//********************************************************************

public class Hourly extends Employee
{
   private int hoursWorked;

   //-----------------------------------------------------------------
   //  Constructor: Sets up this hourly employee using the specified
   //  information.
   //-----------------------------------------------------------------
```

Listing 9.7   continued

```java
public Hourly (String eName, String eAddress, String ePhone,
              String socSecNumber, double rate)
{
   super (eName, eAddress, ePhone, socSecNumber, rate);

   hoursWorked = 0;
}

//-----------------------------------------------------------------
//  Adds the specified number of hours to this employee's
//  accumulated hours.
//-----------------------------------------------------------------
public void addHours (int moreHours)
{
   hoursWorked += moreHours;
}

//-----------------------------------------------------------------
//  Computes and returns the pay for this hourly employee.
//-----------------------------------------------------------------
public double pay()
{
   double payment = payRate * hoursWorked;

   hoursWorked = 0;

   return payment;
}

//-----------------------------------------------------------------
//  Returns information about this hourly employee as a string.
//-----------------------------------------------------------------
public String toString()
{
   String result = super.toString();

   result += "\nCurrent hours: " + hoursWorked;

   return result;
}
}
```

9.3   POLYMORPHISM VIA INTERFACES

Now let's examine how we can create polymorphic references using interfaces. As we've seen many times, a class name can be used to declare the type of an object reference variable. Similarly, an interface name can be used as the type of a reference variable as well. An interface reference variable can be used to refer to any object of any class that implements that interface.

Suppose we declare an interface called Speaker as follows:

```
public interface Speaker
{
    public void speak();
    public void announce (String str);
}
```

The interface name, Speaker, can now be used to declare an object reference variable:

```
Speaker current;
```

The reference variable current can be used to refer to any object of any class that implements the Speaker interface. For example, if we define a class called Philosopher such that it implements the Speaker interface, we can then assign a Philosopher object to a Speaker reference as follows:

```
current = new Philosopher();
```

This assignment is valid because a Philosopher is a Speaker. In this sense the relationship between a class and its interface is the same as the relationship between a child class and its parent. It is an is-a relationship. And that relationship forms the basis of the polymorphism.

The flexibility of an interface reference allows us to create polymorphic references. As we saw earlier in this chapter, using inheritance, we can create a polymorphic reference that can refer to any one of a set of objects as long as they are related by inheritance. Using interfaces, we can create similar polymorphic references among objects that implement the same interface.

For example, if we create a class called Dog that also implements the Speaker interface, it can be assigned to a Speaker reference variable as well. The same reference variable, in fact, can at one point refer to a `Philosopher` object and then later refer to a `Dog` object. The following lines of code illustrate this:

```
Speaker guest;
guest = new Philosopher();
guest.speak();
guest = new Dog();
guest.speak();
```

In this code, the first time the `speak` method is called, it invokes the `speak` method defined in the `Philosopher` class. The second time it is called, it invokes the `speak` method of the `Dog` class. As with polymorphic references via inheritance, it is not the type of the reference that determines which method gets invoked; it is based on the type of the object that the reference points to at the moment of invocation.

Note that when we are using an interface reference variable, we can invoke only the methods defined in the interface, even if the object it refers to has other methods to which it can respond. For example, suppose the `Philosopher` class also defined a public method called `pontificate`. The second line of the following code would generate a compiler error, even though the object can in fact respond to the `pontificate` method:

```
Speaker special = new Philosopher();
special.pontificate();   // generates a compiler error
```

The problem is that the compiler can determine only that the object is a `Speaker`, and therefore can guarantee only that the object can respond to the `speak` and `announce` methods. Because the reference variable `special` could refer to a `Dog` object (which cannot pontificate), it does not allow the invocation. If we know in a particular situation that such an invocation is valid, we can cast the object into the appropriate reference so that the compiler will accept it, as follows:

```
((Philosopher)special).pontificate();
```

As we can with polymorphic references based in inheritance, an interface name can be used as the type of a method parameter. In such situations, any object of any class that implements the interface can be passed into the method. For example, the following method

Key Concept

A parameter to a method can be polymorphic, giving the method flexible control of its arguments.

takes a `Speaker` object as a parameter. Therefore both a `Dog` object and a `Philosopher` object can be passed into it in separate invocations:

```
public void sayIt (Speaker current)
{
    current.speak();
}
```

Using a polymorphic reference as the formal parameter to a method is a powerful technique. It allows the method to control the types of parameters passed into it, yet gives it the flexibility to accept arguments of various types.

9.4   SORTING

Let's examine a problem that lends itself to a polymorphic solution. *Sorting* is the process of arranging a list of items in a well-defined order. For example, you may want to alphabetize a list of names or put a list of survey results into descending numeric order. Many sorting algorithms have been developed and critiqued over the years. In fact, sorting is considered to be a classic area of study in computer science.

This section examines two sorting algorithms: selection sort and insertion sort. Complete coverage of various sorting techniques is beyond the scope of this text. Instead we introduce the topic and establish some of the fundamental ideas involved. We do not delve into a detailed analysis of the algorithms but instead focus on the strategies involved and general characteristics.

Selection Sort

The *selection sort* algorithm sorts a list of values by successively putting particular values in their final, sorted positions. In other words, for each position in the list, the algorithm selects the value that should go in that position and puts it there. Let's consider the problem of putting a list of numeric values into ascending order.

The general strategy of selection sort is: Scan the entire list to find the smallest value. Exchange that value with the value in the first position of the list. Scan the rest of the list (all but the first value) to find the smallest value, then exchange it with the value in the second position of the list. Scan the rest of the list (all but the first two values) to find the smallest value, then exchange it with the value in the third position of the list. Continue this process for all but the last position in the list (which will end up containing the largest value). When the process is complete, the list is sorted. Figure 9.2 demonstrates the use of the selection sort algorithm.

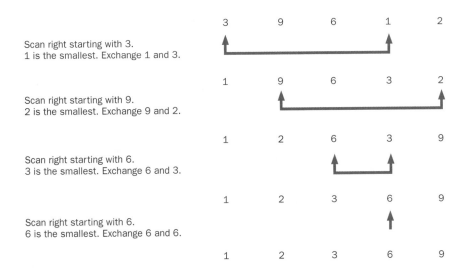

Scan right starting with 3.
1 is the smallest. Exchange 1 and 3.

Scan right starting with 9.
2 is the smallest. Exchange 9 and 2.

Scan right starting with 6.
3 is the smallest. Exchange 6 and 3.

Scan right starting with 6.
6 is the smallest. Exchange 6 and 6.

FIGURE 9.2   Selection sort processing

Let's look at an example. The program shown in Listing 9.8 uses a selection sort to arrange a list of `Contact` objects into ascending order.

Listing 9.9 shows the `Sorting` class. It contains two static sorting algorithms. The `PhoneList` program uses only the `selectionSort` method. The other method is discussed later in this section.

The `selectionSort` method accepts an array of `Comparable` objects to sort. Recall that `Comparable` is an interface that includes only one method, `compareTo`, which is designed to return an integer that is less than zero, equal to zero, or greater than zero if the executing object is less than, equal to, or greater than the object to which it is being compared, respectively.

Any class that implements the `Comparable` interface must define the `compareTo` method. Therefore any such object can be compared to another object to determine their relative order.

The `selectionSort` method is polymorphic. Note that it doesn't refer to `Contact` objects at all, and yet is used to sort an array of `Contact` objects. The `selectionSort` method is set up to sort any array of objects, as long as those objects can be compared to determine their order. You can call `selectionSort` multiple times, passing in arrays of different types of objects, as long as they are `Comparable`.

Listing 9.8

```java
//********************************************************************
//  PhoneList.java        Author: Lewis/Loftus
//
//  Driver for testing a sorting algorithm.
//********************************************************************

public class PhoneList
{
   //-----------------------------------------------------------------
   //  Creates an array of Contact objects, sorts them, then prints
   //  them.
   //-----------------------------------------------------------------
   public static void main (String[] args)
   {
      Contact[] friends = new Contact[8];

      friends[0] = new Contact ("John", "Smith", "610-555-7384");
      friends[1] = new Contact ("Sarah", "Barnes", "215-555-3827");
      friends[2] = new Contact ("Mark", "Riley", "733-555-2969");
      friends[3] = new Contact ("Laura", "Getz", "663-555-3984");
      friends[4] = new Contact ("Larry", "Smith", "464-555-3489");
      friends[5] = new Contact ("Frank", "Phelps", "322-555-2284");
      friends[6] = new Contact ("Mario", "Guzman", "804-555-9066");
      friends[7] = new Contact ("Marsha", "Grant", "243-555-2837");

      Sorting.selectionSort(friends);

      for (Contact friend : friends)
         System.out.println (friend);
   }
}
```

Output

```
Barnes, Sarah    215-555-3827
Getz, Laura      663-555-3984
Grant, Marsha    243-555-2837
Guzman, Mario    804-555-9066
Phelps, Frank    322-555-2284
Riley, Mark      733-555-2969
Smith, John      610-555-7384
Smith, Larry     464-555-3489
```

Listing 9.9

```java
//********************************************************************
//  Sorting.java       Author: Lewis/Loftus
//
//  Demonstrates the selection sort and insertion sort algorithms.
//********************************************************************

public class Sorting
{
   //-----------------------------------------------------------------
   //  Sorts the specified array of objects using the selection
   //  sort algorithm.
   //-----------------------------------------------------------------
   public static void selectionSort (Comparable[] list)
   {
      int min;
      Comparable temp;

      for (int index = 0; index < list.length-1; index++)
      {
         min = index;
         for (int scan = index+1; scan < list.length; scan++)
            if (list[scan].compareTo(list[min]) < 0)
               min = scan;

         // Swap the values
         temp = list[min];
         list[min] = list[index];
         list[index] = temp;
      }
   }

   //-----------------------------------------------------------------
   //  Sorts the specified array of objects using the insertion
   //  sort algorithm.
   //-----------------------------------------------------------------
   public static void insertionSort (Comparable[] list)
   {
      for (int index = 1; index < list.length; index++)
      {
         Comparable key = list[index];
         int position = index;
```

Listing 9.9   **continued**

```
    // Shift larger values to the right
    while (position > 0 && key.compareTo(list[position-1]) < 0)
    {
        list[position] = list[position-1];
        position--;
    }

    list[position] = key;
        }
    }
}
```

Key Concept

Implementing a sort algorithm polymorphically allows it to sort any comparable set of objects.

Each `Contact` object represents a person with a last name, a first name, and a phone number. Listing 9.10 shows the `Contact` class.

The `Contact` class implements the `Comparable` interface and therefore provides a definition of the `compareTo` method. In this case, the contacts are sorted by last name; if two contacts have the same last name, their first names are used.

The implementation of the `selectionSort` method uses two `for` loops to sort the array. The outer loop controls the position in the array where the next smallest value will be stored. The inner loop finds the smallest value in the rest of the list by scanning all positions greater than or equal to the index specified by the outer loop. When the smallest value is determined, it is exchanged with the value stored at the index. This exchange is done in three assignment statements by using an extra variable called `temp`. This type of exchange is often called *swapping*.

Note that because this algorithm finds the smallest value during each iteration, the result is an array sorted in ascending order (that is, smallest to largest). The algorithm can easily be changed to put values in descending order by finding the largest value each time.

Also note that we've set up the sorting methods to sort arrays of objects. Therefore, if your goal is to sort an array of a primitive type, such as an array of integer values, they would have to be put into an array of `Integer` objects to be processed. All of the wrapper classes implement the `Comparable` interface.

Listing 9.10

```java
//********************************************************************
//  Contact.java       Author: Lewis/Loftus
//
//  Represents a phone contact.
//********************************************************************

public class Contact implements Comparable
{
   private String firstName, lastName, phone;

   //-----------------------------------------------------------------
   //  Constructor: Sets up this contact with the specified data.
   //-----------------------------------------------------------------
   public Contact (String first, String last, String telephone)
   {
      firstName = first;
      lastName = last;
      phone = telephone;
   }

   //-----------------------------------------------------------------
   //  Returns a description of this contact as a string.
   //-----------------------------------------------------------------
   public String toString ()
   {
      return lastName + ", " + firstName + "\t" + phone;
   }

   //-----------------------------------------------------------------
   //  Returns a description of this contact as a string.
   //-----------------------------------------------------------------
   public boolean equals (Object other)
   {
      return (lastName.equals(((Contact)other).getLastName()) &&
              firstName.equals(((Contact)other).getFirstName()));
   }
```

Listing 9.10 **continued**

```java
//--------------------------------------------------------------
//  Uses both last and first names to determine ordering.
//--------------------------------------------------------------
public int compareTo (Object other)
{
    int result;

    String otherFirst = ((Contact)other).getFirstName();
    String otherLast = ((Contact)other).getLastName();

    if (lastName.equals(otherLast))
        result = firstName.compareTo(otherFirst);
    else
        result = lastName.compareTo(otherLast);

    return result;
}

//--------------------------------------------------------------
//  First name accessor.
//--------------------------------------------------------------
public String getFirstName ()
{
    return firstName;
}

//--------------------------------------------------------------
//  Last name accessor.
//--------------------------------------------------------------
public String getLastName ()
{
    return lastName;
}
}
```

Insertion Sort

The `Sorting` class also contains a method that performs an insertion sort on an array of `Comparable` objects. If used to sort the array of `Contact` objects in the `PhoneList` program, it would produce the same results as the selection sort did. However, the logic used to put the objects in order is different.

The *insertion sort* algorithm sorts a list of values by repetitively inserting a particular value into a subset of the list that has already been sorted. One at a time, each unsorted element is inserted at the appropriate position in that sorted subset until the entire list is in order.

The general strategy of insertion sort is: Begin with a "sorted" list containing only one value. Sort the first two values in the list relative to each other by exchanging them if necessary. Insert the list's third value into the appropriate position relative to the first two (sorted) values. Then insert the fourth value into its proper position relative to the first three values in the list. Each time an insertion is made, the number of values in the sorted subset increases by one. Continue this process until all values are inserted in their proper places, at which point the list is completely sorted.

The insertion process requires that the other values in the array shift to make room for the inserted element. Figure 9.3 demonstrates the behavior of the insertion sort algorithm with integers.

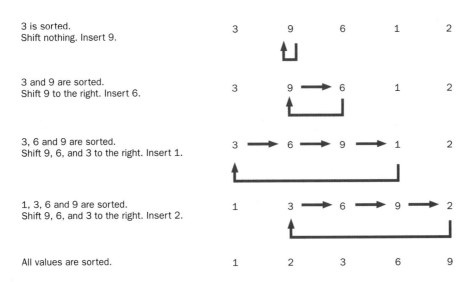

FIGURE 9.3 Insertion sort processing

Similar to the selection sort implementation, the `insertionSort` method uses two `for` loops to sort the array. In the insertion sort, however, the outer loop controls the index in the array of the next value to be inserted. The inner loop compares the current insert value with values stored at lower indexes (which make up a sorted subset of the entire list). If the current insert value is less than the value at `position`, that value is shifted to the right. Shifting continues until the proper position is opened to accept the insert value. Each iteration of the outer loop adds one more value to the sorted subset of the list, until the entire list is sorted.

Comparing Sorts

There are various reasons for choosing one sorting algorithm over another, including the algorithm's simplicity, its level of efficiency, and the amount of memory it uses. An algorithm that is easier to understand is also easier to implement and debug. However, often the simplest sorts are the most inefficient ones. Efficiency is usually considered to be the primary criterion when comparing sorting algorithms. In general, one sorting algorithm is less efficient than another if it performs more comparisons than the other. There are several algorithms that are more efficient than the two we examined, but they are also more complex.

Both selection sort and insertion sort have essentially the same level of efficiency. Both have an outer loop and an inner loop with similar properties, if not purposes. The outer loop is executed once for each value in the list, and the inner loop compares the value in the outer loop with most, if not all, of the values in the rest of the list. Therefore, both algorithms perform approximately n^2 number of comparisons, where n is the number of values in the list. We say that both selection sort and insertion sort are algorithms of *order* n^2. More efficient sorts perform fewer comparisons and are of a smaller order, such as $n \log_2 n$.

Because both selection sort and insertion sort have the same general efficiency, the choice between them is almost arbitrary. However, there are some additional issues to consider. Selection sort is usually easy to understand and will often suffice in many situations. Further, each value moves exactly once to its final place in the list. That is, although the selection and insertion sorts are equivalent (generally) in the number of comparisons made, selection sort makes fewer swaps.

9.5 SEARCHING

Like sorting, searching for an item is another classic computing problem, and also lends itself to a polymorphic solution. *Searching* is the process of finding a designated *target element* within a group of items. For example, we may need to search for a person named Vito Andolini in a club roster.

The group of items to be searched is sometimes called the *search pool*. The search pool is usually organized into a collection of objects of some kind, such as an array.

Whenever we perform a search, we must consider the possibility that the target is not present in the group. Furthermore, we would like to perform a search efficiently. We don't want to make any more comparisons than we have to.

In this section we examine two search algorithms, linear search and binary search. We explore versatile, polymorphic implementations of these algorithms and compare their efficiency.

Linear Search

If the search pool can be examined one element at a time in any order, one straightforward way to perform the search is to start at the beginning of the list and compare each value in turn to the target element. Eventually, either the target element will be found or we will come to the end of the list and conclude that the target doesn't exist in the group.

This approach is called a *linear search* because it begins at one end and scans the search pool in a linear manner. This process is depicted in Figure 9.4. When items are stored in an array, a linear search is relatively simple.

The program shown in Listing 9.11 is similar to the `PhoneList` program from the previous section. It begins with the same, unsorted, array of `Contact` objects. It then performs a linear search for a contact and prints the result. Then it calls the `selectionSort` method, which was discussed in the previous section, to sort the contacts. It then searches for another contact using a binary search, which is discussed later in this section.

Listing 9.12 shows the `Searching` class. It contains two static searching algorithms.

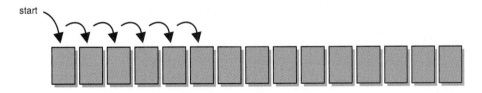

FIGURE 9.4   A linear search

Listing 9.11

```java
//********************************************************************
//  PhoneList2.java        Author: Lewis/Loftus
//
//  Driver for testing searching algorithms.
//********************************************************************

public class PhoneList2
{
   //-----------------------------------------------------------------
   //  Creates an array of Contact objects, sorts them, then prints
   //  them.
   //-----------------------------------------------------------------
   public static void main (String[] args)
   {
      Contact test, found;
      Contact[] friends = new Contact[8];

      friends[0] = new Contact ("John", "Smith", "610-555-7384");
      friends[1] = new Contact ("Sarah", "Barnes", "215-555-3827");
      friends[2] = new Contact ("Mark", "Riley", "733-555-2969");
      friends[3] = new Contact ("Laura", "Getz", "663-555-3984");
      friends[4] = new Contact ("Larry", "Smith", "464-555-3489");
      friends[5] = new Contact ("Frank", "Phelps", "322-555-2284");
      friends[6] = new Contact ("Mario", "Guzman", "804-555-9066");
      friends[7] = new Contact ("Marsha", "Grant", "243-555-2837");

      test = new Contact ("Frank", "Phelps", "");
      found = (Contact) Searching.linearSearch(friends, test);
      if (found != null)
         System.out.println ("Found: " + found);
      else
         System.out.println ("The contact was not found.");
      System.out.println ();
```

Listing 9.11 **continued**

```java
      Sorting.selectionSort(friends);

      test = new Contact ("Mario", "Guzman", "");
      found = (Contact) Searching.binarySearch(friends, test);
      if (found != null)
         System.out.println ("Found: " + found);
      else
         System.out.println ("The contact was not found.");
   }
}
```

Output

```
Found: Phelps, Frank    322-555-2284

Found: Guzman, Mario    804-555-9066
```

Listing 9.12

```java
//********************************************************************
//  Searching.java        Author: Lewis/Loftus
//
//  Demonstrates the linear search and binary search algorithms.
//********************************************************************

public class Searching
{
   //-----------------------------------------------------------------
   //  Searches the specified array of objects for the target using
   //  a linear search. Returns a reference to the target object from
   //  the array if found, and null otherwise.
   //-----------------------------------------------------------------
   public static Comparable linearSearch (Comparable[] list,
                                           Comparable target)
   {
      int index = 0;
      boolean found = false;

      while (!found && index < list.length)
```

Listing 9.12   continued

```
      {
          if (list[index].compareTo(target) == 0)
             found = true;
          else
             index++;
      }

      if (found)
          return list[index];
      else
          return null;
   }

   //-------------------------------------------------------------------
   //   Searches the specified array of objects for the target using
   //   a binary search. Assumes the array is already sorted in
   //   ascending order when it is passed in. Returns a reference to
   //   the target object from the array if found, and null otherwise.
   //-------------------------------------------------------------------
   public static Comparable binarySearch (Comparable[] list,
                                          Comparable target)
   {
      int min=0, max=list.length-1, mid=0;
      boolean found = false;

      while (!found && min <= max)
      {
         mid = (min+max) / 2;
         if (list[mid].compareTo(target) == 0)
            found = true;
         else
            if (target.compareTo(list[mid]) < 0)
               max = mid-1;
            else
               min = mid+1;
      }

      if (found)
         return list[mid];
      else
         return null;
   }
}
```

In the linearSearch method, the while loop steps through the elements of the array, terminating either when the target is found or the end of the array is reached. The boolean variable found is initialized to false and is only changed to true if the target element is located.

Note that we'll have to examine every element before we can conclude that the target doesn't exist in the array. On average, the linear search approach will look through half the data before finding a target that is present in the array.

The linearSearch method is implemented to process an array of Comparable objects. For this algorithm, however, which relies only on the equals method, that restriction is not necessary.

Binary Search

If the elements in an array are sorted, in either ascending or descending order, then our approach to searching can be much more efficient than the linear search algorithm. A *binary search* eliminates large parts of the search pool with each comparison by capitalizing on the fact that the search pool is ordered.

Consider the following sorted array of integers:

0	1	2	3	4	5	6	7	8	9	10	11	12	13	14
10	12	18	22	31	34	40	46	59	67	69	72	82	84	98

Suppose we were trying to determine if the number 67 is in this list. Initially, the target might be anywhere in the list, or not at all. That is, at first, all items in the search pool are *viable candidates*.

Instead of starting the search at one end or the other, a binary search begins in the middle of the sorted list. If the target element is not found at that middle element, then the search continues. The middle element of this list is 46, which is not our target, so we must search on. However, since the list is sorted, we know that if 67 is in the list, it will be in the later half of the array. All values at lower indexes are less than 46. Thus, with one comparison, we've taken half of the data out of consideration, and we are left with the following viable candidates:

Viable Candidates

0	1	2	3	4	5	6	7	8	9	10	11	12	13	14
10	12	18	22	31	34	40	46	59	67	69	72	82	84	98

To search the remaining candidates, we once again examine the "middle" element. The middle element is 72, and thus we have still not found the target. But once again, we can eliminate half of the viable candidates—those greater than 72—and we are left with:

Viable Candidates

0	1	2	3	4	5	6	7	8	9	10	11	12	13	14
10	12	18	22	31	34	40	46	59	67	69	72	82	84	98

Employing the same approach again, we select the middle element, 67, and find the element we are seeking. If it had not been our target, we would have continued with this process until we either found the value or eliminated all possible data.

With each comparison, a binary search eliminates approximately half of the remaining data to be searched (it also eliminates the middle element as well). That is, a binary search eliminates half of the data with the first comparison, another quarter of the data with the second comparison, another eighth of the data with the third comparison, and so on. The binary search approach is pictured in Figure 9.5.

The `binarySearch` method from the `Seraching` class performs a binary search by looping until the target element is found or until the viable candidates drop to zero. Two interger indexes, `min` and `max`, are used to define the portion of the array that is still considered viable. When `min` becomes greater than `max`, then the viable candidates have been exhausted.

On each iteration of the loop, the midpoint is calculated by dividing the sum of `min` and `max` by two. If there are currently an even number of viable candidates, and thus two "middle" values, this calculation discards the fractional remainder and picks the first of the two.

If the target element is not found, the value of `min` or `max` is modified to eliminate the appropriate half of the viable candidates. Then the search continues.

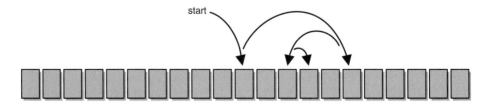

FIGURE 9.5   A binary search

Comparing Searches

As far as the search algorithms go, there is no doubt that the binary search approach is far more efficient than the linear search. However, the binary search requires that the data be sorted. So once again, the algorihtm to choose depends on the situation.

If it's relatively easy to keep the data sorted, or if there will be a lot of searching, it will likely be more appropriate to use a binary search. On the other hand, a linear search is quite simple to implement and may be the best choice when long-term efficiency is not an issue.

9.6   DESIGNING FOR POLYMORPHISM

We've been evolving the concepts underlying good software design throughout this book. For every aspect of object-oriented software, we should make decisions, consciously and carefully, that lead to well-structured, flexible, and elegant code. We want to define appropriate classes and objects, with proper encapsulation. We want to define appropriate relationships among the classes and objects, including leveraging the powerful aspects of inheritance when possible. Now we can add polymorphism to our set of intellectual tools for thinking about software design.

Polymorphism provides a means to create elegant versatility in our software. It allows us to apply a consistent approach to inconsistent but related behaviors. We should try to find opportunities in our software systems that lend themselves to polymorphic solutions. We should seek them out, actively and deliberately, before we begin to write code.

> **Key Concept**
>
> Polymorphism allows us to apply a consistent approach to inconsistent behaviors.

Whenever you find situations in which different types of objects perform the same type of behavior, there is an opportunity for a polymorphic solution. The more experience you get, the easier it will be to detect such situations. See if you recognize the opportunity for polymorphism in the following situations:

> Different types of vehicles move in different ways.
> All business transactions for a company must be logged.
> All products produced by a company must meet certain quality standards.
> A hotel needs to plan their remodeling efforts for every room.
> A casino wants to analyze the profit margin for their games.
> A dispatcher must schedule moving vans and personnel based on the job size.
> A drawing program allows the user to draw various shapes.

> **Key Concept**
>
> We should hone our design senses to identify situations that lend themselves to polymorphic solutions.

The common theme in these examples is that the same basic behavior applies to multiple objects, and those behaviors are accomplished differently depending on the specific type of object. Every circle is drawn using the same basic techniques and information, which is different from the information needed and the steps taken to draw a rectangle. Yet both types of shapes get drawn. Different, but similar. Polymorphic.

The example of a drawing program is explored in more detail in the `PaintBox` case study presented in Appendix J. It follows the refinement of a large program through various stages of its development. The heart of its design is a polymorphic approach to handling the various types of shapes that the user can draw.

Once a polymorphic situation is identified, the specifics of the design can be addressed. In particular, should you use inheritance or interfaces as the mechanism to define polymorphic references? The answer to that question lies in the relationships among the different types of objects involved. If those objects can be related naturally by inheritance, with true is-a relationships, then polymorphism via inheritance is probably the way to go. But if the main thing the objects have in common is their need to be processed in a particular way, then perhaps using an interface to create the polymorphic references is the better solution.

9.7   EVENT PROCESSING

Let's revisit the concept of event processing in a Java GUI and see how it relates to polymorphism. As we've seen many times in previous examples, in order to respond to an event, we must establish a relationship between an event listener object and a particular component that may fire the event. We establish the relationship between the listener and the component it listens to by making a method call that adds the listener to the component.

For example, suppose a class called `MyButtonListener` represents an action listener. To set up a listener to respond to a `JButton` object, we might do the following:

```
JButton button = new JButton();
button.addActionListener (new MyButtonListener());
```

Once this relationship is established, the listener will respond whenever the button fires an action event (because the user pressed it). Now think about the `addActionListener` method carefully. It is a method of the `JButton` class, which was written by someone at Sun Microsystems years ago. On the other hand, we might have written the `MyButtonListener` class today. So how can a method written years ago take a parameter whose class was just written?

The answer is polymorphism. If you examine the source code for the `addActionListener` method, you'll discover that it accepts a parameter of type `ActionListener`, the interface. Therefore, instead of accepting a parameter of only one object type, the `addActionListener` method can accept any object of any class that implements the `ActionListener` interface. All other add listener methods work in similar ways.

> **Key Concept**
>
> Establishing the relationship between a listener and the component it listens to is accomplished using polymorphism.

The `JButton` object doesn't know anything particular about the object that is passed to the `addActionListener` method, except for the fact that it implements the `ActionListener` interface (otherwise the code wouldn't compile). The `JButton` object simply stores the listener object and invokes its `performAction` method when the event occurs.

In Chapter 8 we discussed that we can also create a listener by extending an adaptor class. Well, it turns out that using an adaptor class isn't really a new way to create a listener after all. Each adaptor class is written to implement the appropriate listener interface, providing empty methods for all event handlers. So by extending an adaptor class, the new listener class automatically implements the corresponding listener interface. And that is what really makes it a listener such that it can be passed to an appropriate add listener method.

Thus, no matter how a listener object is created, we are using polymorphism via interfaces to set up the relationship between a listener and the component it listens to. GUI events are a wonderful example of the power and versatility provided by polymorphism.

9.8 FILE CHOOSERS

> **Key Concept**
>
> A file chooser allows the user to browse a disk and select a file to be processed.

Dialog boxes were introduced in Chapter 5. We used the `JOptionPane` class to create several dialog boxes to present information, accept input, and confirm actions.

The `JFileChooser` class represents another specialized dialog box, a *file chooser*, which allows the user to select a file from a hard disk or other storage medium. You have probably run many programs that allow you to open a file using a similar dialog box.

The program shown in Listing 9.13 uses a `JFileChooser` dialog box to select a file. This program also demonstrates the use of another GUI component, a *text*

Listing 9.13

```java
//********************************************************************
//  DisplayFile.java        Author: Lewis/Loftus
//
//  Demonstrates the use of a file chooser and a text area.
//********************************************************************

import java.util.Scanner;
import java.io.*;
import javax.swing.*;

public class DisplayFile
{
   //-----------------------------------------------------------------
   //  Opens a file chooser dialog, reads the selected file and
   //  loads it into a text area.
   //-----------------------------------------------------------------
   public static void main (String[] args) throws IOException
   {
      JFrame frame = new JFrame ("Display File");
      frame.setDefaultCloseOperation (JFrame.EXIT_ON_CLOSE);

      JTextArea ta = new JTextArea (20, 30);
      JFileChooser chooser = new JFileChooser();

      int status = chooser.showOpenDialog (null);

      if (status != JFileChooser.APPROVE_OPTION)
         ta.setText ("No File Chosen");
      else
      {
         File file = chooser.getSelectedFile();
         Scanner scan = new Scanner(file);

         String info = "";
         while (scan.hasNext())
            info += scan.nextLine() + "\n";

         ta.setText (info);
      }
```

Listing 9.13   **continued**

```
        frame.getContentPane().add (ta);
        frame.pack();
        frame.setVisible(true);
    }
}
```

Display

area, which is similar to a text field but can display multiple lines of text at one time. After the user selects a file using the file chooser dialog box, the text contained in that file is displayed in a text area.

The file chooser dialog box is displayed when the showOpenDialog method is invoked. It automatically presents the list of files contained in a particular directory. The user can use the controls on the dialog box to navigate to other directories, change the way the files are viewed, and specify which types of files are displayed.

The showOpenDialog method returns an integer representing the status of the operation, which can be checked against constants defined in the JFileChooser class. In this program, if a file was not selected (perhaps by pressing the Cancel button), a default message is displayed in the text area. If the user chose a file, it is opened and its contents are read using the Scanner class. Note that this program assumes the selected file contains text. It does not catch any exceptions, so if the user selects an inappropriate file, the program will terminate when the exception is thrown.

A text area component is defined by the `JTextArea` class. In this program, we pass two parameters to its constructor, specifying the size of the text area in terms of the number of characters (rows and columns) it should display. The text to display is set using the `setText` method.

A text area component, like a text field, can be set so that it is either editable or noneditable. The user can change the contents of an editable text area by clicking on the text area and typing with the mouse. If the text area is noneditable, it is used to display text only. By default, a `JTextArea` component is editable.

A `JFileChooser` component makes it easy to allow users to specify a specific file to use. Another specialized dialog box—one that allows the user to choose a color—is discussed in the next section.

9.9   COLOR CHOOSERS

In many situations we may want to give the user of a program the ability to choose a color. We could accomplish this in various ways. For instance, we could provide a list of colors using a set of radio buttons. However, with the wide variety of colors available, it's nice to have an easier and more flexible technique to accomplish this common task. A specialized dialog box, often referred to as a *color chooser*, is a graphical component that serves this purpose.

The `JColorChooser` class represents a color chooser. It can be used to display a dialog box that lets the user click on a color of choice from a palette presented for that purpose. The user could also specify a color using RGB values or other color representation techniques.

The program shown in Listing 9.14 uses a color chooser dialog box to specify the color of a panel that is displayed in a separate frame.

After choosing a color, the new color is displayed in the primary frame and another dialog box (this one was created using `JOptionPane` as discussed in Chapter 5) is used to determine if the user wants to change the color again. If so, another color chooser dialog box is displayed. This cycle can continue as long as the user desires.

Invoking the static `showDialog` method of the `JColorChooser` class causes the color chooser dialog box to appear. The parameters to that method specify the parent component for the dialog box, the title that appears in the dialog box

Listing 9.14

```java
//********************************************************************
//  DisplayColor.java       Author: Lewis/Loftus
//
//  Demonstrates the use of a color chooser.
//********************************************************************

import javax.swing.*;
import java.awt.*;

public class DisplayColor
{
   //-----------------------------------------------------------------
   //  Presents a frame with a colored panel, then allows the user
   //  to change the color multiple times using a color chooser.
   //-----------------------------------------------------------------
   public static void main (String[] args)
   {
      JFrame frame = new JFrame ("Display Color");
      frame.setDefaultCloseOperation (JFrame.EXIT_ON_CLOSE);

      JPanel colorPanel = new JPanel();
      colorPanel.setBackground (Color.white);
      colorPanel.setPreferredSize (new Dimension (300, 100));

      frame.getContentPane().add (colorPanel);
      frame.pack();
      frame.setVisible(true);

      Color shade = Color.white;
      int again;

      do
      {
         shade = JColorChooser.showDialog (frame, "Pick a Color!",
                                           shade);

         colorPanel.setBackground (shade);
```

Listing 9.14 **continued**

```
        again = JOptionPane.showConfirmDialog (null,
            "Display another color?");
    }
    while (again == JOptionPane.YES_OPTION);
  }
}
```

Display

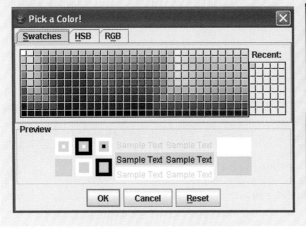 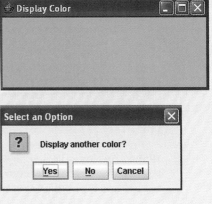

frame, and the initial color showing in the color chooser. By using the variable shade as the third parameter, the color initially showing in the color chooser when it first appears will coincide with the current color of the panel.

9.10 SLIDERS

A *slider* is a component that allows the user to specify a numeric value within a bounded range. A slider can be presented either vertically or horizontally and can have optional tick marks and labels indicating the range of values.

A program called `SlideColor` is shown in Listing 9.15. In one sense, this program is an improvement over the `DisplayColor` program from the previous section in that it allows the user to constantly change the displayed color without using a color chooser each time. This program presents three sliders that control the RGB components of a color. The color specified by the values of the sliders is shown in a square that is displayed to the right of the sliders.

The panel called `colorPanel` defined in the `main` method is used to display the color specified by the sliders by setting its background color. Initially, the settings of the sliders are all zero, which correspond to the initial color displayed (black).

The `SlideColorPanel` class shown in Listing 9.16 is a panel used to display the three sliders. Each is created from the `JSlider` class, which accepts four parameters. The first determines the orientation of the slider using one of two `JSlider` constants (`HORIZONTAL` or `VERTICAL`). The second and third parameters specify the maximum and minimum values of the slider, which are set to 0 and 255 for each of the sliders in the example. The last parameter of the `JSlider` constructor specifies the slider's initial value. In our example, the initial value of each slider is zero, which puts the slider knob to the far left when the program initially executes.

The `JSlider` class has several methods that allow the programmer to tailor the look of a slider. Major tick marks can be set at specific intervals using the `setMajorTickSpacing` method. Intermediate minor tick marks can be set using the `setMinorTickSpacing` method. Neither is displayed, however, unless the `setPaintTicks` method, with a parameter of `true`, is invoked as well. Labels indicating the value of the major tick marks are displayed if indicated by a call to the `setPaintLabels` method.

Note that in this example, the major tick spacing is set to 50. Starting at zero, each increment of 50 is labeled. The last label is therefore 250, even though the slider value can reach 255.

A slider produces a *change event*, indicating that the position of the slider and the value it represents has changed. The `ChangeListener` interface contains a single method called `stateChanged`. In the `SlideColor` program, the same listener object is used for all three sliders. In the `stateChanged` method, which is called whenever any of the sliders is adjusted, the value of each slider is obtained, the labels of all three are updated, and the background color of the display panel is revised. It is actually only necessary to update one of the labels (the one whose corresponding slider changed). However, the effort to determine which slider was adjusted is not warranted. It's easier—and probably more efficient—to update all three labels each time. Another alternative is to have a unique listener for each slider, though that extra coding effort is not needed either.

A slider is often a good choice when a large range of values is possible but strictly bounded on both ends. Compared to alternatives such as a text field, sliders convey more information to the user and eliminate input errors.

Listing 9.15

```java
//********************************************************************
//  SlideColor.java        Author: Lewis/Loftus
//
//  Demonstrates the use of slider components.
//********************************************************************

import java.awt.*;
import javax.swing.*;

public class SlideColor
{
    //----------------------------------------------------------------
    //  Presents a frame with a control panel and a panel that
    //  changes color as the sliders are adjusted.
    //----------------------------------------------------------------
    public static void main (String[] args)
    {
        JFrame frame = new JFrame ("Slide Colors");
        frame.setDefaultCloseOperation (JFrame.EXIT_ON_CLOSE);

        frame.getContentPane().add(new SlideColorPanel());

        frame.pack();
        frame.setVisible(true);
    }
}
```

Display

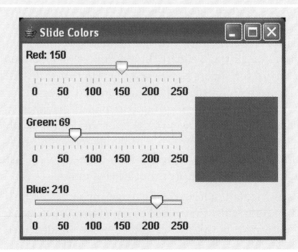

Listing 9.16

```java
//********************************************************************
//  SlideColorPanel.java        Author: Lewis/Loftus
//
//  Represents the slider control panel for the SlideColor program.
//********************************************************************

import java.awt.*;
import javax.swing.*;
import javax.swing.event.*;

public class SlideColorPanel extends JPanel
{
   private JPanel controls, colorPanel;
   private JSlider rSlider, gSlider, bSlider;
   private JLabel rLabel, gLabel, bLabel;

   //-----------------------------------------------------------------
   //  Sets up the sliders and their labels, aligning them along
   //  their left edge using a box layout.
   //-----------------------------------------------------------------
   public SlideColorPanel()
   {
      rSlider = new JSlider (JSlider.HORIZONTAL, 0, 255, 0);
      rSlider.setMajorTickSpacing (50);
      rSlider.setMinorTickSpacing (10);
      rSlider.setPaintTicks (true);
      rSlider.setPaintLabels (true);
      rSlider.setAlignmentX (Component.LEFT_ALIGNMENT);

      gSlider = new JSlider (JSlider.HORIZONTAL, 0, 255, 0);
      gSlider.setMajorTickSpacing (50);
      gSlider.setMinorTickSpacing (10);
      gSlider.setPaintTicks (true);
      gSlider.setPaintLabels (true);
      gSlider.setAlignmentX (Component.LEFT_ALIGNMENT);

      bSlider = new JSlider (JSlider.HORIZONTAL, 0, 255, 0);
      bSlider.setMajorTickSpacing (50);
      bSlider.setMinorTickSpacing (10);
      bSlider.setPaintTicks (true);
      bSlider.setPaintLabels (true);
      bSlider.setAlignmentX (Component.LEFT_ALIGNMENT);
```

Listing 9.16   **continued**

```java
        SliderListener listener = new SliderListener();
        rSlider.addChangeListener (listener);
        gSlider.addChangeListener (listener);
        bSlider.addChangeListener (listener);

        rLabel = new JLabel ("Red: 0");
        rLabel.setAlignmentX (Component.LEFT_ALIGNMENT);
        gLabel = new JLabel ("Green: 0");
        gLabel.setAlignmentX (Component.LEFT_ALIGNMENT);
        bLabel = new JLabel ("Blue: 0");
        bLabel.setAlignmentX (Component.LEFT_ALIGNMENT);

        controls = new JPanel();
        BoxLayout layout = new BoxLayout (controls, BoxLayout.Y_AXIS);
        controls.setLayout (layout);
        controls.add (rLabel);
        controls.add (rSlider);
        controls.add (Box.createRigidArea (new Dimension (0, 20)));
        controls.add (gLabel);
        controls.add (gSlider);
        controls.add (Box.createRigidArea (new Dimension (0, 20)));
        controls.add (bLabel);
        controls.add (bSlider);

        colorPanel = new JPanel();
        colorPanel.setPreferredSize (new Dimension (100, 100));
        colorPanel.setBackground (new Color (0, 0, 0));

        add (controls);
        add (colorPanel);
    }

    //*********************************************************************
    //   Represents the listener for all three sliders.
    //*********************************************************************
    private class SliderListener implements ChangeListener
    {
        private int red, green, blue;
```

Listing 9.16   **continued**

```java
//-----------------------------------------------------------------
//  Gets the value of each slider, then updates the labels and
//  the color panel.
//-----------------------------------------------------------------
public void stateChanged (ChangeEvent event)
{
   red = rSlider.getValue();
   green = gSlider.getValue();
   blue = bSlider.getValue();

   rLabel.setText ("Red: " + red);
   gLabel.setText ("Green: " + green);
   bLabel.setText ("Blue: " + blue);

   colorPanel.setBackground (new Color (red, green, blue));
   }
}
}
```

Summary of Key Concepts

> A polymorphic reference can refer to different types of objects over time.

> The binding of a method invocation to its definition is performed at run time for a polymorphic reference.

> A reference variable can refer to any object created from any class related to it by inheritance.

> The type of the object, not the type of the reference, is used to determine which version of a method to invoke.

> An interface name can be used to declare an object reference variable.

> An interface reference can refer to any object of any class that implements that interface.

> A parameter to a method can be polymorphic, giving the method flexible control of its arguments.

> Implementing a sort algorithm polymorphically allows it to sort any comparable set of objects.

> Polymorphism allows us to apply a consistent approach to inconsistent behaviors.

> We should hone our design senses to identify situations that lend themselves to polymorphic solutions.

> Establishing the relationship between a listener and the component it listens to is accomplished using polymorphism.

> A file chooser allows the user to browse a disk and select a file to be processed.

> A color chooser allows the user to select a color from a palette or using RGB values.

> A slider lets the user specify a numeric value within a bounded range.

Self-Review Questions

SR 9.1   What is polymorphism?

SR 9.2   How does inheritance support polymorphism?

SR 9.3   How is overriding related to polymorphism?

SR 9.4   Why is the StaffMember class in the Firm example declared as abstract?

SR 9.5   Why is the pay method declared in the StaffMember class, given that it is abstract and has no body at that level?

SR 9.6   How can polymorphism be accomplished using interfaces?

SR 9.7   Describe the Comparable interface.

SR 9.8   In what way are the sort methods defined in this chapter polymorphic?

SR 9.9   Which is better: selection sort or insertion sort? Explain.

SR 9.10   Describe the general concept of a binary search.

SR 9.11   What is a file chooser?

SR 9.12   Why is a slider a better choice than a text field in some cases?

Exercises

EX 9.1   Draw and annotate a class hierarchy that represents various types of faculty at a university. Show what characteristics would be represented in the various classes of the hierarchy. Explain how polymorphism could play a role in the process of assigning courses to each faculty member.

EX 9.2   Draw and annotate a class hierarchy that represents various types of animals in a zoo. Show what characteristics would be represented in the various classes of the hierarchy. Explain how polymorphism could play a role in guiding the feeding of the animals.

EX 9.3   Draw and annotate a class hierarchy that represents various types of sales transactions in a store (cash, credit, etc.). Show what characteristics would be represented in the various classes of the hierarchy. Explain how polymorphism could play a role in the payment process.

EX 9.4   What would happen if the pay method were not defined as an abstract method in the StaffMember class of the Firm program?

EX 9.5   Explain how a call to the addMouseListener method represents a polymorphic situation.

EX 9.6   Draw the containment hierarchy tree for the SlideColor program.

Programming Projects

PP 9.1   Modify the `Firm` example from this chapter such that it accomplishes its polymorphism using an interface called `Payable`.

PP 9.2   Modify the `Firm` example from this chapter such that all employees can be given different vacation options depending on their classification. Modify the driver program to demonstrate this new functionality.

PP 9.3   Implement the `Speaker` interface described in Section 9.3, and create three classes that implement `Speaker` in various ways. Create a driver class whose `main` method instantiates some of these objects and tests their abilities.

PP 9.4   Rewrite the `Sorts` class so that both sorting algorithms put the values in descending order. Create a driver class with a `main` method to exercise the modifications.

PP 9.5   Modify the `Tunes` program from Chapter 7 so that it keeps the CDs sorted by title.

PP 9.6   Design and implement a program that graphically displays the processing of a selection sort. Use bars of various heights to represent the values being sorted. Display the set of bars after each swap. Put a delay in the processing of the sort to give the human observer a chance to see how the order of the values changes.

PP 9.7   Repeat Programming Project 9.3 using an insertion sort.

PP 9.8   Design and implement a program that combines the functionality of the `StyleOptions` and `QuoteOptions` programs from Chapter 5. That is, the new program should present the appropriate quote (using radio buttons) whose style can be changed (using checkboxes). Also include a slider that regulates the size of the quotation font. Design the containment hierarchy carefully and use layout managers as appropriate to create a nice interface.

PP 9.9   Design and implement an application that draws the graph of the equation $ax^2 + bx + c$, where the values of a, b, and c are set using three sliders.

Answers to Self-Review Questions

SR 9.1   Polymorphism is the ability of a reference variable to refer to objects of various types at different times. A method invoked through such a reference is bound to different method definitions at different times, depending on the type of the object referenced.

SR 9.2   In Java, a reference variable declared using a parent class can be used to refer to an object of the child class. If both classes contain a method with the same signature, the parent reference can be polymorphic.

SR 9.3   When a child class overrides the definition of a parent's method, two versions of that method exist. If a polymorphic reference is used to invoke the method, the version of the method that is invoked is determined by the type of the object being referred to, not by the type of the reference variable.

SR 9.4   The `StaffMember` class is abstract because it is not intended to be instantiated. It serves as a placeholder in the inheritance hierarchy to help organize and manage the objects polymorphically.

ST 9.5   The `pay` method has no meaning at the `StaffMember` level, so is declared as abstract. But by declaring it there we guarantee that every object of its children will have a `pay` method. This allows us to create an array of `StaffMember` objects, which is actually filled with various types of staff members, and pay each one. The details of being paid are determined by each class as appropriate.

SR 9.6   An interface name can be used as the type of a reference. Such a reference variable can refer to any object of any class that implements that interface. Because all classes implement the same interface, they have methods with common signatures, which can be dynamically bound.

SR 9.7   The `Comparable` interface contains a single method called `compareTo`, which should return an integer that is less than zero, equal to zero, or greater than zero if the executing object is less than, equal to, or greater than the object to which it is being compared, respectively.

SR 9.8   The sorting methods in this chapter all operate on an array of `Comparable` objects. So the sorting method doesn't really "know" what the objects are, other than that they are comparable, and therefore have a `compareTo` method that can be invoked.

SR 9.9   Selection sort and insertion sort are generally equivalent in efficiency, because they both take about n^2 number of comparisons to sort a list of n numbers. Selection sort, though, generally makes fewer swaps. Several sorting algorithms are more efficient than either of these.

SR 9.10   A binary search assumes that the search pool is already sorted and begins by examining the middle element. Assuming the target is not found, approximately half of the data is eliminated as viable candidates. Then the middle element of the remaining candidates is examined, eliminating another quarter of the data. This process continues until the element is found or all viable data has been examined.

SR 9.11   A file chooser is a GUI component that allows the user to navigate a disk or other storage structure and select a file. The program using the file chooser can then use the file as needed.

SR 9.12   If in a specific situation user input should be a numeric value from a bounded range, a slider is probably a better choice than a text field. A slider prevents an improper value from being entered and conveys the valid range to the user.

Exceptions 10

CHAPTER OBJECTIVES

> Discuss the purpose of exceptions.

> Examine exception messages and the call stack trace.

> Examine the `try-catch` statement for handling exceptions.

> Explore the concept of exception propagation.

> Describe the exception class hierarchy in the Java standard class library.

> Explore I/O exceptions and the ability to write text files.

> Create GUIs using mnemonics and tool tips.

> Explore additional GUI components and containers.

Exception handling is an important part of an object-oriented software system. Exceptions represent problems or unusual situations that may occur in a program. Java provides various ways to handle exceptions when they occur. We explore the class hierarchy from the Java standard library used to define exceptions, as well as the ability to define our own exception objects. This chapter also discusses the use of exceptions when dealing with input and output, and examines an example that writes a text file. The Graphics Track sections of this chapter explore some special features of Swing components, as well as a few additional components and containers.

10.1   EXCEPTION HANDLING

As we've discussed briefly in other parts of the text, problems that arise in a Java program may generate exceptions or errors. An *exception* is an object that defines an unusual or erroneous situation. An exception is thrown by a program or the run-time environment and can be caught and handled appropriately if desired. An *error* is similar to an exception except that an error generally represents an unrecoverable situation and should not be caught. Java has a predefined set of exceptions and errors that may occur during the execution of a program.

> **Key Concept**
>
> Errors and exceptions are objects that represent unusual or invalid processing.

Problem situations represented by exceptions and errors can have various kinds of root causes. Here are some examples of situations that cause exceptions to be thrown:

> Attempting to divide by zero.
> An array index that is out of bounds.
> A specified file that could not be found.
> A requested I/O operation that could not be completed normally.
> An attempt was made to follow a null reference.
> An attempt was made to execute an operation that violates some kind of security measure.

These are just a few examples. There are dozens of others that address very specific situations.

As many of these examples show, an exception can represent a truly erroneous situation. But as the name implies, they may simply represent an exceptional situation. That is, an exception may represent a situation that won't occur under usual conditions. Exception handling is set up to be an efficient way to deal with such situations, especially given that they don't happen too often.

We have several options when it comes to dealing with exceptions. A program can be designed to process an exception in one of three ways. It can:

> not handle the exception at all,
> handle the exception where it occurs, or
> handle the exception at another point in the program.

We explore each of these approaches in the following sections.

10.2   UNCAUGHT EXCEPTIONS

If a program does not handle the exception at all, it will terminate abnormally and produce a message that describes what exception occurred and where it was produced. The information associated with an exception is often helpful in tracking down the cause of a problem.

Let's look at the output of an exception. The program shown in Listing 10.1 throws an `ArithmeticException` when an invalid arithmetic operation is attempted. In this case, the program attempts to divide by zero.

Because there is no code in this program to handle the exception explicitly, it terminates when the exception occurs, printing specific information about the exception. Note that the last `println` statement in the program never executes because the exception occurs first.

The first line of the exception output indicates which exception was thrown and provides some information about why it was thrown. The remaining lines are the *call stack trace*; they indicate where the exception occurred. In this case, there is only one line in the call stack trace, but there may be several depending on

---

Listing 10.1

```
//********************************************************************
//   Zero.java          Author: Lewis/Loftus
//
//   Demonstrates an uncaught exception.
//********************************************************************

public class Zero
{
    //-----------------------------------------------------------------
    //   Deliberately divides by zero to produce an exception.
    //-----------------------------------------------------------------
    public static void main (String[] args)
    {
        int numerator = 10;
        int denominator = 0;

        System.out.println (numerator / denominator);

        System.out.println ("This text will not be printed.");
    }
}
```

Output

```
Exception in thread "main" java.lang.ArithmeticException: / by zero
        at Zero.main(Zero.java:17)
```

where the exception originated. The first trace line indicates the method, file, and line number where the exception occurred. The other trace lines, if present, indicate the methods that were called to get to the method that produced the exception. In this program, there is only one method, and it produced the exception; therefore there is only one line in the trace.

The call stack trace information is also available by calling methods of the exception class that is being thrown. The method `getMessage` returns a string explaining the reason the exception was thrown. The method `printStackTrace` prints the call stack trace.

10.3   THE `try-catch` STATEMENT

Let's now examine how we catch and handle an exception when it is thrown. The *try-catch statement* identifies a block of statements that may throw an exception. A *catch clause*, which follows a `try` block, defines how a particular kind of exception is handled. A `try` block can have several `catch` clauses associated with it. Each `catch` clause is called an *exception handler*.

When a `try` statement is executed, the statements in the `try` block are executed. If no exception is thrown during the execution of the `try` block, processing continues with the statement following the `try` statement (after all of the `catch` clauses). This situation is the normal execution flow and should occur most of the time.

If an exception is thrown at any point during the execution of the `try` block, control is immediately transferred to the appropriate catch handler if it is present. That is, control transfers to the first `catch` clause whose exception class corresponds to the class of the exception that was thrown. After executing the statements in the `catch` clause, control transfers to the statement after the entire `try-catch` statement.

Let's look at an example. Suppose a hypothetical company uses codes to represent its various products. A product code includes, among other information, a character in the tenth position that represents the zone from which that product was made, and a four-digit integer in positions 4 through 7 that represents the district in which it will be sold. Due to some reorganization, products from zone R are banned from being sold in districts with a designation of 2000 or higher. The program shown in Listing 10.2 reads product codes from the user and counts the number of banned codes entered.

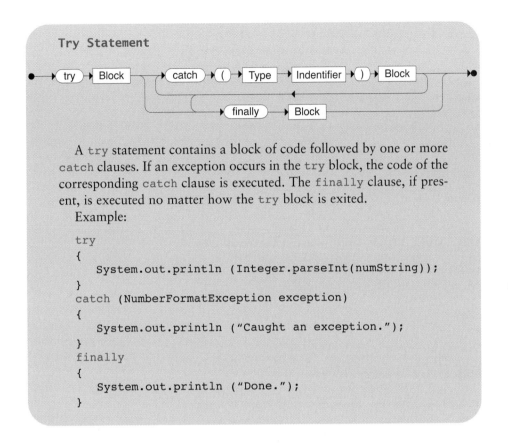

Try Statement

A `try` statement contains a block of code followed by one or more `catch` clauses. If an exception occurs in the `try` block, the code of the corresponding `catch` clause is executed. The `finally` clause, if present, is executed no matter how the `try` block is exited.

Example:

```
try
{
    System.out.println (Integer.parseInt(numString));
}
catch (NumberFormatException exception)
{
    System.out.println ("Caught an exception.");
}
finally
{
    System.out.println ("Done.");
}
```

The programming statements in the `try` block attempt to pull out the zone and district information, and then determine whether it represents a banned product code. If there is any problem extracting the zone and district information, the product code is considered to be invalid and is not processed further. For example, a `StringIndexOutOfBoundsException` could be thrown by either the `charAt` or `substring` methods. Furthermore, a `NumberFormatException` could be thrown by the `parseInt` method if the `substring` does not contain a valid integer. A particular message is printed depending on which exception is thrown. In either case, since the exception is caught and handled, processing continues normally.

Note that, for each code examined, the integer `valid` is incremented only if no exception is thrown. If an exception is thrown, control transfers immediately to the appropriate `catch` clause. Likewise, the zone and district are tested by the `if` statement only if no exception is thrown.

Listing 10.2

```
//********************************************************************
//  ProductCodes.java          Author: Lewis/Loftus
//
//  Demonstrates the use of a try-catch block.
//********************************************************************

import java.util.Scanner;

public class ProductCodes
{
   //-----------------------------------------------------------------
   //  Counts the number of product codes that are entered with a
   //  zone of R and and district greater than 2000.
   //-----------------------------------------------------------------
   public static void main (String[] args)
   {
      String code;
      char zone;
      int district, valid = 0, banned = 0;

      Scanner scan = new Scanner (System.in);

      System.out.print ("Enter product code (XXX to quit): ");
      code = scan.nextLine();

      while (!code.equals ("XXX"))
      {
         try
         {
            zone = code.charAt(9);
            district = Integer.parseInt(code.substring(3, 7));
            valid++;
            if (zone == 'R' && district > 2000)
               banned++;
         }
         catch (StringIndexOutOfBoundsException exception)
         {
            System.out.println ("Improper code length: " + code);
         }
         catch (NumberFormatException exception)
         {
            System.out.println ("District is not numeric: " + code);
         }
```

Listing 10.2   **continued**

```
            System.out.print ("Enter product code (XXX to quit): ");
            code = scan.nextLine();
        }

        System.out.println ("# of valid codes entered: " + valid);
        System.out.println ("# of banned codes entered: " + banned);
    }
}
```

Output

```
Enter product code (XXX to quit): TRV2475A5R-14
Enter product code (XXX to quit): TRD1704A7R-12
Enter product code (XXX to quit): TRL2k74A5R-11
District is not numeric: TRL2k74A5R-11
Enter product code (XXX to quit): TRQ2949A6M-04
Enter product code (XXX to quit): TRV2105A2
Improper code length: TRV2105A2
Enter product code (XXX to quit): TRQ2778A7R-19
Enter product code (XXX to quit): XXX
# of valid codes entered: 4
# of banned codes entered: 2
```

The `finally` Clause

A `try-catch` statement can have an optional *finally clause*. The `finally` clause defines a section of code that is executed no matter how the `try` block is exited. Most often, a `finally` clause is used to manage resources or to guarantee that particular parts of an algorithm are executed.

> **Key Concept**
>
> The `finally` clause is executed whether the `try` block is exited normally or because of a thrown exception.

If no exception is generated, the statements in the `finally` clause are executed after the `try` block is complete. If an exception is generated in the `try` block, control first transfers to the appropriate `catch` clause. After executing the exception-handling code, control transfers to the `finally` clause and its statements are executed. A `finally` clause, if present, must be listed following the `catch` clauses.

Note that a `try` block does not need to have a `catch` clause at all. If there are no `catch` clauses, a `finally` clause may used by itself if that is appropriate for the situation.

10.4 EXCEPTION PROPAGATION

If an exception is not caught and handled where it occurs, control is immediately returned to the method that invoked the method that produced the exception. We can design our software so that the exception is caught and handled at this outer level. If it isn't caught there, control returns to the method that called it. This process is called *propagating the exception*. This propagation continues until the exception is caught and handled or until it is passed out of the main method, which terminates the program and produces an exception message. To catch an exception at an outer level, the method that produces the exception must be invoked inside a try block that has catch clauses to handle it.

> **Key Concept**
>
> If an exception is not caught and handled where it occurs, it is propagated to the calling method.

The Propagation program shown in Listing 10.3 succinctly demonstrates the process of exception propagation. The main method invokes method level1 in the ExceptionScope class (see Listing 10.4), which invokes level2, which invokes level3, which produces an exception. Method level3 does not catch and handle the exception, so control is transferred back to level2. The level2 method does not catch and handle the exception either, so control is transferred back to level1. Because the invocation of level2 is made inside a try block (in method level1), the exception is caught and handled at that point.

Note that the output does not include the messages indicating that the methods level3 and level2 are ending. These println statements are never executed because an exception occurred and had not yet been caught. However, after method level1 handles the exception, processing continues normally from that point, printing the messages indicating that method level1 and the program are ending.

> **Key Concept**
>
> A programmer must carefully consider how and where exceptions should be handled, if at all.

Note also that the catch clause that handles the exception uses the getMessage and printStackTrace methods to output that information. The stack trace shows the methods that were called when the exception occurred.

A programmer must pick the most appropriate level at which to catch and handle an exception. There is no single best answer as to how to do this. It depends on the situation and the design of the system. Sometimes the right approach will be not to catch an exception at all and let the program terminate.

Listing 10.3

```java
//********************************************************************
//   Propagation.java        Author: Lewis/Loftus
//
//   Demonstrates exception propagation.
//********************************************************************

public class Propagation
{
   //-----------------------------------------------------------------
   //   Invokes the level1 method to begin the exception demonstration.
   //-----------------------------------------------------------------
   static public void main (String[] args)
   {
      ExceptionScope demo = new ExceptionScope();

      System.out.println("Program beginning.");
      demo.level1();
      System.out.println("Program ending.");
   }
}
```

Output

```
Program beginning.
Level 1 beginning.
Level 2 beginning.
Level 3 beginning.

The exception message is: / by zero

The call stack trace:
java.lang.ArithmeticException: / by zero
        at ExceptionScope.level3(ExceptionScope.java:54)
        at ExceptionScope.level2(ExceptionScope.java:41)
        at ExceptionScope.level1(ExceptionScope.java:18)
        at Propagation.main(Propagation.java:17)

Level 1 ending.
Program ending.
```

Listing 10.4

```java
//********************************************************************
//  ExceptionScope.java        Author: Lewis/Loftus
//
//  Demonstrates exception propagation.
//********************************************************************

public class ExceptionScope
{
   //-----------------------------------------------------------------
   //  Catches and handles the exception that is thrown in level3.
   //-----------------------------------------------------------------
   public void level1()
   {
      System.out.println("Level 1 beginning.");

      try
      {
         level2();
      }
      catch (ArithmeticException problem)
      {
         System.out.println ();
         System.out.println ("The exception message is: " +
                              problem.getMessage());
         System.out.println ();
         System.out.println ("The call stack trace:");
         problem.printStackTrace();
         System.out.println ();
      }

      System.out.println("Level 1 ending.");
   }

   //-----------------------------------------------------------------
   //  Serves as an intermediate level.  The exception propagates
   //  through this method back to level1.
   //-----------------------------------------------------------------
   public void level2()
   {
      System.out.println("Level 2 beginning.");
      level3 ();
      System.out.println("Level 2 ending.");
   }
```

Listing 10.4   **continued**

```
//----------------------------------------------------------------
//  Performs a calculation to produce an exception.  It is not
//  caught and handled at this level.
//----------------------------------------------------------------
public void level3 ()
{
    int numerator = 10, denominator = 0;

    System.out.println("Level 3 beginning.");
    int result = numerator / denominator;
    System.out.println("Level 3 ending.");
}
}
```

10.5   THE EXCEPTION CLASS HIERARCHY

The classes that define various exceptions are related by inheritance, creating a class hierarchy that is shown in part in Figure 10.1.

The Throwable class is the parent of both the Error class and the Exception class. Many types of exceptions are derived from the Exception class, and these classes also have many children. Though these high-level classes are defined in the java.lang package, many child classes that define specific exceptions are part of several other packages. Inheritance relationships can span package boundaries.

We can define our own exceptions by deriving a new class from Exception or one of its descendants. The class we choose as the parent depends on what situation or condition the new exception represents.

> **Key Concept**
>
> A new exception is defined by deriving a new class from the Exception class or one of its descendants.

The program in Listing 10.5 instantiates an exception object and throws it. The exception is created from the OutOfRangeException class, which is shown in Listing 10.6. Note that this exception is not part of the Java standard class library. It was created to represent the situation in which a value is outside a particular valid range.

After reading in an input value, the main method evaluates it to see whether it is in the valid range. If not, the *throw statement* is executed. A throw statement is used to begin exception propagation. Because the main method does not catch

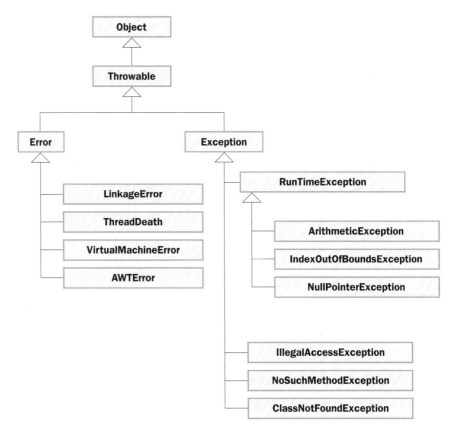

FIGURE 10.1   Part of the `Error` and `Exception` class hierarchy

and handle the exception, the program will terminate if the exception is thrown, printing the message associated with the exception.

We create the `OutOfRangeException` class by extending the `Exception` class. Often, a new exception is nothing more than what you see in this example: an extension of some existing exception class that stores a particular message describing the situation it represents. The important point is that the class is ultimately a descendant of the `Exception` class and the `Throwable` class, which gives it the ability to be thrown using a `throw` statement.

The type of situation handled by this program, in which a value is out of range, does not need to be represented as an exception. We've previously handled such situations using conditionals or loops. Whether you handle a situation using an exception or whether you take care of it in the normal flow of your program is an important design decision.

Listing 10.5

```java
//********************************************************************
//  CreatingExceptions.java        Author: Lewis/Loftus
//
//  Demonstrates the ability to define an exception via inheritance.
//********************************************************************

import java.util.Scanner;

public class CreatingExceptions
{
   //-----------------------------------------------------------------
   //  Creates an exception object and possibly throws it.
   //-----------------------------------------------------------------
   public static void main (String[] args) throws OutOfRangeException
   {
      final int MIN = 25, MAX = 40;

      Scanner scan = new Scanner (System.in);

      OutOfRangeException problem =
         new OutOfRangeException ("Input value is out of range.");

      System.out.print ("Enter an integer value between " + MIN +
                        " and " + MAX + ", inclusive: ");
      int value = scan.nextInt();

      //  Determine if the exception should be thrown
      if (value < MIN || value > MAX)
         throw problem;

      System.out.println ("End of main method.");  // may never reach
   }
}
```

Output

```
Enter an integer value between 25 and 40, inclusive: 69
Exception in thread "main" OutOfRangeException:
        Input value is out of range.
        at CreatingExceptions.main(CreatingExceptions.java:20)
```

Listing 10.6

```java
//********************************************************************
//  OutOfRangeException.java        Author: Lewis/Loftus
//
//  Represents an exceptional condition in which a value is out of
//  some particular range.
//********************************************************************

public class OutOfRangeException extends Exception
{
   //-----------------------------------------------------------------
   //  Sets up the exception object with a particular message.
   //-----------------------------------------------------------------
   OutOfRangeException (String message)
   {
      super (message);
   }
}
```

Checked and Unchecked Exceptions

Some exceptions are checked, whereas others are unchecked. A *checked exception* must either be caught by a method or it must be listed in the *throws clause* of any method that may throw or propagate it. A throws clause is appended to the header of a method definition to formally acknowledge that the method will throw or propagate a particular exception if it occurs. An *unchecked exception* requires no throws clause.

The only unchecked exceptions in Java are objects of type RuntimeException or any of its descendants. All other exceptions are considered checked exceptions. The main method of the CreatingExceptions program has a throws clause, indicating that it may throw an OutOfRangeException. This throws clause is required because the OutOfRangeException was derived from the Exception class, making it a checked exception.

10.6   I/O EXCEPTIONS

Processing input and output is a task that often produces unforseeable situations, leading to exceptions being thrown. Let's explore some I/O issues and the problems that may arise.

A *stream* is an ordered sequence of bytes. The term stream comes from the analogy that as we read and write information, the data flows from a source to a destination (or *sink*) as water flows down a stream. The source of the information is like a spring filling the stream, and the destination is like a cave into which the stream flows.

> **Key Concept**
>
> A stream is a sequential sequence of bytes; it can be used as a source of input or a destination for output.

In a program, we treat a stream as either an *input stream*, from which we read information, or as an *output stream*, to which we write information. That is, a program serves either as the spring filling the stream or as the cave receiving the stream. A program can deal with multiple input and output streams at one time. A particular store of data, such as a file, can serve either as an input stream or as an output stream to a program, but it generally cannot be both at the same time.

There are three streams that are referred to as the *standard I/O streams*. They are listed in Figure 10.2. The System class contains three object reference variables (in, out, and err) that represent the three standard I/O streams. These references are declared as both public and static, which allows them to be accessed directly through the System class.

> **Key Concept**
>
> Three public reference variables in the System class represent the standard I/O streams.

We've been using the standard output stream, with calls to System.out.prinln for instance, in examples throughout this book. We've also used the standard input stream to create a Scanner object when we want to process input read interactively from the user. The Scanner class manages the input read from the standard input stream in various ways that makes our programming tasks easier. It also processes various I/O exceptions internally, creating an InputMismatchException when needed.

The standard I/O streams, by default, represent particular I/O devices. System.in typically represents keyboard input, whereas System.out and System.err typically represent a particular window on the monitor screen. The System.out and System.err streams write output to the same window by default (usually the one in which the program was executed), though they could

Standard I/O Stream	Description
System.in	Standard input stream.
System.out	Standard output stream.
System.err	Standard error stream (output for error messages)

FIGURE 10.2   Standard I/O streams

be set up to write to different places. The System.err stream is usually where error messages are sent.

In addition to the standard input streams, the java.io package of the Java standard class library provides many classes that let us define streams with particular characteristics. Some of the classes deal with files, others with memory,

and others with strings. Some classes assume that the data they handle consists of characters, whereas others assume the data consists of raw bytes of binary information. Some classes provide the means to manipulate the data in the stream in some way, such as buffering the information or numbering it. By combining classes in appropriate ways, we can create objects that represent a stream of information that has the exact characteristics we want for a particular situation.

The broad topic of Java I/O, and the sheer number of classes in the java.io package, prohibits us from covering it in detail in this book. Our focus for the moment is on I/O exceptions.

Many operations performed by I/O classes can potentially throw an IOException. The IOException class is the parent of several exception classes that represent problems when trying to perform I/O.

An IOException is a checked exception. As described earlier in this chapter, that means that either the exception must be caught, or all methods that propagate it must list it in a throws clause of the method header.

Because I/O often deals with external resources, many problems can arise in programs that attempt to perform I/O operations. For example, a file from which we want to read might not exist; when we attempt to open the file, an exception will be thrown because that file can't be found. In general, we should try to design programs to be as robust as possible when dealing with potential problems.

We've seen in previous examples how we can use the Scanner class to read and process input read from a text file. Now let's explore an example that writes data to a text output file. Writing output to a text file requires simply that we use the appropriate classes to create the output stream, then call the appropriate methods to write the data.

Suppose we want to test a program we are writing, but don't have the real data available. We could write a program that generates a test data file that contains random values. The program shown in Listing 10.7 generates a file that contains random integer values within a particular range. It also writes one line of standard output, confirming that the data file has been written.

The FileWriter class represents a text output file, but has minimal method support for manipulating data. The PrintWriter class provides print and println methods similar to the standard I/O PrintStream class.

Listing 10.7

```java
//********************************************************************
//   TestData.java        Author: Lewis/Loftus
//
//   Demonstrates I/O exceptions and the use of a character file
//   output stream.
//********************************************************************

import java.util.Random;
import java.io.*;

public class TestData
{
   //-----------------------------------------------------------------
   //   Creates a file of test data that consists of ten lines each
   //   containing ten integer values in the range 10 to 99.
   //-----------------------------------------------------------------
   public static void main (String[] args) throws IOException
   {
      final int MAX = 10;

      int value;
      String file = "test.dat";

      Random rand = new Random();

      FileWriter fw = new FileWriter (file);
      BufferedWriter bw = new BufferedWriter (fw);
      PrintWriter outFile = new PrintWriter (bw);

      for (int line=1; line <= MAX; line++)
      {
         for (int num=1; num <= MAX; num++)
         {
            value = rand.nextInt (90) + 10;
            outFile.print (value + "    ");
         }
         outFile.println ();
      }

      outFile.close();
      System.out.println ("Output file has been created: " + file);
   }
}
```

Listing 10.7   continued

Output

```
Output file has been created: test.dat
```

Although we do not need to do so for the program to work, we have added a layer in the file stream configuration to include a `BufferedWriter`. This addition simply gives the output stream buffering capabilities, which makes the processing more efficient. While buffering is not crucial in this situation, it is usually a good idea when writing text files.

Note that in the `TestData` program, we have eliminated explicit exception handling. That is, if something goes wrong, we simply allow the program to terminate instead of specifically catching and handling the problem. Because all `IOExceptions` are checked exceptions, we must include the `throws` clause on the method header to indicate that they may be thrown. For each program, we must carefully consider how best to handle the exceptions that may be thrown. This requirement is especially important when dealing with I/O, which is fraught with potential problems that cannot always be foreseen.

The `TestData` program uses nested `for` loops to compute random values and write them to the output file. After all values are printed, the file is closed. Output files must be closed explicitly to ensure that the data is retained. In general, it is good practice to close all file streams explicitly when they are no longer needed.

The data that is contained in the file `test.dat` after the `TestData` program is run might look like this:

```
85  90  93  15  82  79  52  71  70  98
74  57  41  66  22  16  67  65  24  84
86  61  91  79  18  81  64  41  68  81
98  47  28  40  69  10  85  82  64  41
23  61  27  10  59  89  88  26  24  76
33  89  73  36  54  91  42  73  95  58
19  41  18  14  63  80  96  30  17  28
24  37  40  64  94  23  98  10  78  50
89  28  64  54  59  23  61  15  80  88
51  28  44  48  73  21  41  52  35  38
```

10.7   TOOL TIPS AND MNEMONICS

Let's take a look at a some special features that can be used with any Swing component. Appropriate application of these features can enhance the user interface and facilitate the use of the components. This section describes the use of tool tips and mnemonics, as well as the ability to disable components, then explores an example that uses these features.

> **Key Concept**
>
> Tool tips and mnemonics can enhance the functionality of a graphical user interface.

Any Swing component can be assigned a *tool tip*, which is a short line of text that will appear when the cursor is rested momentarily on top of the component. Tool tips are usually used to inform the user about the component, such as the purpose of a button.

A tool tip can be assigned using the `setToolTipText` method of a Swing component. For example:

```
JButton button = new JButton ("Compute");
button.setToolTipText ("Calculates the area under the curve.");
```

When the button is added to a container and displayed, it appears normally. When the user rolls the mouse pointer over the button, hovering there momentarily, the tool tip text pops up. When the user moves the mouse pointer off of the button, the tool tip text disappears.

A *mnemonic* is a character that allows the user to push a button or make a menu choice using the keyboard in addition to the mouse. For example, when a mnemonic has been defined for a button, the user can hold down the ALT key and press the mnemonic character to activate the button. Using a mnemonic to activate the button causes the system to behave just as it would if the user had used the mouse to press the button.

A mnemonic character should be chosen from the label on a button or menu item. Once the mnemonic has been established using the `setMnemonic` method, the character in the label will be underlined to indicate that it can be used as a shortcut. If a letter is chosen that is not in the label, nothing will be underlined and the user won't know how to use the shortcut. You can set a mnemonic as follows:

```
JButton button = new JButton ("Calculate");
button.setMnemonic ('C');
```

When the button is displayed, the letter C in Calculate is underlined on the button label. When the user presses ALT-C, the button is activated as if the user had pressed it with the mouse.

Some components can be *disabled* if they should not be used. A disabled component will appear "grayed out," and nothing will happen if the user attempts to interact with it. To disable and enable components, we invoke the `setEnabled` method of the component, passing it a boolean value to indicate whether the component should be disabled (false) or enabled (true). For example:

```
JButton button = new JButton ("Do It");
button.setEnabled (false);
```

Disabling components is a good idea when users should not be allowed to use the functionality of a component. The grayed appearance of the disabled component is an indication that using the component is inappropriate (and, in fact, impossible) at the current time. Disabled components not only convey to the user which actions are appropriate and which aren't, they also prevent erroneous situations from occuring.

Let's look at an example that uses tool tips, mnemonics, and disabled components. The program in Listing 10.8 presents the image of a light bulb and provides a button to turn the light bulb on and a button to turn the light bulb off.

There are actually two images of the light bulb: one showing it turned on and one showing it turned off. These images are brought in as `ImageIcon` objects. The `setIcon` method of the label that displays the image is used to set the appropriate image, depending on the current status. This processing is controlled in the `LightBulbPanel` class shown in Listing 10.9.

> **Key Concept**
>
> Components should be disabled when their use is inappropriate.

The `LightBulbControls` class shown in Listing 10.10 is a panel that contains the on and off buttons. Both of these buttons have tool tips assigned to them, and both use mnemonics. Also, when one of the buttons is enabled, the other is disabled, and vice versa. When the light bulb is on, there is no reason for the `On` button to be enabled. Likewise, when the light bulb is off, there is no reason for the `Off` button to be enabled.

Each button has its own listener class. The `actionPerformed` method of each sets the bulb's status, toggles the enabled state of both buttons, and causes the panel with the image to repaint itself.

Note that the mnemonic characters used for each button are underlined in the display. When you run the program, note that the tool tips automatically include an indication of the mnemonic that can be used for the button.

Listing 10.8

```java
//********************************************************************
//  LightBulb.java       Author: Lewis/Loftus
//
//  Demonstrates mnemonics and tool tips.
//********************************************************************

import javax.swing.*;
import java.awt.*;

public class LightBulb
{
   //-----------------------------------------------------------------
   //  Sets up a frame that displays a light bulb image that can be
   //  turned on and off.
   //-----------------------------------------------------------------
   public static void main (String[] args)
   {
      JFrame frame = new JFrame ("Light Bulb");
      frame.setDefaultCloseOperation (JFrame.EXIT_ON_CLOSE);

      LightBulbPanel bulb = new LightBulbPanel();
      LightBulbControls controls = new LightBulbControls (bulb);

      JPanel panel = new JPanel();
      panel.setBackground (Color.black);
      panel.setLayout (new BoxLayout(panel, BoxLayout.Y_AXIS));
      panel.add (Box.createRigidArea (new Dimension (0, 20)));
      panel.add (bulb);
      panel.add (Box.createRigidArea (new Dimension (0, 10)));
      panel.add (controls);
      panel.add (Box.createRigidArea (new Dimension (0, 10)));

      frame.getContentPane().add(panel);
      frame.pack();
      frame.setVisible(true);
   }
}
```

Listing 10.8   **continued**

Display

Listing 10.9

```
//********************************************************************
//   LightBulbPanel.java          Author: Lewis/Loftus
//
//   Represents the image for the LightBulb program.
//********************************************************************

import javax.swing.*;
import java.awt.*;

public class LightBulbPanel extends JPanel
{
   private boolean on;
   private ImageIcon lightOn, lightOff;
   private JLabel imageLabel;
```

Listing 10.9   **continued**

```java
//---------------------------------------------------------------
//  Constructor: Sets up the images and the initial state.
//---------------------------------------------------------------
public LightBulbPanel()
{
   lightOn = new ImageIcon ("lightBulbOn.gif");
   lightOff = new ImageIcon ("lightBulbOff.gif");

   setBackground (Color.black);

   on = true;
   imageLabel = new JLabel (lightOff);
   add (imageLabel);
}

//---------------------------------------------------------------
//  Paints the panel using the appropriate image.
//---------------------------------------------------------------
public void paintComponent (Graphics page)
{
   super.paintComponent(page);

   if (on)
      imageLabel.setIcon (lightOn);
   else
      imageLabel.setIcon (lightOff);
}

//---------------------------------------------------------------
//  Sets the status of the light bulb.
//---------------------------------------------------------------
public void setOn (boolean lightBulbOn)
{
   on = lightBulbOn;
}
}
```

Listing 10.10

```java
//********************************************************************
//  LightBulbControls.java       Author: Lewis/Loftus
//
//  Represents the control panel for the LightBulb program.
//********************************************************************

import javax.swing.*;
import java.awt.*;
import java.awt.event.*;

public class LightBulbControls extends JPanel
{
    private LightBulbPanel bulb;
    private JButton onButton, offButton;

    //-----------------------------------------------------------------
    //  Sets up the lightbulb control panel.
    //-----------------------------------------------------------------
    public LightBulbControls (LightBulbPanel bulbPanel)
    {
        bulb = bulbPanel;

        onButton = new JButton ("On");
        onButton.setEnabled (false);
        onButton.setMnemonic ('n');
        onButton.setToolTipText ("Turn it on!");
        onButton.addActionListener (new OnListener());

        offButton = new JButton ("Off");
        offButton.setEnabled (true);
        offButton.setMnemonic ('f');
        offButton.setToolTipText ("Turn it off!");
        offButton.addActionListener (new OffListener());

        setBackground (Color.black);
        add (onButton);
        add (offButton);
    }
```

Listing 10.10 **continued**

```java
//****************************************************************
//  Represents the listener for the On button.
//****************************************************************
private class OnListener implements ActionListener
{
    //------------------------------------------------------------
    //  Turns the bulb on and repaints the bulb panel.
    //------------------------------------------------------------
    public void actionPerformed (ActionEvent event)
    {
        bulb.setOn (true);
        onButton.setEnabled (false);
        offButton.setEnabled (true);
        bulb.repaint();
    }
}

//****************************************************************
//  Represents the listener for the Off button.
//****************************************************************
private class OffListener implements ActionListener
{
    //------------------------------------------------------------
    //  Turns the bulb off and repaints the bulb panel.
    //------------------------------------------------------------
    public void actionPerformed (ActionEvent event)
    {
        bulb.setOn (false);
        onButton.setEnabled (true);
        offButton.setEnabled (false);
        bulb.repaint();
    }
}
}
```

10.8   COMBO BOXES

A *combo box* allows the user to select one of several options from a "drop down" menu. When the user presses a combo box using the mouse, a list of options is displayed from which the user can choose. The current choice is displayed in the combo box. A combo box is defined by the JComboBox class.

A combo box can be either *editable* or *uneditable*. By default, a combo box is uneditable. Changing the value of an uneditable combo box can be accomplished only by selecting an item from the list. If the combo box is editable, however, the user can change the value by either selecting an item from the list or by typing a particular value into the combo box area.

The options in a combo box list can be established in one of two ways. We can create an array of strings and pass it into the constructor of the JComboBox class. Alternatively, we can use the addItem method to add an item to the combo box after it has been created. A JComboBox can also display ImageIcon objects as options as well.

The JukeBox program shown in Listing 10.11 demonstrates the use of a combo box. The user chooses a song to play using the combo box, and then presses the Play button to begin playing the song. The Stop button can be pressed at any time to stop the song. Selecting a new song while one is playing also stops the current song.

The JukeBoxControls class shown in Listing 10.12 is a panel that contains the components that make up the jukebox GUI. The constructor of the class also loads the audio clips that will be played. An audio clip is obtained first by creating a URL object that corresponds to the wav or au file that defines the clip. The first two parameters to the URL constructor should be "file" and "localhost", respectively, if the audio clip is stored on the same machine on which the program is executing. Creating URL objects can potentially throw a checked exception; therefore they are created in a try block. However, this program assumes the audio clips will be loaded successfully and therefore does nothing if an exception is thrown.

Once created, the URL objects are used to create AudioClip objects using the static newAudioClip method of the JApplet class. The audio clips are stored in an array. The first entry in the array, at index 0, is set to null. This entry corresponds to the initial combo box option, which simply encourages the user to make a selection.

Listing 10.11

```java
//********************************************************************
//  JukeBox.java        Author: Lewis/Loftus
//
//  Demonstrates the use of a combo box.
//********************************************************************

import javax.swing.*;

public class JukeBox
{
   //-----------------------------------------------------------------
   //  Creates and displays the controls for a juke box.
   //-----------------------------------------------------------------
   public static void main (String[] args)
   {
      JFrame frame = new JFrame ("Java Juke Box");
      frame.setDefaultCloseOperation (JFrame.EXIT_ON_CLOSE);

      JukeBoxControls controlPanel = new JukeBoxControls();

      frame.getContentPane().add(controlPanel);
      frame.pack();
      frame.setVisible(true);
   }
}
```

Display

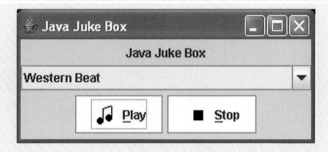

Listing 10.12

```java
//********************************************************************
//  JukeBoxControls.java        Author: Lewis and Loftus
//
//  Represents the control panel for the juke box.
//********************************************************************

import java.awt.*;
import java.awt.event.*;
import javax.swing.*;
import java.applet.AudioClip;
import java.net.URL;

public class JukeBoxControls extends JPanel
{
    private JComboBox musicCombo;
    private JButton stopButton, playButton;
    private AudioClip[] music;
    private AudioClip current;

    //-----------------------------------------------------------------
    //  Sets up the GUI for the juke box.
    //-----------------------------------------------------------------
    public JukeBoxControls()
    {
        URL url1, url2, url3, url4, url5, url6;
        url1 = url2 = url3 = url4 = url5 = url6 = null;

        // Obtain and store the audio clips to play
        try
        {
            url1 = new URL ("file", "localhost", "westernBeat.wav");
            url2 = new URL ("file", "localhost", "classical.wav");
            url3 = new URL ("file", "localhost", "jeopardy.au");
            url4 = new URL ("file", "localhost", "newAgeRythm.wav");
            url5 = new URL ("file", "localhost", "eightiesJam.wav");
            url6 = new URL ("file", "localhost", "hitchcock.wav");
        }
        catch (Exception exception) {}

        music = new AudioClip[7];
        music[0] = null;  // Corresponds to "Make a Selection..."
        music[1] = JApplet.newAudioClip (url1);
        music[2] = JApplet.newAudioClip (url2);
        music[3] = JApplet.newAudioClip (url3);
        music[4] = JApplet.newAudioClip (url4);
```

Listing 10.12 continued

```java
        music[5] = JApplet.newAudioClip (url5);
        music[6] = JApplet.newAudioClip (url6);

        JLabel titleLabel = new JLabel ("Java Juke Box");
        titleLabel.setAlignmentX (Component.CENTER_ALIGNMENT);

        // Create the list of strings for the combo box options
        String[] musicNames = {"Make A Selection...", "Western Beat",
                "Classical Melody", "Jeopardy Theme", "New Age Rythm",
                "Eighties Jam", "Alfred Hitchcock's Theme"};

        musicCombo = new JComboBox (musicNames);
        musicCombo.setAlignmentX (Component.CENTER_ALIGNMENT);

        // Set up the buttons
        playButton = new JButton ("Play", new ImageIcon ("play.gif"));
        playButton.setBackground (Color.white);
        playButton.setMnemonic ('p');
        stopButton = new JButton ("Stop", new ImageIcon ("stop.gif"));
        stopButton.setBackground (Color.white);
        stopButton.setMnemonic ('s');

        JPanel buttons = new JPanel();
        buttons.setLayout (new BoxLayout (buttons, BoxLayout.X_AXIS));
        buttons.add (playButton);
        buttons.add (Box.createRigidArea (new Dimension(5,0)));
        buttons.add (stopButton);
        buttons.setBackground (Color.cyan);

        // Set up this panel
        setPreferredSize (new Dimension (300, 100));
        setBackground (Color.cyan);
        setLayout (new BoxLayout (this, BoxLayout.Y_AXIS));
        add (Box.createRigidArea (new Dimension(0,5)));
        add (titleLabel);
        add (Box.createRigidArea (new Dimension(0,5)));
        add (musicCombo);
        add (Box.createRigidArea (new Dimension(0,5)));
        add (buttons);
        add (Box.createRigidArea (new Dimension(0,5)));

        musicCombo.addActionListener (new ComboListener());
        stopButton.addActionListener (new ButtonListener());
```

Listing 10.12 continued

```
    playButton.addActionListener (new ButtonListener());

    current = null;
  }

  //****************************************************************
  //  Represents the action listener for the combo box.
  //****************************************************************
  private class ComboListener implements ActionListener
  {
    //------------------------------------------------------------
    //  Stops playing the current selection (if any) and resets
    //  the current selection to the one chosen.
    //------------------------------------------------------------
    public void actionPerformed (ActionEvent event)
    {
      if (current != null)
        current.stop();

      current = music[musicCombo.getSelectedIndex()];
    }
  }

  //****************************************************************
  //  Represents the action listener for both control buttons.
  //****************************************************************
  private class ButtonListener implements ActionListener
  {
    //------------------------------------------------------------
    //  Stops the current selection (if any) in either case. If
    //  the play button was pressed, start playing it again.
    //------------------------------------------------------------
    public void actionPerformed (ActionEvent event)
    {
      if (current != null)
        current.stop();

      if (event.getSource() == playButton)
        if (current != null)
          current.play();
    }
  }
```

The list of songs that are displayed in the combo box is defined in an array of strings. The first entry of the array will appear in the combo box by default and is often used to direct the user. We must take care that the rest of the program does not try to use that option as a valid song.

The play and stop buttons are displayed with both a text label and an image icon. They are also given mnemonics so that the jukebox can be controlled partially from the keyboard.

A combo box generates an action event whenever the user makes a selection from it. The `JukeBox` program uses one action listener class for the combo box and another for both of the push buttons. They could have been combined, using code to distinguish which component fired the event.

The `actionPerformed` method of the `ComboListener` class is executed when a selection is made from the combo box. The current audio selection that is playing, if any, is stopped. The current clip is then updated to reflect the new selection. Note that the audio clip is not immediately played at that point. The way this program is designed, the user must press the play button to hear the new selection.

The `actionPerformed` method of the `ButtonListener` class is executed when either of the buttons is pushed. The current audio selection that is playing, if any, is stopped. If it was the stop button that was pressed, the task is complete. If the play button was pressed, the current audio selection is played again from the beginning.

10.9 SCROLL PANES

Sometimes we need to deal with images or information that is too large to fit in a reasonable area. A *scroll pane* is often helpful in these situations. A scroll pane is a container that offers a limited view of a component, and provides vertical or horizontal scroll bars to change that view. At any point, only part of the underlying component can be seen, but the scroll bars allow the user to navigate to any part of the component. Scroll bars are useful when space within a GUI is limited or when the component being viewed is large or can change in size dynamically.

> **Key Concept**
>
> A scroll pane is useful for viewing large objects or large amounts of data.

The program in Listing 10.13 presents a frame that contains a single scroll pane. The scroll pane is used to view an image of a fairly large subway map for Philadelphia and the surrounding areas. The image is put into a label, and the label is added to the scroll pane using the `JScrollPane` constructor.

Listing 10.13

```java
//********************************************************************
//  TransitMap.java        Author: Lewis/Loftus
//
//  Demonstrates the use of a scroll pane.
//********************************************************************

import java.awt.*;
import javax.swing.*;

public class TransitMap
{
   //-----------------------------------------------------------------
   //  Presents a frame containing a scroll pane used to view a large
   //  map of the Philadelphia subway system.
   //-----------------------------------------------------------------
   public static void main (String[] args)
   {
      // SEPTA = SouthEast Pennsylvania Transit Authority
      JFrame frame = new JFrame ("SEPTA Transit Map");

      frame.setDefaultCloseOperation (JFrame.EXIT_ON_CLOSE);

      ImageIcon image = new ImageIcon ("septa.jpg");
      JLabel imageLabel = new JLabel (image);

      JScrollPane sp = new JScrollPane (imageLabel);
      sp.setPreferredSize (new Dimension (450, 400));

      frame.getContentPane().add (sp);
      frame.pack();
      frame.setVisible(true);
   }
}
```

Listing 10.13 continued

Display

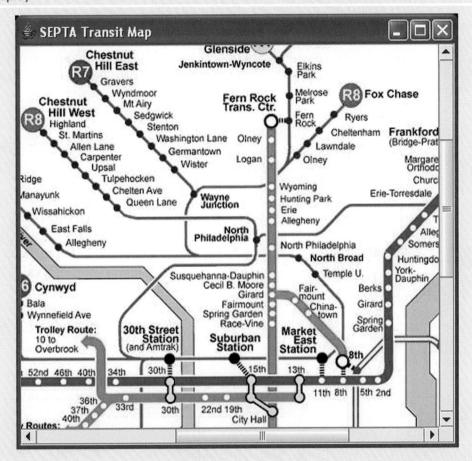

A scroll pane can have a vertical scroll bar on the right of the container as well as a horizontal scroll bar at the bottom of the container. For each of these, the programmer can specify that the scroll bars are always used, never used, or used as needed to view the underlying component. By default, both the vertical and horizontal scroll bars are used as needed. The `TransitMap` program relies on these defaults, and both scroll bars appear because the image is too large in both height and width.

To move a scroll bar, the user can click on and drag the box, called the *knob*, in the scroll bar that indicates its current location (in that dimension: up/down or right/left). Alternatively, the user can click in the bar to the right or left of the knob, or on the arrows at either end of the scroll bar, to adjust the location. The programmer can determine how much each of these actions changes the viewing area.

Note that no event listeners need to be set up to use a scroll pane in this manner. A scroll pane responds automatically to the adjustments of its scroll bars.

10.10 SPLIT PANES

A *split pane* is a container that displays two components separated by a moveable divider bar. Depending on how the split pane is set up, the two components are displayed either side by side or one on top of the other, as shown in Figure 10.3. In Java, we can create a split pane using the JSplitPane class.

> **Key Concept**
>
> A split pane displays two components side by side or one on top of the other.

The orientation of a split pane is set using constants in the JSplitPane class, and can be set when the container is created or explicitly later on. The constant HORIZONTAL_SPLIT specifies that the components be displayed side by side. In contrast, VERTICAL_SPLIT specifies that the components be displayed one on top of the other.

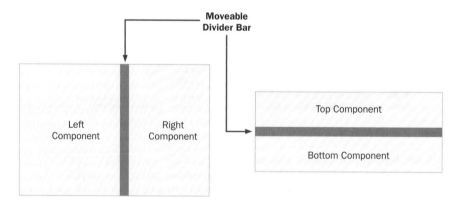

FIGURE 10.3 The configurations of a split pane

The location of the divider bar determines how much visible area is devoted to each component in the split pane. The divider bar can be dragged across the container area using the mouse. As it moves, the visible space is increased for one component and decreased for the other. The total space allotted for both components changes only if the size of the entire split pane changes.

A `JSplitPane` respects the minimum size set for the components it displays. Therefore the divider bar may not allow a section to be reduced in size beyond a particular point. To adjust this aspect, the minimum sizes of the components displayed can be changed.

The divider bar of a `JSplitPane` object can be set so that it can be expanded, one direction or the other, with one click of the mouse. By default, the divider bar does not have this feature and can only be moved by dragging it. If this feature is turned on, the divider bar appears with two small arrows pointing in opposite directions. Clicking either of these arrows causes the divider bar to move fully in that direction, maximizing the space allotted to one of the components. This feature is set using the `setOneTouchExpandable` method, which takes a boolean parameter. The size of the divider bar and the initial location of the divider bar can be set explicitly as well.

Another feature that can be set on a `JSplitPane` is whether or not the components are continuously adjusted and repainted as the divider bar is being moved. If this feature is not set, the components' layout managers will only be consulted after the divider bar stops moving. This feature is off by default, and can be turned on when the `JSplitPane` object is created or using the `setContinuousLayout` method.

Split panes can be nested by putting a split pane into one or both sides of another split pane. For example, we could divide a container into three sections by putting a split pane into the top component of another split pane. There would then be two divider bars, one that separates the total area into two main sections, and another that separates one of those sections into two others. How much visible area is shown in each would depend on where the divider bars are placed.

The program shown in Listing 10.14 presents a list of image file names to the user. When one of the file names is selected, the corresponding image is displayed in the right side of the split pane.

The split pane is created in the `main` method and added to the frame to be displayed. The split pane is oriented, using the `HORIZONTAL_SPLIT` constant, such that the panel containing the list and the label containing the image to be displayed are side by side. The call to the `setOneTouchExpandable` method causes the divider bar of the split pane to display the arrows that permit the user to expand the panes one way or the other with one click of the mouse.

Listing 10.14

```java
//********************************************************************
//  PickImage.java        Author: Lewis/Loftus
//
//  Demonstrates the use of a split pane and a list.
//********************************************************************

import java.awt.*;
import javax.swing.*;

public class PickImage
{
   //-----------------------------------------------------------------
   //  Creates and displays a frame containing a split pane. The
   //  user selects an image name from the list to be displayed.
   //-----------------------------------------------------------------
   public static void main (String[] args)
   {
      JFrame frame = new JFrame ("Pick Image");
      frame.setDefaultCloseOperation (JFrame.EXIT_ON_CLOSE);

      JLabel imageLabel = new JLabel();
      JPanel imagePanel = new JPanel();
      imagePanel.add (imageLabel);
      imagePanel.setBackground (Color.white);

      ListPanel imageList = new ListPanel (imageLabel);

      JSplitPane sp = new JSplitPane(JSplitPane.HORIZONTAL_SPLIT,
                                     imageList, imagePanel);

      sp.setOneTouchExpandable (true);

      frame.getContentPane().add (sp);
      frame.pack();
      frame.setVisible(true);
   }
}
```

Listing 10.14 **continued**

Display

The `ListPanel` class shown in Listing 10.15 defines the panel that contains the list of file names. We use a *list* component, defined by the `JList` class, to display the list of file names. The list contents are set up as an array of `String` objects, which are passed into the `JList` constructor.

In general, all of the options in a `JList` component are visible. When the user selects an item using the mouse, it is highlighted. When a new item is selected, the previously selected item is automatically unhighlighted.

The contents of a `JList` can be specified using an array of objects passed into the constructor. Methods of the `JList` class are used to manage the list in various ways, including retrieving the currently selected item.

Note the similarities and differences between a combo box (described in section 10.8) and a `JList` object. Both allow the user to select an item from a set of choices. However, the choices on a list are always displayed, with the current choice highlighted, whereas a combo box presents its options only when the user presses it with the mouse. The only item displayed all the time in a combo box is the current selection.

Listing 10.15

```java
//********************************************************************
//  ListPanel.java        Author: Lewis/Loftus
//
//  Represents the list of images for the PickImage program.
//********************************************************************

import java.awt.*;
import javax.swing.*;
import javax.swing.event.*;

public class ListPanel extends JPanel
{
   private JLabel label;
   private JList list;

   //-----------------------------------------------------------------
   //  Loads the list of image names into the list.
   //-----------------------------------------------------------------
   public ListPanel (JLabel imageLabel)
   {
      label = imageLabel;

      String[] fileNames = { "circuit.gif",
                             "duke.gif",
                             "hammock.gif",
                             "justin.jpg",
                             "kayla.jpg",
                             "tiger.jpg",
                             "toucan.gif",
                             "worldmap.gif" };

      list = new JList (fileNames);
      list.addListSelectionListener (new ListListener());
      list.setSelectionMode (ListSelectionModel.SINGLE_SELECTION);

      add (list);
      setBackground (Color.white);
   }
```

Listing 10.15   continued

```
//***************************************************************
//   Represents the listener for the list of images.
//***************************************************************
private class ListListener implements ListSelectionListener
{
   public void valueChanged (ListSelectionEvent event)
   {
      if (list.isSelectionEmpty())
         label.setIcon (null);
      else
      {
         String fileName = (String)list.getSelectedValue();
         ImageIcon image = new ImageIcon (fileName);
         label.setIcon (image);
      }
   }
}
}
```

A JList object generates a *list selection event* whenever the current selection of the list changes. The ListSelectionListener interface contains one method called valueChanged. In this program, the private inner class called ListListener defines the listener for the list of file names.

The valueChanged method of the listener calls the isSelectionEmpty method of the JList object to determine if there is any value currently selected. If not, the icon of the label is set to null. If so, the file name is obtained using the getSelectedValue method. Then the corresponding image icon is created and displayed in the label.

A JList object can be set so that multiple items can be selected at the same time. The *list selection mode* can be one of three options, as shown in the table in Figure 10.4.

The list selection mode is defined by a ListSelectionModel object. By default, a list allows multiple interval selection. A call to the setSelectionMode method, using a constant defined in the ListSelectionModel class, will explicitly set the list selection mode.

In the PickImage program, we set the list selection mode to single selection because only one image can be displayed at a time. However, even if multiple

List Selection Mode	Description
Single Selection	Only one item can be selected at a time.
Single Interval Selection	Multiple, contiguous items can be selected at a time.
Multiple Interval Selection	Any combination of items can be selected.

FIGURE 10.4 List selection modes

selections were allowed in this program, the `getSelectedValue` method returns the first item selected, so that would be the image displayed. A similar method called `getSelectedValues` returns an array of objects representing the items selected when multiple selections are permitted.

Instead of an array of `String` objects, the `JList` constructor could be passed an array of `ImageIcon` objects instead. In that case, the images would be displayed in the list.

Summary of Key Concepts

> Errors and exceptions are objects that represent unusual or invalid processing.

> The messages printed when an exception is thrown provide a method call stack trace.

> Each `catch` clause handles a particular kind of exception that may be thrown within the `try` block.

> The `finally` clause is executed whether the `try` block is exited normally or because of a thrown exception.

> If an exception is not caught and handled where it occurs, it is propagated to the calling method.

> A programmer must carefully consider how and where exceptions should be handled, if at all.

> A new exception is defined by deriving a new class from the `Exception` class or one of its descendants.

> The `throws` clause on a method header must be included for checked exceptions that are not caught and handled in the method.

> A stream is a sequential sequence of bytes; it can be used as a source of input or a destination for output.

> Three public reference variables in the `System` class represent the standard I/O streams.

> Output file streams should be explicitly closed or they may not correctly retain the data written to them.

> The Java class library contains many classes for defining I/O streams with various characteristics.

> Tool tips and mnemonics can enhance the functionality of a graphical user interface.

> Components should be disabled when their use is inappropriate.

> A combo box provides a drop down menu of options for the user.

> A scroll pane is useful for viewing large objects or large amounts of data.

> A split pane displays two components side by side or one on top of the other.

Self-Review Questions

SR 10.1   In what ways might a thrown exception be handled?

SR 10.2   What is a catch phrase?

SR 10.3   What happens if an exception is not caught?

SR 10.4   What is a finally clause?

SR 10.5   What is a checked exception?

SR 10.6   What is a stream?

SR 10.7   What are the standard I/O streams?

SR 10.8   What is a tool tip?

SR 10.9   What is a mnemonic and how is it used?

SR 10.10   Why might you want to disable a component?

SR 10.11   Describe the use of scroll bars on a scroll pane.

SR 10.12   What is a combo box?

Exercises

EX 10.1   Create a UML class diagram for the ProductCodes program.

EX 10.2   What would happen if the try statement were removed from the level1 method of the ExceptionScope class in the Propagation program?

EX 10.3   What would happen if the try statement described in the previous exercise were moved to the level2 method?

EX 10.4   Look up the following exception classes in the online Java API documentation and describe their purpose:

a. ArithmeticException
b. NullPointerException
c. NumberFormatException
d. PatternSyntaxException

EX 10.5   Draw the containment hierarchy tree for the LightBulb program.

EX 10.6   Draw the containment hierarchy tree for the PickImage program.

EX 10.7   Draw the containment hierarchy tree for the JukeBox program.

EX 10.8   What effect would removing the call to setSelectionMode in the ListPanel class have? Make the change to test your answer.

Programming Projects

PP 10.1   Design and implement a program that creates an exception class called StringTooLongException, designed to be thrown when a string is discovered that has too many characters in it. In the main driver of the program, read strings from the user until the user enters "DONE". If a string is entered that has too many characters (say 20), throw the exception. Allow the thrown exception to terminate the program.

PP 10.2   Modify the solution to Programming Project 10.1 such that it catches and handles the exception if it is thrown. Handle the exception by printing an appropriate message, and then continue processing more strings.

PP 10.3   Design and implement a program that creates an exception class called InvalidDocumentCodeException, designed to be thrown when an improper designation for a document is encountered during processing. Suppose in a particular business all documents are given a two-character designation starting with either U, C, or P, standing for unclassified, confidential, or proprietary. If a document designation is encountered that doesn't fit that description, the exception is thrown. Create a driver program to test the exception, allowing it to terminate the program.

PP 10.4   Modify the solution to Programming Project 10.3 such that it catches and handles the exception if it is thrown. Handle the exception by printing an appropriate message, and then continue processing.

PP 10.5   Modify the DisplayFile program to add a button labeled Save above the text area. When the button is pushed, write the contents back out to the file.

PP 10.6   Modify the JukeBox program such that it plays a song immediately after it has been selected using the combo box.

PP 10.7   Modify the `StyleOptions` program from Chapter 5 so that it uses a split pane. Orient the split pane such that the label is on the top and the style check boxes are in the bottom. Add tool tips to the check boxes to explain their purpose.

PP 10.8   Modify the `PickImage` program so that it presents several additional image options. Display the list within a scroll pane with a vertical scroll bar that is always displayed. Display the image in a scroll pane that uses both horizontal and vertical scroll bars, but only when necessary.

PP 10.9   Design and implement an application that performs flashcard testing of simple mathematical problems. Allow the user to pick the category. Repetitively display a problem and get the user's answer. Indicate whether the user's answer is right or wrong for each problem, and display an ongoing score.

Answers to Self-Review Questions

SR 10.1   A thrown exception can be handled in one of three ways: it can be ignored, which will cause a program to terminate, it can be handled where it occurs using a `try` statement, or it can be caught and handled higher in the method calling hierarchy.

SR 10.2   A `catch` phrase of a `try` statement defines the code that will handle a particular type of exception.

SR 10.3   If an exception is not caught immediately when thrown, it begins to propagate up through the methods that were called to get to the point where it was generated. The exception can be caught and handled at any point during that propagation. If it propagates out of the `main` method, the program terminates.

SR 10.4   The finally clause of a try-catch statement is executed no matter how the try block is exited. If no exception is thrown, the finally clause is executed after the try block is complete. If an exception is thrown, the appropriate catch clause is executed, then the finally clause is executed.

SR 10.5   A checked exception is an exception that must be either (1) caught and handled or (2) listed in the throws clause of any method that may throw or propagate it. This establishes a set of exceptions that must be formally acknowledged in the program one way or another. Unchecked exceptions can be ignored completely in the code if desired.

SR 10.6   A stream is a sequential series of bytes that serves as a source of input or a destination for output.

SR 10.7   The standard I/O streams in Java are `System.in`, the standard input stream; `System.out`, the standard output stream; and `System.err`, the standard error stream. Usually, standard input comes from the keyboard and standard output and error go to a default window on the monitor screen.

SR 10.8   A tool tip is a small amount of text that can be set up to appear when the cursor comes to rest on a component. It usually gives information about that component.

SR 10.9   A mnemonic is a character that can be used to activate a control such as a button as if the user had used to mouse to do so. The user activates a mnemonic by holding down the ALT key and pressing the appropriate character.

SR 10.10   A component should be disabled if it is not a viable option for the user at a given time. Not only does this prevent user error, it helps clarify what the current valid actions are.

SR 10.11   A scroll pane can have a vertical scroll bar on the right side and/or a horizontal scroll bar along the bottom. The programmer can determine, in either case, whether the scroll bar should always appear, never appear, or appear as needed to be able to view the underlying component.

SR 10.12   A combo box is a component that allows the user to choose from a set of options in a pull-down list. An editable combo box also allows the user to enter a specific value.

Recursion 11

CHAPTER OBJECTIVES

> Explain the underlying concepts of recursion.

> Explore examples that promote recursive thinking.

> Examine recursive methods and unravel their processing steps.

> Define infinite recursion and discuss ways to avoid it.

> Explain when recursion should and should not be used.

> Demonstrate the use of recursion to solve problems.

> Explore the use of recursion in graphics-based programs.

> Define the concept of a fractal and its relationship to recursion.

Recursion is a powerful programming technique that provides elegant solutions to certain problems. This chapter provides an introduction to recursive processing. It contains an explanation of the basic concepts underlying recursion and then explores the use of recursion in programming. Several specific problems are solved using recursion, demonstrating its versatility, simplicity, and elegance.

11.1   RECURSIVE THINKING

We've seen many times in previous examples that one method can call another method to accomplish a goal. What we haven't seen yet, however, is that a method can call itself. *Recursion* is a programming technique in which a method calls itself in order to fulfill its purpose. But before we get into the details of how we use recursion in a program, we need to explore the general concept of recursion. The ability to think recursively is essential to being able to use recursion as a programming technique.

In general, recursion is the process of defining something in terms of itself. For example, consider the following definition of the word *decoration*:

decoration: n. any ornament or adornment used to decorate
something

The word *decorate* is used to define the word *decoration*. You may recall your grade school teacher telling you to avoid such recursive definitions when explaining the meaning of a word. However, in many situations, recursion is an appropriate way to express an idea or definition. For example, suppose we wanted to formally define a list of one or more numbers, separated by commas. Such a list can be defined recursively as either a number or as a number followed by a comma followed by a list. This definition can be expressed as follows:

A *List* is a: `number`
      or a: `number   comma   List`

This recursive definition of *List* defines each of the following lists of numbers:

```
24, 88, 40, 37
96, 43
14, 64, 21, 69, 32, 93, 47, 81, 28, 45, 81, 52, 69
70
```

No matter how long a list is, the recursive definition describes it. A list of one element, such as in the last example, is defined completely by the first (non-recursive) part of the definition. For any list longer than one element, the recursive part of the definition (the part which refers to itself) is used as many times as necessary until the last element is reached. The last element in the list is always defined by the non-recursive part of the definition. Figure 11.1 shows how one particular list of numbers corresponds to the recursive definition of *List*.

```
LIST: number   comma   LIST
        24        ,     88,  40,  37
                       number   comma   LIST
                         88       ,     40,  37
                                number   comma   LIST
                                  40       ,     37
                                                number
                                                  37
```

FIGURE 11.1 Tracing the recursive definition of *List*

Infinite Recursion

Note that the definition of *List* contains one option that is recursive and one option that is not. The part of the definition that is not recursive is called the *base case*. If all options had a recursive component, the recursion would never end. For example, if the definition of *List* was simply "a number followed by a comma followed by a *List*," no list could ever end. This problem is called *infinite recursion*. It is similar to an infinite loop except that the "loop" occurs in the definition itself.

> **Key Concept**
>
> Any recursive definition must have a non-recursive part, called the base case, which permits the recursion to eventually end.

As in the infinite loop problem, a programmer must be careful to design algorithms so that they avoid infinite recursion. Any recursive definition must have a base case that does not result in a recursive option. The base case of the *List* definition is a single number that is not followed by anything. In other words, when the last number in the list is reached, the base case option terminates the recursive path.

Recursion in Math

Let's look at an example of recursion in mathematics. The value referred to as $N!$ (pronounced N *factorial*) is defined for any positive integer N as the product of all integers between 1 and N inclusive. Therefore, 3! is defined as:

    3! = 3*2*1 = 6

and 5! is defined as:

```
5!  =  5*4*3*2*1  =  120.
```

Mathematical formulas are often expressed recursively. The definition of *N*! can be expressed recursively as:

```
1! = 1
N! = N * (N-1)! for N > 1
```

The base case of this definition is 1!, which is defined as 1. All other values of *N*! (for *N* > 1) are defined recursively as *N* times the value (*N*–1)!. The recursion is that the factorial function is defined in terms of the factorial function.

Using this definition, 50! is equal to 50 * 49!. And 49! is equal to 49 * 48!. And 48! is equal to 48 * 47!. This process continues until we get to the base case of 1. Because *N*! is defined only for positive integers, this definition is complete and will always conclude with the base case.

The next section describes how recursion is accomplished in programs.

11.2   RECURSIVE PROGRAMMING

Let's use a simple mathematical operation to demonstrate the concept of recursive programming. Consider the process of summing the values between 1 and *N* inclusive, where *N* is any positive integer. The sum of the values from 1 to *N* can be expressed as *N* plus the sum of the values from 1 to *N*–1. That sum can be expressed similarly, as shown in Figure 11.2.

For example, the sum of the values between 1 and 20 is equal to 20 plus the sum of the values between 1 and 19. Continuing this approach, the sum of the values between 1 and 19 is equal to 19 plus the sum of the values between 1 and 18. This may sound like a strange way to think about this problem, but it is a straightforward example that can be used to demonstrate how recursion is programmed.

As we mentioned earlier, in Java, as in many other programming languages, a method can call itself. Each call to the method creates a new environment in which to work. That is, all local variables and parameters are newly defined with their own unique data space every time the method is called. Each parameter is given an initial value based on the new call. Each time a method terminates, processing returns to the method that called it (which may be an earlier invocation of the same method). These rules are no different from those governing any "regular" method invocation.

$$\sum_{i=1}^{N} i = N + \sum_{i=1}^{N-1} i = N + N-1 + \sum_{i=1}^{N-2} i$$

$$= N + N-1 + N-2 + \sum_{i=1}^{N-3} i$$
$$\vdots$$
$$= N + N-1 + N-2 + \cdots + 2 + 1$$

FIGURE 11.2 The sum of the numbers 1 through N, defined recursively

A recursive solution to the summation problem is defined by the following recursive method called sum:

```java
// This method returns the sum of 1 to num
public int sum (int num)
{
    int result;
    if (num == 1)
        result = 1;
    else
        result = num + sum (num-1);
    return result;
}
```

Note that this method essentially embodies our recursive definition that the sum of the numbers between 1 and N is equal to N plus the sum of the numbers between 1 and N–1. The sum method is recursive because sum calls itself. The parameter passed to sum is decremented each time sum is called until it reaches the base case of 1. Recursive methods invariably contain an if-else statement, with one of the branches, usually the first one, representing the base case, as in this example.

Suppose the main method calls sum, passing it an initial value of 1, which is stored in the parameter num. Since num is equal to 1, the result of 1 is returned to main and no recursion occurs.

Now let's trace the execution of the sum method when it is passed an initial value of 2. Since num does not equal 1, sum is called again with an argument of num-1, or 1. This is a new call to the method sum, with a new parameter num and a new local variable result. Since this num is equal to 1 in this invocation, the result of 1 is returned without further recursive calls. Control returns to the first version of sum that was invoked. The return value of 1 is added to the initial value of num in that call to sum, which is 2. Therefore, result is assigned the value 3, which is returned to the main method. The method called from main correctly calculates the sum of the integers from 1 to 2 and returns the result of 3.

The base case in the summation example is when N equals 1, at which point no further recursive calls are made. The recursion begins to fold back into the earlier versions of the sum method, returning the appropriate value each time. Each return value contributes to the computation of the sum at the higher level. Without the base case, infinite recursion would result. Each call to a method requires additional memory space; therefore infinite recursion often results in a run-time error indicating that memory has been exhausted.

Trace the sum function with different initial values of num until this processing becomes familiar. Figure 11.3 illustrates the recursive calls when main invokes sum to determine the sum of the integers from 1 to 4. Each box represents a copy of the method as it is invoked, indicating the allocation of space to store the formal parameters and any local variables. Invocations are shown as solid lines, and

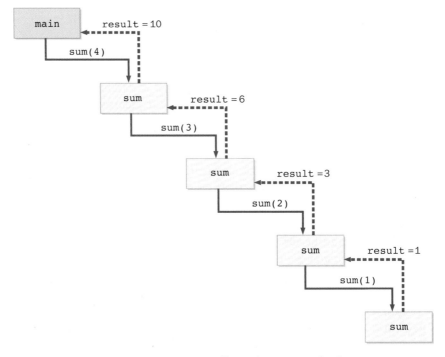

FIGURE 11.3 Recursive calls to the sum method

returns as dotted lines. The return value `result` is shown at each step. The recursive path is followed completely until the base case is reached; the calls then begin to return their result up through the chain.

Recursion vs. Iteration

Of course, there is a non-recursive solution to the summation problem we just explored. One way to compute the sum of the numbers between 1 and num inclusive in an iterative manner is as follows:

```
sum = 0;
for (int number = 1; number <= num; number++)
    sum += number;
```

This solution is certainly more straightforward than the recursive version. We used the summation problem to demonstrate recursion because it is simple, not because you would use recursion to solve it under normal conditions. Recursion has the overhead of multiple method invocations and, in this case, presents a more complicated solution than its iterative counterpart.

> **Key Concept**
>
> Recursion is the most elegant and appropriate way to solve some problems, but for others it is less intuitive than an iterative solution.

A programmer must learn when to use recursion and when not to use it. Determining which approach is best depends on the problem being solved. All problems can be solved in an iterative manner, but in some cases the iterative version is much more complicated. Recursion, for some problems, allows us to create relatively short, elegant programs.

Direct vs. Indirect Recursion

Direct recursion occurs when a method invokes itself, such as when sum calls sum. *Indirect recursion* occurs when a method invokes another method, eventually resulting in the original method being invoked again. For example, if method m1 invokes method m2, and m2 invokes method m1, we can say that m1 is indirectly recursive. The amount of indirection could be several levels deep, as when m1 invokes m2, which invokes m3, which invokes m4, which invokes m1. Figure 11.4 depicts a situation with indirect recursion. Method invocations are shown with solid lines, and returns are shown with dotted lines. The entire invocation path is followed, and then the recursion unravels following the return path.

Indirect recursion requires all of the same attention to base cases that direct recursion requires. Furthermore, indirect recursion can be more difficult to trace because of the intervening method calls. Therefore extra care is warranted when designing or evaluating indirectly recursive methods. Ensure that the indirection is truly necessary and clearly explained in documentation.

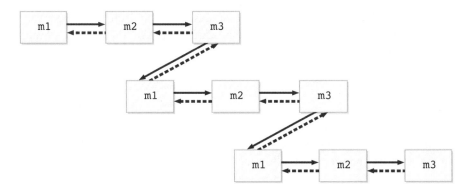

FIGURE 11.4 Indirect recursion

11.3 USING RECURSION

Each of the following sections describes a particular recursive problem. For each one, we examine exactly how recursion plays a role in the solution and how a base case is used to terminate the recursion. As you examine these examples, consider how complicated a non-recursive solution for each problem would be.

Traversing a Maze

Solving a maze involves a great deal of trial and error: following a path, backtracking when you cannot go farther, and trying other untried options. Such activities often are handled nicely using recursion. The program shown in Listing 11.1 creates a `Maze` object and attempts to traverse it.

The `Maze` class shown in Listing 11.2 uses a two-dimensional array of integers to represent the maze. The goal is to move from the top-left corner (the entry point) to the bottom-right corner (the exit point). Initially, a 1 indicates a clear path and a 0 indicates a blocked path. As the maze is solved, these array elements are changed to other values to indicate attempted paths and ultimately a successful path through the maze if one exists.

The only valid moves through the maze are in the four primary directions: down, right, up, and left. No diagonal moves are allowed. In this example, the maze is 8 rows by 13 columns, although the code is designed to handle a maze of any size.

Let's think this through recursively. The maze can be traversed successfully if it can be traversed successfully from position (0, 0). Therefore, the maze can be

Listing 11.1

```java
//********************************************************************
//  MazeSearch.java       Author: Lewis/Loftus
//
//  Demonstrates recursion.
//********************************************************************

public class MazeSearch
{
   //-----------------------------------------------------------------
   //  Creates a new maze, prints its original form, attempts to
   //  solve it, and prints out its final form.
   //-----------------------------------------------------------------
   public static void main (String[] args)
   {
      Maze labyrinth = new Maze();

      System.out.println (labyrinth);

      if (labyrinth.traverse (0, 0))
         System.out.println ("The maze was successfully traversed!");
      else
         System.out.println ("There is no possible path.");

      System.out.println (labyrinth);
   }
}
```

Output

```
1110110001111
1011101111001
0000101010100
1110111010111
1010000111001
1011111101111
1000000000000
111111111111
```

Listing 11.1   continued

```
The maze was successfully traversed!

7770110001111
3077707771001
0000707070300
7770777070333
7070000773003
7077777703333
7000000000000
7777777777777
```

Listing 11.2

```java
//********************************************************************
//   Maze.java        Author: Lewis/Loftus
//
//   Represents a maze of characters. The goal is to get from the
//   top left corner to the bottom right, following a path of 1s.
//********************************************************************

public class Maze
{
   private final int TRIED = 3;
   private final int PATH = 7;

   private int[][] grid = { {1,1,1,0,1,1,0,0,0,1,1,1,1},
                            {1,0,1,1,1,0,1,1,1,1,0,0,1},
                            {0,0,0,0,1,0,1,0,1,0,1,0,0},
                            {1,1,1,0,1,1,1,0,1,0,1,1,1},
                            {1,0,1,0,0,0,0,1,1,1,0,0,1},
                            {1,0,1,1,1,1,1,1,0,1,1,1,1},
                            {1,0,0,0,0,0,0,0,0,0,0,0,0},
                            {1,1,1,1,1,1,1,1,1,1,1,1,1} };

   //-----------------------------------------------------------------
   //   Attempts to recursively traverse the maze. Inserts special
   //   characters indicating locations that have been tried and that
   //   eventually become part of the solution.
   //-----------------------------------------------------------------
```

Listing 11.2   continued

```java
public boolean traverse (int row, int column)
{
    boolean done = false;

    if (valid (row, column))
    {
        grid[row][column] = TRIED;  // this cell has been tried

        if (row == grid.length-1 && column == grid[0].length-1)
            done = true;  // the maze is solved
        else
        {
            done = traverse (row+1, column);     // down
            if (!done)
                done = traverse (row, column+1);  // right
            if (!done)
                done = traverse (row-1, column);  // up
            if (!done)
                done = traverse (row, column-1);  // left
        }

        if (done)  // this location is part of the final path
            grid[row][column] = PATH;
    }

    return done;
}

//-----------------------------------------------------------------
//  Determines if a specific location is valid.
//-----------------------------------------------------------------
private boolean valid (int row, int column)
{
    boolean result = false;

    // check if cell is in the bounds of the matrix
    if (row >= 0 && row < grid.length &&
        column >= 0 && column < grid[row].length)

        //  check if cell is not blocked and not previously tried
        if (grid[row][column] == 1)
            result = true;
```

Listing 11.2 **continued**

```
      return result;
   }

   //---------------------------------------------------------------
   //  Returns the maze as a string.
   //---------------------------------------------------------------
   public String toString ()
   {
      String result = "\n";

      for (int row=0; row < grid.length; row++)
      {
         for (int column=0; column < grid[row].length; column++)
            result += grid[row][column] + "";
         result += "\n";
      }

      return result;
   }
}
```

traversed successfully if it can be traversed successfully from any positions adjacent to (0, 0), namely position (1, 0), position (0, 1), position (–1, 0), or position (0, –1). Picking a potential next step, say (1, 0), we find ourselves in the same type of situation we did before. To successfully traverse the maze from the new current position, we must successfully traverse it from an adjacent position. At any point, some of the adjacent positions may be invalid, may be blocked, or may represent a possible successful path. We continue this process recursively. If the base case, position (7, 12) is reached, the maze has been traversed successfully.

The recursive method in the Maze class is called traverse. It returns a boolean value that indicates whether a solution was found. First the method determines whether a move to the specified row and column is valid. A move is considered valid if it stays within the grid boundaries and if the grid contains a 1 in that location, indicating that a move in that direction is not blocked. The initial call to traverse passes in the upper-left location (0, 0).

If the move is valid, the grid entry is changed from a 1 to a 3, marking this location as visited so that later we don't retrace our steps. The `traverse` method then determines whether the maze has been completed by having reached the bottom-right location. Therefore, there are actually three possibilities of the base case for this problem that will terminate any particular recursive path:

> an invalid move because the move is out of bounds
> an invalid move because the move has been tried before
> a move that arrives at the final location

If the current location is not the bottom-right corner, we search for a solution in each of the primary directions, if necessary. First, we look down by recursively calling the `traverse` method and passing in the new location. The logic of the `traverse` method starts all over again using this new position. A solution is either ultimately found by first attempting to move down from the current location, or it's not found. If it's not found, we try moving right. If that fails, we try up. Finally, if no other direction has yielded a correct path, we try left. If no direction from the current location yields a correct solution, then there is no path from this location, and `traverse` returns false.

If a solution is found from the current location, the grid entry is changed to a 7. The first 7 is placed in the bottom-right corner. The next 7 is placed in the location that led to the bottom-right corner, and so on until the final 7 is placed in the upper-left corner. Therefore, when the final maze is printed, the zeros still indicate a blocked path, a 1 indicates an open path that was never tried, a 3 indicates a path that was tried but failed to yield a correct solution, and a 7 indicates a part of the final solution of the maze.

Note that there are several opportunities for recursion in each call to the `traverse` method. Any or all of them might be followed, depending on the maze configuration. Although there may be many paths through the maze, the recursion terminates when a path is found. Carefully trace the execution of this code while following the maze array to see how the recursion solves the problem. Then consider the difficulty of producing a non-recursive solution.

The Towers of Hanoi

The *Towers of Hanoi* puzzle was invented in the 1880s by Edouard Lucas, a French mathematician. It has become a favorite among computer scientists because its solution is an excellent demonstration of recursive elegance.

The puzzle consists of three upright pegs and a set of disks with holes in the middle so that they slide onto the pegs. Each disk has a different diameter.

Initially, all of the disks are stacked on one peg in order of size such that the largest disk is on the bottom, as shown in Figure 11.5.

The goal of the puzzle is to move all of the disks from their original (first) peg to the destination (third) peg. We can use the "extra" peg as a temporary place to put disks, but we must obey the following three rules:

> We can move only one disk at a time.
> We cannot place a larger disk on top of a smaller disk.
> All disks must be on some peg except for the disk in transit between pegs.

These rules imply that we must move smaller disks "out of the way" in order to move a larger disk from one peg to another. Figure 11.6 shows the step-by-step solution for the Towers of Hanoi puzzle using three disks. In order to ultimately move all three disks from the first peg to the third peg, we first have to get to the point where the smaller two disks are out of the way on the second peg so that the largest disk can be moved from the first peg to the third peg.

The first three moves shown in Figure 11.6 can be thought of as moving the smaller disks out of the way. The fourth move puts the largest disk in its final place. The last three moves then put the smaller disks to their final place on top of the largest one.

Let's use this idea to form a general strategy. To move a stack of N disks from the original peg to the destination peg:

> Move the topmost N–1 disks from the original peg to the extra peg.
> Move the largest disk from the original peg to the destination peg.
> Move the N–1 disks from the extra peg to the destination peg.

This strategy lends itself nicely to a recursive solution. The step to move the N–1 disks out of the way is the same problem all over again: moving a stack of disks. For this subtask, though, there is one less disk, and our destination peg is what we were originally calling the extra peg. An analogous situation occurs after we've moved the largest disk, and we have to move the original N–1 disks again.

FIGURE 11.5 The Towers of Hanoi puzzle

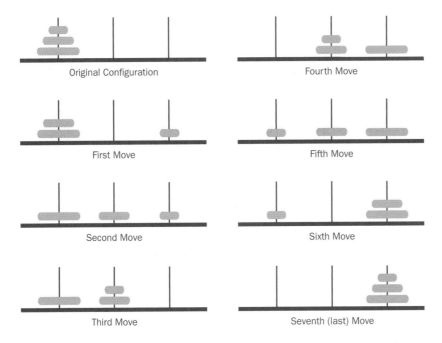

Original Configuration

Fourth Move

First Move

Fifth Move

Second Move

Sixth Move

Third Move

Seventh (last) Move

FIGURE 11.6 A solution to the three-disk Towers of Hanoi puzzle

The base case for this problem occurs when we want to move a "stack" that consists of only one disk. That step can be accomplished directly and without recursion.

The program in Listing 11.3 creates a TowersOfHanoi object and invokes its solve method. The output is a step-by-step list of instructions that describe how the disks should be moved to solve the puzzle. This example uses four disks, which is specified by a parameter to the TowersOfHanoi constructor.

The TowersOfHanoi class shown in Listing 11.4 uses the solve method to make an initial call to moveTower, the recursive method. The initial call indicates that all of the disks should be moved from peg 1 to peg 3, using peg 2 as the extra position.

The moveTower method first considers the base case (a "stack" of one disk). When that occurs, it calls the moveOneDisk method that prints a single line describing that particular move. If the stack contains more than one disk, we call moveTower again to get the N–1 disks out of the way, then move the largest disk, then move the N–1 disks to their final destination with yet another call to moveTower.

Listing 11.3

```
//********************************************************************
//  SolveTowers.java       Author: Lewis/Loftus
//
//  Demonstrates recursion.
//********************************************************************

public class SolveTowers
{
    //-----------------------------------------------------------------
    //  Creates a TowersOfHanoi puzzle and solves it.
    //-----------------------------------------------------------------
    public static void main (String[] args)
    {
        TowersOfHanoi towers = new TowersOfHanoi (4);

        towers.solve();
    }
}
```

Output

```
Move one disk from 1 to 2
Move one disk from 1 to 3
Move one disk from 2 to 3
Move one disk from 1 to 2
Move one disk from 3 to 1
Move one disk from 3 to 2
Move one disk from 1 to 2
Move one disk from 1 to 3
Move one disk from 2 to 3
Move one disk from 2 to 1
Move one disk from 3 to 1
Move one disk from 2 to 3
Move one disk from 1 to 2
Move one disk from 1 to 3
Move one disk from 2 to 3
```

Listing 11.4

```java
//********************************************************************
//  TowersOfHanoi.java       Author: Lewis/Loftus
//
//  Represents the classic Towers of Hanoi puzzle.
//********************************************************************

public class TowersOfHanoi
{
   private int totalDisks;

   //-----------------------------------------------------------------
   //  Sets up the puzzle with the specified number of disks.
   //-----------------------------------------------------------------
   public TowersOfHanoi (int disks)
   {
      totalDisks = disks;
   }

   //-----------------------------------------------------------------
   //  Performs the initial call to moveTower to solve the puzzle.
   //  Moves the disks from tower 1 to tower 3 using tower 2.
   //-----------------------------------------------------------------
   public void solve ()
   {
      moveTower (totalDisks, 1, 3, 2);
   }

   //-----------------------------------------------------------------
   //  Moves the specified number of disks from one tower to another
   //  by moving a subtower of n-1 disks out of the way, moving one
   //  disk, then moving the subtower back. Base case of 1 disk.
   //-----------------------------------------------------------------
   private void moveTower (int numDisks, int start, int end, int temp)
   {
      if (numDisks == 1)
         moveOneDisk (start, end);
      else
      {
         moveTower (numDisks-1, start, temp, end);
         moveOneDisk (start, end);
         moveTower (numDisks-1, temp, end, start);
      }
   }
}
```

Listing 11.4 **continued**

```
//-----------------------------------------------------------------
//  Prints instructions to move one disk from the specified start
//  tower to the specified end tower.
//-----------------------------------------------------------------
private void moveOneDisk (int start, int end)
{
    System.out.println ("Move one disk from " + start + " to " +
                        end);
}
}
```

Note that the parameters to moveTower describing the pegs are switched around as needed to move the partial stacks. This code follows our general strategy and uses the moveTower method to move all partial stacks. Trace the code carefully for a stack of three disks to understand the processing. Compare the processing steps to Figure 11.6.

> **Key Concept**
>
> The Towers of Hanoi solution has exponential complexity, which is very inefficient. Yet the implementation of the solution is incredibly short and elegant.

Contrary to its short and elegant implementation, the solution to the Towers of Hanoi puzzle is terribly inefficient. To solve the puzzle with a stack of N disks, we have to make 2^N-1 individual disk moves. This situation is an example of *exponential complexity*. As the number of disks increases, the number of required moves increases exponentially.

Legend has it that priests of Brahma are working on this puzzle in a temple at the center of the world. They are using 64 gold disks, moving them between pegs of pure diamond. The downside is that when the priests finish the puzzle, the world will end. The upside is that even if they move one disk every second of every day, it will take them over 584 billion years to complete it. That's with a puzzle of only 64 disks! It is certainly an indication of just how intractable exponential algorithmic complexity is.

11.4 **RECURSION IN GRAPHICS**

The concept of recursion has several uses in images and graphics. The following section explores some image and graphics-based recursion examples.

Tiled Pictures

Carefully examine the display for the `TiledPictures` applet shown in Listing 11.5. There are actually three unique images among the menagerie. The entire area is divided into four equal quadrants. A picture of the world (with a circle indicating the Himalayan mountain region) is shown in the bottom-right quadrant. The bottom-left quadrant contains a picture of Mt. Everest. In the top-right quadrant is a picture of a mountain goat.

The interesting part of the picture is the top-left quadrant. It contains a copy of the entire collage, including itself. In this smaller version you can see the three simple pictures in their three quadrants. And again, in the top-left corner, the picture is repeated (including itself). This repetition continues for several levels. It is similar to the effect you can create when looking at a mirror in the reflection of another mirror.

This visual effect is created quite easily using recursion. The applet's `init` method initially loads the three images. The `paint` method then invokes the `drawPictures` method, which accepts a parameter that defines the size of the area in which pictures are displayed. It draws the three images using the `drawImage` method, with parameters that scale the picture to the correct size and location. The `drawPictures` method is then called recursively to draw the upper-left quadrant.

On each invocation, if the drawing area is large enough, the `drawPictures` method is invoked again, using a smaller drawing area. Eventually, the drawing area becomes so small that the recursive call is not performed. Note that `drawPictures` assumes the origin (0, 0) coordinate as the relative location of the new images, no matter what their size is.

The base case of the recursion in this problem specifies a minimum size for the drawing area. Because the size is decreased each time, the base case eventually is reached and the recursion stops. This is why the upper-left corner is empty in the smallest version of the collage.

Listing 11.5

```java
//********************************************************************
//  TiledPictures.java        Author: Lewis/Loftus
//
//  Demonstrates the use of recursion.
//********************************************************************

import java.awt.*;
import javax.swing.JApplet;

public class TiledPictures extends JApplet
{
   private final int APPLET_WIDTH = 320;
   private final int APPLET_HEIGHT = 320;
   private final int MIN = 20;   // smallest picture size

   private Image world, everest, goat;

   //-----------------------------------------------------------------
   //  Loads the images.
   //-----------------------------------------------------------------
   public void init()
   {
      world = getImage (getDocumentBase(), "world.gif");
      everest = getImage (getDocumentBase(), "everest.gif");
      goat = getImage (getDocumentBase(), "goat.gif");

      setSize (APPLET_WIDTH, APPLET_HEIGHT);
   }

   //-----------------------------------------------------------------
   //  Draws the three images, then calls itself recursively.
   //-----------------------------------------------------------------
   public void drawPictures (int size, Graphics page)
   {
      page.drawImage (everest, 0, size/2, size/2, size/2, this);
      page.drawImage (goat, size/2, 0, size/2, size/2, this);
      page.drawImage (world, size/2, size/2, size/2, size/2, this);

      if (size > MIN)
         drawPictures (size/2, page);
   }
```

Listing 11.5   **continued**

```
    //-----------------------------------------------------------------
    //  Performs the initial call to the drawPictures method.
    //-----------------------------------------------------------------
    public void paint (Graphics page)
    {
       drawPictures (APPLET_WIDTH, page);
    }
}
```

Display

Fractals

A *fractal* is a geometric shape that can be made up of the same pattern repeated at different scales and orientations. The nature of a fractal lends itself to a recursive definition. Interest in fractals has grown immensely in recent years, largely due to Benoit Mandelbrot, a Polish mathematician born in 1924. He demonstrated that fractals occur in many places in mathematics and nature. Computers have made fractals much easier to generate and investigate. Over the past quarter century, the bright, interesting images that can be created with fractals have come to be considered as much an art form as a mathematical interest.

One particular example of a fractal is called the *Koch snowflake,* named after Helge von Koch, a Swedish mathematician. It begins with an equilateral triangle, which is considered to be the Koch fractal of order 1. Koch fractals of higher orders are constructed by repeatedly modifying all of the line segments in the shape.

To create the next higher order Koch fractal, each line segment in the shape is modified by replacing its middle third with a sharp protrusion made of two line segments, each having the same length as the replaced part. Relative to the entire shape, the protrusion on any line segment always points outward. Figure 11.7 shows several orders of Koch fractals. As the order increases, the shape begins to look like a snowflake.

The applet shown in Listing 11.6 draws a Koch snowflake of several different orders. The buttons at the top of the applet allow the user to increase and decrease the order of the fractal. Each time a button is pressed, the fractal image is redrawn. The applet serves as the listener for the buttons.

The fractal image is drawn on a canvas defined by the `KochPanel` class shown in Listing 11.7. The `paint` method makes the initial calls to the recursive method

FIGURE 11.7 Several orders of the Koch snowflake

Listing 11.6

```
//********************************************************************
//   KochSnowflake.java        Author: Lewis/Loftus
//
//   Demonstrates the use of recursion.
//********************************************************************

import java.awt.*;
import java.awt.event.*;
import javax.swing.*;

public class KochSnowflake extends JApplet implements ActionListener
{
   private final int APPLET_WIDTH = 400;
   private final int APPLET_HEIGHT = 440;

   private final int MIN = 1, MAX = 9;

   private JButton increase, decrease;
   private JLabel titleLabel, orderLabel;
   private KochPanel drawing;
   private JPanel appletPanel, tools;

   //-----------------------------------------------------------------
   //   Sets up the components for the applet.
   //-----------------------------------------------------------------
   public void init()
   {
      tools = new JPanel ();
      tools.setLayout (new BoxLayout(tools, BoxLayout.X_AXIS));
      tools.setBackground (Color.yellow);
      tools.setOpaque (true);

      titleLabel = new JLabel ("The Koch Snowflake");
      titleLabel.setForeground (Color.black);

      increase = new JButton (new ImageIcon ("increase.gif"));
      increase.setPressedIcon (new ImageIcon ("increasePressed.gif"));
      increase.setMargin (new Insets (0, 0, 0, 0));
      increase.addActionListener (this);
      decrease = new JButton (new ImageIcon ("decrease.gif"));
      decrease.setPressedIcon (new ImageIcon ("decreasePressed.gif"));
      decrease.setMargin (new Insets (0, 0, 0, 0));
```

Listing 11.6   continued

```java
        decrease.addActionListener (this);

        orderLabel = new JLabel ("Order: 1");
        orderLabel.setForeground (Color.black);

        tools.add (titleLabel);
        tools.add (Box.createHorizontalStrut (20));
        tools.add (decrease);
        tools.add (increase);
        tools.add (Box.createHorizontalStrut (20));
        tools.add (orderLabel);

        drawing = new KochPanel (1);

        appletPanel = new JPanel();
        appletPanel.add (tools);
        appletPanel.add (drawing);

        getContentPane().add (appletPanel);

        setSize (APPLET_WIDTH, APPLET_HEIGHT);
    }

    //-----------------------------------------------------------------
    //  Determines which button was pushed, and sets the new order
    //  if it is in range.
    //-----------------------------------------------------------------
    public void actionPerformed (ActionEvent event)
    {
        int order = drawing.getOrder();

        if (event.getSource() == increase)
            order++;
        else
            order--;
```

Listing 11.6   continued

```
    if (order >= MIN && order <= MAX)
    {
        orderLabel.setText ("Order: " + order);
        drawing.setOrder (order);
        repaint();
    }
  }
}
```

Display

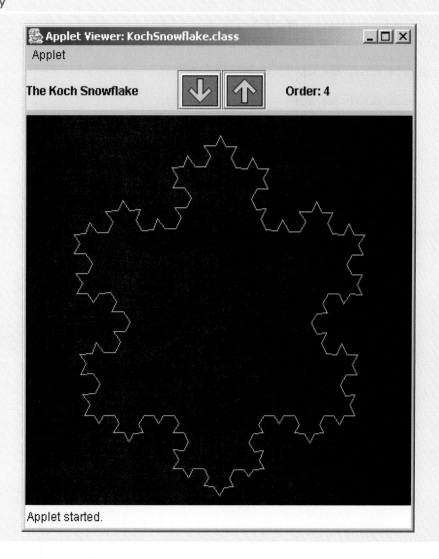

Listing 11.7

```java
//********************************************************************
//  KochPanel.java        Author: Lewis/Loftus
//
//  Represents a drawing surface on which to paint a Koch Snowflake.
//********************************************************************

import java.awt.*;
import javax.swing.JPanel;

public class KochPanel extends JPanel
{
   private final int PANEL_WIDTH = 400;
   private final int PANEL_HEIGHT = 400;

   private final double SQ = Math.sqrt(3.0) / 6;

   private final int TOPX = 200, TOPY = 20;
   private final int LEFTX = 60, LEFTY = 300;
   private final int RIGHTX = 340, RIGHTY = 300;

   private int current; //current order

   //-----------------------------------------------------------------
   //  Sets the initial fractal order to the value specified.
   //-----------------------------------------------------------------
   public KochPanel (int currentOrder)
   {
      current = currentOrder;
      setBackground (Color.black);
      setPreferredSize (new Dimension(PANEL_WIDTH, PANEL_HEIGHT));
   }

   //-----------------------------------------------------------------
   //  Draws the fractal recursively. Base case is an order of 1 for
   //  which a simple straight line is drawn. Otherwise three
   //  intermediate points are computed, and each line segment is
   //  drawn as a fractal.
   //-----------------------------------------------------------------
   public void drawFractal (int order, int x1, int y1, int x5, int y5,
                            Graphics page)
   {
      int deltaX, deltaY, x2, y2, x3, y3, x4, y4;
```

Listing 11.7   **continued**

```java
      if (order == 1)
         page.drawLine (x1, y1, x5, y5);
      else
      {
         deltaX = x5 - x1;   // distance between end points
         deltaY = y5 - y1;

         x2 = x1 + deltaX / 3;   // one third
         y2 = y1 + deltaY / 3;

         x3 = (int) ((x1+x5)/2 + SQ * (y1-y5));   // tip of projection
         y3 = (int) ((y1+y5)/2 + SQ * (x5-x1));

         x4 = x1 + deltaX * 2/3;   // two thirds
         y4 = y1 + deltaY * 2/3;

         drawFractal (order-1, x1, y1, x2, y2, page);
         drawFractal (order-1, x2, y2, x3, y3, page);
         drawFractal (order-1, x3, y3, x4, y4, page);
         drawFractal (order-1, x4, y4, x5, y5, page);
      }
   }

   //-----------------------------------------------------------------------
   //  Performs the initial calls to the drawFractal method.
   //-----------------------------------------------------------------------
   public void paintComponent (Graphics page)
   {
      super.paintComponent (page);

      page.setColor (Color.green);

      drawFractal (current, TOPX, TOPY, LEFTX, LEFTY, page);
      drawFractal (current, LEFTX, LEFTY, RIGHTX, RIGHTY, page);
      drawFractal (current, RIGHTX, RIGHTY, TOPX, TOPY, page);
   }

   //-----------------------------------------------------------------------
   //  Sets the fractal order to the value specified.
   //-----------------------------------------------------------------------
   public void setOrder (int order)
   {
      current = order;
   }
```

Listing 11.7   **continued**

```
//-----------------------------------------------------------------
//  Returns the current order.
//-----------------------------------------------------------------
public int getOrder ()
{
   return current;
}
}
```

drawFractal. The three calls to drawFractal in the paint method represent the original three sides of the equilateral triangle that make up a Koch fractal of order 1.

The variable current represents the order of the fractal to be drawn. Each recursive call to drawFractal decrements the order by 1. The base case of the recursion occurs when the order of the fractal is 1, which results in a simple line segment between the coordinates specified by the parameters.

If the order of the fractal is higher than 1, three additional points are computed. In conjunction with the parameters, these points form the four line segments of the modified fractal. Figure 11.8 shows the transformation.

Based on the position of the two end points of the original line segment, a point one-third of the way and a point two-thirds of the way between them are computed. The calculation of $<x_3, y_3>$, the point at the tip of the protrusion, is more convoluted and uses a simplifying constant that incorporates multiple geometric relationships. The calculations to determine the three new points actually have nothing to do with the recursive technique used to draw the fractal, and so we won't discuss the details of these computations here.

An interesting mathematical feature of a Koch snowflake is that it has an infinite perimeter but a finite area. As the order of the fractal increases, the perimeter grows exponentially larger, with a mathematical limit of infinity. However, a rectangle large enough to surround the second-order fractal for the Koch snowflake is large enough to contain all higher-order fractals. The shape is restricted forever in area, but its perimeter gets infinitely longer.

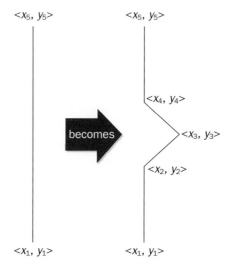

FIGURE 11.8 The transformation of each line segment of a Koch snowflake

Summary of Key Concepts

> Recursion is a programming technique in which a method calls itself. A key to being able to program recursively is to be able to think recursively.

> Any recursive definition must have a non-recursive part, called the base case, which permits the recursion to eventually end.

> Mathematical problems and formulas are often expressed recursively.

> Each recursive call to a method creates new local variables and parameters.

> A careful trace of recursive processing can provide insight into the way it is used to solve a problem.

> Recursion is the most elegant and appropriate way to solve some problems, but for others it is less intuitive than an iterative solution.

> The Towers of Hanoi solution has exponential complexity, which is very inefficient. Yet the implementation of the solution is incredibly short and elegant.

> A fractal is a geometric shape that is defined naturally in a recursive manner.

Self-Review Questions

SR 11.1   What is recursion?

SR 11.2   What is infinite recursion?

SR 11.3   When is a base case needed for recursive processing?

SR 11.4   Is recursion necessary?

SR 11.5   When should recursion be avoided?

SR 11.6   What is indirect recursion?

SR 11.7   Under what conditions does the recursion stop in the MazeSearch program?

SR 11.8   Explain the general approach to solving the Towers of Hanoi puzzle. How does it relate to recursion?

SR 11.9   What is the base case for the TiledPictures program?

SR 11.10   What is a fractal? What does it have to do with recursion?

Exercises

EX 11.1   Write a recursive definition of a valid Java identifier (see Chapter 1).

EX 11.2   Write a recursive definition of x^y (x raised to the power y), where x and y are integers and $y > 0$.

EX 11.3   Write a recursive definition of $i * j$ (integer multiplication), where $i > 0$. Define the multiplication process in terms of integer addition. For example, 4 * 7 is equal to 7 added to itself 4 times.

EX 11.4   Write a recursive definition of the Fibonacci numbers. The Fibonacci numbers are a sequence of integers, each of which is the sum of the previous two numbers. The first two numbers in the sequence are 0 and 1. Explain why you would not normally use recursion to solve this problem.

EX 11.5   Modify the method that calculates the sum of the integers between 1 and N shown in this chapter. Have the new version match the following recursive definition: The sum of 1 to N is the sum of 1 to ($N/2$) plus the sum of ($N/2 + 1$) to N. Trace your solution using an N of 7.

EX 11.6   Write a recursive method that returns the value of $N!$ (N factorial) using the definition given in this chapter. Explain why you would not normally use recursion to solve this problem.

EX 11.7   Write a recursive method to reverse a string. Explain why you would not normally use recursion to solve this problem.

EX 11.8   Design or generate a new maze for the MazeSearch program in this chapter and rerun the program. Explain the processing in terms of your new maze, giving examples of a path that was tried but failed, a path that was never tried, and the ultimate solution.

EX 11.9   Annotate the lines of output of the SolveTowers program in this chapter to show the recursive steps.

EX 11.10   Produce a chart showing the number of moves required to solve the Towers of Hanoi puzzle using the following number of disks: 2, 3, 4, 5, 6, 7, 8, 9, 10, 15, 20, and 25.

EX 11.11   How many line segments are used to construct a Koch snowflake of order N? Produce a chart showing the number of line segments that make up a Koch snowflake for orders 1 through 9.

Programming Projects

PP 11.1   Design and implement a recursive version of the
`PalindromeTester` program from Chapter 5.

PP 11.2   Design and implement a program that implements Euclid's
algorithm for finding the greatest common divisor of two
positive integers. The greatest common divisor is the largest
integer that divides both values without producing a
remainder. An iterative version of this method was part of the
`RationalNumber` class presented in Chapter 6. In a class called
`DivisorCalc`, define a `static` method called `gcd` that accepts
two integers, `num1` and `num2`. Create a driver to test your
implementation. The recursive algorithm is defined as follows:

> `gcd (num1, num2)` is num2 if num2 <= num1 and num2
> divides num1
> `gcd (num1, num2)` is `gcd (num2, num1)` if num1 < num2
> `gcd (num1, num2)` is `gcd (num2, num1%num2)` otherwise

PP 11.3   Modify the `Maze` class so that it prints out the path of the final
solution as it is discovered without storing it.

PP 11.4   Design and implement a program that traverses a 3D maze.

PP 11.5   Modify the `TiledPictures` program so that the repeated
images appear in the lower-right quadrant.

PP 11.6   Design and implement a recursive program that solves the
Non-Attacking Queens problem. That is, write a program to
determine how eight queens can be positioned on an eight-by-
eight chessboard so that none of them are in the same row, column, or diagonal as any other queen. There are no other chess
pieces on the board.

PP 11.7   In the language of an alien race, all words take the form of
Blurbs. A Blurb is a Whoozit followed by one or more
Whatzits. A Whoozit is the character 'x' followed by zero or
more 'y's. A Whatzit is a 'q' followed by either a 'z' or a 'd',
followed by a Whoozit. Design and implement a recursive program that generates random Blurbs in this alien language.

PP 11.8   Design and implement a recursive program to determine
whether a string is a valid Blurb as defined in Programming
Project 11.7.

PP 11.9   Design and implement a recursive program to determine and print the Nth line of Pascal's Triangle, as shown below. Each interior value is the sum of the two values above it. *Hint:* use an array to store the values on each line.

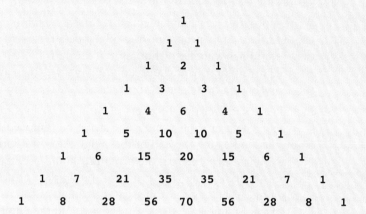

```
                          1
                      1       1
                  1       2       1
              1       3       3       1
          1       4       6       4       1
      1       5      10      10       5       1
  1       6      15      20      15       6       1
1     7      21      35      35      21       7       1
1   8      28      56      70      56      28      8      1
```

PP 11.10   Design and implement an applet that generalizes the KochSnowflake program. Allow the user to choose a fractal design from a menu item and to pick the background and drawing colors. The buttons to increase and decrease the order of the fractal will apply to whichever fractal design is chosen. In addition to the Koch snowflake, include a *C-curve fractal* whose order 1 is a straight line. Each successive order is created by replacing all line segments by two line segments, both half of the size of the original, and which meet at a right angle. Specifically, a C-curve of order N from $<x_1, y_1>$ to $<x_3, y_3>$ is replaced by two C-curves from $<x_1, y_1>$ to $<x_2, y_2>$ and from $<x_2, y_2>$ to $<x_3, y_3>$ where:

```
> x2 = (x1 + x3 + y1 - y3) / 2;
> y2 = (x3 + y1 + y3 - x1) / 2;
```

PP 11.11   Design and implement a graphic version of the Towers of Hanoi puzzle. Allow the user to set the number of disks used in the puzzle. The user should be able to interact with the puzzle in two main ways. The user can move the disks from one peg to another using the mouse, in which case the program should ensure that each move is legal. The user can also watch a solution take place as an animation, with pause/resume buttons. Permit the user to control the speed of the animation.

PP 11.12 Write a program that implements a recursive search of a sorted list of strings. Your program should include a recursive method that determines whether or not a given String is present within a sorted array (or, if you choose, an `ArrayList`) by searching successively smaller segments of the list.

Include a test driver that prompts the user for Strings to be searched. The user should enter one string per line, with an empty line indicating the end of the series. After the sorted list of Strings has been entered, the program should prompt the user for a search string. The program should then print a message stating whether or not the search string was found in the list, the total number of strings in the list, and the number of comparisons made while looking for the search string.

PP 11.13 Write a program that prompts the user for a list of cities, where each city has a name and x and y coordinates. After all cities have been entered, the program should use a recursive algorithm to print the length of all possible routes that start at the first city entered, end at the last city entered, and visit every city in the list. For each route, the program should print the name of each city visited, followed by length of the route.

PP 11.14 A Sierpinski Triangle is a fractal formed by drawing a triangle, and then using the midpoints of each side of triangle to form another triangle. This inner triangle is then removed. The result is three smaller triangles (one at the top and one in each corner) on which the process is repeated. After iteration N, the image will contain 3^N triangles, each of which is similar to the original triangle.

Write a program that implements a recursive algorithm for drawing a Sierpinski Triangle. The user interface for the program should include a `JSlider` that allows the user to select a value for N. The slider should allow the user to pick a value for N between 0 and the maximum value of N possible based on the size of the program window. The maximum slider value should change as appropriate when the window is resized.

Answers to Self-Review Questions

SR 11.1   Recursion is a programming technique in which a method calls itself, solving a smaller version of the problem each time, until the terminating condition is reached.

SR 11.2   Infinite recursion occurs when there is no base case that serves as a terminating condition or when the base case is improperly specified. The recursive path is followed forever. In a recursive program, infinite recursion will often result in an error that indicates that available memory has been exhausted.

SR 11.3   A base case is always required to terminate recursion and begin the process of returning through the calling hierarchy. Without the base case, infinite recursion results.

SR 11.4   Recursion is not necessary. Every recursive algorithm can be written in an iterative manner. However, some problem solutions are much more elegant and straightforward when written recursively.

SR 11.5   Avoid recursion when the iterative solution is simpler and more easily understood and programmed. Recursion has the overhead of multiple method calls and is not always intuitive.

SR 11.6   Indirect recursion occurs when a method calls another method, which calls another method, and so on until one of the called methods invokes the original. Indirect recursion is usually more difficult to trace than direct recursion, in which a method calls itself.

SR 11.7   The `MazeSearch` program recursively processes each of the four positions adjacent to the "current" one unless either (1) the current position is outside of the playing grid or (2) the final destination position is reached.

SR 11.8   The Towers of Hanoi puzzle of N disks is solved by moving $N-1$ disks out of the way onto an extra peg, moving the largest disk to its destination, then moving the $N-1$ disks from the extra peg to the destination. This solution is inherently recursive because, to move the substack of $N-1$ disks, we can use the same process.

SR 11.9   The base case of the `TiledPictures` program is a minimal size for the images to be produced. If the size of the area is smaller than the preset minimum, the recursion terminates.

SR 11.10 A fractal is a geometric shape that can be composed of multiple versions of the same shape at different scales and different angles of orientation. Recursion can be used to draw the repetitive shapes over and over again.

Collections 12

CHAPTER OBJECTIVES

> Explore the concept of a collection.

> Stress the importance of separating the interface from the implementation.

> Examine the difference between fixed and dynamic implementations.

> Define and use dynamically linked lists.

> Introduce classic linear data such as queues and stacks.

> Introduce classic nonlinear data structures such as trees and graphs.

> Discuss the Java Collections API.

> Define the use of generic types and their use in collection classes.

Problem solving often requires techniques for organizing and managing information. This chapter explores objects that store information, called collections, as well as various ways to implement them. Many collections have been developed over the years, and some of them have become classics. This chapter explains how collections can be implemented using references to link one object to another.

12.1   COLLECTIONS AND DATA STRUCTURES

A *collection* is an object that serves as a repository for other objects. It is a generic term that can be applied to many situations, but we usually use it when discussing an object whose specific role is to provide services to add, remove, and otherwise manage the elements that are contained within. For example, the `ArrayList` class (discussed in Chapter 7) represents a collection. It provides methods to add elements to the end of a list or to a particular location in the list based on an index value. It provides methods to remove specific elements as needed.

Some collections maintain their elements in a specific order, while others do not. Some collections are *homogeneous*, meaning that they can contain all of the same type of object; other collections are *heterogeneous*, which means they can contain objects of various types. An `ArrayList` is heterogeneous because it can hold an object of any type. Its heterogeneous nature comes from the fact that an `ArrayList` stores `Object` references, which means it can store any object because of inheritance and polymorphism.

Separating Interface from Implementation

A crucial aspect of collections is that they can be implemented in a variety of ways. That is, the underlying *data structure* that stores the objects can be implemented using various techniques. The `ArrayList` class from the Java standard library, for instance, is implemented using an array. All operations on an `ArrayList` are accomplished by invoking methods that perform the appropriate operations on the underlying array.

An *abstract data type* (ADT) is a collection of data and the particular operations that are allowed on that data. An ADT has a name, a domain of values, and a set of operations that can be performed. An ADT is considered abstract because the operations you can perform on it are separated from the underlying implementation. That is, the details of how an ADT stores its data and accomplishes its methods are separate from the concept that it embodies. Essentially, the terms collection and abstract data type are interchangeable.

Objects are perfectly suited for defining collections. An object, by definition, has a well-defined interface whose implementation is hidden in the class. The way the data is represented, and the operations that manage the data, are encapsulated inside the object. This type of object is reusable and reliable, because its interaction with the rest of the system is controlled.

> **Key Concept**
>
> An object, with its well-defined interface, is a perfect mechanism for implementing a collection.

12.2 DYNAMIC REPRESENTATIONS

An array is only one way in which a list can be represented. Arrays are limited in one sense because they have a fixed size throughout their existence. Sometimes we don't know how big to make an array because we don't know how much information we will store. The ArrayList class handles this by creating a larger array and copying everything over whenever necessary. This is not necessarily an efficient implementation.

A *dynamic data structure* is implemented using links. Using references as links between objects, we can create whatever type of structure is appropriate for the situation. If implemented carefully, the structure can be quite efficient to search and modify. Structures created this way are considered to be dynamic because their size is determined dynamically, as they are used, and not by their declaration.

> **Key Concept**
>
> The size of a dynamic data structure grows and shrinks as needed.

Dynamic Structures

Recall that the variable used to keep track of an object is actually a reference to the object, meaning that it stores the address of the object. A declaration such as

```
House home = new House ("602 Greenbriar Court");
```

actually accomplishes two things: it declares home to be a reference to a House object, and it instantiates an object of class House. Now consider an object that contains a reference to another object of the same type. For example:

```
class Node
{
    int info;
    Node next;
}
```

Two objects of this class can be instantiated and chained together by having the next reference of one Node object refer to the other Node object. The second object's next reference can refer to a third Node object, and so on, creating a *linked list*. The first node in the list could be referenced using a separate variable. The last node in the list would have a next reference that is null, indicating the end of the list. Figure 12.1 depicts this situation.

> **Key Concept**
>
> A dynamically linked list is managed by storing and updating references to objects.

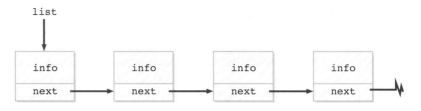

FIGURE 12.1 A linked list

In this example, the information stored in each Node class is a simple integer, but keep in mind that we could define a class to contain any amount of information of any type.

A Dynamically Linked List

The program in Listing 12.1 sets up a list of Magazine objects and then prints the list. The list of magazines is encapsulated inside the MagazineList class shown in Listing 12.2 and is maintained as a dynamically linked list.

The MagazineList class represents the list of magazines. From outside of the class (an external view), we do not focus on how the list is implemented. We don't know, for instance, whether the list of magazines is stored in an array or in a linked list. The MagazineList class provides a set of methods that allows the user to maintain the list of books. That set of methods, specifically add and toString, defines the operations to the MagazineList ADT.

The MagazineList class uses an inner class called MagazineNode to represent a node in the linked list. Each node contains a reference to one magazine and a reference to the next node in the list. Because MagazineNode is an inner class, it is reasonable to allow the data values in the class to be public. Therefore the code in the MagazineList class refers to those data values directly.

The Magazine class shown in Listing 12.3 is well encapsulated, with all data declared as private and methods provided to accomplish any updates necessary. Note that, because we use a separate class to represent a node in the list, the Magazine class itself does not need to contain a link to the next Magazine in the list. That allows the Magazine class to be free of any issues regarding its containment in a list.

Listing 12.1

```java
//********************************************************************
//  MagazineRack.java       Author: Lewis/Loftus
//
//  Driver to exercise the MagazineList collection.
//********************************************************************

public class MagazineRack
{
   //-----------------------------------------------------------------
   //  Creates a MagazineList object, adds several magazines to the
   //  list, then prints it.
   //-----------------------------------------------------------------
   public static void main (String[] args)
   {
      MagazineList rack = new MagazineList();

      rack.add (new Magazine("Time"));
      rack.add (new Magazine("Woodworking Today"));
      rack.add (new Magazine("Communications of the ACM"));
      rack.add (new Magazine("House and Garden"));
      rack.add (new Magazine("GQ"));

      System.out.println (rack);
   }
}
```

Output

```
Time
Woodworking Today
Communications of the ACM
House and Garden
GQ
```

Other methods could be included in the `MagazineList` ADT. For example, in addition to the `add` method provided, which always adds a new magazine to the end of the list, another method called `insert` could be defined to add a node anywhere in the list (to keep it sorted, for instance). A parameter to `insert` could indicate the value of the node after which the new node should be inserted. Figure 12.2 shows how the references would be updated to insert a new node.

> **Key Concept**
>
> Insert and delete operations can be implemented by carefully manipulating object references.

Listing 12.2

```java
//********************************************************************
//  MagazineList.java        Author: Lewis/Loftus
//
//  Represents a collection of magazines.
//********************************************************************

public class MagazineList
{
   private MagazineNode list;

   //-----------------------------------------------------------------
   //  Sets up an initially empty list of magazines.
   //-----------------------------------------------------------------
   public MagazineList()
   {
      list = null;
   }

   //-----------------------------------------------------------------
   //  Creates a new MagazineNode object and adds it to the end of
   //  the linked list.
   //-----------------------------------------------------------------
   public void add (Magazine mag)
   {

      MagazineNode node = new MagazineNode (mag);
      MagazineNode current;

      if (list == null)
         list = node;
      else
      {
         current = list;
         while (current.next != null)
            current = current.next;
         current.next = node;
      }
   }
```

Listing 12.2   continued

```java
//-----------------------------------------------------------------
//  Returns this list of magazines as a string.
//-----------------------------------------------------------------
public String toString ()
{
   String result = "";

   MagazineNode current = list;

   while (current != null)
   {
      result += current.magazine + "\n";
      current = current.next;
   }

   return result;
}

//*****************************************************************
//  An inner class that represents a node in the magazine list.
//  The public variables are accessed by the MagazineList class.
//*****************************************************************
private class MagazineNode
{
   public Magazine magazine;
   public MagazineNode next;

   //-----------------------------------------------------------
   //  Sets up the node
   //-----------------------------------------------------------
   public MagazineNode (Magazine mag)
   {
      magazine = mag;
      next = null;
   }
}
}
```

Listing 12.3

```
//********************************************************************
//  Magazine.java        Author: Lewis/Loftus
//
//  Represents a single magazine.
//********************************************************************

public class Magazine
{
   private String title;

   //------------------------------------------------------------------
   //  Sets up the new magazine with its title.
   //------------------------------------------------------------------
   public Magazine (String newTitle)
   {
      title = newTitle;
   }

   //------------------------------------------------------------------
   //  Returns this magazine as a string.
   //------------------------------------------------------------------
   public String toString ()
   {
      return title;
   }
}
```

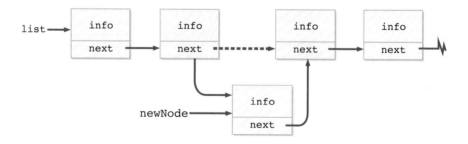

FIGURE 12.2   Inserting a node into the middle of a list

Another operation that would be helpful in the list ADT would be a `delete` method to remove a particular node. Recall from our discussion in Chapter 3 that by removing all references to an object, it becomes a candidate for garbage collection. Figure 12.3 shows how references would be updated to delete a node from a list. Care must be taken to accomplish the modifications to the references in the proper order to ensure that other nodes are not lost and that references continue to refer to valid, appropriate nodes in the list.

Other Dynamic List Representations

You can use different list implementations, depending on the specific needs of the program you are designing. For example, in some situations it may make processing easier to implement a *doubly linked list* in which each node has not only a reference to the next node in the list, but also another reference to the previous node in the list. Our generic `Node` class might be declared as follows:

```
class Node
{
    int info;
    Node next, prev;
}
```

Figure 12.4 shows a doubly linked list. Note that, like a single linked list, the `next` reference of the last node is `null`. Similarly, the previous node of the first node is `null` since there is no node that comes before the first one. This type of structure makes it easy to move back and forth between nodes in the list, but requires more effort to set up and modify.

> **Key Concept**
>
> Many variations on the implementation of dynamically linked lists can be defined.

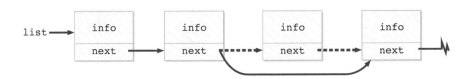

FIGURE 12.3 Deleting a node from a list

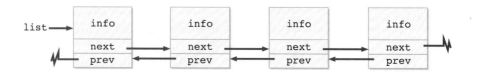

FIGURE 12.4 A doubly linked list

Another implementation of a linked list could include a *header node* for the list that has a reference to the front of the list and another reference to the rear of the list. A rear reference makes it easier to add new nodes to the end of the list. The header node could contain other information, such as a count of the number of nodes currently in the list. The declaration of the header node would be similar to the following:

```
class ListHeader
{
    int count;
    Node front, rear;
}
```

Note that the header node is not of the same class as the Node class to which it refers. Figure 12.5 depicts a linked list that is implemented using a header node.

Still other linked list implementations can be created. For instance, the use of a header can be combined with a doubly linked list, or the list can be maintained

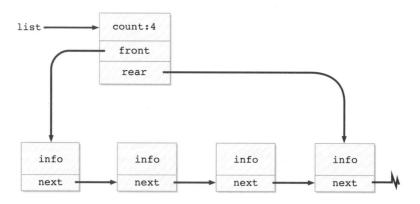

FIGURE 12.5 A list with front and rear references

in sorted order. The implementation should cater to the type of processing that is required. Some extra effort to maintain a more complex data structure may be worthwhile if it makes common operations on the structure more efficient.

12.3   LINEAR DATA STRUCTURES

In addition to lists, some data structures have become classic in that they represent important generic situations that commonly occur in computing. Like lists, a queue and a stack are *linear data structures*, meaning that the data they represent is organized in a linear fashion. This section explores some linear data structures in more detail.

Queues

A *queue* is similar to a list except that it has restrictions on the way you put items in and take items out. Specifically, a queue uses *first-in, first-out* (FIFO) processing. That is, the first item put in the list is the first item that comes out of the list. Figure 12.6 depicts the FIFO processing of a queue.

> **Key Concept**
>
> A queue is a linear data structure that manages data in a first-in, first-out manner.

Any waiting line is a queue. Think about a line of people waiting for a teller at a bank. A customer enters the queue at the back and moves forward as earlier customers are serviced. Eventually, each customer comes to the front of the queue to be processed.

Note that the processing of a queue is conceptual. We may speak in terms of people moving forward until they reach the front of the queue, but the reality might be that the front of the queue moves as elements come off. That is, we are

Items go on the queue
at the rear (enqueue)

Items come off the queue
at the front (dequeue)

FIGURE 12.6 A queue data structure

not concerned at this point with whether the queue of customers moves toward the teller, or remains stationary as the teller moves when customers are serviced.

A queue data structure typically has the following operations:

> enqueue—adds an item to the rear of the queue
> dequeue—removes an item from the front of the queue
> empty—returns true if the queue is empty

Stacks

A *stack* is similar to a queue except that its elements go on and come off at the same end. The last item to go on a stack is the first item to come off, like a stack of plates in the cupboard or a stack of hay bales in the barn. A stack, therefore, processes information in a *last-in, first-out* (LIFO) manner, as shown in Figure 12.7.

A typical stack ADT contains the following operations:

> push—pushes an item onto the top of the stack
> pop—removes an item from the top of the stack
> peek—retrieves information from the top item of the stack without removing it
> empty—returns true if the stack is empty

The `java.util` package of the API contains a class called `Stack` that implements a stack data structure. It contains methods that correspond to the standard stack operations, plus a method that searches for a particular object in the stack.

The `Stack` class has a `search` method that returns an integer corresponding to the position in the stack of the particular object. This type of searching is not usually considered to be part of the classic stack ADT.

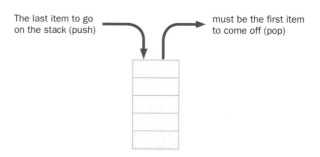

The last item to go on the stack (push)　　must be the first item to come off (pop)

FIGURE 12.7　A stack data structure

Like `ArrayList` operations, the `Stack` operations operate on `Object` references. Because all objects are derived from the `Object` class, any object can be pushed onto a stack. If primitive types are to be stored, they must be treated as objects using the corresponding wrapper class. Unlike the `Stack` class, no class implementing a queue is defined in the Java API.

Let's look at an example that uses a stack to solve a problem. The program in Listing 12.4 accepts a string of characters that represents a secret message. The program decodes and prints the message.

A message that has been encoded has each individual word in the message reversed. Words in the message are separated by a single space. The program uses the `Stack` class to push the characters of each word on the stack. When an entire word has been read, each character appears in reverse order as it is popped off the stack and printed.

Listing 12.4

```java
//********************************************************************
//  Decode.java        Author: Lewis/Loftus
//
//  Demonstrates the use of the Stack class.
//********************************************************************

import java.util.*;

public class Decode
{
   //-----------------------------------------------------------------
   //  Decodes a message by reversing each word in a string.
   //-----------------------------------------------------------------
   public static void main (String[] args)
   {
      Scanner scan = Scanner.create (System.in);

      Stack word = new Stack();

      String message;
      int index = 0;

      System.out.println ("Enter the coded message:");
      message = scan.nextLine();
      System.out.println ("The decoded message is:");
```

Listing 12.4 **continued**

```
    while (index < message.length())
    {
        // Push word onto stack
        while (index < message.length() && message.charAt(index) != ' ')
        {
            word.push (new Character(message.charAt(index)));
            index++;
        }

        // Print word in reverse
        while (!word.empty())
            System.out.print (((Character)word.pop()).charValue());
        System.out.print (" ");
        index++;
    }

    System.out.println();
    }
}
```

Output

```
Enter the coded message:
artxE eseehc esaelp
The decoded message is:
Extra cheese please
```

12.4 NON-LINEAR DATA STRUCTURES

Some data structures are considered to be *non-linear data structures* because their data is not organized linearly. This section examines two types of non-linear structures: trees and graphs.

Trees

A *tree* is a non-linear data structure that consists of a *root node* and potentially many levels of additional nodes that form a hierarchy. All nodes other than the root are called *internal nodes*. Nodes that have no children are called *leaf nodes*.

Figure 12.8 depicts a tree. Note that we draw a tree "upside down," with the root at the top and the leaves at the bottom.

In a general tree like the one in Figure 12.8, each node could have many child nodes. As we mentioned in Chapter 8, the inheritance relationships among classes can be depicted using a general tree structure.

In a *binary tree*, each node can have no more than two child nodes. Binary trees are useful in various programming situations and usually are easier to implement than general trees. Technically, binary trees are a subset of general trees, but they are so important in the computing world that they usually are thought of as their own data structure.

The operations on trees and binary trees vary, but minimally include adding and removing nodes from the tree or binary tree. Because of their non-linear nature, trees and binary trees are implemented nicely using references as dynamic links. However, it is possible to implement a tree data structure using a fixed representation such as an array.

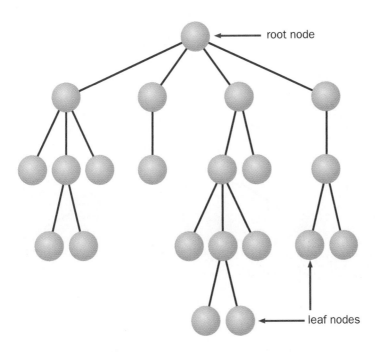

FIGURE 12.8   A tree data structure

Graphs

Like a tree, a *graph* is a non-linear data structure. Unlike a tree, a graph does not have a primary entry point like the tree's root node. In a graph, a node is linked to another node by a connection called an *edge*. Generally there are no restrictions on the number of edges that can be made between nodes in a graph. Figure 12.9 presents a graph data structure.

Graphs are useful when representing relationships for which linear paths and strict hierarchies do not suffice. For instance, the highway system connecting cities on a map and airline connections between airports are better represented as graphs than by any other data structure discussed so far.

In a general graph, the edges are bi-directional, meaning that the edge connecting nodes A and B can be followed from A to B and also from B to A. In a *directed graph*, or *digraph*, each edge has a specific direction. Figure 12.10 shows a digraph, in which each edge indicates the direction using an arrowhead.

A digraph might be used, for instance, to represent airline flights between airports. Unlike highway systems, which are in almost all cases bi-directional,

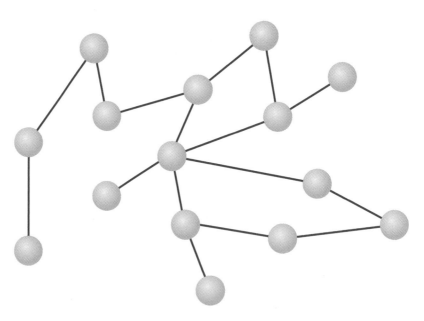

FIGURE 12.9 A graph data structure

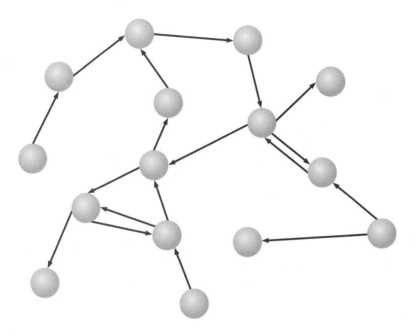

FIGURE 12.10   A directed graph

having a flight from one city to another does not necessarily mean there is a corresponding flight going the other way. Or, if there is, we may want to associate different information with it, such as cost.

Like trees, graphs often are implemented using dynamic links, although they can be implemented using arrays as well.

12.5   THE JAVA COLLECTIONS API

The Java standard class library contains several classes that represent collections of various types. These are often referred to as the *Java Collections API* (Application Programming Interface).

Most of the names of the classes in this set indicate both the collection type and the underlying implementation. One example is the `ArrayList` class, which is discussed in some detail in Chapter 7. It represents a list collection, implemented using an underlying array. Similarly, the `LinkedList` class represents a list collection with a dynamically linked internal implementation.

> **Key Concept**
>
> The Java Collections API defines several collection classes implemented in various ways.

The `Vector` class and the `Stack` class are carried over from earlier Java incarnations, which is why their names aren't consistent with the newer collection classes.

Several interfaces are used to define the collection operations themselves. These interfaces include `List`, `Set`, `SortedSet`, `Map`, and `SortedMap`. A `Set` is consistent with its normal interpretation as a collection of elements without duplicates. A `Map` is a group of elements that can be referenced by a key value.

Generics

> **Key Concept**
>
> The classes of the Java Collections API are implemented as generic types.

As we mentioned in Chapter 7 during the discussion of the `ArrayList` class, the classes in the Java Collections API are implemented as *generic types*, meaning that the type of object that the collection manages can be established when an object of that collection type is instantiated.

For example, to create a `LinkedList` of `String` objects, we would instantiate a collection object in the following way:

```
LinkedList<String> myStringList = new LinkedList<String>();
```

Similarly, to create a `LinkedList` of `Book` objects, we would instantiate the collection as follows:

```
LinkedList<Book> myBookList = new LinkedList<Book>();
```

By specifying the type stored in the collection, we gain two advantages:

> only objects of the appropriate type can be added to the collection
> when an object is removed from the collection, its type is already established, avoiding the need to cast it to an appropriate type

> **Key Concept**
>
> Generic classes ensure type compatibility among the objects stored by the collection.

The `myStringList` object can only store `String` objects, and the `myBookList` collection can only store `Book` objects. Keep in mind that these include objects related to the specified type by inheritance. For example, if a `Dictionary` class is derived from `Book`, then we could store a `Dictionary` object in the `myBookList` collection. After all, if we're using inheritance correctly, a `Dictionary` is-a `Book`.

If no specific type is specified when the collection object is created, the collection is defined as containing references of the `Object` class, which means they can store any type of object. This makes the use of the collections classes consistent with earlier versions of Java that did not include generic specifications.

The details of the collection classes and the techniques for defining a generic class go beyond the scope of this book and so are not explored further here.

Summary of Key Concepts

> An object, with its well-defined interface, is a perfect mechanism for implementing a collection.

> The size of a dynamic data structure grows and shrinks as needed.

> A dynamically linked list is managed by storing and updating references to objects.

> Insert and delete operations can be implemented by carefully manipulating object references.

> Many variations on the implementation of dynamically linked lists can be defined.

> A queue is a linear data structure that manages data in a first-in, first-out manner.

> A stack is a linear data structure that manages data in a last-in, first-out manner.

> A tree is a non-linear data structure that organizes data into a hierarchy.

> A graph is a non-linear data structure that connects nodes using generic edges.

> The Java Collections API defines several collection classes implemented in various ways.

> The classes of the Java Collections API are implemented as generic types.

> Generic classes ensure type compatibility among the objects stored by the collection.

Self-Review Questions

SR 12.1   What is a collection?

SR 12.2   Why are objects particularly well suited for implementing abstract data types?

SR 12.3   What is a dynamic data structure?

SR 12.4   Describe the steps, depicted in Figure 12.2, to insert a node into a list. What special cases exist?

SR 12.5   Describe the steps, depicted in Figure 12.3, to delete a node from a list. What special cases exist?

SR 12.6   What is a doubly linked list?

SR 12.7   What is a header node for a linked list?

SR 12.8   How is a queue different from a list?

SR 12.9   What is a stack?

SR 12.10   What is the Stack class?

SR 12.11   What do trees and graphs have in common?

SR 12.12   What is the Java Collections API?

SR 12.13   What is a generic type and how does it relate to the Java Collections API?

Exercises

EX 12.1   Suppose current is a reference to a Node object and that it currently refers to a specific node in a linked list. Show, in pseudocode, the steps that would delete the node following current from the list. Carefully consider the cases in which current is referring to the first and last nodes in the list.

EX 12.2   Modify your answer to Exercise 12.1 assuming that the list was set up as a doubly linked list, with both next and prev references.

EX 12.3   Suppose current and newNode are references to Node objects. Assume current currently refers to a specific node in a linked list and newNode refers to an unattached Node object. Show, in pseudocode, the steps that would insert newNode behind current in the list. Carefully consider the cases in which current is referring to the first and last nodes in the list.

EX 12.4   Modify your answer to Exercise 12.3 assuming that the list was set up as a doubly linked list, with both next and prev references.

EX 12.5   Would the front and rear references in the header node of a linked list ever refer to the same node? Would they ever both be null? Would one ever be null if the other was not? Explain your answers using examples.

EX 12.6   Show the contents of a queue after the following operations are performed. Assume the queue is initially empty.

```
> enqueue (45);
> enqueue (12);
> enqueue (28);
> dequeue();
> dequeue();
> enqueue (69);
> enqueue (27);
> enqueue (99);
> dequeue();
> enqueue (24);
> enqueue (85);
> enqueue (16);
> dequeue();
```

EX 12.7   In terms of the final state of a queue, does it matter how dequeue operations are intermixed with enqueue operations? Does it matter how the enqueue operations are intermixed among themselves? Explain using examples.

EX 12.8   Show the contents of a stack after the following operations are performed. Assume the stack is initially empty.

```
> push (45);
> push (12);
> push (28);
> pop();
> pop();
> push (69);
> push (27);
> push (99);
> pop();
> push (24);
> push (85);
> push (16);
> pop();
```

EX 12.9   In terms of the final state of a stack, does it matter how the pop operations are intermixed with the push operations? Does it matter how the push operations are intermixed among themselves? Explain using examples.

EX 12.10 Would a tree data structure be a good choice to represent a family tree that shows lineage? Why or why not? Would a binary tree be a better choice? Why or why not?

EX 12.11 What data structure would be a good choice to represent the links between various Web sites? Give an example.

Programming Projects

PP 12.1 Consistent with the example from Chapter 7, design and implement an application that maintains a collection of compact discs using a linked list. In the `main` method of the driver class, add various CDs to the collection and print the list when complete.

PP 12.2 Modify the `MagazineRack` program presented in this chapter by adding delete and insert operations into the `MagazineList` class. Have the `Magazine` class implement the `Comparable` interface, and base the processing of the `insert` method on calls to the `compareTo` method in the `Magazine` class that determines whether one `Magazine` title comes before another lexicographically. In the `driver`, exercise various insertion and deletion operations. Print the list of magazines when complete.

PP 12.3 Design and implement a version of selection sort (from Chapter 9) that operates on a linked list of nodes that each contain an integer.

PP 12.4 Design and implement a version of insertion sort (from Chapter 9) that operates on a linked list of nodes that each contain an integer.

PP 12.5 Design and implement an application that simulates the customers waiting in line at a bank. Use a queue data structure to represent the line. As customers arrive at the bank, customer objects are put in the rear of the queue with an enqueue operation. When the teller is ready to service another customer, the customer object is removed from the front of the queue with a dequeue operation. Randomly determine when new customers arrive at the bank and when current customers are finished at the teller window. Print a message each time an operation occurs during the simulation.

PP 12.6   Modify the solution to the Programming Project 12.5 so that it represents eight tellers and therefore eight customer queues. Have new customers go to the shortest queue. Determine which queue had the shortest waiting time per customer on average.

PP 12.7   Design and implement an application that evaluates a postfix expression that operates on integer operands using the arithmetic operators +, –, *, /, and %. We are already familiar with *infix expressions,* in which an operator is positioned between its two operands. A *postfix expression* puts the operators after its operands. Keep in mind that an operand could be the result of another operation. This eliminates the need for parentheses to force precedence. For example, the following infix expression:

$(5 + 2) * (8 - 5)$

is equivalent to the following postfix expression.

5 2 + 8 5 – *

The evaluation of a postfix expression is facilitated by using a stack. As you process a postfix expression from left to right, you encounter operands and operators. If you encounter an operand, push it on the stack. If you encounter an operator, pop two operands off the stack, perform the operation, and push the result back on the stack. When you have processed the entire expression, there will be one value on the stack, which is the result of the entire expression.

You may want to use a `StringTokenizer` object to assist in the parsing of the expression. You can assume the expression will be in valid postfix form.

PP 12.8   Design and implement a program that prompts the user to enter a string and then performs two palindrome tests. The first should use a single stack to test whether the string is a palindrome. The second should use two stacks to test whether the string is a palindrome when capitalization, spaces, punctuation, and other non-alphanumeric characters are ignored. The program should print the results of both tests.

PP 12.9   Design and implement a class named `StringTree`, a binary tree for storing `String` objects in lexicographic order. Each node in the tree should be represented by a `Node` class, which stores the string value and pointers to the right and left child nodes. For any node value in the tree, the value of its left child should come before that value, and the value of its right child should come after that value. The `StringTree` class should contain a method for adding strings to the tree, and a method for printing the tree's value in lexicographic order. Write a driver program that prompts the user for strings and adds them to the tree. After processing the input, print the tree values.

PP 12.10   Design and implement an application to support a moderated question-and-answer session in which audience members submit questions to a queue. The question at the front of the queue may be answered by the speaker or panel, and a list of answered or unanswered questions may be retrieved at any time.

The program should accept the following simple commands: 'Q' will allow an audience member to submit a question, along with their name; 'A' will allow the speaker to enter an answer to the question currently at the top of the queue; 'P' will allow the speaker to pass on a question, moving it from the front of the queue to the end of the queue; 'R' will allow the speaker to mark a question as rejected, removing it from the queue; 'LA' will print a numbered list of answered questions, along with the answers; 'LU' will print a numbered list of unanswered questions; finally, 'X' will print numbered lists of answered and unanswered questions, then exit the program.

You should create a `Question` class to store each question, its answer, and any other question state information. The answered and unanswered queues should be implemented using the `java.util.LinkedList` class. You must use only the methods in the class that provide Queue functionality: remove the first element, append an element to the end, retrieve the queue size, and iterate over the list.

Answers to Self-Review Questions

SR 12.1   A collection is an object whose purpose is to store and organize primitive data or other objects. Some collections represent classic data structures that are helpful in particular problem solving situations.

SR 12.2   An abstract data type (ADT) is a collection of data and the operations that can be performed on that data. An object is essentially the same thing in that we encapsulate related variables and methods in an object. The object hides the underlying implementation of the ADT, separating the interface from the underlying implementation, permitting the implementation to be changed without affecting the interface.

SR 12.3   A dynamic data structure is constructed using references to link various objects together into a particular organization. It is dynamic in that it can grow and shrink as needed. New objects can be added to the structure and obsolete objects can be removed from the structure at run time by adjusting references between objects in the structure.

SR 12.4   To insert a node into a list, first find the node that comes before the new node (let's call it beforeNode). Then set the new node's next pointer equal to beforeNode's next pointer. Then set beforeNode's next pointer to the new node. A special case exists when inserting a node at the beginning of the list.

SR 12.5   To delete a node from a list, first find the node that comes before the node to be deleted (let's call it beforeNode). Then set beforeNode's next pointer to the deleted node's next pointer. A special case exists when deleting the first node of the list.

SR 12.6   Each node in a doubly linked list has references to both the node that comes before it in the list and the node that comes after it in the list. This organization allows for easy movement forward and backward in the list, and simplifies some operations.

SR 12.7   A header node for a linked list is a special node that holds information about the list, such as references to the front and rear of the list and an integer to keep track of how many nodes are currently in the list.

SR 12.8   A queue is a linear data structure like a list but it has more constraints on its use. A general list can be modified by inserting or deleting nodes anywhere in the list, but a queue only adds nodes to one end (enqueue) and takes them off of the other (dequeue). Thus a queue uses a first-in, first-out (FIFO) approach.

SR 12.9   A stack is a linear data structure that adds (pushes) and removes (pops) nodes from one end. It manages information using a last-in, first-out (LIFO) approach.

SR 12.10   The `Stack` class is defined in the `java.util` package of the Java standard class library. It implements a generic stack ADT. The `Stack` class stores `Object` references, so the stack can be used to store any kind of object.

SR 12.11   Trees and graphs are both non-linear data structures, meaning that the data they store is not organized in a linear fashion. Trees create a hierarchy of nodes. The nodes in a graph are connected using general edges.

SR 12.12   The Java Collections API is a set of classes in the Java standard class library that represents collections of various types, such as `ArrayList` and `LinkedList`.

SR 12.13   A generic type is a collection object that is implemented such that the type of objects it manages can be established when the collection is created. This allows some compile-time control over the types of objects that are added to the collection, and eliminates the need to cast the objects when they are removed from the collection. All collections in the Java Collections API have been implemented as generic types.

abstract—A Java reserved word that serves as a modifier for classes, interfaces, and methods. An `abstract` class cannot be instantiated and is used to specify bodiless abstract methods that are given definitions by derived classes. Interfaces are inherently `abstract`.

abstract class—*See* abstract.

abstract data type (ADT)—A collection of data and the operations that are defined on that data. An abstract data type might be implemented in a variety of ways, but the interface operations are consistent.

abstract method—*See* abstract.

Abstract Windowing Toolkit (AWT)—The package in the Java API (`java.awt`) that contains classes related to graphics and graphical user interfaces. *See also* Swing.

abstraction—The concept of hiding details. If the right details are hidden at the right times, abstraction can significantly help control complexity and focus attention on appropriate issues.

access—The ability to reference a variable or invoke a method from outside the class in which it is declared. Controlled by the visibility modifier used to declare the variable or method. Also called the level of encapsulation. *See also* visibility modifier.

access modifier—*See* visibility modifier.

actual parameter—The value passed to a method as a parameter. *See also* formal parameter.

adaptor class—*See* listener adaptor class.

address—(1) A numeric value that uniquely identifies a particular memory location in a computer's main memory. (2) A designation that uniquely identifies a computer among all others on a network.

ADT—*See* abstract data type.

aggregate object—An object that contains variables that are references to other objects. *See also* has-a relationship.

aggregation—Something that is composed, at least in part, of other things. *See also* aggregate object.

algorithm—A step-by-step process for solving a problem. A program is based on one or more algorithms.

alias—A reference to an object that is currently also referred to by another reference. Each reference is an alias of the other.

analog—A representation that is in direct proportion to the source of the information. *See also* digital.

animation—A series of images or drawings that give the appearance of movement when displayed in order at a particular speed.

API—*See* Application Programming Interface.

applet—A Java program that is linked into an HTML document, then retrieved and executed using a Web browser, as opposed to a standalone Java application.

appletviewer—A software tool that interprets and displays Java applets through links in HTML documents. Part of the Java Development Kit.

application—(1) A generic term for any program. (2) A Java program that can be run without the use of a Web browser, as opposed to a Java applet.

Application Programming Interface (API)—A set of classes that defines services for a programmer. Not part of the language itself, but often relied on to perform even basic tasks. *See also* class library.

arc angle—When defining an arc, the radial distance that defines the arc's length. *See also* start angle.

architectural design—A high-level design that identifies the large portions of a software system and key data structures. *See also* detailed design.

architecture—*See* computer architecture.

architecture neutral—Not specific to any particular hardware platform. Java code is considered architecture neutral because it is compiled into bytecode and then interpreted on any machine with a Java interpreter.

arithmetic operator—An operator that performs a basic arithmetic computation, such as addition or multiplication.

arithmetic promotion—The act of promoting the type of a numeric operand to be consistent with the other operand.

array—A programming language construct used to store an ordered list of primitive values or objects. Each element in the array is referenced using a numerical index from 0 to $N-1$, where N is the size of the array.

array element—A value or object that is stored in an array.

array element type—The type of the values or objects that are stored in an array.

ASCII—A popular character set used by many programming languages. ASCII stands for American Standard Code for Information Interchange. It is a subset of the Unicode character set, which is used by Java.

assembly language—A low-level language that uses mnemonics to represent program commands.

assignment conversion—Some data types can be converted to another in an assignment statement. *See* widening conversion.

assignment operator—An operator that results in an assignment to a variable. The = operator performs basic assignment. Many other assignment operators perform additional operations prior to the assignment, such as the *= operator.

association—A relationship between two classes in which one uses the other or relates to it in some way. *See also* operator association, use relationship.

AWT—*See* Abstract Windowing Toolkit.

background color—(1) The color of the background of a graphical user interface component. (2) The color of the background of an HTML page. *See also* foreground color.

base—The numerical value on which a particular number system is based. It determines the number of digits available in that number system and the place value of each digit in a number. *See also* binary, decimal, hexadecimal, octal, place value.

base 2—*See* binary.

base 8—*See* octal.

base 10—*See* decimal.

base 16—*See* hexadecimal.

base case—The situation that terminates recursive processing, allowing the active recursive methods to begin returning to their point of invocation.

base class—*See* superclass.

behavior—The functional characteristics of an object, defined by its methods. *See also* identity, state.

binary—The base-2 number system. Modern computer systems store information as strings of binary digits (bits).

binary operator—An operator that uses two operands.

binary search—A searching algorithm that requires that the list be sorted. It repetitively compares the "middle" element of the list to the target value, narrowing the scope of the search each time. *See also* linear search.

binary string—A series of binary digits (bits).

binary tree—A tree data structure in which each node can have no more than two child nodes.

binding—The process of associating an identifier with the construct that it represents. For example, the process of binding a method name to the specific definition that it invokes.

bit—A binary digit, either 0 or 1.

bit shifting—The act of shifting the bits of a data value to the left or right, losing bits on one end and inserting bits on the other.

bits per second (bps)—A measurement rate for data transfer devices.

bitwise operator—An operator that manipulates individual bits of a value, either by calculation or by shifting.

black-box testing—Producing and evaluating test cases based on the input and expected output of a software component. The test cases focus on covering the equivalence categories and boundary values of the input. *See also* white-box testing.

block—A group of programming statements and declarations delimited by braces ({}).

boolean—A Java reserved word representing a logical primitive data type that can only take the values `true` or `false`.

boolean expression—An expression that evaluates to a true or false result, primarily used as conditions in selection and repetition statements.

boolean operator—Any of the bitwise operators AND (&), OR (|), or XOR (^) when applied to `boolean` operands. The results are equivalent to their logical counterparts, except that boolean operators are not short-circuited.

border—A graphical edge around a graphical user interface component to enhance its appearance or to group components visually. An empty border creates a buffer of space around a component.

bounding rectangle—A rectangle that delineates a region in which an oval or arc is defined.

boundary values—The input values corresponding to the edges of equivalence categories. Used in black-box testing.

bounds checking—The process of determining whether an array index is in bounds, given the size of the array. Java performs automatic bounds checking.

bps—*See* bits per second.

break—A Java reserved word used to interrupt the flow of control by breaking out of the current loop or `switch` statement.

browser—Software that retrieves HTML documents across network connections and formats them for viewing. A browser is the primary vehicle for accessing the World Wide Web. *See also* Netscape Navigator.

bug—A slang term for a defect or error in a computer program.

build-and-fix approach—An approach to software development in which a program is created without any significant planning or design, then modified until it reaches some level of acceptance. It is a prevalent, but unwise, approach.

bus—A group of wires in the computer that carry data between components such as the CPU and main memory.

button—A graphical user interface component that allows the user to initiate an action, set a condition, or choose an option with a mouse click. There are several kinds of GUI buttons. *See also* check box, push button, radio button.

byte—(1) A unit of binary storage equal to eight bits. (2) A Java reserved word that represents a primitive integer type, stored using eight bits in two's complement format.

byte stream—An I/O stream that manages 8-bit bytes of raw binary data. *See also* character stream.

bytecode—The low-level format into which the Java compiler translates Java source code. The bytecodes are interpreted and executed by the Java interpreter, perhaps after transportation over the Internet.

capacity—*See* storage capacity.

case—(1) A Java reserved word that is used to identify each unique option in a `switch` statement. (2) The orientation of an alphabetic character (uppercase or lowercase).

case sensitive—Differentiating between the uppercase and lowercase versions of an alphabetic letter. Java is case sensitive; therefore the identifier `total` and the identifier `Total` are considered to be different identifiers.

cast—A Java operation expressed using a type or class name in parentheses to explicitly convert and return a value of one data type into another.

catch—A Java reserved word that is used to specify an exception handler, defined after a `try` block.

CD-Recordable (CD-R)—A compact disc on which information can be stored once using a home computer with an appropriate drive. *See also* CD-Rewritable, CD-ROM.

CD-Rewritable (CD-RW)—A compact disc on which information can be stored and rewritten multiple times using a home computer with an appropriate drive. *See also* CD-Recordable, CD-ROM.

CD-ROM—An optical secondary memory medium that stores binary information in a manner similar to a musical compact disc.

central processing unit (CPU)—The hardware component that controls the main activity of a computer, including the flow of information and the execution of commands.

char—A Java reserved word that represents the primitive character type. All Java characters are members of the Unicode character set and are stored using 16 bits.

character font—A specification that defines the distinct look of a character when it is printed or drawn.

character set—An ordered list of characters, such as the ASCII or Unicode character sets. Each character corresponds to a specific, unique numeric value within a given character set. A programming language adopts a particular character set to use for character representation and management.

character stream—An I/O stream that manages 16-bit Unicode characters. *See also* byte stream.

character string—A series of ordered characters. Represented in Java using the `String` class and string literals such as "hello".

check box—A graphical user interface component that allows the user to set a boolean condition with a mouse click. A check box can be used alone or independently among other check boxes. *See also* radio button.

checked exception—A Java exception that must be either caught or explicitly thrown to the calling method. *See also* unchecked exception.

child class—*See* subclass.

class—(1) A Java reserved word used to define a class. (2) The blueprint of an object—the model that defines the variables and methods an object will contain when instantiated.

class diagram—A diagram that shows the relationships between classes, including inheritance and use relationships. *See also* Unified Modeling Language.

class hierarchy—A tree-like structure created when classes are derived from other classes through inheritance. *See also* interface hierarchy.

class library—A set of classes that define useful services for a programmer. *See also* Application Programming Interface.

class method—A method that can be invoked using only the class name. An instantiated object is not required as it is with instance methods. Defined in a Java program by using the `static` reserved word.

CLASSPATH—An operating system setting that determines where the Java interpreter searches for class files.

class variable—A variable that is shared among all objects of a class. It can also be referenced through the class name, without instantiating any object of that class. Defined in a Java program by using the `static` reserved word.

client-server model—A manner in which to construct a software design based on objects (clients) making use of the services provided by other objects (servers).

coding guidelines—A series of conventions that describe how programs should be constructed. They make programs easier to read, exchange, and integrate. Sometimes referred to as coding standards, especially when they are enforced.

coding standard—*See* coding guidelines.

cohesion—The strength of the relationship among the parts within a software component. *See also* coupling.

collision—The process of two hash values producing the same hash code. *See also* hash code, hashing.

color chooser—A graphical user interface component, often displayed as a dialog box, that allows the user to select or specify a color.

combo box—A graphical user interface component that allows the user to select one of several options. A combo box displays the most recent selection. *See also* list.

command-line arguments—The values that follow the program name on the command line. Accessed within a Java program through the `String` array parameter to the `main` method.

comment—A programming language construct that allows a programmer to embed human-readable annotations into the source code. *See also* documentation.

compiler—A program that translates code from one language to equivalent code in another language. The Java compiler translates Java source code into Java bytecode. *See also* interpreter.

compile-time error—Any error that occurs during the compilation process, often indicating that a program does not conform to the language syntax or that an operation was attempted on an inappropriate data type. *See also* logical error, run-time error, syntax error.

component—Any portion of a software system that performs a specific task, transforming input to output. *See also* GUI component.

computer architecture—The structure and interaction of the hardware components of a computer.

concatenation—*See* string concatenation.

condition—A `boolean` expression used to determine whether the body of a selection or repetition statement should be executed.

conditional coverage—A strategy used in white-box testing in which all conditions in a program are executed, producing both `true` and `false` results. *See also* statement coverage.

conditional operator—A Java ternary operator that evaluates one of two expressions based on a condition.

conditional statement—*See* selection statement.

const—A Java reserved word that is not currently used.

constant—An identifier that contains a value that cannot be modified. Used to make code more readable and to facilitate changes. Defined in Java using the `final` modifier.

constructor—A special method in a class that is invoked when an object is instantiated from the class. Used to initialize the object.

container—A Java graphical user interface component that can hold other components. *See also* containment hierarchy.

containment hierarchy—The relationships among graphical components of a user interface. *See also* container.

content pane—The part of a top-level container to which components are added.

control characters—*See* nonprintable characters.

controller—Hardware devices that control the interaction between a computer system and a particular kind of peripheral.

coupling—The strength of the relationship between two software components. *See also* cohesion.

CPU—*See* central processing unit.

data stream—An I/O stream that represents a particular source or destination for data, such as a file. *See also* processing stream.

data structure—Any programming construct, either defined in the language or by a programmer, used to organize data into a format to facilitate access and processing. Arrays, linked lists, and stacks can all be considered data structures.

data type—A designation that specifies a set of values (which may be infinite). For example, each variable has a data type that specifies the kinds of values that can be stored in it.

data transfer device—A hardware component that allows information to be sent between computers, such as a modem.

debugger—A software tool that allows a programmer to step through an executing program and examine the value of variables at any point. *See also* jdb.

decimal—The base-10 number system, which humans use in everyday life. *See also* binary.

default—A Java reserved word that is used to indicate the default case of a `switch` statement, used if no other cases match.

default visibility—The level of access designated when no explicit visibility modifier is used to declare a class, interface, method, or variable. Sometimes referred to as package visibility.

Classes and interfaces declared with default visibility can be used within their package. A method or variable declared with default visibility is inherited and accessible by all subclasses in the same package.

defect testing—Testing designed to uncover errors in a program.

defined—Existing for use in a derived class, even if it can only be accessed indirectly. *See also* inheritance.

delimiter—Any symbol or word used to set the boundaries of a programming language construct, such as the braces ({}) used to define a Java block.

deprecated—Something, such as a particular method, that is considered old-fashioned and should not be used.

derived class—*See* subclass.

design—(1) The plan for implementing a program, which includes a specification of the classes and objects used and an expression of the important program algorithms. (2) The process of creating a program design.

desk check—A type of review in which a developer carefully examines a design or program to find errors.

detailed design—(1) The low-level algorithmic steps of a method. (2) The development stage at which low-level algorithmic steps are determined.

development stage—The software life-cycle stage in which a software system is first created, preceding use, maintenance, and eventual retirement.

dialog box—A graphical window that pops up to allow brief, specific user interaction.

digital—A representation that breaks information down into pieces, which are in turn represented as numbers. All modern computer systems are digital.

digitize—The act of converting an analog representation into a digital one by breaking it down into pieces.

digraph—A graph data structure in which each edge has a specific direction.

dimension—The number of index levels of a particular array.

direct recursion—The process of a method invoking itself. *See also* indirect recursion.

disable—Make a graphical user interface component inactive so that it cannot be used. A disabled component is grayed to indicate its disabled status. *See also* enable.

DNS—*See* Domain Name System.

do—A Java reserved word that represents a repetition construct. A do statement is executed one or more times. *See also* for, while.

documentation—Supplemental information about a program, including comments in a program's source code and printed reports such as a user's guide.

domain name—The portion of an Internet address that specifies the organization to which the computer belongs.

Domain Name System (DNS)—Software that translates an Internet address into an IP address using a domain server.

domain server—A file server that maintains a list of Internet addresses and their corresponding IP addresses.

double—A Java reserved word that represents a primitive floating point numeric type, stored using 64 bits in IEEE 754 format.

doubly linked list—A linked list with two references in each node: one that refers to the next node in the list and one that refers to the previous node in the list.

dynamic binding—The process of associating an identifier with its definition during run time. *See also* binding.

dynamic data structure—A set of objects that are linked using references, which can be modified as needed during program execution.

editor—A software tool that allows the user to enter and store a file of characters on a computer. Often used by programmers to enter the source code of a program.

efficiency—The characteristic of an algorithm that specifies the required number of a particular operation in order to complete its task. For example, the efficiency of a sort can be measured by the number of comparisons required to sort a list. *See also* order.

element—A value or object stored in another object such as an array.

element type—*See* array element type.

else—A Java reserved word that designates the portion of code in an `if` statement that will be executed if the condition is false.

enable—Make a graphical user interface component active so that it can be used. *See also* disable.

encapsulation—The characteristic of an object that limits access to the variables and methods contained in it. All interaction with an object occurs through a well-defined interface that supports a modular design.

equality operator—One of two Java operators that returns a boolean result based on whether two values are equal (==) or not equal (!=).

equivalence category—A range of functionally equivalent input values as specified by the requirements of the software component. Used when developing black-box test cases.

error—(1) Any defect in a design or program. (2) An object that can be thrown and processed by special `catch` blocks, though usually errors should not be caught. *See also* compile-time error, exception, logical error, run-time error, syntax error.

escape sequence—In Java, a sequence of characters beginning with the backslash character (\), used to indicate a special situation when printing values. For example, the escape sequence \t specifies that a horizontal tab should be printed.

exception—(1) A situation that arises during program execution that is erroneous or out of the ordinary. (2) An object that can be thrown and processed by special `catch` blocks. *See also* error.

exception handler—The code in a `catch` clause of a `try` statement, executed when a particular type of exception is thrown.

exception propagation—The process that occurs when an exception is thrown: control returns to each calling method in the stack trace until the exception is caught and handled or until the exception is thrown from the `main` method, terminating the program.

exponent—The portion of a floating point value's internal representation that specifies how far the decimal point is shifted. *See also* mantissa.

expression—A combination of operators and operands that produce a result.

extends—A Java reserved word used to specify the parent class in the definition of a child class.

event—(1) A user action, such as a mouse click or key press. (2) An object that represents a user action, to which the program can respond. *See also* event-driven programming.

event-driven programming—An approach to software development in which the program is designed to acknowledge that an event has occurred and to act accordingly. *See also* event.

false—A Java reserved word that serves as one of the two boolean literals (`true` and `false`).

fetch-decode-execute—The cycle through which the CPU continually obtains instructions from main memory and executes them.

FIFO—*See* first-in, first-out.

file—A named collection of data stored on a secondary storage device such as a disk. *See also* text file.

file chooser—A graphical user interface component, usually displayed as a dialog box, that allows the user to select a file from a storage device.

file server—A computer in a network, usually with a large secondary storage capacity, that is dedicated to storing software needed by many network users.

filtering stream—*See* processing stream.

final—A Java reserved word that serves as a modifier for classes, methods, and variables. A `final` class cannot be used to derive a new class. A `final` method cannot be overridden. A `final` variable is a constant.

finalize—A Java method defined in the `Object` class that can be overridden in any other class. It is called after the object becomes a candidate for garbage collection and before it is destroyed. It can be used to perform "clean-up" activity that is not performed automatically by the garbage collector.

finalizer method—A Java method, called `finalize`, that is called before an object is destroyed. *See also* finalize.

finally—A Java reserved word that designates a block of code to be executed when an exception is thrown, after any appropriate catch handler is processed.

first-in, first-out (FIFO)—A data management technique in which the first value that is stored in a data structure is the first value that comes out. *See also* last-in, first-out; queue.

float—A Java reserved word that represents a primitive floating point numeric type, stored using 32 bits in IEEE 754 format.

flushing—The process of forcing the contents of the output buffer to be displayed on the output device.

font—*See* character font.

for—A Java reserved word that represents a repetition construct. A `for` statement is executed zero or more times and is usually used when a precise number of iterations is known.

foreground color—The color in which any current drawing will be rendered. *See also* background color.

formal parameter—An identifier that serves as a parameter name in a method. It receives its initial value from the actual parameter passed to it. *See also* actual parameter.

fourth-generation language—A high-level language that provides built-in functionality such as automatic report generation or database management, beyond that of traditional high-level languages.

function—A named group of declarations and programming statements that can be invoked (executed) when needed. A function that is part of a class is called a method. Java has no functions because all code is part of a class.

garbage—(1) An unspecified or uninitialized value in a memory location. (2) An object that cannot be accessed anymore because all references to it have been lost.

garbage collection—The process of reclaiming unneeded, dynamically allocated memory. Java performs automatic garbage collection of objects that no longer have any valid references to them.

gigabyte (GB)—A unit of binary storage, equal to 2^{30} (approximately 1 billion) bytes.

goto—(1) A Java reserved word that is not currently used. (2) An unconditional branch.

grammar—A representation of language syntax that specifies how reserved words, symbols, and identifiers can be combined into valid programs.

graph—A non-linear data structure made up of nodes and edges that connect the nodes. *See also* digraph.

graphical user interface (GUI)—Software that provides the means to interact with a program or operating system by making use of graphical images and point-and-click mechanisms such as buttons and text fields.

graphics context—The drawing surface and related coordinate system on which a drawing is rendered or graphical user interface components are placed.

GUI component—A visual element, such as a button or text field, that is used to make up a graphical user interface (GUI).

hardware—The tangible components of a computer system, such as the keyboard, monitor, and circuit boards.

has-a relationship—The relationship between two objects in which one is composed, at least in part, of one or more of the other. *See also* aggregate object, is-a relationship.

hash code—An integer value calculated from any given data value or object, used to determine where a value should be stored in a hash table. Also called a hash value. *See also* hashing.

hash method—A method that calculates a hash code from a data value or object. The same data value or object will always produce the same hash code. Also called a hash function. *See also* hashing.

hash table—A data structure in which values are stored for efficient retrieval. *See also* hashing.

hashing—A technique for storing items so that they can be found efficiently. Items are stored in a hash table at a position specified by a calculated hash code. *See also* hash method.

hexadecimal—The base-16 number system, often used as an abbreviated representation of binary strings.

hierarchy—An organizational technique in which items are layered or grouped to reduce complexity.

high-level language—A programming language in which each statement represents many machine-level instructions.

HTML—*See* HyperText Markup Language.

hybrid object-oriented language—A programming language that can be used to implement a program in a procedural manner or an object-oriented manner, at the programmer's discretion. *See also* pure object-oriented language.

hypermedia—The concept of hypertext extended to include other media types such as graphics, audio, video, and programs.

hypertext—A document representation that allows a user to easily navigate through it in other than a linear fashion. Links to other parts of the document are embedded at the appropriate places to allow the user to jump from one part of the document to another. *See also* hypermedia.

HyperText Markup Language (HTML)—The notation used to define Web pages. *See also* browser, World Wide Web.

icon—A small, fixed-sized picture, often used to decorate a graphical interface. *See also* image.

identifier—Any name that a programmer makes up to use in a program, such as a class name or variable name.

identity—The designation of an object, which, in Java, is an object's reference name. *See also* state, behavior.

IEEE 754—A standard for representing floating point values. Used by Java to represent `float` and `double` data types.

if—A Java reserved word that specifies a simple conditional construct. *See also* else.

image—A picture, often specified using a GIF or JPEG format. *See also* icon.

immutable—The characteristic of something that does not change. For example, the contents of a Java character string are immutable once the string has been defined.

implementation—(1) The process of translating a design into source code. (2) The source code that defines a method, class, abstract data type, or other programming entity.

implements—A Java reserved word that is used in a class declaration to specify that the class implements the methods specified in a particular interface.

import—A Java reserved word that is used to specify the packages and classes that are used in a particular Java source code file.

index—The integer value used to specify a particular element in an array.

index operator—The brackets ([ ]) in which an array index is specified.

indirect recursion—The process of a method invoking another method, which eventually results in the original method being invoked again. *See also* direct recursion.

infinite loop—A loop that does not terminate because the condition controlling the loop never becomes false.

infinite recursion—A recursive series of invocations that does not terminate because the base case is never reached.

infix expression—An expression in which the operators are positioned between the operands on which they work. *See also* postfix expression.

inheritance—The ability to derive a new class from an existing one. Inherited variables and methods of the original (parent) class are available in the new (child) class as if they were declared locally.

initialize—To give an initial value to a variable.

initializer list—A comma-separated list of values, delimited by braces ({}), used to initialize and specify the size of an array.

inline documentation—Comments that are included in the source code of a program.

inner class—A nonstatic, nested class.

input/output buffer—A storage location for data on its way from the user to the computer (input buffer) or from the computer to the user (output buffer).

input/output devices—Hardware components that allow the human user to interact with the computer, such as a keyboard, mouse, and monitor.

input/output stream—A sequence of bytes that represents a source of data (input stream) or a destination for data (output stream).

insertion sort—A sorting algorithm in which each value, one at a time, is inserted into a sorted subset of the entire list. *See also* selection sort.

inspection—*See* walkthrough.

instance—An object created from a class. Multiple objects can be instantiated from a single class.

instance method—A method that must be invoked through a particular instance of a class, as opposed to a class method.

instance variable—A variable that must be referenced through a particular instance of a class, as opposed to a class variable.

instanceof—A Java reserved word that is also an operator, used to determine the class or type of a variable.

instantiation—The act of creating an object from a class.

int—A Java reserved word that represents a primitive integer type, stored using 32 bits in two's complement format.

integration test—The process of testing software components that are made up of other interacting components. Stresses the communication between components rather than the functionality of individual components.

interface—(1) A Java reserved word that is used to define a set of abstract methods that will be implemented by particular classes. (2) The set of messages to which an object responds, defined by the methods that can be invoked from outside of the object. (3) The techniques through which a human user interacts with a program, often graphically. *See also* graphical user interface.

interface hierarchy—A tree-like structure created when interfaces are derived from other interfaces through inheritance. *See also* class hierarchy.

interpreter—A program that translates and executes code on a particular machine. The Java interpreter translates and executes Java bytecode. *See also* compiler.

Internet—The most pervasive wide-area network in the world; it has become the primary vehicle for computer-to-computer communication.

Internet address—A designation that uniquely identifies a particular computer or device on the Internet.

Internet Naming Authority—The governing body that approves all Internet addresses.

invisible component—A graphical user interface component that can be added to a container to provide buffering space between other components.

invocation—*See* method invocation.

I/O devices—*See* input/output devices.

IP address—A series of several integer values, separated by periods (.), that uniquely identifies a particular computer or device on the Internet. Each Internet address has a corresponding IP address.

is-a relationship—The relationship created through properly derived classes via inheritance. The subclass *is-a* more specific version of the superclass. *See also* has-a relationship.

ISO-Latin-1—A 128-character extension to the ASCII character set defined by the International Standards Organization (ISO). The characters correspond to the numeric values 128 through 255 in both ASCII and Unicode.

iteration—(1) One execution of the body of a repetition statement. (2) One pass through a cyclic process, such as an iterative development process.

iteration statement—*See* repetition statement.

iterative development process—A step-by-step approach for creating software, which contains a series of stages that are performed repetitively.

Java Virtual Machine (JVM)—The conceptual device, implemented in software, on which Java bytecode is executed. Bytecode, which is architecture neutral, does not run on a particular hardware platform; instead, it runs on the JVM.

java—The Java command-line interpreter, which translates and executes Java bytecode. Part of the Java Development Kit.

Java—The programming language used throughout this text to demonstrate software development concepts. Described by its developers as object oriented, robust, secure, architecture neutral, portable, high-performance, interpreted, threaded, and dynamic.

Java API—*See* Application Programming Interface.

Java Development Kit (JDK)—A collection of software tools available free from Sun Microsystems, the creators of the Java programming language. *See also* Software Development Kit.

javac—The Java command-line compiler, which translates Java source code into Java bytecode. Part of the Java Development Kit.

javadoc—A software tool that creates external documentation in HTML format about the contents and structure of a Java software system. Part of the Java Development Kit.

javah—A software tool that generates C header and source files, used for implementing `native` methods. Part of the Java Development Kit.

javap—A software tool that disassembles a Java class file, containing unreadable bytecode, into a human-readable version. Part of the Java Development Kit.

jdb—The Java command-line debugger. Part of the Java Development Kit.

JDK—*See* Java Development Kit.

JVM—*See* Java Virtual Machine.

kilobit (Kb)—A unit of binary storage, equal to 2^{10}, or 1024 bits.

kilobyte (K or KB)—A unit of binary storage, equal to 2^{10}, or 1024 bytes.

label—(1) A graphical user interface component that displays text, an image, or both. (2) An identifier in Java used to specify a particular line of code. The `break` and `continue` statements can jump to a specific, labeled line in the program.

LAN—*See* local-area network.

last-in, first-out (LIFO)—A data management technique in which the last value that is stored in a data structure is the first value that comes out. *See also* first-in, first-out; stack.

layout manager—An object that specifies the presentation of graphical user interface components. Each container is governed by a particular layout manager.

lexicographic ordering—The ordering of characters and strings based on a particular character set such as Unicode.

life cycle—The stages through which a software product is developed and used.

LIFO—*See* last-in, first-out.

linear search—A search algorithm in which each item in the list is compared to the target value until the target is found or the list is exhausted. *See also* binary search.

link—(1) A designation in a hypertext document that "jumps" to a new document (or to a new part of the same document) when followed. (2) A connection between two items in a dynamically linked structure, represented as an object reference.

linked list—A dynamic data structure in which objects are linked using references.

list—A graphical user interface component that presents a list of items from which the user can choose. The current selection is highlighted in the list. *See also* combo box.

listener—An object that is set up to respond to an event when it occurs.

listener adaptor class—A class defined with empty methods corresponding to the methods invoked when particular events occur. A listener object can be derived from an adaptor class. *See also* listener interface.

listener interface—A Java interface that defines the methods invoked when particular events occur. A listener object can be created by implementing a listener interface. *See also* listener adaptor class.

literal—A primitive value used explicitly in a program, such as the numeric literal `147` or the string literal `"hello"`.

local-area network (LAN)—A computer network designed to span short distances and connect a relatively small number of computers. *See also* wide-area network.

local variable—A variable defined within a method, which does not exist except during the execution of the method.

logical error—A problem stemming from inappropriate processing in the code. It does not cause an abnormal termination of the program, but it produces incorrect results. *See also* compile-time error, run-time error, syntax error.

logical line of code—A logical programming statement in a source code program, which may extend over multiple physical lines. *See also* physical line of code.

logical operator—One of the operators that perform a logical NOT (`!`), AND (`&&`), or OR (`||`), returning a boolean result. The logical operators are short-circuited, meaning that if their left operand is sufficient to determine the result, the right operand is not evaluated.

long—A Java reserved word that represents a primitive integer type, stored using 64 bits in two's complement format.

loop—*See* repetition statement.

loop control variable—A variable whose value specifically determines how many times a loop body is executed.

low-level language—Either machine language or assembly language, which are not as convenient to construct software in as high-level languages are.

machine language—The native language of a particular CPU. Any software that runs on a particular CPU must be translated into its machine language.

main memory—The volatile hardware storage device where programs and data are held when they are actively needed by the CPU. *See also* secondary memory.

maintenance—(1) The process of fixing errors in or making enhancements to a released software product. (2) The software life-cycle phase in which the software is in use and changes are made to it as needed.

mantissa—The portion of a floating point value's internal representation that specifies the magnitude of the number. *See also* exponent.

megabyte (MB)—A unit of binary storage, equal to 2^{20} (approximately 1 million) bytes.

member—A variable or method in an object or class.

memory—Hardware devices that store programs and data. *See also* main memory, secondary memory.

memory location—An individual, addressable cell inside main memory into which data can be stored.

memory management—The process of controlling dynamically allocated portions of main memory, especially the act of returning allocated memory when it is no longer required. *See also* garbage collection.

method—A named group of declarations and programming statements that can be invoked (executed) when needed. A method is part of a class.

method call conversion—The automatic widening conversion that can occur when a value of one type is passed to a formal parameter of another type.

method definition—The specification of the code that gets executed when the method is invoked. The definition includes declarations of local variables and formal parameters.

method invocation—A line of code that causes a method to be executed. It specifies any values that are passed to the method as parameters.

method overloading—*See* overloading.

mnemonic—(1) A word or identifier that specifies a command or data value in an assembly language. (2) A keyboard character used as a alternative means to activate a graphical user interface component such as a button.

modal—Having multiple modes (such as a dialog box).

modem—A data transfer device that allows information to be sent along a telephone line.

modifier—A designation used in a Java declaration that specifies particular characteristics to the construct being declared.

monitor—The screen in the computer system that serves as an output device.

multidimensional array—An array that uses more than one index to specify a value stored in it.

multiple inheritance—Deriving a class from more than one parent, inheriting methods and variables from each. Multiple inheritance is not supported in Java.

multiplicity—The numeric relationship between two objects, often shown in class diagrams.

NaN—An abbreviation that stands for "not a number," which is the designation for an inappropriate or undefined numeric value.

narrowing conversion—A conversion between two values of different but compatible data types. Narrowing conversions could lose information because the converted type usually has an internal representation smaller than the original storage space. *See also* widening conversion.

native—A Java reserved word that serves as a modifier for methods. A native method is implemented in another programming language.

natural language—A language that humans use to communicate, such as English or French.

negative infinity—A special floating point value that represents the "lowest possible" value. *See also* positive infinity.

nested class—A class declared within another class in order to facilitate implementation and restrict access.

nested if statement—An `if` statement that has as its body another `if` statement.

Netscape Navigator—A popular World Wide Web browser.

network—Two or more computers connected together so that they can exchange data and share resources.

network address—*See* address.

new—A Java reserved word that is also an operator, used to instantiate an object from a class.

newline character—A nonprintable character that indicates the end of a line.

nonprintable characters—Any character, such as escape or newline, that does not have a symbolic representation that can be displayed on a monitor or printed by a printer. *See also* printable characters.

nonvolatile—The characteristic of a memory device that retains its stored information even after the power supply is turned off. Secondary memory devices are nonvolatile. *See also* volatile.

null—A Java reserved word that is a reference literal, used to indicate that a reference does not currently refer to any object.

number system—A set of values and operations defined by a particular base value that determines the number of digits available and the place value of each digit.

object—(1) The primary software construct in the object-oriented paradigm. (2) An encapsulated collection of data variables and methods. (3) An instance of a class.

object diagram—A visual representation of the objects in a program at a given point in time, often showing the status of instance data.

object-oriented programming—An approach to software design and implementation that is centered around objects and classes. *See also* procedural programming.

octal—The base-8 number system, sometimes used to abbreviate binary strings. *See also* binary, hexadecimal.

off-by-one error—An error caused by a calculation or condition being off by one, such as when a loop is set up to access one too many array elements.

operand—A value on which an operator performs its function. For example, in the expression 5 + 2, the values 5 and 2 are operands.

operating system—The collection of programs that provide the primary user interface to a computer and manage its resources, such as memory and the CPU.

operator—A symbol that represents a particular operation in a programming language, such as the addition operator (+).

operator association—The order in which operators within the same precedence level are evaluated, either right to left or left to right. *See also* operator precedence.

operator overloading—Assigning additional meaning to an operator. Operator overloading is not supported in Java, though method overloading is.

operator precedence—The order in which operators are evaluated in an expression as specified by a well- defined hierarchy.

order—The dominant term in an equation that specifies the efficiency of an algorithm. For example, selection sort is of order n^2.

overflow—A problem that occurs when a data value grows too large for its storage size, which can result in inaccurate arithmetic processing. *See also* underflow.

overloading—Assigning additional meaning to a programming language construct, such as a method or operator. Method overloading is supported by Java but operator overloading is not.

overriding—The process of modifying the definition of an inherited method to suit the purposes of the subclass. *See also* shadowing variables.

package—A Java reserved word that is used to specify a group of related classes.

package visibility—*See* default visibility.

panel—A graphical user interface (GUI) container that holds and organizes other GUI components.

parameter—(1) A value passed from a method invocation to its definition. (2) The identifier in a method definition that accepts the value passed to it when the method is invoked. *See also* actual parameter, formal parameter.

parameter list—The list of actual or formal parameters to a method.

parent class—*See* superclass.

pass by reference—The process of passing a reference to a value into a method as the parameter. In Java, all objects are managed using references, so an object's formal parameter is an alias to the original. *See also* pass by value.

pass by value—The process of making a copy of a value and passing the copy into a method. Therefore any change made to the value inside the method is not reflected in the original value. All Java primitive types are passed by value.

PDL—*See* Program Design Language.

peripheral—Any hardware device other than the CPU or main memory.

persistence—The ability of an object to stay in existence after the executing program that creates it terminates. *See also* serialize.

physical line of code—A line in a source code file, terminated by a newline or similar character. *See also* logical line of code.

pixel—A picture element. A digitized picture is made up of many pixels.

place value—The value of each digit position in a number, which determines the overall contribution of that digit to the value. *See also* number system.

pointer—A variable that can hold a memory address. Instead of pointers, Java uses references, which provide essentially the same functionality as pointers but without the complications.

point-to-point connection—The link between two networked devices that are connected directly by a wire.

polyline—A shape made up of a series of connected line segments. A polyline is similar to a polygon, but the shape is not closed.

polymorphism—An object-oriented technique by which a reference that is used to invoke a method can result in different methods being invoked at different times. All Java method invocations are potentially polymorphic in that they invoke the method of the object type, not the reference type.

portability—The ability of a program to be moved from one hardware platform to another without having to change it. Because Java bytecode is not related to any particular hardware environment, Java programs are considered portable. *See also* architecture neutral.

positive infinity—A special floating point value that represents the "highest possible" value. *See also* negative infinity.

postfix expression—An expression in which an operator is positioned after the operands on which it works. *See also* infix expression.

postfix operator—In Java, an operator that is positioned behind its single operand, whose evaluation yields the value prior to the operation being performed. Both the increment (++) and decrement (– –) operators can be applied postfix. *See also* prefix operator.

precedence—*See* operator precedence.

prefix operator—In Java, an operator that is positioned in front of its single operand, whose evaluation yields the value after the operation has been performed. Both the increment (++) and decrement (– –) operators can be applied prefix. *See also* postfix operator.

primitive data type—A data type that is predefined in a programming language.

printable characters—Any character that has a symbolic representation that can be displayed on a monitor or printed by a printer. *See also* nonprintable characters.

private—A Java reserved word that serves as a visibility modifier for methods and variables. Private methods and variables are not inherited by subclasses, and can only be accessed in the class in which they are declared.

procedural programming—An approach to software design and implementation that is centered around procedures (or functions) and their interaction. *See also* object-oriented programming.

processing stream—An I/O stream that performs some type of manipulation on the data in the stream. Sometimes called a filtering stream. *See also* data stream.

program—A series of instructions executed by hardware, one after another.

Program Design Language (PDL)—A language in which a program's design and algorithms are expressed. *See also* pseudocode.

programming language—A specification of the syntax and semantics of the statements used to create a program.

programming language statement—An individual instruction in a given programming language.

prompt—A message or symbol used to request information from the user.

propagation—*See* exception propagation.

protected—A Java reserved word that serves as a visibility modifier for methods and variables. Protected methods and variables are inherited by all subclasses and are accessible from all classes in the same package.

prototype—A program used to explore an idea or prove the feasibility of a particular approach.

pseudocode—Structured and abbreviated natural language used to express the algorithmic steps of a program. *See also* Program Design Language.

pseudo–random number—A value generated by software that performs extensive calculations based on an initial seed value. The result is not truly random because it is based on a calculation, but it is usually random enough for most purposes.

public—A Java reserved word that serves as a visibility modifier for classes, interfaces, methods, and variables. A public class or interface can be used anywhere. A public method or variable is inherited by all subclasses and is accessible anywhere.

pure object-oriented language—A programming language that enforces, to some degree, software development using an object-oriented approach. *See also* hybrid object-oriented language.

push button—A graphical user interface component that allows the user to initiate an action with a mouse click. *See also* check box, radio button.

queue—An abstract data type that manages information in a first-in, first-out manner.

radio button—A graphical user interface component that allows the user choose one of a set of options with a mouse click. A radio button is useful only as part of a group of other radio buttons. *See also* check box.

RAM—*See* random access memory.

random access device—A memory device whose information can be directly accessed. *See also* random access memory, sequential access device.

random access memory (RAM)—A term basically interchangeable with main memory. Should probably be called read-write memory, to distinguish it from read-only memory.

random number generator—Software that produces a pseudo–random number, generated by calculations based on a seed value.

read-only memory (ROM)—Any memory device whose stored information is stored permanently when the device is created. It can be read from, but not written to.

recursion—The process of a method invoking itself, either directly or indirectly. Recursive algorithms sometimes provide elegant, though perhaps inefficient, solutions to a problem.

reference—A variable that holds the address of an object. In Java, a reference can be used to interact with an object, but its address cannot be accessed, set, or operated on directly.

refinement—One iteration of an evolutionary development cycle in which a particular aspect of the system, such as the user interface or a particular algorithm, is addressed.

refinement scope—The specific issues that are addressed in a particular refinement during evolutionary software development.

register—A small area of storage in the CPU of the computer.

relational operator—One of several operators that determine the ordering relationship between two values: less than (<), less than or equal to (<=), greater than (>), and greater than or equal to (>=). *See also* equality operator.

release—A version of a software product that is made available to the customer.

repetition statement—A programming construct that allows a set of statements to be executed repetitively as long as a particular condition is true. The body of the repetition statement should eventually make the condition false. Also called an iteration statement or loop. *See also* do, for, while.

requirements—(1) The specification of what a program must and must not do. (2) An early phase of the software development process in which the program requirements are established.

reserved word—A word that has special meaning in a programming language and cannot be used for any other purpose.

retirement—The phase of a program's life cycle in which the program is taken out of active use.

return—A Java reserved word that causes the flow of program execution to return from a method to the point of invocation.

return type—The type of value returned from a method, specified before the method name in the method declaration. Could be void, which indicates that no value is returned.

reuse—Using existing software components to create new ones.

review—The process of critically examining a design or program to discover errors. There are many types of reviews. *See also* desk check, walkthrough.

RGB value—A collection of three values that define a color. Each value represents the contribution of the primary colors red, green, and blue.

ROM—*See* read-only memory.

run-time error—A problem that occurs during program execution that causes the program to terminate abnormally. *See also* compile-time error, logical error, syntax error.

scope—The areas within a program in which an identifier, such as a variable, can be referenced. *See also* access.

scroll pane—A graphical user interface container that offers a limited view of a component and provides horizontal and/or vertical scroll bars to change that view.

SDK—*See* Software Development Kit.

searching—The process of determining the existence or location of a target value within a list of values. *See also* binary search, linear search.

secondary memory—Hardware storage devices, such as magnetic disks or tapes, which store information in a relatively permanent manner. *See also* main memory.

seed value—A value used by a random number generator as a base for the calculations that produce a pseudo-random number.

selection sort—A sorting algorithm in which each value, one at a time, is placed in its final, sorted position. *See also* insertion sort.

selection statement—A programming construct that allows a set of statements to be executed if a particular condition is true. *See also* if, switch.

semantics—The interpretation of a program or programming construct.

sentinel value—A specific value used to indicate a special condition, such as the end of input.

serialize—The process of converting an object into a linear series of bytes so it can be saved to a file or sent across a network. *See also* persistence.

service methods—Methods in an object that are declared with public visibility and define a service that the object's client can invoke.

shadowing variables—The process of defining a variable in a subclass that supersedes an inherited version.

short—A Java reserved word that represents a primitive integer type, stored using 16 bits in two's complement format.

sibling—Two items in a tree or hierarchy, such as a class inheritance hierarchy, that have the same parent.

sign bit—A bit in a numeric value that represents the sign (positive or negative) of that value.

signed numeric value—A value that stores a sign (positive or negative). All Java numeric values are signed. A Java character is stored as an unsigned value.

signature—The number, types, and order of the parameters of a method. Overloaded methods must each have a unique signature.

slider—A graphical user interface component that allows the user to specify a numeric value within a bounded range by moving a knob to the appropriate place in the range.

software—(1) Programs and data. (2) The intangible components of a computer system.

software component—*See* component.

Software Development Kit (SDK)—A collection of software tools that assist in the development of software. The Java Software Development Kit is another name for the Java Development Kit.

software engineering—The discipline within computer science that addresses the process of developing high-quality software within practical constraints.

sorting—The process of putting a list of values into a well-defined order. *See also* insertion sort, selection sort.

split pane—A graphical user interface container that displays two components, either side by side or one on top of the other, separated by a moveable divider bar.

stack—An abstract data type that manages data in a last-in, first-out manner.

stack trace—The series of methods called to reach a certain point in a program. The stack trace can be analyzed when an exception is thrown to assist the programmer in tracking down the problem.

standard I/O stream—One of three common I/O streams representing standard input (usually the keyboard), standard output (usually the monitor screen), and standard error (also usually the monitor). *See also* stream.

start angle—When defining an arc, the angle at which the arc begins. *See also* arc angle.

state—The state of being of an object, defined by the values of its data. *See also* behavior, identity.

statement—*See* programming language statement.

statement coverage—A strategy used in white-box testing in which all statements in a program are executed. *See also* condition coverage.

static—A Java reserved word that serves as a modifier for methods and variables. A static method is also called a class method and can be referenced without an instance of the class. A static variable is also called a class variable and is common to all instances of the class.

static data structure—A data structure that has a fixed size and cannot grow and shrink as needed. *See also* dynamic data structure.

storage capacity—The total number of bytes that can be stored in a particular memory device.

stream—A source of input or a destination for output.

strictfp—A Java reserved word that is used to control certain aspects of floating point arithmetic.

string—*See* character string.

string concatenation—The process of attaching the beginning of one character string to the end of another, resulting in one longer string.

strongly typed language—A programming language in which each variable is associated with a particular data type for the duration of its existence. Variables are not allowed to take on values or be used in operations that are inconsistent with their type.

structured programming—An approach to program development in which each software component has one entry and exit point and in which the flow of control does not cross unnecessarily.

stub—A method that simulates the functionality of a particular software component. Often used during unit testing.

subclass—A class derived from another class via inheritance. Also called a derived class or child class. *See also* superclass.

subscript—*See* index.

super—A Java reserved word that is a reference to the parent class of the object making the reference. Often used to invoke a parent's constructor.

super reference—*See* super.

superclass—The class from which another class is derived via inheritance. Also called a base class or parent class. *See also* subclass.

support methods—Methods in an object that are not intended for use outside the class. They provide support functionality for service methods. As such, they are usually not declared with public visibility.

swapping—The process of exchanging the values of two variables.

swing—The package in the Java API (`javax.swing`) that contains classes related to graphical user interfaces. Swing provides alternative components than the Abstract Windowing Toolkit package, but does not replace it.

switch—A Java reserved word that specifies a compound conditional construct.

synchronization—The process of ensuring that data shared among multiple threads cannot be accessed by more than one thread at a time. *See also* synchronized.

synchronized—A Java reserved word that serves as a modifier for methods. Separate threads of a process can execute concurrently in a method, unless the method is synchronized, making it a mutually exclusive resource. Methods that access shared data should be synchronized.

syntax rules—The set of specifications that govern how the elements of a programming language can be put together to form valid statements.

syntax error—An error produced by the compiler because a program did not conform to the syntax of the programming language. Syntax errors are a subset of compile-time errors. *See also* compile-time error, logical error, run-time error, syntax rules.

tabbed pane—A graphical user interface (GUI) container that presents a set of cards from which the user can choose. Each card contains its own GUI components.

target value—The value that is sought when performing a search on a collection of data.

TCP/IP—Software that controls the movement of messages across the Internet. The acronym stands for Transmission Control Protocol/Internet Protocol.

terabyte (TB)—A unit of binary storage, equal to 2^{40} (approximately 1 trillion) bytes.

termination—The point at which a program stops executing.

ternary operator—An operator that uses three operands.

test case—A set of input values and user actions, along with a specification of the expected output, used to find errors in a system.

testing—(1) The process of running a program with various test cases in order to discover problems. (2) The process of critically evaluating a design or program.

text area—A graphical user interface component that displays, or allows the user to enter, multiple lines of data.

text field—A graphical user interface component that displays, or allows the user to enter, a single line of data.

text file—A file that contains data formatted as ASCII or Unicode characters.

this—A Java reserved word that is a reference to the object executing the code making the reference.

thread—An independent process executing within a program. A Java program can have multiple threads running in a program at one time.

throw—A Java reserved word that is used to start an exception propagation.

throws—A Java reserved word that specifies that a method may throw a particular type of exception.

timer—An object that generates an event at regular intervals.

token—A portion of a string defined by a set of delimiters.

tool tip—A short line of text that appears when the mouse pointer is allowed to rest on top of a particular component. Usually, tool tips are used to inform the user of the component's purpose.

top-level domain—The last part of a network domain name, such as edu or com.

transient—A Java reserved word that serves as a modifier for variables. A transient variable does not contribute to the object's persistent state, and therefore does not need to be saved. *See also* serialize.

tree—A non-linear data structure that forms a hierarchy stemming from a single root node.

true—A Java reserved word that serves as one of the two boolean literals (`true` and `false`).

truth table—A complete enumeration of all permutations of values involved in a boolean expression, as well as the computed result.

try—A Java reserved word that is used to define the context in which certain exceptions will be handled if they are thrown.

two-dimensional array—An array that uses two indices to specify the location of an element. The two dimensions are often thought of as the rows and columns of a table. *See also* multidimensional array.

two's complement—A technique for representing numeric binary data. Used by all Java integer primitive types (`byte`, `short`, `int`, `long`).

type—*See* data type.

UML—*See* Unified Modeling Language.

unary operator—An operator that uses only one operand.

unchecked exception—A Java exception that does not need to be caught or dealt with if the programmer so chooses.

underflow—A problem that occurs when a floating point value becomes too small for its storage size, which can result in inaccurate arithmetic processing. *See also* overflow.

Unicode—The international character set used to define valid Java characters. Each character is represented using a 16-bit unsigned numeric value.

Unified Modeling Language (UML)—A graphical notation for visualizing relationships among classes and objects. Abbreviated UML. There are many types of UML diagrams. *See also* class diagrams.

uniform resource locator (URL)—A designation for a resource that can be located through a World Wide Web browser.

unit test—The process of testing an individual software component. May require the creation of stub modules to simulate other system components.

unsigned numeric value—A value that does not store a sign (positive or negative). The bit usually reserved to represent the sign is included in the value, doubling the magnitude of the number that can be stored. Java characters are stored as unsigned numeric values, but there are no primitive numeric types that are unsigned.

URL—*See* uniform resource locator.

use relationship—A relationship between two classes, often shown in a class diagram, that establishes that one class uses another in some way, such as relying on its services. *See also* association.

user interface—The manner in which the user interacts with a software system, which is often graphical. *See also* graphical user interface.

variable—An identifier in a program that represents a memory location in which a data value is stored.

visibility modifier—A Java modifier that defines the scope in which a construct can be accessed. The Java visibility modifiers are `public`, `protected`, `private`, and `default` (no modifier used).

void—A Java reserved word that can be used as a return value for a method, indicating that no value is returned.

volatile—(1) A Java reserved word that serves as a modifier for variables. A volatile variable might be changed asynchronously and therefore indicates that the compiler should not attempt optimizations on it. (2) The characteristic of a memory device that loses stored information when the power supply is interrupted. Main memory is a volatile storage device. *See also* nonvolatile.

von Neumann architecture—The computer architecture named after John von Neumann, in which programs and data are stored together in the same memory devices.

walkthrough—A form of review in which a group of developers, managers, and quality assurance personnel examine a design or program in order to find errors. Sometimes referred to as an inspection. *See also* desk check.

WAN—*See* wide-area network.

waterfall model—One of the earliest software development process models. It defines a basically linear interaction between the requirements, design, implementation, and testing stages.

Web—*See* World Wide Web.

while—A Java reserved word that represents a repetition construct. A while statement is executed zero or more times. *See also* do, for.

white-box testing—Producing and evaluating test cases based on the interior logic of a software component. The test cases focus on stressing decision points and ensuring coverage. *See also* black-box testing, condition coverage, statement coverage.

white space—Spaces, tabs, and blank lines that are used to set off sections of source code to make programs more readable.

wide-area network (WAN)—A computer network that connects two or more local area networks, usually across long geographic distances. *See also* local-area network.

widening conversion—A conversion between two values of different but compatible data types. Widening conversions usually leave the data value intact because the converted type has an internal representation equal to or larger than the original storage space. *See also* narrowing conversion.

word—A unit of binary storage. The size of a word varies by computer, and is usually two, four, or eight bytes. The word size indicates the amount of information that can be moved through the machine at one time.

World Wide Web (WWW or Web)—Software that makes the exchange of information across a network easier by providing a common user interface for multiple types of information. Web browsers are used to retrieve and format HTML documents.

wrapper class—A class designed to store a primitive type in an object. Usually used when an object reference is needed and a primitive type would not suffice.

WWW—*See* World Wide Web.

Number Systems B

This appendix contains a detailed introduction to number systems and their underlying characteristics. The particular focus is on the binary number system, its use with computers, and its similarities to other number systems. This introduction also covers conversions between bases.

In our everyday lives, we use the *decimal number system* to represent values, to count, and to perform arithmetic. The decimal system is also referred to as the *base-10 number system*. We use 10 digits (0 through 9) to represent values in the decimal system.

Computers use the *binary number system* to store and manage information. The binary system, also called the *base-2 number system*, has only two digits (0 and 1). Each 0 and 1 is called a *bit*, short for binary digit. A series of bits is called a *binary string*.

There is nothing particularly special about either the binary or decimal systems. Long ago, humans adopted the decimal number system probably because we have 10 fingers on our hands. If humans had 12 fingers, we would probably be using a base-12 number system regularly and find it as easy to deal with as we do the decimal system now. It all depends on what you get used to. As you explore the binary system, it will become more familiar and natural.

Binary is used for computer processing because the devices used to manage and store information are less expensive and more reliable if they have to represent only two possible values. Computers have been made that use the decimal system, but they are not as convenient.

There are an infinite number of number systems, and they all follow the same basic rules. You already know how the binary number system works, but you just might not be aware that you do. It all goes back to the basic rules of arithmetic.

Place Value

In decimal, we represent the values of 0 through 9 using only one digit. To represent any value higher than 9, we must use more than one digit. The position of each digit has a *place value* that indicates the amount it contributes to the overall value. In decimal, we refer to the one's column, the ten's column, the hundred's column, and so on forever.

Each place value is determined by the *base* of the number system, raised to increasing powers as we move from right to left. In the decimal number system, the place value of the digit furthest to the right is 10^0, or 1. The place value of the next digit is 10^1, or 10. The place value of the third digit from the right is 10^2, or 100, and so on. Figure B.1 shows how each digit in a decimal number contributes to the value.

The binary system works the same way except that we exhaust the available digits much sooner. We can represent 0 and 1 with a single bit, but to represent any value higher than 1, we must use multiple bits.

The place values in binary are determined by increasing powers of the base as we move right to left, just as they are in the decimal system. However, in binary, the base value is 2. Therefore the place value of the bit furthest to the right is 2^0, or 1. The place value of the next bit is 2^1, or 2. The place value of the third bit from the right is 2^2, or 4, and so on. Figure B.2 shows a binary number and its place values.

The number 1101 is a valid binary number, but it is also a valid decimal number as well. Sometimes to make it clear which number system is being used, the base value is appended as a subscript to the end of a number. Therefore you can distinguish between 1101_2, which is equivalent to 13 in decimal, and 1101_{10} (one thousand, one hundred and one), which in binary is represented as 10001001101_2.

A number system with base N has N digits (0 through $N-1$). As we have seen, the decimal system has 10 digits (0 through 9), and the binary system has two digits (0 and 1). They all work the same way. For instance, the base-5 number system has five digits (0 to 4).

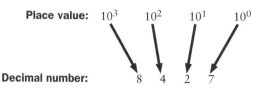

$$
\begin{aligned}
\text{Place value:}\quad & 10^3 \qquad 10^2 \qquad 10^1 \qquad 10^0 \\[4pt]
\text{Decimal number:}\quad & \ 8 \quad\ 4 \quad\ 2 \quad\ 7
\end{aligned}
$$

$$
\begin{aligned}
\text{Decimal number:}\quad & 8 * 10^3 + 4 * 10^2 + 2 * 10^1 + 7 * 10^0 = \\
& 8 * 1000 + 4 * 100 + 2 * 10 + 7 * 1 = 8427
\end{aligned}
$$

FIGURE B.1 Place values in the decimal system

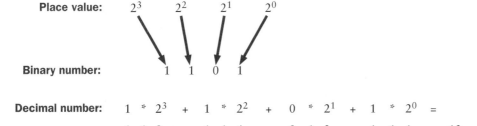

FIGURE B.2 Place values in the binary system

Note that, in any number system, the place value of the digit furthest to the right is 1, since any base raised to the zero power is 1. Also notice that the value 10, which we refer to as "ten" in the decimal system, always represents the base value in any number system. In base 10, 10 is one 10 and zero 1's. In base 2, 10 is one 2 and zero 1's. In base 5, 10 is one 5 and zero 1's.

Bases Higher Than 10

Since all number systems with base N have N digits, then base 16 has 16 digits. But what are they? We are used to the digits 0 through 9, but in bases higher than 10, we need a single digit, a single symbol, that represents the decimal value 10. In fact, in *base 16*, which is also called *hexadecimal*, we need digits that represent the decimal values 10 through 15.

For number systems higher than 10, we use alphabetic characters as single digits for values greater than 9. The hexadecimal digits are 0 through F, where 0 through 9 represent the first 10 digits, and A represents the decimal value 10, B represents 11, C represents 12, D represents 13, E represents 14, and F represents 15.

Therefore the number 2A8E is a valid hexadecimal number. The place values are determined as they are for decimal and binary, using increasing powers of the base. So in hexadecimal, the place values are powers of 16. Figure B.3 shows how the place values of the hexadecimal number 2A8E contribute to the overall value.

All number systems with bases greater than 10 use letters as digits. For example, base 12 has the digits 0 through B and base 19 has the digits 0 through I. However, beyond having a different set of digits and a different base, the rules governing each number system are the same.

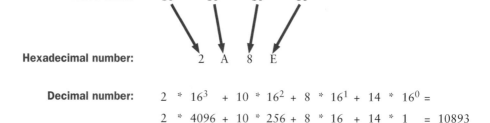

FIGURE B.3 Place values in the hexadecimal system

Keep in mind that when we change number systems, we are simply changing the way we represent values, not the values themselves. If you have 18_{10} pencils, it may be written as 10010 in binary or as 12 in hexadecimal, but it is still the same number of pencils.

Figure B.4 shows the representations of the decimal values 0 through 20 in several bases, including *base 8*, which is also called *octal*. Note that the larger the base, the higher the value that can be represented in a single digit.

Conversions

We've already seen how a number in another base is converted to decimal by determining the place value of each digit and computing the result. This process can be used to convert any number in any base to its equivalent value in base 10.

Now let's reverse the process, converting a base-10 value to another base. First, find the highest place value in the new number system that is less than or equal to the original value. Then divide the original number by that place value to determine the digit that belongs in that position. The remainder is the value that must be represented in the remaining digit positions. Continue this process, position by position, until the entire value is represented.

For example, Figure B.5 shows the process of converting the decimal value 180 into binary. The highest place value in binary that is less than or equal to 180 is 128 (or 2^7), which is the eighth bit position from the right. Dividing 180 by 128 yields 1 with 52 remaining. Therefore the first bit is 1, and the decimal value 52 must be represented in the remaining seven bits. Dividing 52 by 64, which is the next place value (2^6), yields 0 with 52 remaining. So the second bit

Binary (base 2)	Octal (base 8)	Decimal (base 10)	Hexadecimal (base 16)
0	0	0	0
1	1	1	1
10	2	2	2
11	3	3	3
100	4	4	4
101	5	5	5
110	6	6	6
111	7	7	7
1000	10	8	8
1001	11	9	9
1010	12	10	A
1011	13	11	B
1100	14	12	C
1101	15	13	D
1110	16	14	E
1111	17	15	F
10000	20	16	10
10001	21	17	11
10010	22	18	12
10011	23	19	13
10100	24	20	14

FIGURE B.4   Counting in various number systems

is 0. Dividing 52 by 32 yields 1 with 20 remaining. So the third bit is 1 and the remaining five bits must represent the value 20. Dividing 20 by 16 yields 1 with 4 remaining. Dividing 4 by 8 yields 0 with 4 remaining. Dividing 4 by 4 yields 0 with 0 remaining.

Since the number has been completely represented, the rest of the bits are zero. Therefore 180_{10} is equivalent to 10110100 in binary. This can be confirmed by converting the new binary number back to decimal to make sure we get the original value.

Place value	Number	Digit
128	180	1
64	52	0
32	52	1
16	20	1
8	4	0
4	4	1
2	0	0
1	0	0

$$180_{10} = 10110100_2$$

FIGURE B.5 Converting a decimal value into binary

This process works to convert any decimal value to any target base. For each target base, the place values and possible digits change. If you start with the correct place value, each division operation will yield a valid digit in the new base.

In the example in Figure B.5, the only digits that could have resulted from each division operation would have been 1 or 0, since we were converting to binary. However, when we are converting to other bases, any valid digit in the new base could result. For example, Figure B.6 shows the process of converting the decimal value 1967 into hexadecimal.

The place value of 256, which is 16^2, is the highest place value less than or equal to the original number, since the next highest place value is 16^3 or 4096. Dividing 1976 by 256 yields 7 with 175 remaining. Dividing 175 by 16 yields 10 with 15 remaining. Remember that 10 in decimal can be represented as the single digit A in hexadecimal. The 15 remaining can be represented as the digit F. Therefore 1967_{10} is equivalent to 7AF in hexadecimal.

Shortcut Conversions

We have established techniques for converting any value in any base to its equivalent representation in base 10, and from base 10 to any other base. Therefore you can now convert a number in any base to any other base by going through base 10. However, an interesting relationship exists between the bases that are powers of 2, such as binary, octal, and hexadecimal, which allows very quick conversions between them.

Place value	Number	Digit
256	1967	7
16	175	A
1	15	F

$$1967_{10} = 7AF_{16}$$

FIGURE B.6 Converting a decimal value into hexadecimal

To convert from binary to hexadecimal, for instance, you can simply group the bits of the original value into groups of four, starting from the right, then convert each group of four into a single hexadecimal digit. The example in Figure B.7 demonstrates this process.

To go from hexadecimal to binary, we reverse this process, expanding each hexadecimal digit into four binary digits. Note that you may have to add leading zeros to the binary version of each expanded hexadecimal digit if necessary to make four binary digits. Figure B.8 shows the conversion of the hexadecimal value 40C6 to binary.

Why do we section the bits into groups of four when converting from binary to hexadecimal? The shortcut conversions work between binary and any base that is a power of 2. We section the bits into groups of that power. Since $2^4 = 16$, we section the bits in groups of four.

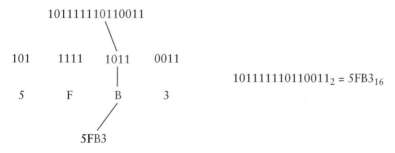

$$101111110110011_2 = 5FB3_{16}$$

FIGURE B.7 Shortcut conversion from binary to hexadecimal

FIGURE B.8 Shortcut conversion from hexadecimal to binary

Converting from binary to octal is the same process except that the bits are sectioned into groups of three, since $2^3 = 8$. Likewise, when converting from octal to binary, we expand each octal digit into three bits.

To convert between, say, hexadecimal and octal is now a process of doing two shortcut conversions. First convert from hexadecimal to binary, then take that result and perform a shortcut conversion from binary to octal.

By the way, these types of shortcut conversions can be performed between any base B and any base that is a power of B. For example, conversions between base 3 and base 9 can be accomplished using the shortcut grouping technique, sectioning or expanding digits into groups of two, since $3^2 = 9$.

The Unicode Character Set

The Java programming language uses the Unicode character set for managing text. A *character set* is simply an ordered list of characters, each corresponding to a particular numeric value. Unicode is an international character set that contains letters, symbols, and ideograms for languages all over the world. Each character is represented as a 16-bit unsigned numeric value. Unicode, therefore, can support over 65,000 unique characters. Only about half of those values have characters assigned to them at this point. The Unicode character set continues to be refined as characters from various languages are included.

Many programming languages still use the ASCII character set. ASCII stands for the American Standard Code for Information Interchange. The 8-bit extended ASCII set is quite small, so the developers of Java opted to use Unicode in order to support international users. However, ASCII is essentially a subset of Unicode, including corresponding numeric values, so programmers used to ASCII should have no problems with Unicode.

Figure C.1 shows a list of commonly used characters and their Unicode numeric values. These characters also happen to be ASCII characters. All of the characters in Figure C.1 are called *printable characters* because they have a symbolic representation that can be displayed on a monitor or printed by a printer. Other characters are called *nonprintable characters* because they have no such symbolic representation. Note that the space character (numeric value 32) is considered a printable character, even though no symbol is printed when it is displayed. Nonprintable characters are sometimes called *control characters* because many of them can be generated by holding down the control key on a keyboard and pressing another key.

The Unicode characters with numeric values 0 through 31 are nonprintable characters. Also, the delete character, with numeric value 127, is a nonprintable character. All of these characters are ASCII characters as well. Many of them have fairly common and well-defined uses, while others are more general. The table in Figure C.2 lists a small sample of the nonprintable characters.

Nonprintable characters are used in many situations to represent special conditions. For example, certain nonprintable characters can be stored in a text document to indicate, among other things, the beginning of a new line. An editor will

Value	Char	Value	Char	Value	Char	Value	Char	Value	Char
32	*space*	51	3	70	F	89	Y	108	l
33	!	52	4	71	G	90	Z	109	m
34	"	53	5	72	H	91	[	110	n
35	#	54	6	73	I	92	\	111	o
36	$	55	7	74	J	93	]	112	p
37	%	56	8	75	K	94	^	113	q
38	&	57	9	76	L	95	–	114	r
39	'	58	:	77	M	96	'	115	s
40	(	59	;	78	N	97	a	116	t
41	)	60	<	79	O	98	b	117	u
42	*	61	=	80	P	99	c	118	v
43	+	62	>	81	Q	100	d	119	w
44	'	63	?	82	R	101	e	120	x
45	–	64	@	83	S	102	f	121	y
46	.	65	A	84	T	103	g	122	z
47	/	66	B	85	U	104	h	123	{
48	0	67	C	86	V	105	i	124		
49	1	68	D	87	W	106	j	125	}
50	2	69	E	88	X	107	k	126	~

FIGURE C.1 A small portion of the Unicode character set

process these characters by starting the text that follows it on a new line, instead of printing a symbol to the screen. Various types of computer systems use different nonprintable characters to represent particular conditions.

Except for having no visible representation, nonprintable characters are essentially equivalent to printable characters. They can be stored in a Java character variable and be part of a character string. They are stored using 16 bits, can be converted to their numeric value, and can be compared using relational operators.

The first 128 characters of the Unicode character set correspond to the common ASCII character set. The first 256 characters correspond to the ISO-Latin-1 extended ASCII character set. Many operating systems and Web browsers will handle these characters, but they may not be able to print the other Unicode characters.

Value	Character
0	null
7	bell
8	backspace
9	tab
10	line feed
12	form feed
13	carriage return
27	escape
127	delete

FIGURE C.2 Some nonprintable characters in the Unicode character set

Java Operators D

Java operators are evaluated according to the precedence hierarchy shown in Figure D.1. Operators at low precedence levels are evaluated before operators at higher levels. Operators within the same precedence level are evaluated according to the specified association, either right to left (R to L) or left to right (L to R). Operators in the same precedence level are not listed in any particular order.

The order of operator evaluation can always be forced by the use of parentheses. It is often a good idea to use parentheses even when they are not required, to make it explicitly clear to a human reader how an expression is evaluated.

For some operators, the operand types determine which operation is carried out. For instance, if the + operator is used on two strings, string concatenation is performed, but if it is applied to two numeric types, they are added in the arithmetic sense. If only one of the operands is a string, the other is converted to a string, and string concatenation is performed. Similarly, the operators &, ^, and | perform bitwise operations on numeric operands but boolean operations on boolean operands.

The boolean operators & and | differ from the logical operators && and || in a subtle way. The logical operators are "short-circuited" in that if the result of an expression can be determined by evaluating only the left operand, the right operand is not evaluated. The boolean versions always evaluate both sides of the expression. There is no logical operator that performs an exclusive OR (XOR) operation.

Java Bitwise Operators

The Java *bitwise operators* operate on individual bits within a primitive value. They are defined only for integers and characters. They are unique among all Java operators because they let us work at the lowest level of binary storage. Figure D.2 lists the Java bitwise operators.

Three of the bitwise operators are similar to the logical operators !, &&, and ||. The bitwise NOT, AND, and OR operations work basically the same way as their logical counterparts, except they work on individual bits of a value. The

Precedence Level	Operator	Operation	Associates
1	[ ] . (*parameters*) ++ --	array indexing object member reference parameter evaluation and method invocation postfix increment postfix decrement	L to R
2	++ -- + - ~ !	prefix increment prefix decrement unary plus unary minus bitwise NOT logical NOT	R to L
3	new (*type*)	object instantiation cast	R to L
4	* / %	multiplication division remainder	L to R
5	+ + -	addition string concatenation subtraction	L to R
6	<< >> >>>	left shift right shift with sign right shift with zero	L to R
7	< <= > >= instanceof	less than less than or equal greater than greater than or equal type comparison	L to R
8	== !=	equal not equal	L to R

FIGURE D.1 Java operator precedence

Precedence Level	Operator	Operation	Associates
9	& &	bitwise AND boolean AND	L to R
10	^ ^	bitwise XOR boolean XOR	L to R
11	| |	bitwise OR boolean OR	L to R
12	&&	logical AND	L to R
13	||	logical OR	L to R
14	?:	conditional operator	R to L
15	= += += -= *= /= %= <<= >>= >>>= &= &= ^= ^= |= |=	assignment addition, then assignment string concatenation, then assignment subtraction, then assignment multiplication, then assignment division, then assignment remainder, then assignment left shift, then assignment right shift (sign), then assignment right shift (zero), then assignment bitwise AND, then assignment boolean AND, then assignment bitwise XOR, then assignment boolean XOR, then assignment bitwise OR, then assignment boolean OR, then assignment	R to L

FIGURE D.1 Java operator precedence, continued

rules are essentially the same. Figure D.3 shows the results of bitwise operators on all combinations of two bits. Compae this chart to the truth tables for the logical operators in Chapter 5 to see the similarities.

The bitwise operators include the XOR operator, which stands for *exclusive OR*. The logical || operator is an *inclusive OR* operation, which means it returns true if both operands are true. The | bitwise operator is also inclusive and yields a 1 if both corresponding bits are 1. However, the exclusive OR operator (^) yields a 0 if both operands are 1. There is no logical exclusive OR operator in Java.

Operator	Description
~	bitwise NOT
&	bitwise AND
|	bitwise OR
^	bitwise XOR
<<	left shift
>>	right shift with sign
>>>	right shift with zero fill

FIGURE D.2 Java bitwise operators

a	b	~ a	a & b	a | b	a ^ b
0	0	1	0	0	0
0	1	1	0	1	1
1	0	0	0	1	1
1	1	0	1	1	0

FIGURE D.3 Bitwise operations on individual bits

When the bitwise operators are applied to integer values, the operation is performed individually on each bit in the value. For example, suppose the integer variable number is declared to be of type byte and currently holds the value 45. Stored as an 8-bit byte, it is represented in binary as 00101101. When the bitwise complement operator (~) is applied to number, each bit in the value is inverted, yielding 11010010. Since integers are stored using two's complement representation, the value represented is now negative, specifically –46.

Similarly, for all bitwise operators, the operations are applied bit by bit, which is where the term "bitwise" comes from. For binary operators (with two operands), the operations are applied to corresponding bits in each operand. For example, assume num1 and num2 are byte integers, num1 holds the value 45, and num2 holds the value 14. Figure D.4 shows the results of several bitwise operations.

The operators &, |, and ^ can also be applied to boolean values, and they have basically the same meaning as their logical counterparts. When used with boolean

num1 & num2	num1 | num2	num1 ^ num2
00101101	00101101	00101101
& 00001110	| 00001110	^ 00001110
= 00001100	= 00101111	= 00100011

FIGURE D.4 Bitwise operations on bytes

values, they are called *boolean operators*. However, unlike the operators && and || , which are "short-circuited," the boolean operators are not short-circuited. Both sides of the expression are evaluated every time.

Like the other bitwise operators, the three bitwise shift operators manipulate the individual bits of an integer value. They all take two operands. The left operand is the value whose bits are shifted; the right operand specifies how many positions they should move. Prior to performing a shift, byte and short values are promoted to int for all shift operators. Furthermore, if either of the operands is long, the other operand is promoted to long. For readability, we use only 16 bits in the examples in this section, but the concepts are the same when carried out to 32- or 64-bit strings.

When bits are shifted, some bits are lost off one end, and others need to be filled in on the other. The *left-shift* operator (<<) shifts bits to the left, filling the right bits with zeros. For example, if the integer variable number currently has the value 13, then the statement

```
number = number << 2;
```

stores the value 52 into number. Initially, number contains the bit string 0000000000001101. When shifted to the left, the value becomes 0000000000110100, or 52. Notice that for each position shifted to the left, the original value is multiplied by 2.

The sign bit of a number is shifted along with all of the others. Therefore the sign of the value could change if enough bits are shifted to change the sign bit. For example, the value –8 is stored in binary two's complement form as 1111111111111000. When shifted left two positions, it becomes 1111111111100000, which is –32. However, if enough positions are shifted, a negative number can become positive and vice versa.

There are two forms of the right-shift operator: one that preserves the sign of the original value (>>) and one that fills the leftmost bits with zeros (>>>).

Let's examine two examples of the *right-shift-with-sign-fill* operator. If the `int` variable `number` currently has the value 39, the expression `(number >> 2)` results in the value 9. The original bit string stored in `number` is 0000000000100111, and the result of a right shift two positions is 0000000000001001. The leftmost sign bit, which in this case is a zero, is used to fill from the left.

If `number` has an original value of –16, or 1111111111110000, the right-shift (with sign fill) expression `(number >> 3)` results in the binary string 1111111111111110, or –2. The leftmost sign bit is a 1 in this case and is used to fill in the new left bits, maintaining the sign.

If maintaining the sign is not desirable, the *right-shift-with-zero-fill* operator (>>>) can be used. It operates similarly to the >> operator but fills with zero no matter what the sign of the original value is.

Java Modifiers E

This appendix summarizes the modifiers that give particular characteristics to Java classes, interfaces, methods, and variables. For discussion purposes, the set of all Java modifiers is divided into two groups: visibility modifiers and all others.

Java Visibility Modifiers

The table in Figure E.1 describes the effect of Java visibility modifiers on various constructs. Some relationships are not applicable (N/A). For instance, a class cannot be declared with protected visibility. Note that each visibility modifier operates in the same way on classes and interfaces and in the same way on methods and variables.

Default visibility means that no visibility modifier was explicitly used. Default visibility is sometimes called *package visibility,* but you cannot use the reserved word `package` as a modifier. Classes and interfaces can have default or public visibility; this visibility determines whether a class or interface can be referenced outside of its package. Only an inner class can have private visibility, in which case only the enclosing class may access it.

Modifier	Classes and interfaces	Methods and variables
default (no modifier)	Visible in its package.	Visible to any class in the same package as its class.
public	Visible anywhere.	Visible anywhere.
protected	N/A	Visible by any class in the same package as its class.
private	Visible to the enclosing class only	Not visible by any other class.

FIGURE E.1 Java visibility modifiers

A Visibility Example

Consider the situation depicted in the Figure E.2. Class P is the parent class that is used to derive child classes C1 and C2. Class C1 is in the same package as P, but C2 is not. Class P contains four methods, each with different visibility modifiers. One object has been instantiated from each of these classes.

The `public` method a() has been inherited by C1 and C2, and any code with access to object x can invoke x.a(). The `private` method d() is not visible to C1 or C2, so objects y and z have no such method available to them. Furthermore, d() is fully encapsulated and can only be invoked from within object x.

The `protected` method b() is visible in both C1 and C2. A method in y could invoke x.b(), but a method in z could not. Furthermore, an object of any class in package One could invoke x.b(), even those that are not related to class P by inheritance, such as an object created from class Another1.

Method c() has `default` visibility, since no visibility modifier was used to declare it. Therefore object y can refer to the method c() as if it were declared locally, but object z cannot. Object y can invoke x.c(), as can an object instantiated from any class in package One, such as Another1. Object z cannot invoke x.c().

These rules generalize in the same way for variables. The visibility rules may appear complicated initially, but they can be mastered with a little effort.

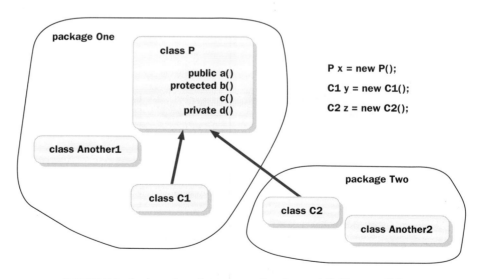

FIGURE E.2 A situation demonstrating Java visibility modifiers

Other Java Modifiers

Figure E.3 summarizes the rest of the Java modifiers, which address a variety of issues. Furthermore, a modifier has different effects on classes, interfaces, methods, and variables. Some modifiers cannot be used with certain constructs and therefore are listed as not applicable (N/A).

The `transient` modifier is used to indicate data that need not be stored in a persistent (serialized) object. That is, when an object is written to a serialized stream, the object representation will include all data that is not specified as transient.

Modifier	Class	Interface	Method	Variable
abstract	The class may contain abstract methods. It cannot be instantiated.	All interfaces are inherently abstract. The modifier is optional.	No method body is defined. The method requires implementation when inherited.	N/A
final	The class cannot be used to drive new classes.	N/A	The method cannot be overridden.	The variable is a constant, whose value cannot be changed once initially set.
native	N/A	N/A	No method body is necessary since implementation is in another language.	N/A
static	N/A	N/A	Defines a class method. It does not require an instantiated object to be invoked. It cannot reference non-static methods or variables. It is implicitly final.	Defines a class variable. It does not require an instantiated object to be referenced. It is shared (common memory space) among all instances of the class.
synchro-nized	N/A	N/A	The execution of the method is mutually exclusive among all threads.	N/A
transient	N/A	N/A	N/A	The variable will not be serialized.
volatile	N/A	N/A	N/A	The variable is changed asynchronously. The compiler should not perform optimizations on it.

FIGURE E.3 The rest of the Java modifiers

Java Coding Guidelines F

This appendix contains a series of guidelines that describe how to organize and format Java source code. They are designed to make programs easier to read and maintain. Some guidelines can be attributed to personal preferences and could be modified. However, it is important to have some standard set of practices that make sense and to follow them carefully. The guidelines presented here are followed in the example code throughout the text and are consistent with the Java naming conventions.

Consistency is half the battle. If you follow the same rules throughout a program, and follow them from one program to another, you make the effort of reading and understanding your code easier for yourself and others. It is not unusual for a programmer to develop software that seems straightforward at the time, only to revisit it months later and have difficulty remembering how it works. If you follow consistent development guidelines, you reduce this problem considerably.

When an organization adopts a coding standard, it is easier for people to work together. A software product is often created by a team of cooperating developers, each responsible for a piece of the system. If they all follow the same development guidelines, they facilitate the process of integrating the separate pieces into one cohesive entity.

You may have to make tradeoffs between some guidelines. For example, you may be asked to make all of your identifiers easy to read yet keep them to a reasonably short length. Use common sense on a case-by-case basis to embrace the spirit of all guidelines as much as possible.

You may choose, or be asked, to follow this set of guidelines as presented. If changes or additions are made, make sure they are clear and that they represent a conscious effort to use good programming practices. Most of these issues are discussed further in appropriate areas of the text but are presented succinctly here, without elaboration.

Design Guidelines

A. Design Preparation

    1. The ultimate guideline is to develop a clean design. Think before you start coding. A working program is not necessarily a good program.

    2. Express and document your design with consistent, clear notation.

B. Structured Programming

    1. Do not use the `continue` statement.

    2. Only use the `break` statement to terminate cases of a `switch` statement.

    3. Have only one `return` statement in a method, as the last line, unless it unnecessarily complicates the method.

C. Classes and Packages

    1. Do not have additional methods in the class that contains the `main` method.

    2. Define the class that contains the `main` method at the top of the file it is in, followed by other classes if appropriate.

    3. If only one class is used from an imported package, import that class by name. If two or more are imported, use the * symbol.

D. Modifiers

    1. Do not declare variables with `public` visibility.

    2. Do not use modifiers inside an interface.

    3. Always use the most appropriate modifiers for each situation. For example, if a variable is used as a constant, explicitly declare it as a constant using the `final` modifier.

E. Exceptions

    1. Use exception handling only for truly exceptional conditions, such as terminating errors, or for significantly unusual or important situations.

    2. Do not use exceptions to disguise or hide inappropriate processing.

    3. Handle each exception at the appropriate level of design.

F. Miscellaneous

    1. Use constants instead of literals in almost all situations.

    2. Design methods so that they perform one logical function. As such, the length of a method will tend to be no longer than 50 lines of code, and usually much shorter.

3. Keep the physical lines of a source code file to less than 80 characters in length.

4. Extend a logical line of code over two or more physical lines only when necessary. Divide the line at a logical place.

Style Guidelines

A. Identifier Naming

1. Give identifiers semantic meaning. For example, do not use single letter names such as `a` or `i` unless the single letter has semantic meaning.

2. Make identifiers easy to read. For example, use `currentValue` instead of `curval`.

3. Keep identifiers to a reasonably short length.

4. Use the underscore character to separate words of a constant.

B. Identifier Case

1. Use UPPERCASE for constants.

2. Use Title Case for class, package, and interface names.

3. Use lowercase for variable and method names, except for the first letter of each word other than the first word. For example, `minTaxRate`. Note that all reserved words must be lowercase.

C. Indentation

1. Indent the code in any block by three spaces.

2. If the body of a loop, `if` statement, or `else` clause is a single statement (not a block), indent the statement three spaces on its own line.

3. Put the left brace (`{`) starting each new block on a new line. Line up the terminating right brace (`}`) with the opening left brace. For example:

```
while (value < 25)
{
   value += 5;
   System.out.println ("The value is " + value);
}
```

4. In a `switch` statement, indent each `case` label three spaces. Indent all code associated with a `case` three additional spaces.

D. Spacing

1. Carefully use white space to draw attention to appropriate features of a program.

2. Put one space after each comma in a parameter list.

3. Put one space on either side of a binary operator.

4. Do not put spaces immediately after a left parenthesis or before a right parenthesis.

5. Do not put spaces before a semicolon.

6. Put one space before a left parenthesis, except before an empty parameter list.

7. When declaring arrays, associate the brackets with the element type, as opposed to the array name, so that it applies to all variables on that line. For example:

```
int[30] list1, list2;
```

8. When referring to the type of an array, do not put any spaces between the element type and the square brackets, such as `int[]`.

E. Messages and Prompts

1. Do not condescend.

2. Do not attempt to be humorous.

3. Be informative, but succinct.

4. Define specific input options in prompts when appropriate.

5. Specify default selections in prompts when appropriate.

F. Output

1. Label all output clearly.

2. Present information to the user in a consistent manner.

Documentation Guidelines

A. The Reader

1. Write all documentation as if the reader is computer literate and basically familiar with the Java language.

2. Assume the reader knows almost nothing about what the program is supposed to do.

3. Remember that a section of code that seems intuitive to you when you write it might not seem so to another reader or to yourself later. Document accordingly.

B. Content

   1. Make sure comments are accurate.

   2. Keep comments updated as changes are made to the code.

   3. Be concise but thorough.

C. Header Blocks

   1. Every source code file should contain a header block of documentation providing basic information about the contents and the author.

   2. Each class and interface, and each method in a class, should have a small header block that describes its role.

   3. Each header block of documentation should have a distinct delimiter on the top and bottom so that the reader can visually scan from one construct to the next easily. For example:

```
//****************************************
//              header block
//****************************************
```

D. In-Line Comments

   1. Use in-line documentation as appropriate to clearly describe interesting processing.

   2. Put a comment on the same line with code only if the comment applies to one line of code and can fit conveniently on that line. Otherwise, put the comment on a separate line above the line or section of code to which it applies.

E. Miscellaneous

   1. Avoid the use of the /* */ style of comment except to conform to the javadoc (/** */) commenting convention.

   2. Don't wait until a program is finished to insert documentation. As pieces of your system are completed, comment them appropriately.

Java Applets

In Chapter 2 we presented the basic concept of an applet, including how an applet differs from an application and how an applet is referenced in an HTML page so that it can be executed in a browser. The applet examples in Chapter 2 present simple drawings. We revisited the concept of an applet in Chapter 8, exploring how applets are a good example of inheritance. This appendix fills in some other details about Java applets.

The example applets in Chapter 2 override the `paint` method of the `JApplet` class. An applet has several other methods that perform specific duties. Because an applet is designed to work with Web pages, some applet methods are specifically designed with that concept in mind. Figure G.1 lists several applet methods.

```
public void init ()
    Initializes the applet. Called just after the applet is loaded.

public void start ()
    Starts the applet. Called just after the applet is made active.

public void stop ()
    Stops the applet. Called just after the applet is made inactive.

public void destroy ()
    Destroys the applet. Called when the browser is exited.

public URL getCodeBase ()
    Returns the URL at which this applet's bytecode is located.

public URL getDocumentBase ()
    Returns the URL at which the HTML document containing this applet is
    located.

public AudioClip getAudioClip (URL url, String name)
    Retrieves an audio clip from the specified URL.

public Image getImage (URL url, String name)
    Retrieves an image from the specified URL.
```

FIGURE G.1 Some methods of the `Applet` class

The `init` method is executed once when the applet is first loaded, such as when the browser or appletviewer initially views the applet. Therefore the `init` method is the place to initialize the applet's environment and permanent data.

The `start` and `stop` methods of an applet are called when the applet becomes active or inactive, respectively. For example, after we use a browser to initially load an applet, the applet's `start` method is called. We may then leave that page to visit another one, at which point the applet becomes inactive and the `stop` method is called. If we return to the applet's page, the applet becomes active again and the `start` method is called again.

Note that the `init` method is called once when the applet is loaded, but `start` may be called several times as the page is revisited. It is good practice to implement `start` and `stop` for an applet if it actively uses CPU time, such as when it is showing an animation, so that CPU time is not wasted on an applet that is not visible.

Also note that reloading the Web page in the browser does not necessarily reload the applet. To force the applet to reload, most browsers provide some key combination for that purpose. For example, in Netscape Navigator, holding down the Shift key while clicking the Reload button with the mouse not only reloads the Web page, but also reloads (and reinitializes) all applets linked to that page.

The `getCodeBase` and `getDocumentBase` methods are useful to determine where the applet's bytecode or HTML document resides. An applet could use the appropriate URL to retrieve additional resources, such as an image or audio clip by using the applet method `getImage` or `getAudioClip`, respectively.

Security is an issue with applets. As you browse Web pages, you may open a page containing an applet, and suddenly an unknown program is executing on your machine. Because of the dangers inherent in that process, applets are restricted in the kinds of operations they can perform. For instance, an applet cannot write data to a local drive.

In the Graphics Track sections throughout this book, we explored issues related to the development of programs that use graphical user interfaces (GUIs). The examples in those sections are presented as Java applications, using `JFrame` components as the primary heavyweight container. An applet can also be used to present GUI-based programs. Like a `JFrame`, a `JApplet` is a heavyweight container.

Applets are useful for small, isolated programs, such as a game or calculator. Because of their security restrictions and processing overhead, they are not frequently used for larger systems. Generally, other technologies are used to support fully integrated, dynamic Web sites.

Regular Expressions H

Throughout the book we've used the Scanner class to read interactive input from the user and parse strings into individual tokens such as words. In Chapter 5 we also used it to read input from a data file. Usually we used the default whitespace delimiters for tokens in the scanner input.

The Scanner class can also be used to parse its input according to a *regular expression*, which is a character string that represents a pattern. A regular expression can be used to set the delimiters used when extracting tokens, or it can be used in methods like findInLine to match a particular string.

Some of the general rules for constructing regular expressions include:

> The dot (.) character matches any single character.
> The * character, which is called the Kleene star, matches zero or more characters.
> A string of characters in brackets ([]) matches any single character in the string.
> The \ character followed by a special character (such as the ones in this list) matches the character itself.
> The \ character followed by a character matches the pattern specified by that character (see the following table).

For example, the regular expression B.b* matches Bob, Bubba, and Baby. The regular expression T[aei]*ing matches Taking, Tickling, and Telling.

These examples are just a few of many. Figure H.1 specifies some of the patterns that can be matched in a Java regular expression, and this list is not complete. See the online documentation for the Pattern class for a complete list.

Regular Expression	Matches
x	The character x
.	Any character
[abc]	a, b, or c
[^abc]	Any character except a, b, or c (negation)
[a-z][A-Z]	a through z or A through Z, inclusive (range)
[a-o[m-p]]	a through d or m through p (union)
[a-z&&[def]]	d, e, or f (intersection)
[a-z&&[^bc]]	a through z, except for b and c (subtraction)
[a-z&&[^m-p]]	a through z but not m through p (subtraction)
\d	A digit: [0–9]
\D	A non-digit: [^0–9]
\s	A whitespace character
\S	A non-whitespace character
^	The beginning of a line
$	The end of a line

FIGURE H.1 Some patterns that can be matched in a Java regular expression

Javadoc
Documentation
Generator

Javadoc is a tool for creating documentation in HTML format from Java source code. The utility examines the source code, extracts specially marked information in the documentation, and then produces Web pages that summarize the software.

Documentation comments, also referred to as doc comments, specify the format for comments to be processed by the javadoc tool. Special labels called *tags* are also parsed by javadoc. Together, doc comments and tags can be used to construct a complete Java application programming interface (API) specification. A Java API is a specification of how to work with a class.

Javadoc can be run on packages or individual files (or both). It produces a well-structured, single document each time. However, javadoc does not support incremental additions.

Javadoc comes as a standard part of the Java Software Development Kit (SDK). The tool executable, javadoc.exe, resides in the bin folder of the installation directory along with the javac compiler and java execution tool. Therefore, if you are able to compile and execute your code using the command line, javadoc should also work.

Using javadoc is simple in its plain form; it is very much like compiling a java source file. For example:

```
javadoc myfile.java
```

The javadoc command may also specify options and package names. The source file name must contain the .java extension (similar to the javac compiler command).

Doc Comments

The document comments are subdivided into descriptions and tags. Descriptions should provide an overview of the functionality of the explained code. Tags address the specifics of the functionality such as code version (for classes or interfaces) or return types (for methods).

Javadoc processes code comments placed between /**, the beginning tag, and */, the end tag. The comments are allowed to span multiple lines where each line begins with a * character, which are, along with any white space before them, discarded by the tool. These comments are allowed to contain HTML tags. For example:

```
/**
 *    This is an <strong>example</strong> document comment.
 */
```

Comment placement should be considered carefully. The javadoc tool automatically copies the first sentence from each doc to a summary at the top of the HTML document. The sentence begins after any white space following the * character and ends at the first period. The description that follows should be concise and complete. Document comments are recognized only if they are placed immediately before a class, constructor, method, interface, or field declaration.

The use of HTML inside the description should be limited to proper comment separation and display rather than styling. Javadoc automatically structures the document using certain tags, for example heading tags. Appropriate use of paragraph or list tags (ordered/unordered) should provide satisfactory formatting.

Tags

Tags are included in a doc comment. Each tag must start on a separate line, hence it must be preceded by the * character. Tags are case sensitive and begin with the @ symbol.

Certain tags are required in some situations. The @param tag must be supplied for every parameter and is used to describe the purpose of the parameter. The @return tag must be supplied for every method that returns anything other than void, to describe what the method returns. The @author class and the @version tags are required for classes and interfaces only.

Figure I.1 lists the various tags used in javadoc comments.

Note the two different types of tags listed in Figure I.1. The *block tags,* which begin with the @ symbol (e.g., @author), must be placed in the tag section

Tag Name	Description
`@author`	Inserts an "Author" entry with the specified text.
`{ @code}`	Same as `<code>{@literal}</code>`.
`@deprecated`	Inserts a bold "Deprecated" entry with the specified text.
`{ @docRoot}`	Relative link to the root of the document.
`@exception`	See `@throws`.
`{ @inheritDoc}`	Copies documentation from the closest inherited class or implemented interface where used allowing for more general comments of hierarchically higher classes to be reused.
`{ @link}`	Inserts a hyperlink to an HTML document. Use: `{@link name url}`.
`{ @linkPlain}`	Same as `{ @link}` but is displayed as plain text. Use: `{@linkPlain link label}`.
`{ @literal}`	Text enclosed in the tag is denoted literally, as containing any HTML. For example, `{@literal <td> TouchDown}` would be displayed as `<td> TouchDown` (`<td>` not interpreted as a table cell).
`@param`	Inserts a "Parameters" section, which lists and describes parameters for a particular constructor/method.
`@return`	Inserts a "Returns" section, which lists and describes any return values for a particular constructor/method. Use: `@return description`. An error will be thrown if included in a comment of a method with the void return type.
`@see`	Included a "See Also" comment with a link pointing to a document with more information. Use: `@see link`.
`@serial`	Used for a serializable field. Use: `@serial text`.
`@serialData`	Used to document used to describe data written by the `writeObject`, `readObject`, `writeExternal`, and `readExternal` methods. Use: `@serialdata text`.
`@serialField`	Used to comment on the `ObjectStreamField`. Use: `@serialField name type description`.
`@since`	Inserts a new "Since" heading that is used to denote when particular features were first introduced. Use: `@since text`.
`@throws`	Includes a "Throws" heading. Use: `@throws name description`.
`{ @value}`	Returns the value of a code element it refers to. Use: `@value code-member` label.
`@version`	Add a "Version" heading when the `–version` command–line option is used. Use: `@version text`.

FIGURE I.1 Various tags used in javadoc comments

following the main description. The *inline tags,* enclosed in the { and } delimiters, can be placed anywhere in the description section or in the comments for block tags. For example:

```
/**
 * This is an <strong>example</strong> document comment.
 * The {@link Glossary} provides definitions of types used.
 *
 * @author Sebastian Niezgoda
 */
```

Files Generated

The javadoc tool analyzes a java source file or package and produces a three-part HTML document for each class. The HTML file is often referred to as a documentation file. It contains cleanly organized information about the class file derived from the doc comments included in the code.

The first part of the document contains an overall description of the class. The class name appears first followed by a graphical representation of the inheritance relationships. A general description is displayed next, which is extracted from the first sentence of each doc comment entity (as discussed previously).

Next, a list of constructors and methods is provided. The signatures of all the constructors and methods included in the source file are listed along with one-sentence descriptions. The name of the constructor/method is a hyperlink to a more detailed description in the third part of the document.

Third, complete descriptions of the methods are provided. Again, the signature is provided first followed by an explanation of the entity, this time without the one-sentence limit, which is obtained from the doc comments. If applicable, a list of parameters and return values, along with their descriptions, is provided in the respective sections.

The HTML document makes extensive use of hyperlinks to provide necessary additional information, using the @see tag for example, and for navigational purposes. The header and the footer of the page are navigation bars, with the following links:

> *Package* provides a list of classes included in the package along with a short purpose and description of each class.
> *Tree* presents a visual hierarchy of the classes within the package. Each class name is a link to the appropriate documentation HTML file.
> *Deprecated* lists functionality that is considered deprecated that is used in any of the class files contained in the package.

> *Index* provides an alphabetical listing of classes, constructors, and methods in the package. The class name is also associated with a short purpose and description of the class. Each appearance of the class name is a link to the appropriate HTML documentation. The signature of every constructor and method is a link to the appropriate detailed description. A one-sentence description presented next to the signature listing associates the constructor/method with the appropriate class.
> *Help* loads a help page with how-to instructions for using and navigating the HTML documentation.

All pages could be viewed with or without frames. Each class summary has links that can be used to quickly access any of the parts of the document (as described above).

The output content could be somewhat generated by command-line options (see above) used when executing the javadoc tool. By default, if no options are specified, the output returned is equivalent to using the —protected option. The options include:

> private shows all classes, methods, and variables.
> public shows only public classes, methods, and variables.
> protected shows only protected and public classes, methods, and variables.
> help presents the online help.
> keywords includes HTML meta tags to the output file generated to assist with searching.

The `PaintBox` Project J

In this appendix we examine a software development project that is larger than any other described in this text. As we explore this program, we will walk through most of the steps in the evolutionary development model that are described in previous sections of this chapter.

Our example program allows the user to create drawings with various shapes and colors. This type of project encompasses a variety of issues that are commonly found in large-scale software development and provides a good basis for exploring our development model. We call this example the `PaintBox` project.

`PaintBox` Requirements

Suppose the client provides the following set of initial requirements. The program will:

> Present a graphical user interface that is primarily mouse driven for all user actions.
> Allow the user to draw lines, ovals, circles, rectangles, and squares.
> Allow the user to change the drawing color.
> Display the current drawing color.
> Allow the user to fill a shape, except for a line, with a color.
> Allow the user to select a shape in order to move it, modify its color, or reshape it.
> Allow the user to cut, copy, and paste individual shapes in a drawing.
> Allow the user to save a drawing in a file and load a previously stored drawing from a file for further editing.
> Allow the user to begin a new drawing at any time.

After examining these general requirements, we might sit down with the client and discuss some of the details to ensure that there are no misunderstandings. We might create a new requirements document that gets much more specific about the issues involved.

During these interactions with the client, we might create a sketch, such as the one shown in Figure J.1, of a user interface for the system. This sketch serves as

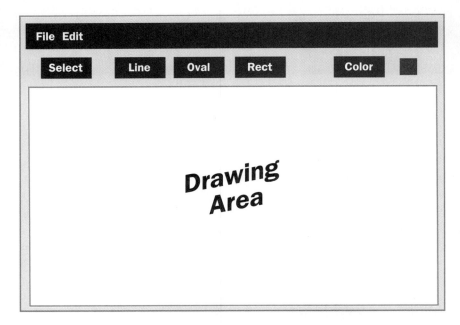

FIGURE J.1 A sketch of the user interface for the `PaintBox` program

a basic prototype of the interface, and gives us something to refer to in our discussions with the client. For other systems there may be many such sketches for each screen of the program.

The interface sketch shows a main drawing area where the user will create a drawing. The top edge contains a set of buttons used to select various tools, such as the oval tool to draw an oval or circle, the color tool to change the current drawing color, and a select tool to select a previously drawn shape to modify or move it. Two menu headings are shown along the top edge. The File menu contains operations to begin a new drawing, save a drawing, and exit the program. The Edit menu contains editing operations such as cut, copy, and paste.

As a result of the discussions with the client, several additional requirements issues are established:

> There is no need to have separate user interactions for circles or squares because they are subsets of ovals and rectangles, respectively.
> The user should also be able to create polyline shapes.
> The buttons used to select drawing tools should have icons instead of words.

> The system should make a distinction between the stroke color (the outline) and the fill color (the interior) of a shape. Therefore, each shape will have a separate stroke and fill color. Lines and polylines will have only a stroke color because they cannot be filled.
> An option to save a drawing under a particular name should be provided (the traditional "save as" operation).
> Traditional keyboard shortcuts for operations such as cut, copy, and paste should be included.
> The system should perform checks to ensure that the user does not lose unsaved changes to a drawing.
> The system should present an initial "splash screen" to introduce the program when it is executed.

These issues must be integrated into the formal description of the requirements document for the project. Several discussions with the client, with additional screen sketches, may be necessary before we have an accurate and solid set of program requirements.

PaintBox Architectural Design

After we have clarified the requirements with the client, we can begin to think about some of the elements of the high-level *architectural design* of the system. For example, many of the classes needed for the user interface can come from the Java standard class library in the Swing package.

It also seems reasonable that a separate class could be used to represent each shape type. Further, each individually drawn shape should be an instantiation of the appropriate shape class. For example, we could define an Oval class to represent an oval, a Line class to represent a line, and so on. Each class should be responsible for keeping track of the information it needs to define it, and it should provide methods to draw itself.

A drawing may be composed of many shapes, so we need a way to keep track of all of them. An ArrayList might be a good choice for this. As each new shape is drawn, we can add the object that represents it to the list. The list will also inherently define the order in which shapes are drawn. Since some shapes will be drawn on top of others, the list will also keep track of the order in which shapes are "stacked."

The process of defining an architectural design could take a while. The key is to make the most important and fundamental decisions that will affect the entire system without skipping ahead to decisions that are better left to individual refinements of the system.

`PaintBox` Refinements

After some consideration, we might decide that the evolution of the `PaintBox` project could be broken down into the following refinement steps:

> Establish the basic user interface.
> Allow the user to draw basic shapes using different stroke colors.
> Allow the user to cut, copy, and paste shapes.
> Allow the user to select, move, and fill shapes.
> Allow the user to modify the dimensions of shapes.
> Allow the user to save and reload drawings.
> Include final touches such as the splash screen.

Note, first of all, that these refinements focus on breaking down the functionality of the system. Additional refinements may be necessary as we get into the iterative process. For instance, we may decide that we need a refinement to address problems that were discovered in previous refinements.

The listed refinements could have been broken down further. For example, one refinement could have been devoted to the ability to draw one particular type of shape. The level of refinement, just like many other decisions when developing a software system, is a judgment call. The developer must decide what is best in any particular situation.

The order in which we tackle the refinements is also important. The user interface refinement seems to be a logical first step because all other activity relies on it. We may decide that the ability to save and reload a drawing would be nice to have early for testing purposes. We might also note that being able to select an object is fundamental to operations such as move and cut/copy/paste. After further analysis, we end up with the set of refinements shown in Figure J.2.

`PaintBox` Refinement #1

Most of the classes used for the interface come from predefined libraries. We use Swing technology whenever reasonable. For example, we can use a `JPanel` for the overall interface space, as well as separate `JPanel` objects to organize the button tools and the drawing area. The `JButton` class will serve well for the buttons. Classes such as `JMenuBar` and `JMenuItem` will serve to implement the menus.

Figure J.3 shows a class diagram that represents the classes that are important to the first refinement of the `PaintBox` project. Note that it does not include all classes that might be needed, nor does it address anything other than the needs of this one refinement. We'll create additional diagrams that augment our understanding of the system design as further refinements are developed.

Refinement	Description
1	Present the basic graphical user interface, including the main frame, buttons, menus, menu items, and the drawing area. The select and shape buttons work together as a radio button set (only one can be chosen at a time). No functionality for these interface elements is included at this time. Exiting the program is provided only by the frame's window close button.
2	Add support for drawing the four basic shapes: lines, ovals, rectangles, and polylines. The chosen shape button determines what shape is drawn. The stroke color button can be used to set the stroke color for the next shape drawn. The color button causes a separate dialog box to appear to allow color selection.
3	Add support for saving and loading drawings. This includes the functionality of the *open, save,* and *save as* File menu items. When the *open, new,* or *exit* File menu options are chosen, check to see if the current drawing has been modified since last saved, and if so prompt to see if the user wants to save the drawing.
4	Provide the ability to select and move shapes on the drawing surface. Simple graphic selection blocks should be presented on the shape's outline to indicate the currently selected shape. Once selected, the mouse can be used to drag the shape to another location on the drawing surface.
5	Add the functionality for the *cut, copy* and *paste* Edit menu items. Once selected, a shape can be cut or copied. Once a shape has been cut or copied, it can be pasted (perhaps multiple times) onto the drawing surface at a fixed offset to the original position. Edit menu items that are not valid at any given time are disabled. For example, unless a shape is selected, the cut and copy menu items cannot be chosen.
6	Add support for filling and reshaping a shape. Once a shape has been selected, the fill color button can be used to determine its fill color. A menu item on the Edit menu can be used to remove the fill of any filled object (make it transparent). The currently selected shape will now have a reshape handle that can be used to change the dimensions of the shape.
7	Add some extra functionality to the program. These additions include a splash screen that appears when the system is initially executed, an *about* dialog box, keyboard shortcuts for all menu items, and packaging the application into an executable JAR file.

FIGURE J.2 Functional refinements for the PaintBox project

The detailed design and implementation for the interface refinement might develop similarly to other graphical projects we've developed in previous chapters. We can create listener objects and methods as appropriate but not concern ourselves with their inner workings at this time. That is, our focus in this refinement is to present the user interface, not create any of the functionality behind

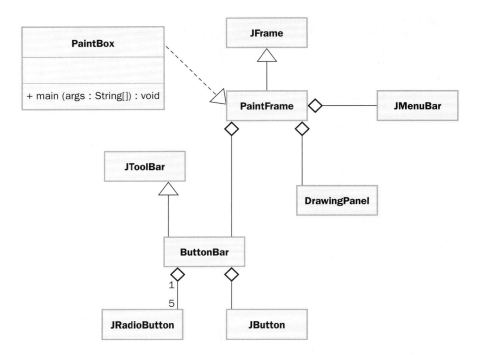

FIGURE J.3 A class diagram for the interface refinement of the `PaintBox` project

the interface. During the development of this refinement, we modify the details of the user interface until it appears just the way we'd like it.

At the end of the first refinement, we are left with a completely implemented program that presents only the user interface. The buttons do nothing when pushed and the menu items do nothing when selected. We have no way of creating a drawing yet.

What we do have, however, is a complete entity that has been debugged and tested to the level of this refinement. We may show it to the client at this point and get further input. Any changes that result from these discussions can be incorporated into future refinements. Figure J.4 shows the `PaintBox` program after the first refinement has been completed.

`PaintBox` Refinement #2

The next refinement to address is the ability to draw basic shapes, because all other operations use drawn shapes in one way or another. Therefore, in this

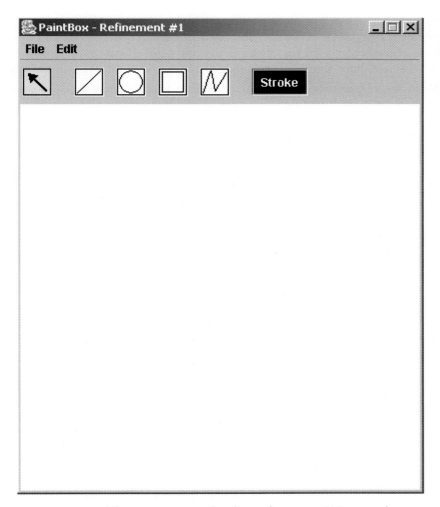

FIGURE J.4 The PaintBox code after refinement #1 is complete

refinement we focus on providing the processing power behind the buttons that draw shapes and specify color.

Most of the objects and classes that we will use in this refinement are not predefined as they were in the interface refinement. We might consider using the Rectangle class from the Java standard class library, but on further investigation we realize that its role is not really consistent with our goals. In addition, no other classes are defined for the other shapes we need.

So, as we envisioned in our architectural design, we consider having one class per shape type: Line, Oval, Rect, and Poly. Remember that circles and squares will just be specific instances of the Oval and Rect classes, respectively. Each shape class will have a draw method that draws that kind of shape on the screen.

Now let's consider the kind of information that each shape needs to store to be able to draw itself. A line needs two points: a starting point and an ending point. Each polyline, on the other hand, needs a list of points to define the start and end points of each line segment. Both ovals and rectangles are defined by a bounded rectangle, storing an upper-left corner and the width and height of the shape.

This analysis leads to the conclusion that Oval and Rect objects have some common characteristics that we could exploit using inheritance. They could both, for instance, be derived from a class called BoundedShape. Furthermore, because all shapes have to be stored in the ArrayList object that we'll use to keep track of the entire drawing, it would simplify the refinement to have a generic Shape class from which all drawn shapes are derived.

The Shape and BoundedShape classes are used for organizational purposes. We do not intend to instantiate them; therefore they probably should be abstract classes. In fact, if we define an abstract method called draw in the Shape class, we could capitalize on polymorphism to simplify the drawing of the shapes in the drawing area. A loop can move through the ArrayList, having each shape (whatever it may be) draw itself.

After some consideration, we achieve the class diagram shown in Figure J.5. This diagram specifically represents the classes that are important to the second refinement of the PaintBox project.

Selecting a current color can be relegated to the JColorChooser component provided by the Swing package. The color button will bring up the JColorChooser dialog box and respond accordingly to the user's selection.

Multiple shapes will accumulate on the drawing surface. We could define a class to serve as a collection of the drawn shape objects. It could use an ArrayList to keep track of the list of shapes. Whenever the drawing area needs to be refreshed, we can iterate through the list of shapes and draw each one in turn.

Figure J.6 shows the PaintBox program after the first two refinements have been completed. Once again, we could visit with the client at this point to determine whether the evolution of the system meets with his or her satisfaction.

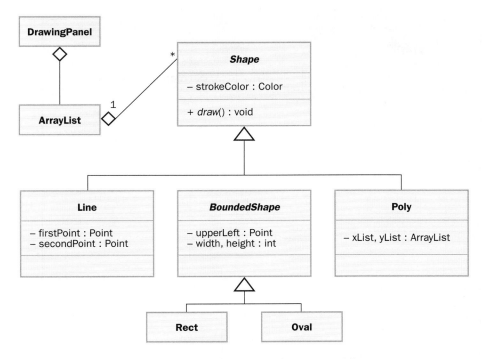

FIGURE J.5 A class diagram for the second refinement of the PaintBox project

Remaining PaintBox Refinements

For space reasons, the code for the various PaintBox refinements is not presented in the text. The full implementation of the first two refinements can be downloaded with the rest of the book's examples. The remaining refinements are left as projects.

The refinements of the PaintBox program continue until all requirements issues and problems have been addressed. This type of evolutionary development is crucial for medium- and large-scale development efforts. Figure J.7 shows the PaintBox program after all of the seven refinements have been completed.

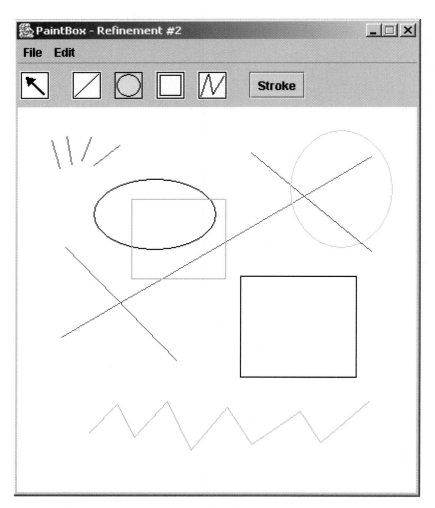

FIGURE J.6 The PaintBox program after the interface and shapes refinements

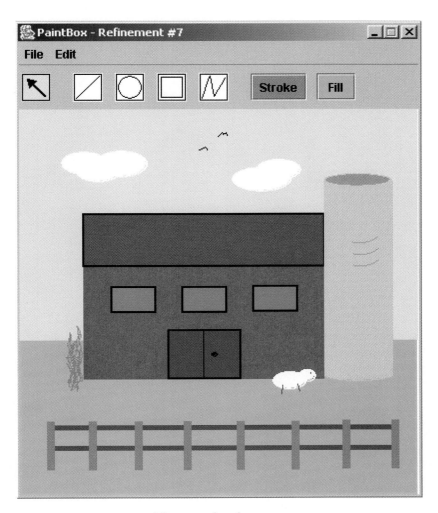

FIGURE J.7 The completed PaintBox program

Throughout the Graphics Track sections of this book, we've discussed various events that components might generate. The goal of this appendix is to put the event/component relationship into context.

The events listed in Figure K.1 are generated by every Swing component. That is, we can set up a listener for any of these events on any component.

Some events are generated only by certain components. The table in Figure K.2 maps the components to the events that they can generate. Keep in mind that these events are in addition to the ones that all components generate. If a component does not generate a particular kind of event, a listener for that event cannot be added to that component.

We have discussed some of the events in Figures K.1 and K.2 at appropriate points in this text; we have left others for your independent exploration. Applying the basic concept of component/event/listener interaction is often just a matter of knowing which components generate which events under which circumstances.

Of course, many events occur in a GUI that have no bearing on the current program. For example, every time a mouse is moved across a component, many mouse motion events are generated. However, this doesn't mean we must listen for them. A GUI is defined in part by the events to which we choose to respond.

Event	Represents
Component Event	Changing a component's size, position, or visibility.
Focus Event	Gaining or losing the keyboard focus.
Key Event	Pressing, releasing, and clicking keyboard keys.
Mouse Event	Clicking the mouse button and moving the mouse into and out of a component's drawing area.
Mouse Motion Event	Moving or dragging a mouse over a component.

FIGURE K.1 Events that are generated by every Swing component

Component	Action	Caret	Change	Document	Item	List Selection	Window	*Other*
JButton	✓		✓		✓			
JCheckBox	✓		✓		✓			
JColorChooser			✓					
JComboBox	✓				✓			
JDialog							✓	
JEditorPane		✓		✓				✓
JFileChooser	✓							
JFrame							✓	
JInternalFrame								✓
JList						✓		✓
JMenu								✓
JMenuItem	✓		✓		✓			✓
JOptionPane								
JPasswordField	✓	✓		✓				
JPopupMenu								✓
JProgessBar			✓		✓			
JRadioButton	✓		✓					
JSlider			✓					
JTabbedPane			✓					
JTable						✓		✓
JTextArea		✓		✓				
JTextField	✓	✓		✓				
JTextPane		✓		✓				✓
JToggleButton	✓		✓		✓			
JTree								✓

FIGURE K.2 Specific events generated by specific components

Despite our heavy coverage of GUI development in this book, we've still only scratched the surface. The following list describes a few other Java GUI containers and components that are not covered in depth in this text:

> A *tool bar* is a container that groups several components into a row or column. A tool bar usually contains buttons that correspond to tasks that can also be accomplished in other ways. Tool bars can be dragged away from the container in which they initially exist into their own window.

> An *internal frame* is a container that operates like a regular frame but only within another window. An internal frame can be moved around within the window and overlapped with other internal frames. Internal frames can be used to create the feel of a GUI desktop in which components can be arranged as the user chooses.

> A *layered pane* is a container that takes into account a third dimension, depth, for organizing the components it contains. When a component is added to a layered pane, its depth is specified. If components overlap, the depth value of each component determines which is on top.

> A *progress bar* can be used to indicate the progress of a particular activity. The user does not generally interact with a progress bar other than to view it to determine how far along a task, such as the loading of images, has progressed.

> A *table* is a Java GUI component that displays data in a table format. A Java table can be completely tailored to provide a precise organization and presentation. It can allow the user to edit the data as well. A Java table does not actually contain or store the data; it simply presents it to the user in an organized manner.

> A *tree* is a component that presents a hierarchical view of data. Like a table, it doesn't actually store the data; it provides an organized view that allows the user to traverse the data from a high-level root node down through the various branches.

> Another area for which Java provides rich support is *text processing*. We've made use of basic text components such as text fields and text areas, but that's only the beginning. The Java standard class library, and particularly the Swing API, has a huge number of classes that support the display, editing, and manipulation of text.

As with all topics introduced in this book, we encourage you to explore these issues in more detail. The world of Java GUIs, in particular, has many opportunities still to discover.

Java Syntax L

This appendix contains syntax diagrams that collectively describe the way in which Java language elements can be constructed. Rectangles indicate something that is further defined in another syntax diagram, and ovals indicate a literal word or character.

Compilation Unit

Package Declaration

Import Declaration

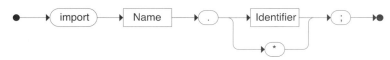

Type Declaration

Class Declaration

Class Associations

Class Body

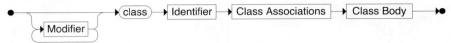

Class Member

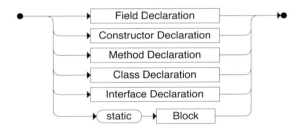

Interface Declaration

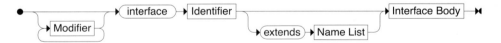

Interface Body

Interface Member

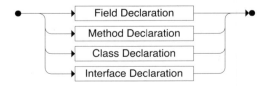

Field Declaration

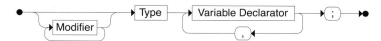

Variable Declarator

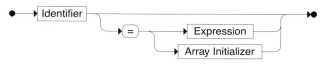

Type

Modifier   **Primitive Type**

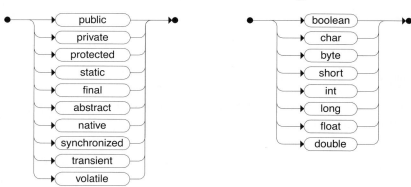

Array Initializer

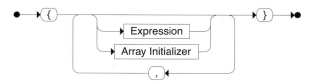

Name   **Name List**

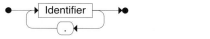
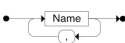

Method Declaration

Parameters

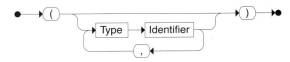

Throws Clause

Method Body

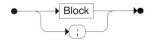

Constructor Declaration

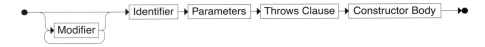

Constructor Body

Constructor Invocation

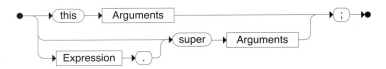

Block

Block Statement

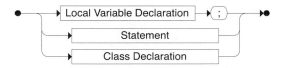

Local Variable Declaration

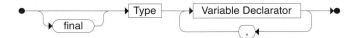

Statement

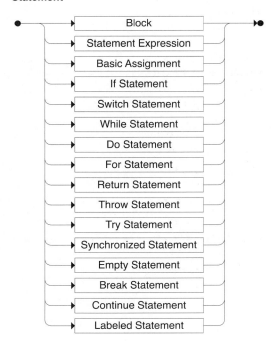

If Statement

Switch Statement

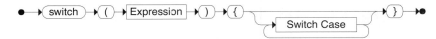

Switch Case

While Statement

Do Statement

For Statement

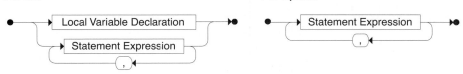

For Init   **For Update**

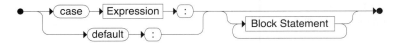

Basic Assignment

Return Statement

Throw Statement

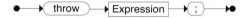

Try Statement

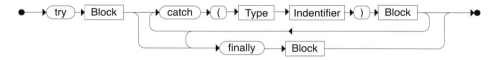

Synchronized Statement

Empty Statement

Break Statement

Continue Statement

Labeled Statement

Expression

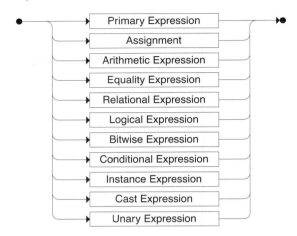

Primary Expression

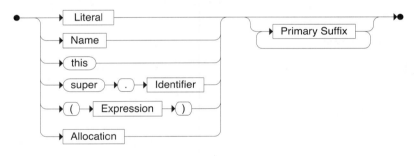

Primary Suffix

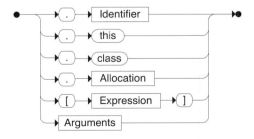

Arguments

Allocation

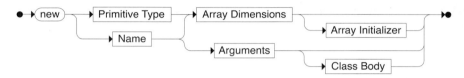

Array Dimensions

Statement Expression

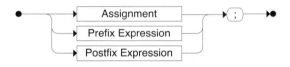

Assignment

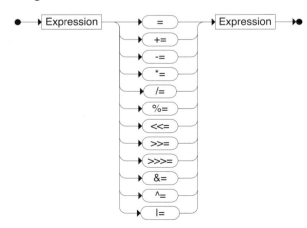

Arithmetic Expression

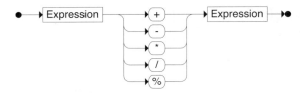

Equality Expression

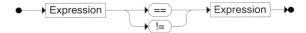

Relational Expression

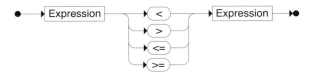

Logical Expression

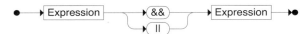

Bitwise Expression

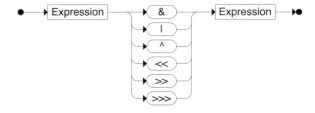

Conditional Expression

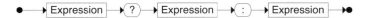

Instance Expression

Cast Expression

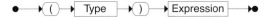

Unary Expression

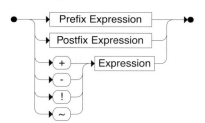

Prefix Expression

Postfix Expression

Literal

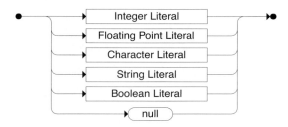

Integer Literal

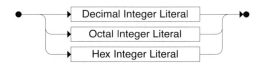

Decimal Integer Literal

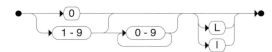

Octal Integer Literal

Hex Digit

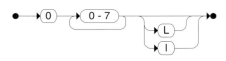

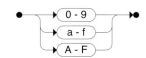

Hex Integer Literal

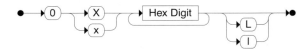

Floating Point Literal

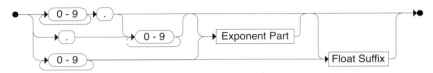

Exponent Part

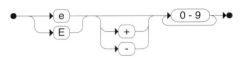

Float Suffix

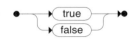

Character Literal

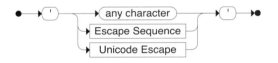

Boolean Literal

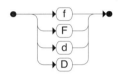

String Literal

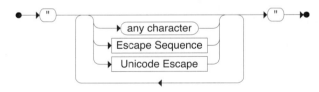

Escape Sequence

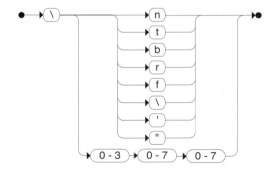

Identifier

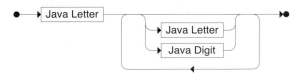

Java Letter

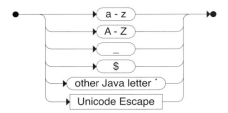

* The "other Java letter" category includes letters
from many languages other than English.

Java Digit

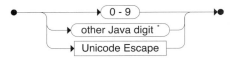

* The "other Java digit" category includes
additional digits defined in Unicode.

Unicode Escape*

* In some contexts, the character represented
by a Unicode Escape is restricted.

The Java Class Library M

In previous editions of this book, this appendix included abbreviated reference material for the Java API Specification, including several classes and interfaces from the Java standard class library. This appendix is still available at **www.aw.com/cssupport/LewisLoftus.html** for anyone who would like to download and make use of it.

A better solution, however, is to get familiar with the official and complete online API documentation available at **java.sun.com/j2se/5.0/docs/api**. It contains a description of every class, interface, and method available to every Java development environment.

We encourage you to spend some time getting familiar with the organization and layout of that documentation. It is a valuable tool to rely on during program development.

Index

Sun Microsystems, Inc. Binary Code License Agreement for the JAVA 2 PLATFORM STANDARD EDITION DEVELOPMENT KIT 5.0

SUN MICROSYSTEMS, INC. ("SUN") IS WILLING TO LICENSE THE SOFTWARE IDENTIFIED BELOW TO YOU ONLY UPON THE CONDITION THAT YOU ACCEPT ALL OF THE TERMS CONTAINED IN THIS BINARY CODE LICENSE AGREEMENT AND SUPPLEMENTAL LICENSE TERMS (COLLECTIVELY "AGREEMENT"). PLEASE READ THE AGREEMENT CAREFULLY. BY DOWNLOADING OR INSTALLING THIS SOFTWARE, YOU ACCEPT THE TERMS OF THE AGREEMENT. INDICATE ACCEPTANCE BY SELECTING THE "ACCEPT" BUTTON AT THE BOTTOM OF THE AGREEMENT. IF YOU ARE NOT WILLING TO BE BOUND BY ALL THE TERMS, SELECT THE "DECLINE" BUTTON AT THE BOTTOM OF THE AGREEMENT AND THE DOWNLOAD OR INSTALL PROCESS WILL NOT CONTINUE.

1. DEFINITIONS. "Software" means the identified above in binary form, any other machine readable materials (including, but not limited to, libraries, source files, header files, and data files), any updates or error corrections provided by Sun, and any user manuals, programming guides and other documentation provided to you by Sun under this Agreement. "Programs" mean Java applets and applications intended to run on the Java 2 Platform Standard Edition (J2SE platform) platform on Java-enabled general purpose desktop computers and servers.

2. LICENSE TO USE. Subject to the terms and conditions of this Agreement, including, but not limited to the Java Technology Restrictions of the Supplemental License Terms, Sun grants you a non-exclusive, non-transferable, limited license without license fees to reproduce and use internally Software complete and unmodified for the sole purpose of running Programs. Additional licenses for developers and/or publishers are granted in the Supplemental License Terms.

3. RESTRICTIONS. Software is confidential and copyrighted. Title to Software and all associated intellectual property rights is retained by Sun and/or its licensors. Unless enforcement is prohibited by applicable law, you may not modify, decompile, or reverse engineer Software. You acknowledge that Licensed Software is not designed or intended for use in the design, construction, operation or maintenance of any nuclear facility. Sun Microsystems, Inc. disclaims any express or implied warranty of fitness for such uses. No right, title or interest in or to any trademark, service mark, logo or trade name of Sun or its licensors is granted under this Agreement. Additional restrictions for developers and/or publishers licenses are set forth in the Supplemental License Terms.

4. LIMITED WARRANTY. Sun warrants to you that for a period of ninety (90) days from the date of purchase, as evidenced by a copy of the receipt, the media on which Software is furnished (if any) will be free of defects in materials and workmanship under normal use. Except for the foregoing, Software is provided "AS IS". Your exclusive remedy and Sun's entire liability under this limited warranty will be at Sun's option to replace Software media or refund the fee paid for Software. Any implied warranties on the Software are limited to 90 days. Some states do not allow limitations on duration of an implied warranty, so the above may not apply to you. This limited warranty gives you specific legal rights. You may have others, which vary from state to state.

5. DISCLAIMER OF WARRANTY. UNLESS SPECIFIED IN THIS AGREEMENT, ALL EXPRESS OR IMPLIED CONDITIONS, REPRESENTATIONS AND WARRANTIES, INCLUDING ANY IMPLIED WARRANTY OF MERCHANTABILITY, FITNESS FOR A PARTICULAR PURPOSE OR NON-INFRINGEMENT ARE DISCLAIMED, EXCEPT TO THE EXTENT THAT THESE DISCLAIMERS ARE HELD TO BE LEGALLY INVALID.

6. LIMITATION OF LIABILITY. TO THE EXTENT NOT PROHIBITED BY LAW, IN NO EVENT WILL SUN OR ITS LICENSORS BE LIABLE FOR ANY LOST REVENUE, PROFIT OR DATA, OR FOR SPECIAL, INDIRECT, CONSEQUENTIAL, INCIDENTAL OR PUNITIVE DAMAGES, HOWEVER CAUSED REGARDLESS OF THE THEORY OF LIABILITY, ARISING OUT OF OR RELATED TO THE USE OF OR INABILITY TO USE SOFTWARE, EVEN IF SUN HAS BEEN ADVISED OF THE POSSIBILITY OF SUCH DAMAGES. In no event will Sun's liability to you, whether in contract, tort (including negligence), or otherwise, exceed the amount paid by you for Software under this Agreement. The foregoing limitations will apply even if the above stated warranty fails of its essential purpose. Some states do not allow the exclusion of incidental or consequential damages, so some of the terms above may not be applicable to you.

7. TERMINATION. This Agreement is effective until terminated. You may terminate this Agreement at any time by destroying all copies of Software. This Agreement will terminate immediately without notice from Sun if you fail to comply with any provision of this Agreement. Either party may terminate this Agreement immediately should any Software become, or in either party's opinion be likely to become, the subject of a claim of infringement of any intellectual property right. Upon Termination, you must destroy all copies of Software.

8. EXPORT REGULATIONS. All Software and technical data delivered under this Agreement are subject to US export control laws and may be subject to export or import regulations in other countries. You agree to comply strictly with all such laws and regulations and acknowledge that you have the responsibility to obtain such licenses to export, re-export, or import as may be required after delivery to you.

9. TRADEMARKS AND LOGOS. You acknowledge and agree as between you and Sun that Sun owns the SUN, SOLARIS, JAVA, JINI, FORTE, and iPLANET trademarks and all SUN, SOLARIS, JAVA, JINI, FORTE, and iPLANET-related trademarks, service marks, logos and other brand designations ("Sun Marks"), and you agree to comply with the Sun Trademark and Logo Usage Requirements currently located at http://www.sun.com/policies/trademarks. Any use you make of the Sun Marks inures to Sun's benefit.

10. U.S. GOVERNMENT RESTRICTED RIGHTS. If Software is being acquired by or on behalf of the U.S. Government or by a U.S. Government prime contractor or subcontractor (at any tier), then the Government's rights in Software and accompanying documentation will be only as set forth in this Agreement; this is in accordance with 48 CFR 227.7201 through 227.7202-4 (for Department of Defense (DOD) acquisitions) and with 48 CFR 2.101 and 12.212 (for non-DOD acquisitions).

11. GOVERNING LAW. Any action related to this Agreement will be governed by California law and controlling U.S. federal law. No choice of law rules of any jurisdiction will apply.

12. SEVERABILITY. If any provision of this Agreement is held to be unenforceable, this Agreement will remain in effect with the provision omitted, unless omission would frustrate the intent of the parties, in which case this Agreement will immediately terminate.

13. INTEGRATION. This Agreement is the entire agreement between you and Sun relating to its subject matter. It supersedes all prior or contemporaneous oral or written communications, proposals, representations and warranties and prevails over any conflicting or additional terms of any quote, order, acknowledgment, or other communication between the parties relating to its subject matter during the term of this Agreement. No modification of this Agreement will be binding, unless in writing and signed by an authorized representative of each party.

SUPPLEMENTAL LICENSE TERMS

These Supplemental License Terms add to or modify the terms of the Binary Code License Agreement. Capitalized terms not defined in these Supplemental Terms shall have the same meanings ascribed to them in the Binary Code License Agreement . These Supplemental Terms shall supersede any inconsistent or conflicting terms in the Binary Code License Agreement, or in any license contained within the Software.

A. Software Internal Use and Development License Grant. Subject to the terms and conditions of this Agreement and restrictions and exceptions set forth in the Software "README" file, including, but not limited to the Java Technology Restrictions of these Supplemental Terms, Sun grants you a non-exclusive, non-transferable, limited license without fees to reproduce internally and use internally the Software complete and unmodified for the purpose of designing, developing, and testing your Programs.

B. License to Distribute Software. Subject to the terms and conditions of this Agreement and restrictions and exceptions set forth in the Software README file, including, but not limited to the Java Technology Restrictions of these Supplemental Terms, Sun grants you a non-exclusive, non-transferable, limited license without fees to reproduce and distribute the Software, provided that (i) you distribute the Software complete and unmodified and only bundled as part of, and for the sole purpose of running, your Programs, (ii) the Programs add significant and primary functionality to the Software, (iii) you do not distribute additional software intended to replace any component(s) of the Software, (iv) you do not remove or alter any proprietary legends or notices contained in the Software, (v) you only distribute the Software subject to a license agreement that protects Sun's interests consistent with the terms contained in this Agreement, and (vi) you agree to defend and indemnify Sun and its licensors from and against any damages, costs, liabilities, settlement amounts and/or expenses (including attorneys' fees) incurred in connection with any claim, lawsuit or action by any third party that arises or results from the use or distribution of any and all Programs and/or Software.

C. License to Distribute Redistributables. Subject to the terms and conditions of this Agreement and restrictions and exceptions set forth in the Software README file, including but not limited to the Java Technology Restrictions of these Supplemental Terms, Sun grants you a non-exclusive, non-transferable, limited license without fees to reproduce and distribute those files specifically identified as redistributable in the Software "README" file ("Redistributables") provided that: (i) you distribute the Redistributables complete and unmodified, and only bundled as part of Programs, (ii) the Programs add significant and primary functionality to the Redistributables, (iii) you do not distribute additional software intended to supersede any component(s) of the Redistributables (unless otherwise specified in the applicable README file), (iv) you do not remove or alter any proprietary legends or notices contained in or on the Redistributables, (v) you only distribute the Redistributables pursuant to a license agreement that protects Sun's interests consistent with the terms contained in the Agreement, (vi) you agree to defend and indemnify Sun and its licensors from and against any damages, costs, liabilities, settlement amounts and/or expenses (including attorneys' fees) incurred in connection with any claim, lawsuit or action by any third party that arises or results from the use or distribution of any and all Programs and/or Software.

D. Java Technology Restrictions. You may not create, modify, or change the behavior of, or authorize your licensees to create, modify, or change the behavior of, classes, interfaces, or subpackages that are in any way identified as "java", "javax", "sun" or similar convention as specified by Sun in any naming convention designation.